SECOND EDITION

TEN STEPS
TO
ADVANCED
READING

SECOND EDITION

TEN STEPS
to
ADVANCED
READING

John Langan

ATLANTIC CAPE COMMUNITY COLLEGE

Books in the Townsend Press Reading Series:

Groundwork for College Reading with Phonics
Groundwork for College Reading
Ten Steps to Building College Reading Skills
Ten Steps to Improving College Reading Skills
Ten Steps to Advancing College Reading Skills
Ten Steps to Advanced Reading

Books in the Townsend Press Vocabulary Series:

Vocabulary Basics
Groundwork for a Better Vocabulary
Building Vocabulary Skills
Building Vocabulary Skills, Short Version
Improving Vocabulary Skills
Improving Vocabulary Skills, Short Version
Advancing Vocabulary Skills
Advancing Vocabulary Skills, Short Version
Advanced Word Power

Supplements Available for Most Books:

Instructor's Edition
Instructor's Manual and Test Bank
Online Exercises
PowerPoint Slides

Copyright © 2013 by Townsend Press, Inc.
Printed in the United States of America
9 8 7 6 5 4 3 2 1

ISBN-13 (Student Edition): 978-1-59194-295-5
ISBN-10 (Student Edition): 1-59194-295-0
ISBN-13 (Instructor's Edition): 978-1-59194-296-2
ISBN-10 (Instructor's Edition): 1-59194-296-9

Send book orders and requests for desk copies or supplements to:
Townsend Press Book Center
439 Kelley Drive
West Berlin, New Jersey 08091

For even faster service, contact us in any of the following ways:
By telephone: 1-800-772-6410
By fax: 1-800-225-8894
By e-mail: cs@townsendpress.com
Through our website: www.townsendpress.com

To my competitors, for inspiring me to try harder.
May I do the same for you, and may all our students benefit.

Selections by Content Area

Contents

Preface: To the Instructor

We all know that many students entering college today do not have the reading skills needed to do effective work in their courses. A related problem, apparent even in class discussions, is that students often lack the skills required to think in a clear and logical way.

The purpose of *Ten Steps to Advanced Reading* is to develop effective reading and clear thinking. To do so, **Part One** presents a sequence of ten reading skills that are widely recognized as essential for basic and advanced comprehension. The first five skills concern the more literal levels of comprehension:

- Recognizing main ideas
- Identifying supporting details
- Recognizing implied main ideas and the central point
- Understanding relationships that involve addition and time
- Understanding relationships that involve illustration, comparison and/or contrast, cause and/or effect, and problem and solution

The remaining skills cover more advanced, critical levels of comprehension:

- Making inferences
- Identifying an author's purpose and tone
- Evaluating arguments
- Separating fact from opinion, detecting propaganda, and recognizing errors in reasoning
- Using a study and notetaking system

In every chapter in Part One, the key aspects of a skill are explained and illustrated clearly and simply. Explanations are accompanied by a series of practices, and each chapter ends with two review tests. The second review test consists of a reading selection so that students can apply the skill just learned to real-world reading materials, including newspaper and magazine articles and textbook selections. Together, the ten chapters provide students with the skills needed for both basic and advanced reading comprehension.

Following each chapter in Part One are **six mastery tests for the skill in question**. The tests progress in difficulty, giving students the additional practice and challenge they may need for the solid learning of each skill. While designed for quick grading, the tests also require students to think carefully before answering each question.

Part Two is made up of ten additional reading selections that will improve both reading and thinking skills. Each selection is followed by *Reading Comprehension Questions* so that students can practice all ten skills presented in Part One. Each reading also includes *Discussion Questions* that engage students in a variety of thinking skills and deepen their understanding of a selection. In addition, for the first six readings, an activity titled *Active Reading and Study of a Textbook Selection* improves students' skill in learning and taking notes on textbook material. For the final four readings, an activity in *Outlining* or *Summarizing* helps students think carefully about the content and organization of a selection.

Part Three consists of a set of three relationships tests and a series of twenty-five combined-skills tests that review the skills in Part One and help students prepare for the standardized reading test that is often a requirement at the end of a semester.

Part Four provides tips that will help students deal effectively with science and mathematics courses and includes both a science and a math textbook selection.

The appendixes that follow include a pronunciation guide and a limited answer key as well as writing assignments for the twenty readings in Parts One and Two of the text. When time permits, asking students to write about a selection will help reinforce the reading and thinking skills they have practiced in the book.

Important Features of the Book

- ● **Focus on the basics.** The book is designed to explain, in a clear, step-by-step way, the essential elements of each skill. Many examples are provided to ensure that students understand each point. In general, the focus is on teaching the skills—not just on explaining or testing them.

- ● **Frequent practice and feedback.** Because abundant practice and careful feedback are essential to learning, this book includes numerous activities. Students can get immediate feedback on the practice exercises in Parts One and Four by turning to the limited answer key at the back of the book. The answers to the review and mastery tests in Part One, the reading questions in Part Two, and the relationships and combined-skills tests in Part Three are in the *Instructor's Manual*.

The limited answer key increases the active role that students take in their own learning. They are likely to use the answer key in an honest and positive way if they know they will be tested on the many activities and selections for which answers are not provided. (Answers not in the book can be easily copied from the *Instructor's Edition* or the *Instructor's Manual* and passed out at the teacher's discretion.)

● **High interest level.** Dull and unvaried readings and exercises work against learning. Students need to experience genuine interest and enjoyment in what they read. Teachers as well should be able to take pleasure in the selections, for their own good feeling can carry over favorably into class work. The readings in the book, then, have been chosen not only for the appropriateness of their reading level but also for their compelling content. They should engage teachers and students alike.

● **Ease of use.** The logical sequence in each chapter—from explanation to example to practice to review test to mastery test—helps make the skills easy to teach. The book's organization into distinct parts also makes for ease of use. Within a single class, for instance, teachers can work on a new skill in Part One, review other skills with one or more mastery tests, and provide variety by having students read one of the selections in Part Two. The limited answer key at the back of the text also makes for versatility: the teacher can assign some chapters for self-teaching. Finally, the mastery tests—each on its own tear-out page—and the combined-skills tests make it a simple matter for teachers to test and evaluate student progress.

● **Integration of skills.** Students do more than learn the skills individually in Part One. They also learn to apply the skills together through the reading selections in Parts One and Two as well as the combined-skills tests in Part Three. They become effective readers and thinkers through repeated practice in applying a combination of skills.

● **Integrated online resources.** Through the use of TP's acclaimed Learning Center, *Ten Steps to Advanced Reading,* 2/e, features powerful online components to enhance learning, including:

 1 **Web-based instructional videos.** The Learning Center hosts hands-on video lessons which provide students with introductions to each of the ten chapters in Part One.

 2 **Online practice exercises and mastery tests.** Each chapter of the book is supported by additional practice exercises and online versions of the book's mastery tests. These materials can be used to reinforce skills taught in the chapter or to assess students' learning.

3   **Helpful PowerPoint files.** A comprehensive collection of PowerPoint files covering the book's ten key chapters is available for immediate downloading.

4   **Downloadable supplements.** Electronic (PDF) versions of the instructor's manual and test bank can be downloaded directly from the Learning Center. These files give you the resources you need whenever and wherever you are—24 hours a day.

5   **Class management controls.** The Learning Center allows you to control which assignments and tests your students can access. It also allows you to create unique assignments for each class you teach, track students' progress, and simplify grading. To learn more, e-mail cs@townsendpress.com or visit the Learning Center at www.townsendpress.net.

● **Thinking activities.** Thinking activities—in the form of outlining, mapping, summarizing, and taking study notes—are a distinctive feature of the book. While educators agree that such organizational abilities are important, these skills are all too seldom taught. From a practical standpoint, it is almost impossible for a teacher to respond in detail to entire collections of class outlines, summaries, or study notes. This book then, presents activities that truly involve students in outlining, mapping, summarizing, and taking study notes—in other words, that truly make students *think*—and yet enable a teacher to give immediate feedback. Again, it is through continued practice and feedback on challenging material that a student becomes a more effective reader and thinker.

● **Supplementary materials.**

Print Supplements

The two helpful supplements listed below are available at no charge to instructors who have adopted the text. They can be obtained quickly by writing or calling Townsend Press (439 Kelley Drive, West Berlin, New Jersey 08091; 1-800-772-6410), by sending a fax to 1-800-225-8894, or by e-mailing Customer Service at cs@townsendpress.com.

1   An *Instructor's Edition*—chances are that you are holding it in your hand—is identical to the student book except that it also provides hints for teachers (see the front of the book), answers to all the practices and tests, and comments on selected items. *No other book on the market has such detailed and helpful annotations.*

2 A combined *Instructor's Manual and Test Bank* includes suggestions for teaching the course, a model syllabus, and readability levels for the text and the reading selections. The test bank contains four additional mastery tests for each of the ten skills and four additional combined-skills tests—all on letter-sized sheets so they can be copied easily for use with students.

Online Supplements

As indicated above, online supplements are available through the TP website by going to the "Supplements" area for instructors at **www.townsendpress.net**.

1 PowerPoint presentations.

2 Online exercises.

3 Instructional videos.

● **One of a sequence of books.** This is the most advanced text in a series that includes five other books.

> *Groundwork for College Reading with Phonics* and *Groundwork for College Reading* are the basic texts in the series. They are suitable for ESL students and basic adult learners.
>
> *Ten Steps to Building College Reading Skills* is often the choice for a first college reading course.
>
> *Ten Steps to Improving College Reading Skills* is an intermediate text appropriate for the core developmental reading course offered at most colleges.
>
> *Ten Steps to Advancing College Reading Skills* is a higher developmental text than the *Improving* book. It can be used as the core book for a more advanced class, as a sequel to the intermediate book, or as a second-semester alternative to it. *Ten Steps to Advanced Reading* can be used as a sequel or alternative to the *Advancing* book.
>
> A companion set of vocabulary books, listed on the copyright page, has been designed to go with the *Ten Steps* books. Recommended to accompany this book is *Advancing Vocabulary Skills* (300 words and word parts), *Advancing Vocabulary Skills, Short Version* (200 words), or *Advanced Word Power* (300 words).
>
> Together, the books and all their supplements form a sequence that should be ideal for any college reading program.

To summarize, *Ten Steps to Advanced Reading*, Second Edition, teaches and reinforces ten essential reading skills. Through an appealing collection of readings and a carefully designed series of activities and tests, students receive extensive guided practice in the skills. The result is an integrated approach to learning that will, by the end of a course, produce better readers and stronger thinkers.

Changes in the Second Edition

Following are changes in this edition of the book:

- **A full-color design.** Color has been carefully used throughout, not as window dressing but to add clarity and readability to the different parts of the book.

- **More cartoons and other graphics.** Because so many students today are visual learners, there are additional illustrations to help introduce or reinforce points made in the book.

- **Many new practice materials and readings.** The book includes **ten** new readings, and practice materials have been freshened throughout. For example, in Part Three there are now five additional "Combined-Skills Tests" as well as three new tests, each made up of twenty-five items, that give students additional practice in mastering relationships. (Such items are a common feature of such standardized tests as the College Board Accuplacer Placement Test.)

- **A greater variety of textbook selections.** Content areas include psychology, history, interpersonal communications, sociology, business, health, criminal justice, literature, speech, mathematics, biology, and anatomy and physiology. (See the list of all textbook selections on page vi, which faces the table of contents.)

- **Expanded online support.** See "Integrated online resources" on pages xi–xii.

Acknowledgments

I owe special thanks for the valuable input provided by Diane Schellack and Jennifer Martin of Burlington County College and by Joanne Nelson of Hillsborough Community College as I worked on this new edition.

At Townsend Press, I thank Kathryn Bernstein, Bill Blauvelt, Denton Cairnes, Beth Johnson, Paul Langan, Ruth A. Rouff, and Hal Taylor for the help they provided along the way. I particularly want to acknowledge two TP editors who once again have brought their special talents to this revision. Barbara Solot is responsible for a layout and full-color text design that are as clear as they are inviting. The result of her artistry is a strikingly attractive book that both students and teachers will appreciate. Janet Goldstein has provided design input along with her usual peerless editorial skills. Her insights, coupled with her many years of classroom teaching, have strengthened the clarity and pedagogy of the book.

It is always a special pleasure to work with people who aspire toward excellence. With help from my colleagues in the teaching profession and at Townsend Press, I have been able to create a much better book than I could have managed on my own.

John Langan

Introduction

1 How to Become a Better Reader and Thinker

The chances are that you are not as good a reader as you should be to do well in college. If so, it's not surprising. You live in a culture where people watch an average of *over seven hours of television every day!!!* All that passive viewing does not allow much time for reading. Reading is a skill that must be actively practiced. The simple fact is that people who do not read very often are not likely to be strong readers.

● How much TV do you guess you watch on an average day? _____

Another reason besides TV for not reading much is that you may have a lot of responsibilities. You may be going to school and working at the same time, and you may have a lot of family duties as well. Given a hectic schedule, you're not going to have much time to read. When you do have free time, you're exhausted, and it's easier to turn on the TV than to open up a book.

● Do you do any regular reading (for example, a daily newspaper, weekly

magazines, occasional novels)? _____

● When are you most likely to do your reading? _____

A third reason for not reading is that school may have caused you to associate reading with worksheets and drills and book reports and test scores. Experts agree that many schools have not done a good job of helping students discover the pleasures and rewards of reading. If reading was an unpleasant experience in school, you may have concluded that reading in general is not for you.

● Do you think that school made you dislike reading, rather than enjoy it?

_____

_____

Here are three final questions to ask yourself:

- Do you feel that perhaps you don't need a reading course, since you "already know how to read"? _____

- If you had a choice, would you be taking a reading course? (It's okay to be honest.) _____

- Do you think that a bit of speed reading may be all you need? _____

Chances are that you don't need to read *faster* as much as you need to read *smarter*. And it's a safe bet that if you don't read much, you can benefit enormously from the reading course in which you are using this book.

One goal of the book is to help you become a better reader. You will learn and practice ten key reading comprehension skills. As a result, you'll be better able to read and understand the many materials in your other college courses. The skills in this book have direct and practical value: they can help you perform better and more quickly—giving you an edge for success—in all of your college work.

The book is also concerned with helping you become a stronger thinker, a person able not just to *understand* what is read but to *analyze* and *evaluate* it as well. In fact, reading and thinking are closely related skills, and practice in thoughtful reading will also strengthen your ability to think clearly and logically. To find out just how the book will help you achieve these goals, read the next several pages and do the brief activities as well. The activities are easily completed and will give you a quick, helpful overview of the book.

How the Book Is Organized

The book is organized into six parts:

Introduction (pages 1–19)

In addition to this first section, "How to Become a Better Reader and Thinker," which will give you a good sense of the book, there are three other parts to the introduction. The second part, "Some Quick Study Tips," presents four hints that can make you a better student. If I had time to say just four things to incoming college students based on my thirty years of teaching experience, these are the things I would say. Turn to page 10 and then write, below, the second of these tips:

_____

_____

There is also a third section titled "Notes on Vocabulary in Context," which will review the importance of using context clues to figure out the meanings of unfamiliar words. And finally, there is a section titled "A Reading Challenge," which will give you a chance to earn some free books.

Part One: Ten Steps to Advanced Reading Skills (pages 21–408)

To help you become a more effective reader and thinker, this book presents a series of ten key reading skills. They are listed in the table of contents on pages vii and viii. Turn to those pages to fill in the skills missing below:

1 Main Ideas

2 _____

3 Implied Main Ideas
4 Relationships I

5 _____

6 Inferences
7 Purpose and Tone

8 _____

9 Critical Reading
10 Active Reading and Study

Each chapter is developed in the same way:

First of all, clear explanations and examples help you *understand* each skill. Practices then give you the "hands-on" experience needed to *learn* the skill.

● How many practices are there for the first chapter, "Main Ideas" (pages 23–62)? _____

Closing each chapter are two review tests. The first review test provides a check of the information presented in the chapter.

● On which page is the first review test for "Main Ideas"? _____

The second review test consists of a story, essay, or textbook selection that both gets you reading and gives you practice in the skill learned in the chapter as well as skills learned in previous chapters.

● What is the title of the reading selection in the "Main Ideas" chapter?

_____

Following each chapter are six mastery tests which gradually increase in difficulty.

● On what pages are the mastery tests for the "Main Ideas" chapter? _____

The tests are on tear-out pages and so can be easily removed and handed in to your instructor. So that you can track your progress, there is a score box at the top of each test. Your score can also be entered into the "Reading Performance Chart" on the inside back cover of the book.

Part Two: Ten Reading Selections (pages 409–533)

The ten reading selections that make up Part Two are followed by activities that give you practice in all the skills studied in Part One. Each reading begins in the same way. Look, for example, at "Understand Your Nervousness," which starts on page 411. What are the headings of the two sections that come before the reading itself?

● _____

● _____

Note that the vocabulary words in "Words to Watch" are followed by the numbers of the paragraphs in which the words appear. Look at the first page of "Understand Your Nervousness" and explain how each vocabulary word is marked in the reading itself.

● _____

Activities Following Each Reading Selection

After each selection, there are three kinds of activities to improve the reading and thinking skills you learned in Part One of the book.

1 The first activity consists of **reading comprehension questions**—questions involving vocabulary in context, main ideas (including implied main ideas and the central point), supporting details, relationships, inferences, purpose and tone, argument, fact and opinion, propaganda devices, and logical thinking.

    ● Look at the reading comprehension questions for "Understand Your Nervousness" on pages 415–419. Note that the questions are labeled so you know which skill you are practicing in each case. How many questions deal with understanding vocabulary in context? _____

    ● How many questions deal with critical reading? _____

2 The second activity involves **outlining, summarizing,** or **taking study notes**. Each of these activities will sharpen your ability to get to the heart of a piece and to think logically and clearly about what you read.

- What kind of activity is provided for "Understand Your Nervousness" on pages 420–421? _____

- What kind of activity is provided for the reading titled "In My Day" on pages 519–520? _____

3 The third activity consists of **discussion questions**. These questions provide a chance for you to deepen your understanding of each selection.

- How many discussion questions are there for "Understand Your Nervousness" (page 422)—and indeed for every other reading? _____

Part Three: Relationships and Combined-Skills Tests (pages 535–606)

The first chapter in Part Three contains three tests that provide additional practice with the relationships you studied in Chapters 4 and 5.

- How many items are in each test? _____

The second chapter in Part Three consists of short passages that give you practice in all the reading skills taught in the book.

- How many such tests are there in all? _____

Part Four: Readings in Science and Mathematics (pages 607–628)

This part of the book presents tips that will help you do well in your science and math courses. It also contains a sample chapter in each of these fields.

- What is the title of the selection from a science textbook?

_____

Appendixes (pages 629–650)

Following Part Four are appendixes that include a pronunciation guide, a limited answer key, and writing assignments for all twenty of the reading selections in the book. Reading and writing are closely connected skills, and writing practice will improve your ability to read closely and to think carefully.

Helpful Features of the Book

1   The book centers on *what you really need to know* to become a better reader and thinker. It presents ten key comprehension skills and explains the most important points about each one.

2   The book gives you *lots of practice.* We seldom learn a skill only by hearing or reading about it; we make it part of us by repeated practice. There are, then, numerous activities in the text. They are not "busywork," but carefully designed materials that should help you truly learn each skill.

Notice that after you learn each skill in Part One, you progress to review tests and mastery tests that enable you to apply the skill. And as you move from one skill to the next, the reading selections help you practice and reinforce the skills already learned.

3   The selections throughout the book are *lively and appealing.* Dull and unvaried readings work against learning, so subjects have been carefully chosen for their high interest level. Almost all of the selections here are good examples of how what we read can capture our attention. For instance, if you, like many Americans, have some sleep problems, you will probably read with great interest the article from *Time* magazine on "Getting a Good Night's Sleep" (page 46). Or look at the textbook selection on page 385; its title, "Personal Conflict Styles," may seem unpromising, but you will be intrigued to compare the way you react to conflict with how other people react. Or read "A Civil War Soldier's Letter to His Wife" on page 502 and try not to shake your head and shed a tear at the heartbreak of war.

4   The readings include *thirteen selections from college textbooks.* Therefore, you will be practicing on materials very much like those in your other courses. Doing so will increase your chances of transferring what you learn in your reading class to your other college courses.

How to Use the Book

1   A good way to proceed is to read and review the explanations and examples in a given chapter in Part One until you feel you understand the ideas presented. Then carefully work through the practices. As you finish each one, check your answers with the "Limited Answer Key" that starts on page 645.

For your own sake, *don't just copy in the answers without trying to do the practices!* The only way to learn a skill is to practice it first and then use the answer key to give yourself feedback. Also, take whatever time is needed to figure out just why you got some answers wrong. By using the answer key to help teach yourself the skills, you will prepare yourself for the review and mastery tests at the end of each chapter as well as the other reading tests in the book. Your instructor can supply you with answers to those tests.

If you have trouble catching on to a particular skill, stick with it. In time, you will learn each of the ten skills.

2   Read the selections first with the intent of simply enjoying them. There will be time afterward for rereading each selection and using it to develop your comprehension skills.

3   Keep track of your progress. Fill in the charts at the end of each chapter in Part One and each reading in Part Two. And in the "Reading Performance Chart" on the inside back cover, enter your scores for all of the review and mastery tests as well as the reading selections. These scores can give you a good view of your overall performance as you work through the book.

In summary, *Ten Steps to Advanced Reading* has been designed to interest and benefit you as much as possible. Its format is straightforward, its explanations are clear, its readings are appealing, and its many practices will help you learn through doing. *It is a book that has been created to reward effort*, and if you provide that effort, you will make yourself a better reader and a stronger thinker. I wish you success.

John Langan

2 Some Quick Study Tips

While it's not my purpose in this book to teach study skills, I do want to give you four quick hints that can make you a better student. The hints are based on my thirty years of experience working with first-year college students and teaching reading and study skills.

 TIP 1   The most important steps you can take to succeed in school are to *go to every class* and *take a lot of notes*. If you don't go to class, or you go but just sit there without taking notes, chances are you're heading for a heap of trouble.

 TIP 2   Let me ask you a question: Which is more important—learning how to read a textbook or learning how to read your professor? Write your answer here:

_____

You may be surprised at the answer: What is far more important is learning how to read your professor—to understand what he or she expects you to learn in the course and to know for tests.

I remember becoming a good student in college only after I learned the truth of this statement. And I have interviewed hundreds of today's students who have said the same thing. Let me quote just one of them:

> *You absolutely have to be in class. Then you learn how to read the teacher and to know what he or she is going to want on tests. You could read an entire textbook, but that wouldn't be as good as being in class and writing down a teacher's understanding of ideas.*

TIP 3   Many teachers base their tests mainly on the ideas they present in class. But when you have to learn a textbook chapter, do the following:

First, read the first and last few paragraphs of the chapter; they may give you a good overview of what the chapter is about.

Second, as you read the chapter, look for and mark off definitions of key terms and examples of those definitions.

Third, as you read the chapter, number any lists of items; if there are series of points and you number them *1, 2, 3,* and so on, it will be easier to understand and remember them.

Fourth, after you've read the chapter, take notes on the most important material and test yourself on those notes until you can say them to yourself without looking at them.

TIP 4 **Here's another question: Are you an organized person?** Do you get out of bed on time, do you get to places on time, do you keep up with school work, do you allow time to study for tests and write papers?

If you are *not* an organized person, you're going to have trouble in school. Here are three steps to take to control your time:

First, pay close attention to the course outline, or *syllabus,* your instructors will probably pass out at the start of a semester. Chances are that syllabus will give you the dates of exams and tell you when papers or reports are due.

Second, move all those dates onto a *large monthly calendar*—a calendar that has a good-sized block of white space for each date. Hang the calendar in a place where you'll be sure to see it every day—perhaps above your desk or on a bedroom wall.

Third, buy a small notebook and write down every day a *"to do" list* of things that need to get done that day. Decide which items are most important, and focus on them first. (If you have classes that day, going to those classes will be "A" priority items.) Carry your list with you during the day, referring to it every so often and checking off items as you complete them.

Questions

1. Of the four hints listed above, which is the most important one for you? Why?

2. Which hint is the second most important for you, and why?

3. You may not realize just how quickly new information can be forgotten. For example, how much class material do you think most people forget in just two weeks? Check (✓) the answer you think is correct.

    _____ 20 percent is forgotten within two weeks

    _____ 40 percent is forgotten within two weeks

    _____ 60 percent is forgotten within two weeks

    _____ 80 percent is forgotten within two weeks

    The truth is that within two weeks most people forget almost 80 percent of what they have heard! Given that fact, what should you be sure to do in all your classes?

3 Notes on Vocabulary in Context

In this advanced reading skills book, there is no separate chapter on the skill of understanding vocabulary in context. Instead, this section will review the skill, and many of the readings in the book will include vocabulary-in-context questions.

Understanding vocabulary in context is an inference skill that most of us learn in the course of reading. For example, if you were asked to define the words *hyperbole*, *querulous*, and *surreptitious*, you might have some difficulty. On the other hand, if you saw these words in sentences, you might be able to infer their meanings by looking at the other words in the sentence.

See if you can define the words in *italics* in the three sentences below. In the space provided, write the letter of the meaning you think is correct in each case.

____ Marcella uses a lot of *hyperbole* to express herself: a restaurant is never just "good"—it's "the most fabulous food in the universe"; her boyfriend isn't just "good-looking"—he's "divine beyond belief."

Hyperbole (hī-pûr′bə-lē) means

A. overstatement.   B. compliment.   C. accuracy.

____ People who work in the complaint department of a store must get used to dealing with lots of *querulous* customers.

Querulous (kwĕr′ə-ləs) means

A. shaky.   B. dishonest.   C. dissatisfied.

____ Students naturally want to know what will be covered on a test. Instead of trying to find out by *surreptitious* means, it is often better to simply ask the instructor a direct question.

Surreptitious (sûr′əp-tĭsh′əs) means

A. straightforward.   B. useless.   C. secret.

In each sentence above, the *context*—the words surrounding the unfamiliar word—provides clues to the word's meaning. You may have guessed from the context that *hyperbole* means "overstatement," that *querulous* means "dissatisfied," and that *surreptitious* means "secret."

Using context clues to understand the meaning of unfamiliar words will help you save time when reading. You will not have to stop to look up words in the dictionary. (Of course, you won't always be able to understand a word from its context, so you should always have a dictionary nearby as you read.)

Types Of Context Clues

There are four common types of context clues:

1 Examples

2 Synonyms

3 Antonyms

4 General Sense of the Sentence or Passage

Following are brief practices that will give you a sense of each type of clue.

1 Examples

If you are given **examples** that relate to an unknown word, you can often figure out its meaning. For instance, note the examples in the sentence "Marcella uses a lot of *hyperbole* to express herself: a restaurant is never just 'good'—it's 'the most fabulous food in the universe'; her boyfriend isn't just 'good-looking'—he's 'divine beyond belief.'" The examples help you figure out that the word *hyperbole* means "overstatement."

Now read the items that follow. An *italicized* word in each sentence is followed by examples that serve as context clues for that word. These examples, which are in **boldfaced** type, will help you figure out the meaning of each word. On the answer line, write the letter of each meaning you think is correct.

Note that examples are often introduced with signal words and phrases like *for example, for instance, including,* and *such as.*

_C___ 1. Jean is a difficult roommate because her moods are so *volatile.* **One day she's on top of the world; the next day she's in the depths of despair.**

Volatile (vŏl′ə-tl) means
A. insensitive.   B. indirect.   C. changeable.

_B___ 2. The boss, a *parsimonious* man, **keeps the office lights dimmed, frowns upon coffee breaks, and seldom turns on the heating or air conditioning**.

Parsimonious (pär′sĭ-mō′nē-əs) means
A. mischievous.   B. stingy.   C. moody.

_____ 3. My father has a *voracious* appetite for news. **He gets two morning papers, listens to an "all news" program in the car, and watches CNN every night**.

Voracious (vô-rā′shəs) means
A. all-consuming.   B. small.   C. unconcerned.

In the first sentence, the examples show that *volatile* means "changeable." In the second sentence, the examples show that *parsimonious* means "stingy." Finally, the examples in the third sentence indicate that a *voracious* appetite is an "all-consuming" one.

2 Synonyms

Context clues are often found in the form of **synonyms**: one or more words that mean the same or almost the same as the unknown word. In the sentence "People who work in the complaint department of a store must get used to dealing with lots of querulous customers," the word *complaint* suggests that *querulous* must mean "complaining" or "dissatisfied." A synonym may appear anywhere in a sentence as a restatement of the meaning of the unknown word.

Each of the following items includes a word or phrase that is a synonym of the italicized word. Underline the synonym for each italicized word. Then, on the answer line, write the letter of each meaning you think is correct.

_____ 1. The heat wave *enervated* the kids. They were too tired to play outside.

Enervated (ĕn′ər-vā′tĭd) means
A. frightened.   B. exhausted.   C. awakened.

_____ 2. Children may believe they are the only ones who are happy to see summer vacation arrive, but their teachers feel *exuberant* also.

Exuberant (ĭg-zōō′bər-ənt) means
A. fearful.   B. bored.   C. overjoyed.

_____ 3. Larry always becomes *morose* when he drinks. Since alcohol makes him so dreary and blue, you'd think he'd give it up.

Morose (mə′rōs) means
A. confused.   B. frantic.   C. gloomy.

You should have underlined *tired* as a synonym for *enervated*, *happy* as a synonym for *exuberant*, and *dreary and blue* as synonyms for *morose*. These synonym clues tell you that *enervated* means "exhausted," *exuberant* means "overjoyed," and *morose* means "gloomy."

3 Antonyms

Antonyms—words and phrases that mean the opposite of a word—are also useful as context clues. Antonyms are sometimes signaled by words and phrases such as *however, but, yet, on the other hand,* and *in contrast.* In the sentences "Students naturally want to know what will be covered on a test. Instead of trying to find out by *surreptitious* means, it is often better to simply ask the instructor a direct question," the antonym *direct* helps you figure out the meaning of *surreptitious.*

In each of the following sentences, underline the word or phrase that means the *opposite* of the italicized word. Then, on the answer line, write the letter of the meaning of the italicized word.

_____ 1. Who says that cats and dogs are enemies? Our dog and two cats live together in the most *amicable* way.

Amicable (ăm′ĭ-kə-bəl) means
A. hostile. B. friendly. C. cute.

_____ 2. I enjoyed the speaker's easygoing, *colloquial* style. She made the topic more interesting than a stiff, formal speaker could have done.

Colloquial (kə-lō′kwē-əl) means
A. deceptive. B. unclear. C. informal.

_____ 3. The two women who were waiting to hear the results of their mammograms were quite different. One was a bundle of nerves while the other seemed quite *placid.*

Placid (plăs′ĭd) means
A. tense. B. untroubled. C. sad.

In the first sentence, the opposite of *amicable* creatures is *enemies;* thus *amicable* means "friendly." In the second sentence, *colloquial* is the opposite of *stiff* and *formal*, so *colloquial* means "informal." Last, someone who is "a bundle of nerves" is the opposite of someone who is placid, so *placid* means "untroubled."

4 General Sense of the Sentence or Passage

Sometimes it takes a bit more detective work to puzzle out the meaning of an unfamiliar word. In such cases, you must draw conclusions based on the information given.

By considering carefully the general sense of each of the following sentences, see if you can decide what the italicized word means in each case.

_____ 1. The students asked if they could use their notes during the test. They were pleased when the teacher *acquiesced.*

Acquiesced (ăk′wē-ĕst′) means
A. consented. B. refused. C. was puzzled.

_____ 2. A person suspected of a crime has the *prerogative* of refusing to answer questions unless his or her lawyer is present.

Prerogative (prĭ-rŏg′ə-tĭv) means
A. choice.   B. duty.   C. belief.

_____ 3. An introductory music course in college can *engender* a lifelong love of music.

Engender (ĕn-jĕn′dər) means
A. endanger.   B. complete.   C. begin.

The first sentence provides enough evidence for you to guess that *acquiesced* means "consented." *Prerogative* in the second sentence means "choice." And *engender* means "begin." (You may not hit on the exact dictionary definition of a word by using context clues, but you will often be accurate enough to make good sense of what you are reading.)

An Important Point about Textbook Definitions

You don't always have to use context clues or the dictionary to find definitions. Very often, textbook authors provide definitions of important terms. They usually follow a definition with one or more examples to ensure that you understand the word being defined. Moreover, they may set off their definitions in *italic* or **boldfaced** type. When an author takes the time to define and illustrate a word, you can generally assume that the material is important enough to learn.

More about textbook definitions and examples appears on pages 178–180 in the "Relationships II" chapter.

4 A Reading Challenge

It's no secret. Reading reseachers, teachers and people with common sense everywhere know that the best way to become a better reader is to do a lot of reading. Here's why:

1. **Reading provides language power.** Research has shown *beyond any question* that frequent reading improves vocabulary, spelling, and reading speed and comprehension, as well as grammar and writing style. If you become a regular reader, all of these language and thinking abilities develop almost automatically!

2. **Reading increases job power.** In today's world more than ever before, jobs involve the processing of information, with words being the tools of the trade. Studies have found that the better your command of words, the more success you are likely to have. *Nothing will give you a command of words like regular reading.*

3. **Reading creates human power.** Reading enlarges the mind and the heart. It frees us from the narrow confines of our own experience. Knowing how other people view important matters helps us decide what we ourselves think and feel. Reading also helps us connect with others and realize our shared humanity. Someone once wrote, "We read in order to know that we are not alone." We become less isolated as we share the common experiences, emotions, and thoughts that make us human. We grow more sympathetic and understanding because we realize that others are like us.

With all the above in mind, Townsend Press is going to offer you a reading challenge. Send us $50. We will then send you the 40 paperback books shown on the next page, with no charge for shipping or handling. Read all 40 books and then email us at **cs@townsendpress.com**. We'll send you a toll-free phone number you can use to speak to a person on our staff, who will ask you questions to confirm that you've really read the books. If you've read all 40, we'll return your $50 and award you an Advanced Reading Achievement Certificate.

What happens if you read just 5 or 10 or so of the 40 books? You will have the benefit of having read those books, and you have a lot of good paperbacks in your house to eventually read yourself or to give to others. One of the best ways to clutter up your living space is with a lot of books.

To get the 40 books, you must currently be taking a college reading course. You must tear out **this original page** (a copy will not do) and send it with the completed order form below. You must then call us no later than three months after completing the course.

ORDER FORM

YES! Please send me the 40 books pictured. Enclosed is fifty dollars to cover the cost of shipping and handling and to partly offset the cost of the books.

Please PRINT the following very clearly. It will be your shipping label.

Name _____

Address _____

City _____ *State* _____ *Zip* _____

Please provide the following information as well:

My school _____

Title of the reading course I am currently taking _____

Name of my instructor _____

MAIL TO:
Townsend Press Book Center, 439 Kelley Drive, West Berlin, NJ 08091.

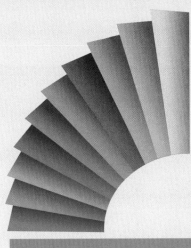

Part One

Ten Steps to Advanced Reading Skills

1 Main Ideas

What Is the Main Idea?

"You're a terrible pet owner. You keep me on a chain, you make me eat on the floor, and you never let me go out in public alone."

"What's the point?" You've probably heard these words before. It's a question people ask when they want to know the main idea that someone is trying to express. The same question can guide you as you read. Recognizing the **main idea**, or point, is the most important key to good comprehension. Sometimes a main idea is immediately clear, as in the above cartoon. The point—that the man is a terrible pet owner—is vividly supported by the dog's reasons: the dog is kept on a chain, must eat on the floor, and is never allowed out in public alone.

To find a point in a reading selection, ask yourself, "What's the main point the author is trying to make?" For instance, read the paragraph on the following page, asking yourself as you do, "What is the author's point?"

[1]Social psychologists have found that almost everyone gossips. [2]Male or female, young or old, blue-collar or professional, humans love to talk about one another. [3]All too often, such gossip is viewed as a frivolous waste of time. [4]However, it actually serves several important functions in the human community. [5]For one thing, gossip is a form of networking. [6]Talking with our friends and coworkers about each other is our most effective means of keeping track of the ever-changing social dynamic. [7]It tells us who is in, who is out, and who can help us climb the social or professional ladder. [8]A second function of gossip is the building of influence. [9]When we engage in gossip, we are able to shape people's opinions of ourselves. [10]We tell stories that show ourselves in a good light—wise, compassionate, insightful, clever. [11]And when we listen sympathetically to the gossip of other people, they perceive us as warm and likable. [12]A final and very powerful function of gossip is the creating of social alliances. [13]There are few quicker ways to form a bond with another person than to share private information with him or her. [14]The words "I wouldn't tell most people this, but . . ." instantly interest and flatter the listener. [15]To talk about a third party, especially in a critical way, creates a bond with our listener and gives a feeling of shared superiority.

A good way to find an author's point, or main idea, is to look for a general statement. Then decide if that statement is supported by most of the other material in the paragraph. If it is, you have found the main idea.

✔ Check Your Understanding

Following are four statements from the passage. Pick out the general statement that is supported by the other material in the passage. Write the letter of that statement in the space provided. Then read the explanation that follows.

Four statements from the passage

A. Social psychologists have found that almost everyone gossips.

B. However, it [gossip] actually serves several important functions in the human community.

C. For one thing, gossip is a form of networking.

D. There are few quicker ways to form a bond with another person than to share private information with him or her.

The general statement that expresses the main idea of the passage is _____.

Explanation

Sentence A: Only the second sentence supports the idea that everyone gossips—not the entire paragraph. While sentence A cannot be the main idea, it does introduce the topic of the paragraph: gossip.

Sentence B: The statement "However, it [gossip] actually serves several important functions in the human community," is a general one. And the rest of the passage goes on to describe three important functions of gossip. Sentence B, then, is the sentence that expresses the main idea of the passage.

Sentence C: This sentence refers only to the first function of gossip. It is not general enough to include the other two functions that are cited in the paragraph.

Sentence D: This sentence simply provides a detail that supports the third function of gossip. It does not cover the other material in the paragraph.

The Main Idea as an "Umbrella" Idea

Think of the main idea as an "umbrella" idea. The main idea is the author's general point; all the other material of the paragraph fits under it. That other material is made up of **supporting details**—specific evidence such as examples, causes, reasons, or facts. The diagram below shows the relationship.

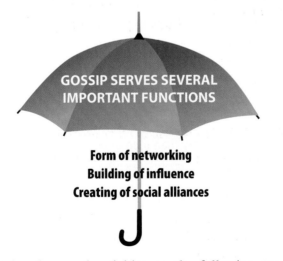

GOSSIP SERVES SEVERAL IMPORTANT FUNCTIONS

Form of networking
Building of influence
Creating of social alliances

The explanations and activities on the following pages will deepen your understanding of the main idea.

Recognizing a Main Idea

As you read through a passage, you must **think as you read**. If you merely take in words, you will come to the end of the passage without understanding much of what you have read. Reading is an active process, as opposed to watching television, which is passive. You must actively engage your mind, and, as you read, keep asking yourself, "What's the point?"

Here are three strategies that will help you find the main idea:

1 Look for general versus specific ideas.

2 Use the topic to lead you to the main idea.

3 Use key words to lead you to the main idea.

Each strategy is explained on the following pages.

1   Look for General versus Specific Ideas

You saw in the paragraph on gossip that the main idea is a *general* idea supported by *specific* ideas. The following practices will improve your skill at separating general from specific ideas. Learning how to tell the difference between general and specific ideas will help you locate the main idea.

> **PRACTICE 1**

In each of the following groups—many based on textbook selections—one statement is the general point, and the other statements are specific support for the point. Identify each point with a **P** and each statement of support with an **S**.

Example

_S_ Women are less likely than men to become full professors.

_S_ Women who become professors are generally paid less than their male counterparts.

_P_ Women often face discrimination in the field of education.

_S_ Female professors are not given an equal number of important committee assignments.

(The third statement is the general idea. It is supported by three examples of discrimination against women.)

1. ___ A. Lottery winners have been known to use their winnings to feed their addictions to gambling and/or drugs.

   ___ B. Other lottery winners report squandering their money to help out a never-ending stream of "hard luck" relatives and friends.

   ___ C. Some lottery winners invest large sums on business ventures they know nothing about and wind up losing all they have invested.

   ___ D. Winning the lottery can create as many problems as it solves.

2. ___ A. People like to interact with other people as they shop.

   ___ B. People like to see, touch, try on, and sometimes even smell the items they intend to buy.

   ___ C. Many people still use shopping as simply an excuse to get out of the house.

   ___ D. Despite its growing popularity, Internet shopping will never entirely replace shopping in stores.

3. ___ A. For much of the 1900s, people regarded cancer as a death sentence.

   ___ B. Attitudes toward cancer used to be very different from those of today.

   ___ C. Few people with cancer were willing to speak openly about battling the disease.

   ___ D. Many people thought that having cancer was contagious.

4. ___ A. Instead of simply offering printed material on loan, modern libraries now allow patrons to borrow CDs, videos, and DVDs.

   ___ B. Even very small libraries now provide computers, which patrons may use to access the Internet.

   ___ C. Libraries have changed drastically in the past decade to keep up with the demands of an ever-changing society.

   ___ D. Some libraries even feature refreshment stands that sell beverages and snacks.

5. ___ A. By age 14, 81 percent of young people have tried drinking.

   ___ B. By the time they graduate from high school, more than 43 percent of teenagers have experimented with illegal drugs.

   ___ C. In the United States, teenage drug and alcohol use is especially common.

   ___ D. About one-third of teenagers who have tried illegal drugs have also tried at least one highly addictive and toxic substance, such as cocaine or heroin.

6. ____ A. Female wigs sometimes rose as much as two and a half feet, making the average wearer roughly seven and a half feet tall.

____ B. Wigs were so valuable that people often willed them to their descendants.

____ C. When traveling, women wearing large wigs often had to sit on the floor of their carriages or ride with their heads sticking out of the windows.

____ D. In the 1700s, it was considered the height of fashion among the European upper classes to wear elaborate wigs.

7. ____ A. Many infant girls are given up for adoption by couples in other countries.

____ B. The traditional Chinese preference for boys, coupled with that country's "one child" policy, has led to some disturbing consequences.

____ C. Other infant girls are not given adequate medical care.

____ D. The development of ultrasound technology to determine a child's gender prior to birth has led to the death by abortion of hundreds of thousands of unborn Chinese girls.

8. ____ A. Before Abraham Lincoln was nominated for president, he provided material for a biography that helped to solidify his image as "Honest Abe, the rail-splitter."

____ B. A number of presidential candidates have written or co-written books in order to bypass the press and speak directly to voters, giving their viewpoint about events and policies.

____ C. John F. Kennedy's *Profiles in Courage*, which won the 1955 Pulitzer Prize for biography, helped Kennedy impress voters as a high-minded public servant.

____ D. *The Audacity of Hope* and *Dreams from My Father* introduced a little-known candidate named Barack Obama to the American public.

9. ____ A. The number of Category 4 and Category 5 hurricanes has nearly doubled in the past three decades, fulfilling some scientists' predictions that global warming will lead to more severe weather.

____ B. There is growing evidence that global warming is real.

____ C. In the past 100-plus years of record-keeping, eight of the ten hottest years have occurred since 1996.

____ D. According to scientists who study the movement of fields of ice, the ice surrounding the North Pole has entered a state of accelerating, long-term decline.

10. ___ A. The separation stage involves the removal of the individual from his or her former status.

___ B. The third stage is the rite of aggregation, which is the readmission of the individual into society in the newly acquired status.

___ C. Rites of passage, which mark the transition of an individual from one stage of life to another, involve three crucial stages.

___ D. The rite of marginality is a period of transition involving specific rituals and often suspension from normal social contact.

2 Use the Topic to Lead You to the Main Idea

You already know that to find the main idea of a selection, you look first for a general statement. You then check to see if that statement is supported by most of the other material in the paragraph. If it is, you've found the main idea. Another approach that can help you find the main idea of a selection is to find its topic.

The **topic** is the general subject of a selection. It can often be expressed in one or more words. Knowing the topic can help you find a writer's main point about that topic.

Textbook authors use the title of each chapter to state the overall topic of that chapter. They also provide many topics and subtopics in boldface headings within the chapter. For example, here is the title of a chapter in a sociology textbook, followed by a topic within the chapter and subtopics under that topic:

Socialization (29 pages)

    Agents of Socialization

        The Family

        The Neighborhood

        Religion

        Day Care

        The School

        Peer Groups

If you were studying the above chapter, you could use the headings to help find the main ideas—one of which is that there are six different agents of socialization.

But there are many times when you are not given topics—with standardized reading tests, for example, or with individual paragraphs in articles or textbooks. To find the topic of a selection when the topic is not given, ask this simple question:

Who or what is the selection about?

For example, look again at the beginning of the paragraph that started this chapter:

> [1]Social psychologists have found that almost everyone gossips. [2]Male or female, young or old, blue-collar or professional, humans love to talk about one another. [3]All too often, such gossip is viewed as a frivolous waste of time.

What, in a phrase, is the above paragraph about? On the line below, write what you think is the topic.

Topic: _____

You probably answered that the topic is "gossip." As you reread the paragraph, you saw that, in fact, every sentence in it is about gossip.

The next step after finding the topic is to decide what main point the author is making about the topic. Authors often present their main idea in a single sentence. (This sentence is also known as the **main idea sentence** or the **topic sentence**.) As we have already seen, the main point about gossip is "it actually serves several important functions in the human community."

✔ ## Check Your Understanding

Let's look now at another paragraph. Read it and then see if you can answer the questions that follow.

> [1]Since 1883, most American schools have used the A–F grading system. [2]But many experts believe that the current letter grading system is bad for students. [3]One problem is that letter grades are too simplistic. [4]A student who gets feedback in the form of a letter may not understand how to improve. [5]An "A" doesn't tell a student what she did right, nor does an "F" tell a student what she did wrong. [6]Another flaw is that schools and teachers are inconsistent in their use of letter grades. [7]An "A" might be easy to get at one school and very difficult to get at another school. [8]It is not fair to give students the same grade for different amounts of work. [9]Finally, grades may be inaccurate, with some teachers giving good marks because they don't want to hurt their students' feelings or because they want to help students improve their self-esteem. [10]This sends a confusing message to students who don't do their work. [11]It is also unfair to the students who actually try hard to earn good grades.

1. What is the *topic* of the paragraph? In other words, what is the paragraph about? (It often helps as you read to look for and even circle a word, term, or idea that is repeated in the paragraph.)

   _____

2. What is the *main idea* of the paragraph? In other words, what point is the author making about the topic? (Remember that the main idea will be supported by the other material in the paragraph.)

_____

Explanation

As the first sentence of the paragraph suggests, the topic is "the A–F grading system." As you continue to read the paragraph, you see that, in fact, everything in it is about this grading system. And the main idea is clearly that "the current letter grading system is bad for students." This idea is a general one that sums up what the entire paragraph is about. It is an "umbrella" statement under which all the other material in the paragraph fits. The parts of the paragraph could be shown as follows:

Topic: A–F grading system

Main idea: The current letter grading system is bad for students.

Supporting details:
1. Too simplistic.
2. Used inconsistently.
3. Inaccurate.

PRACTICE 2

The following practice will sharpen your sense of the difference between a topic, the point about the topic (the main idea), and supporting details.

Read each paragraph below and do the following:

1 Ask yourself, "What seems to be the topic of the paragraph?" (It often helps to look for and even circle a word or idea that is repeated in the paragraph.)

2 Next, ask yourself, "What point is the writer making about this topic?" This will be the main idea. It is stated in one of the sentences in the paragraph.

3 Then test what you think is the main idea by asking, "Is this statement supported by most of the other material in the paragraph?"

> *Hint:* When looking for the topic, make sure you do not pick one that is either **too broad** (covering a great deal more than is in the selection) or **too narrow** (covering only part of the selection). The topic and the main idea of a selection must include everything in that selection—no more and no less.

Paragraph 1

¹Halloween is often associated with ancient, pagan festivals or with the Catholic observance of All Saint's Day. ²But the truth is that Halloween as we celebrate it today is mostly an American invention. ³The Irish and Scottish, who may have first observed the holiday, didn't even carve pumpkins before coming to the United States. ⁴Because the pumpkin is an American fruit, they carved their jack-o'-lanterns only out of turnips and potatoes. ⁵So it wasn't until immigrants brought the holiday to the United States around 1840 that scary, glowing orange faces became a regular sight on Halloween. ⁶Observers of Halloween didn't dress up in scary costumes, either, until the holiday had been American for over sixty years. ⁷That practice originated around 1900, when communities started organizing costume parties to prevent children from taking part in the vandalism that was then the tradition. ⁸Before 1900, people were more likely to see children tipping over outhouses than walking around in costumes on Halloween. ⁹Finally, even "trick-or-treating" was an American invention. ¹⁰It was the Boy Scouts of America who popularized the practice in the 1930s, as an even more appealing alternative to getting into mischief. ¹¹Many Americans might be surprised to learn that their own grandparents were some of the first people in history to go door-to-door asking for candy on Halloween.

1. What is the *topic* of the paragraph? In other words, what (in one or more words) is the paragraph about? __Halloween__

__2__ 2. What *point* is the writer making about the topic? In other words, which sentence states the *main idea* of the paragraph? In the space provided, write the number of the sentence containing the main idea.

Paragraph 2

¹The American criminal justice system is often unjust. ²Many of the poor spend months awaiting trial, while those with money are able to use bonds to secure their release. ³Defense attorneys encourage plea bargaining or pleading guilty (whether or not one committed the crime) in return for being charged with a lesser offense. ⁴Judges dislike "unnecessary trials," and they impose harsher sentences on those who insist on going to trial. ⁵Judges also have biases which influence their sentencing. ⁶Factors that have nothing to do with the offense, but which affect sentencing, include age, employment, and the number of previous arrests. ⁷Even when the offense is the same, older defendants receive more lenient sentences, as do those with higher-status jobs and those with a better employment history.

1. What is the *topic* of the paragraph? __Criminal justice system is unfair__

due friday

___1___ 2. What *point* is the writer making about the topic? In the space provided, write the number of the sentence containing the main idea.

Paragraph 3

¹The ability to empathize seems to exist in a rudimentary form in even the youngest children. ²Research sponsored by the National Institute of Mental Health revealed what many parents know from experience: Virtually from birth, infants become visibly upset when they hear another baby crying, and children who are a few months old cry when they observe another child in tears. ³Young children have trouble distinguishing others' distress from their own. ⁴If, for example, one child hurts his finger, another baby might put her own finger into her mouth as if she were feeling pain. ⁵Researchers report cases in which children who see their parents in tears wipe their own eyes, even though they might not be crying.

1. What is the *topic* of the paragraph? Children can feel each others pain.

___2___ 2. What *point* is the writer making about the topic? In the space provided, write the number of the sentence containing the main idea.

Paragraph 4

¹Popular during the 1950s, the drive-in movie disappeared for a number of reasons. ²The most important was land value. ³Drive-ins were built on undeveloped edges of cities and towns. ⁴When these areas expanded in the 1960s and 1970s, it didn't make sense for a business used only after dark and mostly in warm weather to take up valuable space. ⁵Drive-ins were replaced by industrial parks, tract housing, and shopping malls with indoor theaters. ⁶Another reason was daylight savings time, which became standardized in most areas by the late 1960s. ⁷Theaters had to synchronize their first show with the setting sun. ⁸In the summer, they couldn't get started until nine o'clock, too late for families that had to get up early. ⁹Also, moviegoers began to expect more sophisticated projection and sound than those offered by drive-ins. ¹⁰Furthermore, people lost interest in drive-ins for family entertainment as movies became more violent and sexually explicit. ¹¹The last of the drive-ins vanished when cable television and VCRs came on the scene. ¹²People could now see recent movies without leaving their homes.

1. What is the *topic* of the paragraph? drive-ins movies

___5___ 2. What *point* is the writer making about the topic? In the space provided, write the number of the sentence containing the main idea.

3   Find and Use Key Words to Lead You to the Main Idea

Sometimes authors make it fairly easy to find their main idea. They announce it by using **key words**—verbal clues that are easy to recognize. First to note are **list words**, which tell you a list of items is to follow. For example, the main idea in the paragraph about gossip was stated like this: "However, it actually serves several important functions in the human community." The expression *several important functions* helps you zero in on your target: the main idea. You realize that the paragraph will be about specific functions of gossip.

Here are examples of some common word groups that often announce a main idea. Note that each of them contains a word that ends in *s*—a plural that suggests the supporting details will be a list of items.

Stated main idea

explicited main idea

List Words

several **kinds** (or **ways**) of	several **causes** of	some **factors** in
three **advantages** of	five **steps**	among the **results**
various **reasons** for	a number of **effects**	a **series** of

When expressions like these appear in a sentence, look carefully to see if that sentence might be the main idea. Chances are a sentence containing list words will be followed by a list of major supporting details.

> *Note* Many other list-word expressions are possible. For example, a writer could begin a paragraph with a sentence containing "four kinds of" or "some advantages of" or "three reasons for." So if you see a sentence with a word group like the ones above, you've probably found the main idea.

✓ Check Your Understanding

Underline the **list words** in the following sentences.

> *Hint:* Remember that list words usually contain a word that ends in *s*.

Example   Children become unpopular for <u>several common reasons</u>.

1. Researchers have identified two factors that play a significant role in our dreams.

2. Several steps can help you overcome the fear of speaking and become an effective speaker.

3. Three key differences exist between the House and the Senate.

4. Money is a strong priority for people—even for those with plenty of it—for a number of reasons.   ← *cause + effect*

5. There are four ways that we often express our thoughts by body language rather than by speaking.

Explanation

You should have underlined the following groups of words: *two factors, Several steps, Three key differences, a number of reasons,* and *four ways.*

In addition to list words, <u>addition words can alert you to the main idea.</u> **Addition words** are generally used right before supporting details. When you see this type of clue, you can assume that the detail it introduces fits under <u>the umbrella of a main idea.</u>

Here are some of the addition words that often <u>introduce supporting details and help you discover the main idea.</u>

major supporting details

Addition Words

one	to begin with	also	further
first (of all)	for one thing	in addition	furthermore
second(ly)	other	next	last (of all)
third(ly)	another	moreover	final(ly)

✓ *Check Your Understanding*

Reread the paragraph about gossip, underlining the **addition words** that alert you to supporting details.

¹Social psychologists have found that almost everyone gossips. ²Male or female, young or old, blue-collar or professional, humans love to talk about one another. ³All too often, such gossip is viewed as a frivolous waste of time. ⁴However, it actually serves several important functions in the human community. ⁵For one thing, gossip is a form of networking. ⁶Talking with our friends and coworkers about each other is our most effective means of keeping track of the ever-changing social dynamic. ⁷It tells us who is in, who is out, and who can help us climb the social or professional ladder. ⁸A second function of gossip is the building of influence. ⁹When we engage in gossip, we are able to shape people's opinions of ourselves. ¹⁰We tell stories that show ourselves in a good light—wise, compassionate, insightful, clever. ¹¹And when we listen sympathetically to the gossip of other people, they perceive us as warm and likable. ¹²A final and very powerful function of gossip is the creating of social alliances. ¹³There are few quicker ways to form a bond with another person than to share private information with him or her. ¹⁴The words "I wouldn't tell most people this, but . . ." instantly interest and flatter the listener. ¹⁵To talk about a third party, especially in a critical way, creates a bond with our listener and gives a feeling of shared superiority.

Explanation

The words that introduce each new supporting detail for the main idea are *For one thing*, *second*, and *final*. These addition words introduce each of the three functions of gossip.

Note also that the main idea includes the list words *several important functions*, which signal that the supporting details will be a list of the functions of gossip. In this and many paragraphs, list words and addition words often work hand in hand.

The following chapter, "Supporting Details," includes further information about words that alert you to the main idea and the details that support it. But what you have already learned here will help you find main ideas.

Locations of the Main Idea

Now you know how to recognize a main idea by 1) distinguishing between the general and the specific, 2) identifying the topic of a passage, and 3) using verbal clues. You are ready to find the main idea no matter where it is located in a paragraph.

A main idea may appear at any point within a paragraph. Very commonly, it shows up at the beginning, as either the first or the second sentence. However, main ideas may also appear further within a paragraph or even at the very end.

Main Idea at the Beginning

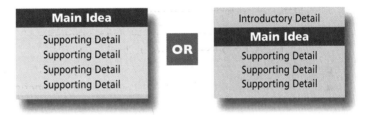

In textbooks, it is very common for the main idea to be either the first or the second sentence of a paragraph.

See if you can underline the main idea in the following paragraph.

> [1]As a result of more than sixty years of election surveys, we now know a great deal about American voters. [2]The wealthier and more educated they are, the more likely people are to support Republican candidates. [3]Men are a bit more likely to vote for Republicans, while women slightly favor Democrats. [4]African Americans vote for Democrats by a margin of more than four to one. [5]For generations, Catholics voted for Democrats, and Protestants (outside the South) favored Republicans; but today, Catholics and Protestants have similar party preferences, and Southern voters have swung from the Democrats to the Republicans. [6]But perhaps the most significant fact has to do with the general lack of interest in politics. [7]Most Americans say politics is not an important part of their lives. [8]Less than 50 percent of Americans bothered to vote in the fall 2010 elections.

In this paragraph, the main idea is in the *first* sentence. All the following sentences in the paragraph provide details about American voters.

Check Your Understanding

Now read the following paragraph and see if you can underline its main idea:

> ¹Today, most people in the Western world use a fork to eat. ²But before the 1700s, using a fork was highly discouraged. ³Most people in Europe ate with their hands. ⁴People from the upper class used three fingers, while the commoners ate with five. ⁵When an inventor from Tuscany created a miniature pitchfork for eating, Europeans thought that it was a strange utensil. ⁶Men who used a fork were often ridiculed and considered feminine. ⁷Priests called out against the fork, claiming that only human hands were worthy to touch the food God had blessed them with. ⁸One wealthy noblewoman shocked clergymen by eating with a fork she designed herself. ⁹Over dinner, they accused her of being too excessive. ¹⁰When the woman died from the plague a few days later, the priests claimed her death was a punishment from the heavens. ¹¹They warned others that using a fork could bring them the same fate.

Explanation

In the above paragraph, the main idea is stated in the *second* sentence. The first sentence introduces the topic, using a fork, but it is the idea in the second sentence—that before the 1700s, using a fork was highly discouraged—that is supported in the rest of the paragraph. So keep in mind that the first sentence may simply introduce or lead into the main idea of a paragraph.

> *Hint:* Very often, a contrast word like *however, but, yet,* or *though* signals the main idea, as in the paragraph you have just read.

Main Idea in the Middle

The main idea at times appears in the middle of a paragraph.

✓ *Check Your Understanding*

Here is an example of a paragraph in which the main idea is somewhere in the middle. Try to find it and underline it. Then read the explanation that follows.

> ¹Each year, as days grow shorter and nights grow colder, animals take action to survive the winter. ²Many animals fly, swim, or walk hundreds or thousands of miles to the south in search of a warm winter home. ³Earthworms travel too slowly to make a long journey to warmer regions. ⁴But they will die if they get trapped in the frozen ground. ⁵To survive a brutal winter, earthworms practice vertical migration. ⁶They move from dirt that's close to the surface to dirt that's deeper down. ⁷Each fall, the same instinct that sends geese flying south causes earthworms to start moving downward. ⁸As little barbs that stick out of their bodies poke into the dirt, the earthworms contract their muscles. ⁹This moves them downward to a point where they're below the soil that will freeze in the winter. ¹⁰Only after winter passes and soil overhead warms up to 36 degrees or more do the earthworms tunnel back upward.

Explanation

If you thought the fifth sentence gives the main idea, you were correct. The first four sentences introduce the topic of migrating for the winter and the challenge faced by earthworms. The fifth sentence then presents the writer's main idea, which is that earthworms practice vertical migration. The rest of the paragraph develops that idea.

Main Idea at the End

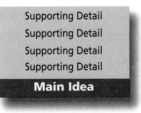

Supporting Detail
Supporting Detail
Supporting Detail
Supporting Detail
Main Idea

Sometimes all the sentences in a paragraph will lead up to the main idea, which is presented at the end. Here is an example of such a paragraph.

¹Throughout history, a pinch of arsenic has been known as the weapon of choice for murderers who wished to discreetly do away with their victims. ²Yet, in 1910, scientists created a compound containing a microscopic amount of arsenic that became the first effective remedy for the treatment of syphilis. ³Today it remains an effective chemotherapy agent for acute forms of leukemia. ⁴Botulinum toxin is another potent poison. ⁵But in extremely diluted form, delivered as the drug Botox, it has proven effective in softening wrinkles, relieving migraine headaches, and lessening the spastic contractions caused by multiple sclerosis and cerebral palsy. ⁶These are but two examples of the medical maxim that the difference between a substance being a poison or a medicine lies in the dosage.

Main Idea at the Beginning and the End

At times an author may choose to state the main idea near the beginning of the paragraph and then emphasize it (as a conclusion) by restating it in other words later in the paragraph. In such cases, the main idea is at both the beginning and the end. Such is the case in the following paragraph.

¹Stress is a part of everyday life. ²So much so that the term *stress* has become part of our colloquial speech. ³It is a noun *(We have stress)*. ⁴It is an adjective *(He has a stressful job)*. ⁵And it is a verb *(Writing a paper stresses me)*. ⁶Indeed, a recent poll by the American Psychological Association shows that, for many of us, stress levels are high and on the rise. ⁷One-third of Americans surveyed reported "living with extreme stress," and nearly half believe that their stress had "increased over the past 5 years." ⁸It seems that being "stressed out" has become a hallmark of modern life.

Note that the main idea—stress is part of everyday life—is expressed in different words in the first and last sentences.

A Note on the Central Point

Just as a paragraph may have a main idea, a longer selection may have a **central point**, also known as a **central idea** or **thesis**. The longer selection might be an essay, a reading, or a section of a textbook chapter. You can find a central point in the same way that you find a main idea—by identifying the topic (which is often suggested by the title of the selection) and then looking at the supporting material. The paragraphs within the longer reading will provide supporting details for the central point.

A Final Thought

Whether we are readers, writers, listeners, or speakers, the "heart" of clear communication is the main idea, or point, and the support for the main idea. Look at the following diagram:

The diagram underscores the importance of the most important of all reading skills: the ability to identify main ideas. The diagram also shows that the ability to identify supporting details for the main idea is an almost equally important skill.

CHAPTER REVIEW

In this chapter, you learned the following:

- Recognizing the main idea is the most important key to good compre-hension. The main idea is a general "umbrella" idea; all the specific supporting material of the passage fits under it.

- Three strategies that will help you find the main idea are to 1) look for general versus specific ideas; 2) use the topic (the general subject of a selection) to lead you to the main idea; 3) use key words—verbal clues that lead you to the main idea.

- The main idea often appears at the beginning of a paragraph, though it may appear elsewhere in a paragraph.

The next chapter—Chapter 2—will sharpen your understanding of the specific details that authors use to support and develop their main ideas.

On the Web: If you are using this book in class, you can go to our website for more practice in recognizing main ideas. Visit our Learning Center at **www.townsendpress.net** for additional activities and an instructional video on this skill.

REVIEW TEST 1

To review what you've learned in this chapter, answer each of the following questions by filling in the blank.

1. To become an active reader, you need to think as you read a paragraph or selection by constantly asking yourself the question, "What is the _____?"

2. To help decide if a certain sentence is the main idea, ask yourself, "Is this statement _____ by most or all of the other sentences in the paragraph?"

3. One strategy that will help you find the main idea is to look for the _____—the general subject of a selection.

4. Addition words such as *first, second, also,* and *finally* often introduce key supporting _____s for a main idea.

5. While a main idea may appear at any place within a paragraph, in textbooks it most often appears at the _____.

REVIEW TEST 2

Here is a chance to apply your understanding of main ideas to a full-length selection. Read the article from *Time* magazine below, and then answer the questions that follow on main ideas. There are also vocabulary questions to help you practice the skill of understanding vocabulary in context.

Preview

Are you starving? Not for food; for sleep. If you're like many Americans, you've been sleep-deprived so long you no longer know how tired you are. Maybe you even take pride in being able to "get by" on little sleep. But as this article explains, sleep is not a luxury you can afford to be without.

Words to Watch

plummet (2): fall
mimic (5): imitate
circadian rhythm (6): recurring naturally on a twenty-four-hour cycle

homework

GETTING A GOOD NIGHT'S SLEEP

Sora Song

It's important that we get a good nights sleep so that we are able to rest our minds.

Americans are not renowned for their powers of self-deprivation; doing without is not something we do particularly well. But experts say there is one necessity of life most of us consistently fail to get: a good night's sleep. The recommended daily requirements should sound familiar: eight hours of sleep a night for adults and at least an hour more for adolescents. Yet 71 percent of American adults and 85 percent of teens do not get the suggested amount, to the detriment of body and mind. "Sleep is sort of like food," says Robert Stickgold, a cognitive neuroscientist at Harvard Medical School. But, he adds, there's one important difference: "You can be quite starved and still alive, and I think we appreciate how horrible that must be. But many of us live on the edge of sleep starvation and just accept it."

Part of the problem is we are so used to being chronically sleep-deprived—and have become so adept at coping with that condition—that we no longer notice how exhausted we really are. In 2003, sleep expert David Dinges and colleagues at the University of Pennsylvania School of Medicine tested the effects of restricting slumber to eight, six, or four hours a night for two weeks. During the first few days, subjects sleeping less than eight hours admitted to being fatigued and lacking alertness. But by Day 4, most people had adapted to their new baseline drowsiness and reported feeling fine—even as their cognitive performance continued to plummet°.

Over time, the experiment's sleep-restricted subjects became so impaired that they had difficulty concentrating on even the simplest tasks, like pushing a button in response to a light. "The human brain is only capable of about 16 hours of wakefulness [a day]," says Dinges. "When you get beyond that, it can't function as efficiently, as accurately or as well."

In the real world, people overcome their somnolence—at least temporarily—by drinking coffee, taking a walk around the block or chatting with office mates. But then they find themselves nodding off in meetings or, worse, behind the wheel. Those short snatches of unconsciousness are what researchers call microsleep, a sure sign of sleep deprivation. "If people are falling asleep because 'the room was hot' or 'the meeting was boring,' that's not coping with sleep loss. I would argue that they're eroding their productive capability," says Dinges.

What most people don't realize 5

is that the purpose of sleep may be more to rest the mind than to rest the body. Indeed, most of the benefits of eight hours' sleep seem to accrue to the brain: sleep helps consolidate memory, improve judgment, promote learning and concentration, boost mood, speed reaction time and sharpen problem solving and accuracy. According to Sonia Ancoli-Israel, a psychologist at the University of California at San Diego who has done extensive studies in the aging population, lack of sleep may even mimic° the symptoms of dementia. In recent preliminary findings, she was able to improve cognitive function in patients with mild to moderate Alzheimer's simply by treating their underlying sleep disorder. "The need for sleep does not change a lot with age," says Ancoli-Israel, but often because of disruptive illnesses and the medications used to treat them, "the ability to sleep does."

If you're one of the otherwise healthy yet perpetually under-rested, there's plenty you can do to pay back your sleep debt. For starters, you can catch up on lost time. Take your mom's advice, and get to bed early. Turn off the TV half an hour sooner than usual. If you can't manage to snooze longer at night, try to squeeze in a midday nap. The best time for a siesta is between noon and 3 p.m., for about 30 to 60 minutes, according to Timothy Roehrs, director of research at the Sleep Disorders and Research Center at Henry Ford Hospital in Detroit. He advises against over-

sleeping on weekend mornings to make up for a workweek of deprivation; later rising can disrupt your circadian rhythm°, making it even harder later to get a full night's rest.

According to Dinge's analysis of data from the 2003 American Time Use Survey, the most common reason we shortchange ourselves on sleep is work. (The second biggest reason, surprisingly, is that we spend too much time driving around in our cars.) But consider that in giving up two hours of bedtime to do more work, you're losing a quarter of your recommended nightly dose and gaining just 12 percent more time during the day. What if you could be 12 percent more productive instead? "You have to realize that if you get a good night's sleep, you will actually be more efficient and get more done the next day. The more you give up on sleep, the harder it is to be productive," says Ancoli-Israel. "What is it going to be?"

8   If mental sharpness is your goal, the answer is clear: stop depriving yourself, and get a good night's sleep.

Reading Comprehension Questions

Vocabulary in Context

____ 1. In the sentence below, the word *detriment* (dĕt′rə-mənt) means
   A. consideration.
   B. harm.
   C. influence.
   D. benefit.

   "Yet 71 percent of American adults and 85 percent of teens do not get the suggested amount, to the detriment of body and mind." (Paragraph 1)

____ 2. In the sentence below, the word *baseline* (bās′līn) means
   A. a baseball term which refers to the area within which a runner must stay when running between bases.
   B. a line bounding each back end in a tennis court.
   C. a line serving as a base, as for purposes of measurement.
   D. caused by extreme boredom.

   "But by Day 4, most people had adapted to their new baseline drowsiness and reported feeling fine—even as their cognitive performance continued to plummet." (Paragraph 2)

____ 3. In the excerpt below, the word *somnolence* (sŏm′nə-ləns) means
   A. lack of sensitivity.
   B. laziness.
   C. boredom.
   D. sleepiness.

   "In the real world, people overcome their somnolence—at least temporarily—by drinking coffee, taking a walk around the block or chatting with office mates." (Paragraph 4)

A 4. In the sentence below, the words *accrue to* (ə-krōō′tōō) mean
   A. improve.
   B. put pressure on.
   C. wear away.
   D. communicate to.

> "Indeed, most of the benefits of eight hours' sleep seem to accrue to the brain: sleep helps consolidate memory, improve judgment, promote learning and concentration, boost mood, speed reaction time and sharpen problem solving and accuracy." (Paragraph 5)

Main Ideas

C 5. The central idea of this selection is that
   A. Americans are willing to deprive themselves of sleep in order to complete more work.
   B. Americans use unsuccessful strategies in order to compensate for lack of sleep.
   C. Americans may not realize it, but chronic sleep deprivation is actually harming them and lowering their productivity.
   D. the need for sleep does not change a lot with age.

B 6. The main idea of paragraph 1 is stated in the
   A. first sentence.
   B. second sentence.
   C. third sentence.
   D. fourth sentence.

A 7. The main idea of paragraph 2 is stated in the
   A. first sentence.
   B. second sentence.
   C. third sentence.
   D. fourth sentence.

A 8. The main idea of paragraph 5 is stated in the
   A. first sentence.
   B. second sentence.
   C. third sentence.
   D. fourth sentence.

C 9. The topic of paragraph 6 is
   A. sleep-deprived people.
   B. oversleeping on weekends.
   C. paying back your sleep debt.
   D. midday naps.

_____A_____ 10. The main idea of paragraph 6 is stated in the
          A. first sentence.
          B. second sentence.
          C. sixth sentence.
          D. seventh sentence.

Discussion Questions

1. How much sleep do you typically get in a night? Do you feel that you sleep enough? If not, what do you think are the major reasons you aren't sleeping more? What are some ways in which you could restructure your life in order to get a full eight hours of sleep a night?

2. A scientist quoted in paragraph 1 compares sleep with food, but notes that while we would not accept being deprived of food, we accept being sleep-deprived. Why do you think so many people simply accept the fact that they don't get enough sleep?

3. The selection mentions nodding off at meetings and falling asleep at the wheel as two potential consequences of sleep deprivation. What are some other negative consequences that you can think of? Conversely, what might some positive consequences be if people got more sleep?

4. In your view, are there any factors which contribute to Americans' sleep deprivation other than those mentioned in the selection? If so, what are they, and what—if anything—could be done to counteract them?

   Note: Writing assignments for this selection appear on page 635.

Check Your Performance   MAIN IDEAS

Activity	Number Right	Points	Score
Review Test 1 (5 items)	_____	× 6 =	_____
Review Test 2 (10 items)	_____	× 7 =	_____
	TOTAL SCORE	=	_____ %

Enter your total score into the **Reading Performance Chart: Review Tests** on the inside back cover.

MAIN IDEAS: Mastery Test 1

A. In each of the following groups, one statement is the general point, and the other statements are specific support for the point. Write the letter of each point in the space provided.

_____ 1. A. German immigrants added such words as *kindergarten, hoodlum,* and *delicatessen* to the American vocabulary.

B. We owe common phrases like *to bad-mouth, a high five,* and *jam session* to African speech patterns.

C. If you've eaten spaghetti, pizza, or lasagna, you've eaten a dish named by Italians.

D. Various ethnic groups and races have contributed to the English language as Americans speak it.

_____ 2. A. Most tall buildings in the United States are struck, on average, 100 times per year.

B. In one recorded incident, the Empire State Building was struck 15 times in 15 minutes.

C. The old saying that lightning never strikes twice is far from true.

D. The exceptions don't just apply to buildings: Roy Sullivan, a U.S. forest ranger, was struck by lightning seven times over the course of 40 years.

_____ 3. A. While many people fear a piranha will bite off their finger, in fact the majority of a piranha's diet is vegetable matter.

B. Although piranhas are most notorious as fearsome killers, they actually make good pets.

C. Although piranhas will attack other types of fish in an aquarium, they don't attack one another and can coexist peacefully.

D. Piranhas are very hardy and adaptable to different types of water, so they require a minimum of tank maintenance.

(Continues on next page)

B. The main idea may appear at any place within each of the two paragraphs that follow. Write the number of each main idea sentence in the space provided.

_____3___ 4. [1]Thoughts are forever coming into and going out of our minds. [2]They are a lot like an ongoing movie. [3]There are a number of types or categories of thoughts that are commonly featured in the movies of our minds. [4]Planning thoughts are those in which we try to decide exactly what to do, specifically ("I'll go to Burger King for lunch today") or generally ("I really should quit this job"). [5]Desire thoughts include wishes for anything, from sex to world peace. [6]Fear thoughts include any type of worry: unhealthy eating, money, work, you name it. [7]Happy or appreciative thoughts are often noting pleasurable sensations such as the sun on one's face or the smell of freshly brewed coffee. [8]Judging thoughts are those in which we approve of, or, more likely, criticize anything or anyone. [9]Righteous thoughts are those in which we are right and other people are wrong. [10]Angry thoughts can be self-hating thoughts or feelings of hatred for the behavior of others.

_____2___ 5. [1]One of the contradictions of humanity is that people long for peace while at the same time they glorify war. [2]War is so common that a cynic might say it is the normal state of society. [3]Sociologist Pitirim Sorokin counted the wars in Europe from 500 B.C. to A.D. 1925. [4]He documented 967 wars, an average of one war every two or three years. [5]Counting years or parts of a year in which a country was at war, at 28 percent Germany had the lowest record of warfare. [6]Spain's 67 percent gave it the dubious distinction of being the most war-prone. [7]Sorokin found that Russia, the land of his birth, had experienced only one peaceful quarter-century during the entire previous thousand years. [8]Since the time of William the Conqueror, who took power in 1066, England was at war an average of 56 out of each 100 years. [9]Spain fought even more often. [10]It is worth noting the history of the United States in this regard: Since 1850, it has intervened militarily around the world about 160 times, an average of once a year.

MAIN IDEAS: Mastery Test 2

A. In each of the following groups—all based on textbook selections—one statement is the general point, and the other statements are specific support for the point. Write the letter of each point in the space provided.

_____ 1. A. Appalachian children of eastern Kentucky typically fall asleep with their parents for the first two years of their life.
B. Japanese children usually lie next to their mothers throughout infancy and early childhood and continue to sleep with a parent or other family member until adolescence.
C. Among the Maya of rural Guatemala, mother-infant co-sleeping is interrupted only by the birth of a new baby, at which time the older child is moved beside the father or to another bed in the same room.
D. Parent and infant bed sharing is common around the globe, in industrialized and unindustrialized countries alike.

_____ 2. A. About 45 million years ago, the subcontinent of India collided with the continent of Asia to form the spectacular Himalaya Mountains.
B. The Alps are thought to have formed as a result of a collision between Africa and Europe many millions of years ago.
C. Some mountain ranges have formed as the result of collisions between continents.
D. The European continent collided with the Asian continent to produce the Ural Mountains, which extend in a north-south direction through present-day Russia.

_____ 3. A. Hunting and gathering societies tend to have fewer social divisions than other societies.
B. Because what they hunt and gather is perishable, hunters and gatherers accumulate few personal possessions.
C. There is no money and no way to become wealthier than anyone else in hunting and gathering societies.
D. Hunters and gatherers place a high value on sharing their food resources, which are essential to their survival.

(Continues on next page)

B. The main idea may appear at any place within each of the two paragraphs that follow. Write the number of each main idea sentence in the space provided.

_____ 4. ¹Data across time, cultures, and methodologies strongly support the notion that people lose their cool and behave more aggressively in hot temperatures. ²More violent crimes occur in the summer than in the winter, during hot years than in cooler years, and in hot cities than in cooler cities at any given time of year. ³The numbers of political uprisings, riots, homicides, assaults, rapes, and reports of violence all peak in the summer months. ⁴Indirect acts of aggression also increase in excessive heat. ⁵As temperatures rise to uncomfortable levels, laboratory participants become more likely to interpret ambiguous events in hostile terms, and drivers in cars without air conditioning become more likely to honk their horns at motorists whose cars are stalled in front of them. ⁶Researchers have also found that as the temperature rises, major-league baseball pitchers are significantly more likely to hit batters with a pitch.

_____ 5. ¹Is it really possible to convince people that they are guilty of a crime they did not commit? ²To search for an answer, researchers recruited pairs of college students to work on a fast- or slow-paced computer task. ³At one point, the computer crashed, and students were accused of having caused the damage by pressing a key that they had been specifically instructed to avoid. ⁴All students were actually innocent and denied the charge. ⁵In half the sessions, however, the second student (who was really an actor, posing as a participant) said that she had seen the student hit the forbidden key. ⁶Demonstrating the process of compliance, many students confronted by this false witness agreed to sign a confession handwritten by the experimenter. ⁷Next, demonstrating the process of internalization, some students later "admitted" their guilt to a stranger (also an actor) after the experiment was supposedly over and the two were alone. ⁸In short, innocent people who are vulnerable to suggestion can be induced to confess and to internalize guilt by the presentation of false evidence.

MAIN IDEAS: Mastery Test 3

A. In each of the following groups—all based on textbook selections—one statement is the general point, and the other statements are specific support for the point. Write the letter of each point in the space provided.

_____ 1. A. In the 1950s, more than 75 percent of American households owned sewing machines, but now that figure is under 5 percent.
B. As more women began working outside the home, fewer and fewer undertook unpaid volunteer work.
C. Women who work outside the home are too busy to do the things they used to do.
D. Women used to clip manufacturers' coupons—today less than 3 percent of manufacturers' coupons are ever redeemed.

_____ 2. A. In many preindustrial societies in which children are of particular importance, sterility or impotence are primary grounds for divorce.
B. In some traditional patriarchal Islamic societies, husbands needed only to proclaim "I divorce thee" three times in front of two witnesses for marriages to end.
C. Throughout most of American history, cruelty, desertion, or adultery were the most common legal grounds for divorce.
D. Just as norms regulate marriage and family relationships, they also specify conditions under which marriages may be dissolved.

_____ 3. A. Contrary to what some animal lovers believe, the natural world is not particularly moral.
B. Infanticide, siblicide (killing of siblings), and rape can be observed in many kinds of animals.
C. Infidelity is common in so-called pair-bonded species.
D. Cannibalism can be expected in all species that are not strictly vegetarians.

(Continues on next page)

B. The main idea may appear at any place within each of the two paragraphs that follow. Write the number of each main idea sentence in the space provided.

_____ 4. ¹Married people are more likely than those who are single, divorced, or widowed to survive cancer for five years; gay men infected with HIV are less likely to contemplate suicide if they have close ties than if they do not; and people who have a heart attack are less likely to have a second one if they live with someone than if they live alone. ²Among students stressed by schoolwork, and among the spouses of cancer patients, more social support is also associated with a stronger immune response. ³Based on a review of eighty-one studies, researchers have concluded that in times of stress, having social support lowers blood pressure, lessons the secretion of stress hormones, and strengthens the immune system. ⁴On the flip side of the coin, people who are lonely exhibit greater age-related increases in blood pressure and have more difficulty sleeping at night. ⁵There's no doubt about it: Being isolated from other people can be hazardous to your health.

_____ 5. ¹Individuals vary widely in what they dream about, the feelings associated with their dreams, and how often they remember dreams. ²Nevertheless, there are some patterns that seem to apply to all dreams. ³One pattern found in dream content relates to gender. ⁴For example, although the dreams of men and women have become more similar over the last several decades, men more often dream about weapons, unfamiliar characters, male characters, aggressive interactions, and failure outcomes, whereas women are more likely to dream about being the victims of aggression. ⁵Dream content also varies by age. ⁶Very young children (ages 2 to 5) tend to have brief dreams, many of which involve animals; but the images are usually unrelated to each other, and there is seldom any emotional narrative or story line. ⁷It is not until the child is 7 to 9 years old that dreams take on a narrative, sequential form. ⁸Feelings and emotions also make their appearance in dreams in the years between 7 and 9, and children more often appear as characters in their own dreams at that age. ⁹Between ages 9 and 15, dreams become more adult-like: Narratives follow well-developed story lines, other people play important roles, and there are many verbal exchanges in addition to motor activity. ¹⁰Finally, cross-cultural studies have shown that people from different cultures report dream content consistent with the unique cultural patterns inherent in their respective cultures.

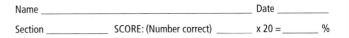

MAIN IDEAS: Mastery Test 4

The main idea may appear at any place within each of the five paragraphs that follow. Write the number of each main idea sentence in the space provided.

_____ 1. ¹Less than a hundred years ago, many people saw adolescence as a time of great instability and strong emotions. ²For example, G. Stanley Hall, one of the first developmental psychologists, portrayed adolescence as a period of "storm and stress," fraught with suffering, passion, and rebelliousness. ³Recent research, however, suggests that the "storm and stress" view greatly exaggerates the experience of most teenagers. ⁴The great majority of adolescents do not describe their lives as filled with turmoil and chaos. ⁵Most adolescents manage to keep stress in check, experience very little disruption in their everyday lives, and generally develop more positively than is commonly believed. ⁶For instance, a cross-cultural study that sampled adolescents from ten countries, including the United States, found that over 75 percent of them had healthy self-images, were generally happy, and valued the time they spent at school and work.

_____ 2. ¹Scientists have calculated that in the year 2029, there is a 1 in 38 chance that an asteroid will smash into our planet. ²That may not be a high probability, but when that probability represents a hole the size of several European countries, 1 in 38 is still cause for concern. ³Luckily, scientists have developed an effective strategy for avoiding an asteroid collision. ⁴Rather than blow up the asteroid and risk its fragments chaotically raining down on the Earth, the best strategy is to slowly deflect the asteroid's path. ⁵Using a nuclear-powered engine that consumes very little fuel, a spacecraft would hover beside the asteroid for as many as twenty years. ⁶Since the force of gravity is such that any object exerts a pull on the objects around it, the spacecraft's mass would slowly pull the asteroid off course. ⁷Although the pull would be very weak, space would offer no resistance, and the asteroid could be safely pulled away from its collision course over a period of many years.

_____ 3. ¹AIDS is an excellent example of the relationship between behavior, environment, and disease. ²This disease was first noted in male homosexuals. ³One person, Gaetan Dugas, an airline steward from Canada, played a key role in its rapid transmission, for he or one of his sex partners had sex with 40 of the first 248 AIDS cases reported in the United States. ⁴The disease then hit another group whose lifestyle also encouraged its transmission—

(Continues on next page)

intravenous drug users who shared needles. ⁵The third of the groups that were the hardest hit represents an environmental risk: Hemophiliacs, who need regular blood transfusions, were exposed to the disease through contaminated blood. ⁶Lifestyle was also central to how the disease entered the general population; the bridge was prostitutes who had sex with intravenous drug users and with bisexual and heterosexual men. ⁷Lifestyle and environment continue to be significant: AIDS is more common among drug users who share needles and among people who have multiple sexual partners.

_____ 4. ¹Today, people who find themselves with too much debt can get help from the government. ²But before the mid-1800s, Americans who couldn't pay their debts were often given harsh punishments. ³Some people were put in a jail called "debtors' prison." ⁴They were forced to sit in their cells until they had the money to pay back their debts. ⁵However, since they couldn't go to work, there was no way for them to get the money unless someone gave it to them. ⁶Many people died in debtors' prison because they could not afford to leave. ⁷Some people were required to give away everything they had, except for their bedding, in order to pay back a debt. ⁸Other people were forced to become indentured servants. ⁹Indentured servants were forced to do work without a salary until their debt was paid. ¹⁰Sometimes even the children of people who owed money were required to work in order to pay off their parents' debt.

_____ 5. ¹Religion sometimes teaches that the existing social arrangements of a society represent what God desires. ²For example, during the Middle Ages, Christian theologians decreed the "divine right of kings." ³That doctrine meant that God determined who would become a king, and set him on the throne. ⁴The king ruled in God's place, and it was the duty of a king's subjects to be loyal to him (and pay their taxes). ⁵To disobey the king would be to disobey God. ⁶The religion of ancient Egypt claimed that the Pharaoh himself was a god. ⁷The Emperor of Japan was similarly declared divine. ⁸In India, Hinduism supports the caste system by teaching that an individual who tries to change caste will come back in the next life as a member of a lower caste—or even as an animal. ⁹In the decades before the Civil War, Southern ministers used Scripture to defend slavery, saying that it was God's will—while Northern ministers legitimated their religion's social structure by using Scripture to denounce slavery as evil.

MAIN IDEAS: Mastery Test 5

The main idea may appear at any place within each of the five paragraphs that follow. Write the number of each main idea sentence in the space provided.

___2___ 1. [1]In speaking and writing, the best language is often the simplest. [2]Your words should be immediately understandable to your audience. [3]Don't try to impress them with jargon and inflated language full of multi-syllable words. [4]For example, instead of *utilize*, say *use*; instead of *alternative*, say *other*; instead of *augment*, say *increase*; instead of *adequate number*, say *enough*. [5]As linguist Paul Roberts advises, "Decide what you want to say and say it as vigorously as possible . . . and in plain words." [6]In his classic essay, "Politics and the English Language," George Orwell lists rules for clear writing, including this prescription for simplicity: "Never use a long word where a short one will do. [7]If it is possible to cut a word out, always cut it out. [8]Never use a foreign phrase, a scientific word, or a jargon word if you can think of an everyday English equivalent." [9]And James J. Kilpatrick has said, "Use familiar words— words that your readers will understand, and not words they will have to look up. [10]No advice is more elementary, and no advice is more difficult to accept. [11]When we feel an impulse to use a marvelously exotic word, let us lie down until the impulse goes away."

___2___ 2. [1]Humans breathe automatically every few seconds. [2]Dolphins, by contrast, breathe only voluntarily and can hold their breath for longer than thirty minutes. [3]So how do they go to sleep without risking oversleeping and drowning? [4]To maintain control of their breathing during sleep, dolphins sleep with only half of their brain at a time. [5]Electroencephalograms, measuring the electric levels in dolphins' brains, show that the left side of a dolphin's mind shuts down while the right side powers its basic life functions. [6]Later, the right side sleeps while the left side takes over. [7]In this way, the dolphin achieves a full eight hours of sleep while still maintaining the ability to swim to the surface and take a breath of air. [8]The strange sleep habits of dolphins might explain a behavior known as "logging" that sailors commonly observe, in which dolphins swim very slowly near the surface of the ocean.

___3___ 3. [1]We've all heard stories about people whose spectacular abilities are apparent at an early age. [2]Mozart started composing music at the age of five, Picasso turned out masterly paintings by the time he was ten, and some mathematicians have enrolled in college before entering their teens. [3]Yet a significant number of famous people were thought to be "slow" rather than gifted when they were children. [4]Thomas Alva Edison was a prime example of this. [5]Little Tom Edison did not learn to talk until he was almost

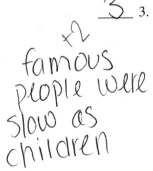

(Continues on next page)

four years of age. [6]When Tom was seven, his teacher lost patience with the boy's persistent questioning and lack of interest in the rote lessons he was supposed to be learning, and expressed his belief that the boy's brains were "addled," or scrambled. [7]Albert Einstein was another example of a genius who started off slowly. [8]In the primary grades, he was considered to be a slow learner, possibly due to dyslexia, shyness, or simply a lack of interest in formal schooling. [9]Another future scientist who made great contributions to the atomic age, Ernest Rutherford, was not able to read until the age of eleven, and even then he still could not write.

4. [1]When a specimen of pure radium was first isolated in 1902, people failed to realize that the glowing radioactive substance could be deadly. [2]Radium in extremely diluted form was added to face creams, health tonics, cosmetics, bath salts, and so on. [3]One drink, Radithor, which contained one part radium salts to 60,000 parts zinc sulfide, was said to cure cancer and mental illness, as well as restore sexual vigor and vitality. [4]Upper-class men and women carried small vials of radium bromide around with them as the latest "status symbol." [5]Watches with glowing, radium-painted numbers and dials were also extremely popular. [6]Eventually, radium became linked with an alarming rise in incidences of cancer.

5. [1]Aside from admitting to a bad back, young, dynamic President John F. Kennedy appeared the picture of health. [2]Yet several years after his assassination, the truth came out that he had suffered from Addison's disease, a debilitating disorder involving the adrenal glands. [3]Kennedy was not the only president to keep his health problems a secret. [4]The first president to lie about his health was Chester A. Arthur, our 21st president, who was diagnosed with Bright's disease, a fatal kidney disorder, shortly after he took office. [5]Unwilling to jeopardize what he wanted to accomplish, Arthur kept his disease a secret, struggled on for four years, then died shortly after he left office. [6]President Grover Cleveland also kept the true state of his health a secret. [7]In 1893, when the country was experiencing an economic depression, doctors secretly operated on Cleveland to cut out a large cancerous growth on the roof of his mouth. [8]A cover story about the removal of two bad teeth kept the suspicious press from learning the rather alarming truth. [9]In October 1919, President Woodrow Wilson suffered a serious stroke which incapacitated him until the end of his term in 1921. [10]The public was never informed of this situation, and Wilson's wife, Edith, virtually ran the government for more than a year. [11]Our 32nd president, Franklin D. Roosevelt, failed to reveal the fact that he had been diagnosed with life-threatening hypertension before he ran for and was elected to a fourth term.

MAIN IDEAS: Mastery Test 6

The main idea may appear at any place within each of the five paragraphs that follow. Write the number of each main idea sentence in the space provided.

_1_ 1. [¹As you might anticipate, research clearly shows that economic hardships are a huge source of stress for individuals and their families.] ²Few events are more stressful than watching one's retirement accounts shrivel up, losing one's job, or, worse yet, losing one's home to foreclosure. ³A recent study of people going through foreclosure found that 29 percent were burdened by medical bills they could not afford, 58 percent had to skip meals due to lack of money, 47 percent suffered from minor to major depression, and a substantial portion had increased their smoking or drinking since their foreclosure. ⁴Other research has shown that prolonged economic setbacks typically send families into a downward emotional spiral marked by anxiety, depression, anger, alienation, and marital conflict. ⁵The stress on parents often spills over to affect their children, who act out and struggle in school. ⁶Another line of research, looking at the effects of unemployment and underemployment, has shown that these afflictions are associated with anxiety, depression, hostility, paranoia, pessimism, helplessness, social isolation, and a host of physical maladies.

economics affect families & individuals

x2

_11_ 2. ¹While the telephone is associated with Alexander Graham Bell, Elisha Grey of Chicago filed for a patent for the same invention within hours of Bell on the same day in 1876. ²After extensive litigation, Bell was awarded the patent. ³In fact, neither of them may have been first. ⁴Italian Antonio Meucci had a successful working model years earlier. ⁵Orville and Wilbur Wright are forever associated with the invention of the airplane in 1903. ⁶However, there is evidence that in New Zealand, a farmer named Richard Pearse made a successful flight some months ahead of the Wright brothers. ⁷Others claim that Gustave Whitehead flew a homemade plane two years earlier in Bridgeport, Connecticut. ⁸The invention of the television is usually credited to Philo Farnsworth of San Francisco in 1926. ⁹In Scotland, also in 1926, John Logie Baird demonstrated a machine he called the "televisor." ¹⁰When Baird and Farnsworth met and compared inventions some months later, Baird admitted Farnsworth had the better design. ¹¹Clearly, while famous inventions usually come to be associated with one person, there are often competing claims for the same invention.

famous inventions

x2

_3_ 3. ¹Most of us, when we are in a depressed mood, are able to relieve it through our own thoughts and actions. ²After a certain period of gloom, we grab our bootstraps and pull ourselves up, using such means as positive

(Continues on next page)

thinking, problem solving, talking with friends, or engaging in activities that we especially enjoy. ³However, severely depressed people have patterns of thought and action that work against their recovery, rather than for it. ⁴Imagine severe depression as a vicious triangle in which a person's mood, thoughts, and actions interact in such a way as to keep him or her in a depressed state. ⁵Depressed mood promotes negative thinking and withdrawal from enjoyable activities; negative thinking promotes depressed mood and withdrawal from enjoyable activities; and withdrawal from enjoyable activities promotes depressed mood and negative thinking. ⁶Each corner of the triangle supports the others.

depressed people

4. ¹Most of us assume that color is "out there," in the environment; our eyes simply take it in. ²While many animals—including some reptiles, fish, and insects—have color vision, what colors they see vary. ³Humans and most other primates perceive a wide range of colors. ⁴Most other mammals experience the world only in reds and greens or blues and yellows. ⁵Hamsters, rats, squirrels, and other rodents are completely colorblind. ⁶So are owls, nocturnal birds of prey that have only rods in their eyes. ⁷At the same time, however, other animals can see colors that we can't. ⁸Bees, for example, see ultraviolet light. ⁹To a bee's eyes, flowers with white petals that look drab to us flash like neon signs pointing the way to nectar. ¹⁰Birds, bats, and moths find red flowers irresistible, but bees pass them by. ¹¹Tradition notwithstanding, bulls can't see red either; they are red-green colorblind. ¹²The matador's cape is bright red to excite the humans in the audience, who find red arousing, perhaps especially when they expect to see blood.

animals seeing in color

5. ¹Have you ever wondered what on earth some of those strange nursery rhymes you learned as a child were supposed to mean? ²Rhymes such as "Jack and Jill" and "Three Blind Mice" have fairly gruesome explanations, but the seemingly innocent "Ring Around the Rosy" takes the prize for its ghastly meaning. ³Written around 1348, this brief song refers to the bubonic plague—a horrifying epidemic that killed 25 million people in Europe in the mid-1300s. ⁴Because contracting the illness meant almost certain death, those who fell ill were simply sent home to die and were instructed to pray continuously with their rosary beads ("Ring around the rosy"). ⁵And because people were dying faster than they could be buried, a little bundle of flowers known as a "posy" was carried in one's pocket and held up to the nose in order to mask the smell of rotting bodies ("A pocket full of posies"). ⁶In time, churches resorted to burning the dead instead of burying them when the corpses began piling up too high in the streets ("Ashes, ashes. We all fall down"). ⁷Ultimately, the plague killed one-third of Europe's inhabitants, leading Europeans at that time to understandably imagine that, in the end, everyone would be killed.

nursery rhymes

2 Supporting Details

In Chapter 1 you worked on the most important reading skill—finding the main idea. A closely related reading skill is locating supporting details. Supporting details provide the added information that is needed for you to make sense of a main idea.

This chapter describes supporting details and presents three techniques that will help you take study notes on main ideas and their supporting details: outlining, mapping, and summarizing.

What Are Supporting Details?

Copyright 2004 by Randy Glasbergen.
www.glasbergen.com

GLASBERGEN

"Reading the morning paper is bad for your health. The political news raises your blood pressure. The business news makes you depressed. And the sports page makes you mad."

Supporting details are reasons, examples, facts, steps, or other kinds of evidence that explain a main idea. In the cartoon shown above, the main idea is that reading the morning paper is bad for the man's health. The supporting reasons are that the political news raises his blood pressure, the business report makes him depressed, and the sports page makes him mad.

On the next page is a paragraph with strong support for its point.

63

hw

Supporting Reasons

Annotate

In the paragraph below, three major details in the form of *reasons* support the main idea that women are underrepresented in U.S. politics. As you read the paragraph, try to identify and check (✓) the three major details.

[1]Eight million more women than men are of voting age, and more women than men vote in U.S. national elections. [2]However, men greatly outnumber women in political office. [3]Since 1789, over 1,800 men have served in the U.S. Senate, but only 39 women have served. [4]Women are underrepresented in U.S. politics for a number of reasons. [5]First, women are still underrepresented in law and business, the careers from which most politicians emerge. [6]In addition, most women find that the irregular hours kept by those who run for office are incompatible with their role as mother. [7]Fathers, in contrast, whose ordinary roles are more likely to take them away from home, are less likely to feel this conflict. [8]Last, preferring to hold on to their positions of power, men have been reluctant to incorporate women into centers of decision-making or to present them as viable candidates.

main idea

subject women being treated unfair in U.S politics

✓ Check Your Understanding

Now see if you can complete the basic outline below that shows the three major reasons supporting the main idea.

Main idea: Women are underrepresented in U.S. politics.

Supporting detail 1: _____

_____

Supporting detail 2: _____

_____

Supporting detail 3: _____

Explanation

You should have added 1) women are still underrepresented in law and business, the usual starting place for politicians; 2) a politician's irregular hours are incompatible with the role of a mother; and 3) men have been reluctant to give women power. These major supporting reasons help you fully understand the main idea.

Supporting Facts

In the paragraph above, the supporting details are *reasons*. Now look at the paragraph below, in which the main idea is explained by a series of *facts*.

[1]Several factors contribute to our pickiness about eating certain foods. [2]One factor which influences what foods we find tasty is how old we are. [3]In young people, taste buds die and are replaced about every seven days. [4]As we age, the buds are replaced more slowly, so taste declines as we grow older. [5]Thus children, who have abundant taste buds, often dislike foods with strong or unusual tastes (such as liver and spinach), but as they grow older and lose taste buds, they may come to like these foods. [6]Pickiness is also related to our upbringing. [7]Many food and taste preferences result from childhood experiences and cultural influences. [8]For example, Japanese children eat raw fish and Chinese children eat chicken feet as part of their normal diet, whereas American children consider these foods "yucky." [9]A third factor relating to pickiness over food is our built-in sense of taste, which enables us to discriminate between foods that are safe to eat and foods that are poisonous. [10]Because most plants that taste bitter contain toxic chemicals, we are more likely to survive if we avoid bitter-tasting plants. [11]We have a preference, then, for sweet foods because they are generally nonpoisonous.

✔ Check Your Understanding

Put a check (✓) by the number of separate factors that contribute to our pickiness about eating certain foods.

___ One fact   ___ Two facts   ___ Three facts

Explanation

There are three supporting facts for why we are picky about eating certain foods: 1) our age and how it affects our taste buds; 2) our upbringing; and 3) our built-in sense of taste. The supporting details give the added information we need to fully understand the main idea.

Supporting Example(s)

Now look at the paragraph below, where the supporting details are in the form of an extended *example*.

Subject
Old Chinese
Story

¹An old Chinese story illustrates the emotional healing power of touch. ²A woman went to a traditional herbal healer, asking for a potion to kill her cruel mother-in-law. ³The herbalist gave her some tea, telling her to make some for her mother-in-law every day for three months. ⁴In addition, he told her to massage the older woman every day, claiming that the poison would enter the woman's system more effectively that way. ⁵At the end of the three months, the mother-in-law would die, apparently of natural causes. ⁶The daughter-in-law did as she was told. ⁷But at the end of two and a half months, she had come to know and understand her mother-in-law through giving her massage. ⁸In turn, her mother-in-law had started to love her. ⁹The young woman ran back to the wise old doctor to ask for an antidote to the poison. ¹⁰He told her the tea was not poison at all, only flower water.

✓   *Check Your Understanding*

Which sentence contains the main idea?   1

Which sentence starts the extended example?   2

Explanation

The first sentence presents the main idea, and the second sentence starts the extended example.

Outlining

Preparing an outline of a passage often helps you understand and see clearly the relationship between a main idea and its supporting details. Outlines start with a main idea (or a heading that summarizes the main idea) followed by supporting details. There are often two levels of supporting details—major and minor. The **major details** explain and develop the main idea. In turn, the **minor details** help fill out and make clear the major details.

On the following page is the paragraph on gossip that appeared in Chapter 1. Reread the paragraph, and put a check (✓) next to each of the three major supporting details.

[1]Social psychologists have found that almost everyone gossips. [2]Male or female, young or old, blue-collar or professional, humans love to talk about one another. [3]All too often, such gossip is viewed as a frivolous waste of time. [4]However, it actually serves several important functions in the human community. [5]For one thing, gossip is a form of networking. [6]Talking with our friends and coworkers about each other is our most effective means of keeping track of the ever-changing social dynamic. [7]It tells us who is in, who is out, and who can help us climb the social or professional ladder. [8]A second function of gossip is the building of influence. [9]When we engage in gossip, we are able to shape people's opinions of ourselves. [10]We tell stories that show ourselves in a good light—wise, compassionate, insightful, clever. [11]And when we listen sympathetically to the gossip of other people, they perceive us as warm and likable. [12]A final and very powerful function of gossip is the creating of social alliances. [13]There are few quicker ways to form a bond with another person than to share private information with him or her. [14]The words "I wouldn't tell most people this, but . . ." instantly interest and flatter the listener. [15]To talk about a third party, especially in a critical way, creates a bond with our listener and gives a feeling of shared superiority.

Subject
gossip

✓ ## Check Your Understanding

Now see if you can fill in the missing items in the following outline of the paragraph, which shows both major and minor details.

Main idea: Gossip serves several important functions in the human community.

Major detail: 1. Form of networking.

   Minor detail: Networking is the best way to know who's out, who's in, and who can help us socially or professionally.

Major detail: 2. Gossip builds influence

   Minor detail: By gossiping we can impress others as clever and compassionate, warm and likable.

Major detail: 3. Creating social alliances

   Minor detail: from form bonds with other people

Explanation

You should have added two major supporting details: (2) Building of influence; (3) Creating of social alliances. And to the third major supporting detail, you should have added the minor detail that sharing private information creates a bond with our listener and gives a feeling of shared superiority.

Notice that just as the main idea is more general than its supporting details, major details are more general than minor ones. For instance, the major detail "Form of networking" is more general than the minor details about talking with friends or coworkers to keep track of what's going on and to climb the social or professional ladder.

Outlining Tips

The following tips will help you prepare outlines:

 TIP 1   Look for words that tell you a list of details is coming. Here are some common list words:

List Words

several **kinds** of	various **causes**	a few **reasons**
a number of **effects**	a **series** of	three **factors**
four **steps**	among the **results**	several **advantages**

For example, look again at the main ideas in two paragraphs already discussed and underline the list words:

- However, it [gossip] actually <u>serves several important functions</u> in the human community.

- Women are underrepresented in U.S. politics for a <u>number of reasons.</u>

Here the words *several important functions* and *a number of reasons* each tell us that a <u>list of major details</u> is coming. But you <u>will not always be given such helpful signals</u> that a list of details will follow. For example, there are no list words in the paragraph on the reasons people are "picky" about eating certain foods. Simply remember to note list words when they are present, as they help you to understand quickly the basic organization of a passage.

TIP 2   Look for words that signal major details. Such words are called **addition words**, and they will be explained further on page 136. Here are some common addition words:

Addition Words

one	to begin with	also	further
first (of all)	for one thing	in addition	furthermore
second(ly)	other	next	last (of all)
third(ly)	another	moreover	final(ly)

✓ ## *Check Your Understanding*

Now look again at the selection on gossip on page 67:

1. The word *one* (in *For one thing*) signals the first major supporting detail.

2. What addition word introduces the second major supporting detail? _A second function_

3. What addition word introduces the third major supporting detail? _A final_

And look again at the selection on underrepresentation of women on page 64:

1. What word introduces the first major detail? _first_
2. What words introduce the second major detail? _in addition_
3. What word introduces the third major detail? _last_

Also look again at the selection on page 65 about pickiness in eating:

1. What word introduces the first major detail? _one factor_
2. What word introduces the second major detail? _but also_
3. What word introduces the third major detail? _a third factor_

Explanation

In the selection on gossip, the second major detail is introduced by the word *second*, and the third major detail by the word *final*. In the selection on the underrepresentation of women, the first major detail is introduced by the word *First*, the second major detail by the words *In addition*, and the third major detail by the word *Last*. In the selection on pickiness about eating certain foods, the first major detail is introduced by the word *One*, the second major detail by the word *also*, and the third major detail by the word *third*.

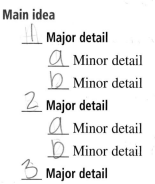

TIP 3   When making an outline, put all supporting details of equal importance at the same distance from the left margin. In the outline of the paragraph on the functions of gossip, on page 67, the three major supporting details all begin at the margin. Likewise, the minor supporting details are all indented at the same distance from the margin. You can therefore see at a glance the main idea, the major details, and the minor details.

✓ *Check Your Understanding*

Put appropriate numbers *(1, 2, 3)* and letters *(a, b)* in front of the items in the following outline.

> **Main idea**
> > _1_ **Major detail**
> > > _a_ Minor detail
> > > _b_ Minor detail
> > _2_ **Major detail**
> > > _a_ Minor detail
> > > _b_ Minor detail
> > _3_ **Major detail**

Explanation

You should have put a *1, 2,* and *3* in front of the major details and an *a* and *b* in front of the minor details. Note that an outline proceeds from the most general to the most specific, from main idea to major details to minor details.

The practice that follows will give you experience in finding major details, in separating major details from minor details, and in preparing outlines.

PRACTICE 1

Read and then outline each passage. Begin by writing in the main idea, and then fill in the supporting details. The first outline requires only major details; the second calls for you to add minor details as well.

A. ¹Although only human beings communicate through words, other animals also communicate in their own ways. ²First, animals can communicate by means of nonverbal sounds, such as chirps and birdsong, mews, barks, howls, and roars. ³Next, animals communicate through chemical signals: male dogs, for instance, use urine to mark their own turf. ⁴A third means of animal communication is touch, such as nuzzling and licking—as well as grooming among, for example, monkeys. ⁵Last of all, animals communicate by visual signals. ⁶Dogs, of course, wag their tails; also, they and some other furry animals raise their hackles (the hairs between the shoulders) when threatened, in order to appear larger. ⁷Baring the teeth is another visual signal. ⁸And honeybees perform a famous "wiggle dance" to inform each other about sources of food.

Main idea: _Animals communicate in their own ways_

Major detail: 1. _They use nonverbal sounds_

Major detail: 2. _Talk through chemical signals_

Major detail: 3. _They touch to talk_

Major detail: 4. _They use visual signs._

B. ¹The diseases that afflict humans can be classified into a number of basic types. ²Infectious diseases are probably what most of us have in mind when we think of "getting sick." ³These are the illnesses that are caused by bacteria, viruses, and other tiny organisms and that we can "catch" from another person, or from an infected animal. ⁴Examples include colds, flu, and tuberculosis. ⁵Another category is hereditary diseases, such as sickle-cell anemia, which are passed on from parent to child in the genes. ⁶A third category, degenerative diseases, includes disorders that result from aging and wear and tear on the body; one example is arthritis. ⁷Still another category, hormonal disorders, are caused by having too much or too little of certain body chemicals. ⁸Diabetes is one hormonal disease. ⁹The category of environmental diseases is becoming a matter of increasing concern. ¹⁰Environmental diseases—which include some allergies and lead poisoning—

are caused by chemical and physical substances in air, water, and food. ¹¹Finally, deficiency diseases are the type caused by a lack of certain nutrients, such as vitamins. ¹²Scurvy and pellagra are vitamin-deficiency disorders.

Main idea: *There are different diseases that afflict humans.*

Major detail: 1. Infectious

  Minor detail: Examples—colds and flu

Major detail: 2. *hereditary*

  Minor detail: Examples— *sickle-cell anemia*

Major detail: 3. *degenerative*

  Minor detail: Examples— *arthritis*

Major detail: 4. *hormonal*

  Minor detail: Examples— *diabetes*

Major detail: 5. *environmental*

  Minor detail: Examples— *air, water, and food*

Major detail: 6. *deficiency*

  Minor detail: Examples— *scurvy and pellagra*

Study Hint: At times you will want to include minor details in your study notes; at other times, it may not be necessary to do so. If you are taking notes on one or more textbook chapters, use your judgment. It is often best to be aware of minor details but to concentrate on writing down the main ideas and major details.

Mapping

Students sometimes find it helpful to use maps rather than outlines. **Maps,** or diagrams, are highly visual outlines in which circles, boxes, or other shapes show the relationships between main ideas and supporting details. Each major detail is connected to the main idea, often presented in the form of a title. If minor details are included, each is connected to the major detail it explains.

✓ ## Check Your Understanding

Read the following passage, and then see if you can complete the map and the questions that follow.

¹With the possible exception of very small, isolated, primitive groups, every human society has had some sort of class system. ²In ancient Rome, there were four major social classes. ³To begin with, at the top of the heap were the aristocrats, called "patricians." ⁴This term derived from the word for father—*pater*—and is still sometimes used today; it also survives in the name Patricia. ⁵Second, as a practical matter if not in principle, were the soldiers, an enormously powerful group. ⁶One Roman emperor, on his deathbed, advised his son: "Enrich the soldiers; nothing else matters." ⁷Next came the common people, called the plebeians. ⁸(This term too survives today: a freshman at a military academy is called a plebe.) ⁹The plebeians were artisans, shopkeepers, and laborers. ¹⁰Fourth, at the bottom, were slaves. ¹¹They could work as domestic servants, manual laborers, and so on; but some slaves were educated and served as teachers.

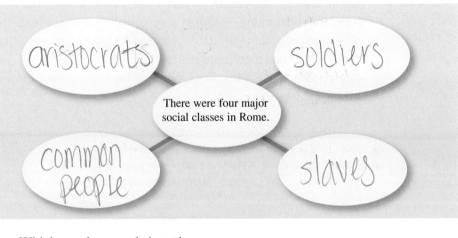

aristocrats   soldiers

There were four major
social classes in Rome.

common
people   slaves

Which word or words introduce:
1. The first major detail? _to begin with_
2. The second major detail? _Second_
3. The third major detail? _Next_
3. The last major detail? _fourth_

Explanation

The map sets off the major details in a very visual way. You see at a glance that the four major social groups were aristocrats, soldiers, common people, and slaves. The words that introduce the major details are *To begin with, Second, Next,* and *Fourth.*

PRACTICE 2

Read each passage, and then complete the maps that follow. The main ideas are given so that you can focus on finding the supporting details. The first passage requires only major details. The second passage calls for you to add both major and minor details.

A. [1]Today, most people smile when someone takes a picture of them. [2]Look at a few of the earliest American photographs, however, and you'll see a batch of frowning grumps staring back at you. [3]But that doesn't mean our ancestors were angry all the time. [4]There are several reasons why early photographic subjects never smiled in pictures. [5]For one thing, photography was a serious business back then. [6]Not everyone was lucky enough to be in a picture, and those who were wanted to do it right. [7]People expected their photos to be passed on from generation to generation. [8]They wanted their posterity to remember them as being serious and dignified. [9]Second, people could not keep smiling for the length of time required to take a picture. [10]People had to stay perfectly still for ten or twenty minutes while the camera took the photo. [11]If they moved at all during that time, the picture would come out blurry. [12]Holding a smile that long would be quite difficult, not to mention uncomfortable. [13]Third, most people did not want to show their teeth. [14]Since no one had toothpaste and few brushed their teeth at all, dental problems were commonplace. [15]No one wanted to be remembered for a mouth full of cavities and rot.

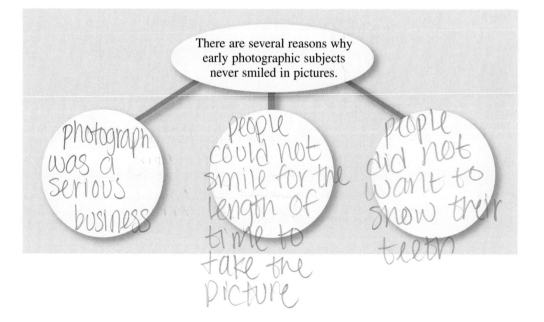

There are several reasons why early photographic subjects never smiled in pictures.

photograph was a serious business

people could not smile for the length of time to take the picture

people did not want to show their teeth

B. ¹Contrary to popular assumption, ancient slavery was not usually based on racism, but on one of three other factors. ²The first was debt. ³In some societies, creditors could enslave people who could not pay their debts. ⁴The second was crime. ⁵Instead of being killed, a murderer or thief might be enslaved by the family of the victim as a compensation for their loss. ⁶The third was war and conquest. ⁷When one group of people conquered another, they often enslaved some of the vanquished. ⁸Historian Gerda Lerner notes that the first people enslaved through warfare were women. ⁹When tribal men raided a village or camp, they killed the men, raped the women, and then brought the women back as slaves. ¹⁰The women were valued for sexual purposes, for reproduction, and for their labor. ¹¹Roughly twenty-five hundred years ago, when Greece was but a collection of city-states, slavery was common. ¹²A city that became powerful and vanquished another city would enslave some of the vanquished. ¹³Both slaves and slaveholders were Greek. ¹⁴Similarly, when Rome became the supreme power about two thousand years ago, following the custom of that time, the Romans enslaved some of the Greeks they had conquered. ¹⁵More educated than their conquerors, some of these slaves served as tutors in Roman homes.

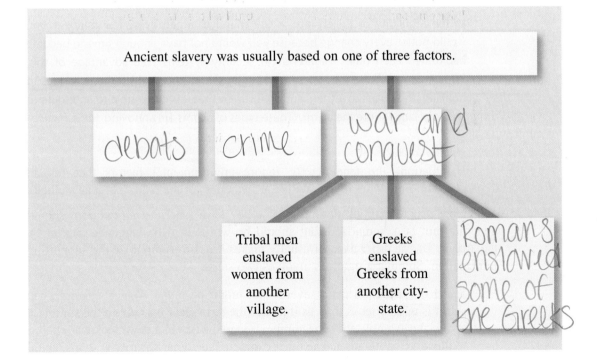

Ancient slavery was usually based on one of three factors.

debts | crime | war and conquest

Tribal men enslaved women from another village.

Greeks enslaved Greeks from another city-state.

Romans enslaved some of the Greeks

Summarizing

In addition to outlining and mapping, summarizing will help you take effective notes on main ideas and supporting details. A **summary** is the reduction of a large amount of information to its most important points. The length and kind of summary will depend upon one's purpose as well as the material in question. Often, a summary will consist of a main idea and its major supporting details. As a general guideline, a paragraph might be reduced to a sentence or two, an article might be reduced to a paragraph, and a textbook chapter might be reduced to about three pages of notes.

One of the most common types of summarizing occurs when you are taking study notes on textbook material. Very often you will find it helpful to summarize examples of key terms. For instance, look at the following textbook passage and the summary that follows.

> [1]**Habituation** is the tendency to ignore environmental factors that remain constant. [2]The brain seems "prewired" to pay more attention to changes in the environment than to stimuli that remain constant. [3]Have you ever gotten a new clock and thought it had a very loud tick, but in a short time you realized you weren't aware of its ticking at all? [4]This happens because you become habituated to the regularity of the sound. [5]If the sound changed every few minutes, you would notice every change because you would not have enough time to become habituated each time. [6]High-end car security systems take advantage of this. [7]When activated, the security system begins with a siren, which then changes to honking, then back to a siren, and so forth, so that it is impossible to habituate to the noise and ignore the alarm. [8]These types of alarms are annoying, but effective.

Summary

Habituation—the tendency to ignore environmental factors that remain constant. For example, you will lose awareness of the ticking of a new clock.

Note that a textbook definition of a key term (such as *habituation*) should generally not be summarized, but should be worded in the language chosen by the author. On the other hand, it usually makes sense to summarize the supporting information. Summarizing often involves two steps:

1   *Select* one example from several that might be given. Which example you select is up to you, as long as it makes the term clear for you. In the summary above, the example about becoming used to the tick of a new clock was chosen to illustrate habituation. The other example, about car security systems, could have been chosen as well.

2 *Condense* the example if it's not already very brief. Notice that the example about the new clock has been condensed from a long sentence to a short one.

A definition of a key term followed by one condensed example is a very useful way to take notes—especially in introductory college courses, where many terms are defined and illustrated.

> *Study Hint:* If you have a textbook chapter to learn, very often you can get the information you need by doing two things: 1) writing down the definitions in the chapter and summarized examples of the definitions, and 2) writing down lists of major supporting details and any minor details that you think are important.

Summarizing a Passage

Read the selection below, taken from an introductory textbook for a college social science course. As is often the case in such introductory texts, a new term is presented and then followed by an extended example. Complete the study notes by circling the answer choice that best summarizes that example.

> [1]Soon after birth, some animals will follow and become attached to the first thing they see or hear that happens to move, a behavior known as **imprinting**. [2]Ordinarily, the "thing" on which the animal imprints is its mother, but experience can dictate otherwise. [3]When animal behaviorist Konrad Lorenz hatched young geese in an incubator, they imprinted on him, following him around and responding to his calls as if he were their mother. [4]In the laboratory, ducklings have imprinted on decoys, rubber balls, and wooden blocks. [5]Once imprinting has occurred, it is usually hard to reverse, even when the "mother" is an inanimate object that can offer neither food nor affection. [6]These facts suggest that imprinting is a special type of perceptual learning that occurs because at a particular stage in development, the animal's nervous system is geared to respond to a conspicuous moving object in a certain way.

Study notes

Imprinting—some animals soon after birth follow and become attached to the first moving thing they see or hear.

Example—

A. Imprinting is hard to reverse even if the "mother" is an inanimate object.
B. An animal's nervous system is geared to respond to a conspicuous moving object in a certain way.
C. Young geese hatched in an incubator followed around and responded to an animal behaviorist as if he were their mother.

Explanation

Useful study notes should include a clear example of a new term. In the case of the paragraph above, answer C summarizes a specific example that helps us clearly understand the term. Neither of the other two answers provides an example of the term.

PRACTICE 3

Read each of the following textbook selections. Then complete the study notes by circling the letter of the answer that best summarizes an example of the term being defined.

A. [1]**Displacement** involves the redirection of repressed motives and emotions from their original objects to substitute objects. [2]The woman who has always wanted to be a mother may feel inadequate when she learns that she cannot have children. [3]As a result, she may become extremely attached to a pet or to a niece or nephew. [4]Perhaps the most familiar example of displacement is the person who must smile and agree with a difficult boss, then comes home and "blows up" at family members for no reason.

Study notes

Displacement—the redirection of repressed motives and emotions from their original objects to substitute objects.

Example—

A. A woman who has always wanted to be a mother feels inadequate when she learns that she cannot have children.

B. A man must smile and agree with a difficult boss.

C. A man comes home and "blows up" at family members for no reason.

B. [1]How do we explain cultural differences in emotional expressions? [2]Each culture has its own **display rules**—rules that govern how, when, and where to express emotions. [3]Parents teach their children display rules by responding angrily to some outbursts, by being sympathetic to others, and on occasion by simply ignoring them. [4]In this way, children learn which emotions they may express in certain situations and which emotions they are expected to control. [5]There are almost as many variations in display rules as there are cultures in the world. [6]In Japanese culture, for instance, children learn to conceal negative emotions with a stoic expression or polite smile. [7]Young males in the Masai culture are similarly expected to conceal their emotions in public by appearing stern and stony-faced. [8]Public physical contact is also governed by display rules. [9]North Americans and Asians are generally not touch-oriented, and only the closest family and friends might hug in greeting or farewell. [10]In contrast, Latin Americans and Middle Easterners often embrace and hold hands as a sign of casual friendship.

Study notes

Display rules—rules which govern how, when, and where to express emotions.

Example—

A. There are many variations in display rules in cultures all over the world.
B. In Japan, children are taught to conceal negative emotions with a stoic expression or polite smile.
C. Parents teach their children display rules by varying their response to the child's behavior.

A Final Note

This chapter has centered on supporting details as they appear in well-organized paragraphs. But keep in mind that supporting details are part of readings of any length, including selections that may not have an easy-to-follow list of one major detail after another. Starting with the reading at the end of this chapter (page 82), you will be given practice in answering all kinds of questions about key supporting details. These questions will develop your ability to pay close, careful attention to what you are reading.

CHAPTER REVIEW

In this chapter, you learned the following:

- Major and minor details provide the added information you need to make sense of a main idea.

- List words and addition words can help you to find major and minor supporting details.

- Outlining, mapping, and summarizing are useful note-taking strategies.

- Outlines show the relationship between the main idea, major details, and minor details of a passage.

- Maps are very visual outlines.

- Writing a definition and summarizing an example is a good way to take notes on a new term.

The next chapter—Chapter 3—will show you how to find implied main ideas and central points.

On the Web: If you are using this book in class, you can go to our website for more practice in recognizing supporting details. Visit our Learning Center at **www.townsendpress.net** for additional activities and an instructional video on this skill.

 REVIEW TEST 1

To review what you've learned in this chapter, answer each of these questions about supporting details by filling in the blank.

1. Two key reading skills that go hand in hand are finding the main idea and identifying the major and minor _____ that support the main idea.

2. **List words**—phrases such as *several types of*, *three steps*, and *four reasons*—are important words to note because they alert you that a list of _____ is coming.

3. Outlining is a way to show at a glance the relationship between a main idea and its _____. It is a helpful way to take study notes on what you have read.

4. Another good way to take study notes is to use a _____ — a highly visual outline that uses circles, boxes, and other shapes to set off main ideas and supporting details.

5. When taking notes on textbook material, you will often find it useful to write out each definition in full and then select and _____ one example of that definition.

REVIEW TEST 2

Here is a chance to apply your understanding of supporting details to a selection from a college textbook, *Understanding Psychology*, by Charles G. Morris and Albert A. Maisto. Read the selection and then answer the supporting-detail questions that follow. There are also questions that involve finding main ideas.

Preview

Unlike many other recreational drugs, alcohol is legal, inexpensive, widely available, and socially acceptable. These factors make it easy to overlook the effects of alcohol—effects as devastating as those of any street drug.

Words to Watch

psychoactive (1): affecting the mind
chronic (2): long-lasting
impairments (2): damages
myopia (5): nearsightedness
correlated with (6): related to

ALCOHOL

Charles D. Morris and Albert A. Maisto

1   The most frequently used psychoactive° drug in Western societies is alcohol. In spite of, or perhaps because of, the fact that it is legal and socially approved, alcohol is America's number-one drug problem. A large-scale survey of adults in the United States found that nearly 9 percent of those surveyed reported alcohol dependence or abuse in the previous 12 months. More than 30 percent reported alcohol dependence or abuse sometime in the course of their lives. More than 25 percent of high school seniors say that they got drunk sometime in the past 30 days, and alcohol is also a significant problem among middle-school students. At least 14 million Americans (more than 7 percent of the population aged 18 and older) have problems with drinking, including more than 8 million alcoholics, who are addicted to alcohol. Three times as many men as women are problem drinkers. For both sexes, alcohol abuse and addiction is highest in the 18- to 29-year-old age group.

2   Excessive chronic° alcohol use can harm virtually every organ in the body, beginning with the brain, and is associated with impairments° in perceptual-motor skills, visual-spatial processing, problem solving, and abstract reasoning. Alcohol is the leading cause of liver disease and kidney damage, is a major factor in cardiovascular disease, increases the risk of certain cancers, and can lead to sexual dysfunction and infertility. Alcohol is particularly damaging to the nervous system during the teenage years. The total economic cost of alcohol abuse and dependence in American is estimated at nearly $200 billion annually. In addition, alcohol abuse is directly involved in more than 20,000 deaths annually, and the number is rising.

3   The social costs of abusing alcohol are high as well. Alcohol is involved in a substantial proportion of violent and accidental deaths, including suicides, which makes it the leading contributor (after AIDS) to death among young people. Alcohol is implicated in more than two-thirds of all fatal automobile accidents, two-thirds of all murders,

two-thirds of all spouse beatings, and more than half of all cases of violent child abuse. Moreover, the use of alcohol during pregnancy has been linked to a variety of birth defects, the most notable being fetal alcohol syndrome. More than 40 percent of all heavy drinkers die before the age of 65 (compared with less than 20 percent of nondrinkers). In addition, there is the untold cost in psychological trauma suffered by the nearly 30 million children of alcohol abusers.

4   What makes alcohol so powerful? Alcohol first affects the frontal lobes of the brain, which figure prominently in inhibitions, impulse control, reasoning, and judgment. As consumption continues, alcohol impairs functions of the cerebellum, the center of motor control and balance. Eventually, alcohol consumption affects the spinal cord and medulla, which regulate such involuntary functions as breathing, body temperature, and heart rate. A blood-alcohol level of 0.25 percent or more may cause this part of the nervous system to shut down and may severely impair functioning; slightly high levels can cause death from alcohol poisoning.

5   Even in moderate quantities, alcohol affects perception, motor processes, memory, and judgment. It diminishes the ability to see clearly, to perceive depth, and to distinguish the difference between bright lights and colors, and it generally affects spatial-cognitive functioning—all clearly necessary for driving a car safely. Alcohol

interferes with memory storage: Heavy drinkers may also experience blackouts, which make them unable to remember anything that occurred while they were drinking; but even long-term alcoholics show improvement in memory, attention, balance, and neurological functioning after three months of sobriety. Heavy drinkers have difficulty focusing on relevant information and ignoring inaccurate, irrelevant information, thus leading to poor judgments, a condition called alcoholic myopia°.

6   Dozens of studies demonstrate that alcohol use is correlated with° increases in aggression, hostility, violence, and abusive behavior. Thus, intoxication makes people less aware of and less concerned about the negative consequences of their actions, increasing their likelihood to engage in risky behavior. The same principle applies to potential victims. For instance, when women are intoxicated, their ability to accurately evaluate a dangerous situation with a potential male aggressor is diminished, so that their risk of being sexually assaulted increases. Not surprisingly, people who are intoxicated are more likely to engage in unprotected sex than if they were sober. The dangers of alcohol notwithstanding, alcohol continues to be popular because of its short-term effects. As a depressant, it calms the nervous system, much like a general anesthetic. Thus, people consume alcohol to relax or to enhance their mood.

Reading Comprehension Questions

Main Ideas

_____ 1. The central idea of the selection is that
   A. the most frequently used psychoactive drug in Western societies is alcohol.
   B. although it is legal, alcohol is America's number-one drug problem.
   C. alcohol can harm both the brain and the body in a number of ways.
   D. despite the fact that alcohol use is correlated with increases in aggression, hostility, violence, and abusive behavior, it continues to be popular.

_____ 2. The main idea of paragraph 3 is stated in the
   A. first sentence.
   B. second sentence.
   C. third sentence.
   D. fourth sentence.

_____ 3. The main idea of paragraph 5 is stated in the
   A. first sentence.
   B. second sentence.
   C. third sentence.
   D. final sentence.

Supporting Details

_____ 4. Alcohol abuse and dependence cost America about how much annually?
   A. $50 billion.
   B. $150 billion.
   C. $200 billion.
   D. $400 billion.

_____ 5. According to the authors, blackouts among heavy drinkers are an example of
   A. alcoholic myopia.
   B. problems with impulse control.
   C. psychological trauma.
   D. alcohol's interference with memory storage.

_____ 6. According to the authors, having unprotected sex while intoxicated is an example of
   A. memory storage.
   B. impaired functions of the cerebellum.
   C. alcoholic myopia.
   D. problems in spatial-cognitive functioning.

_____ 7. After three months of sobriety, even long-term alcoholics
    A. report a decline in their craving for alcohol.
    B. show an improvement in liver and kidney function.
    C. show improvement in memory, attention, balance, and neurological functioning.
    D. all of the above.

8–10. Add the details missing in the following partial outline of the reading. Do so by filling in each blank with the letter of one of the sentences in the box below.

Details Missing from the Outline

    A. Alcohol is implicated in a large proportion of violent deaths.
    B. Alcohol causes liver disease and kidney damage; it also contributes to cardiovascular disease, cancer, sexual dysfunction, and infertility.
    C. Alcohol is linked to increases in aggression, hostility, violence, and abusive behavior.

Central point: **Alcohol abuse harms Americans in a number of ways.**

    A. Alcohol causes a number of physical impairments.

        1. Alcohol abuse harms the brain.

        2. _____

    B. Alcohol abuse has high social costs.

        1. _____

        2. Use of alcohol during pregnancy has been linked to a variety of birth defects (fetal alcohol syndrome).

        3. More than 40% of all heavy drinkers die before the age of 65.

        4. Children of alcohol abusers suffer psychological trauma.

    C. Alcohol affects behavior.

        1. Perception, motor processes, memory, and judgment are all affected by alcohol.

        2. _____

        3. Alcohol abusers are more likely to engage in risky behavior, such as unprotected sex.

Discussion Questions

1. Were you surprised by some of the facts mentioned in this reading? If so, which ones surprised you?

2. Why, in your opinion, is alcohol abuse highest in the 18-to-29-year-old age group? What is it about this age group that makes it most likely to abuse alcohol?

3. Given all we know about the harmful effects of alcohol abuse, why do you think alcohol use is still socially approved while other harmful drugs are not?

4. From 1920 to 1933, the manufacture, transportation, and sale of alcohol was prohibited in the United States. Despite this period of prohibition, many Americans continued to consume alcohol. Given the failure of prohibition and the current widespread consumption of alcohol, is there *anything* Americans can do to lessen alcohol abuse, especially among the young?

Note: Writing assignments for this selection appear on pages 635–636.

Check Your Performance		**SUPPORTING DETAILS**	
Activity	*Number Right*	*Points*	*Score*
Review Test 1 (5 items)	_____	× 6 =	_____
Review Test 2 (10 items)	_____	× 7 =	_____
		TOTAL SCORE =	_____ %

Enter your total score into the **Reading Performance Chart: Review Tests** on the inside back cover.

SUPPORTING DETAILS: Mastery Test 1

A. Answer the supporting-detail questions that follow the passage below.

¹The other day I heard someone say, "I wish I'd known then what I know now." ²The statement made me ask myself what I *do* know now that I didn't know when I was a teenager, still in high school, living at home with my parents. ³I eventually decided that I have learned several important lessons. ⁴The first is that almost any decision is better than no decision. ⁵Gather the best information you can, make a decision, and then show up and do your best. ⁶No matter what happens next, you will learn and grow from the experience. ⁷Another lesson I've learned is that life is not fair. ⁸Good people sometimes suffer unimaginable hardships; bad people sometimes live seemingly charmed lives. ⁹You can protest, "But that's not fair!" until you're blue in the face, but it won't change a thing. ¹⁰All you can do is to try to be fair and just in your own life and not be embittered by the reality around you. ¹¹A final lesson I've learned is that people are very complex. ¹²The worst of us are capable of moments of generosity and compassion; the best of us can be petty, small-minded, and hurtful. ¹³To decide that you know everything about someone is to set yourself up for a shock. ¹⁴We are all full of surprises; we are wonderfully and maddeningly complicated.

lessons learned

____A____ 1. Sentence 3 provides
   A. the main idea.
   B. a major detail.
   C. a minor detail.

____B____ 2. Sentence 7 provides
   A. the main idea.
   B. a major detail.
   C. a minor detail.

____C____ 3. Sentences 12–14 provide
   A. the main idea.
   B. a major detail.
   C. minor details.

____B____ 4. How many major supporting details does the paragraph include?
   A. Two
   B. Three
   C. Four

5. *Fill in the blank:* One addition word that introduces a major supporting detail is _____another_____.

(Continues on next page)

B. (6–10.) Complete the outline of the following textbook passage by adding the main idea and the missing major details.

[1]Advertising fulfills four basic functions in society. [2]For one thing, it serves a marketing purpose by helping companies that provide products or services sell their products. [3]Personal selling, sales promotions, and advertising work together to help market the product. [4]In addition, advertising is educational. [5]People learn about new products and services, or improvements in existing ones, through advertising. [6]Advertising also plays an economic role. [7]The ability to advertise allows new competitors to enter the business arena. [8]Competition, in turn, encourages product improvements and can lead to lower prices. [9]Last of all, advertising performs a definite social function. [10]By vividly displaying the material and cultural opportunities available in a free-enterprise system, advertising helps increase productivity and raises the standard of living.

functions of advertising

Main idea: _Advertising fulfills four basic functions in society._

1. _Serves a marketing purpose_
2. _educational_
3. _performs a definite social function_
4. _helps increase productivity_

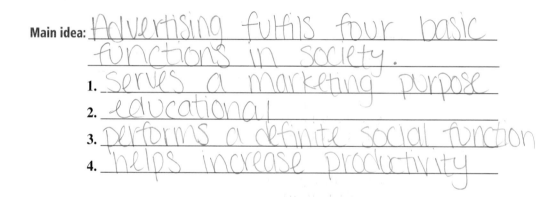

SUPPORTING DETAILS: Mastery Test 2

A. Answer the supporting-detail questions that follow the passage below.

¹Although hunger is clearly a motive that is tied to biological needs, psychological factors are also involved in the regulation of food intake. ²Learning plays a powerful role in determining *what* we eat, *when* we eat (we are often ready to eat at our customary times for eating, even if we have just had a snack), and even *how much* we eat (many families encourage and model overeating). ³Studies of nonhuman animals show that even rats and chimpanzees learn what to eat by watching older animals. ⁴Emotions also play a role in eating. ⁵People who are anxious often eat more than usual, and people who are depressed may lose their appetite for long periods of time. ⁶Perhaps the most troublesome psychological factor to those who are trying to control their eating, however, is incentives— external clues that activate motives. ⁷The smell of freshly baked bread makes you hungry; passing a fast-food joint on your way home from school creates a craving for french fries; and the sight of the dessert creates a desire to eat even when you are way past the point of biological hunger. ⁸Laboratory research with animals has shown that incentives can be powerful enough under some circumstances to push weight above the natural set point. ⁹All rats will overeat to the point of obesity if they have easy access to large quantities of a variety of tasty high-calorie foods.

_____ 1. Sentence 1 provides
    A. the main idea.
    B. a major detail.
    C. a minor detail.

_____ 2. Sentence 2 provides
    A. the main idea.
    B. a major detail.
    C. a minor detail.

_____ 3. Sentences 7–9 provide
    A. the main idea.
    B. a major detail.
    C. minor details.

_____ 4. How many major supporting details does the paragraph include?
    A. Two
    B. Three
    C. Four

5. *Fill in the blank:* One addition word that introduces a major supporting detail is _____.

(Continues on next page)

B. (6–10.) Complete the outline of the following textbook passage by adding the main idea and the missing major details.

¹For many adolescents, finding an identity requires a period of intense self-exploration called an identity crisis. ²Psychologists have identified four possible outcomes of this process. ³One is *identity achievement*. ⁴Adolescents who have reached this status have passed through the identity crisis and succeeded in making personal choices about their beliefs and goals. ⁵They are comfortable with those choices because the choices are their own. ⁶In contrast are adolescents who have taken the path of *identity foreclosure*. ⁷They have prematurely settled on an identity that others provided for them. ⁸They have become what those others want them to be without ever going through an identity crisis. ⁹Other adolescents are in *moratorium* regarding the choice of an identity. ¹⁰They are in the process of actively exploring various role options, but they have not yet committed to any of them. ¹¹Finally, there are teens who are experiencing *identity diffusion*. ¹²They avoid considering role options in any conscious way. ¹³Many are dissatisfied with this condition, but are unable to start a search to "find themselves." ¹⁴Some resort to escapist activities such as drug or alcohol abuse.

Main idea: <u>Psychologists have identified four possible outcomes</u>

1. <u>identity achievement</u>

2. <u>identity foreclosure</u>

3. <u>moratorium</u>

4. <u>identity diffusion</u>

SUPPORTING DETAILS: Mastery Test 3

A. Answer the supporting-detail questions that follow the passage below.

¹Because family violence is a difficult and even taboo subject, the reality surrounding it has become shrouded in myths and misperceptions. ²A first widespread myth is that family violence occurs only among the poor. ³It is true that among families living at or below the poverty level, domestic violence occurs five times as frequently as in more affluent families. ⁴While this does mean that poor people are more likely to experience family violence, it does not mean that most, let alone all, poor families are violent. ⁵A second myth is that violence cannot happen in families where genuine affection exists. ⁶Unfortunately, people who have not learned constructive ways of dealing with anger or frustration may well lash out violently at people whom they love. ⁷Parents can become violent while disciplining their beloved children, and a spouse can resort to violence against a spouse that he or she loves. ⁸While such violence is always unacceptable, it does not prove that love does not exist in the relationship. ⁹An additional common myth is that abused children grow up to be abusive parents. ¹⁰Again, this myth represents a misrepresentation of data. ¹¹While it is true that abused children are more likely to become abusive parents, the majority of child-abuse victims do not grow up to abuse their own children. ¹²A last myth is that alcohol and drug use cause family violence. ¹³It is true that people who drink heavily or use drugs are more likely to abuse their spouses and children. ¹⁴It does not follow, however, that the drug or alcohol use is the cause of the violence. ¹⁵While abusers often use their drinking or drug use as the excuse for their loss of control, personal problems and choices are at the root of their violent actions.

family violence

_____ 1. The main idea is expressed in sentence
   A. 1.   B. 2.   C. 3.

_____ 2. The major supporting details of this paragraph are
   A. causes of myths.   B. types of myths.   C. results of myths.

_____ 3. The second major detail of the paragraph is introduced in sentence
   A. 4.   B. 5.   C. 7.

_____ 4. The third major detail of the paragraph is introduced in sentence
   A. 9.   B. 10.   C. 12.

_____ 5. The fourth major detail is signaled with the addition word
   A. *also.*   B. *while.*   C. *last.*

(Continues on next page)

B. (6–10.) Complete the map of the following textbook passage by adding the main idea and the missing major details.

¹It's a rare person who hasn't at one point worked for a "difficult" boss. ²Difficult bosses have their own personal quirks, but many of them fall into the following categories. ³One common "bad boss" is the bully. ⁴Like a schoolyard bully, this boss thrives on domination. ⁵He will attempt to intimidate everyone around him by shouting and blustering. ⁶Attempting to mollify a bully boss by being super-nice and cooperative rarely works; he perceives the behavior as weakness, and will be more abusive than ever. ⁷On the other end of the bad boss spectrum is the jellyfish. ⁸Unlike the bully, who loves to tell people what they've done wrong, the jellyfish hates conflict so much that he won't correct anyone. ⁹Tasks are done badly or not at all, damaging the workflow and the morale of other employees, while he looks the other way. ¹⁰He refuses to accept responsibility for being the boss. ¹¹The next common difficult boss is the workaholic. ¹²He lives for his job, and he expects his employees to do so as well. ¹³He feels no qualms about calling workers at home in the evenings or on weekends, assuming that they, too, will consider the job more important than their personal lives. ¹⁴Still another difficult boss is the aloof boss. ¹⁵No one knows what he is thinking except him. ¹⁶He makes what appear to be sudden, arbitrary decisions without consulting anyone. ¹⁷Workers have no idea from day to day whether he is satisfied with their performance or planning to fire them.

difficult bosses

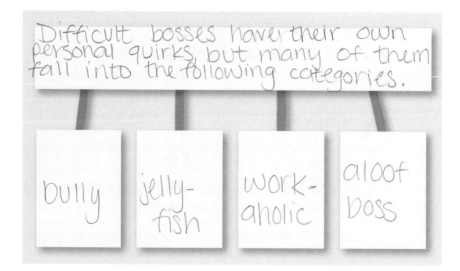

Difficult bosses have their own personal quirks, but many of them fall into the following categories.

| bully | jelly-fish | work-aholic | aloof boss |

SUPPORTING DETAILS: Mastery Test 4

A. Answer the supporting-detail questions that follow the passage below.

¹While criminal acts may seem random and unpredictable, in fact they, like almost everything, follow their own patterns. ²Robbery, for instance, has several very distinctive characteristics. ³To begin with, the majority of robberies occur in the cold winter months. ⁴There are several reasons for this. ⁵Around the holiday season, stores are taking in more money and shoppers are likely to be carrying more cash than usual, making both tempting targets. ⁶The cold weather makes it look natural for the robber to wear a heavy coat, which makes it easier to conceal a weapon. ⁷And the cold weather keeps most people off the street, thereby making it less likely that anyone will witness a holdup. ⁸Secondly, most robberies take place outdoors, on or near a highway. ⁹Such easy access to a highway enables the robber to make a quick escape from the scene of the crime. ¹⁰Yet another characteristic of robberies is that most are committed by people carrying weapons. ¹¹While purse-snatchings and the like may be committed unarmed, the great majority of robberies are planned ahead of time and involve a weapon, usually a gun. ¹²A final characteristic of robbery is that it usually occurs between strangers. ¹³Unlike other violent crimes such as murder and rape, which usually involve people who know each other, a robber and his victim or victims are rarely acquainted.

characteristic of robby

___B___ 1. The main idea is expressed in sentence
A. 1.   B. 2.   C. 3.

___B___ 2. The major supporting details of this paragraph are
A. results.   B. characteristics.   C. reasons.

___A___ 3. The first major detail of the paragraph is introduced in sentence
A. 3.   B. 4.   C. 8.

___A___ 4. The second major detail of the paragraph is introduced in sentence
A. 8.   B. 10.   C. 12.

___B___ 5. Sentences 4–7 contain
A. major supporting details.   B. minor supporting details.

6. *Fill in the blank:* One addition word that introduces a major supporting detail is _____Secondly_____.

(Continues on next page)

B. (7–10.) Complete the outline of the following textbook passage by adding the main idea, the missing major details (definitions), and one summarized example of a definition.

> [1]David Elkind used Piaget's notion of adolescent egocentrism to account for two fallacies of thought he noticed in this age group. [2]The first is the imaginary audience—the tendency of teenagers to feel they are constantly being observed by others, that people are always judging them on their appearance and behavior. [3]This feeling of being perpetually "onstage" may be the source of much self-consciousness, concern about personal appearance, and showing off in adolescence.
>
> [4]The other fallacy of adolescent thinking is the personal fable—adolescents' unrealistic sense of their own uniqueness. [5]For instance, a teenager might feel that others couldn't possibly understand the love he or she feels toward a boyfriend or girlfriend because that love is so unique and special. [6]This view is related to the feeling of invulnerability we mentioned earlier. [7]Many teenagers believe they are so different from other people that they won't be touched by the negative things that happen to others. [8]This feeling of invulnerability is consistent with the reckless risk-taking among people in this age group.

Main idea: _____

_____

Major detail 1: _____

_____

Major detail 2: _____

_____

    Example: _____

_____

_____

_____

SUPPORTING DETAILS: Mastery Test 5

A. Answer the supporting-detail questions that follow the passage below.

[1]Managers don't always do a good job of evaluating their employees. [2]The halo effect, the Hawthorne effect, and uniformity are three common problems in employee performance reviews. [3]The halo effect is one of the most well-known threats to the accuracy of performance reviews. [4]In the classic situation, a person is given a good rating solely because all previous evaluations have been good. [5]A good evaluation is given on faith in previous reviews and without paying attention to the current work habits of the worker. [6]A further threat to reviews is the Hawthorne effect, which says that the act of measuring something changes that thing, so one can never exactly predict anything by relying on observation alone. [7]In other words, if you observe people to evaluate them, they will change their behavior. [8]Because people change their behavior when they are observed, we don't really know what their typical performance is; and not knowing that, we can't really predict if it will continue in the future. [9]Uniformity, or giving everyone in a team or department the same evaluation, is also a problem in performance reviews. [10]When everyone is rated the same despite differing achievements, there is a serious de-motivating effect. [11]In addition to being unfair, if managers rate everyone high or average, they will have a much more difficult time trying to fire someone who deserves to be released.

_____ 1. The main idea is expressed in sentence
      A. 1.   B. 2.   C. 3.

_____ 2. The paragraph is made up of a series of
      A. types.   B. reviews.   C. definitions.

_____ 3. The first major detail of the paragraph is introduced in sentence
      A. 3.   B. 4.   C. 5.

_____ 4. The second major detail of the paragraph is introduced in sentence
      A. 6.   B. 7.   C. 9.

_____ 5. The third major detail of the paragraph is introduced in sentence
      A. 8.   B. 9.   C. 11.

(Continues on next page)

B. (6–10.) Complete the map of the following textbook passage by adding the main idea and the missing major details.

> [1]America has always been a nation of immigrants. [2]Unlike old countries with a homogenous population, America has defined what it is to be an American in terms of a political tradition. [3]Ideally, American political culture is thought to include the following beliefs. [4]First is the American principle of liberty. [5]This holds that people should be free to act as they choose, providing that they do not interfere unreasonably with the well-being of others. [6]A second component of the political culture is the principle of self-government. [7]It proclaims that the people are the ultimate source of authority, and that their general welfare is the only legitimate purpose of government. [8]A third component is equality—the belief that all individuals have moral worth, are entitled to fair treatment under the law, and should have equal opportunity for material gain and political influence. [9]Finally there is unity: the principle that despite our individual differences, Americans are one people that form an indivisible union.

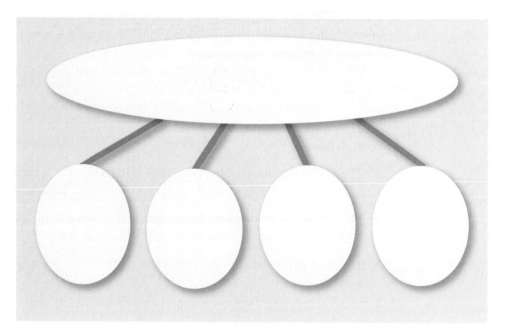

SUPPORTING DETAILS: Mastery Test 6

A. (1–7.) Outline the following textbook passage, which includes two main ideas and supporting details for each of those main ideas.

¹People use birth control for different reasons. ²Many career-minded individuals carefully plan the timing and spacing of children to best provide for their children's financial support without sacrificing their job status. ³Others choose methods of birth control to ensure that they will never have children.

⁴In the choice of birth control methods, financial and legal considerations are one significant factor. ⁵Many people must of necessity take the cost of a method into account when selecting appropriate birth control. ⁶The cost of sterilization and abortion can prohibit some low-income people from choosing these alternatives, especially because federal funds do not support such procedures. ⁷A number of states have established statutes and policies that make contraceptive information and medical services relatively difficult to obtain.

⁸Another important consideration in the use of birth control methods is the availability of professional services. ⁹For instance, some colleges and universities provide contraceptive services through their student health centers. ¹⁰Students in colleges that do not provide such services may find that access to accurate information and clinical services is difficult to obtain and that private professional services are expensive.

¹¹For many people, religious doctrine will be a factor in their selection of a birth control method. ¹²One example is the opposition of the Roman Catholic Church and other religious groups to the use of contraception other than natural family planning.

Main idea: _____

_____

1. _____

2. _____

Main idea: _____

_____

1. _____

2. _____

3. _____

(Continues on next page)

B. (8–10.) Complete the map of the following textbook passage by filling in the missing major supporting details.

¹In the 1800s, millions of Americans moved from the country to the city. ²Big cities had the allure of jobs, entertainment, and socialization. ³However, city life also had its drawbacks. ⁴Sanitation was a serious problem in big cities. ⁵Whereas free-roaming scavengers—chickens, hogs, dogs, and birds—handily cleaned up the garbage in small towns, and backyard latrines were adequate for disposing of human wastes, neither worked when a hundred people lived in a building and shared a single toilet. ⁶City governments provided for waste collection, but even when honestly administered (which was the exception), sanitation departments simply could not keep up. ⁷In addition, health was a major problem in the city. ⁸Crowding led to epidemic outbreaks of serious diseases like smallpox, cholera, measles, typhus, and scarlet fever. ⁹Even less dangerous illnesses like chicken pox, mumps, whooping cough, and influenza were killers in crowded cities. ¹⁰Furthermore, increased crime was a significant urban problem. ¹¹With 14,000 homeless people in New York in 1890, and work difficult to get and unsteady in the best of times, many found the temptations of sneak thievery, pocket picking, purse snatching, and even violent robbery too much to resist. ¹²Whereas the rate of homicide and other serious crimes declined in German and British cities as they grew larger, it tripled in American cities during the 1880s.

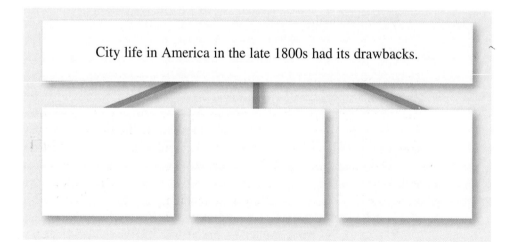

City life in America in the late 1800s had its drawbacks.

3 Implied Main Ideas

In Chapters 1 and 2, you learned the two basic parts of anything you read: a main idea and the supporting details that explain and develop that idea. As you have seen, the main idea may be clearly stated in one sentence of a selection. (topic sentence)

However, sometimes the main idea is **implied**—only suggested by the supporting details and not clearly stated in one sentence. The reader must figure out such an implied main idea by considering the supporting details. In the above cartoon, you can figure out the main idea by noting the details: the newlyweds' car has broken down; and since they are hitchhiking in opposite directions, the implied point is that their marriage has broken down as well.

This chapter offers practice in finding implied main ideas, whether in paragraphs or in longer selections.

Implied Main Ideas

Sometimes a selection lacks a sentence that directly states the main idea. In such cases, the author has simply decided to let the details of the selection suggest the main idea. You must figure out what that implied idea is by deciding upon the point all the details support. For example, read the following paragraph.

[handwritten: Diffences of Men & Women Shopping]

¹Researchers who study the "science" of shopping note that men always move faster than women through a store's aisle. ²Men spend less time looking, too. ³They usually don't like asking where things are, or any other questions. ⁴When a man takes clothing into a dressing room, the only thing that stops him from buying it is if it doesn't fit. ⁵Women, on the other hand, try things on as only part of the consideration process, and garments that fit just fine may still be rejected on other grounds. ⁶Here's another contrast: 86 percent of women look at price tags when they shop. ⁷Only 72 percent of men do. ⁸For a man, ignoring the price tag is almost a measure of his masculinity. ⁹As a result, men are far more easily encouraged to buy more expensive versions of the same product than are women shoppers. ¹⁰They are also far more suggestible than women—men seem so anxious to get out of the store that they'll say yes to almost anything.

You can see that no sentence in the paragraph is a good "umbrella" statement that covers all of the other sentences. To decide on the main idea, we must ask the same three questions we've already used to find main ideas:

- "Who or what is this paragraph about?" That will be the topic.
- "What is the main point the author is trying to make about that topic?"
- And when we think we know the main point, we can test it by asking, "Does *all or most* of the material in the paragraph support this idea?"

In the paragraph above, all of the details are about men and women shoppers, so that must be the topic. Which of the following statements expresses the general point that the author is trying to make about the topic? Check (✓) the answer you think is correct.

_____ A. Men always move faster than women when shopping.

_____ B. Women look at price tags more than men.

__✗__ C. Men and women behave differently when shopping.

_____ D. Men make more expensive choices when shopping.

The details reveal the author's general point to be answer C: men and women behave differently when shopping. All the other statements above are supporting details for this main idea—each tells of a way in which men and women shoppers behave differently. Although the main idea is not directly stated, it is clearly implied by all the material in the paragraph.

Figuring Out Implied Main Ideas in Paragraphs

Remember, to find implied main ideas, it often helps to decide on the topic first. Do so by asking yourself, "Who or what is the selection about?" After you find the topic, then ask yourself, "What is the author's main point about the topic?"

✔ *Check Your Understanding*

Read the following selection and try to answer the questions that follow.

¹You're in your car headed home from school, but traffic is barely moving and, according to the radio report, getting worse by the minute. ²Suddenly, another motorist nearly removes your fender trying to cut into your lane. ³Your pulse accelerates as you shout insults at the driver, who cannot even hear you. ⁴Your stomach tenses as you contemplate the term paper that you have to work on tonight. ⁵If you don't finish the paper soon, you won't have time to study for your math test, not to mention your biology quiz. ⁶Then you remember that you promised the person you're dating that the two of you would get together tonight, but there's no way that can happen; another fight looms on the horizon. ⁷Your classmate asks your opinion of the tuition increase the college announced yesterday, which you've been trying not to think about. ⁸You're already in debt, and your parents are bugging you about changing schools, but you don't want to leave your friends. ⁹Your heartbeat quickens as you contemplate the debate you'll have to wage with your parents. ¹⁰You feel wired with tension at all this stress in your life.

_____ 1. What is the topic of the above paragraph?
- A. Stress in traffic situations
- B. Dealing with personal relationships
- C. Challenges in schoolwork
- D. Stress

_____ 2. Which statement best expresses the unstated main idea of the paragraph?
- A. To deal with stress, people must work to simplify their lives.
- B. Traffic situations and college debt are major causes of tension in life.
- C. Many different circumstances can create stress in people's lives.
- D. The demands of college study can interfere with personal relationships.

Explanation

The topic, referred to directly or indirectly in several sentences, is "Stress." The implied main idea is statement C, that many different circumstances—in this case, traffic situations, schoolwork, personal relationships, and debt—can create stress in people's lives. Statement A is not covered in the paragraph, and statements B and D are too narrow, each referring only to one or two of the causes of stress.

When you think you have determined an implied main idea, be sure to test yourself by asking, *"Does all or most of the material in the paragraph support this idea?"* Only statement C covers all of the content of the above paragraph.

PRACTICE 1

Read each paragraph and then answer the questions that follow. Remember to find a topic by asking "Who or what is the selection about?" and to find an implied main idea by asking "What is the author's point about the topic?"

Hint: Noticing addition words (such as *first, another, also, moreover,* and *finally*) will help you identify the major supporting details that can suggest the main idea.

Paragraph 1

¹Pet owners like to assume that the cat's purr is an expression of pleasure, but this assumption is only partly true. ²Originally, the purr probably evolved as a homing device. ³Because newly born kittens cannot see, hear, or smell, they need some signal to help them feed. ⁴Since they can feel vibratory movement, they can locate their mother through her purring. ⁵Cats may also use the purr as self-comfort. ⁶Felines that are anxious, injured, or ill often issue the same low, continuous, rattling hum. ⁷Like submissive posturing among dogs, purring may be a signal of appeasement to other cats or to people. ⁸In this case, it communicates that the purring cat is not a threat. ⁹Recently, scientists have discovered that cats may purr to help themselves get better when they're injured. ¹⁰In this theory, purring is actually a low-energy mechanism that stimulates muscle and bones. ¹¹The healing power of their purring may even explain their "nine lives." ¹²Then again, the purring cat may simply be reminding its owner to keep stroking.

____ 1. What is the topic of the above paragraph?
   A. Pet owners
   B. A cat's purr
   C. The purr as a homing device
   D. Science and a cat's purr

____ 2. Which statement best expresses the unstated main idea?
   A. There are actually a number of theories about why cats purr.
   B. A cat's purr is both homing signal and signal of appeasement.
   C. There are many false assumptions about why cats purr.
   D. When cats purr, they comfort themselves as well as their owners.

Paragraph 2

¹The family introduces children to the physical world through the opportunities it provides for play and exploration of objects. ²It also creates bonds between people that are unique. ³The attachments children form with parents and siblings usually last a lifetime, and they serve as models for relationships in the wider world of neighborhood and school. ⁴Within the family, children also experience their first social conflicts. ⁵Discipline by parents and arguments with siblings provide children with important lessons in compliance and cooperation as well as opportunities to learn how to influence the behavior of others. ⁶Finally, within the family, children learn the language, skills, and social and moral values of their culture.

_B_ 1. What is the topic of the above paragraph?
    A. Family histories
    B. The family and children
    C. Children
    D. Children's attachments

_D_ 2. Which statement best expresses the unstated main idea?
    A. The family teaches children compliance and cooperation.
    B. The family has a profound effect on child development.
    C. The bonds that children form with their parents last a lifetime.
    D. Through the family, children first learn about the world.

Paragraph 3

¹Today, a football team in possession of the ball has four plays to make a ten-yard first down, but during the late 1800s and early 1900s, the offensive team had three plays to make a five-yard first down, and passing was severely restricted, both by the rules and by tradition. ²As a result, coaches emphasized "mass plays" that directed the maximum amount of force against one isolated player or point on the field. ³The flying wedge was the most notorious mass play. ⁴It entailed players grouping themselves into a V formation and starting to run before the ball was put into play. ⁵At the last moment, the ball was snapped and passed to a player within the wall of the wedge. ⁶The wedge of runners then crashed into their stationary opponents. ⁷Given that their equipment was crude—players often played without helmets, and no helmet had a facemask—this use of a massed brute force injured hundreds of players a year. ⁸If such plays were not bad enough, referees rarely enforced rules against slugging, kicking, and piling on. ⁹During the 1909 season, such allowances resulted in 30 deaths and 216 serious injuries. ¹⁰Victory was the supreme object, and any method seemed justified in pursuit of that goal.

_B_   1. What is the topic of the above paragraph?
    A. Football
    B. Violence in football
    C. Football a hundred years ago
    D. The flying wedge

_A_   2. Which statement best expresses the unstated main idea?
    A. Football was a dangerous sport during the late 1800s and early 1900s.
    B. Schools should enforce strict safety measures with their football teams.
    C. The flying wedge is a brutal and dangerous football play that often leads to injury.
    D. During the late 1800s and early 1900s, no one was concerned about the safety of football players.

PRACTICE 2

The main idea of each of the following paragraphs is unstated, and each paragraph is followed by four sentences. In the space provided, write the letter of the sentence that best expresses each unstated main idea.

Remember to ask yourself, "What is the implied main idea?" Then test your answer by asking, *"Does all or most of the material in the paragraph support this idea?*

Paragraph 1

¹Although many schools have increased funding for girls' sports (volleyball, softball, and basketball) and some have created coeducational teams (usually in volleyball or swimming), few have opened up the "rough sports" to girls. ²Football, hockey, and wrestling continue to be male-dominated activities. ³Generally, the lion's share of spending goes to these exclusively male sports. ⁴When female athletes participate in sports as aggressive and fierce competitors, they face social stigma for demonstrating the same attributes that bring male athletes praise. ⁵There is a widespread myth that competing in sports masculinizes females and may even cause them physical harm. ⁶Consequently, many female athletes attempt to emphasize their "femininity" while competing by wearing hair ribbons, jewelry, or makeup.

_____ Which statement best expresses the unstated main idea of the paragraph?
    A. Schools need to provide equal funding for male and female sports.
    B. Participating in sports does not make women more masculine.
    C. Women must deal with gender stereotypes on a daily basis.
    D. In sports, women still have not achieved equal status with men.

Paragraph 2

[1]A hungry wasp flies over to investigate an enormous burgundy flower. [2]It has one stalk that stretches up to two feet tall and has a giant flower at the tip. [3]The wasp discovers the smell of nectar coming from the large, curled green leaves that surround the stem at ground level. [4]The sides of each leaf wrap together and stick closed, forming a container shaped like a water pitcher, giving the pitcher plant its name. [5]These hollow leaves hold rainwater, dew, and something else—an enzyme that helps digest food. [6]The wasp lands on a leaf edge and begins to drink nectar from the red vein of the leaf. [7]As it drinks, it follows the vein downward to get more nectar. [8]Soon the wasp has gone too far; it lands in the water in the bottom of the leaf, and it can't crawl back up. [9]That's because the thick hairs on the leaf point downward, making the leaf easy to climb down but almost impossible to climb up. [10]The wasp has fallen prey to the pitcher plant's deadly design. [11]It struggles in the water, but the enzyme soon kills and dissolves the wasp. [12]The plant then absorbs phosphorus, nitrogen, and other vitamins and minerals from the waspy water. [13]Wasps are not the only victims. [14]Pitcher plants trap and dissolve ants, bees, butterflies, spiders, and even small frogs.

_____ Which statement best expresses the unstated main idea of the paragraph?
  A. Insects can become victims of a deadly design.
  B. The pitcher plant gets its name from the way its leaves curl together.
  C. The pitcher plant is a deadly trap for insects and other small prey.
  D. The design of the pitcher plant's leaves makes it impossible for insects to escape.

Paragraph 3

[1]By the late 1920s, Americans' food preparation became easier because a variety of foods were now available in cans. [2]This meant that the typical housewife no longer had to shop daily for fresh food. [3]Instead, she could store everything from tuna to pineapple. [4]Soon, ready-made foods like drink mixes, gelatin desserts, cheese, and peanut butter were staples in the kitchen. [5]Even men and children could now prepare meals if they used these foods. [6]Then, in 1949, Clarence Birdseye, a biologist, made a startling discovery. [7]He noticed that meat exposed to the Arctic air tasted as good cooked as fresh meat, even when it was cooked several months later. [8]He noticed that the speed at which something was frozen made the difference. [9]The faster the freeze, the less chance that ice crystals would tear apart cell walls and release natural juices. [10]Birdseye soon applied his methods to poultry, fruits, and vegetables. [11]People could now eat a wide variety of seasonal foods any time during the year. [12]Eating became even easier when Carl Swanson, owner of a food-processing plant, thought of a way to package

complete meals. ¹³In 1954, he introduced the first frozen TV dinner in a three-compartment aluminum tray. ¹⁴People who didn't own freezers could buy TV dinners and eat them the same day.

_____ Which statement best expresses the unstated main idea of the paragraph?
   A. The development of convenience foods freed women from daily shopping.
   B. Frozen foods allowed people to eat a wide variety of seasonal foods all year long.
   C. Convenience foods changed cooking and eating habits in America.
   D. Americans are indebted to Clarence Birdseye and Carl Swanson.

Putting Implied Main Ideas into Your Own Words

When you read, you often have to **infer**—figure out on your own—an author's unstated main idea. The implied main idea that you come up with should cover all or most of the details in the paragraph.

✓   *Check Your Understanding*

See if you can find and write the topic of the paragraph below. Then write the implied main idea in your own words. Finally, read the explanation that follows.

> *Hints:* Remember that you can help yourself identify the topic and main idea if you 1) look for repeated words as you read and 2) try to mark major supporting details. Major details are often signaled by such common addition words as the following:

Addition Words

one	to begin with	also	further
first (of all)	for one thing	in addition	furthermore
second(ly)	other	next	last (of all)
third(ly)	another	moreover	final(ly)

¹All people have a strong need to belong to groups, stemming from evolutionary pressures that increased people's chance of survival and reproduction when in groups rather than in isolation. ²This need may also be driven by the desire to feel protected against threat and uncertainty in everyday life or to gain a greater sense of personal and social identity. ³Moreover, people join specific groups in order to accomplish things that they cannot accomplish as individuals. ⁴Neither symphonies nor football games can be played by one

person alone, and many types of work require team effort. ⁵Further, people join groups because of the social status and identity that they offer. ⁶An important part of people's feelings of self-worth comes from their identification with particular groups. ⁷Even a relatively low-status group can be a source of pride for individuals who are held in high esteem within the group; being big fish in small ponds can make people feel good about themselves, particularly people from individualist cultures. ⁸Finally, people may join groups simply because they like the members and want to have the opportunity to interact with them.

What is the topic of this paragraph? _____

What is the implied main idea of this paragraph? _____

_____

Explanation

One key to the topic here is the words *join groups*, which are repeated through the paragraph. The other key to the topic is the major details in the paragraph. Many of the details are signaled by addition words *(also, Moreover, Further,* and *Finally)*. Each major detail is one of the reasons why people join groups. The author's main point about the topic can simply be stated like this: *People join groups for a number of reasons.*

type question + answer process

PRACTICE 3

In the spaces provided, fill in the topic of each paragraph. Then, using your own words, write the implied main ideas of the paragraphs.

> **Hints:**
>
> **1.** To find the topic, it often helps to look for repeated words in a paragraph.
>
> **2.** To identify the topic and main idea, mark major supporting details as you read. These major details are often signaled by such common addition words as the ones shown in the box on the previous page.

A. ¹Because most students are unmarried, high schools and colleges serve as matchmaking institutions. ²It is at school that many young people find their future spouses. ³Schools also establish social networks. ⁴Some adults maintain friendships from high school and college; others develop networks that benefit their careers. ⁵Another function of schools is to provide employment. ⁶With 53 million students in grade and high schools, and another 15 million enrolled in colleges, U.S. education is big business. [7]Primary and secondary schools provide jobs for 2.9 million teachers, while another million work in colleges and universities. [8]Schools also help stabilize employment. [9]To keep millions of young people in school is to keep them out of the labor market, protecting the positions of older workers. [10]Last of all, schools help stabilize society by keeping these millions off the streets, where they might be marching and protesting in search of unskilled jobs long lost to other nations.

Topic: how schools impact our lives

Implied main idea: Schools impact our lives in five ways.

B. [1]Do you sometimes feel cold, or hot, while others around you seem comfortable? [2]Don't worry—you are not alone. [3]Weight is one of many biological factors that affect how warm or cold you feel: the more body fat you have, the greater the amount of insulation, so you tend not to be as cold. [4]Muscle mass is another factor affecting our body temperature. [5]The more muscular you are, the better your body will be at regulating temperature. [6]Moreover, diet affects body temperature. [7]People who don't get enough essential nutrients may find themselves feeling cold and tired because their body is not getting the "fuel" it needs to work efficiently. [8]In addition, gender plays a part in one's body temperature. [9]Women generally have less muscle mass than men do, which reduces their average body temperature. [10]Age is yet one more biological factor to consider. [11]As people age, their hormonal systems don't produce as many hormones as when they were younger. [12]As a result, the elderly often feel colder. [13]Finally, stress is a factor affecting people's body temperature: tension could reduce your circulation, making you feel colder.

Topic: body temperature

Implied main idea: There are six biological factors that affect our body temperature

C. [1]For the economic crisis we are living with today, the popular press has placed most of the blame on greedy bankers, sleazy Wall Street investors, and shortsighted government regulators. [2]All these culprits surely deserve an enormous amount of blame. [3]But consider the role played by regular folks from Main Street America. [4]We have contributed to the economic crisis by, for example, trading up to houses we could not really afford. [5]We have maxed out our credit cards on luxury goods, and we have reduced our saving to historically low levels. [6]In his book *The Culture of Excess*, J. R. Slosar argues that we live in a world that nurtures a sense of entitlement to material goods, emphasizes immediate gratification, and fails to instill self-discipline. [7]He attributes the current economic disaster to a cultural climate that encourages self-indulgence, overconsumption, and excessive risk-taking. [8]In a similar vein, Peter Whybrow asserts that "the debt-fueled consumptive frenzy that has gripped the American psyche for the past few decades was a nightmare in the making—a seductive, twisted, and commercially conjured version of the American dream that now threatens our environmental, individual, and civic health." [9]Characterizing the American public as addicted to materialism, Whybrow notes that "shopping became the national pastime, and at all levels of society we hungered for more—more money, more power, more food, more stuff."

Topic: economic crisis

Implied main idea: Here are three reasons why regular American folks should be blamed for economic crisis too.

Implied Central Ideas in Longer Passages

When you read, you may have to infer an author's unstated central idea (also called a **thesis**) in a longer passage. The implied central idea that you come up with should cover all or most of the details in the passage. For example, read the following passage.

[1]Commonsense views about abortion include the ideas that abortion is a last resort, that women who get abortions do not know how to use contraceptives, and certainly, that women who get abortions did not want to get pregnant. [2]Consider, however, that abortion is not always a last resort. [3]In Russia, abortion is a major means of birth control, and the average Russian woman has six abortions during her lifetime. [4]Abortion is so common in Russia that there are twice as many abortions as births.

[5]Nor is it true that women who have abortions don't know how to use contraceptives. [6]Sociologist Kristen Luker, who studied an abortion clinic in California, found that many women did not use contraceptives, even though they knew how to use them and did not want to get pregnant. [7]They avoided contraceptives, Luker discovered, because they interfered with intimacy, were expensive, were disapproved of by their boyfriends, or caused adverse side effects. [8]Some even avoided contraceptives to protect their self-concept. [9]If they used contraceptives, they would think of themselves as "available" or sexually

promiscuous, but without them they looked at sex as something that "just happened." [10]Luker's study shows that some women take chances—and then get pregnant and have abortions.

[11]Sociologist Leon Dash, who studied pregnancy among teenagers in Washington, D.C., found that the third commonsense idea is not necessarily true. [12]Some girls get pregnant deliberately. [13]Some want children so that, as they said, "I can have something to hold onto that I can call my own." [14]Some boyfriends also urge their girlfriends to get pregnant. [15]They say that this will make them "feel like a man." [16]And, as Luker discovered, some women get pregnant to test their boyfriends' commitment. [17]Often the relationship sours, and the young women decide not to bear the child. [18]In short, contrary to a middle-class perspective, many poor, young, unmarried women get pregnant because they want to.

You can see that no sentence in the passage is a good "umbrella" statement that covers all of the other sentences. To decide on the implied central idea, we must ask the same three questions we've already used to find main ideas:

- "Who or what is this passage about?" That will be the topic.

- "What is the central point the author is trying to make about that topic?"

- And when we think we know the central idea, we can test it by asking, "Does all or most of the material in the passage support this idea?"

✓ Check Your Understanding

In the passage above, all of the details concern commonsense views about abortion, so that must be the topic. Which of the following statements expresses the central point that the author is trying to make about the topic? Check (✓) the answer you think is correct.

_____ A. Abortion is not always a last resort.

_____ B. Abortion is not always the result of a lack of knowledge about contraceptives.

_____ C. Abortion is not always the result of accidental pregnancy.

_____ D. Commonsense views about abortion are not necessarily true.

The details reveal the author's central idea to be answer D: Commonsense views about abortion are not necessarily true. All the other statements above are supporting details for this central idea—each tells of a view about abortion that is not necessarily true. Although the central idea is not directly stated, it is clearly implied by all the material in the passage.

PRACTICE 4

The central idea of each of the following passages is unstated, and each passage is followed by four sentences. In the space provided, write the letter of the sentence that best expresses each unstated central idea.

Remember to first ask yourself, "What is the implied central idea?" Then test your answer by asking, "Does all or most of the material in the passage support this idea?"

Passage 1

¹In New England, chicken farmers realized that chickens born in the spring fetched better prices than the older, tougher birds that had lived through a winter. ²Sometimes they tried to pass the older chickens off as young, tender birds. ³But smart buyers learned to reject these birds, complaining that they were "no spring chickens." ⁴The phrase has come to mean anyone who is past his youth.

⁵Today, a "white elephant" means an unwanted item you have lying around the house. ⁶White elephants are often the subject of gag gift exchanges. ⁷But the original "white elephant" was no gag at all. ⁸In Burma, albino elephants were considered sacred. ⁹They could not be used for work, and they had to be lavished with the best food and great attention. ¹⁰Eventually a "white elephant" meant something that was costly to maintain and provided few benefits.

¹¹Did you ever wonder where the phrase "to bite the bullet" came from? ¹²In the days before anesthesia, amputations and other surgeries were agonizing affairs. ¹³The surgeon could offer a patient little pain relief other than to give him an object, often a bullet, to clench between his teeth. ¹⁴Today "to bite the bullet" means to pay a painful price in order to get an ordeal over with.

¹⁵When we suspect we know what's going to happen next, we sometimes say we "see the writing on the wall." ¹⁶This phrase is Biblical in its origin. ¹⁷In the book of Daniel in the Old Testament, the wrongdoing of a corrupt king was revealed by a mysterious hand which appeared and wrote a message on the wall, warning that the king's days were numbered.

_____ Which sentence best expresses the implied central idea of the entire selection?
   A. Long ago, life was much simpler than it is today.
   B. Some of today's common phrases have surprising origins.
   C. Some common phrases have come down to us as the result of old-time customs.
   D. Long ago, people entertained each other by making up humorous expressions.

Passage 2

[1]Between one-third and one-half of all adolescents and adults regularly fail to get enough sleep. [2]According to the National Sleep Foundation, adolescents need at least 9 hours of sleep a night, but 80% of them get less sleep than that. [3]As a result, at least once a week 28% of high school students fall asleep in class. [4]Another 22% fall asleep while doing homework, and 14% arrive late or miss school entirely because they oversleep. [5]Thus it is not surprising that chronic sleep deprivation among adolescents results in diminished attention, reduced arousal, and lower test scores.

[6]Sleep deprivation negatively affects reaction time, memory, judgment, and the ability to pay attention. [7]Experts estimate that sleep loss is a contributing factor in more than 200,000 automobile accidents each year in the United States, resulting in more than a thousand deaths and tens of thousands of injuries. [8]Research suggests that driving while sleepy is as dangerous as driving while drunk.

[9]Sleep deprivation may also affect the performance of people in high-risk positions such as nuclear power plant operators, who often have to make critical decisions on short notice. [10]For example, there was an accident at the nuclear power plant at Three Mile Island, Pennsylvania, in which human error transformed a minor mishap into a major nuclear disaster. [11]And certain hospital residents, who work long hours without rest, experience twice as many failures of attention while working at night compared to residents who work shorter shifts. [12]They make over one-third of serious medical errors regarding patients, including five times as many serious diagnostic mistakes that could be life-threatening. [13]To put the state of exhaustion into further perspective, residents working heavy schedules perform similarly on cognitive tasks to people with blood alcohol levels between 0.04% and 0.05%—the level reached when an average-sized man consumes three beers in a single hour.

[14]The lack of sleep also contributes to such diseases as heart attacks, asthma, strokes, high blood pressure, and diabetes. [15]In children, insufficient sleep is associated with increased risk of being overweight. [16]Sleep deprivation is also clearly related to depression in high school and college students. [17]According to Mary Alice Carskadon, a leading researcher in the area of sleep among college students, "Every study we have done over the past decade on high school and college students shows that the less sleep they get, the more depressed moods they report." [18]Even for college students who are not depressed, research shows that a lack of sleep results in lower academic performance.

_____ Which sentence best expresses the implied central idea of the entire selection?

A. Businesses must require their employees to get enough sleep.

B. Chronic sleep loss is widespread in America today.

C. Not getting enough sleep has significant drawbacks.

D. Sleep deprivation is a challenge faced by adolescents and adults alike.

CHAPTER REVIEW

In this chapter, you learned the following:

- At times authors imply, or suggest, a main idea without stating it clearly in one sentence. In such cases, you must figure out that main idea by considering the supporting details. When you think you know the main idea, test it by asking, "Does *all or most* of the material support this idea?"

- To find implied central ideas in longer reading selections, you must again look closely at the supporting material.

The next two chapters—Chapters 4 and 5—will explain common ways that authors organize their material.

 On the Web: If you are using this book in class, you can go to our website for more practice in recognizing implied main ideas. Visit our Learning Center at **www.townsendpress.net** for additional activities and an instructional video on this skill.

REVIEW TEST 1

To review what you've learned in this chapter, answer each of the following questions by filling in the blank.

1. When a paragraph has no sentence that states the main idea, we say the main idea is suggested, or _____.

2. To figure out an implied idea, it often helps to first determine the _____ of the paragraph by asking, "Who or what is this paragraph about?"

3. After you figure out what you think is the implied main idea of a paragraph, test yourself by asking, "Does all or most of the material in the paragraph _____ this idea?"

4. Just as a paragraph has a main idea, a longer selection has a central _____, or thesis, that is supported by all or most of the material in the selection.

5. The central point of a long selection may be stated directly, or it may be _____.

REVIEW TEST 2

The essay below is followed by questions on implied ideas and also on vocabulary in context, stated main ideas, and supporting details.

Preview

Americans are getting fatter. The statistics keep coming out, and they are steadily worse. As a people, our weight keeps climbing, while our physical fitness is declining. What is going on? In this essay, the author encourages us to look at the point where most obesity begins: childhood.

Words to Watch

diabetes (4): a chronic health condition in which the body is unable to break down sugar in the blood
coma (12): a state of prolonged unconsciousness
staple (14): a basic item or feature

"EXTRA LARGE, PLEASE"

Alice M. Davies

1   School lunches have always come in for a lot of criticism. When I was a kid, we complained about "mystery meat" and "leftover surprise casserole." Half a canned pear in a shaky nest of Jell-O didn't do much to excite our taste buds. I hid my share of limp green beans under my napkin, the better to escape the eagle eye of lunchroom monitors who encouraged us to eat our soggy, overcooked vegetables.

2   But the cafeteria lunches were there, and so we ate them. (Most of them. OK, I hid the gooey tapioca pudding, too.) I think we accepted the idea that being delicious was not the point. The meals were reasonably nutritious, and they fueled our young bodies for the mental and physical demands of the day. In my case, that demand included walking a quarter mile to and from school, enjoying three recesses a day, and taking part in gym class a couple of times a week. After-school hours, at least when the weather was good, were spent outdoors playing kickball or tag with neighbor kids.

3   You're thinking, "Who cares?"—aren't you? I don't blame you. My memories of school days in northern Indiana forty-some years ago aren't all that fascinating, even to me. And yet I think you should care, because of one fact I haven't mentioned yet. When I was a kid and looked around at other kids my age, I saw all kinds of differences. There were tall ones and short ones and black and white and brown ones, rude ones and polite ones, popular ones and geeky ones, athletic ones and uncoordinated ones. But you know what? There weren't many heavy ones. The few there were stood out because they were unusual. I think that if you had asked me at the time, I would have told you that kids are just naturally skinny.

4   Flash forward to the present. Walk down any city street in America. Sit in a mall and watch the people stream by. You don't need to be a pediatrician to notice something's changed. Whether you call them big-boned, chubby, husky, or plus-sized, kids are heavy, lots of them. If your own eyes don't convince you, here are the statistics: Since 1980, the number of American kids who are dangerously overweight has tripled. Nearly one-third of American kids qualify as "overweight" or "obese." In 2011, the U.S. military released a study showing that 27 percent of young people ages 17 to 24 are too fat to join the armed forces. Hordes of kids are developing Type-2 diabetes°, a diet-related disease that used to be called "adult onset diabetes" because it was virtually never seen in children. When Texas schools conducted a statewide physical fitness test in 2010, two-thirds of the students failed. The same test in California showed similar results—only one child in three scored in the "physically fit" range. Schools are ordering larger desks to accommodate extra-big kids. Clothing stores for plus-

size kids—from toddlers on up—are multiplying.

5   Part of the problem is that many kids don't have good opportunities to exercise. They live in neighborhoods without sidewalks or paths where they can walk, bike, or skate safely. Drug activity and violent crime may make playing outside dangerous. They can reach their schools only by car or bus. Many of those schools are so short of money they've scrapped their physical-fitness classes. Too few communities have athletic programs in place.

6   Electronic entertainment also plays a role in the current state of affairs. Kids used to go outside to play with other kids because it was more fun than sitting around the house. Today, kids who sit around the house have access to hundreds of cable TV channels, YouTube, Facebook, Hulu, instant streaming movies, DVD players, and a dizzying assortment of video games.

7   Still another cause is the lack of parental supervision. When I was a kid, most of us had a mom or an older sibling at home telling us to get off our butts and go outside. (The alternative was often to stay inside and do chores. We chose to go out and play.) Now, most American parents work outside the home. During the daylight hours, those parents just aren't around to encourage their kids to get some exercise. A related problem is that parents who can't be home much may feel guilty about it. One way of relieving that guilt is to buy Junior the game system of his dreams

and a nice wide-screen TV to play it on.

8   These are all complicated problems whose solutions are equally complicated. But there is one cause of the fattening of America's kids that can be dealt with more easily. And that cause is the enormous influence that fast-food restaurants and other sources of calorie-laden junk have gained over America's kids.

9   I'm no health nut. I like an occasional Quarter Pounder as well as the next mom. When my kids were young, there was no quicker way to their hearts than to bring home a newly-released DVD, a large pepperoni pie, and a bag of Chicken McNuggets. But in our home, an evening featuring extra mozzarella and bottles of 7-Up was a once-in-a-while treat—sort of a guilty pleasure.

10   To many of today's kids, fast food is not a treat—it's their daily diet. Their normal dinnertime equals McDonalds, Pizza Hut, Domino's, Burger King, Taco Bell, or KFC, all washed down with Pepsi. And increasingly, lunchtime at school means those foods too. About 20 percent of our nation's schools have sold chain restaurants the right to put their food items on the lunch line. A majority of middle schools and high schools allow snack and soft-drink vending machines on their campuses. The National Soft Drink Association reports that 60 percent of public and private middle schools and high schools make sodas available for purchase.

11   Believe me, when I was a kid, if the lunch line had offered me a

couple of slices of double-crust stuffed pepperoni-sausage pizza instead of a Turkey Submarine, I would have said yes before you could say the words "clogged arteries." And when I needed a mid-afternoon pick-me-up, I would have gladly traded a couple of bucks for a sugar-and-caffeine-laden "energy drink" like Red Bull or Monster and a Snickers bar.

12   And then I would have gone back into algebra class and spent the hour bouncing between a sugar high and a fat-induced coma°.

13   Advertising for fast foods has also sneaked its way into many schools, increasingly giving kids the idea that junk food is their friend. In one notorious example in Seminole, Florida, kids' report cards came enclosed in Ronald McDonald envelopes. Inside was a promise for a free Happy Meal for good grades. (Concerned parents soon put an end to that particular promotion.) Pizza Hut's "Book It" program rewards frequent readers with Pizza Hut products. McDonald's sponsors a popular "Passport to Play" program, which brings Ronald McDonald into elementary schools to introduce games, dances, and other physical activities from foreign lands.

14   All these factors help hook kids on what's become the Standard American Diet, which is indeed SAD. It's one thing to stop off at Taco Bell for an occasional Seven-Layer Burrito. But when fast food becomes the staple° of young people's diets, it's the kids

who become Whoppers. And it has become the staple for many. According to researchers at Children's Hospital in Boston, during any given week, three out of four children eat a fast-food meal one or more times a day. The beverages they chug down are a problem, too. The U.S. Department of Agriculture says that every day, the average adolescent drinks enough soda, "energy drinks," and fruit beverages to equal the sugar content of 50 chocolate-chip cookies.

15   The problem isn't only that burgers, fries, and sodas aren't nutritious to begin with—although they aren't. What has made the situation much worse is the increasingly huge portions sold by fast-food restaurants. Back when McDonald's began business, its standard meal consisted of a hamburger, two ounces of French fries, and a 12-ounce Coke. That meal provided 590 calories. But today's customers don't have to be satisfied with such modest portions. For very little more money, diners can end up with a Double Quarter Pounder with cheese (730 calories), large fries (570), and a 32-ounce Coke (310). That adds up to 1,610 calories. A whole generation of kids is growing up believing that this massive shot of fat, sugar, and sodium equals a "normal portion." As a result, they're becoming extra large themselves.

16   As kids sit down to watch the after-school and Saturday-morning shows designed for them, they aren't just taking in the programs themselves. They're seeing at least an hour of commercials for every five hours of

programming. On Saturday mornings, nine out of ten of those commercials are for sugary cereals, fast food, and other non-nutritious junk. Many of the commercials are tied in with popular toys or beloved cartoon characters or movies aimed at children. Watching those commercials makes the kids hungry—or at least they *think* they're hungry. (Thanks to all the factors mentioned here, many children can no longer tell if they're genuinely hungry or not. They've been programmed to eat for many reasons other than hunger.) So they snack as they sit in front of the TV set. Then at mealtime, they beg to go out for more junk food. And they get bigger, and bigger, and bigger.

17   There is no overnight solution to the problem of American children's increasing weight and decreasing level of physical fitness. But can anything be done?

18   Yes. Let's start with the good news. With major input from First Lady Michelle Obama, the federal government has begun paying serious attention to increasing physical activity and decreasing obesity in children. Mrs. Obama's "Let's Move!" campaign and the Partnership for a Healthier America, a nonprofit working with the private sector and the Obama administration, have helped raise awareness that childhood obesity is a problem that affects everyone. In 2010, Congress passed the Healthier, Hunger-Free Kids Act. Under this bill, the United States Department of Agriculture released new school meal regulations—the first significant changes to school meals in fifteen years. As the regulations are put into place, school lunches will contain more fruits and vegetables, less fat and salt, and more whole grains than ever before. Eventually, new nutritional guidelines will be released for all foods sold on a school campus, including those obtained from vending machines or available in the à la carte section of the cafeteria.

19   These changes are an excellent beginning. Fast-food meals and junk-food vending machines have no place in our schools. (One study in Florida showed that about one in five middle-school kids routinely skipped the school lunch altogether and instead ate a snack and beverage from a school vending machine.)   Our educational system should be helping children acquire good nutritional habits, not assisting them in committing slow nutritional suicide.

20   In addition, commercials for junk food should be banned from TV during children's viewing time, specifically Saturday mornings.

21   And finally, fast-food restaurants should be required to do what tobacco companies—another manufacturer of products known to harm people's health—have to do. They should display in their restaurants, and in their TV and print ads as well, clear nutritional information about their products. For instance, a young woman at Burger King who was considering ordering a Double Whopper with Cheese, a king-size order

of fries and a king-size Dr. Pepper could read something like this:

— *Your meal will provide 1860 calories, 880 of those calories from fat.*

— *Your recommended daily intake is 2000 calories, with no more than 600 of those calories coming from fat.*

22   At a glance, then, the customer could see that in one fast-food meal, she was taking in almost as many calories and more fat than she should consume in an entire day.

23   There are opponents to many if not all of these measures. Such opponents say that eating well and staying healthy and active are personal responsibilities; that government intervention in the obesity epidemic is an example of a "nanny state" intruding where it does not belong.

They are wrong.   24

The well-funded, well-researched   25 efforts of junk food producers have, in just a couple of generations, contributed to a public health crisis whose effects are only now beginning to be felt—all in the name of a quick profit. If a foreign invader had damaged the health of as many American children, we would be at war.

Overweight kids today become   26 overweight adults tomorrow. Overweight adults are at increased risk for heart disease, diabetes, stroke, and cancer. Schools, fast-food restaurants, and the media are contributing to a public-health disaster in the making. Anything that can be done to decrease the role junk food plays in kids' lives needs to be done, and done quickly.

Reading Comprehension Questions

Vocabulary in Context

_____ 1. In the excerpt below, the word *hordes* (hôrdz) means
  A. small groups.
  B. large groups.
  C. selected groups.
  D. concerned groups.

> "Since 1980, the number of American kids who are dangerously overweight has tripled. . . . Hordes of kids are developing Type-2 diabetes°, a diet-related disease that used to be called 'adult onset diabetes' because it was virtually never seen in children." (Paragraph 4)

Main Ideas

_____ 2. The main idea of paragraph 10 is stated in the
   A. first sentence.
   B. second sentence.
   C. third sentence.
   D. last sentence.

_____ 3. The main idea of paragraph 15 is stated in the
   A. first sentence.
   B. second sentence.
   C. third sentence.
   D. last sentence.

Supporting Details

_____ 4. Which of the following is **not** presented as a reason that kids are growing heavier?
   A. Lack of exercise
   B. Overly large portions of food
   C. Genetics
   D. Overconsumption of soda

_____ 5. The Healthier, Hunger-Free Kids Act requires that
   A. TV stations broadcast public service messages that promote healthy eating.
   B. school lunches contain more fruits and vegetables, less salt and fat, and more whole grains.
   C. schools ban vending machines that sell junk food and sugary soft drinks.
   D. commercials for junk food be banned from TV during children's viewing time.

Implied Main Ideas

_____ 6. Which sentence best expresses the implied main idea of paragraph 4?
   A. Kids today spend too much time in malls.
   B. Diabetes is the most serious health threat today.
   C. Kids today are heavier and less physically fit than ever before.
   D. Kids in California and Texas are heavier and less fit than children elsewhere.

_____ 7. Which sentence best expresses the implied main idea of paragraphs 5–7?

A. Moms should stay home and supervise their kids rather than join the work force.

B. Electronic entertainment influences kids to stay inside and get less physical exercise than they need.

C. Kids are only going to get heavier and less fit as the years go on.

D. There are at least three major reasons for young people's increased obesity.

_____ 8. The implied main idea of paragraph 16 is that

A. kids are pushed to overeat by the commercials that they see.

B. children's television has one hour of commercials for every five hours of programs.

C. many commercials aimed at children feature tie-ins with toys and movies.

D. children do not always realize when they are genuinely hungry.

_____ 9. The implied main idea of paragraphs 17–22 is that

A. First Lady Michelle Obama has started a campaign to help raise awareness of the problem of childhood obesity.

B. the federal government has taken steps to counteract the damaging effects of fast food and junk food, but more needs to be done.

C. fast food has no place in schools.

D. if people realized how unhealthy a fast-food meal is, they might think twice about eating it.

_____ 10. Which sentence best expresses the implied central point of the selection?

A. This generation of children is heavier than previous generations.

B. Our kids' growing obesity is a serious public health problem that has several causes.

C. The fast-food industry should be more closely regulated.

D. Nothing is more important for today's generation of children than getting more exercise.

Discussion Questions

1. When you were a child, how much—and what kinds of—exercise did you typically get? Did you grow up in a place where kids could and did play outside? If not, were you able—or encouraged—to find opportunities to exercise?

2. The author of the selection proposes that fast-food restaurants should be required to display clear nutritional information about their products. Do you think that the presentation of this information would result in a significant reduction in the amount of fast food that people consume? Would it change your eating habits? Why or why not?

3. The author of the selection believes that it's a good idea for the federal government to get involved in trying to get Americans, especially kids, to eat healthier. Do you agree with her? Or do you believe, as opponents of government intervention say, that staying healthy and active are personal responsibilities with which the government should not interfere? Explain your reasoning.

4. The author admits that when she was a kid, she probably would have preferred pizza to something more nutritious. She also mentions that two-thirds of Texas students failed a state-wide physical fitness test. Given the fact that most kids prefer fast foods and passive entertainment, what can be done to promote healthier lifestyles to young people?

Note: Writing assignments for this selection appear on page 636.

Check Your Performance   IMPLIED MAIN IDEAS

Activity	Number Right	Points	Score
Review Test 1 (5 items)	_____	× 6 =	_____
Review Test 2 (10 items)	_____	× 7 =	_____
	TOTAL SCORE	=	_____ %

Enter your total score into the **Reading Performance Chart: Review Tests** on the inside back cover.

IMPLIED MAIN IDEAS: Mastery Test 1

In the space provided, write the letter of the sentence that best expresses the implied main idea of each of the following paragraphs.

_____ 1. [1]Teen girls are often told, "If you just say 'no,' you'll never have to worry about an unwanted pregnancy." [2]But if you're in love—or at least think you are—you don't want to say "no" to your boyfriend, about sex or anything else. [3]You want to please him, make him happy, and above all, not lose him. [4]Furthermore, you may be as interested in sex as he is. [5]Even if you don't have a steady boyfriend, it's not always easy to say "no" to sex. [6]You hear rumors about other girls who are popular because they are sexually available. [7]You reason that boys might like you better, too, if you would sleep with them. [8]If you make out with a boy, he may make you feel guilty about not going further. [9]He may blame you for "leading him on" and making him feel frustrated, or even grow angry with you. [10]What do you do?

    A. Teen girls who are in love with their boyfriends often run the risk of unwanted pregnancy.

    B. Those who encourage teen girls to just say 'no' to sex usually have the best interests of the girls in mind.

    C. Teenage girls who refuse to have sex with their boyfriends may lose them to girls who are sexually available.

    D. While "just saying no" sounds like the perfect solution, sometimes it may not be as simple as it seems.

_____ 2. [1]Most healthy people are able to tell if something is sweet or salty within .1 second of its touching their tongue. [2]They are able to taste .04 ounces of salt dissolved in 550 quarts of water. [3]Normal people can distinguish among anywhere from 4,000 to 10,000 different odors. [4]They can even smell a single drop of perfume let loose anywhere in a three-bedroom apartment. [5]They can see millions of colors. [6]They can even spot a small candle flame from up to thirty miles away on a dark night. [7]They can feel a tiny bee's wing fall on a cheek. [8]They can decide if something is hot or cold almost immediately after it touches their skin. [9]Most people can hear a pin drop across the room or hear a baby cry on another floor of a house.

    A. Human senses are remarkably sensitive.

    B. Some people have a better sense of smell, hearing, and sight than others.

    C. Most people use their senses to detect slight variations in their environment.

    D. Human senses are as sensitive as those of animals.

(Continues on next page)

_____ 3. [1]Consider a pesticide aimed at insects that are attacking a crop. [2]The pesticide may kill almost 100 percent of them, but thanks to the genetic variability of large populations, some insects are likely to survive exposure. [3]The resistant insects can then multiply free of competition and produce many offspring that are resistant to the pesticide and can attack the crop with new vigor. [4]To control these resistant insects, a new and more powerful pesticide must be applied, and this leads to the appearance of a population of still more resistant insects. [5]Consequently, still more pesticides and herbicides must be used.

  A. No pesticide can kill 100 percent of insects that are attacking a crop.
  B. The genetic variability of large populations of insects ensures their survival.
  C. Because of genetic resistance in insects, more powerful pesticides must be used over time.
  D. Harmful insects will continue to vigorously attack crops in the future.

_____ 4. [1]If your roommate is washing the dishes and says acidly, "I hope you're enjoying your novel," the literal meaning of his words is quite clear, but you probably know very well that he is not expressing a concern about your reading pleasure. [2]He is really saying, "I am furious that you are not helping to clean up after dinner." [3]Other emotions can be expressed through voice quality as well. [4]When Mae West, a once famous film star and master of sexual innuendo, asked, "Why don't you come up and see me sometime?" her voice oozed sensuality. [5]Similarly, if you receive a phone call from someone who has very good or very bad news, you will probably know how she feels before she has told you what happened. [6]In the same way, we can literally hear the fear in a person's voice, as we do when we listen to a nervous student give an oral report.

  A. People don't always mean what they say.
  B. Human beings are able to sense each other's fear.
  C. Information may be contained not in the words people use, but in the way they express those words.
  D. In order to truly communicate with those around them, people must practice interpreting subtle linguistic cues.

IMPLIED MAIN IDEAS: Mastery Test 2

In the space provided, write the letter of the sentence that best expresses the implied main idea of each of the following paragraphs.

_A_ 1. [1]As a general rule, if it tastes good, it must be bad for you. [2]So when the artificial sweetener saccharin—the chemical in Sweet'N Low—first appeared on the market, it's no wonder that many healthy eaters thought it too good to be true. [3]In fact, saccharin is indigestible, so it passes through our bodies without providing any of the energy that is often converted into fat. [4]Likewise, the bacteria that form together to become plaque don't receive any nutritional benefit from saccharin, so the sweet substitute doesn't attract tooth-decaying microbes the way that sugar does. [5]Some have claimed that saccharin causes cancer, leading to the warnings you see on Sweet'N Low products. [6]But the study that led to these warnings has been debunked: it's been revealed that the rats in this study that developed bladder cancer were receiving ridiculously high doses of the chemical. [7]To ingest an equivalent amount, a human would have to drink hundreds of cans of diet soda every day for his or her entire life.

Even though saccharin is bad in some ways, it's still better than sugar.

A. Despite initial doubts, saccharin is a good substitute for sugar.
B. Unlike sugar, saccharin won't make you gain weight or rot your teeth.
C. The scientific study that linked saccharin consumption to bladder cancer was later debunked.
D. A human being would have to consume ridiculously high doses of saccharin to develop bladder cancer.

_D_ 2. [1]During World War II, more adolescents worked than ever before. [2]Over a million students dropped out of school to contribute to the war effort. [3]By 1943 almost three million boys and girls were working on farms and in factories. [4]In the new prosperity following the war, their jobs gave them freedom and spending money. [5]They soon became an important new segment of the consumer economy as they snapped up records and clothing. [6]Before long, advertisers aimed marketing campaigns at them, magazines were dedicated to their interests, and even newspapers ran columns about teen news and views. [7]The result was an emergence of a distinct youth subculture that helped shape the nation. [8]Their dances, their rigidly conforming clothing, and their choice of recreation set them apart from adults. [9]The word *teenager* was added to the vocabulary, confirming the importance of those thirteen through nineteen years of age.

A. As a result of World War II, teenagers worked at jobs which gave them freedom and spending money.
B. Because of World War II, advertisers, magazines, and newspapers began catering to a distinct youth subculture.
C. In World War II, adolescents made a major contribution to the war effort by working on farms and in factories.
D. World War II led to changes in the status and lifestyle of young people.

(Continues on next page)

_B_ 3. ¹Parents tend to discipline their firstborns more than their later children and to give them more attention. ²When the second child arrives, the firstborn competes to remain the focus of attention. ³Researchers suggest that this situation instills in firstborns a greater drive for success, which is why they are more likely than their siblings to earn higher grades in school, to attend college, and to go further in college. ⁴Firstborns are even more likely to become astronauts, to appear on the cover of *Time* magazine, and to become president of the United States. ⁵Although subsequent children may not go as far, most are less anxious about being successful and are more relaxed in their relationships. ⁶Firstborns are also more likely to defend the status quo and to support conservative causes, with later-borns tending to upset the apple cart and support liberal causes.

A. Because parents give them more attention, firstborns are able to develop more fully than later children.

B. Birth order plays an important role in determining a person's traits and accomplishments.

C. Firstborns tend to be conservatives, while later-borns tend to be liberals.

D. Giving a child more discipline is likely to make him or her more successful later in life.

_____ 4. ¹Thomas Jefferson's inaugural on March 4, 1801, was the first to take place in the nation's new capital on the Potomac. ²If Washington, D.C., was a symbol of the nation's future, or even the future of the federal government, the prospects looked grim indeed. ³There was no sign there of the prosperity that touched the government's previous homes in New York and Philadelphia: Washington was a backwater, a "city" with unpaved streets that turned to dust in the dry days of summer and into mud streams when it rained. ⁴The executive residence, first occupied by the Adamses, remained, like the Capitol, unfinished. ⁵What was built had been constructed so poorly that chunks of ceiling fell and pillars split within a few years of their installation. ⁶There were no streetlights, no street signs; grand avenues became cow paths. ⁷The city was home to flies and mosquitoes, frogs, and also hogs, which happily gobbled up garbage in the roadways. ⁸An uninformed visitor witnessing the scene could only wonder whether some disaster had occurred. ⁹Was Washington half built—or half destroyed?

A. The major problem with Washington, D.C., back in 1801 was that its streets had not yet been paved.

B. In 1801, Washington, D.C., was an unimpressive place because no one made any effort to control the insects and animals which lived there.

C. Washington, D.C., at the time of Jefferson's inaugural, was a very unimpressive place.

D. Due to the poor construction of its buildings, in 1801 Washington, D.C., appeared to be either half built or half destroyed.

IMPLIED MAIN IDEAS: Mastery Test 3

In the space provided, write the letter of the sentence that best expresses the implied main idea of each of the following paragraphs.

_____ 1. [1]Some people will drink heavily even though they know they're eroding their liver, or they'll eat all the wrong foods even though they know they're increasing their risk for a heart attack. [2]One explanation for self-destructive habits is that they creep up on people slowly. [3]Drug use may grow imperceptibly over years, or exercise habits may decline ever so gradually. [4]Another reason for health-impairing habits is that they are quite pleasant at the time. [5]Actions such as eating favorite foods, smoking cigarettes, and getting "high" are potent reinforcing events. [6]Also, the risks associated with most self-destructive habits are chronic diseases such as cancer that usually take ten, twenty, or thirty years to develop. [7]It is easier to ignore risks that lie in the distant future. [8]Finally, it appears that people have a tendency to underestimate the risks associated with their own bad health habits. [9]They know about the dangers associated with certain habits but often engage in denial when it is time to apply this information to themselves.

    A. Dangerous health habits may develop slowly and imperceptibly.
    B. People often deny the risks associated with their own destructive health habits.
    C. Health-impairing habits often continue because they can be quite pleasant.
    D. There are several reasons why people behave in self-destructive ways.

_____ 2. [1]It has been demonstrated that moviegoers will eat 50 percent more popcorn if given an extra-large tub of popcorn instead of a container one size smaller, even if the popcorn is stale. [2]If a tabletop in the office is stocked with cookies and candy, coworkers tend to nibble their way through the workday, even if they are not hungry. [3]One study showed that if the candy was in plain sight on workers' desks, they ate an average of nine pieces each. [4]Storing candy in a desk drawer reduced consumption to six pieces, as compared to putting the candy a couple of yards from the desk, cutting the number to three pieces per person. [5]In response to these and other findings, many public schools have begun offering only healthy foods in their cafeterias, replacing soft drinks, candy, and chips with juice, milk, fruit, and granola bars.

    A. The average person loves to snack while working.
    B. Reducing people's consumption of snacks depends in large part on making the snacks harder to obtain.
    C. People will eat whatever is readily available, even if they're not hungry.
    D. Students in public schools will consume whatever food is readily available.

(Continues on next page)

_____ 3. ¹In the American colonies, hot chocolate became the preferred drink of aristocrats, who consumed it at intimate gatherings in mansions. ²Coffee, by contrast, became the preeminent morning beverage of colonial businessmen, who praised its caffeine for keeping drinkers sober and focused. ³Coffee was served in the new public coffeehouses, patronized only by men, where politics and business were the topics of conversation. ⁴By the mid-1700s, though, tea had supplanted coffee as the preferred hot, caffeinated beverage in upper-class America. ⁵It was consumed in the afternoons, in private homes, at tea tables presided over by women. ⁶Tea embodied genteel status and polite conversation. ⁷In contrast, rum was the drink of the masses. ⁸This inexpensive, potent distilled spirit, made possible by new technology and the increasing production of sugar, was devoured by free working people everywhere.

A. The demand for hot chocolate, coffee, and tea decreased when rum became available.
B. Hot chocolate, coffee, tea, and rum were each consumed by different segments of society in colonial America.
C. Hot chocolate, coffee, tea, and rum were not the only popular drinks in colonial America.
D. Hot chocolate, coffee, tea, and rum were all considered luxury drinks in colonial America.

_____ 4. ¹Due to the increasing concern about contaminated meat and meat products, the first irradiated meat, ground beef, arrived in American supermarkets in early 2000. ²Irradiated frozen chicken was introduced more recently. ³Irradiation is a process that causes damage to the DNA of disease-causing bacteria such as salmonella and E. coli as well as insects, parasites, and other organisms so that they can't reproduce. ⁴While irradiated meat has much lower bacteria levels than regular meat, irradiation doesn't destroy all bacteria in meat. ⁵In fact, irradiation actually destroys fewer bacteria than does proper cooking. ⁶There is also some concern that irradiation will lull consumers into a false sense of security so that they erroneously believe that they don't have to take the usual precautions in food handling. ⁷For example, under-cooking, unclean work surfaces or cooking utensils, or improper storage can still cause contamination in the meat. ⁸Some also claim that irradiated meat has a distinct off-taste and smell, likening it to "singed hair."

A. Despite the introduction of irradiated food in early 2000, bacterial contamination of meat has not been eliminated in the United States.
B. The irradiation of food has both advantages and disadvantages.
C. Even though food has been irradiated, consumers should still take the usual precautions in food handling.
D. Some people prefer the smell and taste of meat that has not been irradiated to the smell and taste of meat that has been irradiated.

IMPLIED MAIN IDEAS: Mastery Test 4

A. In the space provided, write the letter of the sentence that best expresses the implied main idea of each of the following paragraphs.

_____ 1. [1]Most young girls are more likely to see their fathers reading magazines and watching TV programs about sports than they are to see their mothers doing the same. [2]Additionally, most participants in public sports are men. [3]Although girls may be encouraged to participate in sports, parents are likely to believe that their sons are better at athletics and to feel that sports are more critical for the development of boys. [4]A recent study of over 800 elementary school pupils found that parents hold higher expectations for boys' athletic performance, and children absorb these social messages at an early age. [5]Kindergartners through third-graders of both sexes viewed sports in a gender-stereotyped fashion—as much more important for boys. [6]Boys were also more likely to indicate that it was important to their parents that they participate in athletics. [7]These attitudes affected children's physical self-images as well as their behavior. [8]Girls saw themselves as having less talent at sports, and by the sixth grade they devoted less time to athletics than did their male classmates.

   A. Parents tend to believe that their sons are better athletes than their daughters.
   B. Females spend less time participating in sports than do males.
   C. Schools and parents should work together to encourage girls to participate in sports.
   D. Social expectations and stereotypes often influence girls' participation in athletics.

_____ 2. [1]The higher that people are on the social class ladder, the more likely they are to vote for Republicans. [2]In contrast, most members of the working class believe that the government should intervene in the economy to make citizens financially secure. [3]The majority of these working-class citizens are Democrats. [4]Although the working class is more liberal on economic issues (policies that increase government spending), it is more conservative on social issues (and is likely to oppose, for example, abortion, gay marriage, and the banning of prayer in schools). [5]People toward the bottom of the class structure are also less likely to be politically active—to campaign for candidates, or even to vote.

   A. Social class tends to influence political beliefs.
   B. Rich people are usually Republicans.
   C. The less money someone has, the less likely he or she is to participate in politics.
   D. Money is the sole determiner of a person's political attitudes.

(Continues on next page)

_____ 3. ¹At the beginning of the twentieth century, families often hired older women to keep watch over their daughters. ²When a young man asked a girl on a date, he automatically invited her chaperone as well. ³If a young lady entertained her boyfriend in the parlor, the chaperone did not budge from the room. ⁴Because of her responsibilities, the chaperone had the power to make courtship pleasurable or miserable. ⁵Some chaperones had soft hearts and gave young lovers some privacy. ⁶Others were such sticklers for appearances that they prevented the young couple even from exchanging personal remarks. ⁷In addition to being guardians, chaperones sometimes functioned as private eyes. ⁸They investigated the backgrounds of gentlemen who called on their charges to see which one would make the best match. ⁹The chaperone could be a nuisance, but she could also be a good excuse for avoiding unwanted courtships.

   A. The role of chaperones was to keep a close watch over their charges.
   B. At one time, chaperones played an important role in courtship.
   C. In the past, families hired older women to keep watch over their daughters.
   D. Some chaperones actually helped their charges by investigating the backgrounds of gentlemen and providing excuses for avoiding unwanted courtships.

B. (4.) Write out, in your own words, the implied main idea of the following paragraph.

¹At a former poultry market in New York City, pest control authorities could not understand how rats were stealing eggs without breaking them, so one night an exterminator sat in hiding to watch. ²What he saw was that one rat would embrace an egg with all four legs, then roll over on his back. ³A second rat would then drag the first rat by its tail to their burrow, where they could share their prize in peace. ⁴In a similar manner, workers at a packing plant discovered how sides of meat, hanging from hooks, were knocked to the floor and devoured night after night. ⁵An exterminator named Irving Billig watched and found that a swarm of rats formed a pyramid underneath a side of meat, and one rat scrambled to the top of the heap and leaped onto the meat from there. ⁶It then climbed to the top of the side of meat and gnawed its way through it around the hook until the meat dropped to the floor, at which point hundreds of waiting rats fell upon it.

Implied main idea: _____

_____

strategies

IMPLIED MAIN IDEAS: Mastery Test 5

A. In the space provided, write the letter of the sentence that best expresses the implied main idea of each of the following paragraphs.

_____ 1. [1]In virtually all rich nations, schooling is mandatory through high school, and illiteracy rates of 5 percent or less of the population are common. [2]By contrast, in most low-income nations, less than half of eligible school-age children are enrolled in school. [3]Further, most schools in low-income nations are poorly funded. [4]A recent study showed that high-income nations spent an average of $769 per child on education. [5]By contrast, low-income countries spent about $33 per pupil. [6]With poor school facilities, and farm and other work to perform, most children in low-income countries drop out of school before the fourth grade. [7]Consequently, in many poor countries, illiteracy rates are often as high as 80 percent or more.

[handwritten: Subject -schooling for poor kids]

A. Poor nations spend less on students.
B. Rich nations should help fund educational programs for poor nations.
C. A country's wealth has a significant effect on its educational programs and literacy rates.
D. Poor school facilities in poor nations are a common cause of high illiteracy rates.

_____ 2. [1]Low-income parents often feel a sense of powerlessness and lack of influence in their relationships beyond the home. [2]For example, at work they must obey the rules of others in positions of power and authority. [3]When they get home, their parent-child interaction seems to mirror these experiences, only with them in the authority roles. [4]In contrast, middle-class parents have a greater sense of control over their own lives. [5]At work, they are used to making independent decisions and convincing others of their point of view. [6]At home, they teach these same skills to their children.

[handwritten: Subject - how parents from different classes are at work + home]

A. Parents often duplicate within their own families the class-related social experiences they encounter beyond the home.
B. Because low-income parents must obey their supervisors at work, they demand that their children obey them at home.
C. Parents learn all their child-rearing skills from their work.
D. People from the middle class make the best parents.

_____ 3. [1]Should marketers tell their audiences only the good points about their products, or should they also tell them the bad (or the commonplace)? [2]Should they pretend that their products are the only ones of their kind, or should they acknowledge competing products? [3]These are very real strategy questions that marketers face every day. [4]If the audience is friendly (for example, if it uses the advertiser's products), if it initially favors the

(Continues on next page)

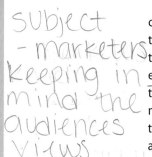

*subject
— marketers
keeping in
mind the
audiences
views*

communicator's position, or if it is not likely to hear an opposing argument, then a *one-sided (supportive) message* that stresses only favorable information is most effective. ⁵However, if the audience is critical or unfriendly (for example, if it uses competitive products), if it is well-educated, or if it is likely to hear opposing claims, then a *two-sided (refutational) message* is likely to be more effective. ⁶Two-sided advertising messages tend to be more credible than one-sided advertising messages because they acknowledge that the advertised brand has shortcomings. ⁷Two-sided messages can also be very effective when consumers are likely to see competitors' negative counterclaims or when consumer attitudes toward the brand are already negative.

A. In promoting their products, marketers must keep in mind the educational level of the audience and whether or not it is friendly.

B. Marketing decisions depend on the nature of the audience and the nature of the competition.

C. When consumers are likely to see competitors' negative counterclaims or when consumers' attitudes toward the brand are already negative, marketers should use two-sided messages.

D. There are two types of advertising messages—supportive and refutational.

B. (4.) Write out, in your own words, the implied central idea of the following textbook passage.

*subject
— locking
up drug
dealers*

¹Some just shake their heads and say that if we can't stop the drugs from coming in, we at least can lock up the dealers and users. ²But there are so many dealers and users that we don't have enough jails and prisons to lock them up. ³Consider these statistics: Several million Americans use cocaine each year, while other millions use heroin, hallucinogens, barbiturates, and inhalants. ⁴During just the past month, about 13 million Americans smoked marijuana. ⁵How could we possibly lock all of these people up? ⁶How many dealers does it take to supply just the marijuana smokers? ⁷If each dealer has 25 customers, there are a half million dealers.

⁸And consider this: To build one prison cell costs about $100,000. ⁹To keep one inmate locked up for one year costs a minimum of $25,000. ¹⁰If we were going to lock up just the drug dealers, where would we get the money? ¹¹If we put two drug dealers in a cell, a half million new cells would run $50 billion. ¹²It would then cost another $25 billion a year to keep those million people in prison.

¹³Not yet mentioned is the fact that there are people waiting in line to take the places of dealers who are arrested. ¹⁴Get rid of one dealer, and two fight to take his or her place.

Implied main idea: Eventhough drug dealers should be locked up, there's reasons why its cheaper to keep than on the streets. A it wont ultimately solve the problem

IMPLIED MAIN IDEAS: Mastery Test 6

A. In the space provided, write the letter of the sentence that best expresses the implied main idea of each of the following paragraphs.

_____ 1. [1]Scientists once believed that large meat-eating dinosaurs lived and hunted alone. [2]Recent discoveries of the buried remains of a dozen large carnivores in the same riverbed in western Canada, however, tell researchers that the dinosaurs may have hunted in packs. [3]For a long time, scientists thought dinosaurs were slow-moving, cold-blooded creatures like crocodiles and lizards. [4]Some scientists changed their thinking when, in 2000, CT scans of a dinosaur's petrified heart showed that it was remarkably similar to that of mammals. [5]The scientists then decided that dinosaurs, too, may have been warm-blooded. [6]Up until recently, scientists thought that all dinosaurs had scaly skin resembling modern-day lizards and snakes. [7]Recent discoveries of numerous feathered dinosaur remains make them look more like weird birds than giant lizards.

[handwritten: subject — Scientists discovering new things about dinosaurs]

A. People hold a number of mistaken beliefs about dinosaurs.
B. Scientists now know that some dinosaurs may have hunted in packs and had scaly skin.
C. Scientists' thinking about dinosaurs has changed in recent years.
D. Scientists now know that not all dinosaurs resembled lizards, crocodiles, or other cold-blooded animals.

_____ 2. [1]In the early 1900s, most inmates in state poorhouses were older people, and almost one-third of Americans age 65 and older depended financially on someone else. [2]Few employers, including the federal government, provided for retired employees. [3]Noting that the government fed retired horses until they died, one postal worker complained, "For the purpose of drawing a pension, it would have been better had I been a horse than a human being." [4]Resistance to pension plans finally broke at the state level in the 1920s. [5]Reformers persuaded voluntary associations, labor unions, and legislators to endorse old-age assistance through pensions, insurance, and retirement homes. [6]By 1933 almost every state provided at least minimal support to needy elderly people, and a path had been opened for a national program of old-age insurance.

[handwritten: subject — Old-age insurance]

A. Between the early 1900s and 1933, America made progress in providing for its elderly.
B. In the early 1900s, America failed to provide for the financial welfare of its elderly citizens.
C. In the early 1900s, the U.S. government treated its retired horses better than it treated its retired human beings.
D. By 1933, a national program of old-age insurance appeared likely to happen, due to the efforts of reformers.

(Continues on next page)

subject
— elders
in
preindustrial
societies

___D___ 3. [1]In preindustrial societies that rely on hunting and gathering, physical strength and good health are important. [2]Consequently, the elderly (who in those societies may be people as young as in their late 30s or 40s) may be viewed as burdens to the family and society. [3]In desperate circumstances, where the survival of the group is at stake, the elderly may be literally abandoned, as in the case of the North American Eskimo. [4]Conversely, in preindustrial societies that rely on growing food or raising animals, physical possessions are regarded as more important than health and strength. [5]In such societies, the elderly, who are the most likely to own land, may be held in higher esteem than younger members of society. [6]For example, among the Berbers of Morocco, elderly tribesman are accorded the highest status because they generally own more land, larger herds, and more material possessions than younger society members.

A. In some preindustrial societies, abandoning the elderly is common.
B. In many societies, the elderly are given respect only if they have material possessions.
C. Elderly people deal with death and aging in different ways.
D. Preindustrial societies tend to value the elderly according to their contributions to the community.

B. (4.) Write out, in your own words, the implied central idea of the following passage.

subject
— dangers
of boxing

[1]Defenders of boxing like to point out that serious injury is more common in such sports as horse racing, skydiving, mountaineering, and college football than in the sport they love. [2]Yet even boxing fans must admit that boxing is the only sport where the goal of the participants is to inflict bodily injury on one another. [3]If you've ever, even briefly, watched a boxing match on TV, you've probably seen boxers give and receive blows to the head. [4]What you might not realize is that when a boxer's gloved hand slams with brute force against his opponent's head, the brain is literally pushed against the skull bone. [5]This action, over time, results in the neurological impairment known as being "punch drunk."

[6]Such boxing greats as Muhammad Ali, Sugar Ray Robinson, and Wilfred Benitez all suffered permanent neurological damage due to their years in the ring. [7]Symptoms include slurred speech, loss of memory, and loss of coordination. [8]In worst-case scenarios, fighters have been hit so hard that they died in the ring, or soon after. [9]A particularly chilling outcome: on March 24, 1962, at Madison Square Garden, Emile Griffith beat Benny "Kid" Paret so brutally that Paret crumpled to the canvas and never regained consciousness. [10]He died ten days later.

[11]From 1920 until the present day, there have been over 900 fatalities due to injuries in the ring. [12]In 2005, 34-year-old Becky Zerlentes was knocked out during a bout at a Colorado boxing event. [13]She died shortly afterward when blood pooled on the surface of her brain.

Implied main idea:

Boxings causes many injuries but a common injury is neurological impairment.

4 Relationships I

Authors use two common methods to show relationships and make their ideas clear. The two methods—**transitions** and **patterns of organization**—are explained in turn in this chapter. The chapter also explains two common types of relationships:

- Relationships that involve **addition**
- Relationships that involve **time**

Transitions

Look at the following items and put a check (✓) by the one that is easier to read and understand:

____ Most people choose a partner who is about as attractive as themselves. Personality and intelligence affect their choice.

____ Most people choose a partner who is about as attractive as themselves. Moreover, personality and intelligence affect their choice.

You probably found the second item easier to understand. The word *Moreover* makes it clear that the writer is presenting several factors in choosing a romantic partner. **Transitions** are words or phrases (like *moreover*) that show relationships between ideas. They are like signs on the road that guide travelers. Or they can be seen as "bridge" words, carrying the reader across from one idea to the next:

Most people choose a partner about as attractive as themselves.  personality and intelligence affect their choices.

Two major types of transitions are words that show addition and words that show time.

Words That Show Addition

Once again, put a check (✓) beside the item that is easier to read and understand:

____ There are several reasons not to fill babies' bottles with sugary juice. It can rot their teeth.

____ There are several reasons not to fill babies' bottles with sugary juice. First of all, it can rot their teeth.

As you probably noted, the second item is easier to understand. The words *first of all* make it clear that the writer plans on giving a series of reasons why babies should not be fed sugary juice. *First of all* and words like it are known as addition words.

Addition words signal added ideas. These words tell you a writer is presenting one or more ideas that continue along the same line of thought as a previous idea. Like all transitions, addition words help writers organize their information and present it clearly to readers. Here are some common words that show addition:

Addition Words

one	to begin with	also	further
first (of all)	for one thing	in addition	furthermore
second(ly)	other	next	last (of all)
third(ly)	another	moreover	final(ly)

Examples

The following examples contain addition words. Notice how these words introduce ideas that *add to* what has already been said.

- Depression can be eased through therapy and medication. Physical exercise has *also* been shown to help.
- Bananas are the most frequently purchased fruit in the U.S. Why are bananas so popular? *To begin with*, they are convenient to carry around and to eat.
- It is annoying to have to sort through a pile of junk mail every day. *Moreover*, junk mail represents a waste of trees and other natural resources.

PRACTICE 1

Complete each sentence with a suitable addition word from the box on the previous page. Try to use a variety of transitions.

> *Hint:* Make sure that each addition word or phrase that you choose fits smoothly into the flow of the sentence. Test each choice by reading the sentence aloud.

1. Computers have affected the lives of people in positive ways, providing all kinds of information and making it easy to keep in touch with loved ones.

   But computers have _____ touched people's lives in hurtful ways, such as by contributing to identity theft and sex crimes.

2. Scolding children too often is actually counterproductive. The kids get used to being scolded and stop taking it seriously. Frequent scoldings, _____, can encourage a child to act aggressive and bully-like.

3. There are various reasons homeless people resist moving to a shelter. For one thing, they may dislike being compelled to follow a shelter's rules. A _____ reason is fear of being robbed while they sleep with people around them.

4. Antarctica is a place of extremes. _____ to being the coldest place on earth, it is also both the wettest and the driest place. How can this be? It is wettest because it contains 70 percent of the world's fresh water, in the form of ice. It is driest because it receives only about two inches of precipitation per year.

5. Typically, men and women have different styles of communication. Women frequently talk about people, while men are more likely to talk about things. _____ difference in styles is that men tend to lecture, while women are more likely to listen and ask questions.

Words That Show Time

Put a check (✓) beside the item that is easier to read and understand:

____ The dog begins to tremble and hide under the couch. A thunderstorm approaches.

____ The dog begins to tremble and hide under the couch when a thunderstorm approaches.

The word *when* in the second item makes clear the relationship between the sentences. It is when a thunderstorm approaches that the dog's behavior changes. *When* and words like it are time words.

Time words tell us *at what point* something happened in relation to when something else happened. They help writers organize and make clear the order of events, stages, and steps in a process. Here are some common words that show time:

Time Words

before	immediately	when	until
previously	next	whenever	often
first (of all)	then	while	frequently
second (ly)	following	during	eventually
third (ly)	later	as (soon as)	final(ly)
now	after (ward)	by	last (of all)

Note: Some additional ways of showing time are dates ("In 1890 . . . ," "Throughout the 21st century . . . ," "By 2020 . . .") and other time references ("Within a week . . . ," "by the end of the month . . . ," "in two years . . .").

Examples

The following examples contain time words. Notice how these words show us *when* something takes place.

● The old woman on the park bench opened a paper bag, and a flock of pigeons *immediately* landed all around her.

● *After* completing medical school, a future doctor continues her training as a "resident" in a hospital.

● *In March 2011,* a massive earthquake caused tremendous devastation in northern Japan.

Helpful Tips about Transitions

Here are two points to keep in mind about transitions:

 TIP 1 **Some transition words have the same meaning.** For example, *also, moreover,* and *furthermore* all mean "in addition." Authors typically use a variety of transitions to avoid repetition.

 TIP 2 **Certain words can serve as two different types of transitions, depending on how they are used.** For example, the word *first* may be used as an addition word to show that the author is beginning to list a series of ideas, as in the following:

> There are a number of reasons not to share personal information on the Internet. *First*, you can't be sure of the identity of the person you're talking to. *Moreover*, . . .

First may also be used to signal a time sequence, as in this sentence:

> Follow these instructions for daily use of the nasal spray. *First*, shake the bottle gently for a few seconds and remove the protective tip.

 **PRACTICE 2**

Complete each sentence with a suitable time word from the box on the previous page. Try to use a variety of transitions.

> *Hint:* Make sure that each time word or phrase that you choose fits smoothly into the flow of the sentence. Test each choice by reading the sentence aloud.

1. Three years _____ signing the Emancipation Proclamation, President Abraham Lincoln was assassinated by an angry Southern sympathizer.

2. _____ the school announced that several students had lice, many parents nervously inspected their own children.

3. The first human heart transplant occurred in 1967. _____ 2012, approximately 5,000 transplants were being performed every year.

4. _____ going to a job interview, it's a wise idea to anticipate questions the interviewer might ask and prepare answers for them.

5. American women were not allowed to vote _____ 1920, when the 19th Amendment to the Constitution was passed.

Patterns of Organization

You have learned that transitions show the relationships between ideas in sentences. In the same way, **patterns of organization** show the relationships between supporting details in paragraphs, essays, and chapters. It is helpful to recognize the common patterns in which authors arrange information. You will then be better able to understand and remember what you read.

The rest of this chapter discusses two major patterns of organization:

● The **list of items pattern**
(Addition words are often used in this pattern of organization.)
● The **time order pattern**
(Time words are often used in this pattern of organization.)

Noticing the transitions in a passage can often help you become aware of its pattern of organization. Transitions can also help you locate the major supporting details.

1   The List of Items Pattern

To get a sense of the list of items pattern, try to arrange the following sentences in a logical order. Put a *1* in front of the sentence that should come first, a *2* in front of the sentence that comes next, a *3* in front of the third sentence, and a *4* in front of the sentence that should come last. The result will be a short paragraph. Use the addition words as a guide.

____ Next is moderate poverty, defined as living on $1 to $2 a day, which refers to conditions in which basic needs are met, but just barely.

____ Nearly half of the six billion people in the world experience one of three degrees of poverty.

____ Last, relative poverty, defined by a household income level below a given proportion of the national average, means lacking things that the middle class now takes for granted.

____ First is extreme poverty, defined by the World Bank as getting by on an income of less than $1 a day, which means that households cannot meet such basic needs for survival as food, clothing, and shelter.

This paragraph begins with the main idea: "Nearly half of the six billion people in the world experience one of three degrees of poverty." The next three sentences go on to describe the three degrees of poverty. The transitions *First, Next,* and *Last* each introduce one of the kinds of poverty. Here is the whole paragraph in its correct order:

[handwritten: G vs. degrees of poverty]

[handwritten: Pattern of Addition]

[1]Nearly half of the six billion people in the world experience one of three degrees of poverty. [2]First is extreme poverty, defined by the World Bank as getting by on an income of less than $1 a day, which means that households cannot meet such basic needs for survival as food, clothing, and shelter. [3]Next is moderate poverty, defined as living on $1 to $2 a day, which refers to conditions in which basic needs are met, but just barely. [4]Last, relative poverty, defined by a household income level below a given proportion of the national average, means lacking things that the middle class now takes for granted.

A **list of items** refers to a series of reasons, examples, facts, or other supporting details that support an idea. The items have no time order, but are listed in whatever order the author prefers. Addition words are often used in a list of items to tell us that other supporting points are being added to a point already mentioned. Textbook authors frequently organize material into lists of items, such as a list of the sources of knowledge, types of diseases, or the kinds of families that exist today.

Addition Words Used in the List of Items Pattern

[handwritten: addition pattern (list)]

one	to begin with	also	further
first (of all)	for one thing	in addition	furthermore
second(ly)	other	next	last (of all)
third(ly)	another	moreover	final(ly)

✓ Check Your Understanding

The paragraph below is organized as a list of items. Complete the outline of the list by first filling in the missing part of the main idea. Then add to the outline the three major details listed in the paragraph.

To help you find the major details, do two things:

- Underline the addition words that introduce the major details in the list.
- Number (*1, 2, . . .*) each item in the list.

[1]Because women were not allowed to act in English plays during Shakespeare's time, young male actors pretended to be women. [2]Acting companies had to work hard to make boys sound and look like women. [3]To begin with, they chose teenage boys who had not reached puberty. [4]They found boy

actors who had high-pitched voices and didn't need to shave. ⁵Next, they dressed the boys in women's clothing. ⁶An upper cloth called a bodice was tightened with string so that the boys looked as if they had feminine waists. ⁷The boys wore dresses and high-heeled shoes that matched their characters. ⁸A long-haired wig completed the costumes. ⁹Finally, they added makeup. ¹⁰A white paste made the boys look pale, and red blush gave them rosy lips and cheeks. ¹¹The boy actors would step on stage looking like ladies.

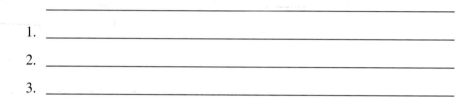

Main idea: Shakespearian acting companies had to work hard to _____

_____

1. _____

2. _____

3. _____

Explanation

The main idea is that Shakespearian acting companies had to work hard to make boys sound and look like women. Following are the three items you should have added to the outline:

1. Chose boys who had not reached puberty. (This item is signaled with the addition phrase *To begin with*).

2. Dressed boys in women's clothing. (This element is signaled by the addition word *Next*).

3. Added makeup. (This element is signaled by the addition word *Finally*.)

PRACTICE 3

A. The following passage uses a listing pattern. Outline the passage by filling in the main idea and the major details.

> *Hint:* Underline the addition words that introduce the items in the list, and number the items. *[handwritten: Pattern of Addition]*

[handwritten left margin: making a list before going to the doctors office]

¹Most people visit a doctor's office when they are concerned about one health issue or another. ²They are often too distracted to prepare for their visit. ³However, there are three important lists that people should make before visiting a doctor's office. ⁴For one thing, they should make a list of all the medications that they are taking. ⁵Many drugs, even over-the-counter remedies, can have dangerous side effects when combined with new prescriptions, so it is important to let the doctor know what pills are being taken on a regular basis. ⁶In addition, people visiting a doctor's office should make a list of their symptoms. ⁷The list should start with whatever symptoms—nausea, fever, joint pain, etc.—have been most troubling, but should include everything that's been bothering them since their last visit to the doctor. ⁸Such lists can aid the doctor in making a diagnosis, and they will also ensure that patients don't forget any important complaints. ⁹Last of all, people visiting their doctor should bring along a short list of questions. ¹⁰A typical doctor sees at least twenty patients every day and can't devote a lot of time to explaining every detail involved in a diagnosis or a treatment. ¹¹So patients who bring specific questions are more likely to have all of their major concerns addressed. ¹²It may seem tiresome to sit down and prepare such lists, but the proactive patients who do so will get the most out of their visits.

Main idea: *[handwritten: However, there are 3 important list that people should make before visiting the doctors]*

1. *[handwritten: list of medicine]*
2. *[handwritten: list of symptoms]*
3. *[handwritten: list of questions]*

B. The following passage uses a listing pattern. Complete the map of the passage by completing the main idea and filling in the missing major details.

¹While getting a tattoo hurts, the sting of a tattoo needle is nothing compared to the sting of regret felt later in life by nearly half of those who have tattoos. ²Luckily, modern medicine has developed a variety of techniques for tattoo removal. ³In the most basic method, dermabrasion, a high-speed buffing tool is used to literally "sand" off several layers of skin. ⁴Another technique, and a less painful one, is cryosurgery, in which skin is frozen to render it numb before removal. ⁵If the tattoo is small enough, surgeons simply snip off the skin and sew the area closed or even graft a "patch" of skin borrowed from elsewhere on the body. ⁶While these methods may all leave scars, the most advanced method, laser removal, leaves virtually no trace. ⁷Lasers are calibrated to pass harmlessly through the surface layers of the skin, breaking apart the tattoo's pigments so that they can be naturally removed by the body's immune system. ⁸While the process feels similar to being snapped with a small rubber band or spattered with tiny drops of hot oil, the pain is considerably less than the discomfort of seeing a tattoo that features, say, the name of a person who is no longer in one's life.

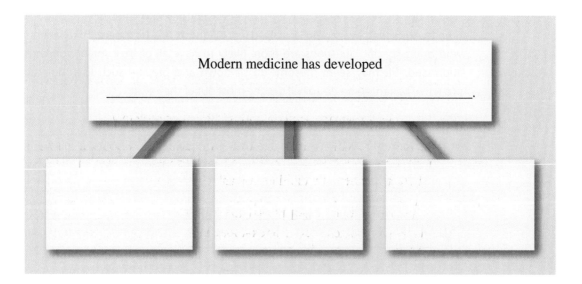

2 The Time Order Pattern

To get a sense of the time order pattern, try to arrange the following sentences in a logical order. Put a *1* in front of the sentence that should come first, a *2* in front of the sentence that comes next, a *3* in front of the third sentence, and a *4* in front of the sentence that should come last. The result will be a short paragraph. Use the time words as a guide.

__2__ Then, in 1638, a press in Cambridge, Massachusetts printed a book of psalms that became an instant bestseller.

__1__ The first books in the United States were imports, brought by the new settlers.

__4__ Eventually, in 1731, Benjamin Franklin asked fifty subscribers to help him start America's first circulating library.

__3__ During the years that followed, booksellers emerged in the Boston area, and by 1685 the leading bookseller offered over three thousand books.

Authors usually present events and processes in the order in which they happen, resulting in a pattern of organization known as **time order**. Clues to the pattern of the above sentences are the transitions *(Then, in 1638, first, Eventually, in 1731, During,* and *by 1685)* that show time. The sentences should read as follows:

> [1]The first books in the United States were imports, brought by the new settlers. [2]Then, in 1638, a press in Cambridge, Massachusetts printed a book of psalms that became an instant bestseller. [3]During the years that followed, booksellers emerged in the Boston area, and by 1685 the leading bookseller offered over three thousand books. [4]Eventually, in 1731, Benjamin Franklin asked fifty subscribers to help him start America's first circulating library.

As a student, you will see time order used frequently. Textbooks in all fields describe events and processes, such as the events leading to the start of the Civil War, the important incidents in the life of Franklin Roosevelt, the steps in looking for a job, the process involved in financial planning, or the stages in biological aging.

In addition, most fiction and biography—and virtually any communication that tells a story—uses time order. (For example, look at the opening paragraphs of the autobiographical selection that starts on page 510 of this book.)

The two most common kinds of time order are 1) a series of events or stages and 2) a series of steps (directions for how to do something). Both kinds of time order are discussed on the following pages.

Series of Events or Stages

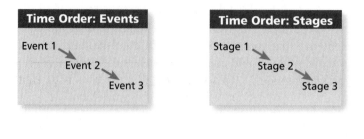

✓ Check Your Understanding

Here is a paragraph that is organized according to time order. Complete the outline of the paragraph by listing the missing stages in the order in which they happen.

To help you find the stages, do two things:

- Underline the time words that introduce each stage in the process.
- Number (*1, 2, . . .*) each stage.

¹People who move into affordable city neighborhoods may not realize it, but they are often part of a process that ends in the change of a community. ²The first stage of this "gentrification" process begins when young artists move into a low-income working-class neighborhood. ³These artists, who generally have little income themselves, are often attracted by the low rents, the availability of studio space, and the proximity to the urban centers where they can't afford to live. ⁴In the next stage, young professionals follow the artists into the neighborhood. ⁵These city-dwellers tend to be between the ages of 25 and 35, are single or at least childless, and are often attracted to the trendy restaurants, galleries, and nightclubs that open in neighborhoods popular with artists. ⁶The final stage of the gentrification process occurs when upper-class families take over the neighborhood. ⁷The fancy restaurants and stores that have grown up around the young professionals draw wealthier people and businesses into the community. ⁸The end result is a neighborhood where the rising rents are too costly for both the original working-class inhabitants and for the artists who started the process of gentrification to begin with. ⁹The artists, therefore, are forced to move on to another working-class neighborhood, where they will start this transformative process all over again.

Main idea: The process of gentrification can transform a community.

Stage 1 _____

Stage 2 _____

Stage 3 _____

Stage 4—The artists are forced to move on to another working-class neighborhood, and the process begins all over again.

Explanation

You should have added these points to the outline:

1. Stage 1—Young artists move into a low-income working-class neighborhood.

2. Stage 2—Young professionals follow the artists into the neighborhood.

3. Stage 3—Upper-class families take over the neighborhood.

As signaled by the transitions *The first stage, In the next stage,* and *The final stage,* the relationship between the points is one of time, with one stage in the process of change leading to the next. A series of stages or events is a common kind of time order.

PRACTICE 4

The following passage describes a sequence of events. Outline the paragraph by filling in the major details.

> *Hint:* Underline the time word or words that introduce each major detail, and number each major detail.

¹In World War II, Sir Winston Churchill refused to bargain with Hitler. ²Defiantly, he told his people that he would resist any German assault: "We shall fight on the beaches . . . we shall fight in the fields and in the streets . . . we shall never surrender." ³A furious Hitler quickly went on the attack against Britain. ⁴First, he unleashed German submarines against British shipping. ⁵A short while later, he sent his air force, the Luftwaffe, to destroy Britain's military defenses from the air. ⁶At the time the assault began, the Royal Air Force (RAF) had just 704 serviceable planes, while Germany had 2,682 bombers and fighters ready for action. ⁷Throughout July and August, the Luftwaffe attacked airfields and radar stations on Britain's southern and eastern coasts. ⁸Then, in September, Hitler shifted strategy and began to bomb civilian targets in London and other British cities.

⁹These air raids, known collectively as the blitz, continued through the fall and winter. ¹⁰In May 1941, the blitz ended. ¹¹The RAF, while outnumbered, had won the Battle of Britain. ¹²Churchill expressed his nation's gratitude with these famous words: "Never in the field of human conflict was so much owed by so many to so few."

Main idea: A furious Hitler quickly went on the attack against Britain.

1. _____

2. _____

3. _____

Series of Steps (Directions)

Time Order: Steps

Step 1

Step 2

Step 3

When authors give directions, they use time order. They explain step 1, then step 2, and so on through the entire series of steps that must be taken toward a specific goal.

✓ Check Your Understanding

Below is a paragraph that gives directions. Complete the outline of the paragraph that follows by filling in the main idea and listing the missing steps in the correct sequence. To help yourself identify each step, do two things:

- Underline the time words that introduce each item in the sequence.
- Number (*1, 2, . . .*) each step in the sequence.

    ¹It's important to take time to reflect upon your goals in life. ²To begin with, take out a sheet of paper and label it "My Lifetime Goals." ³Imagine that you are very old, looking back at your life. ⁴What did you want to accomplish? ⁵What do you feel best about? ⁶Write down anything that pops into your mind. ⁷Next, take a second sheet of paper and write "My Three-Year Goals." ⁸On this, write what you would like to accomplish within the next three years. ⁹Third, take a sheet of paper

and title it "What I Would Do If I Knew I Had Six Months to Live." [10]Assume that you would be in good health and have the necessary resources, and list everything you might like to squeeze into those six months. [11]Now go back over all three lists, and rate each item as A (very important), B (somewhat important), or C (least important.) [12]Finally, evaluate the "A" items on your lists and select the goals that are most important to you.

Main idea: It's important to take time to reflect upon your goals in life.

1. _____

_____

2. _____

_____

3. _____

_____

4. _____

_____

5. _____

_____

Explanation

You should have added the following steps to the outline:

1. Take out a sheet of paper and write down "My Lifetime Goals." (The author signals this step with the time phrase *To begin with*.)

2. Take a second sheet and write down "My Three-Year Goals." (The author signals this step with the time word *Next*.)

3. Take a third sheet and list "What I Would Do If I Knew I Had Six Months to Live." (This step is signaled with the time word *Third*.)

4. On the three lists, rate each item as A, B, or C. (This step is marked by the time word *Now*.)

5. Evaluate the "A" items and select the goals that are most important to you. (*Finally* signals this last step.)

PRACTICE 5

The following passage gives directions involving several steps that must be done in order. Complete the map below by filling in the main idea in the top box and the four missing steps.

¹To write effectively, practice four rules of thumb. ²First of all, decide what point you want to make in your paper. ³Your main idea is often best expressed at the beginning of your paper. ⁴It is a guide for both you and your reader as to what your paper is about. ⁵Next, be sure to provide sufficient support for your point. ⁶To do so, you need to provide specific reasons, examples, and other details that explain and develop the point. ⁷The more precise and particular your supporting details are, the better your readers can "see," "hear," and "feel" them. ⁸The third rule of thumb is to organize your support. ⁹You can often use a listing order in which you present and explain your first supporting detail and then your second and perhaps finally a third or fourth. ¹⁰The last rule of thumb is to write clear, error-free sentences. ¹¹If you spell correctly and follow grammar, punctuation, and usage rules, your sentences will be clear and well written. ¹²To find errors, read your sentences aloud and make whatever changes are needed so they read smoothly and clearly. ¹³If you have questions, refer to a dictionary or a grammar handbook as needed.

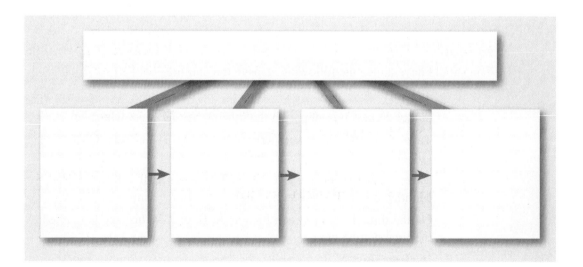

A Note on Main Ideas and Patterns of Organization

A paragraph's main idea may indicate its pattern of organization. For example, here is a sentence from this chapter that suggests a list of items will follow:

> Luckily, modern medicine has developed a variety of techniques for tattoo removal.

And here is a sentence from the chapter that suggests the paragraph will have a time order:

> People who move into affordable city neighborhoods may not realize it, but they are often part of a process that ends in the change of a community.

Paying close attention to the main idea, then, can often give you a quick sense of a paragraph's pattern of organization. Try, for instance, to guess the pattern of the paragraph with this main idea:

> Research has uncovered a number of possible explanations for the link between hostility and heart disease.

The phrase "a number of possible explanations" is a strong indication that the paragraph will list those explanations. The main idea helps us guess that the paragraph will be a list of explanations.

PRACTICE 6

Most of the main ideas below have been taken from college textbooks. In the space provided, write the letter of the pattern of organization that each main idea suggests.

_B_ 1. A woman's pregnancy is usually divided into trimesters, each with its own developmental milestones.
   A. List of items   B. Time order

_A_ 2. Various tests have been developed specifically to measure the intelligence of infants and children.
   A. List of items   B. Time order

_A_ 3. Almost any food item you find in a supermarket will be dated in one of several ways.
   A. List of items   B. Time order

_B_ 4. Widowed adults often go through a series of stages as they adjust to their loss.
   A. List of items   B. Time order

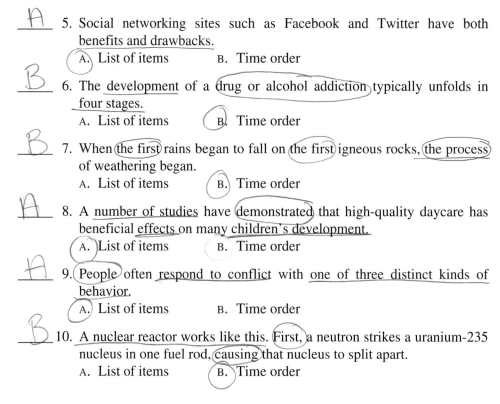

_A_ 5. Social networking sites such as Facebook and Twitter have both benefits and drawbacks.
A. List of items   B. Time order

_B_ 6. The development of a drug or alcohol addiction typically unfolds in four stages.
A. List of items   B. Time order

_B_ 7. When the first rains began to fall on the first igneous rocks, the process of weathering began.
A. List of items   B. Time order

_A_ 8. A number of studies have demonstrated that high-quality daycare has beneficial effects on many children's development.
A. List of items   B. Time order

_A_ 9. People often respond to conflict with one of three distinct kinds of behavior.
A. List of items   B. Time order

_B_ 10. A nuclear reactor works like this. First, a neutron strikes a uranium-235 nucleus in one fuel rod, causing that nucleus to split apart.
A. List of items   B. Time order

Two Final Points

1 While many passages have just one pattern of organization, often the patterns are mixed. For example, you may find that part of a passage uses a list of items pattern, and another part of the same passage uses a time pattern. In the passage below, sentences 8 and 9 list two ways to complete the third step in the series of directions:

> [1]Do you know what to do if you lose a tooth in an accident, fall, or fight? [2]Doctors can replace a knocked-out tooth, but only if you act quickly. [3]First, find the loose tooth. [4]Pick it up by the top part, and don't touch the roots. [5]Second, rinse the tooth with milk. [6]Don't use tap water, soap, or chemicals because they could cause harm. [7]Third, keep the tooth from getting dry. [8]If possible, put the tooth back in its socket. [9]If you cannot do this, store it in milk or keep it between your tongue and cheek, taking care not to swallow it. [10]Finally, go as quickly as possible to a dentist's office or an emergency room. [11]If more than an hour or so passes, your tooth will become unusable.

2 Remember that not all relationships between ideas are signaled by transitions. An author may present a list of items, for example, without using addition words. So as you read, watch for the relationships themselves, not just the transitions.

CHAPTER REVIEW

In this chapter, you learned how authors use transitions and patterns of organization to make their ideas clear. Just as transitions show relationships between ideas in sentences, patterns of organization show relationships between supporting details in paragraphs and longer pieces of writing.

You also learned two common kinds of relationships that authors use to make their ideas clear:

- ● **Addition relationships**

    — Authors often present a list or series of reasons, examples, or other details that support an idea. The items have no time order, but are listed in whatever order the author prefers.

    — Transition words and phrases that signal such addition relationships include *for one thing, second, also, in addition,* and *finally.*

- ● **Time relationships**

    — Authors usually discuss a series of events or steps in the order in which they happen, resulting in a time order.

    — Transition words that signal such time relationships include *first, next, then, after,* and *last.*

The next chapter—Chapter 5—will help you learn four other important kinds of relationships: definition-example, comparison and/or contrast, cause-effect, and problem-solution.

On the Web: If you are using this book in class, you can go to our website for more practice in understanding relationships that involve addition and time. Visit our Learning Center at **www.townsendpress.net** for additional activities and an instructional video on this skill.

REVIEW TEST 1

To review what you've learned in this chapter, answer each of the following questions by filling in the blank.

1. Transitions are words or phrases (like *first of all* or *another* or *then* or *finally*) that show the _____ between ideas. They are like signs on the road that guide travelers.

2. Words such as *for one thing, also,* and *furthermore* are known as addition words. They tell us the writer is presenting one or more _____ that add to the same line of thought as a previous idea.

3. Words such as *then, next,* and *after* are known as time words. They tell us _____ something happened in relation to when something else happened.

4. Just as transitions show the relationships between ideas in sentences, patterns of _____ show the relationships between supporting details in a paragraph or longer passage.

5. Sometimes the _____ of a paragraph may suggest the paragraph's pattern of organization.

The selection that follows is from the college textbook *Communicate!* by Rudolph F. Verderber and Kathleen S. Verderber. Read it and then answer the relationships questions that follow. There are also questions on understanding vocabulary in context, finding main ideas, identifying supporting details, and recognizing implied main ideas.

Preview

Good conversationalists are not born; they are made. If you cringe at the thought of having to make "small talk," this excerpt from a communications textbook will give you some very concrete tips about how to keep the conversational ball rolling smoothly.

Words to Watch

initiator (before paragraph 3): the person who begins
filibuster (13): prolonged speechmaking
paraphrases (18): rewordings

SKILLS OF EFFECTIVE FACE-TO-FACE CONVERSATIONALISTS

Rudolph F. Verderber and Kathleen S. Verderber

1 Regardless of how well we think we converse, almost all of us can learn to be more effective. In this section, we discuss several skills that are basic to effective conversationalists.

Have Quality Information to Present

2 The more you know about a range of subjects, the greater the chance that you will be an interesting conversationalist. Here are some suggestions for building a high-quality information base:

- Read a newspaper every day (not just the comics or the sports).
- Read at least one weekly news or special-interest magazine.
- Watch television documentaries and news specials as well as entertainment and sports programs. (Of course, sports and entertainment are favorite topics of conversation too—but not with everyone.)
- Attend the theater and concerts as well as going to movies.
- Visit museums and historical sites.

Following these suggestions will provide you with a foundation of quality information you can share in social conversations.

As an Initiator°, Ask Meaningful Questions

3   What happens in the first few minutes of a conversation will have a profound effect on how well a social conversation develops. Although asking questions comes easy to some, many people seem at a loss for what to do to get a conversation started. These four question lines will usually help to get a conversation started. Notice that none of them is a yes or no question— each calls for the person to share some specific information.

- *Refer to family:* How is Susan getting along this year at college? How is your dad feeling?
- *Refer to the person's work:* What projects have you been working on lately?
- *Refer to a sporting activity:* How was the fishing trip you went on last week? What is it about Tiger Woods that enables him to be near his best at major tournaments?
- *Refer to a current event:* What do you think is driving people back to more conservative stocks? What do you think we can do to get kids more interested in reading?

Perhaps just looking at these four suggestions will bring other ideas to mind that you can use to start conversations with various acquaintances.

As a Responder, Provide Free Information

4   Effective conversationalists provide a means of enabling others to continue a conversation by providing free information with their responses. Free information is extra information offered during a message that can be used by the responder to continue the conversation.

5   Many people have difficulty building conversations because of a tendency to reply to questions with one-word responses. If, for instance, Paul asks Jack, "Do you like tennis?" and Jack answers "Yes" and then just looks at Paul, Paul has nowhere to go. To keep the conversation going (or to get it started), Paul has to think of a new line to pursue.

6   Suppose, however, that after Jack answers "Yes," he goes on to say "I've only been playing for about a year, but I really enjoy it." Now, Paul has a direction to follow. He might turn the conversation to his own experience: "I haven't been playing long myself, but I'm starting to get more confidence, especially with my forehand." Or he might use the information to ask another question: "Are you able to play very often?"

7   As a respondent, it is important to give free information. As the initiator, it is important to listen for free information. The better the quality of the free

information, the more likely it is that the conversation will grow and prove rewarding to both participants.

Credit Sources

8   Crediting sources means verbally footnoting the source from which you have drawn your information and ideas. In a term paper, you give credit to authors you have quoted or paraphrased by footnoting the sources. Similarly, when you use other people's words or ideas in your oral communication, you can credit the source verbally.

9   By crediting you enable the participants to evaluate the quality of the information you are sharing. Moreover, by crediting ideas from people who are acquaintances, you make people feel better about themselves and avoid hard feelings. For instance, if a friend presents a creative idea and verbally acknowledges you as the source, you probably feel flattered. If, however, the person acts as though the idea were his own, you are probably hurt or angry. So, when you repeat ideas that you have gotten from others, make sure you give proper credit.

10   Crediting is easy enough. To give credit where it is due and avoid possible hard feelings, just include the name of the person you got the idea from. For example, in a discussion about course offerings, you might say, "I like the list of courses we have to choose from, but, you know, we should

really have a course in attitude change. Laura was the one who put me on to the idea, and I can see why it's a good idea."

Balance Speaking and Listening

11   Conversations are most satisfying when all participants feel that they have had their fair share of speaking time. We balance speaking and listening in a conversation by practicing turn-taking techniques.

12   **1. Effective conversationalists take the appropriate number of turns.** In any conversation, the idea is for all to have approximately the same number of turns. If you discover that you are speaking more than your fair share, try to restrain yourself by mentally checking whether everyone else has had a chance to talk once before you talk a second time. Similarly, if you find yourself being inactive in a conversation, try to increase your

participation level. Remember, if you have information to contribute, you are cheating yourself and the group when you do not share it.

13   **2. Effective conversationalists speak an appropriate length of time on each turn.** People are likely to tune out or become annoyed with those conversational partners who make speeches, filibuster°, or perform monologues rather than engaging in the ordinary give-and-take of conversation. Similarly, it is difficult to carry on a conversation with someone who gives one- or two-word replies to questions that are designed to elicit meaningful information. Turns do, of course, vary in length depending on what is being said. If your average statements are much longer or shorter than those of your conversational partners, however, you need to adjust.

14   **3. Effective conversationalists recognize and heed turn-exchanging cues.** Patterns of vocal tone, such as a decrease of loudness or a lowering of pitch, and use of gestures that seem to show obvious completion of a point are the most obvious turn-taking cues. When you are trying to get into a conversation, look for them.

15   By the same token, be careful of giving inadvertent turn-exchanging cues. For instance, if you tend to lower your voice when you are not really done speaking, or take long pauses for emphasis when you expect to continue, you are likely to be interrupted, because these are cues that others are likely to act on. If you find yourself getting interrupted frequently, you might ask people whether you tend to give false cues. Moreover, if you come to recognize that another person has a habit of giving these kinds of cues inadvertently, try not to interrupt when speaking with that person.

16   **4. Effective conversationalists use conversation-directing behavior and comply with the conversation-directing behavior of others.** In general, a person who ends his or her turn may define who speaks next. For instance, when Paul concludes his turn by saying, "Susan, did you understand what he meant?" Susan has the right to the floor. Skillful turn takers use conversation-directing behavior to balance turns between those who freely speak and those who may be more reluctant to speak. Similarly, effective turn takers remain silent and listen politely when the conversation is directed to someone else.

17   Of course, if the person who has just finished speaking does not verbally or nonverbally direct the conversation to a preferred next speaker, then the turn is up for grabs and goes to the first person to speak.

18   **5. Effective conversationalists rarely interrupt.** Although interruptions are generally considered inappropriate, interrupting for "clarification" and "agreement" (confirming) are interpersonally acceptable. For instance, interruptions that are likely to include relevant questions or paraphrases°

intended to clarify, such as "What do you mean by 'presumptuous'" or "I get the sense that you think presumptuous behavior is especially bad," and reinforcing statements such as "Good point, Max" or "I see what you mean, Suzie." The interruptions that are likely to be viewed as disruptive or incomplete include those that change the subject or that seem to minimize the contribution of the interrupted person.

Reading Comprehension Questions

Vocabulary in Context

_____ 1. In the sentence below, the word *elicit* (ĭ-lĭs′ĭt) means
   A. bring out.
   B. describe.
   C. do away with.
   D. challenge.

"Similarly, it is difficult to carry on a conversation with someone who gives one or two-word replies to questions that are designed to elicit meaningful information." (Paragraph 13)

_____ 2. In the excerpt below, the word *inadvertent* (ĭn′əd-vûr′tnt) means
   A. intentional.
   B. obvious.
   C. rude.
   D. accidental.

"By the same token, be careful of giving inadvertent turn-exchanging cues. For instance, if you tend to lower your voice when you are not really done speaking or take long pauses for emphasis when you expect to continue, you are likely to be interrupted because these are cues that others are likely to act on." (Paragraph 15)

Central Point and Main Ideas

_____ 3. Which sentence best expresses the implied central point of the selection?
   A. Many people fail to provide enough free information and therefore cannot be considered skilled conversationalists.
   B. The key to becoming a skilled conversationalist is to have something interesting to say and to know how to say it.
   C. By following some simple suggestions, people can improve their skills as conversationalists.
   D. To become an effective conversationalist, one must heed turn-exchanging cues and comply with the conversation-directing behavior of others.

_____ 4. The implied main idea of paragraphs 4–7 is that
   A. if responders don't provide enough free information, the conversation may end.
   B. all conversationalists need to be aware of the need to provide and listen for free information.
   C. initiators need to listen for free information in order to keep a conversation going.
   D. some conversations can reward both initiators and responders.

_____ 5. The main idea of paragraphs 16–17 is stated in
   A. the first sentence of paragraph 16.
   B. the second sentence of paragraph 16.
   C. the last sentence of paragraph 16.
   D. paragraph 17.

Supporting Details

_____ 6. According to the authors, free information is
   A. information available in any newspaper or magazine.
   B. information that doesn't require an oral response.
   C. extra information offered during a message that can be used by the responder to continue the conversation.
   D. information about carefree topics such as tennis and other sports.

_____ 7. According to the article, two appropriate reasons to interrupt a speaker are
   A. to express disapproval and disgust.
   B. for clarification and agreement.
   C. to dispute the speaker's facts and to ask for elaboration.
   D. to change the subject and to minimize the contribution of the interrupted person.

Transitions

_____ 8. The relationship of the second sentence below to the first sentence is one of
   A. addition.
   B. time.

> "Suppose, however, that after Jack answers 'Yes,' he goes on to say 'I've only been playing for about a year, but I really enjoy it.' Now, Paul has a direction to follow." (Paragraph 6)

_____ 9. The relationship of the second sentence below to the first sentence is one of
   A. addition.
   B. time.

> "By crediting you enable the participants to evaluate the quality of the information you are sharing. Moreover, by crediting ideas from people who are acquaintances, you make people feel better about themselves and avoid hard feelings." (Paragraph 9)

Patterns of Organization

_____ 10. The pattern of organization in this selection is mainly
   A. a list of items.
   B. time order.

Discussion Questions

1. Do you consider yourself a talkative person—or a quiet person? Which of the specific skills mentioned in this essay would be valuable for you to work on? Which of them do you think would work less well for you? Explain.

2. Think of the last time you had an extremely interesting conversation with someone. What was it about the conversation, or the conversationalist, that made it so interesting?

3. Have you ever been in a conversation with someone who dominated the conversation? Conversely, have you ever tried to carry on a conversation with a person who failed to provide any "free information," or who demonstrated other inappropriate conversational behaviors? If so, how did you react in each situation?

4. In your opinion, what advantages do people who are skilled conversationalists have over people who are not?

Note: Writing assignments for this selection appear on page 636.

Check Your Performance   RELATIONSHIPS I

Activity	Number Right	Points	Score
Review Test 1 (5 items)	_____	× 6 =	_____
Review Test 2 (10 items)	_____	× 7 =	_____
	TOTAL SCORE	=	_____ %

Enter your total score into the **Reading Performance Chart: Review Tests** on the inside back cover.

Name _____ Date _____

Section _____ SCORE: (Number correct) _____ x 10 = _____ %

RELATIONSHIPS I: Mastery Test 1

Print 3 docs from Blackboard
course context → patterns 0 →

A. Fill in each blank with an appropriate transition from the box. Use each transition once. Then, in the space provided, write the letter of the transition you have chosen.

A. also A	**B. finally** T	**C. in addition** A
D. next T, A	**E. then**	

_____ 1. [1]A butterfly goes through <u>four stages of life</u>. [2]First, it is an egg; next, it becomes a caterpillar; after that, a pupa inside a cocoon; and _____, an adult butterfly.

_____ 2. [1]Identifying a true food allergy requires a thorough health history, physical examination, and diagnostic tests to eliminate other diseases. [2]Skin pricks with food extracts are a common test for food allergies, even though the high incidence of false positive results can complicate diagnosis. [3]Physicians _____ conduct dietary trials in which they eliminate the offending food and reintroduce it in small quantities to substantiate that reactions occur only when that particular food is eaten.

_____ 3. [1]When administering a lie-detector test, the tester begins by asking general, non-threatening questions. [2]He _____ moves on to questions that may cause the subject to feel anxious or guilty.

_____ 4. [1]People today communicate in ways that earlier generations could have never dreamed of. [2]They can now speak to each other almost anywhere using cell phones. [3]_____, they communicate via fax machines, e-mail, text and instant messaging, Skype, Facebook, and Twitter.

_____ 5. [1]On the sunny Tuesday morning of September 11, 2001, nineteen hijackers seized control of commercial jets that had taken off from East Coast airports. [2]At 8:46 a.m., one plane crashed into the 110-story North Tower of the World Trade Center in New York City, causing a huge explosion and a fire. [3]_____, at 9:03 a.m., a second plane flew into the South Tower. [4]In less than two hours, both buildings collapsed, killing thousands of office workers, firefighters, and police officers.

(Continues on next page)

B. (6–9.) Fill in each blank with an appropriate transition from the box. Use each transition once.

A. finally T , A	B. first T , A	C. then T
D. while T		

¹There has been an overwhelming interest in the story of King Kong from its first appearance in a 1933 movie to the popular remake of that film in 2005. ²The basic story is pretty simple. ³The _____ thing that happens is that filmmakers go to a mysterious island to make a movie about an enormous ape. ⁴The ape _____ snatches the leading lady, with whom he falls in love. ⁵After the ape is captured, he is taken back to the United States and put on display in New York. ⁶The next turn in the plot is that he escapes, grabs the girl again, rampages through the city, and climbs to the top of the Empire State Building. ⁷_____ all of this action is happening, he manages to tenderly protect the girl. ⁸_____, he is mortally wounded by fighter planes, and the massive creature falls to his death. ⁹The story will probably be around forever, having a grip, for whatever mysterious reasons, on our collective imagination.

_____10. The pattern of organization of the above selection is
    A. list of items.
    B. time order.

RELATIONSHIPS I: Mastery Test 2

A. Fill in each blank with an appropriate transition from the box. Use each transition once. Then, in the space provided, write the letter of the transition you have chosen.

A. before ⊤	**B.** for one thing A	**C.** in addition A
D. later ⊤	**E.** second ⊤, A	

_____ 1. ¹"Functional literacy" does not refer only to a person's ability to read words. ²_____, it has to do with a person's ability to understand a map and do simple arithmetic.

_____ 2. ¹Right _____ the pain of a migraine headache begins, many people experience a visual "aura" consisting of flashing or wavy lights.

_____ 3. ¹Some peace movements include no more than a dozen dedicated pacifists. ²Others have widespread popular appeal and the ability to mobilize thousands or even millions of citizens. ³In 1828, Quakers, evangelical preachers, and intellectuals joined to form the American Peace Society, a national organization that promoted world peace as well as abolitionism and women's rights. ⁴_____ in the century, they were joined by feminists, suffragettes, and social reformers.

_____ 4. ¹Forget the spanking clean, neat, freshly painted houses in "colonial villages" constructed for modern tourists. ²Most 17th- and 18th-century colonial homes looked nothing like them. ³_____, few were painted on the outside. ⁴Most were made of split or sawed boards that, like modern wooden garden benches, faded into a gray that blended into the landscape. ⁵Secondly, they were small affairs, often consisting of a single room measuring perhaps eighteen by twenty feet on the inside with a chimney at the end. ⁶And some, but by no means all, had white-washed interior walls; otherwise, the interiors went unfinished.

_____ 5. ¹An early method of writing was sign writing, in which each symbol was based on a picture that resembled what it stood for. ²Thus, a circle with wavy lines radiating from it might stand for the sun, while a horizontal series of wavy lines might stand for water. ³One early form of this style of writing developed in Sumeria (present-day Iraq) around 3500 B.C. ⁴A _____, more familiar form developed in Egypt a few hundred years later and came to be known as hieroglyphics. ⁵The most durable form of sign writing blossomed in China about 2000 to 1500 B.C. ⁶This method required learning thousands of different pictographs that represented various objects and actions. *(Continues on next page)*

B. (6–9.) Fill in each blank with an appropriate transition from the box. Use each transition once.

A. first	B. last of all	C. next
D. second		

~~Either one~~

¹To give first aid for severe external bleeding, one should __first__ place direct pressure on the wound with a sterile gauze pad or any clean cloth, such as a washcloth, towel, or handkerchief. ²Press hard. ³Using a pad or cloth will help keep the wound free from germs and aid clotting. ⁴If you do not have a pad or cloth available, have the injured person apply pressure with his or her hand. ⁵__Second__, elevate the injured area above the level of the heart if you do not suspect a broken bone. ⁶__Next__, apply a pressure bandage to hold the gauze pads or cloth in place. ⁷If blood soaks through the bandage, add more pads and bandages to help absorb the blood. ⁸Do not remove any blood-soaked pads because doing so can interfere with the blood-clotting process. ⁹__Last of all__, if bleeding continues, call EMS personnel and see if you can apply pressure at a pressure point to slow the flow of blood.

__B__ 10. The pattern of organization of the above selection is
    A. list of items.
    B. time order.

RELATIONSHIPS I: Mastery Test 3

A. Fill in each blank with an appropriate transition from the box. Use each transition once. Then, in the space provided, write the letter of the transition you have chosen.

A. **also**	B. **another**	C. **during**
D. **furthermore**	E. **until**	

_____ 1. ¹Premarital sex does not always result from a desire for intimacy. ²_____ important factor is peer pressure. ³For young males, sexual experience is seen as a way to prove their manliness. ⁴For young females, especially ones with a poor self-image, sexual intimacy is regarded as a way to prove they are sexy and desirable.

_____ 2. ¹The most extreme form of social control is capital punishment, that is, the execution of the criminal offender. ²_____ the 1960s, capital punishment was an integral part of the British criminal justice system. ³In the 1700s in particular, there were over two hundred crimes, ranging from high treason to petty thievery, for which people could be executed. ⁴These executions were held in full public view in the belief that the witnesses would be deterred from committing similar acts.

_____ 3. ¹Up to a hundred years ago, people believed tomatoes to be poisonous. ²This is because the tomato belongs to a family of plants, the Nightshade, which does have some poisonous members. ³People _____ assumed the tomato to be poisonous because of the unpleasantly strong odor given off by the stem and leaves of the plant. ⁴The stem and leaves give off this odor because they are, in fact, toxic; but the fruit itself is not.

_____ 4. ¹More than 22,000 pieces of man-made junk are now orbiting in space, mostly left over from old launch vehicles and exploded satellites. ²More space junk is being added all the time. ³_____, the number of pieces is increasing as they bump into one another and break into smaller bits.

(Continues on next page)

_____ 5. ¹At the heart of the technological revolution was the microprocessor. ²First introduced in 1970 by Intel, the microprocessor miniaturized the central processing unit of a computer, enabling small machines to perform calculations that previously only large machines could do. ³_____ the next decades, the power of these integrated circuits increased by a factor of seven thousand. ⁴Computing chores that took a week in the early 1970s took only one minute by the year 2000, while the cost of storing one megabyte of information, or enough for a 320-page book, fell from more than $5,000 in 1975 to 17 cents in 2000. ⁵The implications for business were enormous.

B. (6–9.) Fill in each blank with an appropriate transition from the box. Use each transition once.

A. first	**B. last**	**C. next**
D. third		

¹If you mention the word *prom* to people, they are going to think of a high-school rite of passage. ²In fact, PROM is also the name of a proven study method. ³The _____ step in this system is to preview a reading assignment. ⁴Note the title and read the first and last paragraphs; also look quickly at headings and subheads and anything in **boldface** or *italic*. ⁵_____, read a selection straight through while marking off important ideas such as definitions, examples, and lists of items. ⁶The _____ step is to organize the material you've read by taking study notes on it. ⁷Get all the important ideas down on paper in outline form, relating one idea to another as much as possible. ⁸_____, memorize the study notes that you will need to remember for tests. ⁹Do this by writing key words in the margins of your study outline and turning those words into questions. ¹⁰For instance, the key words "three types of rocks" can be converted into the question "What are the three types of rocks?" ¹¹Recite the answers to these and other key questions until you can answer them without referring to your notes.

_____ 10. The pattern of organization of the above selection is
   A. list of items.
   B. time order.

RELATIONSHIPS I: Mastery Test 4

A. (1–5.) Fill in each blank with an appropriate transition from the box. Use each transition once.

A. **after**	B. **later**	C. **next**
D. **then**	E. **when**	

[1]_____ a string of defeats which forced the Continental Army to retreat down through New Jersey, General George Washington was in despair. [2]He managed to bring his troops across the Delaware River into Pennsylvania on December 11, 1776. [3]The _____ day, Congress, fearing a British attack, fled Philadelphia for Baltimore. [4]But _____ Washington broke the string of defeats on December 30–31, _____ he recrossed the Delaware and surprised a British garrison at Trenton, New Jersey, taking 918 prisoners and killing 30 of the king's soldiers, while the American troops suffered only five casualties. [5]Three days _____, he won another victory at Princeton. [6]The battles of Trenton and Princeton were among the most important of the war. [7]They restored morale and allowed Washington to take his troops into winter camp—war in the 1700s was primarily a summer and fall activity, since the guns of the day fired poorly in cold weather—at Morristown, New Jersey. [8]That meant the Continental Army would be around to fight again in 1777.

_____ 6. The pattern of organization of the above selection is
    A. list of items.
    B. time order.

(Continues on next page)

B. Read the textbook passage below. Then answer the question and complete the outline that follows.

[handwritten: Subject Lottery system]

¹Throughout history, political leaders have used lottery systems to benefit society in several ways. ²One function of lotteries was to fund military projects. ³Ancient Chinese warlord Cheung Leung made up a lottery system to pay for his army. ⁴The system he created is now known as the popular game Keno. ⁵American leader Benjamin Franklin used a lottery to buy the Continental Army a cannon during the Revolutionary War. ⁶Lotteries have also been used to pay for public works. ⁷China's Great Wall was funded in part by a lottery. ⁸The Romans used a lottery system approved by Augustus Caesar to pay for the construction of public buildings. ⁹Boston's Faneuil Hall was rebuilt with the money from a lottery organized by American revolutionary John Hancock. ¹⁰Many of today's American state lotteries fund public education. ¹¹A further use of lotteries has been to help the poor. ¹²Bruges, a Belgian town of the 15th century, created lotteries solely to help support the needy. ¹³The profits from today's New Zealand lotteries are also donated directly to charities and other nonprofit organizations.

[handwritten: A]   7. The pattern of organization of the above selection is
   A. list of items.
   B. time order.

8–10. Complete the outline of the passage.

   Main idea: Throughout history, political leaders have used lottery systems to benefit society in several ways.

   1. [handwritten: military projects]

   2. [handwritten: public education]

   3. [handwritten: help the poor]

RELATIONSHIPS I: Mastery Test 5

A. (1–5.) Fill in each blank with an appropriate transition from the box. Use each transition once.

A. after	B. during	C. eventually
D. next	E. then	

[handwritten left margin: subject biography of Franklin Roosevelt]

[1]Franklin Roosevelt, the twentieth-century president most beloved by America's "common people," had been born into a world of old money and upper-class privilege. [2]The talented son of a politically prominent family, he seemed destined for political success. [3] _After_ graduating from Harvard College and Columbia Law School, he had married Eleanor Roosevelt, Theodore Roosevelt's niece and his own fifth cousin, once removed. [4]He served in the New York state legislature; was appointed Assistant Secretary of the Navy by Woodrow Wilson; and, at the age of thirty-eight, ran for vice-president in 1920 on the Democratic Party's losing ticket.

[5] _Then_ , in 1921, Roosevelt was stricken with polio. [6] _During_ the next two years he was bedridden, fighting one of the most feared diseases of the first half of the twentieth century. [7]He _eventually_ lost the use of his legs, but gained, according to his wife Eleanor, a new strength of character that would serve him well as he reached out to depression-scarred America. [8]As Roosevelt explained it, "If you had spent two years in bed trying to wiggle your big toe, after that anything would seem easy." [9]In 1928 Roosevelt was sufficiently recovered to run for—and win—the governorship of New York. [10]The _next_ step in his remarkable political career was to accept the Democratic Party's presidential nomination in 1932.

_B_ 6. The pattern of organization of the above selection is
  A. list of items.
  B. time order.

[handwritten notes: event 1, event 2, event 3]

(Continues on next page)

+1

B. Read the textbook passage below. Then answer the question and complete the map that follows.

baby's learning about object permanence

¹One of a baby's major accomplishments during its first year of life is learning about **object permanence,** the understanding that something continues to exist even if you can't see it or touch it. ²In the first few months of life, infants are very fickle. ³"Out of sight, out of mind" seems to be their motto. ⁴They will look intently at a little toy, but if you hide it behind a piece of paper, they will not look behind the paper or make an effort to get the toy. ⁵By about six months, infants begin to grasp the idea that objects exist "out there"; a toy is a toy, and the cat is the cat, whether or not they can see the toy or the cat. ⁶If a baby of this age drops a toy from her playpen, she will look for it; she also will look under a cloth for a toy that is partially hidden. ⁷By one year of age, most babies have developed an awareness of the permanence of some objects. ⁸That is when they love to play peek-a-boo.

B 7. The pattern of organization of the above selection is
   A. list of items.   Step 1
   B.) time order.   Step 2   Step 3

G
▽
S

8–10. Complete the map of the paragraph by writing in the missing supporting details.

A baby learns about object permanence in the first year of life.

1ˢᵗ few months infants are very fickle

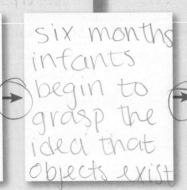

six months infants begin to grasp the idea that objects exist

1 year they've developed awareness

RELATIONSHIPS I: Mastery Test 6

A. Read the passage below, and then answer the question and complete the map that follows.

+1

[1]If parents decide to use punishment to control their children, its effectiveness can be increased in several ways. [2]The first involves consistency. [3]Punishment that is unpredictable is related to especially high rates of disobedience in children. [4]When parents permit children to act inappropriately on some occasions but scold them on others, children are confused about how to behave, and the unacceptable act persists. [5]Second, a warm relationship with children increases the effectiveness of an occasional punishment. [6]Children of involved and caring parents find the interruption in parental affection that accompanies punishment to be especially unpleasant. [7]As a result, they want to regain the warmth and approval of parents as quickly as possible. [8]Third, punishment works best when it is accompanied by an explanation. [9]Explanations increase the effectiveness of punishments because they help children recall the misdeed and relate it to expectations for future behavior.

_____ 1. The pattern of organization of the above selection is
  A. list of items.
  B. time order.

2–4. Complete the map of the paragraph by writing in the missing supporting details.

handwritten notes in margin: parents punishing their kids; G↓S; √ D1 √ D2 √ D3; A; H

Parents can increase the effectiveness of punishment in several ways.

consistency   increases effectiveness   explanation

(Continues on next page)

B. Read the passage below, and then answer the question and complete the outline.

how to deal with verbal abuse

¹Are you living with a person who verbally abuses you? ²If so, you owe it to yourself to change your situation. ³The way to succeed is to break the process into manageable steps. ⁴First and most important, you must believe that you are not to blame for the abuse. ⁵No doubt your abuser has convinced you that if only you would do A, B, or C differently, he or she would not "have" to become abusive. ⁶This is a lie. ⁷No one "has" to be abusive. ⁸Secondly, educate yourself about verbal abuse. ⁹Use books or the Internet to read about verbal abuse and how to deal with it. ¹⁰You'll find you are not alone, and that leads to the next step: Find a support group. ¹¹Identify people (friends, relatives, a teacher or minister or counselor) you can speak frankly to about your situation and who will give you help. ¹²With increased confidence, you are ready for the next step: Talk to your partner. ¹³As calmly and firmly as possible, state that you are a person who deserves respect and civil behavior, and that you will accept no less. ¹⁴Offer to go with your partner to a counselor who will help both of you learn new ways to communicate. ¹⁵If your partner does not respond, you must consider the final step: Leaving. ¹⁶You were not put here on earth to have your self-esteem destroyed by serving as someone else's verbal punching bag.

×1

_B_ 5. The pattern of organization of the above selection is
    A. list of items.
    B. time order.

Step 1
↓ step 2
↓ step 3

6–10. Complete the outline of the passage.

Main idea: To deal with verbal abuse, break the process into manageable steps.

    1. *believe you are not to blame*
    2. *educate yourself*
    3. *find support*
    4. *talk to your partner*
    5. *leave*

5 Relationships II

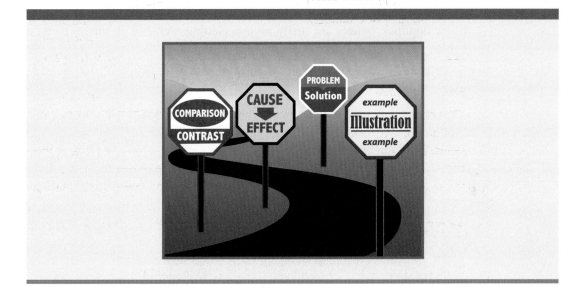

In Chapter 4, you learned how authors use transitions and patterns of organization to show relationships and make their ideas clear. You also learned about two common types of relationships:

- Relationships that involve **addition**
- Relationships that involve **time**

In this chapter you will learn about four other types of relationships:

- Relationships that involve **illustration**
- Relationships that involve **comparison and contrast**
- Relationships that involve **cause and effect**
- Relationships that involve a **problem and solution**

Most of these relationships involve transitional words and phrases, which are like signs on the road that guide travelers.

1 Illustration

Words That Show Illustration

Put a check (✓) beside the item that is easier to understand:

____ Some common beliefs are really myths. Getting a chill will not give you a cold.

____ Some common beliefs are really myths. For instance, getting a chill will not give you a cold.

The second item is easier to follow. The words *for instance* make it clear that the belief a chill will lead to a cold is a myth. *For instance* and other words and phrases like it are illustration words.

Illustration words indicate that an author will provide one or more *examples* to develop and clarify a given idea. Here are some common words that show illustration:

Illustration Words

(for) example	including	(as an) illustration	one
(for) instance	specifically	to illustrate	once
such as	to be specific		

Examples

The following items contain illustration words. Notice how these words signal that one or more *examples* are coming.

- Although they are children's stories, famous fairy tales *such as* "Little Red Riding Hood" and "Snow White" are clearly filled with dark symbolic meanings.

- A number of famous historical figures, *including* Beethoven, Charles Dickens, and Winston Churchill, suffered from depression.

- Some of the world's languages are written right to left, or from the top of the page to the bottom. *For example,* Arabic, Hebrew, and Japanese are all written in something other than left-to-right form.

PRACTICE 1

Complete each item with a suitable illustration word or phrase from the box on the previous page. Try to use a variety of transitions.

Hint: Make sure that each word or phrase that you choose fits smoothly into the flow of the sentence. Test each choice by reading the sentence aloud.

1. Body language often gives clues to a person's feelings about him or herself. Keeping one's arms crossed, _for example_, indicates a sense of low status or anxiety.

2. Technological advances _such as_ the Internet, cell phones, and fax machines have made working from home a practical reality for many people.

3. The definition of "deviant behavior" depends greatly on prevailing social norms. _For instance_, a man who wears women's clothing is considered deviant, while a woman wearing men's clothing is not.

4. Certain personal characteristics— _including_ a strong sense of competition, hostility, and impatience—have been linked to an increased chance of heart attack.

5. Some common phrases have meanings that are nearly forgotten. An _illustration_ is "mad as a hatter." The poisonous mercury that hat-makers used would cause them to lurch around, twitch, and otherwise act "mad."

Illustration words are common in all types of writing. One way they are used in textbooks is in the pattern of organization known as the definition and example pattern.

The Definition and Example Pattern

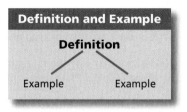

To get a sense of the definition and example pattern, try to arrange the following sentences in an order that makes sense. Put a *1* in front of the sentence that should come first, a *2* in front of the sentence that comes next, and a *3* in front of the sentence that should be last. The result will be a short paragraph. Then read the explanation that follows.

2 For instance, anyone who has ever played a card game such as hearts is familiar with the heuristic to "Get rid of high cards first."

1 Informal problems often call for a **heuristic**—a rule of thumb that suggests a course of action without guaranteeing an optimal solution.

3 Another example is the situation in which a student tries to decide whether to take a particular course and follows the advice to "Ask friends how they liked the instructor."

You should have put a 1 in front of the second sentence, which presents the term *heuristic* and defines the term. That term is then supported by the example in the sentence beginning "For instance" and then the sentence that begins "Another example." As you can see, the definition and example pattern of organization includes just what its name suggests: a definition and one or more examples.

An Important Study Hint: Good textbook authors want to help readers understand the important ideas and terms in a subject—whether it is psychology, sociology, business, biology, or any other field. Such authors often take time, then, to include key definitions. The ideas and terms being defined are usually set off in *italic* or **boldface** type, and the definitions are signaled by such words as *is, are, is called, termed*, and *refers to.* Here are some definitions from a variety of textbooks:

● **Sound bites** are short snippets of information aimed at dramatizing a news story rather than explaining its meaning in a substantive way.

● A decline in attention that occurs because a stimulus has become familiar is called **habituation.**

● **Tracking** refers to the smooth movements of the eye used to follow the track of a moving object.

- A unit of 1000 watts is called a **kilowatt** and is a commonly used measurement of electrical power.

- **Procedural liberties** are restraints on how the government is supposed to act; for example, citizens are guaranteed the due process of law.

- Physicists use the term **half-life** to describe the average time it takes for half of a batch of radioactive isotopes to undergo decay.

- **Gerrymandering** can be defined as the apportionment of voters in districts in such a way as to give unfair advantage to one racial or ethnic group or political party.

- Currently, the term **conservative** refers to those who generally support the social and economic status quo and are suspicious of efforts to introduce new economic arrangements.

- **Seismology**—the study and measurement of vibrations within the Earth—is dedicated to deducing our planet's inner structure.

(**Note:** Sometimes a dash or dashes are used to signal a definition.)

If an author defines a term, you can assume that it is important enough to learn. So when reading a textbook, always do two things:

1) Underline key definitions.

2) Put an "Ex" in the margin next to a helpful example for each definition. When a definition is general and abstract, examples are often essential to make its meaning clear.

✔ Check Your Understanding

Identify the definition and example in the following paragraph.

¹The planning fallacy refers to the fact that people consistently overestimate how quickly and easily they will achieve a goal and underestimate the amount of time or effort that will be required to reach that goal. ²In a study that examined the planning fallacy, college students were asked to list an academic project that had to be completed within the next week and to estimate when they intended to begin the project, when they expected to complete the project, and how many hours they expected to put into it. ³A week later, the students were asked if they had completed the project and when. ⁴Although all the students had estimated that they would complete the project comfortably in the time indicated, one week later more than half the projects remained incomplete. ⁵Those that had been

completed had typically taken, on average, nearly five days longer than had been estimated. ⁶So much for planning!

What term is being defined? _____

Which sentence contains the definition? _____

In which sentence does the example begin? _____

Explanation

The term *planning fallacy* is defined in the first sentence, and the example begins in the second sentence and continues to the end.

PRACTICE 2

Each of the following passages includes a definition and one or more examples. Underline the term being defined. Then, in the spaces provided, write the number of the definition sentence and the number of the sentence where an example begins.

A.   ¹As children engage in routine daily activities, they construct scripts of these activities. ²Scripts represent the typical sequence of actions related to an event and guide future behaviors in similar settings. ³For instance, children who have been to a fast-food restaurant might have a script like this: Wait in line, tell the person behind the counter what you want, pay for the food, carry the tray of food to a table, open the packages and eat the food, gather the trash and throw it away before leaving. ⁴With this script in mind, children can act effectively in similar settings.   2

Definition Scripts *Example*   3

B.   ¹All human beings are, to a large extent, the product of enculturation. ²This refers to the idea that our values, to a significant extent, are the result of the conditioning and shaping influences of our particular culture. ³Specifically, if I had grown up in India a hundred years ago, there is a good chance that I would be a Hindu and worship gods such as Shiva and Vishnu. ⁴If I had grown up in France in the 1400s, there is a good chance that I would have been taught to distrust and dislike the English. ⁵And if I had grown up in many parts of modern-day Africa, I might well view female circumcision as either something for the woman's own good or something worth little or no attention on my part.

Definition   2   *Example 1*   3   *Example 2* 4   *Example 3*   5

2 Comparison and Contrast

Words That Show Comparison

Put a check (✓) beside the item that is easier to understand:

___ As a fish swims, it moves its tail, applying force against the water. The water, in turn, propels the fish forward. In a rocket motor, forces are exerted by hot gases that accelerate out the tail end, propelling the rocket forward.

___ As a fish swims, it moves its tail, applying force against the water. The water, in turn, propels the fish forward. Similarly, in a rocket motor, forces are exerted by hot gases that accelerate out the tail end, propelling the rocket forward.

In the second item, the transition word *similarly* makes it clear that the author is comparing two forces. *Similarly* and words like it are comparison words.

Comparison words signal similarities. Authors use a comparison transition to show that a second idea is *like* the first one in some way. Here are some common words that show comparison:

Comparison Words

(just) as	both	in like fashion	in a similar fashion
(just) like	equal(ly)	in like manner	in a similar manner
alike	resemble	similar(ly)	(in) the same way
same	likewise	similarity	(in) common

Examples

The sentences below contain comparison words. Notice how these words show that things are *alike* in some way.

- During the American Civil War, people in the North and the South were *equally* anguished by the bloody division of their country.

- Very young and very old people *resemble* one another in their dependence upon those around them.

- Car manufacturers often show beautiful women with their products, as if to suggest that owning the car will bring social rewards. *In the same way,* alcohol ads typically show people in fun or romantic settings.

PRACTICE 3

Complete each sentence with a suitable comparison word or phrase from the box on the previous page. Try to use a variety of transitions.

1. The flu is particularly hazardous for babies, the elderly, and people in compromised health. _____, pneumonia is a special danger for those three groups.

2. Many people now do all their banking online, _____ they tend to do much of their shopping on the Internet.

3. _____ Japanese and Korean cultures warn against smiling too much, believing that excessive smiling is silly and undignified.

4. The original computers were so large that they filled enormous rooms. _____ telephones, radios, and electronics of every kind, they are shrinking in size every year.

5. Lions, tigers, and other jungle cats are most active at night, when they do their hunting. The _____ trait can be seen in domesticated cats, who often spend the night prowling around their owners' houses.

Words That Show Contrast

Put a check (✓) beside the item that is easier to understand:

____ The movie was boring and pointless. It featured a talented cast and an award-winning screenwriter.

____ The movie was boring and pointless even though it featured a talented cast and an award-winning screenwriter.

The first item is puzzling. What connection does the writer intend between the first and second sentences? The words *even though* in the second item make it clear that the writer is disappointed that the movie fell short despite its cast and screenwriter. *Even though* and words and phrases like it are contrast words.

Contrast words signal that an author is pointing out differences between subjects. A contrast word shows that two things *differ* in one or more ways. Contrast words also inform us that something is going to *differ from* what we might expect. Here are some common words that show contrast:

Contrast Words

but	instead (of)	even though	difference
yet	in contrast	as opposed to	different(ly)
however	on the other hand	in spite of	differ (from)
although	(on the) contrary	despite	unlike
nevertheless	converse(ly)	rather than	while
still	opposite		

Examples

The sentences below contain contrast words. Notice how these words signal that one idea is *different from* another idea.

- In most Western cultures, it is considered normal to marry for love. *However,* in places where arranged marriages are the norm, it is assumed that love will follow marriage.

- *While* mammals have internal mechanisms that regulate body temperature, cold-blooded animals such as lizards must regulate their temperature by external means, such as basking on warm sunny rocks.

- Corporate executives urged employees to buy the company's stock *despite* the fact that they were selling it themselves.

PRACTICE 4

Complete each sentence with a suitable contrast word or phrase from the above box. Try to use a variety of transitions.

1. The comedian Robin Williams explains that his parents helped him become a cautious optimist. His mother would say "People are basically good" _____ his father would be in the background saying, "There are still those who would throw you under a bus for a nickel."

2. A wise man explained that when he was young, he admired clever people. _____, by the time he was old, he most admired kind people.

3. Many people believe that lava is the primary material ejected from a volcano, _____ this is not always true. Explosive eruptions that eject huge quantities of gas, broken rock, and fine ash and dust occur just as frequently.

4. _____ parents who use physical punishment may think they are practicing good discipline, their children are likely to become violent and aggressive rather than well-behaved.

5. What makes one person seem warm and friendly, whereas another comes across as cold and aloof? One important ingredient appears to be having a positive outlook. People appear warm when they like things, praise them, and approve of them—in other words, when they have a positive attitude toward people and things. _____, people seem cold when they dislike things, disparage them, say they are awful, and are generally critical.

Comparison and contrast transitions often signal the comparison and/or contrast pattern of organization.

The Comparison and/or Contrast Pattern

To get a sense of the comparison and/or contrast pattern, arrange the following group of sentences into an order that makes sense. Put a *1* in front of the sentence that should come first, a *2* in front of the sentence that comes next, and a *3* in front of the sentence that should be last. The result will be a short paragraph. Then read the explanation that follows.

____ However, gender differences remain in career choice and development.

____ Women's labor force participation is approaching that of men's, with 60 percent of adult women (versus 74 percent of men) in the labor force.

____ At present, married women still subordinate their career goals to their husbands', especially when children are involved.

You should have put a *1* in front of the second sentence, which is an introductory statement—that women's labor force participation is becoming comparable to that of men's. The main idea, that gender differences remain, is then presented in the sentence beginning with the contrast word *However*. And the sentence that starts with *At present* gives an example of a significant gender difference—that women will subordinate their career choices to their husbands'.

You will find authors using a **comparison** pattern to show how two things are alike and a **contrast** pattern to show how they are different. Sometimes an author will compare and contrast in the same paragraph, pointing out both similarities and differences between two things. Comparison or contrast transitions will signal what an author is doing.

✓ *Check Your Understanding*

In the following paragraph, the main idea is stated in the first sentence. As is often the case, the main idea suggests a paragraph's pattern of organization. Here the transition *different* is a hint that the paragraph may be organized as comparison or contrast (or both). Read the paragraph and answer the questions below. Then read the explanation that follows.

[handwritten in margin: men & women & dreams, compare & contrast]

¹Men and women, of course, often have different concerns, so we might expect the content of their dreams to differ—and until recently, at least, that has been true. ²Typically, women have been more likely than men to dream about children, family members, familiar characters, friendly interactions, household objects, clothes, and indoor events. ³In contrast, men have been more likely than women to dream about strangers, weapons, violence, sexual activity, achievement, and outdoor events. ⁴But as the lives and concerns of the two sexes have become more similar, so have their dreams. ⁵In one recent study, the content of men's and women's dreams bore a close resemblance. ⁶Only two differences showed up: Men were more likely to dream about behaving aggressively, while women were more likely to dream about their anxieties.

1. Is this paragraph comparing, contrasting, or both? _____Both_____

2. What two things are being compared and/or contrasted? _____dreams of women & men,_____

3. What are three of the comparison and/or contrast signal words used in the paragraph? _____

Explanation

This paragraph is both comparing and contrasting: how the traditional content of men's and women's dreams differs (contrasting), but how that content is now becoming similar (comparing). Two comparison transitions are used—*similar* and *resemblance*. Six contrast transitions are used—*different, differ, In contrast, But, differences,* and *while*.

PRACTICE 5

The following passages use the pattern of comparison *or* the pattern of contrast. Read each passage and answer the questions that follow.

A. ¹Abraham Lincoln and Frederick Douglass shared many common interests. ²Both loved music and literature and educated themselves (Douglass on the sly while a slave) by reading the same books: *Aesop's Fables,* the Bible, Shakespeare, and especially *The Columbian Orator,* a popular anthology of speeches for boys. ³Both were athletic, strong and tall: Douglass was about six feet tall; Lincoln, six feet, four inches, when the average height for men was five feet, seven inches. ⁴Both refrained from alcohol and tobacco at a time when many politicians "squirted their tobacco juice upon the carpet" and drank on the job. ⁵They were equally ambitious and had great faith in the moral and technological progress of their nation. ⁶And they were alike in calling slavery a sin. ⁷"If slavery is not wrong, nothing is wrong," Lincoln stated. ⁸For Douglass, slavery was not only a sin but also "piracy and murder."

Check (✓) the pattern which is used in this passage:

__✓__ Comparison

____ Contrast

What two things are being compared or contrasted?

1. ____Lincoln____   2. ____Douglass____

B. ¹**Personal distress** means our own emotional reactions to the plight of others— our feelings of shock, horror, alarm, concern, or helplessness. ²Personal distress occurs when people who witness an event are preoccupied with their own emotional reactions. ³On the other hand, **empathy** means feelings of sympathy and caring for others, in particular, sharing vicariously or indirectly in the suffering of others. ⁴Empathy occurs when the observer focuses on the needs and emotions of the victim. ⁵While personal distress leads us to feel anxious and apprehensive, empathy leads us to feel sympathetic and compassionate. ⁶Research suggests that the different emotions generated by personal distress and empathy may actually be accompanied by distinctive physiological reactions, including heart rate patterns and facial expressions.

Check (✓) the pattern which is used in this passage:

____ Comparison

__✓__ Contrast

What two things are being compared or contrasted?

1. ____personal distress____   2. ____empathy____

3 Cause and Effect

Words That Show Cause and Effect

Put a check (✓) beside the item that is easier to understand:

_____ The best time to buy a car is near the end of the month. Car dealers often have a monthly quota of cars to sell.

__✓__ The best time to buy a car is near the end of the month because car dealers often have a monthly quota of cars to sell.

In the second item, the word *because* makes very clear just why the end of the month is the best time to buy a car. *Because* and words like it are cause and effect words.

Cause and effect words signal that the author is explaining the *reason* that something happened or the *result* of something happening. Here are some common words that show cause and effect:

Cause and Effect Words

therefore	so	owing to	because (of)
thus	(as a) result	effect	reason
(as a) consequence	results in	cause	explanation
consequently	leads (led) to	if . . . then	accordingly
due to	since	affect	depend(s) on

Examples

The following examples contain cause and effect words. Notice how these words introduce a *reason* for something or the *results* of something.

● Young babies have weak necks and relatively heavy heads. *Consequently,* it is important to support the baby's head firmly when you hold him or her.

● Do not refrigerate potatoes. The *reason* is that a potato's starch will turn to sugar at low temperatures, making the vegetable taste odd.

● The student wanted to concentrate on studying for exams. *Therefore,* he silenced his cell phone and put it in a drawer.

PRACTICE 6

Complete each sentence with a suitable cause and effect word or phrase from the box on the previous page. Try to use a variety of transitions.

1. A Greek philosopher observed that we should always try to be kind to each other _____because_____ everyone we meet is fighting a great battle.

2. Contrary to some beliefs, tanning is not necessarily healthy. Prolonged exposure to the sun can _____led to_____ problems such as sunburn, skin cancer, and early aging.

3. The gecko is a small lizard that can detach its tail. _____Since_____, predators often end up holding the wriggling tail while the gecko escapes.

4. In medieval times, people believed that ringing church bells would dissipate lightning during thunderstorms. This unfortunate superstition _____caused_____ the deaths of over 100 bell ringers in a period when lightning struck 386 church steeples.

5. Meat requires special handling. It contains bacteria, and its moist, nutrient-rich environment favors microbial growth. Ground meat is especially susceptible _____thus_____ it receives more handling than other kinds of meat and has more surface exposed to bacterial contamination.

Cause and effect transitions often signal the cause and effect pattern of organization.

The Cause and Effect Pattern

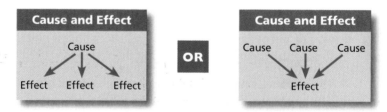

To get a sense of the cause and effect pattern, try to arrange the following sentences in an order that makes sense. Put a *1* in front of the sentence that should come first, a *2* in front of the sentence that comes next, and a *3* in front of the sentence that should be last. The result will be a short paragraph. Then read the explanation that follows.

3 Also, unemployment leads to an increased rate of attempted and completed suicides.

2 Not only can it cause economic distress; it can result in health problems and psychological difficulties as well.

1 Losing one's job is difficult at best and devastating at worst.

As the words *leads to, cause,* and *result in* suggest, this paragraph is organized in a cause and effect pattern. The paragraph begins with the general idea: "Losing one's job is difficult at best and devastating at worst." Next comes a detailed explanation of the results: "Not only can it cause economic distress; it can result in health problems and psychological difficulties as well. Also, unemployment leads to an increased rate of attempted and completed suicides."

Information in a **cause-effect pattern** addresses the questions "Why does a behavior or event happen?" and/or "What are the results of a behavior or event?" An author may then discuss causes, or effects, or both causes and effects.

Authors usually don't just tell what happened. They try to tell about events in a way that explains both *what* happened and *why.* A textbook section on the burning of the rain forests, for example, would be incomplete without a detailed account of all the consequences to the Earth of the destruction of these forests. Or if housing sales across the country go into a decline, journalists would not simply report the decrease in sales. They would also explore the reasons for and effects of that decline.

✔ ## *Check Your Understanding*

Read the paragraph below and see if you can answer the questions about cause and effect. Then read the explanation to see how you did.

¹During the 1950s and 1960s, airports, bus terminals, and train stations often charged patrons to use the toilet. ²People would have to pay a ten- to twenty-five-cent fee before they entered a stall. ³Owners hoped that the fee would help pay for the cost of keeping the restrooms clean. ⁴But for several reasons, pay toilets failed miserably. ⁵For one thing, they angered patrons. ⁶People accustomed to accessing a restroom for free became upset when they discovered they had to pay. ⁷Many outraged bathroom-users vandalized the stalls and trashed the rooms in response, making cleanup even more expensive. ⁸In addition, pay toilets caused more trouble than they were worth. ⁹Employees had to be called in so often to fix broken locks that companies gradually realized the extra work wasn't worth a few more dollars. ¹⁰A final explanation of why pay toilets failed is that they triggered lawsuits from women's groups who claimed the toilets were unfair because females were forced to pay to use a stall, while males could use the urinals for free. ¹¹Therefore, rather than spending money on high maintenance and lawsuits, companies opened the bathrooms for free use.

1. What is the single *effect* being discussed in the paragraph?

   paying to use the toilets

2. What are the three *causes* discussed?
   A. *angered patrons*
   B. *caused more trouble*
   C. *triggered lawsuits from womens*

3. What three cause and effect transitions are used in the paragraph?

   reasons, caused, because

Explanation

The paragraph's main idea is that "But for several reasons, pay toilets failed miserably." That point, or effect, is then supported by three causes: 1) they angered patrons; 2) they caused more trouble than they were worth; and 3) they triggered lawsuits from women's groups. The cause and effect transitions used are *reasons, caused,* and *explanation.*

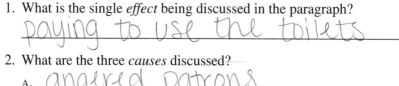

PRACTICE 7

A. Read the paragraph below, looking for the one effect and the two causes. Then complete the outline that follows.

cause-n-effect

list pattern

[1]Fainting was commonplace in Victorian England. [2]Women were often seen falling into the arms of a nearby suitor if it was too warm outside, they became sad, or someone said something offensive. [3]One explanation was the unusual dress of Victorian women. [4]Females were expected to wear a corset underneath their clothes, and the corset was wrapped around their bodies and secured with ribbons. [5]Made to make women's waists look smaller, corsets were often pulled so tight that internal organs became damaged and women could hardly breathe. [6]Since their air supply and blood flow were limited, any physical activity could cause them to faint. [7]The second reason women fell to the floor was cultural roles. [8]Ladies pretended to faint because doing so was seen as delicate and feminine. [9]Victorian women were expected to be weak and to rely on men to be the strong ones. [10]The staging of fainting episodes helped them demonstrate they were fragile and ladylike.

Main idea *(the effect):* *woman fainting was common in Victorian England*

Major supporting details *(the causes):*

1. _corsets were too tight_
2. _in made them look delicate and feminine._

B. Read the paragraph below, looking for the one cause and the three effects. Then complete the map that follows.

cause-n-effect

list pattern

[1]If our planet's sea levels were to rise, the result would be global problems. [2]Rising sea levels would first cause problems by making a drastic change in existing coastlines. [3]Specifically, a rise in sea levels of as little as 5 feet could move coastlines 150 feet inland, displacing coastal communities and flooding low-lying cities all over the world. [4]Next, rising sea levels would create threats to dikes and sea walls, making coastal areas more vulnerable to natural disasters. [5]As seen in New Orleans after Hurricane Katrina, existing dikes and sea walls might be insufficient to defend against the increased storm surges, and disasters could become a yearly phenomenon. [6]The most dangerous effect of a rise in sea levels would be an increase in global warming. [7]Since liquid water absorbs more sunlight than frozen water does, a rise in sea level would eventually cause the oceans to warm, contributing to higher temperatures everywhere—and causing our polar ice caps to melt even faster. [8]The problems created by a rising ocean could then quickly spiral out of control.

Cause: rising sea levels

Effect:

Effect: create threats to dikes + sea walls

Effect:

4 Problem and Solution

What is the relationship between the two sentences below?

problem   Speaking in front of a class is something that terrifies many students.

solution   Practicing in front of friends or with a video camera may prevent you from freezing up on the day of the presentation.

You are correct if you wrote that the relationship between the two sentences is one of problem and solution. The first sentence states a problem—that many students become terrified when required to speak in front of a class. The second sentence offers a solution. It suggests that if a student first practices in front of friends or a video camera, he or she will feel less nervous about the actual presentation.

Unlike the relationship patterns we have studied so far, the relationship of problem to solution does not involve transitional words or phrases. Rather, the relationship usually involves an action that is taken to correct or resolve a negative situation.

Examples

The following items illustrate the problem and solution relationship. Notice how the second sentence offers a solution to the negative situation (problem) stated in the first sentence.

- Every year, tens of millions of trees have to be cut down to provide the paper that goes into book manufacturing.

  Electronic readers such as the Kindle, Nook, and iPad have decreased the need for paper in the book publishing industry.

- Many people who need to exercise suffer from joint problems that make walking, jogging, or running painful.

  Swimming is a low-impact form of exercise that provides an excellent cardiovascular workout for people who experience joint pain.

- During the War of 1812, the British burned Washington, D.C., destroying the Library of Congress.

  Thomas Jefferson immediately offered his entire library of 6,487 books to create a new national library.

PRACTICE 8

In the following items, match each problem in the left column with the appropriate solution in the right column.

__D__ 1. It can be extremely difficult to purchase fresh fruits and vegetables in low-income communities.

__A__ 2. At the end of World War II, the return of tens of thousands of American veterans led to a serious housing shortage.

__B__ 3. Every 43 seconds in the United States, another vehicle is stolen.

__E__ 4. In 1982, seven people died after taking pain-relief capsules that had been laced with cyanide, a deadly poison.

__C__ 5. Elderly people who live at home are often unable to shop and cook for themselves.

A. Using mass production techniques, developers such as William Levitt quickly built tens of thousands of affordable houses.

B. Vehicle tracking systems cut into auto theft rates by using global positioning satellites to keep track of cars.

C. Some volunteer organizations deliver hot meals to the homes of seniors whose mobility is limited.

D. Supermarket chains are receiving property or sales tax breaks to open stores in neighborhoods that currently lack them.

E. The drug industry replaced capsules with caplets and added tamper-evident safety seals to medicine bottles.

The Problem and Solution Pattern

To get a sense of the problem and solution pattern, arrange the following group of sentences into an order that makes sense. Put a *1* in front of the sentence that should come first, a *2* in front of the sentence that comes next, and a *3* in front of the sentence that should be last.

__2__ Most try to quit "cold turkey"—that is, they decide simply not to smoke again.

__1__ Smokers who decide to quit must break through both the physical addiction to nicotine and the habit of lighting up at certain times of day.

__3__ Others use nicotine replacement products such as nicotine chewing gum and the nicotine patch.

You should have put a *1* in front of the second sentence, which introduces the problem—that it is difficult to quit smoking. A *2* should go in front of the first sentence—one solution to the problem of quitting smoking. And a *3* should go in front of another solution to the problem, presented in the third sentence.

Information in a problem-solution pattern addresses the questions "What problem is occurring or has occurred?" and "What action or actions have been taken to solve the problem?"

✓ *Check Your Understanding*

Read the paragraph below and see if you can answer the questions about problem and solutions. Then read the explanation that follows.

[1]During major earthquakes, most casualties occur when buildings collapse. [2]There are two ways to keep buildings from collapsing during earthquakes. [3]One way is to make them stronger, using higher-grade building materials. [4]Another way is to make them more flexible, so they sway and slide above the shaking ground rather than crumbling. [5]The latter technology employs an idea called "base isolation." [6]With base isolation, buildings don't sit directly on the ground, but rather float on systems of ball bearings, springs, and padded cylinders. [7]In the event of a major earthquake, they sway up to a few feet rather than collapse. [8]The buildings are surrounded by "moats," or buffer zones, so they don't swing into other structures. [9]Earthquake-resistant buildings save lives. [10]When an 8.8-magnitude earthquake struck Chile in February 2010, it killed far fewer people (about 700) than a 7.0-magnitude earthquake that struck Haiti a month earlier. [11]The reason was that Chile, a richer and more industrialized nation, had far more buildings that were built to withstand earthquakes than did Haiti.

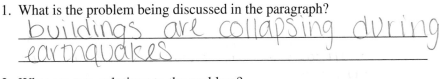

1. What is the problem being discussed in the paragraph?

   buildings are collapsing during earthquakes

2. What are two solutions to the problem?

   A. _make them stronger_

   B. _make them flexible_

Explanation

This paragraph discusses the problem of buildings that collapse during earthquakes, causing injury and death. In sentence 3, the author presents one solution to the problem—constructing buildings out of higher-grade materials. In sentence 4, the author presents another solution to the problem—making buildings more flexible. The rest of the paragraph elaborates on the second method of making buildings earthquake-resistant. It also provides an example of how buildings that were constructed to withstand earthquakes saved lives in Chile, while buildings that were not built to withstand earthquakes led to great loss of life in Haiti.

PRACTICE 9

A. The following passage includes a problem and one or more solutions. In the space provided, write the number of the sentence that states the problem. Then write the number of the first sentence introducing the solutions.

¹The California condor, a type of vulture, is the largest land bird in North America. ²Observing this magnificent bird with its nine-foot wingspan soaring over the countryside is an unforgettable experience. ³Yet in the 1980s, there were only 22 condors left in the wild, and they were on the verge of extinction. ⁴Their numbers had been greatly reduced due to illegal hunting, lead poisoning, contact with power lines, and habitat destruction. ⁵To save the birds, the federal government put in place a plan to capture all 22 remaining wild condors. ⁶The captured birds were then bred at the San Diego Wild Animal Park and the Los Angeles Zoo. ⁷Since 1994, captive-bred California condors have been trained to avoid power lines and people. ⁸As the number of condors grew, some were released back into the wild. ⁹As a result, the number of condor deaths due to power lines has greatly decreased. ¹⁰Furthermore, California hunters are now required to use non-lead bullets when hunting in the condor's range, so the birds no longer run the risk of consuming fragmented lead bullets in large game waste. ¹¹As of April 2011, there are 394 condors known to be living, including 180 wild condors.

Problem ___4___   *Solution* ___5___

B. Read the paragraph below, identify the problem and solution, and complete the map that follows.

> [1]For decades, relief workers had been frustrated in their ability to effectively help victims of famine throughout the world. [2]In villages without electricity, it was useless to give people supplies of milk because there was no way to keep the milk from spoiling. [3]Powered milk or grain was equally useless because most villagers didn't have clean water with which to mix it. [4]Then a few years ago, a French nutritionist developed a paste made of peanut butter, vegetable oil, powdered milk, and powdered sugar, and enriched with vitamins and minerals. [5]Since the paste didn't need refrigeration, water, or cooking, mothers simply squeezed it out of plastic packages to feed their children. [6]The results have been miraculous: children who consume the peanut paste add pounds rapidly, often going from a near-death state to relative health in a month. [7]Not surprisingly, some are calling the paste the greatest health breakthrough since the antibiotic penicillin.

Problem: food went bad b/c villages had no eletricity

Solution: French nutritionist made a paste that didn't need to be refrigerated

A Note on Main Ideas and Patterns of Organization

As mentioned in Chapter 4, a paragraph's main idea often indicates its pattern of organization. For example, here's the main idea of the paragraph you read on page 191:

> If our planet's sea levels were to rise, the result would be global problems.

The word *result* indicates that this paragraph will be organized according to a cause-and-effect pattern.

Paying close attention to the main idea can often give you a quick sense of a paragraph's pattern of organization and can be a helpful step in your understanding of the paragraph.

annotate key transition

PRACTICE 10

Most of the main ideas below have been taken from college textbooks. In the space provided, write the letter of the pattern of organization that each suggests.

_B_   1. Contrary to popular stereotypes, being single is not always more difficult for women than for men.
   A. Definition and   B. Comparison and/or   C. Cause and effect
       example   contrast

_C_   2. The author of _The Paradox of Choice_ argues that people in modern, affluent societies suffer depression and anxiety because they face an overabundance of choices in their personal lives.
   A. Definition and   B. Comparison and/or   C. Cause and effect
       example   contrast

_A_   3. The ineffective study strategy of cramming will strain your memorization capabilities, tax your energy level, and stoke the fires of test anxiety. To avoid the pitfalls of cramming, you need to learn time management techniques.
   A. Problem and   B. Comparison and/or   C. Cause and effect
       solution   contrast

_A_   4. What scientists call the "terrestrial planets" are the relatively small, rocky, high-density worlds: Mercury, Venus, Earth, Mars, and (although it isn't really a planet) Earth's moon.
   A. Definition and   B. Comparison and/or   C. Cause and effect
       example   contrast

_C_   5. The phenomenon of static electricity, including lightning, static cling, and the small sparks produced when walking across a wool rug on a cold winter day, is caused by electrical charges.
   A. Problem and   B. Comparison and/or   C. Cause and effect
       solution   contrast

_B_   6. The differences between the salary and benefit packages given to some chief executives and the low pay and cuts in pension and health benefits forced on low-level workers are striking.
   A. Problem and   B. Comparison and/or   C. Cause and effect
       solution   contrast

_A_   7. Mass hysteria, a type of group behavior that involves a widely held and contagious anxiety, is exemplified by the witch-hunts of medieval times.
   A. Definition and   B. Comparison and/or   C. Cause and effect
       example   contrast

_____ 8. Loneliness exists inside a person and cannot be detected simply by looking at the person, while aloneness is the objective state of being apart from other people.
- A. Problem and solution
- B. Comparison and/or contrast
- C. Cause and effect

_____ 9. One-third of Americans surveyed reported that they "live with extreme stress," and nearly half believed that their stress "had increased over the past five years." Studies have also shown that one of the best ways to deal with everyday stress is to rely on friends and others in one's social network.
- A. Problem and solution
- B. Comparison and/or contrast
- C. Cause and effect

_____ 10. Declining support for the death penalty may be due to heightened awareness of cases in which innocent people have been sentenced to death and subsequently cleared, often by DNA evidence.
- A. Definition and example
- B. Comparison and/or contrast
- C. Cause and effect

A Final Point

Keep in mind that a paragraph or passage may often be made up of more than one pattern of organization. For instance, consider the following passage:

> ¹The gestation period (length of pregnancy) of mammals depends on two factors. ²The first is the mammal's size. ³In general, smaller animals experience shorter pregnancies. ⁴For example, a female rat gives birth only twenty-one days after becoming pregnant; a hamster's gestation period is only sixteen days; a horse, however, is pregnant for about forty-eight weeks. ⁵The second factor that determines the gestation period is life span—longer-lived animals have longer pregnancies. ⁶The gestation period of a lion, which can live up to twenty-eight years, is fifteen weeks. ⁷Dolphins, which have lived as long as forty years, are pregnant for thirty-nine weeks. ⁸You can see the relationship between gestation period and life span when you compare a possum to a cat. ⁹Although the possum is slightly larger than a cat, it has a much shorter gestation period (thirteen days to the cat's sixty-two days). ¹⁰But cats can live up to twenty years, while possums are elderly at 3.

The paragraph uses a cause-effect pattern: The length of pregnancy of mammals is caused by two factors. It also uses a list of items pattern (the two factors) as well as a bit of comparison and contrast.

CHAPTER REVIEW

In this chapter, you learned about four kinds of relationships that authors use to make their ideas clear:

● **Definitions and examples**

— To help readers understand the important ideas and terms in a subject, textbook authors often take time to include key definitions (often setting them off in *italic* or **boldface**) and examples of those definitions. When reading a textbook, it is usually a good idea to mark off both definitions and examples. (Underline each definition, and put *Ex* in the margin next to each example.)

— Transition words that signal the definition and example pattern include *for example, for instance, to illustrate*, and *such as*.

● **Comparison and/or contrast**

— Authors often discuss how two things are alike or how they are different, or both.

— Transition words that signal comparisons include *alike* and *similar*.

— Transition words that signal contrasts include *but, however*, and *in contrast*.

● **Cause and effect**

— Authors often discuss the reasons why something happens or the effects of something that has happened.

— Transition words that signal causes include *reason* and *because*.

— Transition words that signal effects include *therefore, consequently*, and *as a result*.

● **Problem and solution**

— Authors may state a problem (a negative situation) and then offer a solution.

— No transition words are used in this pattern.

Note that pages 222–226 list and offer practice in all the transitions and patterns of organization you have studied in "Relationships I" and "Relationships II."

The next chapter—Chapter 6—will sharpen your ability to make inferences in reading.

On the Web: If you are using this book in class, you can go to our website for more practice in understanding relationships that involve examples, comparison or contrast, cause and effect, and problem and solution. Visit our Learning Center at **www.townsendpress.net** for additional activities and an instructional video on this skill.

REVIEW TEST 1

To review what you've learned in this chapter, answer each of the following questions by filling in the blank or writing the letter of the correct answer.

1. When authors present a term or idea, they often provide one or more _examples_ to help make that definition clear.

_B_ 2. Words such as *likewise, just as*, and *similarly* are known as
   A. illustration words.
   B. comparison words.
   C. contrast words.

_B_ 3. Words such as *but, however,* and *on the other hand* are known as
   A. definition words.
   B. contrast words.
   C. cause and effect words.

_C_ 4. A cause and effect paragraph may include
   A. reasons.
   B. results.
   C. reasons and/or results.

_T_ 5. TRUE OR FALSE? In a problem and solution paragraph, the writer first presents a negative situation and then states one or more ways of resolving it.

REVIEW TEST 2

The selection that follows is from the college textbook *A People and a Nation*, by Mary Beth Norton and others. Read it and then answer the relationships questions that follow. There are also questions on understanding vocabulary in context, finding main ideas, identifying supporting details, and recognizing implied main ideas.

Preview

The generation touched by the Great Depression never forgot its impact. Effects of the economic depression were felt in every corner of the country. Those effects, however, took different forms depending on one's occupation, race, gender, and geographical location. This reading provides a vivid description of hard times across America.

Words to Watch

bolstered (4): supported
marginal (5): very small in scale or importance
coerced (6): forced
affluent (10): well off

HOOVER AND HARD TIMES: 1929–1933

Mary Beth Norton and others

1   By the early 1930s, as the depression continued to deepen, tens of millions of Americans were desperately poor. In the cities, hungry men and women lined up at soup kitchens. People survived on potatoes, crackers, or dandelion greens; some scratched through garbage cans for bits of food. In West Virginia and Kentucky, hunger was so widespread—and resources so limited—that the American Friends Service Committee distributed food only to those who were at least 10 percent below the normal weight for their height. Reports of starvation and malnutrition spread. In November 1932, *The Nation* told its readers that one-sixth of the American population risked starvation over the coming winter. Social workers in New York reported there was "no food at all" in the homes of many of the city's black children. In Albany, New York, a ten-year-old girl died of starvation in her elementary school classroom.

Families, unable to pay rent, were 2 evicted from houses and apartments.

The new homeless poured into shantytowns, called "Hoovervilles" in ironic tribute to the formerly popular president, that had sprung up in most cities. Over a million men took to the road or the rails in desperate search for any sort of work. Teenage boys and girls (the latter called "sisters of the road") also left destitute families to strike out on their own. With uncertain futures, many young couples delayed marriage. The average age at which people married rose by more than two years during the 1930s. Married people put off having children, and in 1933, the birth rate sank below replacement rates. (Contraceptive sales, with condoms costing at least $1 per dozen, did not fall during the depression.) More than 25 percent of women who were between the ages of twenty and thirty during the Great Depression never had children.

3   Farmers were hit especially hard by the economic crisis. The agricultural sector, which employed almost a quarter of American workers, had never shared in the good times of the 1920s. But as urbanites cut back on spending and foreign competitors dumped their own agricultural surpluses into the global market, prices for agricultural products hit rock bottom. Individual farmers tried to make up for lower prices by producing more, thus adding to the surplus and depressing prices even further. By 1932, a bushel of wheat that cost North Dakota farmers 77 cents to produce brought only 33 cents. Throughout the nation, cash-strapped farmers could not pay their property taxes or mortgages. Banks, facing their own ruin, refused to extend deadlines and foreclosed on the mortgages. In Mississippi, it was reported in 1932, on a single day in April approximately one-fourth of all the farmland in the state was being auctioned off to meet debts. By the middle of the decade, the ecological crisis of the Dust Bowl would drive thousands of farmers from their land.

4   Unlike farmers, America's industrial workers had seen a slow but steady rise in their standard of living during the 1920s, and their spending on consumer goods had bolstered° the nation's economic growth. In 1929, almost every urban American who wanted a job had one. But as Americans had less money to spend, sales of manufactured goods

plunged and factories closed—more than 70,000 had gone out of business by 1933. As car sales dropped from 4.5 million in 1929 to 1 million in 1933, Ford laid off more than two-thirds of its workers in Detroit. All of the remaining workers at U.S. Steel, America's first billion-dollar corporation, were put on "short hours"; the huge steel company had no full-time workers in 1933. Almost a quarter of industrial workers were unemployed, and those who managed to hang onto a job saw the average wage fall by almost one-third.

5   For workers who had long been marginal°, discriminated against, or relegated to the lowest rungs of the employment ladder, the depression was a crushing blow. In the South, where employment opportunities for African Americans were already most limited, pressure for "Negro removal" grew. The jobs that most white men had considered below their dignity before the depression—street cleaners, bellhops, garbage collectors—seemed suddenly desirable as other jobs disappeared. African Americans living in the North did not fare much better. As industry cut production, African Americans were the first fired. An Urban League survey of 106 cities found black employment rates averaged 30 to 60 percent higher than rates for whites. By 1932, African American unemployment reached almost 50 percent.

6   Mexican Americans and Mexican nationals trying to make a living in the American Southwest also felt the twin impacts of economic depression and racism. Concentrated in agricultural work, they saw their wages at California farms fall from a miserable 35 cents an hour in 1929 to a cruel 14 cents an hour by 1932. Throughout the Southwest, Anglo-Americans claimed that foreign workers were stealing their jobs. Campaigns against "foreigners" hurt not only Mexican immigrants but also American citizens of Hispanic background whose families had lived in the Southwest for centuries, long before the land belonged to the United States. In 1931, the Labor Department announced that the United States would deport illegal immigrants to free jobs for American citizens. This policy fell hardest on people of Mexican origin. Even those who had immigrated legally often lacked full documentation. Officials often ignored the fact that children born in the United States were U.S. citizens. The U.S. government officially deported 82,000 Mexicans between 1929 and 1935, but a much larger number—almost half a million people—repatriated to Mexico during the 1930s. Some left voluntarily, but many were coerced° or tricked into believing they had no choice.

7   Women of all classes and races shared status as marginalized workers. Even before the economic crisis, women were barred altogether from many jobs and paid at significantly lower rates than men. As the economy worsened, working women faced heightened discrimination. Most

Americans already believed that men should be breadwinners and women homemakers. With widespread male unemployment, it was easy to believe that women took jobs from men. In fact, men laid off from U.S. Steel would not likely have been hired as elementary school teachers, secretaries, "sales girls," or maids. The job market was heavily segregated. Nonetheless, when a 1936 Gallup poll asked whether wives should work if their husbands had jobs, 82 percent of the respondents (including 75 percent of the women) answered no. Such beliefs translated into policy. Of 1500 urban school systems surveyed by the National Education Association in 1930 and 1931, 77 percent refused to hire married women as teachers, and 63 percent fired female teachers who married while employed.

8   The depression had a mixed impact on women workers. At first, women lost jobs more quickly than men. Women in low-wage manufacturing jobs were laid off before male employees, who were presumed to be supporting families. Hard times hit domestic workers especially hard, as middle-class families economized by dispensing with household help. Almost a quarter of women in domestic service—a high percentage of them African American— were unemployed by January 1931. And as jobs disappeared, women of color lost even these poorly paid positions to white women who were newly willing to do domestic labor. Despite discrimination and a poor economy, however, the number of women working outside the home rose during the 1930s. "Women's jobs," such as teaching, clerical work, and switchboard operators, were not hit so hard as "men's jobs" in heavy industry, and women—including married women who previously did not work for wages—increasingly sought employment to keep their families afloat during hard times. Still, by 1940 only 15.2 percent of married women worked outside the home.

9   Though unemployment rates climbed to 25 percent, most Americans did not lose their homes or their jobs during the depression. Professional and white-collar workers did not fare as badly as industrial workers and farmers. Many middle-class families, however, while never hungry or homeless, "made do" with less. "Use it up, wear it out, make it do, or do without," the saying went, and middle-class women cut back on household expenses by canning food or making their own clothes; newspapers offered imaginative suggestions for cooking cheap cuts of meat ("Liver-burgers") or for using "extenders," cheap ingredients to make food go further ("Cracker-Stuffed Cabbage"). Though most families' incomes fell, the impact was cushioned by the falling cost of consumer goods, especially food. In early 1933, for example, a café in Omaha offered a ten-course meal, complete with a rose for ladies and a cigar for gentlemen, for sixty cents.

10   As housewives scrambled to make do, men who could no longer

provide well for their families often blamed themselves for their "failures." But even for the relatively affluent°, the psychological impact of the depression was inescapable. The human toll of the depression was visible everywhere, and no one took economic security for granted anymore. Suffering was never equal, but all Americans had to contend with years of uncertainty and with fears about the future of their families and their nation.

Reading Comprehension Questions

Vocabulary in Context

_____ 1. In the excerpt below, the word *destitute* (dĕs′tĭ-tōōt′) means
   A. abusive.
   B. reluctant.
   C. extremely poor.
   D. very large.

   "Over a million men took to the road or the rails in desperate search for any sort of work. Teenage boys and girls (the latter called 'sisters of the road') also left destitute families to strike out on their own." (Paragraph 2)

_____ 2. In the sentence below, the word *relegated* (rĕl′ĭ-gāt′ĭd) means
   A. lifted.
   B. transferred.
   C. attracted.
   D. assigned downward.

   "For workers who had long been marginal, discriminated against, or relegated to the lowest rungs of the employment ladder, the depression was a crushing blow." (Paragraph 5)

Central Point and Main Ideas

_____ 3. Which sentence best expresses the implied central point of the selection?

    A. Farmers were hit especially hard by the Great Depression.

    B. Although some groups suffered more than others, the Great Depression forced virtually all Americans to contend with fear and uncertainty about the future.

    C. During the Great Depression, many Americans were forced to "make do" with less.

    D. Although minority groups and farmers were especially hard hit by the Great Depression, most Americans did not lose their homes or their jobs.

_____ 4. The main idea of paragraph 3 is stated in the

    A. first sentence.

    B. second sentence.

    C. third sentence.

    D. final sentence.

_____ 5. The implied main idea of paragraphs 5–7 is that during the depression,

    A. the U.S. government established a policy of deporting illegal immigrants to free jobs for American citizens.

    B. most white Americans believed that women should not compete with men for jobs.

    C. minority groups and women faced economic discrimination.

    D. African Americans faced growing competition from whites for low-status jobs.

Supporting Details

_____ 6. Large corporations such as Ford and U.S. Steel responded to the Great Depression by

    A. investing in new and more efficient methods of production.

    B. demanding that their female employees take extended leaves of absence.

    C. laying off workers, reducing work hours, and lowering the wages of those still employed.

    D. seeking loans from the federal government in order to keep from going bankrupt.

_____ 7. The prices for agricultural products fell during the depression because
A. the supply of agricultural products far exceeded the demand for them.
B. farmers weren't producing enough crops.
C. the Dust Bowl, an ecological disaster, drove thousands from their land.
D. bankers refused to extend credit to needy farmers.

Transitions

_____ 8. Which word in the following sentence indicates a cause and effect transition?
A. *make*
B. *more*
C. *thus*
D. *further*

"Individual farmers tried to make up for lower prices by producing more, thus adding to the surplus and depressing prices even further." (Paragraph 3)

_____ 9. The relationship of the second sentence below to the first sentence is one of
A. contrast.
B. cause and effect.
C. comparison.
D. illustration.

"And as jobs disappeared, women of color lost even these poorly paid positions to white women who were newly willing to do domestic labor. Despite discrimination and a poor economy, however, the number of women working outside the home rose during the 1930s." (Paragraph 8)

Patterns of Organization

_____ 10. The pattern of organization in this selection is mainly one of
A. definition and example.
B. comparison.
C. contrast.
D. cause and effect.

Discussion Questions

1. This reading provides a great many facts about how the Great Depression affected various parts of the U.S. population. What did you learn from the reading that surprised you most?

2. The selection mentions that African Americans and people of Mexican origin were particularly hard hit during the depression, often facing discrimination as the competition for jobs became desperate. In your opinion, has the position of African Americans and Latinos improved since the depression, worsened, or stayed about the same? Explain your reasoning.

3. The authors spend most of their time describing the economic impact of the depression. In the final paragraph, however, they mention "the psychological impact of the depression." From what you have read here, what psychological effects would you infer the depression had on various groups?

4. The Great Depression led to economic hardship and social upheaval, yet somehow our system of government remained stable. How do you think Americans would respond today if we experienced a depression? For instance, how might the government respond if the unemployment rate reached 25 percent? How might the American public respond to even more widespread unemployment and reduction in wages?

Note: Writing assignments for this selection appear on page 637.

Check Your Performance   **RELATIONSHIPS II**

Activity	Number Right	Points	Score
Review Test 1 (5 items)	_____	× 6 =	_____
Review Test 2 (10 items)	_____	× 7 =	_____
		TOTAL SCORE =	_____%

Enter your total score into the **Reading Performance Chart: Review Tests** on the inside back cover.

RELATIONSHIPS II: Mastery Test 1

A. Fill in each blank with an appropriate transition from the box. Use each transition once. Then, in the space provided, write the letter of the transition you have chosen.

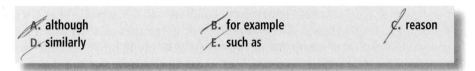

A. although	B. for example	C. reason
D. similarly	E. such as	

Hint: Make sure that each word or phrase that you choose fits smoothly into the flow of the sentence. Test each choice by reading the sentence to yourself.

B 1. ¹Repression involves keeping distressing thoughts and feelings buried in the subconscious. ²_for example_, when you forget a dentist appointment or the name of someone you don't like, repression may be at work.

C 2. ¹Aging is incredibly difficult for women. ²They must compete with models on billboards who are 20 years old and perfect. ³And they must also compete with not only younger women but also their younger selves. ⁴It's the ___reason___ why there is so much plastic surgery and cosmetic dermatology.

D 3. ¹When you stretch a thick, strong rubber band and release it, it snaps painfully back against your hand. ²_similarly_, an earthquake occurs when rock suddenly breaks along a more or less flat surface called a fault.

E 4. ¹The "new politics" of today depends upon key operatives who charge hefty fees for their services—campaign consultants, pollsters, media producers, and fundraising specialists. ²Over the years, some of these operatives, _such as_ James Carville for the Democrats and Karl Rove for the Republicans, have developed almost legendary reputations.

A 5. ¹Times have changed, and I know this because I have children, two of them, one born in the old days and one in modern times. ²The older child grew up inhaling clouds of secondhand smoke, and the younger one lives in a house in which nobody ever thinks about smoking, _although_ sometimes a guest has lurked in the backyard, like a convicted sex offender, and consumed a cigarette.

(Continues on next page)

209

B. Label each item with the letter of its main pattern of organization.

    A Definition and example   C Contrast   E Problem and
    B Comparison   D Cause and effect   solution

C 6. [1]In the typical fairy tale, a dashing young man and a beautiful young woman marry, have children, and live happily ever after. [2]However, that scenario does not match the realities of love and marriage in the 21st century. [3]Today, it is just as likely that the man and woman would first live together, then get married and have children, but end up getting divorced.

D 7. [1]The presence of others often results in making people work more efficiently. [2]An 1898 study showed that bicyclists rode faster when in a group than when alone. [3]The study also showed that children worked harder to pull in a fishing line when they were in a group than when they were alone.

A 8. [1]One way that psychologists evaluate people is according to their tendency to "self-monitor." [2]Self-monitoring refers to the degree to which people attend to and control the impressions they make on others. [3]For instance, you are a high self-monitor if you are quick to adjust your tone of voice or what you say based on how you think others are responding.

E 9. [1]Although it is impossible to put a monetary value on human life, the economic burden of heart disease on our society is staggering—more than $351.8 billion, according to a recent estimate. [2]This figure includes the cost of physician and nursing services, hospital and nursing home facilities, medications, and lost productivity resulting from disability. [3]The best line of defense against heart disease is to prevent it from developing in the first place. [4]Regular physical checkups, a healthy diet, and regular exercise can all prevent arteries from becoming clogged.

B 10. [1]A human baby and a baby songbird are different in almost every imaginable way. [2]But the two share certain similarities when it comes to learning language—in the baby's case, speech, and in the bird's case, its particular song. [3]Both babies and songbirds learn their language from listening to their parents. [4]Babies and birds raised in isolation do not learn to communicate with sound. [5]Both go through a period of babbling. [6]A baby will string together words and phrases, such as "mama, ball, so big, peekaboo," in ways that make no sense. [7]Later, the baby will sort out those words to form thoughts and sentences. [8]In a similar fashion, a baby songbird will sing tiny segments of its parents' song, but with those segments in the wrong order. [9]As it matures, it will learn to put the segments of song together in the right sequence.

RELATIONSHIPS II: Mastery Test 2

A. Fill in each blank with an appropriate transition from the box. Use each transition once. Then, in the space provided, write the letter of the transition you have chosen.

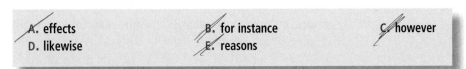

A. effects	B. for instance	C. however
D. likewise	E. reasons	

Hint: Make sure that each word or phrase that you choose fits smoothly into the flow of the sentence. Test each choice by reading the sentence to yourself.

B 1. ¹The names of dog breeds often give a hint about what that dog was bred to do. ²_For instance_, the word *terrier* means "of the earth," suggesting that the dog likes to dig into the earth to hunt for burrowing animals.

C 2. ¹Cohabitation rates have increased dramatically over the past few decades. ²Most cohabiters are young adults who tend to be working couples. ³_However_, about 7 percent of cohabiters are retired adults of age 65 or more.

E 3. ¹As people grow old, they often lose about an inch in height. ²There are two _reasons_. ³First, they have lost some fat and muscle tissue as they age. ⁴And second, the discs between their vertebrae have become slightly compressed.

A 4. ¹The short- and longer-term consequences of childhood sexual abuse can be extremely damaging. ²Victims initially report fear, anxiety, depression, anger, and hostility. ³Long-term _effects_ may include depression, self-destructive behavior, feelings of isolation, poor self-esteem, and substance abuse.

D 5. ¹Even in contemporary industrial societies where women have made great strides in the last hundred years, gender inequality and male privilege persist in marriage and family relationships. ²In America, it is still customary for the bride's family to pay for the wedding, and many wives continue to take their husbands' name. ³_Likewise_, many people believe that even when the husband's and wife's jobs are equal in terms of income and career advancement, the husband's job should take precedence.

(Continues on next page)

B. Label each item with the letter of its main pattern of organization.

> A Definition and example   C Contrast   E Problem and
> B Comparison   D Cause and effect   solution

_E_   6. ¹Researchers have found that 70 to 90% of college students procrastinate before beginning academic assignments, and that 20% of adults are chronic procrastinators. ²People who delay tackling tasks should make and follow a daily "to do" list of specific goals for each day.

_D_   7. ¹In what is now considered a classic experiment, young children saw a film of an adult wildly hitting a five-foot-tall inflatable punching toy called a Bobo doll. ²As a result, when the children were given the opportunity to play with the Bobo doll themselves, most displayed the same kind of behavior, in some cases mimicking the aggressive behavior almost identically.

_A_   8. ¹Self-handicapping is the tendency to sabotage one's performance to provide an excuse for possible failure. ²For example, when a big test is looming, self-handicappers put off studying until the last minute or go out drinking the night before the test. ³If, as is likely, they don't do well on the exam, they explain their poor performance by saying they didn't prepare. ⁴People use a variety of tactics for handicapping their performance: alcohol, drugs, procrastination, a bad mood, a distracting stimulus, anxiety, depression, and being overcommitted.

_B_   9. ¹Researchers were amazed at the similarities they discovered in pairs of identical twins separated early in life. ²Identical twins Oskar Stohr and Jack Yufe were separated soon after birth. ³Oskar was sent to a Nazi-run school in Yugoslavia while Jack was raised in a Jewish home on a Caribbean island. ⁴When they were reunited for the first time in middle age, both showed up wearing similar mustaches, haircuts, shirts, and wire-rimmed glasses. ⁵A pair of previously separated female twins both arrived at the Minneapolis airport wearing seven rings on their fingers. ⁶One had a son named Richard Andrew, and the other had a son named Andrew Richard.

_C_ 10. ¹Some significant gender differences exist in the display of need for power. ²Men with high power needs tend to show unusually high levels of aggression, drink heavily, act in a sexually exploitative manner, and participate more frequently in competitive sports. ³In contrast, women display their power needs with more restraint; this is congruent with traditional societal constraints on women's behavior. ⁴Women with high power needs are more apt than men are to channel those needs in a socially responsible manner, such as by showing concern for others or displaying highly nurturing behavior.

RELATIONSHIPS II: Mastery Test 3

Read each textbook paragraph below. Then answer the questions that follow.

A. ¹In the early 1900s, conditions in America's slaughterhouses and packinghouses were enough to turn one's stomach. ²Since there was no law permitting the federal government to inspect the meat-packing industry, spoiled and diseased food often made its way onto American tables. ³Upton Sinclair's novel *The Jungle* contained graphic descriptions of the slaughter of cattle infected with tuberculosis, of meat covered with rodent droppings, and of men falling into cooking vats. ⁴When President Theodore Roosevelt received a copy of *The Jungle*, he was sickened by what he read. ⁵So was the public. ⁶Spurred by public outrage, The Pure Food and Drug Act of 1906 sailed through Congress; the law prohibited allowing diseased and spoiled food in interstate and foreign commerce.

_____ 1. In the space provided, write the number of the sentence that states the problem in this paragraph.

_____ 2. In the space provided, write the number of the sentence that presents the solution.

B. ¹Are you one of the millions of people who need a jolt from a caffeinated drink to do your job? ²If you are, you may be interested to know that drinks with caffeine in them first became widespread at the same time humanity was switching from farm to factory work. ³It seems that prior to the Industrial Revolution, the work schedule was basically a matter of following natural rhythms: sunrise, sunset, and the cycle of the seasons. ⁴The drink of choice was beer, which can interfere with completing tasks requiring coordinated movement. ⁵When the nature of work changed from relatively slow-paced farm work to one timed by clocks and aided by fast-paced machinery, humans had to adapt. ⁶Caffeinated beverages such as coffee, tea, and, later, colas helped people adjust to this new, faster-paced world. ⁷Imagine what the consequences would be if you drank beer while performing factory work. ⁸You might fall asleep, or worse! ⁹But legions of workers stayed wide awake and energetic due partly to the aid of caffeinated drinks.

_____ 3. The main pattern of organization of the paragraph is
    A. definition and example.   C. comparison.
    B. cause and effect.   D. contrast.

    4. One transition that signals the pattern of organization of this paragraph is _____.

(Continues on next page)

C. ¹A social dilemma exists when behavior that is advantageous for one party leads to disadvantageous outcomes for others. ²The classic illustration is to imagine yourself as a criminal and that you and your partner in crime have been taken to the police station on suspicion of having committed a crime. ³The police believe both of you are guilty, but they lack sufficient evidence to turn the case over to the district attorney for prosecution. ⁴The police officers place you and your partner in separate rooms, where each of you may confess or maintain your innocence. ⁵The police inform you that if both you and your partner remain silent, each of you will get off with three-year sentences. ⁶If both of you confess, you both will serve seven years. ⁷However, should you confess and implicate your partner while your coconspirator maintains his innocence, you will be released, but your partner will receive a fifteen-year prison term. ⁸The situation will be reversed should you maintain your innocence and your partner confesses.

_____ 5. The main pattern of organization of the paragraph is
      A. definition and example.   C. comparison.
      B. cause and effect.   D. contrast.

      6. One transition that signals the pattern of organization of this paragraph

        is _____.

D. ¹When adults in the United States meet for the first time, one of the first questions they ask each other is, "What do you do?" ²A person's occupation—doctor, lawyer, garbage collector, police officer, or mortician—affects how he or she is perceived by others and the nature of the interaction that will follow. ³In the same way, when college students meet, they often ask, "What's your major?" ⁴This is essentially the same question, in that it implies, "What occupation do you plan to enter after you graduate?"

_____ 7. The main patterns of organization of the paragraph are cause and effect
      and
      A. definition and example.   C. contrast.
      B. comparison.   D. comparison and contrast.

      8. One transition that signals the second pattern of organization of this

        paragraph is _____.

RELATIONSHIPS II: Mastery Test 4

Read each textbook paragraph below. Then answer the questions that follow.

A. [1]One of the most stressful times for most people occurs when we begin a conversation with a complete stranger. [2]If you find talking to strangers difficult, you might use one of several conversational openers to help overcome anxiety. [3]One is to simply introduce yourself and ask the other person's name. [4]Another is to refer to the physical context. [5]For instance, you might say something like, "This is awful weather for a game, isn't it?" or "Kim did a great job of remodeling. [6]Did you see the apartment before she began?" [7]You might also ask a semi-personal question such as "Do you live here in town also?" [8]A cheerful response to one of your openers suggests that the person is interested in continuing. [9]Refusal to answer or a curt reply may simply mean that the person is not really interested in talking with you at this time.

_____ 1. In the space provided, write the number of the sentence that states the problem in this paragraph.

_____ 2. In the space provided, write the number of the sentence that presents the solution.

B. [1]*Doublespeak* is a term applied to the use of words that are evasive, ambiguous, or stilted for the purpose of deceiving or confusing the reader or listener. [2]The ethical use of doublespeak is highly questionable, but many organizational managers and politicians make use of it as a means, they hope, to soften the harsh blows of reality and to cover up bad news or mislead the public. [3]For instance, would you rather be "fired" from your job or be "downsized," "outsourced," or "offered a career-change opportunity"? [4]Would you prefer to be "laid off" or to be "transitioned" because the company you've been working for is being "reorganized" or "reengineered," or is engaging in "decruitment" (the opposite of recruitment)? [5]If you had participated in the Gulf War or the Iraqi War, would you have preferred to hear that your organization's "massive bombing attacks killed thousands of civilians" or that your "force packages" successfully "visited a site" and "degraded," "neutralized," or "sanitized" targets? [6]As you become "chronologically gifted" (i.e., old), maybe you will learn the meaning of these terms and phrases, but it seems new ones are constantly being developed.

_____ 3. The main pattern of organization of the paragraph is
    A. definition and example.   C. comparison.
    B. cause and effect.   D. contrast.

    4. One transition that signals the pattern of organization of this paragraph is _____.

(Continues on next page)

C. [1]According to psychologists, boys gain independence from their mothers more easily than girls do. [2]In the first place, society expects boys to be more self-reliant. [3]As children, they have more physical freedom to explore their environment. [4]They are encouraged to compete, take risks, and achieve. [5]Girls, on the other hand, are kept closer to home. [6]They are taught to win approval from others. [7]Being obedient and passive keeps them dependent longer. [8]Secondly, boys don't have to change the sex of their first and primary love object. [9]They don't have to abandon Mother; they only have to find another female. [10]Girls, however, have to transfer their feelings from their mother to someone of the opposite sex. [11]Rebelling against Mother is essential to test and prove the girl's ability to break away.

_____ 5. The main patterns of organization of the paragraph are list of items and
   A. definition and example.   C. contrast.
   B. comparison.   D. comparison and contrast.

6. One transition that signals the second pattern of organization of this

   paragraph is _____.

D. [1]Frogs may be cute little amphibians to some and a nuisance to others, but they actually play an important role in nature. [2]Known as environmental or bio-indicators, these creatures have the capability of revealing the environmental health of an area. [3]The reason for this is that frogs have permeable skin, which allows toxins or pollutants to move freely into their bodies, where the poisons can concentrate. [4]This sensitivity is heightened since frogs spend their life cycle both on land and in the water. [5]So if an area is abundant with frogs, chances are that the environment is healthy in terms of air and water quality. [6]If the frog population in an area is dwindling, it could be an early indicator that the environment is unhealthy, or that it is changing. [7]Thus, frogs provide an early warning signal that undesirable changes either have occurred or are looming.

_____ 7. The main pattern of organization of the paragraph is
   A. definition and example.   C. comparison.
   B. cause and effect.   D. contrast.

8. One transition that signals the pattern of organization of this paragraph

   is _____.

RELATIONSHIPS II: Mastery Test 5

A. Read the textbook paragraph below. Then answer the question and complete the outline that follows.

[handwritten notes in margin: "cause & effect", "list pattern"]

¹Prior to the 1960s, almost everyone in America wore some type of hat. ²But due to a number of lifestyle changes, few of today's Americans wear hats. ³For one thing, America changed from an outdoor culture to an indoor culture. ⁴When Americans used to spend so much time traveling and working outdoors, hats helped them keep the warmth in during the winter and the sun out during the summer. ⁵Since most of today's Americans have heated homes and spend little time outside, there is no longer a need to wear hats for protection. ⁶In addition, the widespread use of cars made wearing hats awkward. ⁷While it used to be more popular to walk or take public transportation to a job site, the majority of today's workers drive their own cars. ⁸The low ceiling in most cars makes it difficult to wear any sort of headgear, and few drivers want to keep putting their hats on and taking them off. ⁹Last, because fewer people wear hats, wearing them has become socially unacceptable in many situations. ¹⁰While it used to be considered proper to wear a hat, today's schools and offices often have dress codes that prohibit headgear.

[handwritten: B] 1. The main patterns of organization of the paragraph are list of items, contrast, and
   A. definition and example.
   B. cause and effect. *[circled]*
   C. comparison.

2–5. Complete the outline of the paragraph by writing in the main idea and the three major supporting details.

Main idea: *In 1960s, almost everyone in America wore some type of hat.*

1. *outside to inside*

2. *wearing them in the car*

3. *fewer people wear hats*

(Continues on next page)

B. Read the textbook paragraph below. Then answer the question and complete the map that follows.

(handwritten margin notes: definition & example / comparison / list pattern)

¹Psychologists distinguish between two types of loneliness: emotional and <u>social</u>. ²Both types of loneliness can cause considerable distress, but they are not the same. ³<u>Emotional</u> loneliness occurs when an intimate attachment figure is absent. ⁴An example would be a child missing a parent; an adult, his or her spouse; or an individual missing an intimate friend. ⁵Or a widow might feel intense emotional loneliness after the death of her husband, but still have social ties to her friends and family. ⁶<u>Social loneliness,</u> on the other hand, occurs when a person is lacking a sense of being integrated into a community. ⁷To illustrate, a young couple moving to a new state might not feel emotional loneliness, as they have each other. ⁸But they are likely to experience social loneliness until they put down roots in their new community. ⁹It is quite possible to experience one type of loneliness without the other.

___A___ 6. The main organizational patterns of the paragraph are contrast and
    (A.) definition and example.
    B. cause and effect.
    C. comparison.

7–10. Complete the map of the paragraph by writing in the major and minor supporting details.

Psychologists distinguish between two types of loneliness: emotional and social.

emotional	social
Ex. — *a child missing a parent*	Ex. — *couple moving to a different state*

RELATIONSHIPS II: Mastery Test 6

A. Read the textbook paragraph below. Then answer the question and complete the outline that follows.

contrast

*cause &
effect*

¹An experiment with surgery patients shows how touching can have different meanings. ²A nurse whose job it was to tell patients about their upcoming surgery purposely touched the patients twice, once briefly on the arm when she introduced herself, and then for a full minute on the arm during the instruction period. ³When she left, she also shook the patient's hand. ⁴The nurse's touches affected women and men differently. ⁵For the women patients, the touching was soothing. ⁶It lowered their blood pressure and anxiety both before the surgery and for more than an hour afterward. ⁷The touching upset the men, however. ⁸Their blood pressure and anxiety increased. ⁹Experimenters have suggested that the men found it harder to acknowledge dependency and fear. ¹⁰Instead of a comfort, the touch was a threatening reminder of their vulnerability.

___D___ 1. One organizational pattern of the paragraph is
    A. definition and example.   C. comparison.
    B. cause and effect.   (D.) contrast.

2. A transition that signals this pattern of organization is *differently*.
    however instead   .

___B___ 3. A second organizational pattern of the paragraph is
    A. definition and example.   C. comparison.
    (B.) cause and effect.   D. contrast.

4. A transition that signals this pattern of organization is _____.
    suggested   .

5–6. Complete the outline of the paragraph by writing in the two major supporting details.

Main idea: An experiment with surgery patients showed how touching can have different meanings.

    1. *lowered womans blood
pressure*

    2. *increased mens blood pressure
& made them angry*

(Continues on next page)

B. Read the textbook paragraph below. Then answer the question and complete the map that follows.

cause & *effect* (handwritten note, left margin)

¹The triumph of the Union in the Civil War led to several fundamental changes in the nature of the American republic. ²No consequence of the Civil War was as basic as the abolition of slavery in the United States. ³The Emancipation Proclamation made it possible for many slaves to gain freedom. ⁴Once hundreds of thousands of blacks left their masters to flee to the Union lines, it was ridiculous to imagine a return to the old ways.

time *order* (handwritten note, left margin)

⁵The Civil War also created a new political majority. ⁶Since the founding of the republic, Southerners played a role in the national government out of proportion to their numbers. ⁷By seceding from the Union, the South opened the way for the northern Republican Party to take its place in the position of political power. ⁸Another momentous innovation of the Civil War years was the ability of citizens to acquire free land. ⁹Before the war, Southern fear of new free states in the territories paralyzed every attempt to liberalize the means by which the federal government disposed of its western lands. ¹⁰Without the influence of Southern congressmen, the Homestead Act was passed, providing every head of family with the opportunity to receive 160 acres of public land for free.

___B___ 7. The main pattern of organization of the paragraph is
    A. definition and example.   C. comparison.
    B. cause and effect.   D. contrast.

8–10. Complete the map of the paragraph by writing in the three major supporting details.

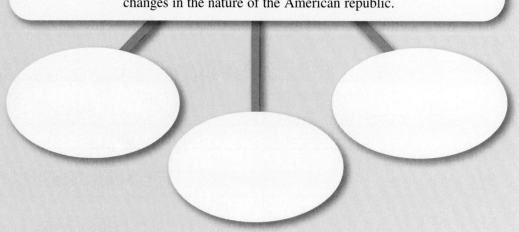

Union victory in the Civil War led to several fundamental changes in the nature of the American republic.

TO THE STUDENT

The pages that follow contain two mastery tests that offer additional practice in the skills covered in Chapters 4 and 5:

- Relationships that involve **addition**

- Relationships that involve **time**

- Relationships that involve **illustration**

- Relationships that involve **comparison and/or contrast**

- Relationships that involve **cause and effect**

- Relationships that involve **problem and solution**

For ease in reference, the lists of words that show these relationships have been reprinted on the next page.

Addition Words

one	to begin with	also	further
first (of all)	for one thing	in addition	furthermore
second(ly)	other	next	last (of all)
third(ly)	another	moreover	final(ly)

Time Words

before	immediately	when	until
previously	next	whenever	often
first (of all)	then	while	frequently
second(ly)	following	during	eventually
third(ly)	later	as (soon as)	final(ly)
now	after (ward)	by	last (of all)

Illustration Words

Deifinition r General

(for) example	including	(as an) illustration	one
(for) instance	specifically	to illustrate	once
such as	to be specific		

Comparison Words

(just) as	both	in like fashion	in a similar fashion
(just) like	equal(ly)	in like manner	in a similar manner
alike	resemble	similar(ly)	(in) the same way
same	likewise	similarity	(in) common

Contrast Words

but	instead (of)	even though	difference
yet	in contrast	as opposed to	different(ly)
however	on the other hand	in spite of	differ (from)
although	on the contrary	despite	unlike
nevertheless	converse(ly)	rather than	while
still	opposite		

Cause and Effect Words

therefore	so	owing to	because (of)
thus	(as a) result	effect	reason
(as a) consequence	results in	cause	explanation
consequently	leads (led) to	if . . . then	accordingly
due to	since	affect	depend(s) on

RELATIONSHIPS I AND II: Mastery Test 1

A. Fill in each blank with an appropriate transition from the box. Use each transition once. Then, in the spaces provided, write the letter of the transition you have chosen

> **A.** conversely   **B.** due to   **C.** for example
> **D.** later   **E.** other

_E_ 1. [1]The war on drugs consists of two basic strategies. [2]One is punitive: using law enforcement to stop the supply of drugs and punish drug sellers and users. [3]The ___other___ is supportive: using drug prevention (or education) and treatment to reduce the demand for drugs and help drug addicts.

_C_ 2. [1]The nutritional needs of a baby change over the first year of life. [2]Most babies do best if they are fed a diet of only breast milk and/or formula for the first four to six months. [3]At that time, parents can begin to offer a single-grain cereal, such as rice cereal, with added iron. [4]___For example___, the baby should be offered no more than one new food every week, with the parent watching for signs of an allergic reaction to any food.

_B_ 3. [1]It has long been noted that students in most Asian countries score higher in tests of math and science than do American students. [2]In all probability, this is ___due to___ a basic difference in cultural beliefs. [3]North American parents and teachers emphasize innate ability—the idea that some people are just naturally "good at math." [4]Asian parents and teachers believe strongly that any student can do better by working harder.

_A_ 4. [1]Cancer seems to occur in different degrees in different ethnic and gender groups. [2]_____, African American men have the world's highest rate of prostate cancer. [3]Native American men are more likely than white American men to develop lung cancer or colorectal cancer. [4]And Vietnamese American and Hispanic American women have higher than average rates of cervical cancer.

_D_ 5. [1]When life's end is near, more and more people and their families are turning to some form of hospice care, rather than traditional hospitalization. [2]In a hospital, medical professionals are in charge, with the patient and family members often feeling pushed aside and somewhat bewildered by all that is going on. [3]_____, in a hospice setting, the patient and family are in charge. [4]They decide what medical treatments they will ask for or accept, and friends and family members are deeply involved in the dying person's care.

(Continues on next page)

+16

B. Fill in each blank with an appropriate transition from the box. Use each transition once. Then, in the spaces provided, write the letter of the transition you have chosen.

| A. after | B. for instance | C. for one thing |
| D. however | E. in contrast | |

B 6. ¹Researchers find that adults who call themselves "very religious" are less afraid of death than those who describe themselves as "less religious." ²This would suggest that the more religious one is, the less afraid one is of death. ³_____, this pattern breaks down when people who describe themselves as "completely non-religious" are questioned. ⁴They report themselves as equally unafraid of death as the "very religious."

x2 **A** 7. ¹Early in childhood, children are likely to connect moral judgments with adult observation. ²They feel guilty or ashamed only if a parent or teacher sees them violating a moral rule. ³A 7-year-old candy thief, for instance, is unlikely to feel guilty unless he is caught in the act. ⁴But _____ the age of 10 or 11, that same child is likely to make behavioral choices based on how guilty, ashamed, or proud he thinks he will feel.

E 8. ¹When you notice "the man in the moon," you are demonstrating a phenomenon called pareidolia. ²Pareidolia is the name psychologists give to people's tendency to mistake a vague, random stimulus for a recognizable image—most often a human face. ³_____, people often think they perceive faces in clouds, wallpaper designs, geologic formations, paint swirls, and other meaningless formations.

+2

D 9. ¹The usual standard for good vision in an adult is "20/20," meaning that subject can see something 20 feet away as well as the average person. ²_____, a person with "20/100" vision has to be as close as 20 feet to see something that the ordinary person can see at 100 feet. ³In other words, the higher the second number, the poorer the person's vision.

x2

C 10. ¹The sales of fur tumbled to an all-time low in the late 1980s, thanks largely to the efforts of groups like People for the Ethical Treatment of Animals (PETA). ²But in recent years, fur has made a fashion comeback. ³Why? ⁴_____, designers have been incorporating fur into blended fabrics, making it less obvious that it is real fur. ⁵For another, the anti-fur movement is simply less novel and chic than it was in years past.

x2

RELATIONSHIPS I AND II: Mastery Test 2

Read each selection and answer the questions that follow. Note that paragraphs D and E have **two** patterns of organization.

A. ¹The "psychological consequences" of product use are internal, personal outcomes, such as how a product makes you feel. ²For instance, using Nexxus shampoo might make you feel more attractive; wearing Gap sportswear might make you feel more (or less) stylish; and eating an ice cream cone from Baskin-Robbins might make you feel happy. ³Consumers may also think in terms of the "social consequences" of product use, which might include "My friends will like/respect/envy me if I buy an iPod; my mother will think I am a smart shopper if I buy this jacket on sale."

_____ 1. The main pattern of organization of the selection is
    A. comparison and/or contrast.
    B. time order.
    C. definition and example.

2. One transition that signals the pattern of organization of this paragraph is

_____.

B. ¹A growing body of evidence shows that living in a concentrated pocket of poverty intensifies all the ill effects of family poverty. ²When the whole neighborhood is poor, parents have fewer other resources to rely on, and children have more violent adult models and fewer supportive ones. ³Rates of child abuse rise, along with rates of aggression and delinquency in children. ⁴When the whole neighborhood also lacks what sociologists call connectedness and stability—when the adults do not collaborate to monitor the children and do not provide practical or emotional support to one another—the results are still worse.

_____ 3. The main pattern of organization of the selection is
    A. time order.
    B. definition and example.
    C. cause and effect.

4. One transition that signals the pattern of organization you selected is

_____.

C. ¹Crispus Attucks was born in about 1723, the son of a slave and a Native American woman. ²He is thought to have escaped from slavery in 1750. ³After that he worked as a sailor and laborer in Boston. ⁴Like many Colonial sailors, he hated the presence of the occupying British troops because they could force sailors to serve in the Royal Navy. ⁵On March 5, 1770, a crowd gathered to protest the presence of the British. ⁶Attucks spoke to the crowd, waving a club and urging other colonists to attack the British. ⁷The British soldiers then opened fire, killing Attucks as well as four white men. ⁸Attucks's death in the Boston Massacre was an important milestone along the road to the American Revolution.

(Continues on next page)

_____ 5. The main pattern of organization of the selection is
    A. time order.
    B. contrast.
    C. definition and example.

6. One transition that signals the pattern of organization you selected is

_____.

D. ¹According to a recent *Consumer Reports* article, as much as 25 percent of Americans' expenditures on medical care are wasted on unnecessary treatments, procedures, tests, or hospitalization. ²Several possible explanations can be suggested for this waste of time, money, and resources. ³One possible explanation is the profit motive. ⁴The more medical services provided, the greater the income for members of the medical-care industry. ⁵Another possible reason is the desire of doctors and hospitals to avoid being sued by patients for undiagnosed or improperly treated sickness or injury. ⁶Finally, because most U.S. patients do not pay directly for medical care, they probably are less interested in keeping costs down. ⁷They may demand treatments that are not appropriate or necessary. ⁸In any case, we clearly are not making the most efficient use of our medical-care resources.

_____ 7. The main patterns of organization of the selection are list of items and
    A. comparison and/or contrast.
    B. cause and effect.
    C. definition and example.

8. One transition that signals the pattern of organization you selected is

_____.

E. ¹Epidemiology is the study of the origin and spread of disease in a given population. ²Epidemiology emerged as an applied science in 1854, when the English physician John Snow discovered the source of one of London's periodic cholera epidemics. ³Specifically, he had gone to the neighborhoods where the patients lived and asked them what they did every day, where they worked, what they ate and drank, and many other questions about their lives and activities. ⁴Finally, after sifting through a huge pile of information, Snow hit upon the clue to the origin of the disease. ⁵He found that they all had one thing in common: They had drunk water from a particular pump on Broad Street. ⁶Snow simply shut off the pump and, with that simple act, stopped the epidemic in its tracks. ⁷Not until many years later, with the discovery of germs, could anyone explain why shutting down the pump was effective. ⁸Dr. Snow had removed the source of the cholera bacterium.

_____ 9. The main patterns of organization of the selection are time order, problem and solution, and
    A. definition and example.
    B. comparison.
    C. contrast.

10. One transition that signals the pattern of organization you selected is

_____.

6 Inferences

You have probably heard the expression "to read between the lines." When you "read between the lines," you pick up ideas that are not directly stated in what you are reading. These implied ideas are often important for a full understanding of what an author means. Discovering the ideas in writing that are not stated directly is called **making inferences**, or **drawing conclusions**.

Look at the cartoon below. What inferences can you make about it? Check (✓) the **two** inferences that are most logically based on the information suggested by the cartoon.

____ A. The dog requires more than one leash to keep it securely tied to the parking meter.

⨉ B. The dog has eaten the other dogs tied up at the parking meter.

____ C. The dog is ordinarily a friendly dog.

⨉ D. The dog is waiting for its owner to return.

Explanation

A. *The dog requires more than one leash to keep it securely tied to the parking meter.*

The owner has used only one leash to tie the dog to the parking meter. The other leashes are in the dog's mouth. You should not have checked this item.

B. *The dog has eaten the other dogs tied up at the parking meter.*

Three other leashes are in the mouth of this big, hostile-looking dog. You should have checked this item.

C. *The dog is ordinarily a friendly dog.*

It may or may not ordinarily be a friendly dog, but it doesn't look friendly here, and it obviously has not been friendly to other dogs. You should not have checked this item.

D. *The dog is waiting for its owner to return.*

It is a reasonable inference that the owner who tied up the dog will return—and will be in for a surprise!

Inferences in Reading

In reading, we make logical leaps from information stated directly to ideas that are not stated directly. As one scholar has said, inferences are "statements about the unknown made on the basis of the known." To make inferences, we use all the clues provided by the writer, our own experience, and logic.

You have already practiced making inferences in this book. Do you remember the following sentence on page 12 of the introductory chapter?

Marcella uses a lot of *hyperbole* to express herself: a restaurant is never just "good"—it's "the most fabulous food in the universe"; her boyfriend isn't just "good-looking"—he's "divine beyond belief."

That sentence does not tell the meaning of *hyperbole*, but the examples help us infer that *hyperbole* means "overstatement."

You also made inferences in the chapter on implied main ideas. There you used the evidence in selections to figure out main ideas that were implied rather than stated directly. In this chapter, you will get a good deal of practice in making a variety of inferences about reading selections and other material.

Inferences in Short Passages

> ✓ *Check Your Understanding*
>
> Read the following passage and then check (✓) the **two** inferences most logically based on the information provided.
>
> > Mark Twain said: "When I was a boy of 14, my father was so ignorant I could hardly stand to have the old man around. But when I got to be 21, I was astonished at how much the old man had learned in seven years."
>
> _✗_   A. Teenagers tend to think they know it all and that adults do not.
>
> ____   B. Even old people are capable of learning a great deal.
>
> ____   C. The older fathers get, the less foolish they become.
>
> _✗_   D. As a young person matures, he learns to respect the knowledge of adults.
>
> *Explanation*
>
> A. Experience tells us that teenagers often think they know more than their parents' generation. Twain's observation is a humorous statement of this truth. You should have checked this item.
>
> B. Twain's age (14) when he thought his father was ignorant and the age (21) at which he is astonished at the "old man's" learning are clues that it is Twain who has changed, not his father. You should not have checked this item.
>
> C. There is nothing in the statement to support the inference that Twain's father was actually foolish. Again, it is Twain's viewpoint that has changed, not his father. You should not have checked this item.
>
> D. Experience tells us that when young people begin to face the same life challenges that adults face, they gain new respect for the knowledge adults possess. Clearly, as Twain reached manhood, he began to respect his father. You should have checked this item.

PRACTICE 1

For each of the following passages, check (✓) the **two** inferences most logically based on the information provided.

1. "When will people understand that words can cut as sharply as any blade, and that those cuts leave scars upon our souls." —Unknown author

   ___X___ A. People seldom reflect on how deeply their words can wound others.

   ___X___ B. Emotional wounds can be just as painful as physical ones.

   _____ C. Sometimes we fail to listen to the words of others.

   _____ D. People do not always understand each other's words.

2. "I can't imagine I could have become the person I am now without books. How could I know there was another world beyond my small, isolated, feeling-abandoned world? Books became synonymous with freedom. They showed that you can open doors and walk through." —Oprah Winfrey

   ___X___ A. The author of this statement probably had a difficult childhood.

   _____ B. Everyone who reads can accomplish great things.

   ___X___ C. Books can open doors to new possibilities in one's life.

   _____ D. Reading can show people how to achieve success.

3. "It is inaccurate to say I hate everything. I am strongly in favor of common sense, common honesty, and common decency. This makes me forever ineligible for public office." —H.L. Mencken

   _____ A. The author regrets the fact that he will never be elected to office.

   _____ B. The author must be a very unhappy man.

   ___X___ C. The author believes that many politicians are liars or crooks.

   ___X___ D. The author has probably been accused of being overly critical.

4. "The only devils in this world are those running around in our own hearts, and that is where all our battles should be fought." —Mahatma Gandhi

   _____ A. Devils can defeat the best efforts of good people.

   ___X___ B. People should try to overcome their own worst impulses.

   _____ C. There are no really evil people in the world.

   ___X___ D. Rather than blame others, we should instead seek ways to improve ourselves.

5. "One reads books in order to gain the privilege of living more than one life. People who don't read are trapped in a mine shaft, even if they think the sun is shining. Most New Yorkers wouldn't travel to Minnesota if a bright star shone in the west and hosts of angels were handing out plane tickets, but they might read a book about Minnesota, and thereby form some interesting and

useful impression of us. This is the benefit of literacy. Life is lonely; it is less so if one reads." —Garrison Keillor

____ A. Reading is a sure antidote for loneliness.

____ B. People who do not read do not realize how much they limit their view of the world.

____ C. The author considers Minnesotans to be superior to New Yorkers.

____ D. Reading enables people to establish connections with people and places they might otherwise look down upon or fear.

Inferences in Paragraphs

✓ Check Your Understanding

Read the following textbook passage and then check (✓) the **three** inferences that can most logically be drawn from the information provided.

> ¹Let's suppose that you have a ticket to fly to some exotic destination. ²There will be 200 passengers plus crew on board your plane. ³You are excited about your trip, but on the way to the airport, the radio program you are listening to is interrupted by an announcement that five U.S. jets will be hijacked that day. ⁴All will crash—and all passengers and crew will die. ⁵There is no doubt that five planes will go down, that 1,000 terrified passengers and crew will plunge to their deaths. ⁶The reporter adds that the airlines have decided to stay open for business. ⁷Do you still fly? ⁸After all, the chances are good that *yours* will not be one of the five planes. ⁹My best guess is that you turn around and go home, that U.S. airports will be eerily silent that day. ¹⁰Nicotine—with its progressive emphysema and several types of cancer—kills about 400,000 Americans each year. ¹¹This is the equivalent of five fully loaded, 200-passenger jets with full crews crashing each and every day—leaving no survivors. ¹²Who in their right mind would take the risk that *their* plane will not be among those that crashed? ¹³Yet that is the risk that smokers take.

____ A. The author implies that many Americans don't like to think about the harmful effects of smoking.

____ B. The author implies that chances are good that fewer Americans will smoke in the future.

____ C. The author suggests that too many people risk their lives by smoking.

____ D. The author suggests that people would be willing to take their chances on a plane crash if the odds are in their favor.

____ E. This excerpt is probably from a business textbook.

____ F. This excerpt is probably from a textbook that deals with social problems.

Explanation

A. This is a logical inference. The author presents statistics showing the harmful effects of smoking. Life experience tells us that few people like to think about the negative consequences of their behavior.

B. This is not a logical inference. There is nothing in the passage to indicate that fewer Americans will smoke in the future.

C. This is a logical inference. The author presents statistical evidence that the nicotine in cigarettes kills about 400,000 Americans each year.

D. This is not a logical inference. The author says that airports would be inactive and silent on a day when five jets were to be hijacked.

E. This is not a logical inference. The focus of the passage is health, not business.

F. This is a logical inference. Clearly any behavior that kills 400,000 Americans each year is a social problem.

Guidelines for Making Inferences in Reading

The paragraphs that follow will give you practice in making careful inferences when you read. Here are three guidelines to that process:

1 **Never lose sight of the available information.** As much as possible, base your inferences on the facts. For instance, in the passage about the risks of smoking, we are told that most Americans would refuse to fly if they knew that jets were to be hijacked, but that many Americans continue to risk their lives despite the known dangers of smoking. On the basis of those facts, we would not conclude that fewer Americans will smoke in the future.

It's also important to note when a conclusion lacks support. For instance, the conclusion that the smoking passage is from a business textbook has no support in the passage, which focuses on the health costs of smoking rather than the economic costs.

2 **Use your background information and experience to help you in making inferences.** For instance, life experience tells us that people don't like to dwell on the negative consequences of their behavior. Therefore, you can conclude that American smokers don't like to think about the harmful effects of smoking.

The more you know about a subject, the better your inferences are likely to be. So keep in mind that if your background in an area is weak, your inferences may be shaky. If your car suddenly develops a tendency to stall, an auto mechanic's inferences about the cause are likely to be more helpful than your inferences.

3 **Consider the alternatives.** Don't simply accept the first inference that comes to mind. Instead, consider all of the facts of a case and all the possible explanations. For example, the mechanic analyzing why your car stalls may first think of and then eliminate several possibilities before coming to the right conclusion.

PRACTICE 2

Read the following textbook passages. Then, in the space provided, write the letter of the most logical answer to each question, based on the information given in the passage.

A. [1]If your roommate is washing the dishes and says acidly, "I hope you're enjoying your novel," the literal meaning of his words is quite clear, but you probably know very well that he is not expressing a concern about your reading pleasure. [2]He is really saying, "I am furious that you are not helping to clean up after dinner." [3]Other emotions can be expressed through tone of voice as well. [4]When Mae West, a once famous film star and master of sexual innuendo, asked, "Why don't you come up and see me sometime?" her voice oozed sensuality. [5]Similarly, if you receive a phone call from someone who has very good or very bad news, you will probably know how she feels before she has told you what happened. [6]In the same way, we can literally hear the fear in a person's voice, as we do when we listen to a nervous student give an oral report.

_B_ 1. Which of the following would be a good title for this passage?
  A. Humans Can Sense Fear
  B. It's Not What You Say; It's How You Say It
  C. Getting Along with Others

_C_ 2. The author uses the example of Mae West in order to suggest that
  A. movie stars used to be far sexier than they are now.
  B. Mae West probably never experienced a moment of nervousness in her life.
  C. people are capable of conveying much meaning through voice quality.

_B_ 3. The author probably mentions the fear in a nervous student's voice because she feels
  A. that students are needlessly nervous about giving oral reports.
  B. it is an experience that many people are familiar with.
  C. that students should not be forced to give oral reports.

B. ¹When sociologists first examined children's picture books in the 1970s, they found that it was unusual for a girl to be the main character. ²Almost all the books featured boys, men, and even male animals. ³The girls, when pictured at all, were passive and doll-like, whereas the boys were active and adventuresome. ⁴While the boys did things that required independence and self-confidence, most girls were shown trying to help their brothers and fathers. ⁵Feminists protested these stereotypes and even formed their own companies to publish books that showed girls as leaders, as active and independent.

⁶The result of these efforts, along with the changed role of women in society, is that children's books now have about an equal number of boy and girl characters. ⁷Girls are also now depicted in a variety of nontraditional activities. ⁸Researchers find, however, that males are seldom depicted as caring for the children or doing grocery shopping, and they never are seen doing housework. ⁹As gender roles continue to change, I assume that this, too, will change.

4. We can infer that the author of this passage believes that
   A. in real life, boys tend to be more active and independent than girls.
   B. the feminist criticisms of children's books in the 1970s had little merit.
   C. girls should be given books that show them acting with self-confidence and a sense of independence.

5. We can infer from the passage that feminists believe that
   A. male authors intentionally tried to harm young girls.
   B. girls should perform only nontraditional tasks.
   C. reading books can influence how girls think and act.

6. We can conclude from this passage that
   A. in real life, males seldom care for children or do housework.
   B. children's books will continue to reflect changing gender roles.
   C. children's books now unrealistically depict girls engaged in non-traditional tasks.

C. ¹I want to tell you about something that happened just a few days ago that gave me a glimpse into what it might feel like for a young person to be bullied because of a physical appearance that is outside the norm. ²On Monday I found an anonymous, typed note in my mailbox at work. ³The note informed me of how bad my clothes look on me and that I really need to get some new ones. ⁴The tone of the note implied that this person cared about me and, therefore, thought I should know this.

⁵I have no idea who wrote the note, and I don't know if this person is aware that I am a cancer survivor. ⁶Perhaps they aren't aware that two surgeries, radiation treatments, and hormone therapy have left me with a body quite different from the cute, petite figure I had a few years ago. ⁷Perhaps they don't

know about the challenges I have in finding clothes that will hide the deformities that will be with me for the rest of my life. [8]And they probably don't understand the financial challenges that come with a cancer diagnosis.

[9]When I read the note, I told myself that as a mature adult, I should just let these cruel comments roll off my back. [10]Instead, I went home and wept. [11]I cried because someone thought my appearance was so bad that they felt compelled to leave me this hurtful note. [12]And I cried because the note was a reminder of the losses and changes that I've seen in my life since cancer moved in.

[13]But, as in all of life's experiences, there was a lesson here. [14]If I, as a 50-year-old woman, could be bothered so much by an anonymous note, then I thought about how a fragile teenager might feel when exposed to hurtful comments, especially when they happen repeatedly.

7. We can infer that the author
   A. believes that bullying among the young is a serious problem.
   B. is the mother of a child who has been bullied.
   C. will complain to her supervisor at work about the anonymous note.

8. On the basis of paragraphs 3 and 4, we can infer that
   A. the author will never recover from receiving the cruel note.
   B. it is even more difficult for teenagers to cope with hurtful comments than it is for mature adults.
   C. the author vowed to find out who sent the anonymous note so she could explain to that person how bad the note made her feel.

9. Which statement can we reasonably infer from the passage?
   A. Sometimes when we suffer, we become more sensitive to the suffering of others.
   B. If you see someone whose appearance needs improvement, you should politely suggest ways he or she can improve it.
   C. It is unusual for teenagers to experience cruel comments.

D. [1]A psychologist employed seven assistants and one genuine subject in an experiment in which they were asked to judge the length of a straight line that they were shown on a screen. [2]The seven assistants, who were the first to speak and report what they saw, had been instructed to report unanimously an evidently incorrect length. [3]The eighth member of the group, the only naïve subject in the lot, did not know that his companions had received such an instruction, and he was under the impression that what they reported was really what they saw. [4]In one-third of the experiments, he reported the same incorrect length as they did. [5]The pressure of the environment had influenced his own reaction and had distorted his vision. [6]When one of the assistants, under the secret direction of the experimenter, started reporting the correct length, it relieved that pressure of the environment, and the perception of the uninformed subject improved accordingly.

_____ 10. We can infer that this passage is probably from
   A. a biology textbook.
   B. a business textbook.
   C. a social science textbook.

_____ 11. This passage suggests that
   A. people tend to be influenced by the actions of others.
   B. people can be forced into saying just about anything.
   C. most people will change their minds when they see that they are in the minority.

_____ 12. The genuine subjects in the experiment can best be described as
   A. bright.
   B. pressured.
   C. foolish.

E.   ¹World War I caught most people by surprise. ²Lulled by a century of peace, many observers had come to regard armed conflict as an anachronism, a dead relic rendered unthinkable by human progress. ³Convinced that the major powers had advanced too far morally and materially to fight, these optimists believed that nation-states would settle disputes through diplomacy. ⁴By the early 1900s, peace societies abounded on both sides of the Atlantic, nurturing visions of a world without war, and the Hague Conferences of 1899 and 1907 seemed to bear out these hopes by codifying international law in order to establish procedures for the peaceful resolution of conflict. ⁵World War I shattered these dreams, demonstrating that death and destruction had not yet been banished from human affairs.

_____ 13. Even if we do not know their definitions, we can infer that the words *anachronism* and *relic* have to do with
   A. the past.
   B. the present.
   C. the future.

_____ 14. Just before World War I, people tended to believe that war
   A. would always be a necessary evil.
   B. was a human vice that could be overcome by decent people.
   C. was beneficial for nations seeking land and power.

_____ 15. The onset of World War I
   A. probably shattered the ideals of many thinkers of the time.
   B. may have grown out of disagreements between international peace societies.
   C. might never had occurred if there had been more laws in place.

Inferences in Literature

Inferences are very important in reading literature. While writers of factual material usually state directly much of what they mean, creative writers often provide verbal pictures that *show* what they mean. It is up to the reader to infer the point of what the creative writer has said. For instance, a nonfiction writer might write the following:

> It would be really hard to feel the pain that others feel. It is better not to know.

Compare the above with the following lines about the pain in human life from George Eliot's *Middlemarch*, considered by many the greatest of English novels:

> If we had a keen vision and feeling of all ordinary human life, it would be like hearing the grass grow and the squirrel's heart beat, and we should die of that roar which lies on the other side of silence. As it is, we walk about well wadded with stupidity.

Eliot uses vivid images that help us infer a profound human truth—that behind the surface we often carry around a great deal of pain—a "roar . . . on the other side of silence." So as to not die from experiencing the pain of others, we protect and wad ourselves with ignorance and stupidity. To get the most out of literature, you must often infer the meanings behind the words.

A Note on Figures of Speech

Creative writers often use comparisons known as **figures of speech** to imply their meanings and give us a fresh and more informed way of looking at something. The two most common figures of speech are similes and metaphors.

Simile—a <u>comparison</u> introduced with *like, as,* or *as if.*

"Your eyes are beautiful," he said.

"Shall I compare them to a summer day? No, even more."

"Your eyes are like two supper dishes."

PEANUTS: © 1995 Peanuts Worldwide LLC. Dist. By UNIVERSAL UCLICK. Reprinted with permission. All rights reserved.

In the cartoon, Snoopy writes about a pair of beautiful eyes that they are "like two supper dishes"! (The joke, of course, is that the comparison is hardly a flattering one.)

In the quotation from *Middlemarch*, George Eliot uses two similes. To see and feel all ordinary human life, Eliot says, would be "like hearing the grass grow and the squirrel's heart beat."

Here's another example. Instead of saying, "The morning after the party, my mouth felt awful," you could express the same idea vividly by saying, "The morning after the party, my mouth felt like a used ashtray." The simile shows just how nasty your mouth felt. It gives us more information than the line that simply tells us your mouth felt awful.

Here are some other <u>similes:</u>

- Abandoned houses lined the city street *like tombstones.*
- That too-thin teenage girl has arms *like matchsticks.*
- The look the hostess gave me was *as welcoming as a glass of ice water in my face.*
- The used car salesman attached himself to prospective customers *like Velcro.*
- My mind was becoming *as calm as the surface of a quiet mountain lake.*

Metaphor—an implied comparison, with *like, as,* or *as if* omitted.

The 23rd Psalm in the Bible is the source of some of the world's best-known metaphors, including "The Lord is my shepherd." The comparison suggests that God is like a shepherd who looks after his sheep.

Here are some other metaphors:

- The candidate waded into *a sea of people* to shake hands.
- The movie was *a bomb.*
- Her disapproval was *an ice pick to my heart.*
- The algebra problems were *a forest of tiny enemies*, jeering at me from the page.
- To people searching for information, the Internet is a vast *candy store* of facts.

PRACTICE 3

Use a check (✓) to identify each figure of speech as either a simile or a metaphor. Then, in the space provided, answer each inference question that follows.

____ 1. To Jennifer, the psychology course was a banquet of ideas.

____ simile   ✗ metaphor

You can infer that Jennifer
A. finds her psychology course rather tedious.
B. likes to eat during her psychology course.
C. finds her psychology course quite interesting.

_B_   2. After I ate that meal, I felt as if I had swallowed a barbell.

___ simile   _X_ metaphor

You can infer that the meal was

A. sweet.
B. heavy.
C. spicy.

_A_   3. When Don started to run track again after his knee operation, he felt like a bus on the racetrack at the Indy 500.

_X_ simile   ___ metaphor

You can infer that Don

A. felt slow and awkward.
B. felt cheerful and optimistic.
C. knew he would never regain his old form.

_A_   4. Tina says that her first boyfriend was an economy car, but her current one is a luxury sedan.

___ simile   _X_ metaphor

You can infer that Tina's current boyfriend

A. is a big improvement over her first one.
B. is an auto mechanic.
C. is a family man.

_C_   5. The CEO of the company gave a talk to his employees that was one part sugar and one part sandpaper.

___ simile   _X_ metaphor

You can infer that the CEO

A. was hard to understand.
B. led a company that sold both groceries and home products.
C. was both encouraging to and critical of his employees.

PRACTICE 4

The following is a true story written by sports columnist and Pulitzer Prize nominee Bill Lyon. In just under 900 words, Lyon describes a memorable event that happened before the start of a professional basketball game in Portland. Read the story and then decide what inferences can be made about it.

One Shining Moment

¹There she stood at center court, this little girl with the big, big voice, poised for the moment of a lifetime, the house lights dimmed, 20,000 people waiting expectantly for her, 20,000 people ready to hear her sing . . .

. . . and the words wouldn't come.

²They lodged in her throat and couldn't be budged, no matter how mightily she strained. ³It was the song she knew by heart, the one she had heard a million times, the one she had sung over and over and over, the very one that she had rehearsed in a dressing room perfectly—every single run-through dead solid perfect—only minutes before, for heaven's sake. ⁴But now the words all tumbled over each other, crazy-quilted in a jumbling, confusing mishmash:

rocket's last gleaming . . . twilight's red glare . . . flag's not there . . . oh, say can you see . . . yet wave . . .

⁵She wanted to disappear, of course. ⁶She wanted the floor to open up and swallow her. ⁷Or a spaceship to beam her up and carry her off. ⁸Natalie Gilbert, a 13-year-old eighth grader, was living the nightmare each of us, in moments of morbid, fearful imagining, has conjured.

⁹And then, suddenly, silent as a shadow, he was there, standing beside her, his left arm protectively, comfortingly around her, and he was whispering the forgotten words and she began to nod her head—*yes, yes, I remember now*—and she began to mouth the words, and then he started to sing them, softly, and she joined in, hesitantly at first, but with a growing confidence, and soon they were a duet, and he was urging the crowd on with his right hand, and soon the duet had 20,000 backups, 20,000 people singing partly out of relief, partly out of compassion, partly out of pride, and rarely has the national anthem of the United States of America been rendered with such heartfelt gusto.

¹⁰It was a glorious, redemptive moment.

¹¹Surely, you thought, sport has never been grander.

¹²In fact, it says here that, for all the acrobatic, aeronautic, pyrotechnic, cruise-o-matic moments that the NBA playoffs have presented to us thus far this spring, all pale in comparison to the night of April 25, in the Rose Garden in Portland, Oregon, shortly before the Trail Blazers met the Dallas Mavericks in the third game of their series.

¹³That is when Maurice Cheeks, once the quintessential point guard, selfless and without ego and pretense, for many meritorious seasons a Philadelphia 76er, and most recently the coach of the Blazers, came to the rescue of Natalie Gilbert.

[14]"I don't know why I did it," he said. [15]"It wasn't something I thought about. [16]It's one of those things you just do."

[17]Except, of course, no one else thought to do it.

[18]Everybody else did precisely what most of us would do in such a situation—study the ceiling, develop a sudden interest in our shoes, shift from side to side, paralyzed, frozen to the spot, embarrassed for the little girl, empathizing furiously, wishing desperately it would all end: *Please, let her remember the words. Please. Somebody do something.*

[19]Maurice Cheeks, himself a father, did what all fathers, and grandfathers, too, in moments of heroic reverie, dream they would do. [20]He tried to make the world go away.

[21]Seeing as how his team was one loss away from elimination, he might have been expected to have other things on his mind than a junior high school girl who had won a contest to sing "The Star-Spangled Banner" before tip-off of the most crucial game of the year.

[22]And yet, there he was, not sure how exactly, walking to center court. [23]And once there, this thought stabbed him:

[24]"I wasn't sure whether I knew the words myself," he said, laughing.

[25]"I just didn't want her to be out there all alone."

[26]For those of us who chronicled Maurice Cheeks during his tenure in Philadelphia, what he did was totally in character. [27]The man was never the self-absorbed prima donna so many have become. [28]He played a spare, bare-bones, beautifully economical game, and wanted very much to disappear as soon as the game was over. [29]He had no more a desire for the spotlight than he did for flamboyance on the court.

[30]The best point guards are sharers and protectors and soothers. [31]The best of them understand how to get the ball to the right people in the right place at the right time. [32]The best of them watch out for everybody else.

[33]Maurice Cheeks is still a point guard at heart.

[34]The Trail Blazers haven't given Portland much to be proud of. [35]It is a dysfunctional team, full of head cases and temperamental malcontents. [36]But in one impromptu moment, Maurice Cheeks gave everyone a reason to be proud.

[37]It has become a touchstone, this act of compassion. [38]There isn't a TV network that hasn't played snippets of the coach coaching the little girl singing the anthem.

[39]There is a reason so many want to show it, to write of it, to celebrate it. [40]Because it resonates so, because it strums one of our most emotional chords, because it reminds us of the stirring capabilities of the human spirit.

[41]"I guess," Maurice Cheeks said, a bit uncomfortable at the thought, "it has become a moment."

[42]Oh, yes. [43]Yes, it has.

[44]One shining moment.

[45]Of grace.

Check (✓) the **five** inferences that can best be made about the story.

    ____ A. Natalie Gilbert will never sing in front of an audience again.

    ✕ B. The audience was inspired by the fact that Maurice Cheeks helped Natalie Gilbert sing the national anthem.

    ____ C. Young people should not be encouraged to perform in front of live audiences.

    ____ D. Natalie always got stage fright when she performed.

    ✕ E. Maurice Cheeks knows that there's more to life than basketball.

    ____ F. Natalie had never sung in public before.

    ✕ G. Professional athletes tend to be so self-involved that they are unable to relate to ordinary people.

    ✕ H. Not all professional athletes and coaches are spoiled and self-centered.

    ✕ I. Bill Lyon thinks that professional sports needs more people like Maurice Cheeks.

    ____ J. Maurice Cheeks is a professional singer as well as an athlete.

Inferences in Tables and Graphs

You have already tried your hand at making inferences about a picture—the cartoon involving the dog at the beginning of this chapter. To understand many of the cartoons in newspapers and magazines, you must use your inference skills. Other "pictures" that require inferences are tables and graphs, which combine words with visual representations. Authors of textbooks, professional and newspaper articles, and other materials often organize large amounts of material into tables and graphs. Very often, the graphs and tables are used to show comparisons and changes that take place over time.

As with other reading material, to infer the ideas presented in tables and graphs, you must consider all the information presented.

Steps in Reading a Table or Graph

To find and make sense of the information in a table or graph, follow a few steps.

1 Read the title. It will tell you what the table or graph is showing in general.

● What is the title of the graph on the next page?_____

_____

2 Check the source. At the bottom of a table or graph, you will usually find the source of the information, an indication of the reliability of its material.

  ● What is the source for the graph below? _____

  _____

3 Read any labels or captions at the top, the side, or underneath that tell exactly what each column, line, bar, number, or other item represents. This information includes such things as quantities, percentages, and years.

✔ *Check Your Understanding*

Study the graph below and then check (✓) the **three** inferences that are most logically based on the information in the graph. Then read the explanation that follows.

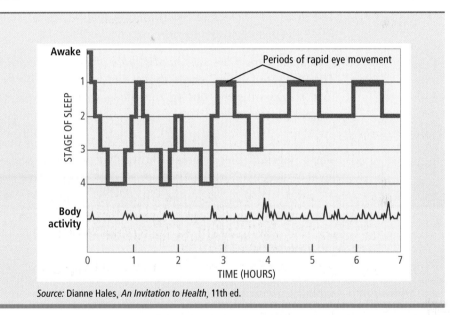

Source: Dianne Hales, *An Invitation to Health*, 11th ed.

  ☒ A. Our deepest sleep occurs early in the sleep cycle.

  ☒ B. Our REM (rapid eye movement) sleep occurs at about the same time as our deepest sleep.

  ☒ C. Our body activity is slowest during the deepest part of our sleep.

  ____ D. We spend over half of our sleep time in REM sleep.

  ____ E. For the most part, we stay in one stage of sleep during the sleep cycle.

  ☒ F. It takes less than an hour to reach the deepest level of sleep.

Explanation

A. *Our deepest sleep occurs early in the sleep cycle.*
The "Stages of Sleep" graph shows that we are in the deepest sleep in the first three hours or so of the sleep cycle. You should have checked item A.

B. *Our REM (rapid eye movement) sleep occurs at about the same time as our deepest sleep.*
The "Stages of Sleep" graph shows that our REM sleep occurs in the second part of our sleep cycle rather than at the same time of our deepest sleep, in the first part of the sleep cycle. You should not have checked this item.

C. *Our body activity is slowest during the deepest part of our sleep.*
The "body activity" is least active during the deepest part of our sleep, in the first part of the sleep cycle, so you should have checked this item.

D. *We spend over half of our sleep time in REM sleep.*
The graph of "Stages of Sleep" shows that we spend about two hours in REM sleep, so you should not have checked item D.

E. *For the most part, we stay in one stage of sleep during the sleep cycle.*
The "Stages of Sleep" graph shows that we move back and forth between four stages of sleep during our sleep cycle, so you should not have checked this item.

F. *It takes less than an hour to reach the deepest level of sleep.*
The "Stages of Sleep" graph shows that we can descend to the deepest level of sleep within a half hour or so. You should have checked item F.

PRACTICE 5

Read the table on the next page, following the steps on pages 242–243. Then check (✓) the **three** inferences that are most logically based on the table.

Occupations with the Largest Projected Employment Growth, 2010–2020

OCCUPATION	PERCENTAGE INCREASE	TYPICAL EDUCATION FOR ENTRY
Personal care aides	71%	Less than high school
Home health aides	69%	Less than high school
Medical Secretaries	41%	High school diploma or GED
Medical Assistants	31%	High school diploma or GED
Registered nurses	26%	Associates Degree
Receptionists and information clerks	24%	High school diploma or GED
Physicians and surgeons	24%	Doctoral or professional degree
Licensed practical and vocational nurses	22%	Postsecondary non-degree
Construction laborers	21%	Less than high school
Truck drivers	21%	High school diploma or GED
Landscaping & groundskeeping workers	21%	Less than high school
Nursing aides, orderlies, & attendants	20%	Postsecondary non-degree
Childcare workers	20%	High school diploma or GED
Carpenters	20%	High school diploma or GED
Security guards	19%	High school diploma or GED
Office clerks, general	17%	High school diploma or GED
Elementary school teachers	17%	Bachelor's degree
Postsecondary teachers	17%	Doctoral or professional degree
Retail salespersons	17%	Less than high school
Sales representatives, wholesale & manufacturing	16%	High school diploma or GED
Customer service representatives	16%	High school diploma or GED
Accountants & auditors	16%	Bachelor's degree
Teacher assistants	15%	High school diploma or GED
Food service workers	15%	Less than high school
Freight, stock and materials movers	15%	Less than high school
First-line office supervisors	14%	High school diploma or GED
Bookkeeping, accounting clerks	14%	High school diploma or GED
Janitors and cleaners, except maids	11%	Less than high school
Waiters and waitresses	9%	Less than high school
Cashiers	7%	Less than high school

Source: U.S. Department of Labor, 2012

_____ A. Most occupations with the largest projected growth in the next few years will require a college degree.

_✗_ B. Healthcare jobs will be abundant in the next few years.

_✗_ C. In coming years, students with high school diplomas will qualify for more jobs than high school dropouts.

_____ D. There will be few job opportunities in the years ahead in the education and sales areas.

_____ E. There will be fewer construction projects started in 2010–2020 than there were in 2000–2010.

_✗_ F. In the years ahead, more people than ever will choose to receive health care services in their homes.

CHAPTER REVIEW

In this chapter, you learned the following:

● Many important ideas in reading are not stated directly, but must be inferred. To make inferences about implied ideas, use the information provided as well as your own experience and logic.

● Inferences are also a key part of reading literature and such visual materials as cartoons, tables, and graphs.

The next chapter—Chapter 7—will help make you aware of an author's purpose and tone.

On the Web: If you are using this book in class, you can go to our website for more practice in making inferences. Visit our Learning Center at **www.townsendpress.net** for additional activities and an instructional video on this skill.

REVIEW TEST 1

To review what you've learned in this chapter, answer each of the following questions by filling in the blank or writing the letter of the correct answer.

1. We make inferences by "reading between the lines" and picking up ideas that are not directly _____stated_____ in what we are reading.

2. A reader must make _____inferences_____ when determining the meaning of words through context and when deciding on implied main ideas.

_____D_____ 3. To make sound inferences, we must use
   A. all the information provided by the writer.
   B. our own experience.
   C. logic.
   D. all of the above.

4. Creative writers often use comparisons to suggest what they mean. _____Similes_____ are direct comparisons introduced with *like* or *as* or *as if*, and metaphors are implied comparisons with *like* or *as* or *as if* omitted.

5. In textbooks we must often ____infer____ the ideas presented in graphs and tables.

REVIEW TEST 2

The essay below is followed by questions on inferences and also on the skills you have practiced in previous chapters.

Preview

Why are women so very critical of the way they look? And why are men so very . . . not? Humorist Dave Barry explores this difference between the sexes in a way that ties together supermodels, lawn care, and a well-known plastic doll.

Words to Watch

bloat (4): swell
regimen (5): process
mutation (8): an organism resulting from a DNA change
bolster (9): make stronger

THE UGLY TRUTH ABOUT BEAUTY

Dave Barry

1   If you're a man, at some point a woman will ask how she looks.

2   "How do I look?" she'll ask.

3   You must be careful how you answer this question. The best technique is to form an honest yet sensitive opinion, then collapse on the floor with some kind of fatal seizure. Trust me, this is the easiest way out. Because you will never come up with the right answer.

4   The problem is that women generally do not think of their looks in the same way that men do. Most men form an opinion of how they look in the seventh grade, and they stick to it for the rest of their lives. Some men form the opinion that they are irresistible stud muffins, and they do not change this opinion even when their faces sag and their noses bloat° to the size of eggplants and their eyebrows grow together to form what appears to be a giant forehead-dwelling tropical caterpillar.

5   Most men, I believe, think of themselves as average-looking. Men will

think this even if their faces cause heart failure in cattle at a range of 300 yards. Being average does not bother them; average is fine, for men. This is why men never ask anybody how they look. Their primary form of beauty care is to shave themselves, which is essentially the same form of beauty care that they give to their lawns. If, at the end of his four-minute daily beauty regimen°, a man has managed to wipe most of the shaving cream out of his hair and is not bleeding too badly, he feels that he has done all he can, so he stops thinking about his appearance and devotes his mind to more critical issues, such as the Super Bowl.

6   Women do not look at themselves in this way. If I had to express, in three words, what I believe most women think about their appearance, those words would be: "not good enough." No matter how attractive a woman may appear to be to others, when she looks at herself in the mirror, she thinks: woof. She thinks that at any moment a municipal animal-control officer is going to throw a net over her and haul her off to the shelter.

7   Why do women have such low self-esteem? There are many complex psychological and societal reasons, by which I mean Barbie. Girls grow up playing with a doll proportioned such that, if it were human, it would be seven feet tall and weigh 81 pounds, of which 53 pounds would be bosoms. This is a difficult appearance standard to live up to, especially when you contrast it with the standard set for little boys by their

dolls . . . excuse me, by their action figures. Most of the action figures that my son played with when he was little were hideous-looking. For example, he was very fond of an action figure (part of the He-Man series) called "Buzz-Off," who was part human, part flying insect. Buzz-Off was not a looker. But he was extremely self-confident. You could not imagine Buzz-Off saying to the other action figures: "Do you think these wings make my hips look big?"

8   But women grow up thinking they need to look like Barbie, which for most women is impossible, although there is a multibillion-dollar beauty industry devoted to convincing women that they must try. I once saw an Oprah show wherein supermodel Cindy

Crawford dispensed makeup tips to the studio audience. Cindy had all these middle-aged women applying beauty products to their faces; she stressed how important it was to apply them in a certain way, using the tips of their fingers. All the women dutifully did this, even though it was obvious to any sane observer that, no matter how carefully they applied these products, they would never look remotely like Cindy Crawford, who is some kind of genetic mutation°.

9   I'm not saying that men are superior. I'm just saying that you're not going to get a group of middle-aged men to sit in a room and apply cosmetics to themselves under the instruction of Brad Pitt, in hopes of looking more like him. Men would realize that this task was pointless and demeaning. They would find some way to bolster° their self-esteem that did not require looking like Brad Pitt. They would say to Brad: "Oh *yeah*? Well, what do you know about *lawn care*, pretty boy?"

10   Of course many women will argue that the reason they become obsessed with trying to look like Cindy Crawford is that men, being as shallow as a drop of spit, *want* women to look that way. To which I have two responses:

11   1. Hey, just because *we're* idiots, that does not mean *you* have to be; and

12   2. Men don't even notice 97 percent of the beauty efforts you make anyway. Take fingernails. The average woman spends 5,000 hours per year worrying about her fingernails; I have never once, in more than 40 years of listening to men talk about women, heard a man say, "She has a nice set of fingernails!" Many men would not notice if a woman had upward of four hands.

13   Anyway, to get back to my original point: If you're a man, and a woman asks you how she looks, you're in big trouble. Obviously, you can't say she looks bad. But you also can't say that she looks great, because she'll think you're lying, because she has spent countless hours, with the help of the multi-billion-dollar beauty industry, obsessing about the differences between herself and Cindy Crawford. Also, she suspects that you're not qualified to judge anybody's appearance. This is because you have shaving cream in your hair.

Reading Comprehension Questions

Vocabulary in Context

_____ 1. In the excerpt below, the word *demeaning* (dǐ-mēn'ǐng) means
   A. insulting.
   B. difficult.
   C. strange.
   D. disgusting.

> "I'm just saying that you're not going to get a group of middle-aged men to sit in a room and apply cosmetics to themselves under the instruction of Brad Pitt, in hopes of looking more like him. Men would realize that this task was pointless and demeaning." (Paragraph 9)

Central Point and Main Ideas

_____ 2. Which sentence best expresses the implied central point of the selection?
   A. Women have been brought up to believe that they should look like real-life Barbie dolls, even though this is impossible.
   B. In our society, women tend to have lower self-esteem than men.
   C. Because of the way they have been brought up, most women spend far more time worrying about their appearance than men do.
   D. It is impossible for men to tell women the truth about how they look because women will not believe them.

_____ 3. The implied main idea of paragraphs 8 and 9 is that
   A. middle-aged women who try to look like Cindy Crawford are foolish.
   B. men have more important things to do than to compare themselves to Brad Pitt.
   C. the beauty industry convinces many women that they should try to look like Cindy Crawford, an impossible task.
   D. in contrast to women, men have not been led to believe that their looks are the most important thing about them.

Supporting Details

_____ 4. The author's son played with an action figure that was
   A. attractive and self-confident.
   B. hideous-looking but self-confident.
   C. neither attractive nor self-confident.
   D. worried about the size of his hips.

_D_ 5. One thing the author has never heard a man say is
   A. "I'm shallow as a drop of spit."
   B. "Honey, you look bad."
   C. "Honey, you look great."
   D. "She has a nice set of fingernails."

Transitions

_B_ 6. The relationship of the second sentence below to the first sentence is one of
   A. addition.
   B. cause and effect.
   C. time.
   D. comparison.

> "Why do women have such low self-esteem? There are many complex psychological reasons, by which I mean Barbie." (Paragraph 7)

Patterns of Organization

_C_ 7. The selection mainly
   A. defines and illustrates related terms.
   B. narrates a series of events in time order.
   C. compares and contrasts women's attitudes toward their physical appearance with men's.
   D. lists a variety of strategies that women and men can use to change their attitudes toward physical appearance.

Inferences

_C_ 8. We can infer from paragraph 5 that the author believes that
   A. most men are ugly, not average-looking.
   B. most men are afraid to ask people how they really look.
   C. most men don't spend much time grooming themselves or thinking about the way they look.
   D. the Super Bowl is a critical issue.

_D_ 9. On the basis of paragraph 6, we can infer that the author believes that
   A. most women have an unrealistically negative view of their own appearance.
   B. most women waste time in front of mirrors because they're spoiled and lazy.
   C. many women become uncontrollably angry when they see themselves in a mirror.
   D. it is impossible for a woman to ever be pleased with her appearance.

_____ 10. We can conclude from the last two paragraphs that many women

    A. overestimate the amount of attention men pay to women's appearances.

    B. dislike men because they care so little about their own appearance.

    C. are annoyed that the beauty industry forces them to spend countless hours worrying about their appearance.

    D. believe that men with shaving cream in their hair are big trouble.

Discussion Questions

1. Although Barry's piece is written for laughs, he obviously has something serious to say about women and men and their feelings about their appearances. In non-humorous language, how would you rephrase his main points?

2. Think about the women you know. How much time would you say that they devote to clothing, hairstyles, and makeup? On the basis of your answer, do you agree with the author's view that women spend far too much time worrying about how they look? Why or why not?

3. Do you agree or disagree with the author's negative view of the role Barbie dolls play in shaping American girls' image of themselves? Once the girls have grown up, to what extent would you say that external forces, such as the media and the fashion industry, influence their feelings about their own appearances? Explain your reasoning.

4. Do you agree with Barry that men are generally satisfied with their own appearance? Why might their standards be so different from those of women?

Note: Writing assignments for this selection appear on page 637.

Check Your Performance   INFERENCES

Activity	Number Right	Points	Score
Review Test 1 (5 items)	_____	× 6 =	_____
Review Test 2 (10 items)	_____	× 7 =	_____
		TOTAL SCORE =	_____%

Enter your total score into the **Reading Performance Chart: Review Tests** on the inside back cover.

INFERENCES: Mastery Test 1

For each item, put a check (✓) by the **two** inferences most logically based on the information provided.

1. "Success is to be measured not so much by the position that one has reached in life as by the obstacles which he has overcome." —Booker T. Washington

    ____ A. The author considers himself to be a hero.

    ____ B. People can achieve success even if they were born with few, if any, social and economic advantages.

    ____ C. The author is telling us that we should naturally respect the son of a millionaire.

    ____ D. The author does not necessarily admire all successful men.

2. "Our only hope will lie in the frail web of understanding of one person for the pain of another." —John Dos Passos

    ____ A. If we don't learn to better understand each other, we may all be doomed.

    ____ B. Some people are very skillful in hiding their personal pain from others.

    ____ C. It is impossible to comprehend the pain of others.

    ____ D. Everyone needs empathy—the ability to walk in another's shoes.

3. "You must be the change you wish to see in the world." —Mahatma Gandhi

    ____ A. People should lead by setting a good example for others to follow.

    ____ B. Before you can make the world a better place, you must first conquer your own inner demons.

    ____ C. Don't criticize others until you have first attained perfection.

    ____ D. It's harder to change the world than it is to change yourself.

4. "I have decided to stick with love. Hate is too great a burden to bear." —Martin Luther King, Jr.

    ____ A. Martin Luther King, Jr., was tempted to hate his adversaries, but realized that harboring such an emotion would only hurt himself.

    ____ B. Only very strong people can successfully carry the burden of hate.

    ____ C. It takes a strong person to hate someone else.

    ____ D. Hate is a waste of time and energy.

(Continues on next page)

5. "The heart of another is a dark forest, always, no matter how close it has been to one's own." —Willa Cather

____ A. People can never really completely know each other.

____ B. People who have been close friends often become enemies.

____ C. Even the most intimate friends may keep secrets from one another.

____ D. Some people like to keep others in the dark in order to trick them.

INFERENCES: Mastery Test 2

A. (1–4.) Put a check (✓) by the **four** inferences that are most logically based on the details in the cartoon.

_____ A. Something is the matter with the man's remote control.

_____ B. The man thinks his bookshelf is a TV set.

_____ C. The man no longer recognizes books when he sees them.

_____ D. The man is angry because he doesn't have a new book to read.

_____ E. The man in the cartoon is not an American.

_____ F. The man believes that his remote control is not working properly.

_____ G. The man does not own a TV set.

_____ H. The cartoonist believes that watching TV makes people less literate.

B. Read the passages below. Then check the **two** inferences that are most logically supported in each passage.

5–6. [1]Shortly before takeoff, a flight attendant approached boxing legend Muhammad Ali and asked him to fasten his seat belt. [2]Ali gave her his famous smile and said, "Superman don't need no seat belt."

[3]"That may be," said the flight attendant. [4]"But Superman don't need no airplane, either."

_____ A. Ali was a modest man.

_____ B. Ali assumed the flight attendant knew who he was.

_____ C. The flight attendant wasn't going to give a famous passenger special privileges.

_____ D. Ali never did fasten his seat belt.

(Continues on next page)

7–8. ¹Group A of college students was asked to chaperone delinquent juveniles on a field trip to the zoo. ²Only 32 percent said yes. ³Group B of college students was asked to commit to two years' service as volunteer counselors to delinquent children. ⁴All said no. ⁵But when that request was immediately followed up by a request to chaperone the zoo field trip, 56 percent of Group B said yes.

____ A. It is good strategy to ask first for more than you really hope to receive.

____ B. College students in general do not feel any obligation to help others.

____ C. The college students would probably have agreed to volunteer for two years with elderly people.

____ D. A promise to volunteer for two years is a big commitment.

9–10. ¹Personal distress means our own emotional reactions to the plight of others—our feelings of shock, horror, alarm, concern, or helplessness. ²Personal distress occurs when people who witness an event are preoccupied with their own emotional reactions. ³In contrast, empathy means feelings of sympathy and caring for others, in particular, sharing vicariously or indirectly in the suffering of others. ⁴Empathy occurs when the observer focuses on the needs and emotions of the victim. ⁵Personal distress leads us to feel anxious and apprehensive; empathy leads us to feel sympathetic and compassionate. ⁶Research suggests that the distinctive emotions generated by personal distress and empathy may actually be accompanied by distinctive physiological reactions, including heart rate patterns and facial expressions.

____ A. People who experience personal distress in response to the plight of others are less likely to take constructive action than people who feel empathy.

____ B. People who experience personal distress in response to the plight of others will respond in roughly the same way as people who feel empathy.

____ C. The author suggests that feelings of personal distress are more realistic than feelings of empathy.

____ D. The author suggests that empathy is a more positive emotion than personal distress.

INFERENCES: Mastery Test 3

A. (1–4.) Put a check (✓) by the **four** inferences that are most logically based on the details in the cartoon.

© Randy Glasbergen.
www.glasbergen.com

GLASBERGEN

"What fits your busy schedule better, exercising
one hour a day or being dead 24 hours a day?"

____ A. The patient has claimed he is too busy to exercise.

____ B. The patient has an incurable illness.

____ C. The patient will take the doctor's advice and begin exercising.

____ D. The doctor believes the patient needs to exercise more.

____ E. The patient is angry at the doctor.

____ F. Currently, the patient exercises more than an hour a day.

____ G. The doctor has just examined the patient.

____ H. Exercise can help people live longer.

(Continues on next page)

B. (5–10.) Read the passage below from J.R. Moehringer's acclaimed memoir *The Tender Bar*. Then check the **six** statements after the passage which are most logically supported by the information given.

> ¹Mom said that "Grandpa is a real-life Scrooge, and not just with money." ²Grandpa hoarded love, my mother said, as if he were afraid of one day running out. ³He'd ignored her and her sister and brother while they were growing up, giving them no attention or affection whatsoever. ⁴She described one family outing at the beach when she was five. ⁵Seeing how sweetly the father of her cousin played with his children, my mother asked Grandpa to put her on his shoulders in the ocean. ⁶He did, but then carried her past the waves, and when they were out far, when she could barely see the shore, she became frightened and pleaded with him to let her down. ⁷So he threw her. ⁸Down she went, plunging to the bottom, gulping seawater. ⁹She fought her way to the surface, gasped for air, and saw Grandpa—laughing. ¹⁰"You wanted to be let down," he told her, oblivious to her tears. ¹¹Staggering out of the surf, alone, my mother had a precocious epiphany: Her father was not a good man. ¹²In that realization, she told me, came a release. ¹³She felt independent. ¹⁴I asked her what "independent" meant. ¹⁵"Free," she said.

____ A. Mom envied her cousins' personal relationship with their father.

____ B. Grandpa preferred his son to either of his daughters.

____ C. Mom's family never went to the beach again.

____ D. Grandpa was stingy with his money as well as his love.

____ E. Mom wanted her father to love her.

____ F. After dropping his daughter in the water, Grandpa felt ashamed.

____ G. Grandpa didn't help Mom get back to shore.

____ H. Grandpa knew that dropping his daughter would frighten her badly.

____ I. After the incident at the shore, Mom no longer expected Grandpa to be a good father.

____ J. Mom was depressed to realize that her father was not a good man.

INFERENCES: Mastery Test 4

A. Identify the figure(s) of speech in each sentence as either a simile or a metaphor. Then answer each inference question that follows.

B 1. In *The Divine Comedy,* Dante writes that at midlife he found himself "in a dark wood with no clear path through."

   A. simile   B. metaphor

B 2. You can infer that Dante
   A. has been in this spot before.
   B. is hopeful despite doubts.
   C. is bewildered.

A 3. A woman without a man is like a fish without a bicycle.

   A. simile   B. metaphor

A 4. You can infer that a woman
   A. cannot function without a man.
   B. does not need a man to function.
   C. cannot ride a bicycle without a man.

B 5. The accident at the chemical plant released a witch's brew into the atmosphere.

   A. simile   B. metaphor

C 6. You can infer that the chemical company
   A. will quickly explain the cause of the accident.
   B. deliberately planned to get rid of some chemicals.
   C. released a mix of harmful chemicals into the atmosphere.

B. Read the textbook passages below. Then check (✓) the **two** statements after the passage which are most logically supported by the information given.

7–8. ¹Two recent series of studies indicate that the adolescent's biological and cognitive maturation may play a role in unbalancing the family system during early adolescence. ²Several researchers have demonstrated that family relationships change during puberty, with conflict between adolescents and their parents increasing—especially between adolescents and their mothers— and closeness between adolescents and their parents diminishing somewhat. ³Although puberty seems to distance adolescents from their parents, it is not associated with familial "storm and stress." ⁴The conflict is more likely to take the form of bickering over day-to-day issues like household chores than outright fighting. ⁵Similarly, the diminished closeness is more likely to be manifested in

(Continues on next page)

increased privacy on the part of the adolescent and diminished physical affection between teenagers and parents, rather than any serious loss of love or respect between parents and children.

_____ A. Fathers may not notice much change in their relationships with their adolescent children.

_____ B. During adolescence, girls are more likely than boys to bicker with their mothers.

_____ C. Adolescence is a normal but sometimes trying period.

_____ D. Adolescence is the most difficult period of life.

9–10. ¹In the late 1800s and early 1900s, new technologies led to momentous changes in home life. ²Advanced systems of central heating (furnaces), artificial lighting, and modern indoor plumbing resulted in a new kind of consumption, first for middle-class households and later for most others. ³Whereas formerly families bought coal or chopped wood for cooking and heating, made candles for light, and hauled water for bathing, they increasingly connected to outside pipes and wires for gas, electricity, and water. ⁴Moreover, these utilities helped create new attitudes about privacy. ⁵Middle-class bedrooms and bathrooms became comfortable private retreats. ⁶Even children could have their own bedrooms, complete with individualized decoration. ⁷Also, though not affordable for the poor, central heat and artificial light made it possible for the middle class to enjoy a steady, comfortable temperature and turn night into day, while indoor plumbing removed the unpleasant experiences of the outhouse.

_____ A. In the late 1800s and early 1900s, new technologies created unbridgeable gaps between the middle class and the poor.

_____ B. In the late 1800s and early 1900s, new technologies helped reduce the amount of labor associated with housekeeping.

_____ C. The poor were angry that they could not enjoy the new technologies available to the middle class.

_____ D. In the early 1800s, people didn't have as much access to privacy as they would later have.

INFERENCES: Mastery Test 5

A. (1–5.) Read the passage below. Then check the **five** statements after the passage which are most logically supported by the information given.

[1]None of us escapes the changes that the years bring. [2]Lines deepen, jowls sag, chins seem to melt, eyelids droop. [3]We may not greet these changes with joy, but until recent years, we learned to live with them. [4]More than live with them, in fact; many of us learned to cherish the changes that time wrought on the faces of those we loved. [5]A spouse's laugh lines or a parent's furrowed brow became dear to us, as visible signs of the person's evolving inner being. [6]But that is changing. [7]The increasing popularity of cosmetic surgery—ever more drastic and at ever-younger ages—is turning us into a nation of smooth-faced ciphers: personality-challenged masks with unlined brows and wide, surprised eyes. [8]Instead of admiring their elders as models of graceful aging, youngsters today see their grandparents getting nipped and tucked in a never-ending—and unwinnable—battle against nature. [9]Ordinary people are increasingly following the leads of youth-obsessed celebrities, who have been desperately fighting the anti-aging battle for decades. [10]It is to the point where it is surprising to find some brave Hollywood soul who is willing to look his or her years. [11]When an icon like Robert Redford, long admired for allowing his handsome face to grow more craggy and weather-beaten, showed up in public with a shiny new facelift, many hearts sank. [12]Who will stand up for the beauty that comes with age?

_____ A. Signs of aging give people's faces a beauty and dignity which surgically altered faces lack.

_✗_ B. Plastic surgeons now mostly market themselves to the very young.

_____ C. People today celebrate appearance over emotional maturity.

_✗_ D. Our society has an unrealistic obsession with appearing youthful.

_____ E. People no longer treat senior citizens with love and respect.

_____ F. In sharp contrast to his on-screen image, Robert Redford is actually a coward.

_✗_ G. People often appreciate signs of aging in others' faces more than in their own.

_____ H. Robert Redford has found it hard to get movie roles as he has grown older.

_____ I. The writer previously admired Robert Redford more than she does now.

_____ J. Young people today often encourage their elders to get cosmetic surgery.

(Continues on next page)

B. (6–10.) Read the passage below from Frank McCourt's acclaimed memoir *Teacher Man*. Then check the **five** statements after the passage which are most logically supported by the information given.

> ¹Phyllis wrote an account of how her family gathered the night Neil Armstrong landed on the moon, how they shuttled between the living room television and the bedroom where her father lay dying. ²Back and forth. ³Concerned with the father, not wanting to miss the moon landing. ⁴Phyllis said she was with her father when her mother called to come and see Armstrong set foot on the moon. ⁵She ran to the living room, everyone cheering and hugging till she felt this urgency, the old urgency, and ran to the bedroom to find her father dead. ⁶She didn't scream, she didn't cry, and her problem was how to return to the happy people in the living room to tell them Dad was gone.
>
> ⁷She cried now, standing in front of the classroom. ⁸She could have stepped back to her seat in the front row, and I hoped she would because I didn't know what to do. ⁹I went to her. ¹⁰I put my left arm around her. ¹¹But that wasn't enough. ¹²I pulled her to me, embraced her with both arms, let her sob into my shoulder. ¹³Faces around the room were wet with tears till someone called, Right on, Phyllis, and one or two clapped and the whole class clapped and cheered and Phyllis turned to smile at them with her wet face and when I led her to her seat she turned and touched my cheek and I thought, This isn't earthshaking, this touch on the cheek, but I'll never forget it: Phyllis, her dead father, Armstrong on the moon.

_____ A. McCourt was teaching a course that involved writing.

__X__ B. Phyllis did not want to spoil her family's joy at the moon landing.

_____ C. Phyllis's fellow students thought she should have told her family immediately that her dad was dead.

_____ D. Phyllis regretted that she wasn't in the bedroom with her dad when he died, but knew that she wasn't really at fault.

_____ E. Phyllis will continue to feel guilty about missing her dad's death.

_____ F. Phyllis's family did not care about her father.

__X__ G. The events we tend to remember aren't necessarily earthshaking.

_____ H. McCourt should not have embraced a student.

_____ I. McCourt was probably not a very effective teacher.

__X__ J. To McCourt, Phyllis's story shows how life goes on in the midst of death.

INFERENCES: Mastery Test 6

A. (1–5.) Read the graph below. Then check the **five** statements that are most logically based on the graph.

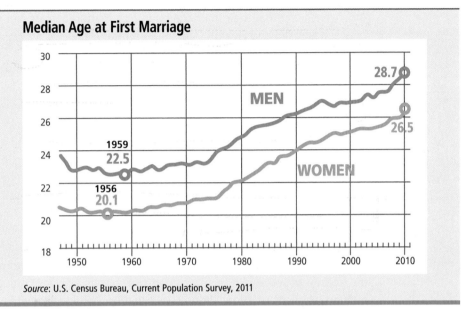

Median Age at First Marriage

1959 22.5

1956 20.1

28.7

26.5

MEN

WOMEN

Source: U.S. Census Bureau, Current Population Survey, 2011

_____ A. The median age for first marriage has been increasing gradually since the mid-1950s.

_X_ B. The median age for first marriage has been increasing gradually since the mid-1960s.

_X_ C. Overall, the median age for first marriage rose steadily from 1960 to 2010.

_____ D. The median age for first marriage has risen with dramatic quickness over the years.

_X_ E. In the period shown, men have always married at an older age than women.

_X_ F. In the 1950s, women married at an age more than five years younger than they did sixty years later.

_____ G. In the 1950s, women married at an age almost ten years younger than they did sixty years later.

_____ H. Based on the graph, there is probably more pressure for young people to marry now than there was over sixty years ago.

_____ I. Based on the graph, remaining single has become a more acceptable lifestyle.

_X_ J. Based on the trends shown, women and men will probably marry at about the same age within the next decade.

(Continues on next page)

B. (6–10.) Read the following textbook passage. Then check the **five** statements after the passage which are most logically supported by the information given.

[A4]

[1]Not the least of President Franklin Roosevelt's assets was his remarkable wife, Eleanor. [2]Only much later, in the age of anything-goes journalism, did Americans learn that their marriage had been shattered years earlier by an affair between Franklin and Eleanor's personal secretary. [3]Eleanor offered a divorce, but Franklin asked that she stay with him. [4]A divorce would have ended Roosevelt's political career short of the presidency. [5]Not until 1952 did a divorced man run for the presidency, unsuccessfully; not until 1980 was one elected. [6]Divorce would also have denied Roosevelt the services of his one aide who may be called indispensable. [7]Eleanor was thought of by friend and foe alike as the president's alter ego. [8]She was his legs, for Roosevelt was paralyzed from the waist down by polio, unable to walk more than a few steps in heavy, painful steel leg braces. [9]Eleanor was a locomotive. [10]With no taste for serving tea and greeting Boy Scouts visiting the White House, she raced around the country, picking through squalid tenements, wading in the mud in Appalachian hollows, and descending into murky coal mines to see how the other half made do. [11]Whereas Franklin was cool, detached, calculating, and manipulative, Eleanor was compassionate, deeply moved by the misery and injustices suffered by the "forgotten" people at the bottom of society. [12]She interceded with her husband to appoint women to high government positions. [13]She supported organized labor when Franklin had to straddle a politically difficult decision. [14]She made the grievances of Americans her particular interest and persuaded her husband to name blacks to high government posts. [15]Much of the affection that came to Franklin in the form of votes was earned by "that woman in the White House."

_X_ A. At the time, few Americans were aware of Franklin and Eleanor's marital problems.

___ B. The press during the Roosevelts' era reported extensively on Franklin's romantic adventures.

___ C. Franklin Roosevelt's affair hurt his chance to become president.

___ D. Attitudes toward divorce have changed significantly since the days of Eleanor and Franklin Roosevelt.

_X_ E. Eleanor Roosevelt believed in gaining firsthand information about the problems of people at the bottom of society.

___ F. Eleanor Roosevelt's activism harmed her husband's election chances.

_X_ G. Eleanor Roosevelt was not very domestic, but she was very involved in national concerns.

_X_ H. Eleanor Roosevelt was in most ways a very traditional First Lady.

___ I. The author of this passage disapproved of Eleanor Roosevelt's activism.

_X_ J. Eleanor Roosevelt's decision to stay with her husband, Franklin, affected the course of American history.

7 Purpose and Tone

tone: authors opinion or attitude about the topic

purpose:

Newspaper photos often have a purpose and tone. The purpose of the photo above, for example, is to inform us of the return of American soldiers killed in the service of their country; the tone is one of solemnity, reverence, and respect. And behind what you read, there are often a purpose and tone as well. Consider that what you read has been written by a person with thoughts, feelings, and opinions. Whether this author is a sportswriter, a newspaper columnist, a novelist, or a friend sending you a letter, he or she works from a personal point of view. That point of view is reflected in (1) the purpose of a piece of writing as well as (2) its tone—the expression of the author's attitude and feeling.

Both purpose and tone are discussed in this chapter.

Purpose

Authors write with a reason in mind, and you can better evaluate their ideas by determining what that reason is. The author's reason for writing is also called the **purpose** of a selection. Three common purposes are as follows:

Objective tone

- To **inform**—to give information about a subject. Authors with this purpose wish to provide facts that will explain or teach something to readers.

  For example, the main idea of an informative paragraph about bosses might be "Bosses have different styles of supervising." The author may then go on to describe an authoritarian boss whose word is law, contrasted with a more democratic boss who welcomes employees' input.

Subjective tone

- To **persuade**—to convince the reader to agree with the author's point of view on a subject. Authors with this purpose may present facts, but their main goal is to argue or prove a point to readers.

  The main idea of a persuasive passage about bosses might read "Bosses should listen to their employees but take ultimate responsibility for making decisions." The author might then go on to support the point with details about problems that result from indecisive bosses.

  Note that words like *should*, *ought*, and *must* are often meant to convince us rather than to inform us.

Subjective tone

- To **entertain**—to amuse and delight; to appeal to the reader's senses and imagination. Authors with this purpose entertain in various ways, through fiction as well as nonfiction.

  The main idea of a humorous paragraph about bosses might be "My boss is so dumb that he once returned a necktie because it was too tight."

While the cover and title of anything you read—books, articles, and so on—don't necessarily suggest the author's main purpose, often they do. Here are the covers of three books. See if you can guess the primary purpose of each of these books.

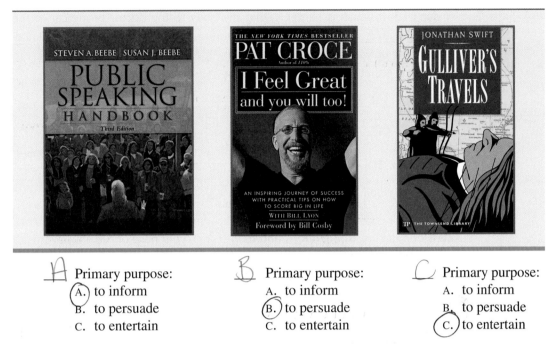

A Primary purpose:
  A. to inform
  B. to persuade
  C. to entertain

B Primary purpose:
  A. to inform
  B. to persuade
  C. to entertain

C Primary purpose:
  A. to inform
  B. to persuade
  C. to entertain

As you probably concluded, the main purpose of the public speaking textbook is to inform; the main purpose of *I Feel Great and You Will Too!* is to persuade; and the main purpose of the timeless story *Gulliver's Travels,* by Jonathan Swift, is to entertain.

✓ Check Your Understanding

Read each of the three paragraphs below and decide whether the author's main purpose is to inform, to persuade, or to entertain. Write in your answers, and then read the explanation that follows.

1. [1]The typical American gobbles three burgers and four orders of fries every week. [2]Toss in the pizzas, the popcorn, the sugary breakfast cereals, the sodas, the snack cakes, candy bars, ice cream and everything else we eat in lieu of real food in this society, and your body is like an eighteen-wheeler roaring down a high-fat highway straight to obesity and an early grave. [3]Fast food is bad food. [4]It's loaded with bad stuff like fat and sugar and sodium. [5]It's packed with chemicals that are in there to make it taste and smell and feel like it's real food. [6]What it lacks is vitamins, minerals, fiber, all the stuff you really need.

    Purpose: persuade

2.   ¹I don't know which is harder, taking my body to the doctor or my car to the garage. ²Both worry me. ³I'm always afraid they'll find something I didn't know about. ⁴The only advantage of taking my body to the doctor over taking my car to the garage is that the doctor never asks me to leave it overnight.

Purpose: ___entertain___

3.   ¹Personal contact is necessary for common cold viruses to spread. ²The viruses must get into the nose, where they can infect the nasal membranes. ³Inhaling contaminated droplets produced when someone else coughs or sneezes may be one way to catch a cold. ⁴Cold viruses can remain infective even if they are outside the body for a few hours. ⁵Therefore, you can also catch a cold if you handle something that is contaminated with a cold virus—for example, the doorknob of a classroom or a restroom door—and then scratch your nose or rub your eyes with your contaminated fingers. ⁶The cold viruses can reach your nose when you rub your eyes because the virus can be passed down the tear ducts that go from the eyes into the nasal cavities.

Purpose: ___inform___

Explanation

In the first paragraph, the writer's purpose is to *persuade* readers that Americans should not indulge in fast food. The purpose of the second paragraph is to *entertain* with its playful and exaggerated details (clearly, the doctor is not going to ask the writer to leave his body overnight). The purpose of the third paragraph is to *inform* readers about how cold viruses spread.

Note: At times, writing may blend two or even three purposes. A persuasive article on the importance of avoiding junk foods, for example, might include a good many facts and even some comic touches. Remember in such cases to focus on the author's primary purpose. Ask yourself, "What is the author's main idea?"

PRACTICE 1

Label each item according to its main purpose: to inform (**I**), to persuade (**P**), or to entertain (**E**).

Obv __I__ 1. The average American household carries $15,799 in credit-card debt.

Sub __P__ 2. High schools should require students to take a course in money management.

Obj / I   3. The pigeon is one of the few birds that drinks by suction, rather than by tipping its head back to let gravity do the work.

Sub / E   4. My doctor told me he had good news and bad news. I said, "Doc, only tell me the good news, all right?" He said, "All right. They're going to name a new disease after you."

Obj / I   5. The writer Edgar Allan Poe married his first cousin, Virginia, when she was only 13.

Sub / P   6. The taboo against marriage between cousins is outdated and should be discarded.

Sub / E   7. Cleaning the house is such a waste of time; a year later, you just have to do it again.

Obj / I   8. Lips often feel chapped and dry because they are protected only by a very thin layer of skin that contains no oil glands.

Sub / P   9. It would be better for students to attend small schools in their own neighborhoods, rather than being bused to large consolidated schools.

Sub / E   10. My dog sleeps on the couch all day while I commute for an hour to a job I hate in order to make money to buy dog food. And I think that *he's* the dumb animal?

PRACTICE 2

In the space provided, indicate whether the primary purpose of each passage is to inform (**I**), to inform *and* persuade (**I+P**), or to entertain (**E**).

I+P   1. [1]The Intrepid Fallen Heroes Fund provides assistance to our nation's military heroes—those who have been critically injured in the performance of duty—and their families. [2]Double and triple amputations, severe head or body trauma, blindness, deafness, and partial or full paralysis are just some of the injuries our heroes have to endure today and for the rest of their lives. [3]Many of our injured military personnel and veterans, who come from all branches of the armed forces, are treated at Brooke Army Medical Center in San Antonio, Texas. [4]The American people, our military constituents, and allies around the world are united in heart for the care and rehabilitation of these men and women, who have sacrificed and are still suffering so much for the freedoms we enjoy today. [5]Providing them with the best possible care is a small price to pay to say "thank you" for a job well done.

[6]This is why I would like to urge you to join this very special effort to help support those brave men and women by contributing to the Fund. [7]100% of your donation goes directly to building this vitally-needed rehabilitation center. [8]Browse our website at www.fallenheroesfund.org and join our effort in supporting our troops!

2. [1]War is a state of widespread conflict between states, organizations, or relatively large groups of people, which is characterized by the use of lethal violence between combatants or upon civilians. [2]Other terms for war, which often serve as euphemisms, include "armed conflict," "hostilities," and "police action." [3]War is contrasted with peace, which is usually defined as the absence of war.

[4]A common perception of war is as a series of military campaigns between at least two opposing sides involving a dispute over sovereignty, territory, resources, religion or a host of other issues. [5]A war to liberate an occupied country is sometimes characterized as a "war of liberation," while a war between internal elements of the same state may constitute a civil war.

3. [1]Only one ticket agent was on duty at the airline counter. [2]As a result, a long line formed, filled with inconvenienced travelers. [3]Suddenly, an irate passenger pushed his way to the front. [4]He threw his ticket down and said, "I *have* to be on this flight, and it has to be *first class.*"

[5]The agent replied, "Sir, I'll be happy to assist you, but I've got to help these folks first."

[6]The passenger was unimpressed. [7]Loudly, he demanded, "Do you have any idea who I am?"

[8]Without hesitating, the gate agent smiled and grabbed the public address microphone. [9]"May I have your attention, please?" she began, her voice sounding throughout the terminal. [10]"We have a passenger here *who does not know who he is.* [11]If anyone can help him find his identity, please come to Gate D2."

Tone

A writer's **tone** reveals the attitude that he or she has toward a subject. Tone is expressed through the words and details the writer selects. Just as a speaker's voice can project a range of feelings, a writer's voice can project one or more tones, or feelings: anger, sympathy, hopefulness, sadness, respect, dislike, and so on. Understanding tone is, then, an important part of understanding what an author has written.

To appreciate the differences in tone that writers can employ, read the following statements by students of a demanding teacher.

She hates students, that's all there is to it. I can't wait until I'm out of her class. (*Tone:* Bitter, angry)

She's tough, but she's also really good. I've learned more from her than I've learned from any other teacher. (*Tone:* Fair, objective)

Yeah, I love her. Just like I love sleeping on a bed of nails or having bamboo slivers pushed under my fingernails. (*Tone:* Sarcastic)

I might as well just stop going to class now. I'm never going to understand the material. It's hopeless. (*Tone:* Pessimistic)

I think if I talk to her and explain what I'm having trouble with, she can help me sort it out. I'm going to figure out a way to deal with this. (*Tone:* Optimistic)

Words That Describe Tone

Below and on the next two pages are two lists of words commonly used to describe tone. With the exception of the words *matter-of-fact* and *objective*, the words reflect a feeling or judgment. The words in the first list are more familiar ones. Brief meanings are given in parentheses for the words in the second list. Refer to these meanings as needed to learn any words you don't know yet.

Some Words That Describe Tone

accepting	cheerful	fearful	self-critical
admiring	conceited	forgiving	self-pitying
affectionate	concerned	frightened	serious
alarmed	critical	grateful	sorrowful
amused	cruel	humorous	sympathetic
angry	curious	insulting	threatening
apologetic	defensive	joyous	tragic
appreciative	determined	loving	warm
approving	disapproving	playful	worried
ashamed	doubtful	praising	
calming	encouraging	regretful	
caring	excited	respectful	

More Words That Describe Tone—With Their Meanings

ambivalent	*uncertain about a choice*
arrogant	*full of self-importance; conceited*
bewildered	*confused; puzzled*
bitter	*angry; full of hate*
compassionate	*deeply sympathetic*
cynical	*distrustful and disbelieving*
depressed	*very sad or discouraged*
despairing	*giving up hope*
detached	*emotionally uninvolved*
disbelieving	*unbelieving*
distressed	*suffering sorrow, misery, or pain*
hypocritical	*false*
impassioned	*filled with strong feeling*
indignant	*angry about something wrong, unfair, or mean*
informal	*casual and friendly*
instructive	*teaching*
ironic	*contrary to what is expected or intended*
lighthearted	*happy and carefree*
malicious	*intending to do harm*
matter-of-fact	*sticking to facts; unemotional*
mocking	*making fun of and/or looking down upon something*
nostalgic	*longing for something or someone in the past*
objective	*not influenced by feelings or personal prejudices*
optimistic	*looking on the bright side of things*
outraged	*fiercely angered and shocked*
pessimistic	*looking on the gloomy, unfavorable side of things*
pleading	*begging*
prideful	*full of pride or exaggerated self-esteem*
remorseful	*guilty over a wrong one has done*
revengeful	*wanting to hurt someone in return for an injury*
reverent	*showing deep respect*
sarcastic	*sharp or wounding; ironic*
scheming	*tricky*
scornful	*looking down on someone or something*
self-mocking	*making fun of or looking down on oneself*

(Continues on next page)

More Words That Describe Tone—With Their Meanings

sentimental	*showing tender feelings; romantic; overly emotional*
solemn	*involved with serious concerns*
straightforward	*direct and honest*
suggestive	*tending to suggest an idea*
superior	*looking down on others*
tolerant	*accepting and respectful of others' views and behavior; patient about problems*
uncertain	*doubting*

✔ Check Your Understanding

Below are five statements expressing five reactions to Wal-Mart moving into a town. Five different tones are used:

A. accepting	**B.** cynical	**C.** indignant
D. threatening	**E.** worried	

Label each statement according to which of these five tones you think is present. Then read the explanation that follows.

E 1. Wal-Mart may create an economic underclass in our town. Its employees aren't paid enough to live on, and they have very poor benefits.

A 2. Wal-Mart is a fact of life. It's going to hurt some people, but at least we'll be able to buy a lot of things at lower prices.

D 3. Wal-Mart had better not ever try to move into our town. They'll run into opposition like they've never seen before. We're not going to just lie down and let them take over.

B 4. Our local government says Wal-Mart will benefit everyone. That's a joke. Wal-Mart is mainly going to benefit itself and our local politicians.

C 5. Wal-Mart is run by a family of billionaire hypocrites who make huge profits by crushing little towns. They wave the flag about how great they are for America and then sell us stuff mostly made in China.

Explanation

The first item has a *worried* tone, as the writer suggests that Wal-Mart's low wages and benefits may have a negative economic effect on the town. In the second item, the writer's statement that "Wal-Mart is a fact of life" indicates *acceptance*, as does her effort to balance the negative aspects of Wal-Mart with the benefit of lower prices. The tone of the third item is *threatening* because of the writer's clearly stated intention to help block Wal-Mart's move. In the fourth item, the writer clearly does not believe local government's claim that Wal-Mart will benefit everyone; her comment "That's a joke" gives the item a *cynical* tone. In the fifth item, the writer is *outraged* and *indignant* at what she perceives as the uncaring greed and hypocrisy of Wal-Mart.

A Note on Irony and Sarcasm   Verbal

One commonly used tone is that of **irony**, which involves a contrast between expectations and reality. This contrast is often humorous. Both language and situations can be ironic.

Following are a few examples of **sarcasm**, an often biting form of verbal irony. Notice that the irony of each quotation lies in the contrast between what is said and what is actually meant.

- A telemarketer interrupts you in the middle of dinner. You say to him, "I'm so glad you've called. I hate eating dinner while it's still hot."

- A friend asks how you like your new boss. You reply, "He's great. It's refreshing working for someone who has half my IQ."

- You break up with your girlfriend, who becomes hysterical and slaps you. You say to yourself afterward, "I think she took that well."

- At a family reunion, an uncle becomes extremely drunk, starts insulting people, and then passes out. You remark, "I simply can't understand why people say he has a drinking problem."

- An instructor has an extremely cold, businesslike manner. You tell a classmate, "I really like the warmth and concern she shows her students."

As you can see, irony is a useful tone for humor and can be used to imply exactly the opposite of what is said or what is done.

Irony also refers to situations that involve a contrast between what is expected or intended and what actually happens. We could call it ironic, for example, if the arsonist responsible for a string of fires turned out to be a city firefighter, or if a bank were robbed by two guards that were hired to protect it. Here are a few more examples of this type of irony:

- While fastening his seat belt to keep himself safe, a man loses control of his car and crashes.

- A preacher who is fiercely critical of gays turns out to have a secret homosexual life.

- Ludwig van Beethoven, perhaps the greatest composer who ever lived, became totally deaf and could not hear his own music.

- Finally losing patience with her chronically unemployed husband, a woman files for divorce. The next week, the husband wins a multi-million-dollar lottery.

- Jerome Rodale, the father of the modern organic food movement, often bragged, "I'm going to live to be 100 unless I'm run down by a sugar-crazed taxi driver." Instead, he dropped dead at age 72 while appearing on a talk show.

The five examples above show that irony also describes meaningful situations that are contrary to what is intended or expected.

✓ *Check Your Understanding*

Explain the irony in the cartoon below.

Frank and Ernest

COMMUNICATION WORKSHOP
————————
SOMETIME TONIGHT IN A ROOM UPSTAIRS

THAVES

- The irony in the sign that a communication workshop will be "sometime tonight in a room upstairs" is that doesn't say when to work or where to go

Explanation

The irony is that the sign advertising the communication workshop fails to communicate just when and where the workshop will be.

PRACTICE 3

A. Below are five statements expressing different attitudes about eating. Five different tones are used:

> A. ambivalent   B. detached   C. humorous
> D. impassioned   E. superior

For each statement, write the letter of the tone that you think is present. Use each tone once.

_____ 1. Eating is just another chore. There should be a protein pill we could simply swallow every day and be done with it.

_____ 2. My husband's idea of a seven-course meal is a steak and a six-pack.

_____ 3. Too many things we eat poison our bodies! People must cut out junk food and empty carbs and white flour and sugar. Eating wisely can make all the difference to our health.

_____ 4. I love to eat, but I hate what food does to my body. After I eat something delicious, I think, "I didn't need that."

_____ 5. I don't understand why people make such a big deal about food. Just eat when you're hungry and don't eat when you aren't. What's so hard about that?

B. Following are five statements expressing different attitudes about exercise. Label each statement with the tone of voice that you think is present. Choose each tone from the following box, and use each tone only once.

> A. humorous   B. matter-of-fact   C. optimistic
> D. pessimistic   E. self-critical

_____ 6. Exercise is just something that is part of my daily routine. I get up in the morning, exercise, shower and shave, eat something, and head off for school. It's all pretty automatic for me.

_____ 7. What's the point of exercising and taking care of yourself? You're always hearing about people who live healthy lifestyles and just drop dead anyway.

_____ 8. I know I ought to exercise more. I just always find an excuse not to. I guess I don't have much self-discipline.

_____ 9. I hate exercise with all my heart. The only reason I do it is because it feels so good when I stop.

_____ 10. I've begun an exercise program that I know I can stick with. I think it's just a matter of weeks before I start seeing some really great results.

PRACTICE 4

Each passage on the pages that follow illustrates one of the tones in the box below. In each space, put the letter of the one tone that best applies. Use each letter only once. Three tones will be left over.

Remember that the tone of a selection reflects the author's attitude. To find the tone of a paragraph, ask yourself what attitude is revealed by its words and phrases.

A. amused	B. appreciative	C. despairing	D. instructive
E. optimistic	F. outraged	G. sentimental	H. sympathetic

_____ 1. ¹Some days I like to stop and think about all the small, wonderful things that grace my ordinary day-to-day existence. ²To begin with, I generally open my eyes to see the adoring face of my dog resting on the pillow beside me. ³No matter how sleep-rumpled, dragon-breathed, and swollen-eyed I am, he always greets with me a look that says, "Good morning, you beautiful thing!" ⁴Next, I swing my feet out of bed and into my soft, comfy sheepskin-lined slippers. ⁵Heaven! ⁶I wander sleepily into the bathroom, and there awaits something else I'm thankful for every day—unlimited hot water. ⁷As I splash it luxuriously over my face, I feel wakefulness, warmth and life beginning to return. ⁸From the bathroom I head to the kitchen, where I encounter the queen of all that is wondrous. ⁹I refer, of course, to coffee. ¹⁰The making of that first cup of the day—the measuring, the aroma, the sound of the dripping water, the anticipation, the taste—*ahhhhhh*. ¹¹Life is so good.

_____ 2. . . . Out, out, brief candle!
Life's but a walking shadow, a poor player
That struts and frets his hour upon the stage
And then is heard no more. It is a tale
Told by an idiot, full of sound and fury,
Signifying nothing.
        (From Shakespeare's *Macbeth*)

_____ 3. ¹While it's common to complain about work, being *without* work is a terrible thing. ²Work gives structure to our days and dignity to our lives. ³One of the first questions we ask new acquaintances is "What do you do?" meaning "What kind of *work* do you do?" ⁴Without work, we lack a very basic part of our identity. ⁵That's why it is so sad to consider the plight of people in this country who are deprived of the comfort and stability of a steady job. ⁶The reasons for their lack of employment are many. ⁷There may not be jobs available in their areas. ⁸Perhaps they cannot afford the transportation or childcare necessary to hold down a job. ⁹Often the jobs for which they are qualified do not pay a living wage. ¹⁰They may have grown up surrounded by beaten-down men and women who have taught them that holding a job is not possible. ¹¹In many cases they have attempted to find work, but the obstacles they had to climb over and their own self-doubt were too much to deal with. ¹²Slowly and steadily, a sense of defeat overwhelmed and poisoned them, leaving them without hope or direction. ¹³In their place, it is doubtful that any one of us would do better.

_____ 4. ¹In *The Catcher in the Rye,* Holden Caulfield yearns to protect children like his younger sister Phoebe. ²He tells Phoebe that when he hears the song about the catcher in the rye, he imagines children playing in a field, innocent and free. ³But somewhere in that field there is a cliff, and sooner or later, the children will come near the cliff. ⁴Holden wants to be there to catch them, to keep them from falling off the field. ⁵He believes that it is his calling to be the catcher, to be their protector. ⁶The rye field becomes a symbol for the freedom and purity of childhood. ⁷Holden wants to shield the children from the hidden cliff, which symbolizes the cruel realities of the adult world.

_____ 5. ¹I hear a lot of complaints about badly behaved children—children who dominate public places with yelling, tantrums, crashing into furniture and other people, and generally acting uncivilized. ²I don't complain about those children, however. ³The people I do complain about are their idiot parents. ⁴The last time I checked, it was a parent's job to teach a child to behave in socially acceptable ways; but many lazy, stupid parents seem to have missed that memo. ⁵It makes me furious, for example, to see a child in a restaurant yelling at the top of his voice and throwing food on the floor while his oblivious mother talks on her cell phone. ⁶When I see a father quiet a crying child by shoving a candy bar and a can of soda at her, I want to pour the sugary drink on top of the moronic dad's head. ⁷Does he really think that stuffing her with junk food is going to make her a happier, healthier child? ⁸I also hate to see a kid screaming for a treat or a toy and hear the parent say, "Oh, all right!" and buy it for him. ⁹Are you kidding, you jerk? ¹⁰Don't you realize that spoiling him by giving in is only going to encourage his bad behavior? **11**Worst of all is the so-called parent who responds to a misbehaving child by shouting at her or hitting her. **12**Such a parent is only teaching the child to be aggressive and violent. **13**Any parent who won't take the time to learn some effective parenting techniques ought to be shot.

CHAPTER REVIEW

In this chapter, you learned that part of reading critically is to do the following:

- Be aware of an author's **purpose**: the reason why he or she writes. Three common purposes are to inform, to persuade, and to entertain.

- Be aware of **tone**—the expression of the author's attitude and feeling about a subject. A writer's tone might be objective—the case in most textbook writing—or it might be lighthearted, sympathetic, angry, affectionate, respectful, or any of the other tones shown on pages 271–273.

    One important tone to recognize is **irony**: saying one thing but meaning the opposite.

The next chapter—Chapter 8—will explain another part of reading critically: recognizing an author's point and evaluating the support for that point.

On the Web: If you are using this book in class, you can go to our website for more practice in identifying an author's purpose and tone. Visit our Learning Center at **www.townsendpress.net** for additional activities and an instructional video on this skill.

REVIEW TEST 1

To review what you've learned in this chapter, answer each of the following questions by filling in the blank or writing the letter of the correct answer.

1. The main purpose of almost any textbook is to _____.

2. Typically the purpose of a news report is to _____, the purpose of an editorial is to _____, and the purpose of a mystery novel or adventure story is to _____.

_____ 3. TRUE OR FALSE? The purpose of some writing may be to persuade as well as to inform, or even to inform, persuade, *and* entertain.

4. The tone of a selection helps reveal the author's _____ toward and feeling about his or her subject.

5. A writer is using an ironic tone if he or she says one thing but means the _____.

REVIEW TEST 2

The selection that follows is from the college textbook *Psychology Applied to Modern Life* by Wayne Weiten, Dana S. Dunn, and Elizabeth Yost Hammer. Read it and then answer the questions on purpose and tone that follow. There are also questions on the skills you have practiced in previous chapters.

Preview

Amazing news! You can gain confidence; lose weight; quit smoking; fix your marriage; find your soul mate; heal your wounded inner child, and triumph over your fears—and you can do it all for the cost of a single book! Or can you? This textbook excerpt explores the question: Are self-help books actually that helpful?

Words to Watch

voracious (1): greedy; unable to be satisfied
serenity (2): calmness
prevalence (2): widespread occurrence
distillation (6): condensed version
exploitive (7): selfish

SELF-HELP BOOKS

Wayne Weiten, Dana S. Dunn, and Elizabeth Yost Hammer

1   Americans spend roughly $650 million annually on "self-help books" that offer do-it-yourself treatments for common personal problems. If you include self-help audiotapes, CDs, DVDs, software, Internet sites, lectures, seminars, and life coaching, self-improvement appears to be a $2.5-billion-a-year industry. This fascination with self-improvement is nothing new. For decades, American readers have displayed a voracious° appetite for self-help books such as *I'm OK—You're OK*; *Your Erroneous Zones*; *The Seven Habits of Highly Effective People*; *Men Are from Mars, Women Are from Venus*; *Ageless Body, Timeless Mind*; *Don't Sweat the Small Stuff . . . and It's All Small Stuff*; *The Purpose-Driven Life*; *The Secret*; and *Become a Better You: Seven Keys to Improving Your Life Every Day*.

2   With their simple recipes for achieving happiness, these books have generally not been timid about promising to change the quality of the reader's life. Unfortunately, merely reading a book is not likely to turn your life around. If only it were that easy! If only someone could hand you a book that would solve all your problems! If the consumption of these literary narcotics were even remotely as helpful as their publishers claim, we would be a nation of serene, happy, well-adjusted people. It is clear, however, that serenity° is not the dominant national mood. Quite the contrary; as already noted, in recent decades Americans' average anxiety level has moved upward, and the prevalence° of depression has increased as well. The multitude of self-help books that crowd bookstore shelves represent just one more symptom of our collective distress and our search for the elusive secret of happiness.

The Value of Self-Help Books

3   It is somewhat unfair to lump all self-help books together for a critique, since they vary widely in quality. Surveys exploring psychotherapists' opinions of self-help books suggest that there are some excellent books that offer authentic insights and sound advice. Many therapists encourage their patients to read carefully selected self-help books. A few books have even been tested in clinical trials with favorable results, although the studies have often had methodological weaknesses. Thus, it would be foolish to dismiss all these books as shallow drivel. Unfortunately, however, the gems are easily lost in the mountains of rubbish. A great many self-help books offer little of real value to the reader. Generally, they suffer from four fundamental shortcomings.

4   First, they are dominated by "psychobabble." The term *psychobabble*, coined by R.D. Rosen, seems appropriate to describe the "hip" but hopelessly vague language used in many of the books. Statements such as "It's beautiful if you're unhappy," "You've got to get in touch with yourself," "You have to be up front," "You gotta be you 'cause you're you," and "You need a real

high-energy experience" are typical examples of this language. At best, such terminology is ill-defined; at worst, it is meaningless. Clarity is sacrificed in favor of a hip jargon that prevents, rather than enhances, effective communication.

5   A second problem is that self-help books tend to place more emphasis on sales than on scientific soundness. The advice offered in these books is far too rarely based on solid, scientific research. Instead, the ideas are frequently based on the authors' intuitive analyses, which may be highly speculative. Even when books are based on well-researched therapeutic programs, interventions that are effective in clinical settings with professional supervision may not be effective when self-administered without professional guidance. More-over, even when responsible authors provide scientifically valid advice and are careful not to mislead their readers, sales-hungry publishers routinely slap outrageous, irresponsible promises on the books' covers, often to the dismay of the authors.

6   The third shortcoming is that self-help books don't usually provide explicit directions about how to change your behavior. These books tend to be smoothly written and "touchingly human" in tone. They often strike responsive chords in the reader by aptly describing a common problem that many of us experience. The reader says, "Yes, that's me!" Unfortunately, when the book focuses on how to deal with the problem, it usually provides only a vague distillation° of simple common sense, which could be covered in 2 rather

than 200 pages. These books often fall back on inspirational cheerleading in the absence of sound, explicit advice.

7   Fourth, many of these books encourage a remarkably self-centered, narcissistic approach to life. *Narcissism* is a personality trait marked by an inflated sense of importance, a need for attention and admiration, a sense of entitlement, and a tendency to exploit others. The term is based on the Greek myth of Narcissus, an attractive young man in search of love who sees himself reflected in water and falls in love with his own image. Although there are plenty of exceptions, the basic message in many self-help books is "Do whatever you feel like doing, and don't worry about the consequences for other people." According to McGee, this mentality began to creep into books in the 1970s, as "bald proposals that one ought to 'look out for #1' or 'win

through intimidation' marked a new ruthlessness in the self-help landscape." This "me first" philosophy emphasizes self-admiration, one's entitlement to special treatment, and an exploitive° approach to interpersonal relationships. Interestingly, research suggests that narcissism levels have increased among recent generations of college students. It is hard to say how much popular self-help books have fueled the rise in narcissism, but surely they have contributed.

What to Look For in Self-Help Books

8   Because self-help books vary so widely in quality, it seems a good idea to provide you with some guidelines about what to look for in seeking genuinely helpful books. The following thoughts give you some criteria for judging books of this type.

9   **1.** Clarity in communication is essential. Advice won't do you much good if you can't understand it. Try to avoid drowning in the murky depths of psychobabble.

10   **2.** This may sound backward, but look for books that do not promise too much in the way of immediate change. The truly useful books tend to be appropriately cautious in their promises and realistic about the challenges of altering your behavior. As Arkowitz and Lilienfeld put it, "Be wary of books that make promises that they obviously cannot keep, such as curing a phobia in five minutes or fixing a failing marriage in a week."

11   **3.** Try to check out the credentials of the author or authors. Book jackets will often exaggerate the expertise of authors, but these days a quick Internet search can often yield more objective biographical information and perhaps some perceptive reviews of the book.

12   **4.** Try to select books that mention, at least briefly, the theoretical or research basis for the program they advocate. It is understandable that you may not be interested in a detailed summary of research that supports a particular piece of advice. However, you should be interested in whether the advice is based on published research, widely accepted theory, anecdotal evidence, clinical interactions with patients, or pure speculation by the author. Books that are based on more than personal anecdotes and speculation should have a list of references in the back (or at the end of each chapter).

13   **5.** Look for books that provide detailed, explicit directions about how to alter your behavior. Generally, these directions represent the crucial core of the book. If they are inadequate in detail, you have been shortchanged.

14   **6.** More often than not, books that focus on a particular kind of problem, such as overeating, loneliness, or marital difficulties, deliver more than those that promise to cure all of life's problems with a few simple ideas. Books that cover everything are usually superficial and disappointing. Books that devote a great deal of thought to a particular topic tend to be written by authors with genuine expertise on that topic. Such books are more likely to pay off for you.

Reading Comprehension Questions

Vocabulary in Context

_____ 1. In the passage below, the word *speculative* (spĕk′yə-lə-tĭv) means
    A. encouraging.   C. realistic.
    B. factual.   D. based on opinion, not fact.

"The advice in these books is far too rarely based on solid, scientific research. Instead, the ideas are frequently based on the authors' intuitive analyses, which may be highly speculative." (Paragraph 5)

Central Point and Main Ideas

_____ 2. Which sentence best expresses the central point of the selection?
    A. In the United States, do-it-yourself treatments for common personal problems have been popular for decades.
    B. Far from offering clear-cut solutions to our problems, self-help books are filled with jargon that prevents effective communication.
    C. Although many self-help books promise far more than they can deliver, it is possible to find helpful information in them.
    D. Most self-help books are better at describing common problems than offering sound, explicit advice.

_____ 3. The implied main idea of paragraph 2 is that
    A. despite the exaggerated claims of publishers, self-help books have done little to make Americans happier.
    B. it's difficult for most people to make positive changes in their lives.
    C. in recent decades, the national mood has only gotten more anxious and depressed.
    D. because self-help books offer simple recipes for achieving happiness, they are highly popular.

Supporting Details

_____ 4. The authors believe that some self-help books have contributed to
    A. greater levels of happiness among the young.
    B. an increase in the use of hopelessly vague language among the young.
    C. increased levels of narcissism in our society.
    D. the belief that solid scientific research is more valuable than intuition.

_____ 5. The authors encourage people who are seeking genuinely helpful books to
    A. select books that are smoothly written and "touchingly human."
    B. select books that devote a great deal of thought to a particular topic.
    C. select books that favor a "me first" approach to life's challenges.
    D. avoid self-help books that were published before the 1970s.

Transitions

_____ 6. The relationship between the second sentence below and the first sentence
is one of
A. illustration.
B. addition.
C. time.
D. cause and effect.

> "Even when books are based on well-researched therapeutic programs,
> interventions that are effective in clinical settings with professional
> supervision may not be effective when self-administered without pro-
> fessional guidelines. Moreover, even when responsible authors provide
> significantly valid advice and are careful not to mislead their readers,
> sales-hungry publishers routinely slap outrageous, irresponsible promises
> on the books' covers, often to the dismay of authors." (Paragraph 5)

Patterns of Organization

_____ 7. In paragraph 7, the authors mainly
A. compare today's college students with college students in the 1970s.
B. contrast self-help books that were published before the 1970s with
self-help books that were published during the 1970s.
C. define _narcissism_ and provide examples of narcissist thinking in self-
help books.
D. illustrate the negative consequences of narcissistic thinking in
American society.

Inferences

_____ 8. We can infer from this selection that the authors believe
A. most self-help authors deliberately try to mislead people.
B. only research scientists should write self-help books.
C. many self-help books are worthless.
D. it is impossible for most people to alter their behavior.

Purpose and Tone

_____ 9. The authors' main purpose is to
A. entertain readers with examples of the outrageous promises made by
self-help books.
B. advise readers how to identify and avoid worthless self-help books
and find genuinely helpful ones.
C. inform readers of common pitfalls to avoid when writing a self-help
book.
D. persuade readers never to buy self-help books.

_____ 10. The authors' tone in paragraphs 8 through 14 is
    A. compassionate.   C. determined.
    B. pleading.   D. instructive.

Discussion Questions

1. Have you ever attempted to make a change in your life by reading a self-help book or consulting other self-help media, such as the _Dr. Phil_ show on TV? If so, were you successful? Would you recommend the book or other "do-it-yourself" treatment to others? Why or why not?

2. Do you agree with the authors that Americans are more anxious and depressed than ever? If so, what do you believe are some of the major causes of our "collective distress"?

3. The authors refer to some self-help books as "literary narcotics." What do these books seem to have in common with actual narcotics, such as heroin and cocaine?

4. Despite the number of self-help books available, the authors feel that "merely reading a book is not likely to turn your life around." Do you agree? If so, why do you think it is so difficult for people to change?

Note: Writing assignments for this selection appear on page 638.

Check Your Performance   PURPOSE AND TONE

Activity	_Number Right_	_Points_	_Score_
Review Test 1 (5 items)	_____	× 6 =	_____
Review Test 2 (10 items)	_____	× 7 =	_____
		TOTAL SCORE =	_____ %

Enter your total score into the **Reading Performance Chart: Review Tests** on the inside back cover.

Name _____ Date _____

Section _____ SCORE: (Number correct) _____ x 10 = _____ %

PURPOSE AND TONE: Mastery Test 1

T3

A. In the space provided, indicate whether the primary purpose of each item is to inform (**I**), to persuade (**P**), or to entertain (**E**).

Sub/E 1. Experts believe that between 3 and 5 percent of American children have some form of Attention Deficit Hyperactivity Disorder (ADHD).

H (H Obj)/I 2. Studies show that boys are three times more likely to develop ADHD than girls.

o ro Obj/I 3. Parents and teachers are too quick to put children on medication for ADHD when the kids are actually just normal and high-spirited.

+ (+1 Sub/E 4. A mother was talking about her son, recently diagnosed with Attention Deficit Disorder. "I don't understand," she said. "We pay plenty of attention to him!"

+1 Sub/P 5. Parents of children with ADHD should experiment with modifying the children's diet rather than putting them on medication.

B. Each of the following passages illustrates better than the others one of the five different tones identified in the box below. In the space provided, put the letter of the tone that best applies to each passage. Use each tone once.

A. admiring	**B.** alarmed	**C.** determined
D. reverent	**E.** sarcastic	

_____ 6. Amazing grace! How sweet the sound
That saved a wretch like me!
I once was lost, but now am found;
Was blind, but now I see.

⁵ 'Twas grace that taught my heart to fear,
And grace my fears relieved;
How precious did that grace appear
The hour I first believed!

Through many dangers, toils and snares,
¹⁰ I have already come;
'Tis grace hath brought me safe thus far,
And grace will lead me home.

_____ 7. ¹The experience I had writing my first college essay was unforgettable. ²I received a C- for the essay. ³Scrawled next to the grade was the comment "Not badly written, but ill-conceived." ⁴I remember going to the instructor after class, asking about his comment as well as the word *Log* that he had

(Continues on next page)

added in the margin at various spots. ⁵"What are all these logs you put in my paper?" I asked, trying to make a joke of it. ⁶He looked at me a little wonderingly. ⁷"Logic," he answered, "logic." ⁸He went on to explain that I had not thought out my paper clearly. ⁹There were actually two ideas rather than one in my thesis, one supporting paragraph had nothing to do with either idea, and so on. ¹⁰I've never forgotten his last words: ¹¹"If you don't think clearly," he said, "you won't write clearly."

¹²I was speechless, and I felt confused and angry. ¹³I didn't like being told that I didn't know how to think. ¹⁴I went back to my room and read over my paper several times. ¹⁵Eventually, I decided that my instructor was right. ¹⁶"No more logs," I said to myself. ¹⁷"I'm going to get these logs out of my papers."

_____ 8.   ¹Let me list some of the reasons I'm happy that my sister Sophie is marrying Tom "Big Shot" Lewis. ²First, Tom is a considerate human being. ³He realizes that doing conventional "nice" things, like remembering his girlfriend's birthday or giving her a Christmas present, would just distract her from the important things in life, like ironing his shirts. ⁴Secondly, he's got such potential. ⁵It's true that he's not working now; in fact, since we've known him he hasn't held a job for more than two months. ⁶But I'm sure any day now his plan to become a traveling disk jockey is going to materialize. ⁷Then he'll be able to pay Sophie back all the money she's lent him.

_____ 9.   ¹Jackie Kennedy knew how to live with grace. ²From her trademark sunglasses to her French-inspired outfits and feminine pumps, she always dressed with a style of her own. ³As the First Lady, she brought a youthful classiness to her role, the likes of which the White House had never before seen. ⁴Americans often remember her smiling and waving gently, as she stepped gracefully from airplane ramps and stage platforms. ⁵As a hostess, she never missed a beat. ⁶Using her charm and wit, she made guests feel right at home. ⁷Even when her husband, the president, was killed, Jackie faced the spotlight with graceful dignity. ⁸In the hearts of many, she will always be an unforgettable American icon.

_____ 10.   ¹In the United States today there are 39 million geriatric patients—defined as over the age of 65. ²Of these, 5.7 million are older than 85, now characterized as the "old old." ³Yet the American Medical Directors Association, which credentials physicians in long-term care, says there are not enough doctors for the aged in our country today; only 2 percent of physicians in training say they want to go into geriatric care. ⁴As we baby boomers go about our lives, frozen into our routines of work and family responsibilities, a vast inland sea of elders is building. ⁵By 2020 there will be an estimated 53 million Americans older than 65, 6.5 million of whom will be "old old." ⁶Many of you will be among them. ⁷How will America possibly cope with this flood of old folks, each with a unique set of medical and financial circumstances?

Part A

PURPOSE AND TONE: Mastery Test 2

A. In the space provided, indicate whether the primary purpose of each item is to inform (**I**), to persuade (**P**), or to entertain (**E**).

_____ 1. With more than 400 billion cups consumed annually, coffee is the world's most popular beverage.

_____ 2. Instead of buying diamonds, people should save their money and buy gorgeous synthetic stones like cubic zirconia.

_____ 3. The bank says that I have no money left in my checking account, but that can't be true. I have plenty of checks left.

_____ 4. Albinism, the lack of color-producing pigment in the skin, hair, and eyes, can affect people of any race.

_____ 5. Telemarketers should be required to immediately identify themselves as such when beginning a phone conversation.

_____ 6. ¹How do these celebrities stay so impossibly thin? ²Simple: They have full-time personal trainers, who advise them on nutrition, give them pep talks, and shoot them with tranquilizer darts whenever they try to crawl, on hunger-weakened limbs, toward the packet of rice cakes that constitutes the entire food supply in their 37,000-square-foot mansions. ³For most celebrities, the biggest meal of the day is toothpaste (they use reduced-fat Crest).

_____ 7. ¹The world today is in the midst of a technology revolution. ²The time is coming when every single person on the planet can be in instant communication with everyone else. ³Investors in the right technology stocks—the Apple computer stocks of tomorrow—will have the potential to profit enormously. ⁴BUT YOU MUST ACT NOW. ⁵It's happened more times than you might believe. . . . ⁶Sometimes just one smart decision—one strategic investment move—can earn you staggering profits. ⁷The key? ⁸Pinpointing the exact tipping point when a smart idea becomes a highly profitable investment vehicle. ⁹For this new market, that time is now! ¹⁰The key is information and timing, and now the world's leading growth stock guru (his investment gains have averaged up to 100% a year) is opening his exclusive advisory service to a few fortunate investors. ¹¹This is your opportunity to capitalize on his expertise.

(Continues on next page)

B. Each of the following passages illustrates better than the others one of the six different tones identified in the box below. In the space provided, put the letter of the tone that best applies to each passage. Use each tone once. (Three tone choices will be left over.)

A. ambivalent	B. angry	C. defensive
D. ironic	E. regretful	F. suggestive

_____ 8. ¹It has been rumored for years that some major league baseball stars were taking steroids to increase their ability to hit home runs. ²But not until early in 2005 did major league baseball finally require mandatory steroid testing and strict penalties for steroid use. ³Why did it take baseball bigwigs so long to clamp down on the illegal substances? ⁴The only answer can be sheer profit-driven hypocrisy.

⁵Players who "bulked up" with the aid of steroids tended to hit more home runs than they otherwise could have. ⁶More home runs generated greater fan excitement. ⁷Greater fan excitement meant higher ticket sales, and more money for owners and players alike. ⁸Who really cared that steroid use could lead to serious side effects? ⁹Who cared that old-time ballplayers were having their records broken by drug-injected Godzillas? ¹⁰Who cared that steroid use by pro ballplayers could set a bad example for the nation's youth? ¹¹Certainly not major league baseball, that is, until a spate of bad publicity forced its hand.

_____ 9. ¹I am a hunter. ²Do you hate me already? ³Probably; most people seem to have made up their minds that hunting is a terrible thing, even if they don't know anything about it. ⁴And if hunting is a bad thing, then I must be a bad person for doing it. ⁵But I don't think I'm a bad person. ⁶I do not go hunting primarily for the kill. ⁷In fact, there have been many more times that I've come home empty-handed from a hunt than otherwise. ⁸The biggest reason that I go hunting is that I love being in the wilderness and in the company of my hunting buddies. ⁹But even if I do manage to bag a deer or a pheasant for my table, I don't feel guilty about it. ¹⁰Hunters kill a fraction of the wild animals that automobiles mow down on our highways every year. ¹¹The hunting licenses we buy help to fund state wildlife management programs. ¹²Responsible hunting helps to keep wildlife populations in check, rather than letting flocks and herds expand to the point that animals are starving and diseased.

_____ 10. ¹Feeling a sense of privacy and comfort, I allow the sound of my own voice to soothe my mind and body, while I speak slowly and softly. ²My body is slowing down as though everything is moving in slow motion. ³With every word I say, I feel more relaxed and at peace. ⁴Moment by moment, my mind is becoming as clear as the surface of a calm and quiet mountain lake.

⁵As my mind clears, I use my imagination to relax more deeply while I read. ⁶I imagine that I am sitting on a comfortable chair on a beautiful beach as I read. ⁷With my peripheral vision I see the golden sand that surrounds me . . . and the waves as they crash on the shore. ⁸I hear the gentle and rhythmic sounds they make.

Part A

PURPOSE AND TONE: Mastery Test 3

A. In the space provided, indicate whether the primary purpose of each item is to inform (**I**), to persuade (**P**), or to entertain (**E**).

_**I**_ 1. When two complete thoughts are combined into one sentence by a joining word like *and, but,* or *so*, a comma is used before the joining word.

_**P**_ 2. Any adult who is convicted of having molested a child should be sentenced to jail without parole for a minimum of twenty years.

_**E**_ 3. I am famous for my backyard weed garden; my children tease me for having a "black thumb."

_**P**_ 4. ¹What's remarkable about us humans is that, unique among creatures, we know we are doomed. ²Yet we stubbornly persist in defying the odds. ³The same DNA that dictates the bell curve of our lives—growth, maturity, decline—also contains a gene for relentless self-improvement. ⁴We insist, and must insist, on continuing to grow.

_**E**_ 5. ¹I'm a very susceptible person, easily influenced, a natural-born follower with no sales resistance. ²When I walk into a store, clerks wrestle one another trying to get to me first. ³My wife won't let me watch infomercials because of all the junk I've ordered that's now piled up in the garage. ⁴My medicine cabinet is filled with vitamins and baldness cures.

_**I**_ 6. ¹When the next diet book comes out promising major weight loss with minor effort, there will be 200 million chubby Americans waiting to believe it. ²Well, tough, but it's not true. ³The dreary, persistent fact is that diets don't work; 95 percent of them fail, which is why setting weight loss as your goal is generally a bum idea. ⁴The almost certain failure can infect your attitude toward fitness, while the yo-yoing up and down actually makes you gain weight. ⁵So don't diet. ⁶Our advice is, basically, forget about it. ⁷Instead, exercise six days a week and make it a rule of your life to quit eating crap.

_**I**_ 7. ¹Abraham Maslow proposed that human motives are organized into a hierarchy of needs—a systematic arrangement of needs, according to priority, in which basic needs must be met before less basic needs are aroused. ²This hierarchical arrangement is usually portrayed as a pyramid, with the needs toward the bottom of the pyramid, such as physiological or security needs, being the most basic. ³Higher levels in the pyramid consist of progressively less basic needs. ⁴When a person manages to satisfy a level of needs reasonably well (complete satisfaction is not necessary), this satisfaction activates needs at the next level.

(Continues on next page)

B. Each of the following passages illustrates better than the others one of the six different tones identified in the box below. In the space provided, put the letter of the tone that best applies to each passage. Use each tone once. (Three tone choices will be left over.)

A. admiring	B. disbelieving	C. fearful
D. indignant	E. optimistic	F. regretful

_____ 8. ¹In the face of busy days, long work hours, and extended after-school activities, the American dinnertime has become all but obsolete. ²The dinner hour used to be a refuge, a time when family members could enjoy each other's company over a warm, nutritious meal. ³But distracted by other obligations, today's families have traded that valuable together time for things of less importance. ⁴Husbands and wives have lost that precious moment of sharing after a hard day's work. ⁵Parents no longer have a built-in opportunity to give valuable counsel and encouragement to their children. ⁶Likewise, children have lost a slot of guaranteed attention time with their parents. ⁷The slow transition to on-the-go fast food and TV dinners may not have been noticed by families adapting to the faster-paced world. ⁸But the close bonds once formed over home-cooked meals will certainly be missed.

_____ 9. ¹It never ceases to astound me that puppies are sold in pet stores. ²And chances are that the unfortunate animals imprisoned in tiny cages have already been mistreated all their lives. ³They are typically born at "puppy mills" whose only aim is to produce many sellable animals as quickly as possible, without regard for the animals' health. ⁴Female dogs are kept pregnant constantly, quickly wearing out their health, and are killed when they lose the ability to reproduce. ⁵Puppies born from such exhausted, worn-out mothers are kept in filthy crates until they are shipped out to a pet store for sale. ⁶Not only are their lives miserable, but their health and temperaments are likely to be poor. ⁷There is no excuse for puppy mills or the pet stores that help support them.

_____10. ¹In the afternoon I fell asleep in the living room with the soft autumn sun coming through the window. ²It was dusk when I awakened, and I could tell that it had gotten cooler. ³As my eyes opened, they glanced out the window into a yard that was now filled with dark shadows. ⁴Out of some instinct, I averted my eyes so they did not scan around the yard. ⁵I half felt I would see something moving out there, something I would not want to see. ⁶I quickly closed the miniblinds to the windows. ⁷Then, as I fumbled to find the wall switch and turn on a light, I was suddenly aware of a faint scratching sound. ⁸It was coming from the door to the basement, and I sensed that someone was trying to break in.

PURPOSE AND TONE: Mastery Test 4

A. In the space provided, indicate whether the primary purpose of each item is to inform (**I**), to persuade (**P**), or to entertain (**E**).

_____ 1. On any given day, approximately 160,000 kids decide to skip school to avoid being bullied by their peers.

_____ 2. For every year he or she is in school, each student should be required to read at least ten books.

_____ 3. In a successful marriage, a bride promises to obey her husband at all times, and the groom promises that his first words to his wife will always be "Yes, dear."

_____ 4. It would benefit students if high-school math departments offered courses in managing a bank account and basic investing as well as algebra and geometry.

_____ 5. ¹To win an argument, one rule is to drink liquor. ²Suppose you are at a party and some hotshot intellectual is expounding on the economy of Peru, a subject you know nothing about. ³If you're drinking some health-fanatic drink like grapefruit juice, you'll hang back, afraid to display your ignorance, while the hotshot enthralls your date. ⁴But if you drink several large martinis, you'll discover you have *strong views* about the Peruvian economy. ⁵You'll be a *wealth* of information. ⁶You'll argue forcefully, offering great insights and even upsetting furniture. ⁷People will be impressed. ⁸Some may leave the room.

_____ 6. ¹Guns are being used more widely than ever in our society and in other parts of the world. ²More than 60 percent of the homicides and 55 percent of the suicides committed each year in the United States involve the use of guns. ³Gun violence is a leading killer of teenagers and young men, especially African American men, and the use of semiautomatic assault weapons by individuals and gang members is common. ⁴Colleges and universities are not immune to gun violence. ⁵A recent study found that 4.3 percent of college students had a working firearm at college. ⁶Of these, nearly half stated that they had the gun for protection.

_____ 7. ¹When asked by his nephew what he ought to do in life, Henry James replied: "Three things in human life are important. ²The first is to be kind. ³The second is to be kind. ⁴And the third is to be kind." ⁵The key to those words is the repetition—the insistence that one find an existence that enables one to be kind. ⁶How to do so? ⁷By wading in, over and over, with that purpose in mind, with a willingness to sail on, tacking and tacking again, helped by those we aim to help, guided by our moral

(Continues on next page)

yearnings on behalf of others, on behalf of ourselves with others: a commitment to others that won't avoid squalls and periods of drift, a commitment that will become the heart of the journey itself.

B. Each of the following passages illustrates better than the others one of the six different tones identified in the box below. In the space provided, put the letter of the tone that best applies to each passage. Use each tone once. (Three tone choices will be left over.)

A. approving	B. bewildered	C. disapproving
D. malicious	E. objective	F. pessimistic

_____ 8. ¹Androgyny, or the blending of both feminine and masculine qualities, is more clearly evident in our society now than ever before. ²Today it is quite common to see men involved in raising children (including changing diapers) and doing routine housework. ³On the other hand, it is also quite common to see women entering the workplace in jobs traditionally managed by men and participating in sports traditionally played by men. ⁴Men are not scoffed at when their eyes tear during a sad movie. ⁵Women are not laughed at when they choose to assert themselves. ⁶The rejection of many sexual stereotypes has probably benefited our society immensely by relieving people of the pressure to be 100 percent "womanly" or 100 percent "macho."

_____ 9. ¹Freedom, in this culture, means that whatever makes you happy is okay. ²This is the freedom of a fourteen-year-old child. ³Freedom to eat a whole box of doughnuts in one sitting. ⁴Freedom to make a mess, to be loud and obnoxious, to blow things up, to inflict injury for the thrill of it, to conceive babies without care or thought for the consequences. ⁵Mostly, it is freedom from authority, particularly parental authority which, when it exists at all now, often functions at a level qualitatively no higher than a child's. ⁶Under this version of freedom, there is no legitimate claim for any authority to regulate human desires—not even the personal conscience—nor any appropriate scale of management, and all supposed authorities are viewed as corrupt, mendacious, and irrelevant. ⁷This view of freedom is not what Hamilton, Jefferson, Madison, and the other founders had in mind.

_____ 10. ¹Human activities are to blame for a dramatic increase in global warming, and the effects are and will continue to be disastrous. ²The average global temperature has risen about 1 degree Fahrenheit since the late 1800s, and scientific models show that it will rise another 2.2 to 10 degrees Fahrenheit in the next decade. ³This will lead to an increase in the frequency and intensity of extreme weather events such as floods, droughts, heat waves, and hurricanes. ⁴Crops will fail, glaciers will melt, sea levels will rise, and animal and plant species will be wiped out. ⁵Political and business leaders who are in a position to work to counteract global warming are too invested in the status quo to take significant actions, so there is little chance that this crisis will be averted.

all

PURPOSE AND TONE: Mastery Test 5

Read the passages below. Then carefully consider the questions that follow, and, in the spaces provided, write the letters of the best responses.

A. [1]I wake up and bounce out of bed in a pleasant mood and then notice that I can see my breath. [2]There is frost on the bathroom mirror and a thin sheet of ice in the toilet. [3]So I trot downstairs and turn up the thermostat. [4]I like the house to be cozy, as if we had a blazing fire in each room, but I am married to Nanook of the North, who feels a person of character can put on a warm sweater and be comfortable at 58 degrees.

[5]The furnace rumbles in the basement, and I make coffee and fetch the paper. [6]Then she appears in the kitchen in her woolens and says, "The thermostat was set at 85. [7]Do we have elderly people coming for breakfast?" [8]I explain that I had found the thermostat set low. [9]"Put on a sweater," she says.

_____ 1. The primary purpose of this passage is to
   A. inform.   B. persuade.   C. entertain.

_____ 2. The predominant tone of this passage can be described as
   A. scornful.   C. conceited.
   B. lighthearted.   D. revengeful.

B. [1]During the Spanish Civil War in the late 1930s, Indiana farmer Dan West was serving as a volunteer relief worker. [2]He grew frustrated with having to decide how to distribute limited food aid. [3]Upon returning home, he founded the remarkable organization now known as Heifer International, whose aim is to provide permanent hunger relief by giving families their own livestock. [4]Donors to Heifer International can purchase an entire animal or a "share" of a gift animal, which is then given to a family in need. [5]A unique feature of Heifer International's program is that recipient families are required to pass at least one of their animal's female offspring along to a neighboring family. [6]That family in turn passes on one of its animals, and so on. [7]As of 2006, Heifer International had distributed sheep, rabbits, honeybees, pigs, llamas, water buffalo, chicks, ducks, goats, geese and trees as well as heifers in 115 countries around the world.

_____ 3. The primary purpose of this paragraph is to
   A. inform readers about the existence and work of Heifer International.
   B. persuade readers to donate to Heifer International.
   C. entertain readers with anecdotes about relief ventures in other countries.

_____ 4. The tone of this paragraph can be described as
   A. critical.   C. admiring.
   B. straightforward.   D. amusing.

(Continues on next page)

C. [1]"Identity theft" sounds like something out of a futuristic movie, but it's very much a problem in the here and now. [2]Identity theft is committed by a person who has gained access to your personal information and is passing himself off as you, usually to make purchases or conduct illegal activity. [3]With the increasing popularity of credit cards and, especially, the rising number of people making purchases over the Internet, identity theft is becoming much more common. [4]Signs that you have been a victim of identity theft include getting letters or phone calls saying you have been approved or turned down for credit you never applied for; seeing charges on your credit card statement for things you didn't buy; failing to receive your credit card statements in the mail; or receiving calls from collection agencies concerning accounts you never opened.

_____ 5. The primary purpose of this paragraph is to
        A. inform.   B. persuade.   C. entertain.

_____ 6. The predominant tone of this paragraph can be described as
        A. sympathetic.   C. instructive.
        B. cheerful.   D. detached.

D. [1]When you adopt a dog from the pound, you have to fill out an application and prove that you will be a suitable owner. [2]When you want to drive a car, you have to pass a driver's test and get a license. [3]When you want to become a citizen of this country, you must prove you know something about the history and government of the U.S. [4]But to become a parent—certainly the hardest and most important job anyone ever does, if it's done right—you don't have to do anything but produce a baby. [5]This state of affairs reflects some awfully messed-up priorities. [6]I am sick of seeing, almost every day, another tragic news story about a helpless infant battered, starved, or otherwise mistreated by ignorant and uninformed parents. [7]At the very minimum, middle-school and high-school students should be required to take classes in parenting and child care. [8]Beyond that, a pregnant couple should be required to show they have a plan to care for and raise their child. [9]Too many children are brought into this world with even less thought than is given to adopting a pet. [10]And once those children get here, they receive far less affection and caring than a dog or cat.

_____ 7. The primary purpose of this paragraph is to
        A. inform.   B. persuade.   C. entertain.

_____ 8. The main tone of this paragraph can be described as
        A. tolerant.   C. disgusted.
        B. apologetic.   D. depressed.

all

PURPOSE AND TONE: Mastery Test 6

Read the paragraphs below. Then carefully consider the questions that follow, and, in the spaces provided, write the letters of the best responses.

A. ¹Someone was drawing water, and my teacher placed my hand under the spout. ²As the cool stream gushed over one hand, she spelled into the other the word *water*, first slowly, then rapidly. ³I stood still, my whole attention fixed upon the motion of her fingers. ⁴Suddenly I felt a misty consciousness as of something forgotten—a thrill of returning thought; and somehow the mystery of language was revealed to me. ⁵I knew that "w-a-t-e-r" meant the wonderful cool something that was flowing over my hand. ⁶The living word awakened my soul, gave it light, hope, joy, set it free! ⁷There were barriers still, it is true, but barriers that could in time be swept away.

—From *The Story of My Life,* by Helen Keller, a blind and deaf woman

_____ 1. The primary purpose of this paragraph is to
  A. inform. B. persuade. C. inform and entertain.

_____ 2. The tone of this paragraph can be described as
  A. optimistic and joyful. C. matter-of-fact.
  B. lighthearted and sentimental. D. warm but self-pitying.

B. ¹In the Civil War, 365,000 Northern soldiers were killed, and 133,000 soldiers from the South died. ²In World War I, 116,000 American soldiers were killed. ³In World War II, 407,000 died; 54,000 died in Korea; 58,000 in Vietnam.

⁴More than a million Americans have died in our wars, each one much loved by someone. ⁵Twelve of my classmates died in World War II, but my memory of them comes at unexpected times—not on Memorial Day—and I would like to see the effort we now put into this one day redirected.

⁶There are men in every country on earth—mostly men—who spend full time devising new ways for us to kill each other. ⁷In the United States alone, we spend seven times as much on war as on education.

⁸There's something wrong here. ⁹On this Memorial Day, we should certainly honor those who have died in war, but we should dedicate this day not so much to their memory, but to the search for a way to end the idiocy of the wars that killed them.

_____ 3. The primary purpose of this paragraph is to
  A. inform. B. persuade. C. entertain.

_____ 4. The tone of this paragraph can be described as
  A. passionate and distressed. C. detached and matter-of-fact.
  B. admiring and sentimental. D. worried but optimistic.

(Continues on next page)

C. ¹We hold these truths to be self-evident, that all men are created equal, that they are endowed by their Creator with certain unalienable rights, that among these are life, liberty and the pursuit of happiness. ²That to secure these rights, governments are instituted among men, deriving their just powers from the consent of the governed. ³That whenever any form of government becomes destructive of these ends, it is the right of the people to alter or to abolish it, and to institute new government, laying its foundations on such principles and organizing its powers in such form, as to them shall seem most likely to effect their safety and happiness. ⁴Prudence, indeed, will dictate that governments long established should not be changed for light and transient causes; and accordingly all experience hath shown that mankind are more disposed to suffer, while evils are sufferable, than to right themselves by abolishing the forms to which they are accustomed. ⁵But when a long train of abuses and usurpations, pursuing invariably the same object, evinces a design to reduce them under absolute despotism, it is their right, it is their duty, to throw off such government, and to provide new guards for their future security.

_____ 5. The primary purpose of this paragraph is to
      A. inform.   B. persuade.   C. inform and entertain.

_____ 6. The tone of this paragraph can be described as
      A. solemn and determined.   C. alarmed and pessimistic.
      B. bitter and indignant.   D. indignant and superior.

D. ¹Go placidly amid the noise and the haste, and remember what peace there may be in silence. ²As far as possible, without surrender, be on good terms with all persons. ³Speak your truth quietly and clearly; and listen to others, even to the dull and the ignorant; they too have their story. . . .

    ⁴Beyond a wholesome discipline, be gentle with yourself. ⁵You are a child of the universe, no less than the trees and the stars; you have a right to be here. ⁶And whether or not it is clear to you, no doubt the universe is unfolding as it should.

    ⁷Therefore, be at peace with God, whatever you conceive Him to be. ⁸And whatever your labors and aspirations in the noisy confusion of life, keep peace in your soul. ⁹With all its sham, drudgery and broken dreams, it is still a beautiful world. ¹⁰Be cheerful. ¹¹Strive to be happy.

_____ 7. The primary purpose of this passage is to
      A. inform.   B. persuade.   C. entertain.

_____ 8. The predominant tone of this passage can be described as
      A. warm but self-pitying.   C. reflective and nostalgic.
      B. worried and sorrowful.   D. optimistic and inspirational.

8 Argument

Many of us enjoy a good argument. A good argument is not an emotional experience in which people allow their anger to get out of control, leaving them ready to start throwing things. Instead, it is a rational discussion in which each person advances and supports a point of view about some matter. We might argue with a friend, for example, about where to eat or what movie to see. We might argue about whether a boss or a parent or an instructor is acting in a fair or an unfair manner. We might argue about whether certain performers or sports stars deserve to get paid as much as they do.

In an argument, the two parties each present their supporting evidence. (In the playful cartoon above, the wife's supporting evidence is simply that the husband has no say about where they will go for Thanksgiving!) The goal is to determine who has the more solid evidence to support his or her point of view.

Argumentation is, then, a part of our everyday dealings with other people. It is also an important part of much of what we read. Authors often try to convince us of their opinions and interpretations. Very often the most important things we must do as critical readers are

1 Recognize the **point** the author is making.

2 Decide if the author's support is **relevant**.

3 Decide if the author's support is **adequate**.

This chapter will give you practice in doing the above, first in everyday arguments and then in textbook material.

The Basics of Argument: Point and Support

A good **argument** is one in which a point is stated and then persuasively and logically supported. Here is a point:

Point: Evidence suggests that men are more romantic than women.

You may well disagree with this, especially if you are a woman. "Why do you say that?" you might legitimately ask. "Give your reasons." Support is needed so you can decide for yourself whether a valid argument has been made. Suppose the point is followed by these three reasons:

1. Studies indicate that men fall in love more easily than women, whereas women fall out of love more easily than men.

2. In interviews, women are more likely than men to say they would marry someone they didn't love.

3. Research shows that men hold more romantic beliefs—such as "Love lasts forever"—than women do.

Clearly, the details provide solid support for the point. They give you a basis for understanding and agreeing with the point. Of course, you may want to see the research. You may question just what is meant by the word "romantic." And based on your personal experience, you might decide to disagree. You could then try to provide evidence that supports your point of view.

Many issues in everyday life are the subject of argument. Is single life preferable to married life? Should abortions be banned? Should gay marriages be legalized? Should the death penalty exist? Should mercy killing be permitted? Should the United States have gotten involved in Afghanistan? Should handguns be banned? Should contraceptives be distributed in schools?

For all these and many other complex issues, there are no easy answers, and arguments about them are bound to persist. Typically, even when one of these issues goes in some form before the U.S. Supreme Court, where all the support is examined in great detail, the judges are often unable to reach a unanimous opinion.

Given the complexity of important issues, we must try our best to think as clearly as we can about them. We must decide what we individually think after close consideration of all the evidence available.

✔ *Check Your Understanding*

Let's look at another example:

Point: Hitting children at times is (*or is not*) a good way to discipline them.

What is your point of view? Is it OK for adults to hit children at times?

_____ OK   _____ Not OK

Circle in the list below the letters of the **three** reasons that you feel solidly support your point of view. And in the space underneath, feel free to add another reason or two that you feel support your point.

A. Hitting a child is the quickest and most effective way to let the child know that he or she has done wrong.

B. Hitting a child teaches him that bigger people are allowed to hurt smaller people. This can lead to the child becoming a bully to smaller children.

C. Disciplinary methods other than spanking, such as a "time out," withdrawing a privilege, or reasoning with the child, just drag out the punishment. It's better to just get it over with.

D. Children who are spanked learn that hitting is the appropriate response to anger. They are likely to become violent adults, to abuse their partners, and to hit and even abuse their own children.

E. It is a parent's job to teach a child to respect and obey those in authority. If a parent doesn't use firm discipline such as hitting, the child will grow up to be a misbehaving, disrespectful adult.

F. Even parents who intend to spank their child only gently can easily lose their temper and hit the child harder than they planned. Many cases of child abuse have begun with "only a spanking."

At your option, write here any other reason(s) you may have in support of your position: _____

_____

_____

Explanation

If you think it's **not** OK to hit kids, you would have chosen B, D, and F as your support. If you think it **is** OK, you would have chosen A, C, and E. The heart of the matter here is that you must determine, by careful and clear thinking, your own point of view about a given issue. Your aim is to construct a valid argument—one supported by what you feel are the most logical facts, examples, reasons, or other evidence.

The Point and Support of an Argument

In everyday life, of course, people don't simply say "Here is my point" and "Here is my support." Even so, the basic structure of point and support is just under the surface of most opinions, and to evaluate an opinion and argument, you need to examine the unspoken support.

The following activity will help sharpen your understanding of a point and its support. The activity may also deepen your sense of the complexity of many everyday issues.

PRACTICE 1

For each statement, choose your point of view by checking "I agree" or "I disagree." Then circle the letters of the **three** items that support your point of view. At your option, add, in the space provided under each item, additional support for your point of view.

> **Note** Be forewarned: People are passionate about many of the following issues. You will probably agree or disagree strongly with some of the evidence. The purpose here is not to endorse either side of a given issue, but rather to sharpen your sense of the point and support that is the backbone of any argument. A secondary purpose is to encourage civilized adult discussion of some important matters in our country today.

1. **Point: The death penalty should exist for certain crimes.**

   ___ I agree   ___ I disagree

   A. Certain crimes, such as the rape and murder of a child, are so heinous that there is no possibility of rehabilitation for the perpetrator. Such a person has given up his right to be treated as a human being and deserves nothing but death. Society should not have to put up with such individuals.

   B. The death penalty does not deter anyone from committing a crime. It is absurd to believe that anyone thinks, "I am willing to risk life in prison, but not execution" before acting.

C. The death penalty acts as a strong deterrent to crime. It serves as a reminder that there are certain acts that society will not tolerate.

D. It is a misuse of taxpayers' money to keep killers alive on death row. The cost of providing prisoners with food, housing and medical care for decades is staggering. Our tax dollars can be put to far better use.

E. The death penalty is inconsistently and unfairly applied. Poor minority criminals without access to good legal representation are far more likely to be executed than more affluent white criminals.

F. The great majority of developed nations have rejected capital punishment as a remnant of a barbaric system of justice. The United States is alone among affluent Western nations in retaining it. By allowing capital punishment, the U.S. has aligned itself philosophically with such countries as Libya, Vietnam, Iran, and China and against countries that include Mexico, Canada, Italy, France, Australia, England, Norway, and Sweden.

Optional additional support for your point of view: _____

_____

_____

Optional minority point of view: Is there one point for the other side that you have some sympathy for? If so, put its letter here: _____. (Some issues are so complex that you may, to some extent, have a divided point of view.)

2. **Point: Contraceptives should be distributed in high schools.**

____ I agree   ____ I disagree

A. Distributing contraceptives in high school amounts to condoning teen sexual activity. High school students should be encouraged to postpone sexual activity until they are older, not given the message that it's OK to be sexually active.

B. Part of having good moral values is to "just say no" and to refrain from sex outside of marriage. Teenage virginity is a virtue that should be promoted, not discouraged. By making contraceptives available, schools will discourage chaste behavior.

C. Most people who would use a contraception-distribution program are sexually active already. The program would help prevent unwanted pregnancies that would happen otherwise.

D. Although sex education should ideally come from one's parents, many parents are not willing or able to do the job. The school is the logical next best source for education about and help with contraception.

E. There can be a lot of confusion and misunderstanding about how to use contraceptives properly, how effective they are, and whether they prevent the spread of STD's. Distributing them at school will just add to that confusion. Medical professionals, not high school personnel, should be the ones to provide people with contraceptives and education about using them properly.

F. Sex is a normal part of life, not something to be hidden away as if it were shameful. Responsible sexuality should be taught at school like any other life skill, and making contraceptives available should be part of that teaching.

Optional additional support for your point of view: _____

_____

_____

Optional minority point of view: Is there one point for the other side that you have some sympathy for? If so, put its letter here: _____. (Some issues are so complex that you may, to some extent, have a divided point of view.)

3. **Point: Abortion should be banned.**

____ I agree   ____ I disagree

A. Abortion is murder. A fetus is a human being from the moment of conception. Just as it is illegal to kill a full-term baby, it should be illegal to kill an unborn baby.

B. Abortion is preferable to having women bear unwanted babies. Every day there are stories in the news about unwanted children being abused and neglected. There are already too many unwanted children in the world. Abortion is a practical solution to that problem.

C. Legal abortion encourages sexual immorality. People are less careful about using contraception if they have the option of abortion.

D. Abortion is a woman's civil right. Almost invariably, it is the woman who ends up bearing most of the responsibility for raising a child. It should be the woman's choice whether or not to bear a child.

E. Abortion cheapens the sanctity of life in all its forms. If abortion is legal, people will soon want to legalize the killing of the sick, the intellectually disabled, the elderly, and other helpless individuals.

F. It is an individual decision whether or not abortion is morally right or wrong. If a person has religious scruples against abortion, she is free not to have an abortion. But someone else's religious beliefs should not be the basis for law.

Optional additional support for your point of view: _____

_____

_____

Optional minority point of view: Is there one point for the other side that you have some sympathy for? If so, put its letter here: _____. (Some issues are so complex that you may, to some extent, have a divided point of view.)

4. **Point: Gay couples should be legally allowed to marry in every state.**

____ I agree   ____ I disagree

A. Throughout history, marriage has been defined as the union of a man and a woman. Centuries of tradition should not be tossed out in order to accommodate gay couples.

B. Many people consider homosexuality to be morally wrong. It is offensive to them to see the state and/or church recognize gay marriages.

C. Gay marriage would represent a strengthening of our society. Marriage of any type encourages "family values" such as commitment and monogamy.

D. Gay people deserve to have their committed relationships recognized and honored as much as straight people. Being able to marry would allow gays to take a further step in "coming out" into full participation in society.

E. The legal and financial protection offered by marriage should be the right of gay couples as well as straight couples.

F. Gay marriage is unnecessary. Gays may be offered "civil unions" that offer some legal protection, but stop short of being called marriage.

Optional additional support for your point of view: _____

_____

_____

Optional minority point of view: Is there one point for the other side that you have some sympathy for? If so, put its letter here: _____. (Some issues are so complex that you may, to some extent, have a divided point of view.)

5. **Point: Physicians should be allowed to assist in suicide.**

___ I agree   ___ I disagree

A. Knowing they have the option of requesting physician-assisted suicide gives many terminally ill patients peace of mind. In fact, many people who have made arrangements for physician-assisted suicide end up not using the option. They still benefit from the knowledge that if their suffering becomes too intense, they can control when and how they die.

B. Life belongs to God. It should end only when God decides to end it. Any form of suicide is wrong.

C. Physician-assisted suicide relieves the patient's family of the heavy responsibility of deciding when to withdraw further care. A person can choose to die when she is ready, knowing that her family will not have to decide to "pull the plug" if she becomes unresponsive and unable to make her wishes known.

D. If physician-assisted suicide is legal, then sick, elderly people will be pressured to make use of it. Instead of honoring and caring for our sick elders, we will become a society that wants to hurry them into death when they become infirm.

E. Physician-assisted suicide allows patients to opt out of suffering through a long, painful death. Enduring such a death is as agonizing for their loved ones as it is painful for the patients themselves.

F. The purpose of a physician is to heal the sick. It is a perversion of the physician's role to ask doctors to assist in suicide.

Optional additional support for your point of view: _____

_____

_____

Optional minority point of view: Is there one point for the other side that you have some sympathy for? If so, put its letter here: _____. (Some issues are so complex that you may, to some extent, have a divided point of view.)

Relevant Support

Once you identify the point and support of an argument, you need to decide if each piece of evidence is **relevant**—in other words, if it really applies to the point. The critical reader must ask, "Is this reason relevant support for the argument?"

In their desire to win an argument, people often bring up irrelevant support. For example, in asking you to vote for him, a political candidate might say,

"I'll vote to lower your taxes." But your town or state might have such financial problems that lowering taxes would not be possible. You would then want to look closely at other reasons why you should or should not vote for this candidate.

An excellent way to develop skill in recognizing relevant support is to work on simple point-support outlines of arguments. By isolating the reasons of an argument, such outlines help you think about whether each reason is truly relevant. Paying close attention to the relevance of support will help you not only in your reading, but also in making and supporting points in your own writing.

✔ Check Your Understanding

Consider the following outline. The point is followed by six facts, only three of which are relevant support for the point. In the spaces, write the letters of the **three** relevant statements of support.

> **Point: Despite their fearsome image, sharks have more to fear from humans than humans do from sharks.**
>
> A. Some species of sharks are able to detect as little as one part per million of blood in seawater.
> B. Shark-fin soup is considered a great delicacy in the Far East, and hundreds of thousands of sharks have been slaughtered simply for their fins.
> C. Sharks can range in size from hand-sized pygmy sharks to plankton-eating whale sharks which grow to a maximum length of 49 feet.
> D. It's estimated that 100 million sharks, skates, and rays are caught and killed each year.
> E. Some populations of large sharks have fallen by as much as 90 percent due to accelerated fishing activities in recent decades.
> F. Large sharks such as great whites, tiger sharks, and bull sharks have been known to attack people, perhaps mistaking them for seals.
>
> *Items that logically support the point:* __B__   __D__   __E__

Explanation

The three statements that support the idea that humans are dangerous to sharks are B, D, and E. The other three statements provide interesting facts about sharks but do not offer relevant support for the point in question. (You could not cite any of these interesting facts about sharks as support for the idea that sharks are dangerous. If you did so, you would be *changing the subject* by introducing irrelevant support.)

due friday (+5)

PRACTICE 2

Each point is followed by three statements that provide relevant support and three that do not. In the spaces, write the letters of the **three** relevant statements of support.

> *Hint:* To help you decide if a sentence is relevant, ask yourself, "Does this provide logical support for the point being argued?"

1. **Point: E-waste, or waste from discarded computers and other electronic equipment, is currently the most rapidly growing waste problem in the world.**

   A. Amounts of electronic waste are increasing nearly three times more quickly than amounts of other municipal wastes.

   B. Discarded electronics equipment contains lead, mercury, cadmium, PCBs, dioxins, and other toxic substances.

   C. Some components in discarded computers can be successfully recycled.

   D. The United States is a world leader in the development of computer software programs.

   E. Environmental, health, and safety regulations make recycling E-waste unprofitable in the United States, so we have been shipping it around the world to countries with inadequate environmental protections.

   F. The United States has been increasingly outsourcing its computer support jobs to India and other developing nations.

   Items that logically support the point: __A__ __B__ __E__

2. **Point: Childhood obesity has a number of causes.**

   A. Overweight children are at risk for a number of health problems throughout their lives.

   B. The increasing popularity of computers, video games, and other electronic entertainment has caused children to become more sedentary.

   C. It is estimated that about 18 percent of American children are overweight.

   D. Many kids live in areas where they cannot safely go outside for physical exercise.

   E. Fatty fast food and high-calorie snacks make up a large portion of many children's diets.

   F. There are a growing number of "fat camps" aimed at helping youngsters lose weight during vacation.

   Items that logically support the point: __B__ __D__ __E__

3. **Point: A major problem with prisons is that they fail to teach their clients to stay away from crime.**

    A. A number of prisoners are suffering from mental illness, addiction, or both.

    B. Three out of every four prisoners have been in prison before.

    C. When prisoners convicted of violent crimes are released, in just three years half are back in prison.

    D. Far more men than women are imprisoned for violent crimes.

    E. Some prisoners earn their GEDs or higher degrees while in prison.

    F. More than seventy percent of those jailed for stealing cars, burglary, and robbery commit similar crimes after they are released.

    Items that logically support the point: ___B___   ___C___   ___F___

4. **Point: Contrary to popular belief, citrus fruits are not the only foods which are high in vitamin C.**

    A. Potatoes provide about 20 percent of all the vitamin C in the U.S. diet.

    B. Florida and California are two states which lead the nation in producing oranges and other citrus fruits.

    C. Sailors once got the disease known as scurvy on long ocean voyages because they were deprived of foods that were high in vitamin C.

    D. A single serving of broccoli, green pepper, or cauliflower provides nearly the entire recommended daily amount of vitamin C.

    E. Cantaloupes and strawberries are high in vitamin C.

    F. Evidence is inconclusive that taking large amounts of vitamin C can prevent colds.

    Items that logically support the point: ___A___   ___D___   ___E___

5. **Point: Social networking sites such as Facebook and Twitter have dramatically expanded opportunities for people to communicate with others in helpful ways.**

    A. When Mark Zuckerberg and his friends founded Facebook in 2004, membership was limited to their fellow Harvard students.

    B. Recently, protesters in Egypt, Libya and other Middle Eastern countries credited social networking sites with enabling them to organize large demonstrations against corrupt rulers.

    C. With a Twitter account, people can almost immediately learn what others are thinking and doing and feeling, even when they're miles apart.

    D. Some students have used social media sites to spread hurtful messages about others; such "cyber bullying" has caused some vulnerable young people to commit suicide.

E. Using social networking sites, it's easy to publicize parties, reunions, concerts, and other social activities.

    F. A market research firm concluded that forty percent of Twitter messages were "pointless babble."

Items that logically support the point: ___B___   ___C___   ___E___

Adequate Support

A valid argument must include not only relevant support but also **adequate** support—substantial enough to prove the point. For example, it would not be valid to argue "Abortion is wrong" if one's only support was "My sister had an abortion and has regretted it ever since." Such an important issue would require more support than the attitude and experience of a single relative. Arguing a point that doesn't have adequate support is called "jumping to a conclusion" or "hasty generalization."

You will seldom see a textbook author jump to a conclusion; instead, the author's approach will be to present the existing data about a given subject and then to draw reasonable conclusions based upon that data. As always, the key to understanding will be to focus on what points the author is making and what support is being provided for those points.

✓ Check Your Understanding

In the argument below, four supporting reasons are given, followed by four possible conclusions. The evidence (that is, the supporting reasons) adequately supports only one of the points; it is insufficient to support the other three. Check (✓) the **one** point that you think is adequately supported.

Support

● A happily married man or woman might attribute a spouse's distracted manner to stress at work.

● An unhappily married man or woman might attribute a distracted manner to a decline in affection.

● A happily married man or woman might attribute a spouse's unexpected gift to a desire to show love.

● An unhappily married man or woman might consider an unexpected gift as evidence of guilt about something.

Which **point** is adequately supported by all the evidence above?

___ A. Men or women who surprise their partners with gifts have probably been cheating on them.

✗ B. Happily and unhappily married spouses tend to interpret their partners' behaviors differently.

___ C. People who are happily married are often deluding themselves about reality.

___ D. Spouses should give each other gifts more often.

Explanation

The correct answer is B. All of the supporting items back up the idea that one partner's interpretation of the other partner's behavior can be influenced by whether they are happy or unhappy in the marriage. None of the other three items, A, C, or D, is backed up by the items of support.

due friday   (+4)

 PRACTICE 3

In each group that follows, the support is from experiments, surveys, studies, and other evidence in textbooks. Check (✓) the **point** in each case that is adequately supported by the evidence.

Group 1

Support

- Ads in magazines such as *Glamour, Ebony,* and *Esquire* are four times more likely to display women's buttocks, legs, stomach, shoulders, or back than to show men's.

- In television beer commercials, the camera shots are significantly more likely to focus on women's bodies than on men's bodies.

- In newspapers, a typical photograph of a man dedicates two-thirds of the space to his face, while the typical photograph of a woman dedicates only one-half of the space to her face.

1. Which **point** is adequately supported by all the evidence above?

    A. The media are responsible for much of the gender inequality in our society.

    B. Exploitation of women is the single greatest problem in American society today.

    C. Media images tend to emphasize men's faces and women's bodies.

    D. Most news and entertainment media are controlled by men.

Group 2

Support

- Engaging in stimulating activities and hobbies can help older adults retain sharp mental abilities.

- Elderly people who remain socially active are by and large happier than those who do not.

- Volunteering to help others tends to increase elderly people's overall sense of life satisfaction.

2. Which **point** is adequately supported by all the evidence above?
   - A. There are steps people can take to make their elder years enjoyable.
   - B. Growing old is a difficult and challenging process.
   - C. A person who is not socially outgoing cannot have an enjoyable life.
   - D. Helping other people is the single most effective way to increase one's life satisfaction.

Group 3

Support

- Neurotic individuals tend to appraise events as more stressful than other individuals and to become more distressed by problems.

- Neurotic people report more health problems and visit the doctor more often than other individuals, although their symptoms are often found to have no physical basis.

- Neurotic individuals often suffer from a range of anxieties that seem exaggerated to others.

3. Which **point** is adequately supported by all the evidence above?
   - A. Neurotic people are seriously mentally ill and need to be institutionalized.
   - B. Neurotic disorders are very rare.
   - C. It is impossible for neurotic people to make friends.
   - D. Being neurotic produces a range of problems that make life difficult.

Group 4

Support

- The Constitution requires that a U.S. president be at least 35 years old.

- As of 2012, every U.S. president has been male.

- The Constitution requires that a U.S. president be a natural-born U.S. citizen.

_C_   4. Which **point** is adequately supported by all the evidence above?

+1

A. No female will ever be elected president of the United States.
B. The U.S. Constitution's requirements for the presidency are unfair.
C. There are both formal requirements and traditional expectations for becoming president of the United States.
D. It is past time for a woman to be president of the United States.

Group 5

Support

- In ancient Rome, wealthy citizens who aspired to political office expanded their influence by donating extremely expensive entertainments to the rest of the population of the city on a regular basis.

- Julius Caesar owed much of his political success to the fact that he was better than his rivals at providing the people with elaborate outdoor entertainment.

- One of Julius Caesar's public shows included a gladiatorial contest, stage-plays for every quarter of Rome performed in several languages, chariot races, athletic competitions, and a mock naval battle.

_B_   5. Which **point** is adequately supported by all the evidence above?

A. Above all, ancient Romans enjoyed chariot races.
B. In ancient Rome, politicians were the ones who provided elaborate outdoor entertainment to the masses.

+1

C. In ancient Rome, leaders wasted their time providing free entertainment to the masses.
D. Julius Caesar's skill at organizing mass entertainment was more important than his skill as a general.

A Note on Argument in Textbook Writing

In most textbook writing, argument takes the form of well-developed ideas or theories (in other words, points) that are supported with experiments, surveys, studies, expert testimony, reasons, examples, or other evidence. Textbook arguments generally have solid support, but recognizing the author's points and asking yourself whether the support is relevant and adequate will help you be an involved and critical reader.

CHAPTER REVIEW

Claim

In this chapter, you learned the following:

support

- A good argument is made up of a point, or a conclusion, and logical evidence to back it up.

(1) ● To critically read an argument, you must recognize the **point** the author is making.

(2) ● To think through an argument, you need to decide if each piece of evidence is **relevant**.

(3) ● To think through an argument, you also need to decide if the author's support is **adequate**.

(4) *check bars*

- Textbook arguments generally have solid support, but recognizing the author's point and watching for relevant and adequate support will help you become a more involved and critical reader.

The next chapter—Chapter 9—will explain other aspects of being a critical reader: separating fact from opinion, detecting propaganda, and recognizing errors in reasoning.

On the Web: If you are using this book in class, you can go to our website for more practice in evaluating arguments. Visit our Learning Center at **www.townsendpress.net** for additional activities and an instructional video on this skill.

REVIEW TEST 1

To review what you've learned in this chapter, answer each of the following questions by filling in the blank.

1. A good argument advances a clear _____point_____ of some kind.

2. The second basic part of a good argument is solid _____support_____.

3. Many issues in everyday life are the subject of continuing argument because the issues are so _____complex_____ that there are no easy answers or solutions.

4. Good thinkers have the ability to look at evidence and decide what logical point or *Conclusion* can be drawn from that evidence.

5. Good thinkers have the ability to decide whether there is a(n) *adequate* amount of evidence to convincingly support a point.

REVIEW TEST 2

The essay below is followed by questions on argument and also the skills covered in previous chapters.

Preview

"Mark and Lindsey are shopping for a ring!" It's a feature of nearly every American engagement—The Ring. And not just any ring, but a *diamond* ring. But why is a diamond ring so necessary? This essay reveals the not-so-romantic truth behind one of the most successful marketing campaigns in history.

Words to Watch

signify (5): symbolize; be a sign of
multi-faceted (6): on several levels; having many aspects
enlisted (6): requested the cooperation of
Spartan (13): frugal; self-denying (after Sparta, a city in ancient Greece known for its focus on discipline and physical fitness)

DIAMONDS AREN'T FOREVER

Ruth A. Rouff

1 It's no secret that we Americans are exposed to advertising virtually from the cradle to the grave. Aside from print advertising, the amount of time we spend watching TV commercials alone is staggering. One source estimated that by the time a person turns sixty, he or she will have "wasted" *three years* watching TV commercials.

2 Of course, advertisers and their

clients don't think of their messages as a waste of time—far from it. They see them as serving the vital purpose of keeping us informed about important goods and services. But it's one thing to convince us to spend money on a particular brand of toothpaste or frozen dinner. It's quite another to manipulate us into feeling as if we must spend large sums of money on things we don't really *need* but have been told that we *should* want.

3   One surefire way advertisers get us to spend lots of money on nonessential items is to hit us where we are most vulnerable—not in the head, but in the heart. What they do is suggest that if we *truly* love a person, we will show it by how much we spend on him or her. And if that statement is true, then its opposite is also true. The less expensive the gift—well, you don't want those you love thinking you're *cheap*, do you?

4   The history of diamond engagement rings is a classic example of the way that advertisers play upon our emotions to stimulate demand for a particular product. As strange as it may now seem, giving diamond rings to symbolize engagement is a fairly recent custom. Oh, in the 1800s and earlier, European royalty exchanged diamond engagement rings, but Americans usually didn't. In fact, back in colonial times, the Puritans frowned upon jewelry and instead gave thimbles as a sign of commitment. The thimble was then used by the bride-to-be as she sewed her wedding clothes and linen.

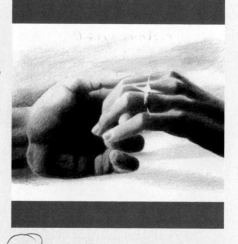

After the wedding, the thimble was cut to show that it was no longer needed. The rim of the thimble was then worn on the finger like a ring.

This charming custom gradually 5 died out, along with Puritanism. By the middle of the 19th century, the practice of giving rings to signify° engagement became commonplace. These engagement rings were usually not diamonds—because diamonds were very rare. However, something happened in 1870 that would forever change the jewelry industry. Huge diamond mines were discovered in South Africa. Since diamonds were literally being scooped out of these mines by the ton, the price of the gems rapidly dropped. By the 1890s, inexpensive diamond engagement rings were well within the reach of many Americans. Mass-market retailers such as Sears and Roebuck began featuring modestly priced rings in their mail-order catalogs. In the late 1930s, the average

diamond rings had a fair price

rings went

price of a diamond engagement ring was only $80. This drop in price was not what the De Beers Company, which had a monopoly on the South African diamond mines, wanted to see.

6   So in 1938, De Beers hired an American advertising agency, N.W. Ayer, to boost diamond prices by changing American attitudes toward diamonds. They wanted to get the message across to young men that diamonds were a gift of love: the larger and finer the diamond, the greater the expression of love. Similarly, young women had to be encouraged to view diamonds as an essential part of romantic courtship. As if waging a great military campaign, N.W. Ayer used a multi-faceted° approach to promote the giving of costly diamond engagement rings:

- Movie stars were given diamonds to use as their symbols of undying love.
- Journalists were paid to write magazine stories that stressed the size of diamonds that celebrities presented to their loved ones. Glossy close-ups of ring-laden hands accompanied the stories.
- Speakers were sent around to high schools across the country to lecture students about diamond engagement rings.
- The British royal family was even enlisted° to wear diamonds rather than other jewels.

As Ayer explained in a 1948 company report, "We spread the word of diamonds worn by stars of screen and stage, by wives and daughters of political leaders, by any woman who can make the grocer's wife and the mechanic's sweetheart say 'I wish I had what she has.'"

7   But the masterstroke of the campaign was the slogan, "A Diamond Is Forever," which is now considered the most recognized advertising slogan of all time. The genius of the slogan was that since "diamonds are forever," they should never be resold. As a result, secondhand diamonds—which would have increased supply and lowered prices—never entered the market.

8   The ad campaign was amazingly successful. By 1941, the retail sale of diamonds had increased over 50%, and nearly everyone viewed a diamond ring as an essential part of an engagement.

9   These days, the price of diamond engagement rings continues to rise. In 2007, the average cost in the United States was $2,100. In 2011, the average cost of a jewelry-store diamond ring was between $3,500 and $4,000, with larger stones selling for even more. And, of course, the matching wedding band is extra.

10   Ironically, given the number of American marriages that end in divorce, a diamond may be forever, but marriages often aren't. The National Center for Health Statistics recently predicted that one-third of new marriages among younger people will end in divorce within 10 years and 43 percent within 15 years.

11   Despite such statistics, we will continue to think of Mother's Day, Valentine's Day, Christmas, anniversaries, and birthdays as days to reaffirm bonds of love. But in the cold, hard eyes of the jewelry industry, these days are golden marketing opportunities.

- "Every Kiss Begins with Kay," proclaims Kay Jewelers.
- "True love has a beginning but no ending," says a slogan on the Tiffany.com website.

The message is that if you *really* love your partner, you'll want to shower her (or him) with jewelry throughout her (or his) life.

12   But what if, after all that spending, true love *isn't* forever? Well, high-powered divorce lawyers now advertise in many of the same magazines that carry ads for jewelry.

13   If you're like most people, you're probably thinking, "But I still want a diamond engagement ring, just like the one my mother had." There's nothing wrong with that. After all, very few of us desire a totally Spartan° lifestyle.

14   But keep in mind that advertisers are doing their best to pressure us into wanting what *they* think we should want. And remember, too: love can't be reduced to dollar signs.

15   If it could, the rich would never get divorced.

Reading Comprehension Questions

Vocabulary in Context

 1. In the following excerpt, the word *masterstroke* (măs'tər-strōk') means
   A. brilliant idea.
   B. major error.
   C. first step.
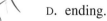 D. ending.

> "But the masterstroke of the campaign was the slogan, 'A Diamond Is Forever,' which is now considered the most recognized advertising slogan of all time. The genius of the slogan was that since 'diamonds are forever,' they should never be resold." (Paragraph 7)

Central Point and Main Ideas

_D_ 2. Which sentence best expresses the central point of the selection?

x1

    A. Despite current beliefs, giving diamond rings to symbolize engagement is a fairly recent custom.

    B. In 1938, De Beers hired the N.W. Ayer advertising agency to change American attitudes toward diamonds.

    C. Given the number of American marriages that end in divorce, a diamond may be forever, but marriages often aren't.

    D. The history of diamond engagement rings is a classic example of the way that advertisers play upon our emotions to stimulate demand for a particular product.

_B_ 3. Which sentence best expresses the main idea of paragraphs 5–6?

x1

    A. After huge diamond mines were discovered in South Africa, the price of diamond engagement rings dropped.

    B. Because the price of diamonds dropped after diamond mines were discovered in South Africa, the De Beers Company hired an ad agency to promote the giving of costly diamonds.

    C. The American ad agency N.W. Ayer tried to convince young people to view diamonds as a gift of love.

    D. The De Beers Company, which had a monopoly on the South African diamond mines, was not happy to see the average price of a diamond engagement ring drop.

Supporting Details

_C_ 4. Which of the following tactics was *not* employed as part of N.W. Ayer's campaign to promote the giving of costly diamond engagement rings?

    A. Movie stars were photographed wearing diamonds.

x

    B. Speakers lectured high school students about diamond engagement rings.

    C. The First Lady of the United States was photographed wearing an expensive diamond ring.

    D. The slogan "A Diamond Is Forever" was created.

Transitions

_____ 5. The relationship between the second sentence below and the first sentence is one of
   A. contrast.
   B. cause and effect.
   C. illustration.
   D. comparison.

> "They wanted to get the message across to young men that diamonds were a gift of love: the larger and finer the diamond, the greater the expression of love. Similarly, young women had to be encouraged to view diamonds as an essential part of romantic courtship." (Paragraph 6)

Patterns of Organization

_____ 6. In general, paragraphs 1 and 2
   A. compare wasting time watching TV commercials with wasting time watching TV programs.
   B. contrast what the author thinks of advertised messages with how advertisers themselves view their messages.
   C. present a time-order relationship.
   D. illustrate how advertisers manipulate us into buying things we don't really need.

Inferences

_____ 7. We can conclude from this selection that
   A. it is natural for most people to prefer diamonds to other precious stones.
   B. diamonds are the rarest precious stones.
   C. the demand for diamonds has been artificially stimulated.
   D. people who purchase expensive diamond rings are less likely to divorce than those who do not.

Purpose and Tone

_____ 8. On the basis of the reading, we might conclude that the author's intention is
   A. only to inform.
   B. to entertain and persuade.
   C. both to inform and to persuade.

_____C_____ 9. The author's tone in the selection may be characterized as
        A. affectionate.
        B. sentimental.
        C. critical.
        D. detached.

Argument

_____A_____ 10. Three of the items below are supporting details for an argument. Write
the letter of the statement that represents the point of this argument.
        A. By the 1890s, inexpensive diamond engagement rings were well within the reach of many Americans.
        B. Contrary to popular belief, diamonds have not always been costly.
        C. Retailers such as Sears and Roebuck began featuring modestly priced diamond engagement rings in their mail-order catalogs.
        D. In the late 1930s, the average price of a diamond engagement ring was only $80.

Discussion Questions

1. As a result of reading this selection, has your attitude toward the giving of expensive jewelry changed or stayed about the same? Explain.

2. The author describes advertisers who suggest that if we truly love a person, we will show it by spending lots of money on her or him. Do you agree that spending money on someone demonstrates love? Why or why not? Have you ever felt guilty or resentful about the amount of money you spent on a gift? Explain.

3. The author describes the Puritan practice of giving a thimble as a sign of commitment as a "charming custom." Do you agree with her? Why or why not? Can you think of any religious groups today that frown upon jewelry? If so, what reasons do they give for doing so?

4. The author describes the N.W. Ayer campaign for De Beers as a classic example of the way advertisers play on our emotions to stimulate demand for a particular product. Can you think of some other examples of advertisements that manipulate our emotions? Do any of them use celebrities to convince us to buy their products? Explain.

Note: Writing assignments for this selection appear on page 638.

Check Your Performance

ARGUMENT

Activity	Number Right	Points	Score
Review Test 1 (5 items)	_____	× 6 =	_____
Review Test 2 (10 items)	_____	× 7 =	_____
	TOTAL SCORE	=	_____ %

Enter your total score into the **Reading Performance Chart: Review Tests** on the inside back cover.

ARGUMENT: Mastery Test 1

A. In each group, one statement is the point of an argument, and the other statements are support for that point. In the space provided, write the letter of the point of each group.

____C____ 1.   A. Debates over who could drive the car created serious conflicts between parents and teenagers.
   B. The use of automobiles for Sunday outings was thought to have led to a decline in church attendance.
   C. The first automobiles were a cause for alarm in many communities.
   D. Autos were seen as giving young people too much freedom and privacy, serving as "portable bedrooms" that couples could take anywhere.

____D____ 2.   A. During the 1920s, banks began offering the country's first home mortgages.
   B. Retail sellers of everything from cars to irons in the 1920s allowed customers to pay in installments.
   C. In the 1920s, about 60 percent of mortgages and 75 percent of all radios were purchased on the installment plan.
   D. The use of installment credit became very popular with banks, retail sellers, and consumers during the 1920s.

____B____ 3.   A. Most women today continue to work in a relatively small number of traditional "women's" jobs, and full-time female workers earn only 68 cents for every $1 paid to men.
   B. Despite all that has been achieved in terms of women's rights, many injustices still remain.
   C. Today, the economic plight of women involved in the 50% of marriages that end in divorce is often grave.
   D. Although female-headed families constitute only 15 percent of the U.S. population, they account for over 50% of the poor population.

____B____ 4.   A. Printed newspapers are limited by the amount of news that can be printed in one edition, but online papers have no such limitations.
   B. More and more people are reading online newspapers because they realize that online papers have certain advantages over traditional newspapers.
   C. Online papers can be updated continuously, since they have no edition deadlines.
   D. Online newspapers are interactive—e-mail addresses, bulletin boards, and chat rooms allow readers to provide quick feedback to the paper.

(Continues on next page)

323

B. Read the three items of support (the evidence) in the group below. Then, in the space provided, write the letter of the point that is adequately supported by that evidence.

> *Support*
>
> ● Eating chocolate releases serotonin in the human brain, resulting in feelings of pleasure.
>
> ● Chocolate contains caffeine, a stimulant that restores alertness.
>
> ● Dark chocolate contains antioxidants that have health benefits such as protecting blood vessels and promoting cardiac health.

_B__ 5. Which **point** is adequately supported by all the evidence above?
   A. Sweet treats are actually good for your health.
   B. Chocolate can have a significant impact on the human body.
   C. Dark chocolate is healthier than milk chocolate.
   D. Chocolate could be considered a drug.

ARGUMENT: Mastery Test 2

A. In each group, one statement is the point of an argument, and the other statements are support for that point. In the space provided, write the letter of the point of each group.

_A_ 1. A. Adult-structured sports promote healthy child development.
B. Adult-structured sports teach children how to accept authority and prepare them for the realistic competition they will face as adults.
C. Practices and games regularly scheduled by adults ensure that children get plenty of exercise.
D. Adult-structured sports enable parents and children to create healthy bonds.

_D_ 2. A. Physicians never hold up cabbies, but many do cheat Medicare.
B. Bookkeepers don't rob convenience stores, but they have been known to take money from their employers' accounts.
C. Instead of mugging, pimping, and burglary, the privileged evade income tax, bribe public officials, and embezzle money.
D. The more privileged social classes can be just as guilty of criminal activity as members of the lower classes.

_C_ 3. A. Only 4 out of every 100,000 men in China die of heart disease each year, compared with 67 of every 100,000 men in the United States.
B. Chinese people eating traditional foods consume three times the fiber of people eating the American way, take in about half the fat, and have blood cholesterol values about half of what they are in the United States.
C. Despite consuming 20 percent more food energy each day than we do, Chinese who eat traditional Chinese foods have a far healthier diet than Americans.
D. Chinese living in China also suffer much less cancer of the colon and rectum than do Chinese who have adopted a Western diet.

(Continues on next page)

B. Read the three items of support (the evidence) in each group below. Then, in the space provided, write the letter of the point that is adequately supported by that evidence.

Support

- Animal researchers tested two crows, Betty and Abel, to see whether they would choose a hooked wire or a straight wire to use for getting some food out of a tube.

- During one session Abel snatched the hooked wire away from Betty, leaving Betty with only the straight wire to use.

- When Betty realized the straight wire wouldn't work, she bent it into a hook with her beak.

_____ 4. Which **point** is adequately supported by all the evidence above?
   A. A crow can construct a simple tool.
   B. Crows have proven themselves to be the smartest birds.
   C. Researchers prefer to work with crows because they are so intelligent.
   D. Research indicates that some crows can construct simple tools.

Support

- In cancer, cells begin to reproduce in a rapid, disorganized fashion.

- As this cell reproduction lurches out of control, the teeming new cells clump together to form tumors.

- If this wild growth continues unabated, the spreading tumors cause tissue damage and begin to interfere with normal functioning in the affected areas.

_____ 5. Which **point** is adequately supported by all the evidence above?
   A. There are a host of new ways that cancer can be treated.
   B. Cancer is a very serious disease because cancer cells tend to over-whelm the body.
   C. There are various types of cancers which attack different organs in the body.
   D. Some but not all tumors are cancerous.

due friday

ARGUMENT: Mastery Test 3   (+8)

A. In each group, one statement is the point of an argument, and the other statements are support for that point. In the space provided, write the letter of the point of each group.

_B_ 1.   A. Although boys in elementary school are developmentally two years behind girls in reading and writing, they are expected to learn the same material in the same way.

×1

B. American schools are failing to meet the needs of their male students.

C. Males are 30% more likely to drop out of school than females.

D. Today's teachers tend to rely on teaching strategies that appeal to the females in their classes, but alienate their male students.

_D_ 2.   A. During certain days of Lent, the period prior to Easter, many Christians refrain from eating meat.

B. Muslims fast from sunup to sundown during the holy month of Ramadan.

×1

C. Dietary restrictions permit Orthodox Jews to eat beef, but not pork; fish but not shellfish; and they dictate special handling methods for permitted foods.

D. Throughout the world, many religions place restrictions on what kind of foods can be consumed and when they can be consumed.

B. Each point is followed by three statements that provide relevant support and three that do not. In the spaces, write the letters of the **three** relevant statements of support.

3–5. **Point: To better provide for their well-being, zoo elephants should be transferred to large nature preserves.**

A. Adult elephants can consume from 300 to 600 pounds of food a day.

B. Elephants in the wild are accustomed to roaming up to thirty miles a day.

C. Zookeepers try to provide their captive elephants with the best possible veterinary care.

×3

D. In zoos, elephants are fed balanced, highly nutritious diets.

E. Zoo elephants often suffer from degenerative joint problems and chronic foot infections which are the result of standing for long periods on concrete or other unnatural surfaces.

F. Small enclosures in zoos often cause behavioral problems in elephants, including repetitive swaying and head-bobbing, as well as increased aggression toward zookeepers and other elephants.

Items that logically support the point: ___B___   ___E___   ___F___

(Continues on next page)

327

6–8. **Point:** People react to stress on <u>three levels:</u> emotional, physiological, and behavioral.

A. Because today's society is so fast-paced, people are subject to a great deal of stress.

B. When you groan in reaction to a traffic report, you're experiencing an emotional response to stress.

C. When your pulse quickens and your stomach knots up, you're exhibiting physiological responses to stress.

D. Working in a hospital emergency room is certainly a highly stressful occupation.

E. Research has demonstrated that some people are better at handling stress than others.

F. When you shout insults at another driver, your verbal aggression is a behavioral response to the stress at hand.

Items that logically support the point: ___B___   ___C___   ___F___

ARGUMENT: Mastery Test 4

A. In the following group, one statement is the point of an argument, and the other statements are support for that point. In the space provided, write the letter of the point of this group.

_____ 1. A. Children whose parents do not use alcohol tend to abstain or to drink only moderately.

B. A recent study suggests that children are more likely to abuse alcohol if their family tolerates deviance in general or encourages indulgent activities and pleasure-seeking.

C. Adolescents who have been physically assaulted or sexually abused in their homes are at an increased risk for drug abuse.

D. The family setting in which a child grows up helps shape his or her attitudes and beliefs about drug and alcohol use.

B. Read the three items of support (the evidence) in each group below. Then, in the space provided, write the letter of the point that is adequately supported by that evidence.

Support

● The atmosphere on Mars is 95% carbon dioxide, with only small traces of oxygen.

● Liquid water, which is necessary to sustain life, does not exist on Mars.

● Dangerous dust storms frequent Mars, sometimes engulfing the entire planet.

_____ 2. Which **point** is adequately supported by all the evidence above?
A. Mars is one of the most dangerous planets.
B. It is not known whether extraterrestrial beings exist on Mars.
C. Mars is a unique planet.
D. It would be impossible for humans to live on Mars.

(Continues on next page)

C. (3–5.) For the following statement, choose your point of view by checking "I agree" or "I disagree." Then circle the letters of the **three** items that logically support your point of view.

> **Point: Prostitution should be legalized.**
>
> ___ I agree   ___ I disagree
>
> A. Prostitutes perform a service for society. They provide sex for people who otherwise cannot find sexual partners. They may even help marriages by reducing sexual demands on wives. There is no way to put an end to the "world's oldest profession."
>
> B. Prostitution is immoral, and we should not legalize immoral activities. The foundation of society is the family, and we should take steps to strengthen the family, not tear it apart by approving sex as a commercial transaction outside the family.
>
> C. The legalization of prostitution will not stop sexually transmitted diseases. For example, the HIV virus can be transmitted before the disease shows up in blood tests. Even though prostitutes are licensed, they will spread AIDS during this interval.
>
> D. If prostitution is declared a legal occupation, the government can regulate it. If the government licenses prostitutes, it can collect taxes and require prostitutes to have regular medical checkups. Prostitutes can be required to display a dated and signed medical certificate stating that they are free of sexually transmitted diseases.
>
> E. Prostitution stigmatizes and marginalizes women who want to work as prostitutes. It corrupts some police officers, who accept bribes to allow prostitutes to work. Some prostitution is run by organized crime, with women held in bondage. Legalization of prostitution will eliminate these problems.
>
> F. Prostitution degrades women. To legalize prostitution is to give society's approval to their degradation. It also would affirm class oppression: Most prostitutes come from the working class and serve as objects to satisfy the sexual desires of men from more privileged classes.

ARGUMENT: Mastery Test 5

A. In each group, one statement is the point of an argument, and the other statements are support for that point. In the space provided, write the letter of the point of each group.

D 1. A. Charity work gives celebrities a chance to escape the strangeness of life in the spotlight and connect with "regular" people.
   B. Modern-day celebrities have found it beneficial to engage in charitable work.
   C. Charity work gives many celebrities a positive public image.
   D. Domestic or international charity work allows celebrities to make a difference in the world without becoming involved in controversial political issues.

B 2. A. The multicultural movement has led to ethnic revivals in many cities and the nation itself.
   B. The new appreciation of cultural diversity is reflected in efforts to bring the language, literature, and perspective of various ethnic groups into classrooms.
   C. Multiculturalism has raised people's consciousness about the importance of gender, disability, sexual orientation, and other differences that were previously neglected.
   D. Multiculturalism has brought fundamental changes to American education and American society as a whole.

B. (3–5.) The point below is followed by three statements that provide relevant support and three that do not. In the spaces, write the letters of the **three** relevant statements of support.

Point: Animal owners should neuter their pets.

   A. Neutering is mainly practiced in first-world countries.
   B. Neutering makes pets less likely to bite people.
   C. Some animal shelters offer more reasonable rates for neutering than others.
   D. Neutering pets makes them less likely to develop illnesses.
   E. Having pets neutered helps ease the burden on crowded animal shelters.
   F. Some people believe that neutering makes animals less protective of their owners.

Items that logically support the point: ____B____   ____D____   ____E____

(Continues on next page)

C. (6–8.) For the following statement, choose your point of view by checking "I agree" or "I disagree." Then circle the letters of the **three** items that logically support your point of view.

> **Point:** High-school students should be required to participate in the daily Pledge of Allegiance.
>
>   ⨉ I agree   ___ I disagree
>
> A. Requiring students to pledge allegiance to the flag is an exercise in respect for authority. It reminds them that as they should show respect to the flag, they should also show respect to their teachers and other figures in authority.
>
> B. Pledging allegiance to the flag is a constructive way of affirming our identity, as a group and as Americans.
>
> C. To require students to pledge their allegiance is a violation of their civil liberties. In America, we are free to hold views that would interfere with our willingness to say the pledge.
>
> D. The Pledge of Allegiance, with its phrase "one nation, under God," represents a violation of the separation of church and state. Students who are non-believers or who do not believe that God favors one country over another should not be asked to recite the pledge.
>
> E. Requiring the recitation of the Pledge of Allegiance is a way to promote blind, simplistic nationalism. Such nationalism has no place in a democratic society.
>
> F. Any person benefiting from living in the United States should be, at the minimum, willing to publicly declare his allegiance to the country.

ARGUMENT: Mastery Test 6

A. In each group below, one statement is the point of an argument, and the other statements are support for that point. In the space provided, write the letter of the point of each group.

_____ 1. A. Half of all American adults are overweight.
  B. Obesity is one of the most pressing health concerns in today's world.
  C. At least 30 percent of all Americans under the age of 19 are over-weight or obese.
  D. Increases in obesity rates have occurred in both sexes, in all social classes and age groups, and in many other countries.

_____ 2. A. In marriage, the assumption is permanence; in cohabitation, couples agree to remain together "as long as it works out."
  B. For marriage, individuals make public vows that legally bind them as a couple; for cohabitation, they simply move in together.
  C. The difference between cohabitation and marriage is spiritual and legal commitment.
  D. Marriage requires a judge to authorize its termination; when a cohabiting relationship sours, the couple simply separates.

B. (3–5.) The point below is followed by three statements that provide relevant support and three that do not. In the spaces, write the letters of the **three** relevant statements of support.

Point: Our society's taste in movies is sometimes influenced by what we fear.

A. The plots of some movies are based on out-of-control computers, such as the science-fiction classic *2001: A Space Odyssey*, in which an evil computer named Hal attempts to sabotage a space mission to Jupiter.
B. Owners of movie theaters fear that the increasing popularity of in-home entertainment centers may cause a drop in theater attendance.
C. Great improvements in digital technology have enabled today's moviegoers to experience special effects unheard of a generation ago.
D. In the 1950s, movies such as *Godzilla* and *The Beast from 20,000 Fathoms* reflected our fear of the effects of radiation on living beings.
E. Generally, women tend to be more interested in movies that feature emotional relationships, whereas men tend to gravitate toward movies with plenty of action.
F. Movies about serial killers such as *The Silence of the Lambs* engage our concern about falling victim to people who appear normal but are secretly homicidal maniacs.

Items that logically support the point: _____ _____ _____

(Continues on next page)

C. (6–8.) For the following statement, choose your point of view by checking "I agree" or "I disagree." Then circle the letters of the **three** items that logically support your point of view.

Point: Affirmative action is a good idea.

____ I agree   ____ I disagree

A. Affirmative action stigmatizes the people who benefit from it. It suggests that they hold their jobs because of race rather than merit.

B. Affirmative action is good for everyone, because it leads to the development of a larger minority middle and upper class. This will result in more stable, self-sufficient minority communities that will act as full participants in society.

C. Affirmative action recognizes that merit alone has never been the basis for people to get ahead. People have always been hired or promoted because of factors such as whom they know (or are related to) or where they went to school. Affirmative action helps "level the playing field" by giving a hand to people not already tied into such influential networks.

D. Affirmative action is discrimination in reverse form. It makes a person's race more important than the individual's training or ability to perform a job.

E. White people have benefited from generations of preferential treatment, and have come to think that they have rightfully earned their place at the top of society. Affirmative action forces them to share benefits that they did not fairly earn.

F. By edging qualified non-minority people out of jobs, affirmative action forces them to pay for past inequalities that they had nothing to do with.

9 Critical Reading

Skilled readers are those who can *recognize* an author's point and the support for that point. **Critical readers** are those who can *evaluate* an author's support for a point and determine whether that support is solid or not. In this book, you have already had practice in evaluating support—deciding when inferences are valid and when they are not (pages 228–245) and determining whether supporting evidence is relevant (pages 306–310) and adequate (pages 310–313). This chapter will extend your ability to read critically in three ways. It will explain and offer practice in each of the following:

- Separating fact from opinion
- Detecting propaganda
- Recognizing errors in reasoning

Separating Fact from Opinion

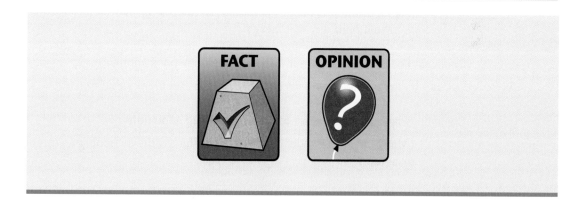

Fact

A **fact** is information that can be proved true through objective evidence. This evidence may be physical proof or the spoken or written testimony of witnesses. Following are some facts—they can be checked for accuracy and thus proved true.

Fact: Abraham Lincoln, whose nickname was "Honest Abe," had no formal education or religion; he was president of the United States from 1861 to 1865 at a salary of $25,000 a year.

(You can look up in historical documents the above facts about Lincoln.)

Fact: At least four out of five adults will experience lower back pain at some point in their lives.

(Extensive medical research confirms that this statement is true.)

Fact: Quitting smoking now greatly reduces serious risks to your health.

(You can look this up in government reports by the U.S. Surgeon General; this fact also appears by law on many cigarette packs and ads.)

Opinion

An **opinion** is a belief, judgment, or conclusion that cannot be objectively proved true. As a result, it is open to question. Following are some opinions:

Opinion: With the exception only of George Washington, Abraham Lincoln was the greatest leader our country has ever had.

(Many people might agree with this statement, but others would not. There is no way to prove it definitively. *Greatest* is a **value word**, a word we use to express a value judgment. Value words are signals that an opinion is being expressed. By their very nature, these words represent opinions, not facts.)

Opinion: The best treatment for lower back pain is physical therapy.

(There is no consensus in the scientific community that this is true.)

Opinion: Smoking is the worst of America's drug addictions.

(Many people, such as those coping with alcoholism, might disagree.)

Points about Fact and Opinion

There are several points to keep in mind when considering fact and opinion.

1 Statements of fact may be found to be untrue.

For example, the United States went to war in Iraq because of the fact that Iraq had weapons of mass destruction. However, this widely accepted "fact" later proved to be untrue. The point is that facts can turn out to be errors, not facts. It is not unusual for evidence to show that a "fact" is not really true. It was once considered to be a fact that the world was flat, for example, but that "fact" also turned out to be an error.

bias

2 **Value words** (ones that contain a judgment) often represent opinions. Here are examples of these words:

Value Words

best	great	beautiful
worst	terrible	bad
better	lovely	good
worse	disgusting	wonderful

Value words are generally subjective, not objective. While factual statements report on observed reality, subjective statements evaluate or interpret reality. For example, the observation that it is cloudy outside is objective. The statement that the weather is bad, however, is subjective, an evaluation of reality. (Some people—for example, farmers whose crops need water—consider rain to be good weather.)

3 The words *should* and *ought to* often signal opinions. Those words introduce what some people think should, or ought to, be done. Other people may disagree.

Adults who molest young children ought to be put to death.

Women with children should not run for public office.

4 Don't mistake widely held opinions for facts. Much information that sounds factual is really opinion. A real estate agent, for example, might say, "At the price listed, this ranch home is a great buy." Buyers would be wise to wonder what the value word *great* means to the agent. Or an ad may claim that a particular automobile is "the most economical car on the road today," a statement that at first seems factual. But what is meant by *economical*? If the car offers the most miles per gallon but the worst record for expensive repairs, you might not agree that it's economical.

As we will see in later parts of this chapter, advertisers and politicians often try to manipulate us by presenting opinions as if they were facts. For instance, one politician may claim that another will be soft on terrorism or will waste our tax dollars. But accusations are often not facts. Clear-thinking citizens must aim to get below the surface of claims and charges and determine as much factual truth as possible.

5   Finally, remember that much of what we read and hear is a mixture of fact and opinion. Our job, then, is to draw upon existing fact and opinion and to arrive at an informed opinion. On our Supreme Court, for example, nine justices deliberate in order to deliver informed opinions about important issues of our time. But even these justices often disagree and deliver split decisions. The reality is that most of what matters in life is very complex and cannot be separated into simple fact and opinion. Our challenge always is to arrive at the best possible informed opinion, and even then there will be people who disagree with us.

combination of both fact/opinion [handwritten annotation]

Fact and Opinion in Reading

In general, textbook authors try to be as factual as possible. Most textbook material is based on scientific observation and study, and textbook authors do their best to present us with all the facts and objective informed opinion. On the other hand, many essays, editorials, political speeches, and advertisements may contain facts, but those facts are often carefully selected to back up the authors' opinions.

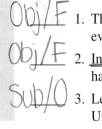

✔ *Check Your Understanding*

To sharpen your understanding of fact and opinion, read the following statements and decide whether each is fact or opinion. Put an **F** (for "fact") or an **O** (for "opinion") beside each statement. Put **F+O** beside the **one** statement that is a mixture of fact *and* opinion. Then read the explanation that follows.

> *Hint:* Remember that opinions are signaled by value words—words such as *great* or *hard* or *beautiful* or *terrible* that express a value judgment. Take care to note such words in your reading.

Obj/F 1. There are so many guns in the United States that if you gave one to every adult, you would run out of adults before you'd run out of guns.

Obj/F 2. In 1828, New York became the first state to restrict abortion; by 1900 it had been made illegal throughout the country.

Sub/O 3. Legalized abortion is the main cause of sexual misbehavior in the United States.

OBJ/F 4. Many people have nightmares in which they are falling and wake up right before they hit the ground.

Sub/O 5. If you have a nightmare in which you are plunging to the ground and you don't wake up before you hit the ground, you'll die.

Sub/O 6. It is a fact that overpopulation is the number one problem facing the world today.

OBJ/F 7. About 250 babies are born worldwide every minute.

OBJ/F 8. The first American animated feature film was *Snow White and the Seven Dwarfs*, released in 1937 by the Disney studio.

Sub/O 9. Today's computer-animated films are not as good as the old hand-drawn animated ones.

F/O 10. The 1940 animated film *Fantasia*, which combined animation with classical music, is the most imaginative movie ever made.

Explanation

1. This is a fact. Statistical records show that there are a greater number of guns in the country than there are adults.

2. These are facts that could be looked up in historical records.

3. This is an opinion. Some people would argue, for example, that sexual misbehavior existed before abortion became an option.

4. This is a fact that can be confirmed by checking medical research on nightmares.

5. This is obviously an opinion—and an old joke!

6. This is an opinion. Just saying that something is a fact doesn't make it so. Other people would say, for example, that global warming is the most immediate problem we face today.

7. This is a fact that can be confirmed by population and census records.

8. This is a fact that can be confirmed by checking film records.

9. This is an opinion. Many people might disagree.

10. The first part of the sentence is a fact that can be confirmed by checking movie records and watching the film. The second part is an opinion; other people might nominate some other film as the most imaginative one ever made.

+a / 10

PRACTICE 1

Read the following statements and label each fact with an **F**, each opinion with an **O**, and the two statements of fact *and* opinion with an **F+O**.

+ *Sub/O* 1. Young people today should spend more time reading and less time on their computers.

+ *Obj/F* 2. 85 percent of households with children aged 8 to 18 own at least one personal computer.

− *Obj/F* 3. Cotton is the world's most widely-used fabric.

+ *Sub/O* 4. Clothes made of cotton are always better choices than other clothes.

+ *F/O* 5. Cotton clothing is often recommended for people with skin allergies, which are the most irritating kind of allergies to have.

+ *Obj/F* 6. A starfish eats by moving its stomach outside its body, then wrapping its stomach around its prey.

+ *Sub/O* 7. No sea creature is more bizarre and interesting than the starfish.

+ *Obj/F* 8. In Las Vegas, there is one slot machine for every 2.5 city residents.

+ *Sub/O* 9. Gambling is a harmless diversion that should be legal everywhere.

+ *F/O* 10. Since the legalization of gambling in Nevada in 1931, Las Vegas has become a hotbed of sin and corruption.

Detecting Propaganda

Advertisers, salespeople, and politicians are constantly promoting their points: "Buy our product," "Believe what I say," and "Vote for me." Often they lack adequate factual support for their points, so they appeal to our emotions by using propaganda techniques.

Part of being a critical reader is having the ability to recognize these propaganda techniques for the emotional fluff that they are. The critical reader strips away the fluff to determine whether there is solid support for the point in question. None of us wants to accept someone else's point as a result of emotional manipulation.

This section will introduce you to six common propaganda techniques:

- Bandwagon
- Plain Folks
- Testimonial
- Name Calling
- Transfer
- Glittering Generalities

While there are other propaganda techniques, the ones described below are among the most common. They all use emotional appeals to distract from the fact they are not providing solid evidence to support their points.

1   Bandwagon

Old-fashioned parades usually began with a large wagon carrying a brass band. Therefore, to "jump on the bandwagon" means to join a parade, or to do what many others are doing. The **bandwagon** technique tells us to buy a product or support a certain issue because, in effect, "everybody else is doing it."

An ad may claim that more and more people are getting their evening news from anchorperson Chet Miller. Or a political ad may feature people from all walks of life speaking out in support of a certain political candidate. The ads imply that if you don't jump on the bandwagon and get on the winning side, the parade will pass you by.

Here are two examples of ads that use the bandwagon appeal:

> An ad announces a sale giving us a chance to buy the most popular SUV in America today.

> In a soft drink ad, a crowd of young people follow a young woman on skates who is drinking a diet soda.

● Check (✓) the ad below that uses bandwagon appeal.

_____ 1. A beautiful woman in a slinky red dress is shown driving the sponsor's car.

_____ 2. An ad for a weight-loss pill features an attractive couple who are "just two of the millions" who have decided to get their bodies back with the new diet formula.

2 Testimonial

Famous athletes often appear as spokespersons for all sorts of products, from soft drinks to automobiles. Movie and TV stars make commercials endorsing products or political issues. The idea behind the **testimonial** approach is that the testimony of famous people influences the viewers that admire these people.

What consumers must remember is that famous people get paid to endorse products. In addition, these people are not necessarily experts about the products or the political issues or candidates they promote.

Here are two examples of real ads that have used the appeal of testimonials:

A famous actor is shown coping with a swarm of photographers in order to get a bottle of his favorite beer.

A popular TV talk show host appears in an ad that indicates she uses a certain credit card.

● Check (✓) the ad below that uses a testimonial.

_____ 1. Numerous people crowd around the department store door, waiting for the store to open.

_____ 2. A famous actress says that she loves to use a certain hair coloring.

3 Transfer

The most common type of propaganda technique is **transfer,** in which products or candidates try to associate themselves with something that people admire or love. In the illustration on page 340, we see a political candidate wearing an American flag and saying "Vote for Me," accompanied by a beauty queen wrapped in a U.S.A. banner.

There are countless variations on this ad, in which a beautiful and sexy woman and/or an American flag or some other symbol of the U.S.A. is used to promote a product or candidate or cause. The hope is that we will *transfer* the positive feelings we have towards a beautiful or sexy-looking person to the product being advertised, or that we will *transfer* the patriotism that we feel to a product or candidate. Over the years, advertisers have found that beauty and sex "sell" and that appeals to patriotism often succeed. In short, transfer often works.

Here are two examples of real ads that have used the appeal of transfer:

An American flag is in the background of an ad for U.S. Savings Bonds.

A tanned blonde in a bikini is stretched out on the beach, holding in her hand a certain suntan lotion.

● Check (✓) the ad below that uses transfer.

_____×_____ 1. A beer company sponsors the Daytona 500 auto race with the line "America's Race and America's Beer."

_____ 2. A picture of a can of soda bears the caption, "You know it's got to be good."

4   Plain Folks

Some people distrust political candidates who are rich or well educated. They feel that these candidates, if elected, will not be able to understand the problems of the average working person. Therefore, candidates often use the **plain folks** technique, presenting themselves as ordinary, average citizens. They try to show they are just "plain folks" by referring in their speeches to hard times in their lives or by posing for photographs while wearing a hard hat or mingling with everyday people.

Similarly, the presidents of some companies appear in their own ads, trying to show that their giant corporations are just family businesses run by ordinary folks.

Here are two examples of real ads that have used the appeal of plain folks:

> Average-looking American kids are shown at home trying and enjoying a cereal.

> The president of a poultry company talks to us as if he's an everyday shopper looking for a quick, easy meal to make, just like us.

● Check (✓) the ad below that uses a plain-folks approach.

_____ 1. A famous basketball player wears the sponsor's sneakers.

_____×_____ 2. The president of a car company is shown playing on the lawn with his young children. He says, "I'm head of this company, but I'm also a dad who is concerned about automobile safety."

5   Name Calling

Name calling is the use of emotionally loaded language or negative comments to turn people against a product or political candidate or cause. An example of name calling would be a political candidate's labeling an opponent "soft," "radical," or "wimpy."

Here are two examples of name calling taken from real life:

> In the 1950s, during the early days of the "cold war" with the Soviet Union, an exaggerated concern about communism in this country brought charges of un-Americanism against many.

> During a taste test, consumers described the other leading brand of spaghetti sauce as "too salty" and "thin and tasteless."

● Check (✓) the ad below that uses name calling.

   ___X___ 1. A political ad implies that a candidate who does not support the war in Afghanistan is anti-American.

   _____ 2. A pastor describes how when his house burned down, his home insurance company responded quickly and helpfully.

6 Glittering Generalities

A **glittering generality** is an important-sounding but unspecific claim about some product, candidate, or cause. An example is saying that a certain television is "simply the best" or having a sign that reads "Sam Slick for Mayor: Integrity, Dedication, Care." A glittering generality uses fine and virtuous words but says nothing definite.

Here are two examples from real ads that use glittering generalities:

A room deodorizer exclaims, "Experience the freshness!"

A canned-food ad boasts of "nutrition that works."

● Check (✓) the ad below that uses a glittering generality.

   ___X___ 1. A car ad claims, "It just feels right."

   _____ 2. A movie star looks over her dark sunglasses and says, "Maybe you can't be a celebrity. But you can look like one in glasses like mine."

PRACTICE 2

In the space provided, write the letter of the propaganda technique that applies to each item.

A. bandwagon	B. testimonial	C. transfer
D. plain folks	E. name calling	F. glittering generalities

   ___B___ 1. A Hall-of-Fame quarterback claims that a certain drug relieves his acid reflux.

   ___C___ 2. A beautiful blonde wearing an evening gown drapes herself against a display of a high-priced brand of luggage.

   ___A___ 3. "Millions of satisfied users can't be wrong," says the announcer of an ad for an anti-acid pill.

   ___D___ 4. In a TV ad, a wealthy politician appears, dressed in a flannel shirt and jeans, at a county fair.

   ___F___ 5. A realtor advertises that she "will always be there for you."

x| __E__ 6. "My opponent is forcing people out of their homes and businesses so that developers can reap huge profits," claims a candidate for mayor.

x| __C__ 7. A local auto dealership runs a newspaper ad featuring images of Abraham Lincoln and George Washington every Presidents' Day.

x| __A__ 8. A magazine ad for a family beach resort advises us to "See for yourself why thousands of families fall in love with Crestwood Beach each year."

x| __B__ 9. A famous golf star appears on the back of a cereal box and promotes it as part of a balanced diet.

x| __D__ 10. A woman whose name is on a line of frozen pizzas is shown in her own kitchen, wearing an apron, chopping tomatoes and onions for pizza sauce. She says, "Before it goes on my pizza, my sauce has to pass my personal test."

Recognizing Errors in Reasoning

So far in this chapter, you have gotten practice in separating fact from opinion and in spotting propaganda. In this section you will learn about some common errors in reasoning—also known as fallacies—that take the place of the real support needed in an argument. As shown in the illustration, a valid point is based on a rock-like foundation of solid support; a fallacious point is based on a house of cards that offers no real support at all. Regrettably, these fallacies appear all too often in political arguments, often as the result of deliberate manipulation, other times as the result of careless thinking.

You've already learned about two common fallacies in Chapter 8, "Argument." One of those fallacies is sometimes called **changing the subject**. Attention is diverted from the issue at hand by presenting irrelevant support— evidence that actually has nothing to do with the argument. The second fallacy covered in Chapter 8 is sometimes called hasty generalization—in which a point is based on inadequate support. To be valid, a point must be based on an adequate amount of evidence. To draw a conclusion on the basis of insufficient evidence is to make a hasty generalization.

Below are six other common fallacies that will be explained in this section.

Three Fallacies That Ignore the Issue

- Circular Reasoning
- Personal Attack
- Straw Man

Three Fallacies That Oversimplify the Issue

- False Cause
- False Comparison
- Either-Or

(claim)   *(no relevent support)*

In all of these fallacies, a point is argued, but no true support is offered for that point.

Fallacies That Ignore the Issue

Circular Reasoning

Part of a point cannot reasonably be used as evidence to support it. The fallacy of including such illogical evidence is called **circular reasoning** or **begging the question**. Here is a simple and obvious example of such reasoning: "Alan Gordon is a great manager because he is so wonderful at managing." The supporting reason ("he is so wonderful at managing") is really the same as the conclusion ("Alan Gordon is a great manager"). We still do not know *why* he is a great manager. No real reasons have been given—the statement has merely repeated itself.

Can you spot the circular reasoning in the following arguments?

1. The climate in California is perfect because it's just beautiful.
2. Hybrid cars are economical because they cost so little to run.

The point is that California's weather is perfect, and the support (it's just beautiful) is simply another way of restating the point. The second claim—that hybrid cars are economical—gets no real support; to say they cost so little to run is just to restate the point. The careful reader should say, "Give me supporting evidence, not a repetition."

- Check (✓) the item that contains an example of the circular reasoning fallacy.

    _____ 1. Exercise is healthful because it improves your well-being.

    _____ 2. Exercise is healthful because it reduces blood pressure, high cholesterol, and body fat.

Personal Attack

This fallacy involves an unfair **personal attack** on an individual rather than on his or her position. Here's an example:

> That woman should not be on a church committee. She just got divorced for the second time.

A woman's divorce or divorces have nothing to do with her ability to contribute to a church committee. Personal attack ignores the issue under discussion and concentrates instead on the character of the opponent.

● Check (✓) the item that contains an example of the personal attack fallacy.

_____ 1. Our school guidance counselor should be asked to resign. She cursed at a student last week.

  2. Our school guidance counselor should be asked to resign. One of her sons is gay.

Straw Man

The **straw man** fallacy suggests that an opponent favors an obviously unpopular cause—when the opponent really doesn't support anything of the kind.

In everyday debates, rather than take on a real opponent, it's tempting to create a man (or woman) of straw and battle it instead. Here is an example:

> Senator Crosley supports a bill to limit the purchase of handguns. She wants to take guns out of the hands of law-abiding citizens and put them into the hands of criminals!

Senator Crosley does not, of course, want to put guns into the hands of criminals. But her opponent wants voters to think that she does and so misrepresents and falsifies her position.

● Check (✓) the item that contains an example of the straw man fallacy.

✗ 1. My neighbors are voting against the new school budget. They want our students to fall behind students in developing nations like India and China.

_____ 2. My neighbors are voting against the new school budget. They oppose the salary increases for the superintendent and his staff.

(valid)

Fallacies That Oversimplify the Issue

False Cause

You have probably heard someone say as a joke, "I know it's going to rain today because I forgot to bring an umbrella." The idea that someone can make it rain by forgetting an umbrella is funny because the two events obviously have nothing to do with each other. However, with more complicated issues, it is easy to make the mistake known as the fallacy of **false cause**. The mistake is to assume that because event B *follows* event A, event B *was caused by* event A.

Consider this argument:

> My favorite TV show was moved to a different time slot this season. No wonder it's now getting canceled.

But there could be reasons other than the move to a new time slot for the program's getting canceled. Perhaps the show has less competent writers; perhaps a favorite actor has left the show; perhaps network executives want a different programming direction. In any case, it's easy but dangerous to assume that just because A *came before* B, A **caused** B.

● Check (✓) the item that contains an example of the fallacy of false cause.

(invalid)

  ✗   1. Many fast-food commercials on TV are hard to resist. That's why I've gained a lot of weight.

      2. Many fast-food commercials on TV are hard to resist. If I'm not careful, I'll eat too many burgers, shakes, and fries.

(valid)

False Comparison

When Shakespeare wrote, "Shall I compare thee to a summer day," he meant that both the woman he loved and a summer day were beautiful. In some ways—such as being a source of humidity or pollen, for example—his love did not resemble a summer day at all. Comparisons are often a good way to clarify a point. But because two things may not be alike in all respects, comparisons (sometimes called **analogies**) often make poor evidence for arguments.

In the error in reasoning known as **false comparison**, the assumption is that two things are more alike than they really are. For example, read the following argument:

> When your brother was your age, he was already married and raising a family. So why aren't you married, Dean?

To judge whether or not this is a false comparison, consider how the two situations are alike and how they differ. They are similar in that both involve persons of the same age. But the situations are different in that Dean is an individual with choices and goals that are different from those of his brother. (For example, perhaps Dean wants to continue his education or focus on his career, or perhaps he has not met the right person yet.) The differences in this case are more important than the similarities, making it a false comparison.

● Check (✓) the item that contains an example of the fallacy of false comparison. (The other item contains an example of false cause.) *(invalid)*

____X____ 1. My dad takes an anti-depressant, so I don't see what's wrong with my smoking marijuana.

_____ 2. My dad takes an anti-depressant, so I'm probably going to have a mood disorder some day. *(valid)*

Either-Or *(Black & White)*

It is often wrong to assume that there are only two sides to a question. Offering only two choices when more actually exist is an **either-or** fallacy. For example, the statement "You are either with us or against us" assumes that there is no middle ground. Or consider the following:

Women must decide whether they want to have a career or have children.

This argument fails to allow for other alternatives, such as working part-time or sharing child-rearing responsibilities with a partner. While some issues have only two sides (Will you take that job, or won't you?), most have several.

● Check (✓) the item that contains an example of the either-or fallacy. (The other item contains an example of false cause.) *(valid)*

_____ 1. You're ignoring my cat. You must be angry with me about something.

____X____ 2. You're ignoring my cat. You must hate all animals. *(invalid)*

due tommorw

PRACTICE 3

A. In the space provided, write the letter of the fallacy contained in each argument. Choose from the three fallacies shown in the box below.

> A **Circular reasoning** (*a statement repeats itself rather than providing a real supporting reason to back up an argument*)
>
> B **Personal attack** (*ignores the issue under discussion and concentrates instead on the character of the opponent*)
>
> C **Straw man** (*an argument is made by claiming an opponent holds an extreme position and then opposing that extreme position*)

_A__ 1. The divorcing couple didn't get along well because they were so incompatible.

_B__ 2. Professor Johnson is up for tenure at the college, but he shouldn't get it. His ex-wife was arrested last week for shoplifting.

_C__ 3. My opponent opposes the Medicare reform bill. Apparently she wants to see the elderly forced to eat cat food in order to pay for their prescription drugs.

_B__ 4. I will not tolerate my child going to a Sunday school class with a teacher who belongs to a motorcycle club.

_C__ 5. The governor disapproves of armed militias patrolling our border with Mexico. Clearly he wants this nation to be overwhelmed by waves of illegal immigrants.

B. In the space provided, write the letter of the fallacy contained in each argument. Choose from the three fallacies shown in the box below.

> A **False cause** (*the argument assumes that the order of events alone shows cause and effect*)
>
> B **False comparison** (*the argument assumes that two things being compared are more alike than they really are*)
>
> C **Either-or** (*the argument assumes that there are only two sides to a question*)

_C__ 6. Are you going to become a vegetarian, or do you intend to eat like a normal person?

A   7. Ever since I switched schools, my grades have gone down. My new teachers are doing a poor job.

B   8. When I was younger, people didn't have to get their cats and dogs vaccinated for rabies, so I don't see why we have to shell out the money to do it now.

A   9. Lisa went out with a guy who lied and said he was single when he was actually married with two kids. She never should have dated someone she met on the Internet.

B 10. The crime rate would drop if we would do what some Middle Eastern countries do and chop off the hands of convicted thieves.

CHAPTER REVIEW

In this chapter, you learned that critical readers evaluate an author's support for a point and determine whether that support is solid or not. Critical reading includes the following three abilities:

- **Separating fact from opinion.** A **fact** is information that can be proved true through objective evidence. An **opinion** is a belief, judgment, or conclusion that cannot be proved objectively true. Much of what we read is a mixture of fact and opinion, and our job as readers is to arrive at at the best possible informed opinion. Textbooks and other effective writing provide informed opinion—opinion based upon factual information.

- **Detecting propaganda.** Advertisers, salespeople, and politicians often try to promote their points by appealing to our emotions rather than our powers of reason. To do so, they practice six common propaganda techniques: bandwagon, testimonial, transfer, plain folks, name calling, and glittering generalities.

- **Recognizing errors in reasoning.** Politicians and others are at times guilty of errors in reasoning—fallacies—that take the place of the real support needed in an argument. Such fallacies include circular reasoning, personal attack, straw man, false cause, false comparison, and either-or.

The final chapter in Part One—Chapter 10—will provide an overall approach to the skill of active reading.

On the Web: If you are using this book in class, you can go to our website for more practice in critical reading. Visit our Learning Center at **www.townsendpress.net** for additional activities and an instructional video on this skill.

REVIEW TEST 1

To review what you've learned in this chapter, answer each of the following questions by filling in the blank.

1. Value or judgment words such as *best, worst, great,* and *beautiful* often represent not facts but ___subjective opinion___

2. Textbook authors work very hard to back up all of their opinions with ___objective evidence___

3. **Propaganda techniques** (*bandwagon, transfer, testimonial, plain folks, name calling,* and *glittering generalities*) are emotional appeals used to distract us from the lack of relevant and adequate ___support___ for a given point.

4. In the most common propaganda technique, ___transfer___, products or candidates try to associate themselves with appealing images such as beautiful people or symbols of America such as the flag.

5. **Fallacies** (*circular reasoning, personal attack, straw man, false cause, false comparison,* and *either-or*) are errors in reasoning also used to distract us from the lack of relevant and adequate ___evidence___ for a given point.

![book icon] **REVIEW TEST 2**

The essay below is followed by questions on critical reading skills as well as on the skills you have practiced in previous chapters.

Preview

When it comes to radically altering your world view, nothing compares with parenthood. Issues that you previously shrugged off are suddenly of tremendous importance because they are going to affect your child. In this reading, newspaper columnist Steve Lopez describes how becoming the father of a baby girl gave him a new and troubling perspective on our sex-saturated society.

Words to Watch

> *tawdry* (3): cheap
> *vapid* (3): dull; meaningless
> *lurid* (5): intended to shock
> *surreptitiously* (15): secretly

A SCARY TIME TO RAISE A DAUGHTER

Steve Lopez

1   Three months ago, with my wife's contractions getting closer and closer, we flicked on the TV as a distraction before going to the hospital.

2   Bad idea.

3   No one expects a great deal of enlightenment from the tube these days. But as we switched from one tawdry° and vapid° reality or dating show to another, I wondered if we should have our heads examined for bringing a child into this world.

4   Especially a girl.

5   It's not just television that scares me. It's the Internet, pop music, radio, advertising. The most lurid° elements of each medium now dominate pop culture, and the incessant, pounding message, directed primarily at young people, is that it's all about sex.

6   Sure, some of us boomers had our flower child days of free love, but that was a social revolution, not a corporate-driven campaign.

7   Today, if you haven't just had it, you're a loser. If you don't expect to have it in the immediate future, try plastic surgery, because sex appeal—the one

true standard of human achievement—is the only thing worth aspiring to.

8   Yes, I'll admit it: I'm frazzled about all of this because I have a baby girl. At my daughter's first checkup, our pediatrician mentioned that he routinely has pregnant patients in their early teens. I shook my head and said it's no wonder, given what kids see on TV and the Internet.

9   Forget that, the doctor said. Go for a drive and take a look at some billboards. Belts are unbuckled. Bras are undone. Everyone is on the make.

10   While contemplating these horrors as a new dad, I got an e-mail one day from actress Susan Dey, who has volunteered at the Rape Treatment Center in Santa Monica for fifteen years.

11   Dey was America's grooviest teenager in a more innocent media era—she played Laurie on *The Partridge Family*. She told me she had gotten an unsolicited email directing her to a Web site with college girls having live sex. Dey checked it out and was horrified at what is essentially a guide for frat boys on how to nail co-eds.

12   "A little alcohol will always loosen up the college chicks!" the site advises, complete with graphic results.

13   "These are the girls we see at the rape center," Dey said with disgust.

14   Gail Abarbanel, director of the center, said 50% of rape victims are 18 or younger, and the rapists are acquaintances 80% of the time.

15   "We see a lot of cases where raped women are incapacitated by drugs or

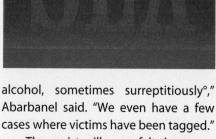

alcohol, sometimes surreptitiously°," Abarbanel said. "We even have a few cases where victims have been tagged."

16   The rapist will use a felt-tip pen to mark his conquest, she said, just as a gangbanger leaves his tag on a wall.

17   When I asked Abarbanel what was going on, she said kids are saturated as never before with marketing and entertainment that's all about sex and violence. Subtlety and restraint are quaint, nostalgic notions, as is attentive parenting.

18   Another factor, I think, is that very little in the culture encourages independent thinking, and that makes peer pressure all the more powerful. "Look at what's happening with oral sex in the bathrooms of middle schools," Abarbanel said, telling me that, in workshops at local schools, they hear stories about how commonplace it's become.

19   I've got friends who told me they turn the radio off while taking their kids to school, because it's routine to hear shock jocks carrying on about oral sex. Next time I was in my car, I flipped through the FM dial and, in nothing flat, found that very thing on two stations.

20   A couple of weeks after we met, Dey called again to say I ought to have a look at the photos in the Abercrombie & Fitch store at the Grove in the Fairfax District. We met there Thursday and took a tour.

21   On both floors of the store, which markets to a young crowd, the walls were plastered with huge blowups of fresh-faced, great-looking teens who are either nude or nearly nude.

22   In one, a topless girl is playing the violin while in the clutches of a shirtless boy, and a carefully placed strand of hair is all that keeps her from being completely revealed.

23   In another, a naked girl is sandwiched by two boys, her breasts completely visible but for a bit of strategic airbrushing. The three of them are holding a blanket over what appear to be nude lower bodies.

24   An odd advertising campaign, you'd have to say—all this nudity being used to sell clothes.

25   It's all about an image, a clerk explained.

26   Yeah, I gathered as much.

27   "The message is, you should be a sexual object," Dey said outside the store. "Like I've been saying, connect the dots."

28   She had been telling me the problem isn't the photos in the store, or billboards on the street, or TV shows, or movies, or the Internet. It's all of those things together.

29   "I taught my daughter to love her body, but that's not what this is about," Dey said. "A boy's not cool if he hasn't just done it. His whole manhood is at stake. I don't think we were ever targeted the way they're targeting this generation, and when does it stop?

30   "I would love it if parents said, 'No, I'm not putting my credit card down for this.' Can you imagine what would happen if parents said to Madison Avenue, 'I want my 13-year-old to be a 13-year-old'?"

Reading Comprehension Questions

Central Point and Main Ideas

_____ 1. Which sentence best expresses the central point of the selection?
  A. The author is disgusted by the idea that our young people are exposed to negative messages.
  B. The author contrasts the free-love social revolution of his day with the corporate-driven campaigns of today.
  C. The author is concerned that his baby daughter may eventually fall victim to the idea, promoted by our sex-saturated culture, that it's good to be a sex object.
  D. The author visits an Abercrombie & Fitch store with an actress and is shocked to see that it is plastered with nude images of young people.

Supporting Details

_____ 2. A startling fact that Lopez's pediatrician mentions is that
  A. he was once a flower child in the days of free love.
  B. he knows actress Susan Dey, once America's grooviest teenager.
  C. his own daughter was drugged and raped by a frat boy.
  D. he routinely has pregnant patients in their early teens.

Patterns of Organization

_____ 3. Paragraphs 20–26 in large part
  A. contrast the clerk's attitude toward sex with that of the author.
  B. narrate a series of events in time order.
  C. provide illustrations of the use of sex to sell products.
  D. discuss the consequences of using sex to sell clothing to teenagers.

Inferences

_____ 4. The last two paragraphs of the selection suggest that parents should
  A. relax and let their 13-year-olds do whatever they want.
  B. encourage their boys to prove their manhood by having sex.
  C. refuse to pay for products which tell teens that it's good to be a sex object.
  D. use cash instead of credit cards to make purchases.

Purpose and Tone

_____ 5. In paragraph 7, the author's tone is
   A. sarcastic.
   B. ambivalent.
   C. detached.
   D. solemn.

Argument

_____ 6. Three of the items below are supporting details for an argument. Write the letter of the statement that represents the point of these supporting details.
   A. Some Web sites encourage frat boys to use alcohol in order to get co-eds to have sex with them.
   B. The director of a rape treatment center says that 50% of rape victims are 18 or younger.
   C. A pediatrician says that he routinely has pregnant patients in their early teens.
   D. Girls and young women are often sexually victimized by males.

Critical Reading

_____ 7. The sentence below is
   A. a fact.
   B. an opinion.
   C. both fact and opinion.

   "But as we switched from one tawdry and vapid reality or dating show to another, I wondered if we should have our heads examined for bringing a child into this world." (Paragraph 3)

_____ 8. The use of a pretty, topless girl to sell clothing is an example of the propaganda technique of
   A. testimonial.   C. bandwagon.
   B. plain folks.   D. transfer.

_____ 9. When a store "plasters the walls with images of fresh-faced, great-looking teens who are either nude or semi-nude," it is using the propaganda technique of
   A. testimonial.   C. bandwagon.
   B. plain folks.   D. name calling.

_B_   10. The statement "If you haven't just had [sex], you're a loser" is an example of the logical fallacy of
   A. circular reasoning.
   B. personal attack.
   C. straw man.
   D. either-or.

Discussion Questions

1. Do you agree with Lopez that this is a particularly challenging time to raise a child? Which of his concerns do you share? Do you think his concerns are groundless or exaggerated?

2. How much effect do you believe that marketing campaigns such as Abercrombie & Fitch's have on young people and their views on sexuality? Do you agree with the author that such messages result in negative consequences for young people, especially girls—or do you disagree? Explain.

3. According to the selection, 50% of rape victims are 18 or younger, and the rapists are acquaintances 80% of the time. In your view, what changes can we make as a society to help ensure that fewer girls and young women fall victim to rape?

4. Why do you think Lopez is particularly concerned about raising a girl in today's society? How is the impact of a sexualized society different for boys than it is for girls?

Note: Writing assignments for this selection appear on page 639.

Check Your Performance   CRITICAL READING

Activity	Number Right	Points	Score
Review Test 1 (5 items)	_____	× 6 =	_____
Review Test 2 (10 items)	_____	× 7 =	_____
	TOTAL SCORE =		_____ %

Enter your total score into the **Reading Performance Chart: Review Tests** on the inside back cover.

+18

CRITICAL READING: Mastery Test 1 (Fact and Opinion)

A. Identify facts with an **F**, opinions with an **O**, and the one combination of fact *and* opinion with an **F+O**.

1. Overpopulation is the number one problem facing the world today.

2. The world population reached 7 billion in the year 2011, and it is projected to be nearly 9 billion by the year 2050.

3. Blood transfusions were dangerous before scientists identified the four different types of human blood, making it possible to match donors and patients according to blood type.

4. The identification of blood types is the most important scientific discovery in recent history.

5. The elephant's closest living relative is an African mammal called the hyrax, which is about the size of a large rabbit.

6. The hunting of elephants is immoral and should be banned completely.

7. Elephants can communicate by making sounds at a lower frequency than the human ear is able to detect.

8. Although not commonly used during the time period, contact lenses were first manufactured in 1887.

9. Most people are more attractive when they wear contact lenses instead of glasses.

10. Heroin is derived from the opium poppy, *Papaver somniferum*, which means "the poppy that brings sleep."

11. Addiction to heroin is not as bad as addiction to crack cocaine.

12. In the United States, heroin is illegal for any purposes, although it should be available as a treatment for pain in those with terminal disease.

B. Following are eight short movie reviews. Identify a factual review with an **F**; identify a review that includes both facts about the movie *and* the reviewer's opinion with an **F+O**.

13. ***Rocky:*** The first, and by far the best, of Sylvester Stallone's "Rocky" franchise. A Philadelphia punk gets a chance to fight the heavyweight champ in an exhibition match. Stallone is memorably awkward and lovable as Rocky Balboa, and Talia Shire shines as Adrian, the shy girl who believes in him.

(Continues on next page)

_____14. ***The Wizard of Oz:*** Winner of the 1939 Academy Awards for Best Original Score and Best Original Song ("Over the Rainbow"). Sixteen-year-old Judy Garland plays the young heroine Dorothy Gale, who is swept away from her home in Kansas to the magical Land of Oz.

_____15. ***The Artist:*** Winner of the 2012 Academy Award for Best Movie. Its setting is Hollywood, 1927. George Valentin is a silent movie superstar. The advent of the talkies means the end of his career and sees him fall into oblivion. For Peppy Miller, a young extra who was in Valentin's silent films, major movie stardom awaits. *The Artist* tells the story of their interlinked destinies.

_____16. ***Night of the Living Dead:*** This 1968 low-budget horror classic still has the power to shock. Groundbreaking both for its gore and its sly comments on racism, *Night of the Living Dead* is a must-see for fans of the genre.

_____17. ***Singin' in the Rain:*** Everybody's favorite romantic musical comedy. If the sight of Gene Kelly joyfully leaping onto a lamppost and splashing through puddles as he dances in the ecstasy of new love doesn't bring a smile to your face, you are beyond hope.

_____18. ***Modern Times:*** Made in 1936, Charlie Chaplin's last silent film is a brilliant protest against the dehumanization of man in the Industrial Age. Playing his famous "Little Tramp" character, Chaplin is seen in a succession of hilarious, sharply satirical scenes as an assembly-line worker, a shipyard worker, a night watchman, and more.

_____19. ***The Godfather:*** Winner of the 1972 Academy Awards for Best Actor (Marlon Brando), Best Picture, and Best Screenplay, *The Godfather* tells the story of the aging patriarch of a crime family (Brando) transferring control to his initially reluctant son (Al Pacino). Runs just under three hours.

_____20. ***On the Waterfront:*** "I coulda been a contender!" This strangled, heartbroken protest from ex-boxer turned longshoreman Terry Malloy (Marlon Brando) has entered the gallery of immortal movie lines. After witnessing a murder ordered by his corrupt union boss, Terry must struggle with his conscience. Stellar performances by a range of Hollywood heavyweights that include Rod Steiger, Karl Malden, Lee J. Cobb, and Eva Marie Saint.

CRITICAL READING: Mastery Test 2 (Fact and Opinion)

A. Identify facts with an **F**, opinions with an **O**, and the one combination of fact *and* opinion with an **F+O**.

free

Sub/O 1. Magicians can often tell when a hidden card comes up by seeing the pupils of the person who put it in the deck dilate in recognition.

Sub/O 2. Magicians aren't as talented as people seem to think they are.

Obj/F 3. At least ten magicians have died trying to perform a "bullet-catching" trick.

Obj/F 4. Overall, human life expectancy is more than twice as long as it was in 1840.

Sub/O 5. These days, most Americans are obsessed with stretching out their lives as far as possible.

Sub/O 6. Many people who suffer from depression are weak and self-pitying.

Obj/F 7. Some 15 million people in the United States suffer from major depression.

Obj/F 8. The percentage of people who regularly watch network news has declined in recent years.

Sub/O 9. CNN is the most reliable source of news.

Obj/F 10. Gutenberg invented the printing press in the 1450s, and the first book ever to be printed on it was the Bible.

F/O 11. In a few short years, books will be obsolete because everyone will be able to access reading material electronically or online.

Obj/F 12. In greyhound racing, which amounts to animal abuse, the dogs chase an artificial rabbit as they speed around the racetrack.

B. Following are eight short book reviews. Identify a factual review with an **F**; identify a review that includes both facts about the book *and* the reviewer's opinion with an **F+O**.

F/O 13. ***Narrative of the Life of Frederick Douglass:*** This book is the most powerful first-person account of slave life ever written. Douglass, a man of fiery temperament and passionate intelligence, makes the reader feel every lash of the whip and suffer every barbarity he witnessed. Highly recommended.

(Continues on next page)

14. ***The Scarlet Letter:*** Hester Prynne is a young woman living in colonial Boston, then under the control of stern Puritans. When she becomes pregnant by an unknown lover, her punishment is to wear the letter A (for adultery) forever. Hester's refusal to name her partner in sin sets in motion a series of events that will change two men's lives forever.

15. ***Black Beauty:*** This first-person account of a horse's life tells of Black Beauty's succession of homes and owners. Along the way he learns of the lives and fortunes of other horses. Set in 19th century London, the book was written as a protest against the maltreatment of animals.

16. ***Pride and Prejudice:*** One of Jane Austen's most popular novels, the book tells the story of the Bennet family, whose five daughters are destined for poverty unless they marry well. Witty Elizabeth Bennet, the second oldest of the daughters, takes such pleasure in disliking rich, proud Mr. Darcy that the reader can only suspect the two will end up together. How this unlikely relationship progresses creates a delightful reading experience.

17. ***The Shame of the Nation:*** Although the racial segregation of America's schools officially ended in 1954, author Jonathan Kozol makes it clear in this devastating book that schools serving black and Hispanic children are woefully inadequate, and getting worse. Kozol's meticulous research contradicts the empty words of those who claim that all America's children have equal opportunity.

18. ***The Grapes of Wrath:*** Winner of the Pulitzer Prize for Fiction in 1940, John Steinbeck's novel is the account of one Depression-era family, the Joads, traveling from the ruins of their Oklahoma farm to what they believe will be an Eden of opportunity in California. The Joads struggle to maintain their hope in the face of the challenges of migrant life.

19. ***The Year of Magical Thinking:*** Essayist Joan Didion and her husband, novelist John Gregory Dunne, were just sitting down to dinner after visiting their seriously ill daughter when Dunne collapsed and died. This book is Didion's account of the next twelve months—adjusting to her husband's absence while dealing with her daughter's critical illness.

20. ***No Ordinary Time: Franklin and Eleanor Roosevelt:*** Historian Doris Kearns Goodwin chronicles how the private lives of the White House occupants have a direct bearing on national policy as she simultaneously explores the often tumultuous marriage of Franklin and Eleanor Roosevelt in a time of international crisis. An invaluable contribution to our understanding of the Roosevelts and their era, this page-turner reads like a skillfully written novel.

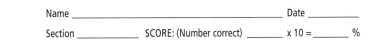
#8

CRITICAL READING: Mastery Test 3 (Propaganda Techniques)

A. Each pair of items below illustrates a particular propaganda technique. On the line next to each item, write the letter of the main technique being used.

___C___ 1. ● An aspirin company says that millions of Americans use its product.

x\   ● A cell phone ad shows a roomful of concertgoers taking their phones out in unison and waving them in the air.

    A. Name calling   C. Bandwagon

    B. Testimonial   D. Plain folks

___B___ 2. ● A milk advertisement shows photographs of A-list celebrities with milk mustaches.

x\   ● A famous singer tells television viewers how she overcame her battle with acne by using a particular brand of skin care products.

    A. Name calling   C. Bandwagon

    B. Testimonial   D. Plain folks

___D___ 3. ● A large chain store uses pictures of actual employees in its advertisements.

x\   ● A presidential candidate appears at a rally in jeans and shirtsleeves.

    A. Name calling   C. Bandwagon

    B. Testimonial   D. Plain folks

___C___ 4. ● A beautiful woman in office attire is seen enjoying a juicy hamburger.

x\   ● A huge American flag is used as a backdrop for a political speech.

    A. Testimonial   C. Transfer

    B. Name calling   D. Glittering generalities

___B___ 5. ● American political leaders refer to a certain part of the world as the "axis of evil."

x\   ● Anti-tobacco advertisers use the term "Big Tobacco" in campaigns to vilify tobacco companies and executives.

    A. Testimonial   C. Transfer

    B. Name calling   D. Glittering generalities

(Continues on next page)

6. ● An ad calls a car "an American revolution."
   ● A cellular phone company ad proclaims, "Dream meets delivery. Promise meets performance."

   A. Testimonial   C. Transfer
   B. Name calling   D. Glittering generalities

B. Below are descriptions of four actual ads. On each line, write the letter of the main propaganda technique that applies to the ad.

A. Bandwagon	B. Testimonial	C. Transfer
D. Plain folks	E. Name calling	F. Glittering generalities

7. An ad for a spicy fast-food premium chicken sandwich shows an attractive young woman on a motorcycle. She explains that when she needs her spice, she goes for this new flavor sandwich. "How can I not like it?" she says. "It's bold, spicy and hot . . . just like me."

8. TV personality Ellen DeGeneres appears in an ad which features a questionnaire she has filled out listing her card as American Express.

9. "Beyond shiny. Beyond beauty. Beyond healthy," reads an ad for a line of hair care products. Above the text, a woman stands next to an elevator. The elevator's top button, titled "Hair Heaven," has been pushed.

10. An ad for chocolate candy shows people giving the chocolates to each other as gifts. A woman hugs her friend after receiving a box of chocolates. A mother accepts a box of chocolates from her grown daughter with a smile. In the office, a boss gives a box of chocolates to each employee. A couple brings chocolates as a hostess gift. A young girl presents a box of chocolates to her teacher. In the last scene, all the people in the ad are shown simultaneously while the announcer says, "It's everyone's way to say thank you."

CRITICAL READING: Mastery Test 4 (Propaganda Techniques)

A. Each pair of items below illustrates a particular propaganda technique. On the line next to each item, write the letter of the main technique being used.

_____ 1. ● A bank advertises "A Return to Better Banking."

     ● "Beyond Precision," claims a car ad.

      A. Testimonial   C. Transfer
      B. Name calling   D. Glittering generalities

_____ 2. ● An ad encouraging women to buy right-hand diamond rings reads: "Women of the world, raise your right hand."

     ● A TV ad claims that more and more people in the region are getting their evening news from a certain anchor team.

      A. Name calling   C. Bandwagon
      B. Testimonial   D. Plain folks

_____ 3. ● A very attractive middle-aged woman wearing a long, flowered dress walks with a cute little girl in a field of wildflowers to advertise a drug which claims to reverse bone loss.

     ● Local retail stores display the American flag in their storefront windows.

      A. Testimonial   C. Transfer
      B. Name calling   D. Glittering generalities

_____ 4. ● An Academy Award-winning actress encourages us to "discover the excitement" of her home state.

     ● In a magazine ad, an Olympic gold medalist ice skater is shown giving her kitchen appliances a score of a perfect ten.

      A. Testimonial   C. Transfer
      B. Name calling   D. Glittering generalities

_____ 5. ● A middle-aged woman in pajamas, bathrobe, and slippers is shown using a new brand of facial tissue.

     ● In a TV commercial, a blue-collar employee of a large corporation tells how much he loves his job.

      A. Name calling   C. Bandwagon
      B. Testimonial   D. Plain folks

(Continues on next page)

_____ 6. ● A politician refers to a candidate in the opposing party as a "girly man."

● An ice cream maker says, "Our vanilla ice cream has four ingredients: Milk, cream, sugar, and vanilla," and that the ingredients in a competitor's vanilla ice cream read like "a chemistry experiment."

A. Testimonial   C. Transfer
B. Name calling   D. Glittering generalities

B. Below are descriptions of four actual ads. On each line, write the letter of the main propaganda technique that applies to the ad.

A. Bandwagon	B. Testimonial	C. Transfer
D. Plain folks	E. Name calling	F. Glittering generalities

_____ 7. A diamond ad shows a picture of a woman with light emanating from her finger, where a ring would be. Below, the text reads: "A diamond is forever. Forever timeless. Forever unique. Forever a force of nature. Forever all the things that make a woman . . ."

_____ 8. An ad for a flower delivery company features a sexy supermodel putting on a low-cut black dress and spike heels while she gazes at the vase of red roses and white lilies on her makeup table. "Guys, Valentine's Day isn't that complicated," she murmurs. "Give . . . and ye shall receive."

_____ 9. Singer Sheryl Crow wears a milk moustache as she tells us, "To keep the crowd on their feet, I keep my body in tune. With milk. Studies suggest that the nutrients in milk can play an important role in weight loss. So if you're trying to lose weight or maintain a healthy weight, try drinking 24 ounces of low-fat or fat-free milk every twenty-four hours as part of your reduced-calorie diet . . . It's a change that'll do you good."

_____10. A commercial shows an average-looking young couple looking unhappily at a bare spot beside their house. An announcer's voice says, "Home improvement projects got you down? Come into McGowan Hardware, and we'll solve your problems together!" We see the couple chatting with a friendly-looking hardware employee, then cheerfully working to build their own patio.

CRITICAL READING: Mastery Test 5 (Errors in Reasoning)

A. Each pair of items below illustrates a particular error in reasoning. On the line next to each item, write the letter of the logical fallacy contained in both items. Choose from the three fallacies shown in the box below.

> A **Circular reasoning** (*a statement repeats itself rather than providing a real supporting reason to back up an argument*)
>
> B **Personal attack** (*ignores the issue under discussion and concentrates instead on the character of the opponent*)
>
> C **Straw man** (*an argument is made by claiming an opponent holds an extreme position and then opposing that extreme position*)

_____ 1. ● Capital punishment is wrong because it is immoral.

● Sports cars will continue to be popular as long as people enjoy driving them.

_____ 2. ● Our biology teacher believes in evolution. He must be one of those godless liberals.

● That senator supports abortion. She has no right calling herself a Christian.

_____ 3. ● Mary McGee would make a terrible governor. She'd probably get irrational because she's middle-aged.

● I suggest you think twice before taking a class with that instructor. He was seen coming out of a gay bar.

_____ 4. ● Scott can't seem to throw anything out because he is a pack rat.

● Coca-Cola is the world's best-selling soft drink for the simple fact that more people buy it than any other soda.

_____ 5. ● Our neighbors say they won't object if minorities buy the house across the street. Evidently it doesn't matter to them if the neighborhood goes downhill.

● The president supports drilling for oil off the Gulf Coast of Florida. Apparently he doesn't care if a huge oil spill wrecks our tourism industry.

(Continues on next page)

B. In the space provided, write the letter of the fallacy contained in each pair of arguments. Choose from the three fallacies shown in the box below.

> A **False cause** (*the argument assumes that the order of events alone shows cause and effect*)
>
> B **False comparison** (*the argument assumes that two things being compared are more alike than they really are*)
>
> C **Either-or** (*the argument assumes that there are only two sides to a question*)

_____ 6. ● My cousin stole a car and wrecked it when he was 15. That's what happens to children of divorced parents.

       ● I woke up in the night feeling sick to my stomach. That restaurant where I had dinner must have served spoiled food.

_____ 7. ● Adults are allowed to have wine or mixed drinks with their meals, so teenagers should have this privilege also.

       ● In nature, the male lion rules over the females, so I believe that men should dominate women.

_____ 8. ● In choosing a car, you need to decide whether to get a safe vehicle or one that's fun to drive.

       ● If Sonya doesn't check want ads and send out at least several resumés every day, then she must not be serious about finding a job.

_____ 9. ● Ever since Ryan started listening to rap music, he's become rude and disrespectful. That music should be banned.

       ● TV shows these days are showing more and more skin. No wonder teenage behavior is so outrageous.

_____ 10. ● I went to State University and did just fine, so I don't understand why my son needs to go to a fancy private college.

       ● Back in my day, when a person got old, his children took care of him. I don't see why my children want to put me in assisted living.

CRITICAL READING: Mastery Test 6 (Errors in Reasoning)

A. Each pair of items below illustrates a particular error in reasoning. On the line next to each item, write the letter of the logical fallacy contained in both items. Choose from the three fallacies shown in the box below.

> A **Circular reasoning** (*a statement repeats itself rather than providing a real supporting reason to back up an argument*)
>
> B **Personal attack** (*ignores the issue under discussion and concentrates instead on the character of the opponent*)
>
> C **Straw man** (*an argument is made by claiming an opponent holds an extreme position and then opposing that extreme position*)

_C_ 1. ● Our senators voted to reduce the nation's defense budget. Why do they want to weaken America?

   ● The mayor is campaigning to legalize gambling in this city. He doesn't seem to mind if poor people blow all their food and rent money at the slots.

_B_ 2. ● Linda Randolph is a recovering alcoholic and should never have been put into a management position.

   ● That man should not be allowed to have a radio show. He was convicted of having a prescription drug addiction.

_C_ 3. ● My opponent voted to raise the minimum wage to $8.00 an hour. He must want many small business owners to go bankrupt.

   ● You want to get your eyebrow pierced? Next you'll want to stay out all night and experiment with heroin, too, and I won't allow you to start down that road.

_A_ 4. ● My brother-in-law just lies around all day because he is so lazy.

   ● Landscaping improves the appearance of a home since it is beautiful to look at.

_B_ 5. ● Even if you're very sick, don't go to the ER at that hospital. Three people died there last week.

   ● That actress is such a conceited person that she is bound to spoil the new movie she is in.

(Continues on next page)

B. In the space provided, write the letter of the fallacy contained in each pair of arguments. Choose from the three fallacies shown in the box below.

> A **False cause** (*the argument assumes that the order of events alone shows cause and effect*)
>
> B **False comparison** (*the argument assumes that two things being compared are more alike than they really are*)
>
> C **Either-or** (*the argument assumes that there are only two sides to a question*)

_____ 6. ● Renee switched to a low-fat diet but still got cancer. Low-fat diets are no healthier than high-fat diets.

● My boyfriend likes to look at other women when we go to the beach. That shows he doesn't really love me.

_____ 7. ● Ever since I broke off with my boyfriend, my life has gone downhill. I need to forgive him and restart our relationship.

● Twelve months after the youth recreation center opened, the crime rate in our town had risen 15 percent. Clearly the center is attracting bad characters.

_____ 8. ● Why should I have to take algebra? I'm not going to be a professional mathematician.

● Nobody helped me pay for college back in the 1980s, and my kids shouldn't expect me to help them, either.

_____ 9. ● This year the murder rate has increased in our city. The police commissioner should be replaced.

● The day their quarterback didn't shave was the day his team broke a three-game losing streak. He's decided not to shave again until they lose.

_____ 10. ● Why did you hire a teenage babysitter? Wouldn't you rather have someone who knows what she's doing?

● Do you support our president's policies, or are you un-American?

10 Active Reading and Study

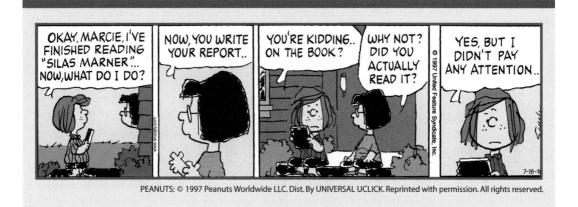

Active readers are involved in what they are reading. They think and ask questions as they read, looking for the author's main points and the support for those points. After—or as—they read, they take notes and use an effective study method to help them master those notes. Active readers are the opposite of passive readers (such as the light-haired girl pictured in the *Peanuts* cartoon above), whose minds do not really pay attention to what they read.

So far in this book you have practiced a number of active reading skills that should help you become a more active reader. In this final chapter, you'll learn how to deepen your active reading by including writing and study.

Here in a nutshell is what you should do to read actively, whether an essay or a textbook chapter or any other material:

- Ask yourself, "What is the point?" and "What is the support for the point?"
- Pay close attention to titles and other headings, and also mark off definitions, examples, and enumerations.

For example, read the following classic essay by the philosopher Bertrand Russell. Have your pen in hand, and see if you can mark off the central point and number the supporting points. Then answer the questions that follow.

Three Passions
Bertrand Russell

[1]Three passions, simple but overwhelmingly strong, have governed my life: the longing for love, the search for knowledge, and unbearable pity for the suffering of mankind. [2]These passions, like great winds, have blown me hither and thither, in a wayward course, over a deep ocean of anguish, reaching to the very verge of despair.

[3]I have sought love, first, because it brings ecstasy—ecstasy so great that I would often have sacrificed all the rest of life for a few hours of this joy. [4]I have sought it, next, because it relieves loneliness—that terrible loneliness in which one shivering consciousness looks over the rim of the world into the cold unfathomable lifeless abyss. [5]I have sought it, finally, because in the union of love I have seen, in a mystic miniature, the prefiguring vision of the heaven that saints and poets have imagined. [6]This is what I sought, and though it might seem too good for human life, this is what—at last—I have found.

[7]With equal passion I have sought knowledge. [8]I have wished to understand the hearts of men. [9]I have wished to know why the stars shine. [10]And I have tried to apprehend the Pythagorean power by which number holds sway above the flux. [11]A little of this, but not much, I have achieved.

[12]Love and knowledge, so far as they were possible, led upward toward the heavens. [13]But always pity brought me back to earth. [14]Echoes of cries of pain reverberate in my heart. [15]Children in famine, victims tortured by oppressors, helpless old people a hated burden to their sons, and the whole world of loneliness, poverty, and pain make a mockery of what human life should be. [16]I long to alleviate the evil, but I cannot, and I too suffer.

[17]This has been my life. [18]I have found it worth living, and would gladly live it again if the chance were offered me.

● What is the author's **point**? Write your answer in the space below.

_____

● What is the author's **support** for his point? Write your answer in the spaces below.

  1. _____

  2. _____

  3. _____

Explanation

The author's point might be expressed as "Three strong passions have governed my life." His support might be summarized as:

1. Love, which brings joy and relieves loneliness.
2. Knowledge, to help understand the hearts of others and the "why's" of the universe, such as why the stars shine.
3. Pity, because there is much suffering and evil in the world.

A passive reader would read the essay once, and that would be it. An active reader reads the essay while at the same time asking the two basic questions, "What is the author's point, and how does he support his point?" (The active reader pays attention to the title "Three Passions" and notes that Russell makes a point about the title in his very first sentence.) The active reader then writes out the answers to the basic questions. *The very act of writing helps an active reader study and master and remember the material.* In a nutshell, the study method to use with your reading is to locate *and then write notes* on the point(s) and support(s) of a selection.

When notetaking, apply, as needed, all three of the writing techniques—outlining, mapping, and summarizing—that have been explained on pages 66–77.

✓ Check Your Understanding

Read the following selection (it's helpful to have your pen in hand to mark off material), and then write down its main point and support in the space provided.

Note that an enumeration and definitions are keys to important ideas here. You can easily mark off the items in the enumeration as 1, 2, and 3.

[1]Humanistic psychologist Carl Rogers believed that people are basically good and are endowed with tendencies to fulfill their potential. [2]Each of us is like an acorn, primed for growth and fulfillment, unless thwarted by an environment that inhibits growth. [3]Rogers theorized that a growth-promoting climate for people required three conditions. [4]The first of those conditions is genuineness. [5]According to Rogers, people nurture our growth by being genuine—by dropping false faces and being open with their own feelings. [6]The second condition, said Rogers, is by offering "unconditional positive regard"—an attitude of total acceptance toward another person. [7]We sometimes enjoy this gratifying experience in a good marriage, a close family, or an intimate friendship in which we no longer feel a need to explain ourselves and are free to be spontaneous without fear of losing another's esteem. [8]Finally, Rogers said that people nurture growth by being empathic—by nonjudgmentally reflecting our feelings and meanings. [9]"Rarely do we listen with real understanding, true empathy," he said. [10]"Yet listening, of this very special kind, is one of the most potent forces for change that I know."

Point: _____

_____

Support:

1. _____

2. _____

3. _____

Explanation

The third sentence expresses the main idea, or point, of the passage. (Note the list words *three conditions* that signal the main idea.) That point is then developed with three supporting details, clearly marked by the addition words *first, second*, and *Finally*.

PRACTICE 1

Read the following short textbook passages from different disciplines (again, it's helpful to have your pen in hand and mark off material) and then write down their main points and support in the spaces provided.

1   Selection from a History Text

> ***Note***: An enumeration (numbered list) is a key to important ideas here.

¹The United States experienced falling birth rates in the nineteenth century. ²Several factors explain this decline in birth rates. ³First, America was becoming an urban nation, and birth rates have historically been lower in cities than in rural areas. ⁴On farms, where young children worked at home or in the fields, each child born represented an addition to the family work force. ⁵In the wage-based urban economy, children could not contribute significantly to the family income for many years, and a new child represented another mouth to feed. ⁶Second, infant mortality fell as diet and medical care improved, and families did not have to bear many children to ensure that some would survive. ⁷Third, awareness that smaller families meant improved quality of life seems to have stimulated decisions to limit family size—either by abstaining from sex during the wife's fertile period or by using contraception and abortion. ⁸Families with six or eight children became rare; three or four became more usual. ⁹Birth control technology—diaphragms and condoms—had been utilized for centuries, but in this era new materials made devices more convenient and dependable.

Point: _____

_____

Support:

1. _____
2. _____
3. _____

2   Selection from a Communications Text

Note: Titles, an enumeration, and definitions and examples are keys to important ideas here.

Three Kinds of Noise

[1]Communications scholars define noise as anything that interferes with the delivery of the message. [2]A little noise might pass unnoticed, while too much noise might prevent the message from reaching its destination in the first place. [3]There are at least three different types of noise: semantic, mechanical, and environmental.

Semantic Noise

[4]Semantic noise occurs when different people have different meanings for different words and phrases. [5]For example, if you ask a New Yorker for a "soda" and expect to receive something that has ice cream in it, you'll be disappointed. [6]The New Yorker will give you a bottle of what is called "pop" in the Midwest.

Mechanical Noise

[7]Noise can also be mechanical. [8]This type of noise occurs when there is a problem with a machine that is being used to assist communication. [9]A TV set with a broken focus knob, a pen running out of ink, a static-filled radio, and a keyboard with a broken space bar are all examples of mechanical noise. [10]In addition, problems that are caused by people encoding messages to machines can also be thought of as a type of environmental noise. [11]Thus typographical and printing errors are examples of mechanical noise.

Environmental Noise

[12]A third form of noise can be called environmental. [13]This type refers to sources of noise that are external to the communication process but that nonetheless interfere with it. [14]Some environmental noise might be out of the communicator's control—a noisy restaurant, for example, where the communicator is trying to hold a conversation. [15]Some environmental noise might be introduced by the source or the receiver; for example, you might try to talk to somebody who keeps drumming his or her fingers on the table. [16]A reporter not getting a story right because of a noisy room is an example of someone subjected to environmental noise.

Point: _____

Support:

1. _____

    Example: _____

2. _____

    Example: _____

3. _____

    Example: _____

3 ˙ Selection from a Biology Text

> *Note:* A title, definition, and examples are keys to important ideas here.

Elements

[1]If all matter could be reduced to its pure states, we would find that there are 92 naturally occurring kinds of matter (and a number that are synthetic). [2]These kinds of matter are the chemical elements.

[3]A *chemical element* is a substance that cannot be separated into simpler substances through ordinary chemical means. [4]Each element has specific properties that make it different from other elements. [5]The properties of elements include their most common physical state (solid, liquid, or gas), color, odor, texture, boiling and freezing points, chemical reactivity, and others. [6]Elements can actually be broken down further, such as by bombarding them with high-energy particles, but then their properties would change and the products would no longer represent that element. [7]This is just another way of saying that the properties define the element.

[8]Familiar elements include sulfur, phosphorus, oxygen, nitrogen, carbon, and hydrogen. [9]These six elements, often referred to by the acronym SPONCH, are important because they make up about 99% of living matter. [10]The SPONCH elements are not the only ones important to life. [11]The remaining elements are rare in organisms and of less interest to biologists.

Point: _____

_____

Support: _____

_____

_____

_____

A Textbook Study System

You have now practiced, in a nutshell, a study system that really works:

1 **Read the material, looking for the main points and supports.**

   Very often the clues to important ideas will be titles, enumerations, definitions, and examples. Note that it helps to have your pen in hand so you can mark off material as you read.

2 **Take written notes on the main points and supports.**

   What has been done above with the short essay by Bertrand Russell and the three short textbook selections can be done with longer essays and textbook selections as well. As you read, look for (and mark off) important ideas, and then take notes on those ideas. The very act of notetaking—of writing ideas out on paper—will help you study and master those ideas. *What many students do not realize is that taking notes on a subject can help in thinking about and understanding the subject. Writing is thinking.* Effective reading often means more than looking for important ideas; it means marking them off and writing them down as well.

A Detailed Study System

There are a variety of very similar "textbook study systems" that are just a larger-scale version of what you have done with the Russell essay and the short textbook selections. Two of these study systems, for example, are SQ3R (the letters stand for *Survey, Question, Read, Recite, Review*) and PRWR. Here is the PRWR system, which directs you to study what you read by taking four steps:

1 **Preview** the chapter to get a general overview and "a lay of the land" before you start reading. Note the title, which is probably a summary of what the whole chapter is about, and quickly read the first and last paragraphs of the chapter, which may introduce or summarize main ideas in the chapter.

2 **Read** and underline or otherwise mark what seem to be the important ideas in the chapter. In particular, look for and underline *definitions,* and set off *examples* of those definitions with an "Ex." Also look for *enumerations*— major lists of items, which may already be numbered 1, 2, 3, etc. or which you can number yourself.

3 **Write** (or type into your computer) study notes on the chapter. *Actual writing and notetaking is a key to successful learning.* In the very act of deciding what is important enough to write down and then writing it down, you begin to learn and master the material.

Organize your notes into a rough outline that shows relationships between ideas. Write main headings at the margin of your notes, and indent subheads about half an inch away from the margin. Print each term being defined, and put an *Ex.* beside each example of a definition. Number items in any list, and be sure to include a heading that tells what each list is about.

4 **Recite** your study notes until you can say them to yourself without looking at them. It helps to put key words in the margin of your notes. For example, if you are studying the three kinds of noise, write the following in the margin:

> *3 kinds of noise*
> > *1. Semantic*
> > *2. Mechanical*
> > *3. Environmental*

Then look at the first, "semantic," and see if you can recite what it means. After you can recite "semantic" and give an example without looking at it, go on to "mechanical." When you can recite it and give an example without looking at it, go back and test yourself on "semantic." ***Repeated self-testing is the key to effective learning.***

After you can recite the definitions and examples of "semantic" and "mechanical," go on and test yourself on "environmental." When you can recite it, go back and test yourself on all three. It is impossible to be passive in your study if you continue this strategy of repeated self-testing.

PRACTICE 2

Read the following textbook selections from different disciplines, and then write down their important ideas in the space provided. Taking notes on these selections will give you the practice you need to take notes on longer textbook selections.

Keep in mind the following:

1. Research has shown that tests are based primarily on material that an instructor presents in class. Never make the mistake of thinking that textbook notetaking will take the place of going to class regularly and taking good notes.

    Your textbook notes and study usually supplement what you are learning in class.

2. When taking notes on textbook material, don't lose sight of the forest for the trees. Here in a nutshell is what you should do to be an active reader and notetaker:

    ● Ask yourself, "What is the point?" and "What is the support for the point?"

    ● Pay close attention to (and write down) titles and other headings, and also mark definitions, examples, and enumerations.

1   Selection from a Health Text

Note: The answer to the question in the title is one of the important ideas in this selection.

Why Is Everyone So Angry?

[1]According to the AAA Foundation for Traffic Safety, violent aggressive driving—which some dub "road rage"—has been rising by 7 percent per year. [2]Sideline rage at amateur and professional sporting events has become so widespread that a Pennsylvania midget football game ended in a brawl involving more than one hundred coaches, players, parents, and fans.

[3]No one seems immune. [4]Women fly off the handle just as often as men, although they're less likely to get physical. [5]The young and the infamous, including several rappers and musicians sentenced to anger management classes for violent outbursts, may seem more volatile, but ordinary senior citizens have erupted into "line rage" and pushed ahead of others simply because they feel they've "waited long enough" in their lives.

[6]"Everyone everywhere seems to be hotter under the collar these days," observes Sybil Evans, a conflict resolution expert who singles out three primary culprits: time, technology, and tension. [7]"Americans are working longer hours than anyone else in the world. [8]The cell phones and pagers that were supposed to make our lives easier have put us on call 24-7-365. [9]Since we're always running, we're tense and low on patience, and the less patience we have, the less we monitor what we say to people and how we treat them."

[10]For years, therapists encouraged people to "vent" their anger. [11]However, recent research shows that letting anger out only makes it worse. [12]"Catharsis is worse than useless," says psychology professor Brad Bushman of Iowa State University, whose research has shown that letting anger out makes people more aggressive, not less. [13]"Many people think of anger as the psychological equivalent of the steam in a pressure cooker that has to be released or it will explode. [14]That's not true. [15]People who react by hitting, kicking, screaming, and swearing aren't dealing with the underlying cause of their anger. [16]They just feel more angry."

[17]Over time, temper tantrums sabotage physical health as well as psychological equanimity. [18]By churning out stress hormones, chronic anger revs the body into a state of combat readiness, multiplying the risk for stroke and heart attack—even in healthy individuals. [19]In one study by Duke University researchers, young women with "Jerry-Springer-type anger," who tended to slam doors, curse, and throw things in fury, had higher cholesterol levels than those who reacted more calmly.

Study notes

Reasons for anger: _____

_____

_____

Danger in venting anger: _____

_____

Results of anger: _____

_____

2   Selection from a Business Text

Note: An enumeration is the key to the important ideas here.

What Is Work?

[1]Most people know when they are working and when they are playing. [2]They often have difficulty explaining what the difference is, though. [3]Stop here and take a moment to see if you can differentiate between work and play. [4]Write a definition of work and play before proceeding.

[5]Some will say that the difference between work and play is that people get paid to work. [6]If payment is the criterion, then mowing one's lawn or dusting one's home can be considered play. [7]So payment cannot be the sole criterion for differentiating between work and play. [8]Some might argue that work is the performance of some task one does not like. [9]Then mowing and dusting would fit with going to work. [10]But many people, if not most, like their work or at least find it tolerable. [11]Therefore, liking or disliking a task is not a criterion for differentiating between work and play. [12]We might next try to examine the task itself, but a professional athlete's work is engaging in sports that nonprofessionals would classify as play. [13]How, then, can we differentiate between work and play?

[14]As shown in Table 1.1, differentiating between work and play requires that three factors be examined:

- the task's purpose
- the attitude of the person performing the task
- the reward or rewards received by the person performing the task

Table 1.1 Differentiating between Work and Play		
	Work	**Play**
Task Purpose	Has a definite purpose	May or may not have a purpose
Personal Attitude	Task viewed as work	Task viewed as play
Task Reward	External and internal	Internal

[15]The difference between work and play is in the person and the person's reason for performing a task.

Purpose. [16]Work has a definite purpose. [17]Something is being accomplished when work is being performed. [18]Some resource, either material, financial, informational, or human, is being transformed. [19]Play, however, does not have to have a purpose. [20]Sometimes people engage in play for its own sake. [21]Other times play, like work, has an outcome, as when people grow gardens for recreation and also produce food.

Attitude. [22]The second criterion to be examined is the attitude of the person performing a task. [23]A task may be work if the person performing it believes it is work. [24]If the person performing a task thinks it is play, then to that person it is play. [25]To a professional athlete, playing baseball feels like work. [26]Therefore, part of the determination of whether a task is work or play resides in the individual.

Reward. [27]The final criterion for whether a task is work or play is whether an internal or an external reward is received for performing the task. [28]External rewards are given for work; internal rewards are received from play. [29]External rewards are given to the task performer from someone else, like an employer. [30]Money may be the most common external reward. [31]Others are promotions, praise, recognition, or status. [32]In contrast, internal rewards (for play) are received from the performance of the task. [33]Internal rewards include curiosity satisfaction, enjoyment, a sense of achievement, or the meeting of charitable, personal, or philanthropic goals.

Study notes

Point: _____

1. _____

   _____

2. _____

   _____

3. _____

   _____

3   Selection from a Sociology Text

Note: An enumeration and examples are keys to important ideas.

[1]Few aspects of social life affect the way people behave and think as much as social class does. [2]For one thing, it largely determines their life chances—the likelihood that individuals and groups will enjoy opportunities for living healthy and long lives. [3]Broadly considered, life chances have to do with people's level of living and their options for choice. [4]For example, social class affects education. [5]The higher the social class of parents, the further their children go in school and the better they perform. [6]Long-term poverty experienced during childhood affects cognitive ability, and poverty experienced during adolescence affects cognitive achievement. [7]By 5 years of age, youngsters who have always lived in poverty have IQs on average 9 points lower than those who were never poor; this gap cannot be explained by differences in mothers' education, divorce rates, or race.

[8]Class also affects health and life expectancy. [9]As a doctor expressed in the *Journal of the American Medical Association*, "Lower socioeconomic status (SES) is probably the most powerful single contributor to premature morbidity and mortality, not only in the United States but worldwide." [10]Health is affected by income, education, and social class in all industrialized societies. [11]As with education, childhood poverty continues to affect health into adulthood. [12]Although health risk factors including obesity, smoking, and lack of exercise are more common among people of low socioeconomic classes, researchers also point to differences in exposure to occupational and environmental health hazards in explaining class differences in morbidity and mortality.

[13]Social class affects life chances in other ways. [14]During the Vietnam War, some 80 percent of the 2.5 million men who served in Southeast Asia came from working-class and impoverished backgrounds. [15]When the *Titanic* sank in 1912, passengers traveling in first class were more than twice as likely to survive as those traveling third class.

[16]Social class also affects people's style of life—the magnitude and manner of their consumption of goods and services. [17]Convenience foods—TV dinners, potato chips, frozen pizza, and Hamburger Helper—are more frequently on the menus of lower-income than those of higher-income households. [18]Lower-class families drink less vodka, Scotch, bourbon, and imported wine but consume more beer and blended whiskey. [19]Social class even affects such things as the styles of furniture people buy and the programs they watch on television.

[20]Social class is associated with various patterns of behavior. [21]For instance, voting increases with socioeconomic status in most Western nations. [22]And people in the lower classes begin sexual activities at a younger age, but people in the upper classes are more tolerant of sexual variations and engage in a wider variety of sexual activities. [23]In sum, one's social class leaves few areas of life untouched.

Study notes

Point: _____

_____

1. _____

   Ex.— _____

2. _____

   Ex.— _____

3. _____

   Ex.— _____

4. _____

   Ex.— _____

5. _____

   Ex.— _____

CHAPTER REVIEW

In this chapter, you learned what it takes to be an active reader as opposed to a passive reader:

- Active readers think and ask questions as they read. Active readers ask, "What is the point?" and "What is the support for the point?" Active readers also pay close attention to titles and other headings, as well as definitions, examples, and enumerations.

- Active readers often have a pen in hand as they read so they can mark off what seem to be the important ideas.

- Active readers often use a reading study system. In a nutshell, they *preview* a selection first; then they *read and mark off* what seem to be the important ideas; next, they *take written notes* on that material; and finally, they *recite their notes* until they can remember them.

On the Web: If you are using this book in class, you can go to our website for more practice in active reading and study. Visit our Learning Center at **www.townsendpress.net** for additional activities and an instructional video on this skill.

REVIEW TEST 1

To review what you've learned in this chapter, answer each of the following questions by filling in the blank.

1. In addition to asking "What is the point?" and "What is the support for the point?" active readers also notice titles, definitions, _____, and enumerations.

2. When you read material, looking for main points and supports, it helps to have a pen in hand so you can _____ off material as you read.

3. When studying material, it is often not enough to just mentally note the points and supports. You should also _____ them down.

4. Textbook study systems typically suggest that before you start reading an essay or chapter, you first _____ it to get an overall sense of the selection.

5. To master important material and avoid passive study, you should _____ your study notes until you can say them to yourself without looking at them.

REVIEW TEST 2

Here is a chance to practice active reading on a selection from a college textbook. Read it and mark off the central point and major supporting details, including enumerations, definitions, and examples. Then answer the questions on the skills you have practiced in previous chapters.

Preview

Nobody gets through life without experiencing conflict. But when faced with conflict, our responses vary. This reading from the communications textbook *Looking Out/Looking In* provides descriptions of common responses to conflict, along with their pros and cons. The descriptions will help you not only identify your own personal style, but also evaluate its effectiveness.

Words to Watch

status quo (4): the existing condition
emblems (8): symbols
amiable (13): friendly

PERSONAL CONFLICT STYLES

Ronald B. Adler, Russell F. Proctor II, and Neil Towne

1 People can act in several ways when their needs aren't met. Each way has very different characteristics, as we can show by describing a common problem. At one time or another almost everyone has been bothered by the neighbor's barking dog. You know the story: Every passing car, distant siren, pedestrian, and falling leaf seems to set off a fit of barking that makes you unable to sleep, socialize, or study. In a description of the possible ways of handling this kind of situation, the differences between nonassertive, directly aggressive, passive-aggressive, indirect, and assertive behavior should become clear.

Nonassertive Behavior

2 Nonassertion is the inability or unwillingness to express thoughts or feelings in a conflict. Sometimes nonassertion comes from a lack of confidence. At other times people lack the awareness or skill to use a more direct means of expression. Sometimes people know how to communicate in an assertive way but choose to behave nonassertively.

3 Nonassertion is a surprisingly common way of dealing with conflicts. One study revealed that dating partners do not express roughly 40 percent of their relational grievances to one another. Another study examined the conflict level of spouses in "non-distressed" marriages. Over a five-day period, spouses reported that their partner engaged in an average of thirteen behaviors that were "displeasurable" to them but that they had only one confrontation during the same period.

4 Nonassertion can take a variety of forms. One is avoidance—either physical (steering clear of a friend after having an argument) or conversational (changing the topic, joking, or denying that a problem exists). People who avoid conflicts usually believe that it's easier to put up with the status quo° than to face the conflict head-on and try to solve it. Accommodation is another nonassertive response. Accommodators deal with conflict by giving in, putting the others' needs ahead of their own.

5 Faced with the annoyance of a barking dog next door, a nonassertive person might try to ignore the noise by closing the windows and turning up the radio. Other nonassertive responses would be to deny that the problem even exists or to hope that it would go away. None of these alternatives sounds very appealing. They probably would lead the nonassertive communicator to grow more and more angry at the neighbors, making a friendly relationship difficult. Nonassertion also can lead to a loss of self-respect. It's hard to respect yourself when you can't cope with even an everyday irritation.

6   Nonassertion isn't always a bad idea. You might choose to keep quiet or give in if the risk of speaking up is too great: getting fired from a job you can't afford to lose, being humiliated in public, or even risking physical harm. You might also avoid a conflict if the relationship that it involves isn't worth the effort. Even in close relationships, though, nonassertion has its logic. If the issue is temporary or minor, you might let it pass. It might even make sense to keep your thoughts to yourself and give in if the issue is more important to the other person than it is to you. These reasons help explain why the communication of many happily married couples is characterized by "selectively ignoring" the other person's minor flaws. This doesn't mean that a key to successful relationships is avoiding all conflicts. Instead, it means that it's smart to save energy for the truly important ones.

7   Like avoidance, accommodation can also be appropriate, especially in cases in which the other person's needs may be more important than yours. For instance, if a friend wants to have a serious talk and you feel playful, you'd most likely honor her request, particularly if the friend is facing some kind of crisis and wants your help. In most cases, however, accommodators fail to assert themselves either because they don't value themselves sufficiently or because they don't know how to ask for what they want.

Direct Aggression

8   In contrast to nonassertion, direct aggression occurs when a communicator expresses a criticism or demand that threatens the face of the person at whom it is directed. Communication researcher Dominic Infante identified several types of direct aggression: character attacks, competence attacks, physical appearance attacks, maledictions (wishing the other ill fortune), and teasing, ridicule, threats, swearing, and nonverbal emblems°.

9   Direct aggression can have a severe impact on the target. Recipients can feel embarrassed, inadequate, humiliated, hopeless, desperate, or depressed. These results can lead to decreased effectiveness in personal relationships, on the job, and in families. There is a significant connection between verbal aggression and physical aggression, but even if the attacks never lead to

blows, the psychological effects can be devastating. For example, siblings who were teased by a brother or sister report less satisfaction and trust than those whose relationships were relatively free of this sort of aggression, and high school teams with aggressive coaches lose more games than those whose coaches are less aggressive.

10   Aggressive behavior can punish the attacker as well as the victim. Men who view conversations as contests and partners as opponents are 60 percent more apt to die earlier than those who are less aggressive. Newly married couples whose disagreements are marked by sarcasm, interruptions, and criticism suffer a drop in the effectiveness of their immune systems.

11   You could handle the barking dog problem with direct aggression by abusively confronting your neighbors, calling them names, and threatening to call the dogcatcher the next time you see their dog running loose. If your town has a leash law, you would be within your legal rights to do so, and thus you would gain your goal of bringing peace and quiet to the neighborhood. Unfortunately, your direct aggression would have other, less productive consequences. Your neighbors and you would probably cease to be on speaking terms, and you could expect a complaint from them the first time you violated even the most inconsequential of city ordinances. If you live in the neighborhood for any time at all, this state of hostilities isn't very appealing. This example shows why research confirms what common sense suggests:

Unlike other conflict styles, direct aggression is judged incompetent by virtually everyone who encounters it.

12   To be fair, there are probably times when direct aggression is the only realistic option. In abusive or life-threatening situations, for instance, it might be necessary to "fight fire with fire." There are also occasions in which all other methods have been exhausted and you decide to go for the "win" no matter what it costs. For instance, after repeated appeals to your neighbors, you might finally call the dogcatcher because you're more concerned with peace and quiet than with maintaining relations with neighbors who don't seem to care about your concerns. Later in this section we'll discuss how being assertive (rather than aggressive) can allow you to "win" without requiring someone else to "lose."

Passive Aggression

13   Passive aggression occurs when a communicator expresses hostility in an obscure or manipulative way—a behavior that might be termed "crazymaking." It occurs when people have feelings of resentment, anger, or rage that they are unable or unwilling to express directly. Instead of keeping these feelings to themselves, a crazymaker sends aggressive messages in subtle, indirect ways, thus maintaining a front of kindness. This amiable° facade eventually crumbles, however, leaving the crazymaker's victim confused and angry at having been fooled. The targets of the crazymaker can either react with

aggressive behavior of their own or retreat to nurse their hurt feelings. In either case, passive aggression seldom has anything but harmful effects on a relationship.

14   You could respond to your neighbors and their barking dog in several crazymaking, passive-aggressive ways. One way would be to complain anonymously to the city pound and then, after the dog has been hauled away, express your sympathy. Or you could complain to everyone else in the neighborhood, hoping that their hostility would force the offending neighbors to quiet the dog or face being social outcasts.

15   There are a number of shortcomings to this sort of approach, each of which illustrates the risks of passive aggression. First, there is the chance that the crazymaking won't work: The neighbors might simply miss the point of your veiled attacks and continue to ignore the barking. On the other hand, they might get your message clearly, but either because of your lack of sincerity or out of sheer stubbornness, they might simply refuse to do anything about it. In either case, it's likely that in this and other instances, passive aggression won't satisfy your unmet need.

16   Even when passive aggression proves successful in the short run, a second shortcoming lies in its consequences over the longer term. You might manage to intimidate your neighbors into shutting up their dog, for instance, but in winning the battle you could lose what would become a war. As a means of revenge, they could wage their own campaign of crazymaking by such tactics as badmouthing your sloppy gardening to other neighbors or phoning in false complaints about your loud parties. It's obvious that feuds such as this one are counterproductive and outweigh the apparent advantages of passive aggression.

Indirect Communication

The clearest communication is not 17 necessarily the best approach. Indirect communication conveys a message in a roundabout manner, in order to save face for the recipient. Although indirect communication lacks the clarity of aggressive or assertive communication, it involves more initiative than nonassertion. It also has none of the hostility of passive-aggressive crazymaking. The goal is to get what you want without arousing the hostility of the other person. Consider the case of the barking dog. One indirect approach would be to strike up a friendly conversation with the owners and ask if anything you are doing is too noisy for them, hoping they would get the hint.

Because it saves face for the other 18 party, indirect communication is often kinder than blunt honesty. If your guests are staying too long, it's probably kinder to yawn and hint about your big day tomorrow than to bluntly ask them to leave. Likewise, if you're not interested in going out with someone who has asked you for a date, it may be more compassionate to claim that you're busy than to say, "I'm not interested in seeing you."

19   At other times we communicate indirectly in order to protect ourselves. You might, for example, test the waters by hinting instead of directly asking the boss for a raise or by letting your partner know indirectly that you could use some affection. At times like these, an indirect approach may get the message across while softening the blow of a negative response.

20   The advantages of self-protection and face-saving for others help explain why indirect communication is the most common way by which people make requests. The risk of an indirect message, of course, is that the other party will misunderstand you or fail to get the message at all. There are also times when an idea is so important that hinting lacks the necessary punch. When clarity and directness are your goals, an assertive approach is in order.

Assertion

21   Assertion occurs when a message expresses the speaker's needs, thoughts, and feelings clearly and directly without judging or dictating to others. A complete assertive message includes a description of the other person's behavior, an interpretation, and statements of feelings, consequences, and intentions.

22   An assertive course of action in the case of the barking dog would be to wait a few days to make sure that the noise is not just a fluke. If the barking continues, you could introduce yourself to your neighbors and explain your problem. You could tell them that although they might not notice it, the dog often plays in the street and keeps barking at passing cars. You could tell them why this behavior bothers you. It keeps you awake at night and makes it hard for you to do your work. You could point out that you don't want to be a grouch and call the pound. Rather than resort to that, you could tell them that you've come to see what kind of solution you can find that will satisfy both of you. This approach may not work, and you might then have to decide whether it is more important to avoid bad feelings or to have peace and quiet. But the chances for a happy ending are best with this assertive approach. And no matter what happens, you can keep your self-respect by behaving directly and honestly.

Reading Comprehension Questions

Vocabulary in Context

_____ 1. In the sentence below, the word *ordinances* (ôr′dn-ən-sĭs) means
   A. organizations.
   B. licenses.
   C. activities.
   D. regulations.

> "Your neighbors and you would probably cease to be on speaking terms, and you could expect a complaint from them the first time you violated even the most inconsequential of city ordinances." (Paragraph 11)

_____ 2. In the excerpt below, the word *facade* (fə-sŏd′) means
   A. determination.
   B. outward appearance.
   C. certainty.
   D. foundation.

> "Instead of keeping these feelings to themselves, a crazymaker sends aggressive messages in subtle, indirect ways, thus maintaining a front of kindness. This amiable facade eventually crumbles, however, leaving the crazymaker's victim confused and angry at having been fooled." (Paragraph 13)

Central Point and Main Ideas

_____ 3. Which sentence best expresses the central point of the selection?
   A. At one time or another, almost everyone has been bothered by neighbors, but most likely handled the situation in different ways.
   B. When confronted with neighbors who have a barking dog, it is best to take an assertive approach.
   C. There are both benefits and drawbacks to using the indirect method to communicate your needs to others.
   D. When communicating one's needs in a conflict situation, there are clear differences between nonassertive, directly aggressive, passive-aggressive, indirect, and assertive behaviors.

_____ 4. The implied main idea of paragraph 5 is that faced with the annoyance of a barking dog next door,
   A. a nonassertive person might act in ways that are unsatisfactory.
   B. some nonassertive people try to ignore the noise by closing the windows and turning up the radio.
   C. another nonassertive response would be to deny that the problem even exists or to hope it will go away.
   D. the nonassertive communicator will grow more and more angry at the neighbors.

_____ 5. The implied main idea of paragraph 11 is that
   A. one way to respond to the barking dog problem would be to abusively confront and threaten your neighbors.
   B. direct aggression can bring peace and quiet to a neighborhood.
   C. direct aggression would probably produce negative consequences.
   D. people who respond with direct aggression to a barking dog are acting within their legal rights.

_____ 6. The implied main idea of paragraph 22 is that, in the case of the barking dog,
   A. an assertive approach should be thought out carefully in advance.
   B. an assertive approach often does not work.
   C. an assertive approach should always be a last resort.
   D. you might have to decide whether it is more important to avoid bad feelings or to have peace and quiet.

Supporting Details

_____ 7. According to the selection, the communication of many happily married couples is characterized by
   A. avoiding all conflicts, both important and unimportant.
   B. indirectly suggesting that the other person correct his or her annoying behavior.
   C. selectively ignoring the other person's minor flaws.
   D. direct assertions which include a description of the other person's behavior, an interpretation, and statements of feelings, consequences, and intentions.

_____ 8. According to the selection, newly married couples whose disagreements are marked by sarcasm, interruptions, and criticism
   A. tend to suffer a loss of self-respect.
   B. tend to die earlier than other couples.
   C. are guilty of crazymaking behavior.
   D. suffer a drop in the effectiveness of their immune systems.

_____ 9. One drawback of indirect communication is that
   A. it can lead to a loss of self-esteem.
   B. it can cause people to seek revenge against you.
   C. it can cause the other party to lose face.
   D. the other party may misunderstand you or fail to get the message at all.

Transitions

_____ 10. The relationship of the second sentence below to the first sentence is one of
   A. comparison.
   B. illustration.
   C. contrast.
   D. cause and effect.

> "The neighbors might simply miss the point of your veiled attacks and continue to ignore the barking. On the other hand, they might get your message clearly, but either because of your lack of sincerity or out of sheer stubbornness, they might simply refuse to do anything about it." (Paragraph 15)

Patterns of Organization

_____ 11. The main pattern of organization of this selection is
   A. list of items.
   B. time order.
   C. comparison.
   D. contrast.

Inferences

_____ 12. On the basis of this selection, we can infer that people who lack self-confidence are most likely to engage in
   A. direct aggression.
   B. nonassertive behavior.
   C. indirect communication.
   D. assertion.

_____ 13. We can infer from this selection that people who communicate indirectly are
   A. sensitive to the feelings of others.
   B. expressing hostility to others.
   C. blunt to the point of rudeness.
   D. sneaky.

Purpose and Tone

_____ 14. The authors' primary purpose in this selection is to
A. inform.
B. persuade.
C. entertain.

_____ 15. The tone of the selection is mainly
A. scornful.
B. sympathetic.
C. humorous.
D. objective.

Argument

_____ 16. Write the letter of the statement that is the point of the following argument. The other statements are support for that point.
A. Targets of direct aggression can feel embarrassed, inadequate, humiliated, hopeless, or depressed.
B. Direct aggression can lead to negative consequences for both the aggressor and the target.
C. Aggressive people are more likely to die earlier than those who are less aggressive.
D. People often react with hostility to those who use direct aggression against them.

_____ 17. Write the letter of the statement that is the point of the following argument. The other statements are support for that point.
A. Nonassertion sometimes comes from a lack of confidence.
B. Some people lack the awareness or skill to use a more direct means of expression.
C. Some people behave nonassertively in certain situations in order to save their energy for more important conflicts.
D. There are various reasons why some people behave nonassertively.

Critical Reading

_____ 18. The statement below is
A. fact.
B. opinion.
C. a mixture of fact and opinion.

"If your guests are staying too long, it's probably kinder to yawn and hint about your big day tomorrow than to bluntly ask them to leave." (Paragraph 18)

_____ 19. The facts of the reading are probably based on

    A. the authors' observations of their own family members.

    B. stories clipped from local newspapers.

    C. a great deal of sociological research.

    D. oral histories of people who have lived in one neighborhood for a long time.

_____ 20. A politician who uses the propaganda technique of name calling to attack his opponent probably has which of the following personal conflict styles?

    A. Nonassertive

    B. Direct aggressive

    C. Passive-aggressive

    D. Assertive

Discussion Questions

1. How would you have handled the barking dog situation? In general, what would you say is your primary style of behavior in a conflict situation?

2. The authors state: "Over a five-day period, spouses reported that their partner engaged in an average of thirteen behaviors that were 'displeasurable' to them but that they had only one confrontation during the same period." Do you believe in the policy of letting most "displeasurable behaviors" go by without mentioning them? Or do you think it is better to immediately let a partner, family member, or colleague know when you are displeased about something? Explain your answer.

3. After reading this selection, do you feel that you might try to change your style of behavior in a conflict situation? If so, what style of behavior might you try now, and why?

4. It seems that every day we hear stories about people who resort to violence in response to conflict situations. Indeed, the United States has one of the highest murder rates in the world. In your view, why do so many Americans resort to an aggressive style of behavior in responding to conflicts?

Note: Writing assignments for this selection appear on page 639.

A Final Activity

Now, using separate paper, take study notes on the selection you have just read, "Personal Conflict Styles." An enumeration, definitions, and examples are keys to important ideas.

Check Your Performance

ACTIVE READING AND STUDY

Activity	Number Right	Points	Score
Review Test 1 (5 items)	_____	× 4 =	_____
Review Test 2 (20 items)	_____	× 4 =	_____
	TOTAL SCORE	=	_____%

Enter your total score into the **Reading Performance Chart: Review Tests** on the inside back cover.

ACTIVE READING AND STUDY: Mastery Test 1

Complete the study notes that follow the selection below, taken from a psychology text.

Phobias

[1]A *phobia* is an intense, unrealistic fear. [2]In this case, the anxiety is focused so intensely on some object or situation that the individual is acutely uncomfortable around it and will often go to great pains to avoid it. [3]There are three types of phobias, as explained below.

[4]*Specific phobia* is the least disruptive of the phobias. [5]Examples include intense fear of heights, dogs, blood, hypodermic injections, and closed spaces. [6]Individuals with a specific phobia generally have no other psychological problems, and their lives are disrupted only if the phobia creates a direct problem in daily living. [7]For example, a fear of elevators would be highly disruptive for a person who works in a skyscraper, but it probably would not be for a vegetable farmer.

[8]Other forms of phobia, by their very nature, frequently cause problems for the individual. [9]The term *social phobia* is used to describe extreme anxiety about social interactions, particularly those with strangers and those in which the person might be evaluated negatively. [10]Job interviews, public speaking, and first dates are extremely uncomfortable for individuals with social phobias. [11]Persons with social phobias usually have unrealistically negative views of their social skills and attempt to avoid evaluation. [12]Because this kind of phobia hampers and limits social interactions, it can seriously disrupt the individual's social and occupational life.

[13]*Agoraphobia* is the most impairing of all the phobias. [14]Literally meaning "fear of open spaces," agoraphobia involves an intense fear of leaving one's home or other familiar places. [15]In extreme cases, the agoraphobic individual is totally bound to his or her home, finding a trip to the mailbox an almost intolerable experience. [16]Other agoraphobic individuals are able to travel freely in their neighborhood but cannot venture beyond it. [17]A 30-year-old German man recounts his experience with agoraphobia in the following passage.

> [18]I start a little walk down the street about a hundred feet from the house. [19]I am compelled to rush back, in horror of being so far away . . . a hundred feet away . . . from home and security. [20]I have never walked or ridden, alone or with others, as a normal man, since that day. . . .

(Continues on next page)

Note: You may put your study notes on this page, or your instructor may ask you to use separate paper.

Study notes

Definition of phobia: _____

Three types of phobias, with descriptions and examples:

1. _____ — _____

   _____

   Ex. — _____

2. _____ — _____

   _____

   _____

   Ex. — _____

3. _____ — _____

   _____

   _____

   Ex. — _____

   _____

ACTIVE READING AND STUDY: Mastery Test 2

Complete the study notes that follow the selection below, taken from a sociology text.

Owning Feelings and Opinions

¹Owning feelings or opinions, or crediting yourself, means making "I" statements to identify yourself as the source of a particular idea or feeling. ²An "I" statement can be any statement that has a first-person pronoun such as *I, my, me,* or *mine.* ³"I" statements help the listener understand fully and accurately the nature of the message. ⁴For example, instead of saying "Advertising is the weakest department in the corporation" (an unsupported assertion), say "I believe advertising is the weakest department in the corporation." ⁵Likewise, instead of saying "Everybody thinks Collins is unfair in his criticism," say "It seems to me that Collins is unfair in his criticism." ⁶Both of these examples contrast a generalized or impersonal account with an "I" statement.

⁷Why do people use vague references to others rather than owning their ideas and feelings? ⁸There are two basic reasons.

1. **To strengthen the power of their statements.** ⁹If listeners doubt the statement "Everybody thinks Collins is unfair in his criticism," they are bucking the collective evaluation of countless people. ¹⁰Of course, not everybody knows and agrees that Collins is unfair. ¹¹In this instance, the statement really means that one person holds the belief. ¹²But people often think that their feelings or beliefs will not carry much power, so they feel the need to cite unknown or universal sources for those feelings or beliefs.

2. **To escape responsibility.** ¹³Similarly, people use collective statements such as "everybody agrees" and "anyone with any sense" to escape responsibility for their own feelings and thoughts. ¹⁴It seems far more difficult for a person to say "I don't like Herb" than it is to say "No one likes Herb."

¹⁵The problem with such generalized statements is that at best they are exaggerations and at worst they are deceitful and unethical. ¹⁶Being both accurate and honest with others requires taking responsibility for our own feelings and opinions. ¹⁷We all have a right to our reactions. ¹⁸If what you are saying is truly your opinion or an expression of how you really feel, let others know and be willing to take responsibility for it. ¹⁹Otherwise, you may alienate people who would have respected your opinions or feelings even if they didn't agree with them.

(Continues on next page)

Study notes

Note: The first item—the definition of "owning feelings"—has been inserted for you.

Definition of "owning feelings": Making "I" statements to identify yourself as the source of a particular idea or feeling. The statement must have a first-person pronoun such as "I", "me," or "mine."

Ex. — _____

_____

_____

Reasons (with examples) why people do not "own" feelings:

1. _____

_____

Ex. — _____

_____

2. _____

_____

Ex. — _____

_____

ACTIVE READING AND STUDY: Mastery Test 3

Complete the study notes that follow the selection below, taken from a health text.

Why Men and Women Drink

[1]In recent years, researchers have been comparing and contrasting the reasons why men and women drink. [2]Undergraduate women and men are equally likely to drink for stress-related reasons; both perceive alcohol as a means of tension relaxation. [3]Both genders may engage in *compensatory drinking*, consuming alcohol to heighten their sense of masculinity or femininity. [4]Some psychologists theorize that men engage in *confirmatory drinking*; that is, they drink to reinforce the image of masculinity associated with alcohol consumption.

[5]Here are some other reasons why men, women, or both drink:

- **Inherited susceptibility.** [6]For both women and men, genetics accounts for 50 to 60 percent of a person's vulnerability to a serious drinking problem. [7]Female alcoholics are more likely than males to have a parent who abused drugs or alcohol, who had psychiatric problems, or who attempted suicide.
- **Childhood traumas.** [8]Female alcoholics often report that they were physically or sexually abused as children or suffered great distress because of poverty or a parent's death.
- **Depression.** [9]Women are more likely than men to be depressed prior to drinking and to suffer from both depression and a drinking problem at the same time. [10]Young men who drink, as well as those who drink heavily, have high levels of depression and distress.
- **Relationship issues.** [11]Single, separated, or divorced men and women drink more—and more often—than married ones.
- **Psychological factors.** [12]Both men and women may drink to compensate for feelings of inadequacy. [13]Women who tend to ruminate or mull over bad feelings may find that alcohol increases this tendency and makes them feel more distressed.
- **Employment.** [14]Women who work outside the home are less likely to become problem drinkers or alcoholics than those without paying jobs. [15]The one exception: women in occupations still dominated by men, such as engineering, science, law enforcement, and top corporate management.
- **Self-medication.** [16]More so than men, some women feel it's permissible to use alcohol as if it were a medicine. [17]As long as they're taking it for a reason, it seems acceptable to them, even if they're drifting into a drinking problem.

(Continues on next page)

Study notes

Why both men and women drink:

1. _____

_____

2. _____

_____

One theory why men drink: _____

_____

_____

Other reasons for drinking:

1. _____

_____

2. _____

_____

3. _____

_____

4. _____

_____

5. _____

_____

6. _____

_____

7. _____

_____

ACTIVE READING AND STUDY: Mastery Test 4

Complete the study notes that follow the selection below, taken from a political science text.

Who Wins Congressional Elections?

¹Everyone in Congress is a politician, and politicians continually have their eyes on the next election. ²The players in the congressional election game are the incumbents and the challengers.

³*Incumbents* are individuals who already hold office. ⁴Sometime during each term, the incumbent must decide whether to run again or to retire voluntarily. ⁵Most decide to run for reelection. ⁶They enter their party's primary, almost always emerge victorious, and typically win in the November general election, too. ⁷Indeed, the most important fact about congressional elections is this: *Incumbents usually win.*

⁸Thus, the key to ensuring an opponent's defeat is not having more money than the opponent, although that helps. ⁹It is not being more photogenic, although that helps, too. ¹⁰The best thing a candidate can have going for him or her is simply to be the incumbent. ¹¹Even in a year of great political upheaval such as 1994, in which the Republicans gained 8 seats in the Senate and 53 seats in the House, 92 percent of incumbent senators and 89 percent of incumbent representatives won their bids for reelection.

¹²Not only do more than 90 percent of the incumbents seeking reelection win, but most of them win with more than 60 percent of the vote. ¹³Perhaps most astonishing is the fact that even when challengers' positions on the issues are closer to the voters' positions, incumbents still tend to win.

A Different Picture in the Senate

¹⁴The picture for the Senate is a little different. ¹⁵Even though senators still have a good chance of beating back a challenge, the odds of reelection are often not as handsome as for House incumbents; senators typically win by narrower margins.

¹⁶One reason for the greater competition in the Senate is that an entire state is almost always more diverse than a congressional district and thus provides a larger base for opposition to an incumbent. ¹⁷At the same time, senators have less personal contact with their constituencies, which on average are nearly ten times larger than those of members of the House of Representatives. ¹⁸Senators also receive more coverage in the media than representatives do and are more likely to be held accountable on controversial issues. ¹⁹Moreover, senators tend to draw more visible challengers, such as governors or members of the House, whom voters already know and who have substantial financial backing—a factor that

(Continues on next page)

lessens the advantages of incumbency. [20]Many of these challengers know that the Senate is a stepping stone to national prominence and sometimes even the presidency.

[21]Despite their success at reelection, incumbents often feel quite vulnerable. [22]As Thomas Mann put it, members of Congress perceive themselves as "unsafe at any margin." [23]Thus, they have been raising and spending more campaign funds, sending more mail to their constituents, visiting their states and districts more often, and staffing more local offices than ever before. [24]They realize that with the decline of partisan loyalty in the electorate, they bear more of the burden of obtaining votes.

Study notes

*Who wins congressional elections?*_____

_____

_____

_____

Why is the picture different in the Senate?

1. _____

_____

_____

2. _____

_____

_____

3. _____

_____

_____

4. _____

_____

_____

ACTIVE READING AND STUDY: Mastery Test 5

Complete the study notes that follow the selection below, taken from a biology text.

The Laws of Thermodynamics

[1]The laws of thermodynamics are time-honored principles that describe the behavior of energy. [2]These laws are based on certain observations about the behavior of matter and energy that are remarkably invariable from one instance to the next. [3]Such consistency leads to predictions. [4]What happens, for example, to objects raised above the ground and then released? [5]What happens to an object that is heated and then set aside, away from the heat? [6]Everyone can predict that the first object will fall to the ground and that the second will cool. [7]Such observations, made time and again, have eventually led to the formulation of laws of nature.

The First Law

[8]The first law of thermodynamics states that *energy can neither be created nor destroyed, but it can be converted from one form to another.* [9]Understandably, the first law is also called the law of conservation of energy. [10]What the first law means is that the total amount of energy present in a system remains constant. [11]The concept refers to idealized conditions that exist only in what is called an "isolated system"—one in which matter and energy cannot enter and leave. [12]Such systems do not really exist (except perhaps as the universe itself) but are contrived as models by scientists who wish to test their ideas under hypothetical conditions that can be limited and controlled.

Energy Transitions: A Case History

[13]Energy changes occur in a variety of ways. [14]When you start your lawnmower engine, you can begin to appreciate the idea of energy conservation. [15]Consider that the gasoline in the lawnmower's tank is a veritable storehouse of chemical energy, locked away in the chemical bonds that hold the carbon and hydrogen of the gasoline molecules together. [16]As you pull the cord, a mix of gasoline vapor and air encounters an electrical discharge from the spark plug, and the engine starts. [17]Chemical energy in the fuel molecules becomes heat energy, and heat then expands the gases in the engine cylinder. [18]The next energy transformation is to mechanical energy, or energy of motion, which comes about when the expanding gases push against the piston. [19]The piston moves up and down, its connecting rod rotating the crankshaft, which spins the lawnmower blade. [20]At certain points in the piston's movement, valves open, and the expanding gases escape into the surroundings, their energy dissipating as heat. [21]The escaping

(Continues on next page)

gases—carbon dioxide and water vapor—are at a considerably lower energy level than gasoline, and the difference between the two energy levels is to be found in exhausted heat and the energy of motion. [22]The latter largely becomes heat as well, as the moving parts of the lawnmower encounter friction.

[23]What we see here is characteristic of energy as it changes form. [24]Energy transformations are accompanied by the formation of heat, and when such heat has dissipated, it is no longer capable of work, at least as far as that system (in this case, the lawnmower) is concerned. [25]The transition of systems with great energy to systems with low energy extends beyond lawnmowers; it is a tendency of the universe at large. [26]Physicists express this general observation in the *second law of thermodynamics*.

The Second Law

[27]The second law of thermodynamics tells us that energy transitions are imperfect—that some energy is always lost, usually as heat, in each transition. [28]Again, in the transitions from the chemical bond energy in gasoline to the mechanical energy in the spinning lawnmower blade, much of the original energy is lost as heat. [29]The energy is not lost from the system; it is just that such heat energy is normally not available to do useful work.

Study notes

The Laws of Thermodynamics— _____

_____

1. *The First Law—* _____

    _____

    _____

    Ex. — _____

    _____

    _____

2. *The Second Law—* _____

    _____

    _____

    Ex. — _____

    _____

    _____

ACTIVE READING AND STUDY: Mastery Test 6

Complete the study notes that follow the selection below, taken from a business text.

Motivational Factors (Satisfiers)

[1]We've all probably seen organizations that function in rundown buildings, yet morale and productivity are high. [2]One researcher (Herzberg) contends that people's attitudes toward their jobs far outweigh the importance of working conditions or environment. [3]Herzberg has provided a list of motivational factors, or satisfiers, that can be said to motivate individuals and to produce job satisfaction.

[4]Achievement is important to many employees. [5]Is it to you? [6]Achievement means feeling that you've accomplished a goal; that is, you've finished something that you've started. [7]Some work situations provide this feeling; others, such as assembly-line work, often make feelings of achievement difficult. [8]This is especially true when cycle times (the time needed to complete one task) are as short as 6 seconds or less. [9]One former student working for a food company that prepared institutional meals had a job that repeated every 2 seconds. [10]His task was to place two slices of white bread on a tray as it passed by on a conveyor belt (later, others added meat, condiments, etc., to produce a sandwich). [11]Thirty times a minute the same task was performed, and he never saw the finished product. [12]Not much of a sense of achievement there.

[13]Many employees appreciate recognition. [14]It gives the employee a feeling of worth and self-esteem. [15]Don't you like to know how you stand in a work situation? [16]When you and other employees know how you are doing, even when the results aren't completely satisfactory, you at least know that your boss is concerned about you. [17]There's a tendency for managers to overlook the need for giving employees recognition and feedback on their performance. [18]Some managers think that it's unnecessary to say anything to an employee when a job has been done well. [19]"Charlie knows he does good work" is a far too typical managerial attitude. [20]Charlie, like most employees, might not be certain what his boss really thinks of his performance without some form of overt recognition.

[21]The job itself is a highly important motivating factor. [22]Have you ever thought about why some employees are chronically late? [23]In many cases, it's because they dread going to their 9-to-5 jobs. [24]They derive little satisfaction from their monotonous jobs and as a result would like to be able to say, as that defiant country song puts it, "Take this job and shove it!" [25]People who like their jobs tend to be far more motivated to avoid absenteeism and lateness.

[26]Growth and advancement opportunities also serve to motivate. [27]In a sense, these are like the old carrot and stick philosophy. [28]Don't you, like many

(Continues on next page)

employees, tend to move in directions that help you obtain the "carrot," for example, a promotion with more salary? [29]However, managers must keep in mind that if employees never get to "taste the carrot" but only feel the "stick," then their interest in carrots will tend to fade. [30]Motivational tools should never be used to manipulate people. [31]They should be used sincerely, with the employee's as well as the organization's interests in mind.

[32]Responsibility is another factor that motivates many employees. [33]Some people will forego taking sick leave when they don't feel well out of a sense of responsibility. [34]It provides a sense of accomplishment and fills an internal need to see things done right. [35]Even the behavior of some so-called troublemakers in organizations has been modified after they have been given added responsibilities.

[36]Herzberg believes that the ideal form of feedback is one that is inherent to the job. [37]In this situation, the person does not have to be told that he or she has done a good job; it is known automatically. [38]For example, when a radiographer examines an x-ray film she has just taken, she knows if it is good or if it needs to be repeated. [39]The feedback is immediate and inherent.

Study notes

Central point: _____

_____

_____

1. _____

_____

2. _____

_____

3. _____

_____

4. _____

_____

5. _____

_____

6. _____

_____

Ex. — _____

_____

Part Two

Ten Reading Selections

Introduction to the Readings

This part of the book is made up of ten reading selections that will help you practice the skills presented in Part One.

The first six readings are from a variety of college textbooks:

- From a speech text: "Understand Your Nervousness"
- From a sociology text: "Consequences of Social Class"
- From a business communications text: "Types of Nonverbal Symbols"
- From a psychology text: "The Roots of Happiness: An Empirical Analysis"
- From a health text: "Cardiovascular Disease Risk Factors"
- From a business text: "Exploring the World of Business and Economics"

Following each of the readings are reading comprehension and discussion questions and an activity titled "Active Reading and Study of a Textbook Selection." The activity will help demonstrate to you that the keys to important ideas in textbook reading are often titles and subtitles, enumerations, and definitions and examples. The activity will also serve to underscore a point already made: *the very act of taking notes helps you understand and master textbook material.*

The remaining four readings represent other kinds of writing you might expect to encounter in college courses:

- A research-based essay: "Abusive Relationships among the Young"
- A historical document: "A Civil War Soldier's Letter to His Wife"
- An excerpt from a famous autobiography: "In My Day" from the Pulitzer-Prize-winning *Growing Up*
- A classic science essay: "The Spider and the Wasp"

Following each of the second group of readings are reading comprehension questions, an activity in either outlining or summarizing, and discussion questions.

Note: Writing assignments for each reading selection may be found in the Appendix, beginning on page 633.

1 Understand Your Nervousness

Steven A. Beebe and Susan J. Beebe

Preview

Do you tremble at the very idea of speaking in public? Would you rather walk barefoot over burning coals than make a speech to your classmates or coworkers? As the authors of the speech textbook *Public Speaking Handbook* explain below, you're not alone—and, surprisingly, your nervousness might actually be good for you.

Words to Watch

octave (1): an interval of eight musical notes
default (2): normal; original
physiological (2): relating to bodily functions
resonated with (3): sounded familiar to
predisposed (4): inclined
enhance (6): improve
confrontational (6): meeting face to face

1   What makes you feel nervous about speaking in public? Why do your hands sometimes shake, your knees quiver, your stomach flutter, and your voice seem to go up an octave°? What is happening to you? Believe it or not, your brain is signaling your body to help you with a difficult task. Sometimes, however, this assistance is not useful because your brain offers more "help" than you need.

2   Your view of the speaking assignment, your perception of your speaking skill, and your own self-esteem interact to create anxiety. You want to do well, but you're not sure that you can or will. Presented with this conflict, your body responds by increasing your breathing rate, pumping more adrenaline, and causing more blood to rush through your veins. In short, your body summons more energy to deal with the conflict you are facing. Your brain switches to its default° fight-or-flight mode: You can either fight to respond to the challenge or flee to avoid the cause of the anxiety. You are experiencing physiological° changes because of your psychological state, which explains why you may have a more rapid heartbeat, shaking knees and hands, a quivering voice, and increased perspiration. You may experience butterflies in your stomach because of changes in your

digestive system. As a result of your physical discomfort, you may make less eye contact with your audience, use more vocalized pauses ("Um," "Ah," "You know"), and speak too rapidly. Although you see your physical responses as hindrances, your body is simply trying to help you with the task at hand.

What Makes People Nervous When Speaking in Public?

3   Researchers found that among the causes of anxiety about public speaking were fear of humiliation, concern about not being prepared, worry about one's looks, pressure to perform, personal insecurity, concern that the audience wouldn't be interested in the speaker or the speech, lack of experience, fear of making mistakes, and an overall fear of failure. Another study found that men are likely to experience more anxiety than women when speaking to people from a culture different from their own. As you read the list, you probably found a reason that resonated with° you—most people feel some nervousness when they speak before others. You're not alone if you are apprehensive about giving a speech.

4   Increasingly, researchers are concluding that communication apprehension may have a genetic or biological basis; some people may inherit a tendency to feel anxious about speaking in public. You may wonder, "So if I have a biological tendency to feel nervous, is there anything I can do to help manage my fear?" The answer is yes. Even if you are predisposed° to

feel nervous because of your genetic makeup, there are strategies you can use to help manage your apprehension. A better understanding of why you feel apprehensive is a good starting point on the journey to speaking with greater confidence.

When Are You Most Likely to Feel Nervous about Giving a Speech?

5   Research suggests that many people feel most nervous right before they give their speech. If you're typical, you'll feel the second-highest level of anxiety when your instructor explains the speech assignment. You'll probably feel the least anxiety when you're preparing your speech. One practical application of this research is that now you can understand when you'll need the most help managing your anxiety—right before you speak. It will also help to remember that as you begin speaking, anxiety begins to decrease—often dramatically. You'll feel less anxious about your speech when you're doing something positive to prepare for it. Don't put off working on your speech; if you prepare well in advance, you'll not only have a better speech; you'll also feel less anxious about presenting it.

6   To identify patterns in how people experience communication apprehension, one researcher measured speakers' heart rates when they were delivering speeches and also asked them several questions about their fear of speaking. After studying the results, he identified four styles of communication apprehension:

- Average—you have a generally positive approach to communicating in public; your overall heart rate when speaking publicly is in the average range. Speakers with this style rated their own speaking performance the highest.

- Insensitive—likely to be your style only if you have had previous experience in public speaking. Perhaps because of your experience, you tend to be less sensitive to apprehension when you speak; you have a lower heart rate when speaking and rate your performance as moderately successful.

- Inflexible—you have the highest heart rate when speaking publicly. Some people use this high and inflexible level of anxiety to enhance° their performance. Their fear motivates them to prepare and be at their best. For others, the anxiety of the inflexible style creates so much tension that their speaking performance is diminished.

- Confrontational°—you have a very high heart rate as you begin presenting a speech, and then your heart rate tapers off to more average levels. This style occurred in people who reported a strong emotional or affective response to speaking and was characteristic of more experienced speakers or people with at least some public-speaking background.

Does Your Style of Communication Apprehension Make a Difference?

First, it may help to know that you are not alone in how you experience apprehension and that others likely share your feelings. Second, having a general idea of your own style may give you greater insight in how to better manage your apprehension. For example, if you know that your apprehension tends to spike upward at the very beginning of speaking to an audience (the confrontational style), you will need to draw on strategies to help manage your anxiety at the outset of your talk. Finally, the research on apprehension styles lends support to the theory that communication apprehension may be a genetic trait or tendency. That doesn't mean that there's nothing you can do to manage your anxiety; what it does mean is that, depending on your own tendencies, you may need more information to help you develop constructive ways of managing your apprehension. 7

You Are Going to Feel More Nervous Than You Look

When she finished her speech, Carmen sank into her seat and muttered, "Ugh, was I shaky up there! Did you see how nervous I was?" 8

"Nervous? You were nervous?" asked Kosta, surprised. "You looked pretty calm to me." 9

Realize that your audience cannot see evidence of everything you feel. If you worry that you are going to appear 10 nervous to others, you may, in fact, increase your anxiety. Your body will exhibit more physical changes to deal with your self-induced state of anxiety.

Almost Every Speaker Experiences Some Degree of Nervousness

11   President Kennedy was noted for his superb public-speaking skills. When he spoke, he seemed perfectly at ease. Former British Prime Minister Winston Churchill was also hailed as one of the twentieth century's great orators. Amazingly, both Kennedy and Churchill were extremely fearful of speaking in public. The list of famous people who admit to feeling nervous before they speak may surprise you: Katie Couric, Conan O'Brien, Jay Leno, Carly Simon, and Oprah Winfrey have all reported feeling anxious and jittery before they speak in public. Almost everyone experiences some anxiety when speaking. It is unrealistic to try to eliminate speech anxiety. Instead, your goal should be to manage your nervousness so that it does not create so much internal noise that it keeps you from speaking effectively.

Anxiety Can Be Useful

12   Extra adrenaline, increased blood flow, pupil dilation, increased endorphins to block pain, increased heart rate, and other physical changes caused by anxiety improve your energy level and help you function better than you might otherwise. Your heightened state of readiness can actually help you speak better, especially if you view the public-speaking event positively instead of negatively.

13   Speakers who label their increased feelings of physiological arousal as "nervousness" are more likely to feel anxious and fearful, but the same physiological feelings are experienced as enthusiasm or excitement by speakers who don't label the increased arousal negatively, as fear, anxiety, or nervousness. You are more likely to gain the benefits of the extra help your brain is trying to give you if you think positively rather than negatively about speaking in public. Don't let your initial anxiety convince you that you cannot speak effectively.

Reading Comprehension Questions

Vocabulary in Context

_____ 1. In the excerpt below, the word *hindrances* (hĭn′drən-sĭs) means
   A. extremely important.
   B. connections.
   C. drawbacks.
   D. sensations.

> "As a result of your physical discomfort, you may make less eye contact with your audience, use more vocalized pauses ("Um," "Ah," "You know"), and speak too rapidly. Although you see your physical responses as hindrances, your body is simply trying to help you with the task at hand." (Paragraph 2)

_____ 2. In the excerpt below, the word *apprehensive* (ăp′rĭ-hĕn′sĭv) means
   A. confused.
   B. disgusted.
   C. uneasy.
   D. excited.

> "As you read the list, you probably found a reason that resonated with you—most people feel some nervousness when they speak before others. You're not alone if you are apprehensive about giving a speech." (Paragraph 3)

Central Point and Main Ideas

_____ 3. Which sentence best expresses the central point of the selection?
   A. Since almost everyone gets nervous about speaking in public, it's unrealistic to try to eliminate speech anxiety.
   B. Anxiety about speaking in public can cause several disturbing physiological changes.
   C. Research has shown that there are four styles of communication apprehension.
   D. Understanding your nervousness about public speaking can help you speak in public with greater confidence.

_____ 4. The implied main idea of paragraph 3 is that
  A. anxiety about public speaking, which affects most people, has a number of causes.
  B. men are more anxious about public speaking than women are.
  C. fear of humiliation and concern about not being prepared are two major reasons why people fear speaking in public.
  D. much research has been done on the causes of anxiety about public speaking.

_____ 5. The main idea of paragraph 4 is stated in its
  A. first sentence.
  B. second sentence.
  C. fourth sentence.
  D. fifth sentence.

Supporting Details

_____ 6. According to the selection, you'll probably feel the least anxiety
  A. right before you speak.
  B. midway through your speech.
  C. when you're preparing your speech.
  D. when your instructor explains the speech assignment.

_____ 7. TRUE OR FALSE? Audiences can generally tell if a speaker is nervous or not.

_____ 8. According to the passage, people who have an inflexible style of communication apprehension
  A. usually have the most experience in public speaking.
  B. tend to rate their own speaking performance the highest.
  C. usually have a very high heart rate that tapers off shortly after they begin their speech.
  D. sometimes become so tense that their speaking performance is harmed.

Transitions

_____ 9. The relationship of the second sentence below to the first sentence is one of
  A. illustration.
  B. addition.
  C. cause and effect.
  D. comparison.

> "One practical application of this research is that now you can understand when you'll need the most help managing your anxiety—right before you speak. It will also help to remember that as you begin speaking, anxiety begins to decrease—often dramatically." (Paragraph 5)

_____10. The relationship of the second sentence below to the first sentence is one of
  A. contrast.
  B. cause and effect.
  C. illustration.
  D. addition.

> "It is unrealistic to try to eliminate speech anxiety. Instead, your goal should be to manage your nervousness so that it does not create so much internal noise that it keeps you from speaking effectively." (Paragraph 11)

Patterns of Organization

_____11. The main pattern of organization of paragraph 2 is
  A. contrast.
  B. list of items.
  C. definition and example.
  D. cause and effect.

_____12. The main pattern of organization of paragraph 7 is
  A. contrast.
  B. list of items.
  C. definition and example.
  D. cause and effect.

Inferences

_____13. On the basis of paragraph 2, we can infer that
   A. the human body tends to react to having to give a speech in the same way it reacts to other conflict situations.
   B. no one really enjoys speaking in public.
   C. some people have actually run out of the room before finishing their speeches.
   D. all of the above.

_____14. We can infer that the authors of this selection
   A. are professional speechwriters.
   B. have studied the techniques of public speaking.
   C. once suffered from extreme anxiety about speaking in public.
   D. have conducted experiments designed to measure communication apprehension.

Purpose and Tone

_____15. The authors' main purpose is to
   A. inform readers of the body's physiological responses to the challenge of speaking in public.
   B. persuade readers that they can become successful public speakers by learning to manage their anxiety.
   C. entertain readers with inspiring stories of famous people who overcame their fear of speaking in public.

_____16. The general tone of the reading is
   A. straightforward and encouraging.
   B. casually humorous.
   C. serious and concerned.
   D. detached.

Argument

17. Label the point of the following argument with a P and the three statements of support with an S.

____ A. Speakers who label their increased feelings of physiological arousal as "enthusiasm" or "excitement" are less likely to feel anxious and fearful than those who do not.

____ B. People who have to speak in public should try to remember certain facts.

____ C. As you begin speaking, anxiety begins to decrease—often dramatically.

____ D. Preparing a speech well in advance will make you feel less anxious about presenting it.

Critical Reading

_____18. The statement below is
A. a fact.
B. an opinion.
C. both fact and opinion.

"Your heightened state of readiness can actually help you speak better, especially if you view the public-speaking event positively instead of negatively." (Paragraph 12)

_____19. A person who states, "If you haven't learned how to speak in public by now, you never will" is illustrating the logical fallacy of
A. false comparison.
B. either-or.
C. straw man.
D. circular reasoning.

_____20. Someone who states that President John F. Kennedy was known as a superb public speaker because he was highly skilled at speaking in public is illustrating the logical fallacy of
A. false comparison.
B. either-or.
C. straw man.
D. circular reasoning.

Active Reading and Study of a Textbook Selection

Complete the following study notes on this selection. Some items and parts of items are already filled in for you.

> *Note:* Headings, examples, enumerations and major details are keys to the important ideas in this selection. The act of deciding which details to pick out and write down will help you get a sense of them all.

Central point: _____

_____

1. You feel nervous about speaking in public because your brain is signaling your body to help you with a difficult task. In other words, your brain switches to its default fight-or-flight mode.

    Ex. — _____

    _____

    _____

2. Causes of anxiety about public speaking include: fear of humiliation, concern about not being prepared, worry about one's looks, pressure to perform, personal insecurity, lack of audience interest, lack of experience, overall fear of failure.

    a. Most people feel some nervousness when they speak before others.
    b. Some people may inherit a tendency to feel anxious about speaking in public.

3. People feel different levels of nervousness at different times about giving a speech.

    a. Most people feel most nervous right before they give their speech—but then anxiety begins to decrease—often dramatically. You'll need the most help managing your anxiety right before you speak.

    b. _____

    _____

    c. Most people feel least level of anxiety while preparing a speech. Preparing your speech well in advance will help you feel less anxious about presenting it.

4. Researchers have identified four styles of communication apprehension:

   a. _____

   b. _____

   c. _____

   d. _____

5. Your style of communication apprehension can make a difference.

   a. _____

   b. Having a general idea of your own style may enable you to manage your apprehension.

     Ex. — _____

   c. Even if your communication apprehension may be a genetic trait, you can develop constructive ways of managing it.

6. You are going to feel more nervous than you look.

7. Almost every speaker experiences some degree of nervousness.

     Ex. — President Kennedy, Oprah Winfrey

8. Anxiety can be useful.

   a. Anxiety can improve your energy level.

   b. _____

Discussion Questions

1. Have you ever had to speak in public? If so, did you experience any of the physiological changes that the authors discuss? Did you use any strategies to help manage your anxiety? Were they successful? Explain.

2. According to paragraph 6, what style of communication apprehension might characterize you? Explain.

3. Take a few minutes to list some professions in which being skilled at speaking in public would be a definite asset. Then present your list to the class. What conclusions can you draw on the basis of everyone's lists?

4. In the selection, the authors state that thinking positively, rather than negatively, about speaking in public can actually help you speak better. Looking back on your life so far, do you believe that the way you viewed a certain task ever influenced the way you performed that task? Explain.

Note: Writing assignments for this selection appear on page 640.

Check Your Performance	UNDERSTAND YOUR NERVOUSNESS		
Activity	*Number Right*	*Points*	*Score*
Reading Comprehension Questions			
Vocabulary in Context (2 items)	_____	x 4 =	_____
Central Point and Main Ideas (3 items)	_____	x 4 =	_____
Supporting Details (3 items)	_____	x 4 =	_____
Transitions (2 items)	_____	x 4 =	_____
Patterns of Organization (2 items)	_____	x 4 =	_____
Inferences (2 items)	_____	x 4 =	_____
Purpose and Tone (2 items)	_____	x 4 =	_____
Argument (1 item)	_____	x 4 =	_____
Critical Reading (3 items)	_____	x 4 =	_____
Active Reading and Study (10 items)	_____	x 2 =	_____
		TOTAL SCORE =	_____ %

Enter your total score into the **Reading Performance Chart: Ten Reading Selections** on the inside back cover.

2 Consequences of Social Class
James M. Henslin

Preview

We've all heard that America is the land of opportunity. And we've been told that no matter who our parents are or what they do for a living, we can become anything we want. However, as James M. Henslin tells us below, the social class we were born into has more to do with our future success than we might like to think.

Words to Watch

subculture (4): separate social group
blighted (5): decaying
outstanding (8): still unpaid
commodity (12): product
docile (21): easy to manage
prestigious (28): high-status

1 The man was a C student throughout school. As a businessman, he ran an oil company (Arbusto) into the ground. A self-confessed alcoholic until age forty, he was arrested for drunk driving. With this background, how did he become president of the United States?

2 Accompanying these personal factors was the power of social class. George W. Bush was born the grandson of a wealthy senator and the son of a businessman who himself became president of the United States after serving as a member of the House of Representatives, director of the CIA, and head of the Republican Party. For high school, he went to an elite private prep school, Andover; to Yale for his bachelor's degree; and for his MBA to Harvard. He was given $1 million to start his own business. When that business (Arbusto) failed, Bush fell softly, landing on the boards of several corporations. Taken care of even further, he was made the managing director of the Texas Rangers baseball team and allowed to buy a share of the team for $600,000, which he sold for $15 million.

3 When it was time for him to get into politics, Bush's connections financed his run for governor of Texas and then for the presidency.

4   Does social class matter? And how! Think of each social class as a broad subculture° with distinct approaches to life, so significant that it affects almost every aspect of our lives—our health, family life, education, religion, politics, and even our experiences with crime and the criminal justice system. Let's look at how social class affects our lives.

Physical Health

5   *If you want to get a sense of how social class affects health, take a ride on Washington's Metro system. Start in the blighted° Southeast section of downtown D.C. For every mile you travel to where the wealthy live in Montgomery County in Maryland, life expectancy rises about a year and a half. By the time you get off, you will find a twenty-year gap between the poor blacks where you started your trip and the rich whites where you ended it.*

6   The principle is simple: As you go up the social-class ladder, health increases. As you go down the ladder, health decreases. Age makes no difference. Infants born to the poor are more likely to die before their first birthday, and a larger percentage of poor people in their old age—whether 75 or 95—die each year than do the elderly who are wealthy.

7   How can social class have such dramatic effects? While there are many reasons, here are three basic ones. First, social class opens and closes doors to medical care. Consider this:

8   *Terry Takewell (his real name), a 21-year-old diabetic, lived in a trailer park in Somerville, Tennessee. When Zettie*

Mae Hill, Takewell's neighbor, found the unemployed carpenter drenched with sweat from a fever, she called an ambulance. Takewell was rushed to Methodist Hospital, where he had an outstanding° bill of $9,400.

9   *When the hospital administrator learned of the admission, he went to Takewell's room, got him out of bed, and escorted him to the parking lot. There, neighbors found him under a tree and took him home.*

10   *Takewell died about twelve hours later.*

11   *Zettie Mae Hill said, "I didn't think a hospital would just let a person die like that for lack of money."*

12   Why was Terry Takewell denied medical treatment and his life cut short? The fundamental reason is that health care in the United States is not a citizens' right but a commodity° for sale. Unlike the middle and upper classes, few poor people have a personal physician, and they often spend hours waiting in crowded public health clinics. When the poor are hospitalized, they are likely to find themselves in understaffed and underfunded public hospitals, treated by rotating interns who do not know them and cannot follow up on their progress. . . .

13   A second reason is lifestyles, which are shaped by social class. People in the lower classes are more likely to smoke, eat a lot of fats, be overweight, abuse drugs and alcohol, get little exercise, and practice unsafe sex. This, to understate the matter, does not improve people's health.

14   There is a third reason, too. Life is hard on the poor. The persistent stresses they face cause their bodies to wear out faster. The rich find life better. They have fewer problems and more resources to deal with the ones they have. This gives them a sense of control over their lives, a source of both physical and mental health.

Mental Health

15   Sociological studies from as far back as the 1930s have found that the mental health of the lower classes is worse than that of the higher classes. Greater mental problems are part of the higher stress that accompanies poverty. Compared with middle- and upper-class Americans, the poor have less job security and lower wages. They are more likely to divorce, to be the victims of crime, and to have more physical illnesses. Couple these conditions with bill collectors and the threat of eviction, and you can see how they can deal severe blows to people's emotional well-being.

16   People higher up the social class ladder experience stress in daily life, of course, but their stress is generally less, and their coping resources are greater. Not only can they afford vacations, psychiatrists, and counselors, but *their class position also gives them greater control over their lives, a key to good mental health.*

17   As is starkly evident from the following Thinking Critically section, social class is also important when it comes to the medical care people receive for their mental problems.

Thinking Critically

Mental Illness and Inequality in Medical Care

18   Standing among the police, I watched as the elderly naked man, looking confused, struggled to put on his clothing. The man had ripped the wires out of the homeless shelter's main electrical box and then led police on a merry chase as he ran from room to room.

19   I asked the officers where they were going to take the man, and they replied, "To Malcolm Bliss" (the state hospital). When I commented, "I guess he'll be in there for quite a while," they said, "Probably just a day or two. We picked him up last week—he was crawling under cars at a traffic light—and they let him out in two days."

20   The police explained that the man must be a danger to himself or to others to be admitted as a long-term patient. Visualizing this old man crawling under cars in traffic and thinking about the possibility of electrocution as he ripped out electrical wires with his bare hands, I marveled at the definition of "danger" that the hospital psychiatrists must be using.

21   Stripped of its veil, the two-tier system of medical care is readily visible. The poor—such

as this confused naked man—find it difficult to get into mental hospitals. If they are admitted, they are sent to the dreaded state hospitals. In contrast, private hospitals serve the wealthy and those who have good insurance. The rich are likely to be treated with "talk therapy" (forms of psychotherapy), the poor with "drug therapy" (tranquilizers to make them docile,° sometimes called "medicinal straitjackets").

For Your Consideration

22   How can we improve the treatment of the mentally ill poor? Take into consideration that the country is in debt and the public does not want higher taxes. What about the more fundamental issue—that of inequality in health care? Should medical care be a commodity that is sold to those who can afford it? Or do all citizens possess a fundamental right to high-quality health care?

Family Life

23   Social class also makes a significant difference in family life, in our choice of spouse, our chances of getting divorced, and how we rear our children.

24   **Choice of Husband or Wife** Members of the capitalist class place strong emphasis on family tradition. They stress the family's history, even a sense of purpose or destiny in life. Children of this class learn that their choice of

husband or wife affects not just them, but the entire family, that it will have an impact on the "family line." These background expectations shrink the field of "eligible" marriage partners, making it narrower than it is for the children of any other social class. As a result, parents in this class play a strong role in their children's mate selection.

25   **Divorce** The more difficult life of the lower social classes, especially the many tensions that come from insecure jobs and inadequate incomes, leads to higher marital friction and a greater likelihood of divorce. Consequently, children of the poor are more likely to grow up in broken homes.

26   **Child Rearing** Lower-class parents focus more on getting their children to follow rules and obey authority, while middle-class parents focus more on developing their children's creative and leadership skills. Sociologists have traced this difference to the parents' occupation. Lower-class parents are closely supervised at work, and they anticipate that their children will have similar jobs. Consequently, they try to teach their children to defer to authority. Middle-class parents, in contrast, enjoy greater independence at work. Anticipating similar jobs for their children, they encourage them to be more creative. Out of these contrasting orientations arise different ways of disciplining children; lower-class parents are more likely to use physical punishment, while the middle classes rely more on verbal persuasion.

27   Working-class and middle-class parents also have different ideas about how children develop. Working-class parents think that children develop naturally—they sort of unfold from within. If parents provide comfort, food, shelter, and other basic support, the child's development will take care of itself. Middle-class parents, in contrast, think that children need a lot of guidance to develop correctly. Among the consequences of these contrasting orientations is that middle-class parents read to their children more, make more efforts to prepare them for school, and encourage play and extracurricular activities that they think will help develop their children's mental and social skills.

Education

28   Education increases as one goes up the social class ladder. It is not just the amount of education that changes, but also the type of education. Children of the capitalist class bypass public schools. They attend exclusive private schools where they are trained to take a commanding role in society. Prep schools such as Andover, Groton, and Phillips Exeter Academy teach upper-class values and prepare their students for prestigious° universities.

29   Keenly aware that private schools can be a key to upward social mobility, some upper-middle-class parents do their best to get their children into the prestigious preschools that feed into these exclusive prep schools. Although some preschools cost $23,000 a year, they have a waiting list. Parents even solicit letters of recommendation for their 2- and 3-year-olds. Such parental involvement and resources are major reasons why children from the more privileged classes are more likely to go to college—and to graduate.

Religion

30   One area of social life that we might think would not be affected by social class is religion. ("People are just religious, or they are not. What does social class have to do with it?") The classes tend to cluster in different denominations. Episcopalians, for example, are more likely to attract the middle and upper classes, while Baptists draw heavily from the lower classes. Patterns of worship also follow class lines: The lower classes are attracted to more expressive worship services and louder music, while the middle and upper classes prefer more "subdued" worship.

Politics

31   As I have stressed throughout this text, people perceive events from their own corner in life. Political views are no exception to this symbolic interactionist principle, and the rich and the poor walk different political paths. The higher that people are on the social class ladder, the more likely they are to vote for Republicans. In contrast, most members of the working class believe that the government should intervene in the economy to provide jobs and to make citizens financially secure. They are more likely to vote for Democrats. Although the working class is more liberal on *economic* issues (policies that

increase government spending), it is more conservative on *social* issues (such as opposing abortion and the Equal Rights Amendment). People toward the bottom of the class structure are also less likely to be politically active—to campaign for candidates or even to vote.

Crime and Criminal Justice

32   If justice is supposed to be blind, it certainly is not when it comes to one's chances of being arrested. The white-collar crimes of the more privileged classes are more likely to be dealt with outside the criminal justice system, while the police and courts deal with the street crimes of the lower classes. One consequence of this class standard is that members of the lower classes are more likely to be in prison, on probation, or on parole. In addition, since those who commit street crimes tend to do so in or near their own neighborhoods, the lower classes are more likely to be robbed, burglarized, or murdered.

Reading Comprehension Questions

Vocabulary in Context

_____ 1. In the excerpt below, the word *orientations* (ôr′ē-ĕn-tā′shəns) means
   A. privileges.
   B. laws.
   C. outlooks.
   D. rewards.

   "Working-class parents think that children develop naturally—they sort of unfold from within. If parents provide comfort, food, shelter, and other basic support, the child's development will take care of itself. Middle-class parents, in contrast, think that children need a lot of guidance to develop correctly. Among the consequences of these contrasting orientations is that middle-class parents read to their children more . . . ." (Paragraph 27)

_____ 2. In the sentence below, the word *subdued* (səb-do͞od′) means
   A. realistic.
   B. energetic and emotional.
   C. long-lasting.
   D. quiet and restrained.

   "Patterns of worship also follow class lines: The lower classes are attracted to more expressive worship services and louder music, while the middle and upper classes prefer more 'subdued' worship." (Paragraph 30)

Central Point and Main Ideas

_____ 3. Which sentence best expresses the central point of the selection?
   A. Poorer mental and physical health is the most striking difference between the poor and the middle class.
   B. In the United States, it's almost impossible for someone to rise above the social class he or she was born into.
   C. Compared to the poor, the rich have fewer problems and more resources to deal with the ones they have.
   D. Social class affects almost every aspect of our lives.

_____ 4. The main idea of paragraph 15 is expressed in its
   A. first sentence.
   B. second sentence.
   C. third sentence.
   D. last sentence.

_____ 5. The main idea of paragraph 31 is expressed in its
   A. first sentence.
   B. second sentence.
   C. third sentence.
   D. last sentence.

Supporting Details

_____ 6. According to the selection, poor people who are seriously mentally ill
   A. often become long-term mental patients.
   B. usually receive "talk therapy" instead of drugs.
   C. are often ignored.
   D. are often given tranquilizers to make them docile.

_____ 7. According to the selection, members of the capitalist class
   A. tend to believe that children sort of unfold from within.
   B. tend to stress the family's sense of destiny or purpose in life.
   C. are generally not as religious as working-class people.
   D. tend to be liberal on economic issues and conservative on social issues.

_____ 8. According to the selection, which of the following is *not* characteristic of the lower social classes?
   A. They are more likely to believe that the government should intervene in the economy.
   B. They are more likely to try to teach their children to defer to authority.
   C. They are more likely to smoke, eat a lot of fats, and be overweight.
   D. They are more likely to encourage their children to be creative.

Transitions

_____ 9. The relationship expressed in the sentences below is one of
   A. contrast.
   B. illustration.
   C. cause and effect.
   D. time.

> "The more difficult life of the lower social classes, especially the many tensions that come from insecure jobs and inadequate incomes, leads to higher marital friction and a greater likelihood of divorce. Consequently, children of the poor are more likely to grow up in broken homes." (Paragraph 25)

_____10. The relationship expressed in the sentence below is one of
   A. comparison.
   B. contrast.
   C. cause and effect.
   D. illustration.

> "Unlike the middle and upper classes, few poor people have a personal physician, and they often spend hours waiting in crowded public health clinics." (Paragraph 12)

Patterns of Organization

_____11. The pattern of organization of paragraphs 2 and 3 is
   A. cause and effect.
   B. time order.
   C. contrast.
   D. addition.

_____12. In general, this selection explains the effects social class has on people's lives and also
   A. contrasts the lives and beliefs of upper-class people with the lives and beliefs of lower-class people.
   B. lists factors that help explain why some people are wealthier than others.
   C. narrates a history of social class from early American times to the present.
   D. defines the term "social class" and provides examples of typical upper-class, middle-class, and lower-class people.

Inferences

_____13. On the basis of paragraphs 1–4, we can infer that the author believes that
   A. attending Andover, Yale, and Harvard made George W. Bush well-qualified to be president.
   B. George W. Bush would probably never have become president if he had not been born rich.
   C. George W. Bush inherited his leadership ability from his grandfather and father.
   D. George W. Bush was an excellent businessman.

_____14. We can infer from paragraphs 8–11 that
   A. Terry Takewell died because he couldn't afford to pay his hospital bill.
   B. Terry Takewell died because his diabetes was left untreated.
   C. Terry Takewell's neighbors cared more about him than did the hospital administrator who escorted him to the parking lot.
   D. all of the above.

_____15. On the basis of paragraphs 18–21, we can infer that the author thinks that
   A. the old man should be admitted as a long-term mental patient.
   B. state-run mental hospitals are just as good as private ones.
   C. "drug therapy" is more effective than "talk therapy."
   D. the old man should be treated quickly and released.

_____16. We can conclude from paragraph 26 that lower-class parents believe that their children will have jobs where they are expected to
   A. invent new ways of doing things.
   B. take orders.
   C. manage others.
   D. work independently.

Purpose and Tone

_____17. The main purpose of this reading is to
   A. entertain readers with colorful stories about the unbelievable situations that poor people get themselves into.
   B. inform readers of ways in which social class determines much about our lives.
   C. persuade readers that we should raise taxes on the rich in order to pay for better health care for the poor.

Argument

18. Label the point of the following argument with a **P** and the two statements of support with an **S**. Label with an **X** the statement that is neither the point nor the support of the argument.

   ____ A. Middle- and upper-class people usually have a personal physician, while poor people often spend hours waiting in crowded public health clinics.

   ____ B. When the poor are hospitalized, they are likely to find themselves in understaffed and underfunded public hospitals.

   ____ C. In the United States, there is a two-tier system of medical care.

   ____ D. The health care reform passed by Congress in 2010 was intended to reduce some of the inequality that has characterized medical care in the United States.

Critical Reading

_____19. The sentence below is
   A. fact.
   B. opinion.
   C. both fact and opinion.

      "Greater mental problems are part of the higher stress that accompanies poverty." (Paragraph 15)

_____20. A person who argues that the President's proposal of a modest tax increase on the wealthiest Americans is actually "class warfare" and that the President wants to get rid of the upper class is committing the fallacy of

A. straw man *(an argument is made by claiming an opponent holds an extreme position and then opposing that extreme position).*

B. either-or *(the argument assumes that there are only two sides to a question).*

C. circular reasoning *(a statement repeats itself rather than providing a real supporting reason to back up the argument).*

D. false comparison *(the argument assumes that two things being compared are more alike than they really are).*

Active Reading and Study of a Textbook Selection

Complete the following study notes on the selection. Some items and parts of items are already filled in for you.

Note: Headings, enumerations, and examples are keys to the important ideas in this selection.

Central point: Social class affects almost every aspect of our lives.

1. Physical health

  a. As you go up the social-class ladder, health increases. As you go down, health decreases.

    Ex. — There is a twenty-year difference in life expectancy between the people who live in southeast Washington, D.C. and those who live in wealthy Montgomery County, Maryland.

  b. _____

    Ex. — Diabetic Terry Takewell died because a hospital administrator forced him to vacate his hospital bed after learning that Takewell had not paid off his previous hospital bill.

  c. _____

    Ex. — People in the lower classes do unhealthy things such as smoke, eat a lot of fats, be overweight, abuse drugs and alcohol, get little exercise, and practice unsafe sex.

d. Life is hard on the poor. Persistent stress causes their bodies to wear out faster.

2. Mental Health

a. The mental health of the lower classes is worse than that of the higher classes because the lower classes experience more stress. Causes of stress include less job security and lower wages. The poor are more likely to divorce, to be the victims of crime, and to have more physical illnesses.

b. _____

_____

_____

_____

c. The poor who are mentally ill do not receive adequate care.

Ex. — The mentally ill man who ripped out electrical wires and was only put in the state hospital for a day or two.

d. The poor are given "drug therapy," while the rich are given "talk therapy."

3. Family Life

a. _____

_____

_____

b. The more difficult life of the lower social classes leads to a higher divorce rate.

c. _____

_____

_____

_____

d. Working-class parents believe children develop naturally. They provide basic support, but then assume that the child's development will take care of itself. Middle-class parents spend more time encouraging activities (like reading) that will help develop their children's mental and social skills.

4. Education

    a. _____

      _____

    b. Parental involvement and resources make it more likely that children from the more privileged classes will go to college and graduate.

5. Religion

    a. Middle- and upper-class people cluster in different denominations from lower-class people.

      Ex. — Episcopalians tend to be middle and upper class. Baptists tend to be lower class.

    b. _____

      Ex.—_____

      _____

      _____

6. Politics

    a. _____

      _____

    b. Lower-class people are more likely to be Democrats who are economically liberal (believe that the government should intervene in the economy to provide jobs and make citizens financially secure) but socially conservative (oppose abortion and the Equal Rights Amendment).

7. Crime and Criminal Justice

    a. The social classes commit different types of crime. The more privileged classes commit white-collar crime, while the lower classes commit street crime.

    b. _____

      _____

      _____

      _____

    c. Lower-class people are more likely to be the victims of crime, such as robbery, burglary, or murder.

Discussion Questions

1. In paragraph 22, the author asks, "Should medical care be a commodity that is sold to those who can afford it? Or do all citizens possess a fundamental right to high-quality health care?" What do you think? Explain your position.

2. The selection compares child-rearing practices of lower-class parents with child-rearing practices of middle- and upper-class parents. Think about how you were raised. Which style of child-rearing did your parents follow? Explain. If you have or are planning to have children, which style of child-rearing would you use? Why?

3. When discussing social class in America, some argue that social classes are fluid in the United States—in other words, that anyone can rise in social class on the basis of his or her willingness to work hard. Do you agree with this argument? Why or why not?

4. Do you think that the author presents an accurate picture of the way social class affects family life, religion and politics? Why or why not? How would you describe your own views of family, religion, and politics? Do they fit what the selection describes as characteristic of your social class? Explain.

Note: Writing assignments for this selection appear on page 640.

Check Your Performance	**CONSEQUENCES OF SOCIAL CLASS**		
Activity	*Number Right*	*Points*	*Score*
Reading Comprehension Questions			
Vocabulary in Context (2 items)	_____	x 4 =	_____
Central Point and Main Ideas (3 items)	_____	x 4 =	_____
Supporting Details (3 items)	_____	x 4 =	_____
Transitions (2 items)	_____	x 4 =	_____
Patterns of Organization (2 items)	_____	x 4 =	_____
Inferences (4 items)	_____	x 4 =	_____
Purpose and Tone (1 item)	_____	x 4 =	_____
Argument (1 item)	_____	x 4 =	_____
Critical Reading (2 items)	_____	x 4 =	_____
Active Reading and Study (10 items)	_____	x 2 =	_____
		TOTAL SCORE =	_____ %

Enter your total score into the **Reading Performance Chart: Ten Reading Selections** on the inside back cover.

3 Types of Nonverbal Symbols

Michael Drafke

Preview

When we think of "communication," we initially think of language. But as this selection from the business communications textbook *The Human Side of Organizations* makes clear, the words we use are only a part—possibly not even the most important part—of how we get our message across. In even the simplest social exchange, our nonverbal behavior does much of our talking for us.

Words to Watch

repertoire (7): types of behavior that a person habitually uses
in conjunction (9): together
rationale (11): set of reasons

1   To be in control of your communications and to always send the message that you want to send, you must first be aware of what type of nonverbal symbols exist. Once you are aware of the types of nonverbal communications that exist, you may focus on the ones that you use. Once you notice the ones you use, you can determine if they are appropriate or not. Here we will explore the following types of nonverbal communication:

- the eyes
- the face and head
- gestures
- touch

Although all of these are important, and they all combine to transmit our total message, some are used more extensively than others. In general, the hands, the face, and especially the eyes are the most expressive.

The Eyes

2   The eyes may be the single most important area for nonverbal communication. People not only attend to the expressions made with the eyes but also to the amount of eye contact being made. Eye contact is the amount of time you look at another person's eyes, whether or not that person is looking back into your eyes. In general, Americans give more eye contact than they receive when they are listening. In other words, when two Americans

are having a conversation, the listener looks at the speaker for a longer time than the speaker looks at the listener. The American speaker glances at the listener for brief periods and then breaks eye contact. The most common way to break eye contact in the United States is to look diagonally down and to the side. As one person speaks, then listens, then speaks, and then listens, the amount of eye contact given to the other person changes from less, to more, to less, to more again. Although the amount of eye contact varies with one's role, it is always of major importance to our communications.

3   Eye contact is important when speaking to individuals or when speaking to groups. Maintaining proper eye contact conveys a message of warmth and concern for the listener. When speaking to a group, give some eye contact to each person (or as many as possible) to show interest in the audience members. In business, making eye contact conveys trust and sincerity. Not making eye contact or making the wrong kind of eye contact can send the wrong message or an undesired one.

4   Eye contact for other than the accepted amount of time can vary from none, to too little, to too much. After reading this section, make a conscious effort to note the eye contact you give others, the eye contact they give you, and the circumstances under which eye contact is made. For example, if someone fails to make eye contact with you, try to determine why he or she did not. It may be that no eye contact is the perfectly acceptable amount.

For example, on the street or in close quarters (for example, in an elevator or while standing in line) or in other situations with strangers, no eye contact is often proper. On the street, anything more than a passing glance can have other meanings (as we shall see in a moment). A concerted effort not to make eye contact on the street can also mean that you do not want to acknowledge someone else's existence (like a beggar). When people you know or work with fail to make eye contact, it could be a signal that they believe they are superior, that they are arrogant, or that they hold you in contempt. Of course, sometimes it just means they are concentrating on a problem or some other thought.

5   Just as no eye contact is sometimes appropriate and other times not, so is a short amount of eye contact. In a room or hall, a short amount of eye contact, two to three seconds, is acceptable. Anything longer can be construed as staring or requires a "hello" or some type of nonverbal substitute. A small amount of eye contact can indicate a withdrawn individual. We may also give less eye contact when asked a question that is embarrassing or one that makes us uncomfortable. When confronted with an accusation, too little eye contact is likely to be perceived as an admission of guilt. However, in some cultures, looking down, and thus giving too little eye contact, is a sign of respect.

6   Giving too much eye contact, in other words, for longer than the accepted time given the situation, sends different messages depending

on the circumstances. When speaking to a large group of people, you may give just about as much eye contact to a person as you wish. Otherwise, staring at someone is a sign of recognition. It is acceptable for friends to look at each other for longer than the situationally acceptable time. If you do not know the person you are staring at, and you both seem to know it, then the message is that you want to know the person (in the case of two members of the opposite sex, or with two women); otherwise you will make that person feel uneasy (it's not polite to stare). Too much eye contact can also be threatening. This is especially true when a man stares at another man. In a work situation, long eye contact indicates anger or defensiveness. An angry subordinate may stare straight into the eyes of his or her boss when speaking, although normally the subordinate would look away. Prolonged eye contact with the boss can also be a challenge to the boss's authority (meaning you either dispute or reject the boss's authority over you). This demonstrates the importance of knowing the message different nonverbal communications send. You would not want to stare at your boss and send a message of anger unless you truly felt that way (and even then you might not want to). Also, as with other levels of eye contact, what is acceptable varies from country to country. Although too much eye contact might be threatening or rude in the United States, in Britain and in other cultures, too little eye contact would be rude or impolite.

The eyes are extremely important for communication, but they are just one part of the repertoire°. The eyes and face combine to send stronger and more varied messages than either one could separately.   7

The Face and Head

Research has identified a minimum of eight eyebrow and forehead positions, a minimum of eight eye and eyelid positions, and at least ten positions for the lower face. All of these are used not only in combination, but in rapid succession. Some of these facial/eye combinations will be described in order to increase your awareness of them.   8

Working in conjunction° with the eyes, the eyebrows are one of the most expressive areas of the face. Quickly raising both eyebrows, an "eyebrow flash," is another way of acknowledging someone. Raising the eyebrows and widening the eyes indicates surprise, astonishment, or even anger. Showing anger with the eyes and eyebrows can be accomplished by lowering the eyebrows and bringing them closer to the middle of the face. An alternative to this is the ability of some people to lower one eyebrow while simultaneously raising the other. More subtle movements and expressions are also possible, as when people squint ever so slightly to indicate interest in something, as if showing their mental focus through their eyes.   9

The mouth is also highly expressive. The most well known of all nonverbal cues involving the mouth is the smile. But the mouth is capable of much more, as most of us know. Tightening   10 the mouth can indicate anger. Biting one side of the lower lip can show apprehension. Opening the mouth and leaving it open can indicate surprise. Turning up one corner of the mouth and tightening the cheek on the same side can be just as effective as saying "Oh, sure" to indicate disbelief. Note two things as you review these nonverbal cues. First, they are commonly used in conjunction with eye, eyebrow, and other gestures. Raising the eyebrows, widening the eyes, and opening the mouth combine to indicate surprise. For more expressiveness we might add movements of the entire head.

11   The most common head movements are nodding and shaking the head to say "Yes" and "No." Nodding the head can mean more than a simple "Yes." When Ray talks and Jeanette listens and nods her head, Jeanette is not only saying "Yes," but she is saying "Yes, I understand you." If Jeanette is now speaking and Ray is listening and nodding his head, then Ray is not only saying "Yes, I understand you"; he is also saying that he agrees. Nodding is so important that it can sometimes be used by you to get a positive reaction from someone who is hesitant to agree with your rationale° or your sales tactics. You cannot, however, just stand there bobbing your head up and down and hope for results. The nod must be used selectively and in conjunction with a persuasive argument; otherwise, you will look like one of those little dogs or figurines some people put in the back windows of their cars. Receiving a head nod is also important and can help you

gauge the agreement, or lack thereof, of individuals and of groups. This is especially helpful when speaking to large groups where other, more subtle NVC (nonverbal communication) is not always available.

12   The head can be used to convey other messages besides "Yes," "No," and "I understand." Simply turning your head toward someone indicates the start of communications, whereas turning your head away can convey the end. Turning the head up and to one side can be a sign of haughtiness or indignation. Simply rotating the head to turn an ear to someone indicates an increased interest in hearing what that person has to say. Rotating the head with a slight frown indicates that you do not understand or do not agree with something. Tilting the head while your arms are crossed in front of your chest indicates that you are skeptical. Add a tightening of the mouth with one corner slightly raised, and you can convey displeasure with what the speaker is saying. Again, different areas can be used in combinations to transmit different messages. As with this last example, the hands and arms are often used in these combinations for added or more varied effects.

Gestures

13   Adding hand and arm gestures to the NVC mix greatly increases our ability to communicate because hand gestures are almost as expressive as facial gestures. Making a fist indicates anger or tension. Wringing your hands shows nervousness. Hands clasped

together in front of a person (with the fingers interlaced) can derail a forceful presentation because this gesture is seen as making an appeal or begging. Holding your fingertips together, kissing them, and immediately moving the hand away from the body in an arc is a sign of praise, especially for well-prepared food. Extending the fingers and then touching the index finger to the thumb is the O.K. or "Everything is all right" sign. Holding the hand up at elbow height with the fingers extended and together means "halt" or "stop." Holding the bridge of the nose with the thumb, index, and middle fingers indicates fatigue or a depressed reluctance at having to hear about or handle a situation. An index finger pointed at the temple and rotated indicates that you think someone is odd or crazy. Sitting back with the fingers separated and the tips of the fingers of both hands touching demonstrates confidence or contemplation. Standing with your palms on your hips with the thumb towards the back indicates confidence or aggressiveness. Poking a finger or object into someone's chest is also an aggressive signal. Hands clasped together behind the back indicates confidence and says, "I am in charge." Wagging the index finger back and forth is the same as saying "You were bad" or "You are wrong." Essentially it's an admonition or a sign of caution. Probably the most common hand gesture involving one person is waving hello or goodbye. Other hand gestures involve the arms or two people.

14   Many hand gestures made during a conversation involve the hands and the arms. Holding both hands out with the palms turned up at a 45-degree angle and shrugging the shoulders is telling someone that you don't know something. For example, Mary asks Don where Kassie is, and Don performs the gesture instead of saying "I don't know." Another hand-arm gesture, one that indicates a closed attitude, is crossing both arms in front of your chest. Raising one hand and arm almost level with one's head indicates that the person is strongly emphasizing a point. Raising both hands and arms over the head indicates victory. Other gestures involving the hands and arms are fairly common and well known, but some people use none. Not knowing what to do with their hands, they often put their hands in their pockets. This is not a positive gesture. Worse yet is to have your hands in your pockets and then jingle the coins or keys in them or to put your hands in your suit coat pockets.

15   Some hand and arm gestures involve two people, the most common of which is the handshake. A proper handshake in the United States is one in which the web at the base of your thumb is in contact with the web at the base of the other person's thumb. There should be a firm grip, the palms should not be sweaty, and the elbow is pumped about three to six times. Disinterest is shown when the handshake is weak and limp. When you offer your hand, your fingers should be extended and your hand should be held vertically. Offering the hand with the palm up is a sign of submissiveness, whereas offering the hand with the palm down is a sign of dominance.

The handshake is only slightly different when it involves women—the elbow is pumped less often or not at all, but the hand is not released too quickly. For women, the hand is held for 2 to 3 seconds. If a man holds a woman's hand for much longer, it can be taken as a sign of sexual interest. Although the handshake is virtually required during introductions, it is also one of the few forms of touch that is uniformly accepted in business situations.

Touch

16   Strict rules govern acceptable ways to touch in organizations. Touch in general is seen as a sign of caring and concern. In business and organizations, touch is generally acceptable when it is to the upper back or to the arm. There are other concerns, though, than where the touch occurs. The length of the touch, the amount of pressure used, any movement while touching, the presence of others, the relationship between the people, and the gender of the person initiating the touch are variables that have subtle distinctions between acceptable and unacceptable.

17   If a man touches a woman and the touch lasts for too long (for more than a few seconds), the touch sends a sexual message. To be safe, a man must also use less pressure than a woman. Touching someone and then moving the hand or rubbing the person sends a sexual message too strong for most business situations. Although a brief, light touch to the forearm is acceptable when others are present, almost any touch between a man and a woman can have a different or sexual undertone when the two are alone. Touching in hallways, in groups, in meetings, and in public, if done acceptably, can be an asset. Touching between genders in private is often too risky unless both are clear on the meaning. Longtime, close friends, and those leaving on long trips may hug, although this is more common with women than men. Another relationship between people that governs touch is rank. Here, people of higher rank can initiate acceptable touch with those of lower rank. In any of these cases, the safest course is to limit touch to handshakes and to the forearm, and only when others are present and it is appropriate and cannot be misinterpreted.

Reading Comprehension Questions

Vocabulary in Context

_____ 1. In the sentence below, the word *concerted* (kən-sûr'tĭd) means
  A. careless.
  B. half-hearted.
  C. surprising.
  D. strong.

  "A concerted effort not to make eye contact on the street can also mean that you do not want to acknowledge someone else's existence (like a beggar)." (Paragraph 4)

_____ 2. In the excerpt below, the word *construed* (kən-strōōd') means
  A. expected.
  B. challenged.
  C. welcomed.
  D. interpreted.

  "In a room or hall, a short amount of eye contact, two to three seconds, is acceptable. Anything longer can be construed as staring or requires a 'hello' or some type of nonverbal substitute." (Paragraph 5)

_____ 3. In the excerpt below, the word *admonition* (ăd'mŏ-nĭsh'ən) means
  A. surprise.
  B. connection.
  C. warning.
  D. gesture.

  "Wagging the index finger back and forth is the same as saying 'You were bad' or 'You are wrong.' Essentially it's an admonition or a sign of caution." (Paragraph 13)

Central Point and Main Ideas

_____ 4. Which point best expresses the central point of the selection?
  A. The eyes are extremely important for communication, but they are only one of many methods of nonverbal communication that can be used in certain situations.
  B. It is important to know that hand gestures are almost as expressive as facial gestures.
  C. Many people are unaware that some of the nonverbal symbols they use to communicate are actually inappropriate in certain situations.
  D. There are four kinds of nonverbal communication, but some of them are used more frequently than others.

_____ 5. The main idea of paragraph 6 is stated in its
   A. first sentence.
   B. second sentence.
   C. third sentence.
   D. last sentence.

_____ 6. The main idea of paragraph 12 is stated in its
   A. first sentence.
   B. second sentence.
   C. third sentence.
   D. last sentence.

_____ 7. The main idea of paragraph 13 is stated in its
   A. first sentence.
   B. second sentence.
   C. third sentence.
   D. last sentence.

_____ 8. The implied main idea of the final two paragraphs of the selection is that
   A. in an organizational setting, a man must be careful when touching a woman.
   B. the rules governing acceptable touching in organizational settings depend on several different factors.
   C. touching, if done acceptably, can be an asset.
   D. rank is an important factor which governs touch in organizational settings.

Supporting Details

_____ 9. According to the selection, prolonged eye contact in a work situation indicates
   A. confusion.
   B. an admission of guilt.
   C. anger or defensiveness.
   D. recognition.

_____ 10. According to the selection, head movements are most commonly used to indicate
   A. surprise.
   B. "yes" or "no."
   C. the start of communications.
   D. disagreement or displeasure.

_____ 11. The selection states that in organizations, touch is generally seen as
    A. an indication of sexual interest.
    B. a way to communicate that one is of a higher rank than another.
    C. inappropriate.
    D. a sign of caring and concern.

Transitions

_____ 12. The relationship between the two parts of the sentence below is one of
    A. illustration.
    B. cause and effect.
    C. time.
    D. comparison.

> "Just as no eye contact is sometimes appropriate and other times not, so is a short amount of eye contact." (Paragraph 5)

_____ 13. The relationship of the second sentence below to the first is one of
    A. illustration.
    B. addition.
    C. time.
    D. cause and effect.

> "You would not want to stare at your boss and send a message of anger unless you truly felt that way (and even then you might not want to). Also, as with other levels of eye contact, what is acceptable varies from country to country." (Paragraph 6)

Patterns of Organization

_____ 14. The main pattern of organization of this selection is
    A. definition and example.
    B. comparison.
    C. list of items.
    D. cause and effect.

Inferences

_____ 15. We can conclude from this selection that
   A. Americans tend to be less aware of the meaning of nonverbal symbols than people in other parts of the world.
   B. when communicating nonverbally, when and where you do something is often just as important as what you do.
   C. the same nonverbal symbols are appropriate for all situations.
   D. skill in communicating nonverbally cannot be taught—-it is something you must be born with.

_____ 16. We can infer from the selection that people who constantly nod in agreement at whatever others say risk being seen as
   A. arrogant and aggressive.
   B. weak-willed and dependent.
   C. depressed and reluctant.
   D. guilty.

Purpose and Tone

_____ 17. The main purpose of this selection is to
   A. inform people of the various types of nonverbal communication and how to use them successfully.
   B. entertain people with stories about how some people use nonverbal communication in inappropriate ways.
   C. persuade people that they need to learn to communicate nonverbally far more effectively than they have done before.

_____ 18. From the tone of the last two paragraphs, we can infer that the author
   A. is critical of the need for strict rules governing acceptable ways to touch in organizations.
   B. is amused by the rules governing acceptable touch in organizations.
   C. accepts the need for strict rules governing acceptable ways to touch in organizations.
   D. rejects the strict rules which govern acceptable touch in organizations.

Argument

19. Label the point of the following argument with a **P** and the two statements of support with an **S**. Label with an **X** the statement that is neither the point nor the support of the argument.

    ____ A. Sometimes people don't make eye contact because they are concentrating on a problem or some other thought.

    ____ B. When people you know or work with fail to make eye contact, it could mean several different things.

    ____ C. When a person fails to make eye contact with you, it could be a signal that he considers himself superior to you.

    ____ D. It is interesting to note the eye contact you give to others, the eye contact they give to you, and the circumstances under which eye contact is made.

Critical Reading

____ 20. The statement below is
    A. fact.
    B. opinion.
    C. both fact and opinion.

    "In general, the hands, the face, and especially the eyes are the most expressive." (Paragraph 1)

Active Reading and Study of a Textbook Selection

Take brief notes on the selection, writing down two or three important ideas under each of the four subheadings.

> *Note:* The overall central point, headings, and an enumeration and major details are keys to the important ideas in this selection. The very act of deciding which details to pick out and write down will help you get a sense of all of them.

Central point: _____

_____

_____

_____

_____

_____

_____

— Beware of giving too much eye contact (to boss or member of opposite sex or someone on the street); it may seem impolite or threatening.

_____

_____

_____

_____

_____

— The most common head movements are nodding and shaking the head to say "Yes" and "No." Use the nod selectively. Many other messages in head movements.

Ex.—Turning the head away can mean the end of a communication.

3. Gestures

_____

_____

_____

_____

— Handshake should be firm with elbow pumped about three to

six times.

4. Touch

_____

_____

_____

— A touch that lasts too long can have sexual overtones. Another

relationship that governs touch is rank, with people of higher rank able

to initiate touch with those of lower rank.

Discussion Questions

1. What are some of the ways that you (or people you know) communicate nonverbally? What are the messages that you (or they) tend most often to convey? Have these nonverbal messages ever been misunderstood? Explain.

2. What differences does the author note between men's and women's nonverbal communication? What other differences have you noticed? In your opinion, what factors account for these differences?

3. Every culture has its own vocabulary of gestures. The author mentions a few common American gestures, such as indicating "OK!" by making a circle with the thumb and first finger. What are some gestures not mentioned here that you are familiar with, and what do they mean? Are they common to a group of friends, an age group, a nationality, a family, or another kind of group?

4. Now that you have read this selection, are there any forms of nonverbal communication that you would like to be able to use more effectively? In what ways might you benefit if you improved your command of nonverbal communication?

Note: Writing assignments for this selection appear on page 641.

Check Your Performance	**TYPES OF NONVERBAL SYMBOLS**		
Activity	*Number Right*	*Points*	*Score*
Reading Comprehension Questions			
Vocabulary in Context (3 items)	_____	x 4 =	_____
Central Point and Main Ideas (5 items)	_____	x 4 =	_____
Supporting Details (3 items)	_____	x 4 =	_____
Transitions (2 items)	_____	x 4 =	_____
Patterns of Organization (1 item)	_____	x 4 =	_____
Inferences (2 items)	_____	x 4 =	_____
Purpose and Tone (2 items)	_____	x 4 =	_____
Argument (1 item)	_____	x 4 =	_____
Critical Reading (1 item)	_____	x 4 =	_____
Active Reading and Study (10 items)	_____	x 2 =	_____
	TOTAL SCORE =		_____ %

Enter your total score into the **Reading Performance Chart: Ten Reading Selections** on the inside back cover.

4 The Roots of Happiness: An Empirical Analysis

Wayne Weiten, Dana S. Dunn, and Elizabeth Yost Hammer

Preview

Do you think you know what matters most in life? If so, see if you can complete the following sentence: "All I need to make me truly happy is _____." Then read the article below from the textbook *Psychology Applied to Modern Life* to find out if most people would agree with you.

Words to Watch

hypotheses (1): possible explanations
abound (1): exist in great number
determinants (2): causes
voracious (6): greedy
allocating (6): assigning
conjectures (15): theories
affluent (16): wealthy
matrix (16): structure within which something else originates, develops, or is contained

1   What exactly makes a person happy? This question has been the subject of much speculation. Commonsense hypotheses° about the roots of happiness abound°. For example, you have no doubt heard that money cannot buy happiness. But do you believe it? A television commercial says, "If you've got your health, you've got just about everything." Is health indeed the key? What if you're healthy, but poor, unemployed, and lonely? We often hear about the joys of parenthood, the joys of youth, and the joys of the simple, rural life. Are these the factors that promote happiness?

2   In recent years, social scientists have begun putting these and other hypotheses to empirical test. Quite a number of survey studies have been conducted to explore the determinants° of ***subjective well-being*—individuals' personal assessments of their overall happiness or life satisfaction.** The

findings of these studies are quite interesting. We review this research because it is central to the topic of adjustment and because it illustrates the value of collecting data and putting ideas to an empirical test. As you will see, many commonsense notions about happiness appear to be inaccurate.

3   The first of these is the apparently widespread assumption that most people are relatively unhappy. Writers, social scientists, and the general public seem to believe that people around the world are predominantly dissatisfied, yet empirical surveys consistently find that the vast majority of respondents—even those who are poor or disabled—characterize themselves as fairly happy. When people are asked to rate their happiness, only a small minority place themselves below the neutral point on the various scales used. When the average subjective well-being of entire nations is computed, based on almost 1000 surveys, the means cluster toward the positive end of the scale. Moreover, these national happiness scores generally have been on the rise since the 1980s. That's not to say that everyone is equally happy. Researchers have found substantial and thought-provoking disparities among people in subjective well-being, which we will analyze momentarily. But the overall picture seems rosier than anticipated.

What Isn't Very Important?

4   Let us begin our discussion of individual differences in happiness by highlighting those things that turn out to be relatively unimportant determinants of subjective well-being. Quite a number of factors that one might expect to be influential appear to bear little or no relationship to general happiness.

5   **Money**. Most people think that if they had more money, they would be happier. There *is* a positive correlation between income and feelings of happiness, but the association is surprisingly weak. For example, one study found a correlation of just .13 between income and happiness in the United States, and another more recent investigation yielded an almost identical correlation of .12. Admittedly, being very poor can make people unhappy, but once people ascend above the poverty level, there is little relation between income and happiness. On the average, even very wealthy people are only marginally happier than those in the middle classes. One reason for this weak association is that a disconnect seems to exist between actual income and how people feel about their financial situation. Recent research suggests that the correlation between actual wealth and people's subjective perceptions of whether they have enough money to meet their needs is surprisingly modest (around .30).

6   Another problem with money is that in this era of voracious° consumption, rising income contributes to escalating material desires. When these growing material desires outstrip what people can afford, dissatisfaction is likely. Thus, complaints about not having enough money are routine even among people who earn hefty six-figure incomes.

Interestingly, there is some evidence that people who place an especially strong emphasis on the pursuit of wealth and materialistic goals tend to be somewhat less happy than others. Perhaps they are so focused on financial success that they derive less satisfaction from other aspects of their lives. Consistent with this view, a study found that higher income was associated with working longer hours and allocating° fewer hours to leisure pursuits. Insofar as money does foster happiness, it appears to do so by reducing the negative impact of life's setbacks, allowing wealthier people to feel like they have a little more control over their lives.

7   **Age**. Age and happiness are consistently found to be unrelated. Age accounts for less than 1% of the variation in people's happiness. The key factors influencing subjective well-being may shift some as people grow older— work becomes less important, health more so—but people's average level of happiness tends to remain remarkably stable over the life span.

8   **Gender.** Women are treated for depressive disorders about twice as often as men, so one might expect that women are less happy on the average. And Lykken notes that "men still tend to have better jobs than women do, and get higher pay for the same jobs . . . but they report well-being levels as high as those of women." Thus, like age, gender accounts for less than 1% of the variation in people's subjective well-being.

9   **Parenthood**. Children can be a tremendous source of joy and fulfillment, but they can also be a tremendous source of headaches and hassles. Compared to childless couples, parents worry more and experience more marital problems. Apparently, the good and bad aspects of parenthood balance each other out, because the evidence indicates that people who have children are neither more nor less happy than people without children.

10   **Intelligence**. Intelligence is a highly valued trait in modern society, but researchers have not found an association between IQ scores and happiness. Educational attainment also appears to be unrelated to life satisfaction.

11   **Physical attractiveness**. Good-looking people enjoy a variety of advantages in comparison to unattractive people. Given that physical attractiveness is an important resource in Western society, we might expect attractive people to be happier than others, but the available data indicate that the correlation between attractiveness and happiness is negligible.

What Is Somewhat Important?

12   Research has identified four facets of life that appear to have a moderate impact on subjective well-being: health, social activity, religious belief, and culture.

13   **Health**. Good physical health would seem to be an essential requirement for happiness, but people adapt to health problems. Research reveals that individuals who develop serious, disabling health conditions aren't as unhappy as one might guess. Good

health may not, by itself, produce happiness, because people tend to take good health for granted. Such considerations may help explain why researchers find only a moderate positive correlation (average = .32) between health status and subjective well-being. While health may promote happiness to a moderate degree, happiness may also foster better health, as recent research has found a positive correlation between happiness and longevity.

14   **Social activity**. Humans are social animals, and people's interpersonal relations *do* appear to contribute to their happiness. People who are satisfied with their friendship networks and who are socially active report above-average levels of happiness. And people who score as exceptionally happy tend to report greater satisfaction with their social relations than others.

15   **Religion**. The link between religiosity and subjective well-being is modest, but a number of surveys suggest that people with heartfelt religious convictions are more likely to be happy than people who characterize themselves as nonreligious. Researchers aren't sure how religious faith fosters happiness, but Myers offers some interesting conjectures.° Among other things, he discusses how religion can give people a sense of purpose and meaning in their lives, help them accept their setbacks gracefully, connect them to a caring, supportive community, and comfort them by putting their ultimate mortality in perspective.

16   **Culture**. Surveys suggest that there are some moderate differences among nations in mean levels of subjective well-being. These differences correlate with economic development, as the nations with the happiest people tend to be affluent° and those with the least happy people tend to be among the poorest. Although wealth is a weak predictor of subjective well-being *within* cultures, comparisons *between* cultures tend to yield rather strong correlations between nations' wealth and their people's happiness. How do theorists explain this paradox? They believe that national wealth is a relatively easy-to-measure marker associated with a matrix° of cultural conditions that influence happiness. Specifically, they point out that nations' economic development correlates with greater recognition of human rights, greater income equality, greater gender equality, and more democratic governance. So, it may not be affluence per se that is the driving force behind cultural disparities in subjective well-being.

What Is Very Important?

17   The list of factors that turn out to be very important ingredients of happiness is surprisingly short. Only a few variables are strongly related to overall happiness.

18   **Love, marriage, and relationship satisfaction.** Romantic relationships can be stressful, but people consistently rate being in love as one of the most critical ingredients of happiness. Furthermore, although people complain a lot about their marriages, the evidence indicates that marital status is a key correlate of happiness. Among both

men and women, married people are happier than people who are single or divorced, and this disparity holds around the world in widely different cultures. And among married people, marital satisfaction predicts personal well-being. The research in this area generally has used marital status as a crude but easily measured marker of relationship satisfaction. In all likelihood, it is relationship satisfaction that fosters happiness. In other words, one does not have to be married to be happy. Relationship satisfaction probably has the same association with happiness in cohabiting heterosexual couples and gay couples.

Work. Given the way people often   19
complain about their jobs, we might not expect work to be a key source of happiness, but it is. Although less critical than relationship satisfaction, job satisfaction is strongly associated with general happiness. Studies also show that unemployment has strong negative effects on subjective well-being. It is difficult to sort out whether job satisfaction causes happiness or vice versa, but evidence suggests that causation flows both ways.

Reading Comprehension Questions

Vocabulary in Context

_____ 1. In the excerpt below, the word *empirical* (ĕm-pîr′ĭ-kəl) means
   A. related to the history of empires, such as those of ancient Greece and Rome.
   B. based on observation and experiment.
   C. long-lasting and unchanging.
   D. hard to define.

"In recent years, social scientists have begun putting these and other hypotheses to empirical test. Quite a number of survey studies have been conducted to explore the determinants of **subjective well-being— individuals' personal assessments of their overall happiness or life satisfaction**." (Paragraph 2)

_____ 2. In the excerpt below, the word *disparities* (dĭ-spăr′ĭ-tēz) means
A. differences.
B. relationships.
C. attitudes.
D. similarities.

> "That's not to say that everyone is equally happy. Researchers have found substantial and thought-provoking disparities among people in subjective well-being . . . ." (Paragraph 3)

Central Point and Main Ideas

_____ 3. Which sentence best expresses the central point of the selection?
A. There is a widespread assumption that most people are more or less unhappy.
B. Over the years, many survey studies have been conducted to determine factors related to personal happiness or life satisfaction.
C. Love, marriage, relationship satisfaction, and job satisfaction are all strongly associated with general happiness.
D. A number of survey studies indicate that many commonsense notions about happiness appear to be inaccurate.

_____ 4. The main idea of paragraph 13 is that
A. good physical health seems to be essential for happiness.
B. even people with serious, disabling health conditions aren't as unhappy as one might guess.
C. happy people tend to live longer than unhappy people.
D. good health is only moderately related to happiness.

Supporting Details

_____ 5. According to the selection,
A. women in general are less happy than men.
B. people's average level of happiness seems to diminish with age.
C. marital satisfaction predicts personal well-being.
D. researchers are convinced that religious faith fosters happiness.

_____ 6. According to the selection, one reason there is only a weak correlation between having money and feelings of happiness is that
   A. people who are physically healthy often believe that they can always earn more money.
   B. the more money people have, the more money and material possessions they want.
   C. wealthy people tend to live in constant fear of losing all their money.
   D. in the United States, even poor people have lots of material possessions.

Transitions

_____ 7. The relationship of the second sentence below to the first sentence is one of
   A. time.   C. addition.
   B. contrast.   D. problem and solution.

   "When the average subjective well-being of entire nations is computed, based on almost 1000 surveys, the means cluster toward the positive end of the scale. Moreover, these national happiness scores generally have been on the rise since the 1980s." (Paragraph 3)

_____ 8. The relationship of the second sentence below to the first sentence is one of
   A. illustration.   C. comparison.
   B. addition.   D. cause and effect.

   "There _is_ a positive correlation between income and feelings of happiness, but the association is surprisingly weak. For example, one study found a correlation of just .13 between income and happiness in the United States ..." (Paragraph 5)

_____ 9. The relationship of the second sentence below to the first sentence is one of
   A. contrast.   C. time.
   B. illustration.   D. cause and effect.

   "When these growing material desires outstrip what people can afford, dissatisfaction is likely. Thus, complaints about not having enough money are routine even among people who earn hefty six-figure incomes." (Paragraph 6)

Patterns of Organization

_____10. The main pattern of organization of the selection is
      A. time order.   C. definition and example.
      B. list of items.   D. contrast.

_____11. The main patterns of organization of paragraph 16 are cause and effect and
      A. list of items.   C. definition and example.
      B. time order.   D. contrast.

Inferences

_____12. On the basis of paragraph 3, we can conclude that
      A. most people experience about the same level of happiness.
      B. few researchers have studied the average subjective well-being of people in other nations.
      C. most people are happier than is generally believed.
      D. most people are about as happy as they were thirty years ago.

_____13. On the basis of paragraphs 5 and 6, we can infer that
      A. very poor people can be just as happy as rich people.
      B. it is impossible for people who work long hours and have little time for leisure to be happy.
      C. the more money some people have, the more money they feel they need.
      D. wealthy people tend to complain more than people with less money.

_____14. On the basis of paragraph 16, we can infer that
      A. in order for a person to be happy, his or her basic human rights must be respected.
      B. people who live in democracies are generally happier than people who live under dictatorships.
      C. women tend to be happier in economically developed nations than they are in nations that are not economically developed.
      D. all of the above.

_____15. On the basis of paragraph 18, we can conclude that
      A. the stressful aspects of romantic relationships balance out the enjoyable aspects.
      B. married heterosexual couples are happier than gay couples who live together.
      C. being in a close, loving relationship brings happiness.
      D. it is impossible to be single and happy.

Purpose and Tone

_____ 16. The purpose of this selection is to
   A. inform.
   B. persuade.
   C. both inform and persuade.

_____ 17. The general tone of the reading is
   A. informal and ironic.
   B. objective and instructive.
   C. admiring and respectful.
   D. critical and caring.

Argument

18. Label the point of the following argument with a **P** and the two statements of support with an **S**. Label with an **X** the statement that is neither the point nor the support of the argument.

   ____ A. Religion connects people to a caring, supportive community.

   ____ B. People with strong religious convictions tend to be happier than nonreligious people.

   ____ C. Researchers aren't sure how religious faith relates to happiness.

   ____ D. Religion helps people deal with setbacks.

Critical Reading

_____ 19. An ad for the new Chevy Camaro that states, "You could live without it. If you call that living" is illustrating the propaganda technique of
   A. testimonial.
   B. transfer.
   C. glittering generalities.
   D. plain folks.

_____ 20. A person who states that gay couples can't be happy because being gay is an unfulfilling lifestyle is committing the logical fallacy of
   A. straw man _(an argument is made by claiming an opponent holds an extreme position and then opposing that extreme position)._
   B. false comparison _(the argument assumes that two things being compared are more alike than they really are)._
   C. either-or _(the argument assumes that there are only two sides to a question)._
   D. circular reasoning _(a statement repeats itself rather than providing a real supporting reason to back up an argument)._

Active Reading and Study of a Textbook Selection

Complete the following study notes on the selection. Some items and parts of items are already filled in for you.

> *Note:* Headings and enumerations are the keys to the important ideas here.

Central point: _____

_____

_____

1. _____

     a. _____

        _____

        People who place a strong emphasis on the pursuit of wealth and

        materialistic goals tend to be somewhat less happy than others.

        Money can foster happiness by reducing the negative impact of

        life's setbacks, allowing wealthier people to feel like they have more

        control over their lives.

     b. *Age—People's average level of happiness tends to remain stable*

        over the life span.

     c. _____

     d. _____

        _____

     e. _____

        _____

     f. *Physical attractiveness—there is little correlation with happiness.*

2. *Four facets of life appear to have a moderate impact on subjective*

    well-being.

     a. _____

        _____

     b. _____

        _____

c. Religion—People with strong religious convictions are more likely to be happy than people who characterize themselves as nonreligious.

d. Culture—The nations with the happiest people tend to be affluent, and those with the least happy people tend to be among the poorest. Nations' economic well-being correlates with greater recognition of human rights, greater income equality, gender equality, and more democratic governance. This matrix of cultural conditions influences happiness.

3. _____

   a. _____
      _____
      _____
      _____
      _____

   b. Work—Job satisfaction is strongly associated with general happiness, and unemployment has strong negative effects on subjective well-being.

Discussion Questions

1. According to the selection, the vast majority of people who respond to surveys characterize themselves as fairly happy. Think of the people you know. Would you say that most of them think of themselves as fairly happy—or unhappy? What factors would you say most contribute to their relative happiness or unhappiness? Explain.

2. On the basis of your observations, would you be inclined to agree that married people (or people who are living together) are happier than single or divorced people? Why or why not?

3. The authors of the selection state that "people's average level of happiness tends to remain remarkably stable over the life span." Would you say that your level of happiness has tended to stay the same over time, or have you been happier at some times and less happy at others? Explain.

4. According to the selection, national happiness scores generally have been on the rise since the 1980s. Do you feel that happiness scores will continue to increase? Why or why not?

Note: Writing assignments for this selection appear on page 641.

Check Your Performance

THE ROOTS OF HAPPINESS: AN EMPIRICAL ANALYSIS

Activity	Number Right	Points	Score
Reading Comprehension Questions			
Vocabulary in Context (2 items)	_____	x 4 =	_____
Central Point and Main Ideas (2 items)	_____	x 4 =	_____
Supporting Details (2 items)	_____	x 4 =	_____
Transitions (3 items)	_____	x 4 =	_____
Patterns of Organization (2 items)	_____	x 4 =	_____
Inferences (4 items)	_____	x 4 =	_____
Purpose and Tone (2 items)	_____	x 4 =	_____
Argument (1 item)	_____	x 4 =	_____
Critical Reading (2 items)	_____	x 4 =	_____
Active Reading and Study (10 items)	_____	x 2 =	_____
		TOTAL SCORE =	_____ %

Enter your total score into the **Reading Performance Chart: Ten Reading Selections** on the inside back cover.

5 Cardiovascular Disease Risk Factors

Wayne A. Payne, Dale B. Hahn, and Ellen B. Lucas

Preview

Do you know if you are at increased risk for heart disease? There are steps you can take to protect yourself—but only once you've identified the factors that put you in danger. Being aware of your risks, as described in this selection from *Understanding Your Health*, is a big step toward living a longer and healthier life.

Words to Watch

cardiovascular (1): of or relating to the heart or blood vessels
epidemiological (14): relating to the control of diseases
debilitating (20): making weak and infirm

1 As you know, the heart and blood vessels are among the most important structures in the human body. By protecting your cardiovascular° system, you lay the groundwork for a more exciting, productive, and energetic life. The best time to start protecting and improving your cardiovascular system is early in life, when lifestyle patterns are developed and reinforced. Of course, it is difficult to move backward through time, so the second-best time to start protecting your heart is today. Improvements in certain lifestyle activities can pay significant dividends as your life unfolds.

The American Heart Association 2 encourages people to protect and enhance their heart health by examining the ten cardiovascular risk factors that are related to various forms of heart disease. A *cardiovascular risk factor* is an attribute that a person has or is exposed to that increases the likelihood that he or she will develop some form of heart disease. Three risk factors are those you will be unable to change. An additional six risk factors are those you can clearly change. One final risk factor is thought to be a contributing factor to heart disease. Let's look at these three groups of risk factors separately.

RISK FACTORS THAT CANNOT BE CHANGED

3 The three risk factors that you cannot change are increasing age, male gender, and heredity. Despite the fact that these risk factors cannot be changed, your knowledge that they might be an influence in your life should encourage you to make a more serious commitment to the risk factors you can change.

Increasing Age

4 Heart disease tends to develop gradually over the course of one's life. Although we may know of a person or two who experienced a heart attack in their twenties or thirties, most of the serious consequences of heart disease become evident as we age. For example, nearly 84 percent of people who die from heart disease are aged 65 and older.

Male Gender

5 Men have a greater risk of heart disease than do women prior to age 55. Yet when women move through menopause (typically in their fifties), their rates of heart disease become similar to men's rates. It is thought that women have a degree of protection from heart disease because of their natural production of the hormone estrogen during their fertile years.

Heredity

6 Obviously, you have no input in determining who your biological parents are. Like increasing age and male gender, this risk factor cannot be changed. By the luck of the draw, some people are born into families where heart disease has never been a serious problem, whereas others are born into families where heart disease is quite prevalent. In this latter case, children are said to have a genetic predisposition (tendency) to develop heart disease as they grow and develop throughout their lives. These people have every reason to be highly motivated to reduce the risk factors they can control.

7 Race is also a consideration related to heart disease. The prevalence of hypertension (high blood pressure) among African Americans is among the highest in the United States. More than one in every three African Americans has hypertension (two out of every three over age 65). Hypertension significantly increases the risk of heart disease, stroke, and kidney disease. Fortunately, as you will soon read, hypertension can be controlled through a variety of methods. It is especially important for African Americans to take advantage of every opportunity to have their blood pressure measured so that preventive measures can be started immediately if necessary.

RISK FACTORS THAT CAN BE CHANGED

8 Six cardiovascular risk factors are influenced, in large part, by our lifestyle choices. These risk factors are tobacco smoke, physical inactivity, high blood cholesterol level, high blood pressure, diabetes mellitus, and obesity and overweight. Healthful behavior changes can help you protect and strengthen your cardiovascular system.

Tobacco Smoke

9   Approximately 46.5 million adults in the United States smoke cigarettes, and 28.5 percent of high school students are smokers. Smokers have a heart attack risk that is more than twice that of nonsmokers. Smoking cigarettes is the major risk factor associated with sudden cardiac death. In fact, smokers have two to four times the risk of dying from sudden cardiac arrest than do nonsmokers. Smokers who experience a heart attack are more likely to die suddenly (within an hour) than are those who don't smoke.

10   Smoking also adversely affects nonsmokers who are exposed to environmental tobacco smoke. Studies suggest that the risk of death caused by heart disease is increased about 30 percent in people exposed to secondhand smoke in the home. The risk of death caused by heart disease may even be higher in people exposed to environmental tobacco smoke in work settings (for example, bars, casinos, enclosed offices, some bowling alleys and restaurants), since higher levels of smoke may be present at work than at home. Because of the health threat to nonsmokers, restrictions on indoor smoking in public areas and business settings are increasing tremendously in every part of the country.

11   For years it was commonly believed that if you had smoked for many years, it was pointless to try to quit; the damage to one's health could never be reversed. However, the American Heart Association now indicates that by quitting smoking, regardless of how long or how much you have smoked, your risk of heart disease declines rapidly.

12   This news is exciting and should encourage people to quit smoking, regardless of how long they have smoked. Of course, if you have started to smoke, the healthy approach would be to quit now . . . before the nicotine controls your life and leads to heart disease or damages your lungs or leads to lung cancer.

Physical Inactivity

13   Lack of regular physical activity is a significant risk factor for heart disease. Regular aerobic exercise helps strengthen the heart muscle, maintain healthy blood vessels, and improve the ability of the vascular system to transfer blood and oxygen to all parts of the body. In addition, physical activity helps lower overall blood cholesterol levels for most people, encourages weight loss and retention of lean muscle mass, and allows people to moderate the stress in their lives.

14   With all the benefits that come with physical activity, it amazes health professionals that so many Americans refuse to become regularly active. The Centers for Disease Control and Prevention reports that 60 percent or more of Americans do not achieve the recommended amount of physical activity each week and that 25 percent of Americans age 18 or older report no leisure-time physical activity. In terms of relative risk for developing cardiovascular disease (CVD), physical inactivity is comparable to high blood pressure, high blood cholesterol, and cigarette

smoking. Critical findings reported in the year 2000 from the highly respected Harvard Alumni Health Study support the contention that physical activity is closely associated with decreased risk of coronary heart disease. After monitoring Harvard alumni for nearly twenty years in a variety of epidemiological° studies, researchers confirmed that sustained, vigorous physical activity produces the strongest reductions in CVD. Light and moderate physical activities such as golf, gardening, and walking are helpful in reducing CVD, but more vigorous activities (such as jogging, swimming, tennis, stair climbing, or aerobics) produce greater reductions in CVD. Additionally, Harvard researchers found that physical activity produces reductions in CVD whether the daily activity comes in one long session or in two shorter sessions of activity. The "bottom line" is this: to reduce your chances of experiencing CVD, you must engage in some form of regular, sustained physical activity.

15   If you are middle-aged or older and have been inactive, you should consult with a physician before starting an exercise program. Also, if you have any known health condition that could be aggravated by physical activity, check with a physician first.

High Blood Cholesterol Level

16   The third controllable risk factor for heart disease is high blood cholesterol level. Approximately 102 million American adults have a total cholesterol level of greater than 200 mg/dl (about 41 million have levels greater than 240 mg/dl). Generally speaking, the higher the blood cholesterol level, the greater the risk for heart disease. The table below shows ranges for cholesterol levels. When high blood cholesterol levels are combined with other important risk factors, the risk becomes much greater.

17   Fortunately, blood cholesterol levels are relatively easy to measure. Many campus health and wellness centers provide cholesterol screenings for employees and students. These screenings help identify people whose cholesterol levels (or profiles) may be dangerous. Medical professionals have linked people's diets to their cholesterol levels. People with high blood cholesterol levels are encouraged to consume a heart-healthy diet and to become physically active. In recent years, researchers have developed a

Classification of Total Cholesterol Levels	
TOTAL CHOLESTEROL LEVEL	**CLASSIFICATION**
<200 mg/dl	Desirable blood cholesterol level
200–239 mg/dl	Borderline-high blood cholesterol level
>240 mg/dl	High blood cholesterol level

variety of drugs that are very effective at lowering cholesterol levels.

High Blood Pressure

18 The fourth of the six cardiovascular risk factors that can be changed is high blood pressure, or hypertension. Approximately 58 million Americans have hypertension, one-third of whom have not been diagnosed. High blood pressure can seriously damage a person's heart and blood vessels. High blood pressure causes the heart to work much harder, eventually causing the heart to enlarge and weaken. High blood pressure increases the risk of stroke, heart attack, congestive heart failure, and kidney disease.

19 When high blood pressure is seen with other risk factors, the risk for stroke or heart attack is increased tremendously. As you will soon see, this "silent killer" is easy to monitor and can be effectively controlled through a variety of approaches.

Diabetes Mellitus

20 Diabetes mellitus is a debilitating° chronic disease that has a significant effect on the human body. Approximately 17 million Americans have diabetes, one-third of whom have not been diagnosed. In addition to increasing the risk of developing kidney disease, blindness, and nerve damage, diabetes increases the likelihood of developing heart and blood vessel diseases. More than 65 percent of people with diabetes die of some type of heart or blood vessel disease. The cardiovascular damage is thought to occur due to the abnormal levels of cholesterol and blood fat found in individuals with diabetes. With weight management, exercise, dietary changes, and drug therapy, diabetes can be relatively well controlled in most people. Despite careful management of this disease, diabetic patients remain quite susceptible to eventual heart and blood vessel damage.

Obesity and Overweight

21 According to the 1999 National Health and Nutrition Survey, approximately 61 percent of American adults are overweight, and 26 percent are obese. Even if they have no other risk factors, obese people are more likely than are nonobese people to develop heart disease and stroke. Obesity, particularly if of the abdominal form, places considerable strain on the heart, and it tends to worsen both blood pressure and blood cholesterol levels. Obese men and women can expect a greater risk of heart disease, diabetes, gallbladder disease, osteoarthritis, respiratory problems, and certain cancers. Maintaining body weight within a desirable range minimizes the chances of obesity ever happening. To accomplish this, you can elect to make a commitment to a reasonably sound diet and an active lifestyle.

ANOTHER RISK FACTOR THAT CONTRIBUTES TO HEART DISEASE

22 The American Heart Association identifies one other risk factor that is associated with an increased risk of heart disease. This risk factor is one's individual response to stress.

Individual Response to Stress

23   Unresolved stress over a long period may be a contributing factor to the development of heart disease. Certainly, people who are unable to cope with stressful life experiences are more likely to develop negative dependence behaviors (for example, smoking, underactivity, poor dietary practices), which can then lead to cardiovascular problems through changes in blood fat profiles, blood pressure, and heart workload.

Reading Comprehension Questions

Vocabulary in Context

_____   1. In the sentence below, the word *prevalent* (prĕ′və-lĕnt) means
   A. rare.
   B. cured.
   C. correct.
   D. common.

   "By the luck of the draw, some people are born into families where heart disease has never been a serious problem, whereas others are born into families where heart disease is quite prevalent." (Paragraph 6)

_____   2. In the sentence below, the word *contention* (kən-tĕn′shən) means
   A. gathering.
   B. contest.
   C. argument.
   D. candidate.

   "Critical findings reported in the year 2000 from the highly respected Harvard Alumni Health Study support the contention that physical activity is closely associated with decreased risk of coronary heart disease." (Paragraph 14)

Central Point and Main Ideas

_____ 3. Which sentence best expresses the central point of the selection?
   A. Even though some cardiovascular disease risk factors cannot be changed, it is still important to learn about them.
   B. There are three cardiovascular disease risk factors you cannot change and six you can.
   C. It is important for people to learn about cardiovascular disease risk factors that can and cannot be changed so they can better ensure their heart health.
   D. The best time to start improving your cardiovascular health is early in life, when lifestyle patterns are developed and reinforced.

_____ 4. The main idea of paragraph 10 is stated in its
   A. first sentence.
   B. second sentence.
   C. third sentence.
   D. fourth sentence.

_____ 5. The implied main idea of paragraph 14 is that
   A. 60 percent of Americans don't achieve the recommended amount of physical activity each week.
   B. light and moderate physical activities are helpful in reducing CVD, but sustained, vigorous physical activity is better.
   C. it does not matter whether daily physical activity comes in one long session or in two shorter sessions.
   D. although the majority of Americans fail to get enough physical activity, it has been proven that regular, sustained physical activity lowers CVD.

Supporting Details

_____ 6. According to the selection, regular aerobic exercise does all of the following *except*
   A. help strengthen the heart muscle.
   B. eliminate the need to measure blood cholesterol levels.
   C. allow people to moderate the stress in their lives.
   D. improve the ability of the vascular system to transfer blood and oxygen to all parts of the body.

_____ 7. The American Heart Association now indicates that
A. if you have smoked for many years, it is pointless to try to quit.
B. people are not adversely affected by secondhand smoke.
C. people who quit smoking lower their risk of heart disease no matter how long they have smoked.
D. the effects of quitting smoking after having smoked for many years are still unknown.

Transitions

_____ 8. The relationship of the second sentence below to the first sentence is one of
A. cause and effect.
B. problem and solution.
C. illustration.
D. addition.

> "Lack of regular physical activity is a significant risk factor for heart disease. Regular aerobic exercise helps strengthen the heart muscle, maintain healthy blood vessels, and improve the ability of the vascular system to transfer blood and oxygen to all parts of the body." (Paragraph 13)

Patterns of Organization

_____ 9. The main pattern of organization in the selection is
A. time order.
B. list of items.
C. definition and example.
D. contrast.

Inferences

_____ 10. On the basis of paragraph 7, we can infer that
A. African Americans are generally unaware of the connection between race and heart disease.
B. people who are not African American seldom suffer from hypertension.
C. African Americans also have high rates of heart disease, stroke, and kidney disease.
D. very few African Americans currently get their blood pressure measured.

_____ 11. On the basis of paragraphs 11–12, we can infer that for years
   A. some smokers never tried to quit smoking because they thought it was pointless.
   B. most people had no idea that smoking could damage their health.
   C. the American Heart Association withheld important information from the American public.
   D. the number of people who smoked increased due to lack of information from the American Heart Association.

_____ 12. The final paragraph of the reading suggests that
   A. people under stress usually have psychological problems.
   B. researchers are certain that unresolved stress leads to heart disease.
   C. stressful life experiences are far more likely to happen to people with heart disease.
   D. people who learn positive ways to cope with stress are at less risk of developing heart disease.

Purpose and Tone

_____ 13. The purpose of this selection is
   A. both to inform and to persuade.
   B. both to persuade and to entertain.
   C. only to persuade.

_____ 14. The authors' tone can be described as
   A. ironic and ambivalent.
   B. sympathetic and lighthearted.
   C. concerned but encouraging.
   D. distressed but informal.

Argument

_____ 15. Which item does **not** support the following point?

   Point: Researchers have found that physical activity is closely associated with decreased risk of coronary heart disease.

   A. Light and moderate physical activities are helpful in reducing cardiovascular disease (CVD).
   B. Twenty-five percent of Americans age 18 or older report no leisure-time physical activity.
   C. Vigorous physical activity produces greater reductions in CVD than does light or moderate activity.
   D. Physical activity produces reductions in CVD whether the daily activity comes in one long session or in two shorter sessions.

16. Label the point of the following argument with a **P** and the two statements of support with an **S**. Label with an **X** the statement that is neither the point nor the support of the argument.

_____ A. High blood pressure causes the heart to work much harder, eventually causing the heart to enlarge and weaken.

_____ B. High blood pressure increases the risk of stroke, heart attack, congestive heart failure and kidney disease.

_____ C. High blood pressure is easy to monitor and can be controlled through a variety of measures.

_____ D. High blood pressure can have severe negative effects on health.

Critical Reading

_____ 17. The statement below is
   A. fact.
   B. opinion.
   C. a mixture of fact and opinion.

   "However, the American Heart Association now indicates that by quitting smoking, regardless of how long or how much you have smoked, your risk of heart disease declines rapidly." (Paragraph 11)

_____ 18. The statement below is
   A. fact.
   B. opinion.
   C. both fact and opinion.

   "This news is exciting and should encourage people to quit smoking, regardless of how long they have smoked." (Paragraph 12)

_____ 19. A person who complains that he must choose between eating healthy foods or foods that taste good is committing the logical fallacy of
   A. straw man *(an argument is made by claiming an opponent holds an extreme position and then opposing that extreme position).*
   B. false comparison *(the argument assumes that two things being compared are more alike than they really are).*
   C. either-or *(the argument assumes that there are only two sides to a question).*
   D. personal attack *(ignores the issue under discussion and concentrates instead on the character of the opponent).*

_____ 20. A person who states that it's useless for him to adopt a healthy lifestyle, since his dad died at the age of 50, is committing the logical fallacy of

    A. straw man *(an argument is made by claiming an opponent holds an extreme position and then opposing that extreme position).*

    B. false comparison *(the argument assumes that two things being compared are more alike than they really are).*

    C. either-or *(the argument assumes that there are only two sides to a question).*

    D. false cause *(the argument assumes that the order of events alone shows cause and effect).*

Active Reading and Study of a Textbook Selection

Complete the following study notes on the selection. Some items and parts of items are already filled in for you.

Note: Headings and enumerations are the keys to the important ideas here.

Central point: To prevent heart disease, everyone should learn about the ten cardiovascular risk factors and eliminate as many of them as possible.

1. Risk Factors That Cannot Be Changed:

    a. _____—nearly 84% of people who die from heart disease are aged 65 or over.

    b. Male Gender—men have greater risk of heart disease than do women prior to age 55.

    c. _____—children may have genetic predisposition (tendency) to develop heart disease. Race is also a related consideration; prevalence of hypertension among African Americans is among the highest in the U.S.

2. _____

    a. _____—About 46.5 million adults and about 28.5% of high school students smoke. Smokers have a heart attack risk more than twice that of nonsmokers.

Heart attack risk is about 30% greater for people exposed to secondhand smoke in the home.

Good news—heart attack risk declines rapidly when a person stops smoking.

b. _____ —Regular aerobic exercise strengthens heart muscle, lowers blood cholesterol, moderates stress, and more.

60% of Americans are not physically active enough.

Sustained, vigorous physical activity produces strong reduction in CVD.

c. _____ —About 102 million American adults have a total cholesterol level of greater than 200 mg/dl. The higher the level, the greater the risk for heart disease. Drugs and diet can control.

d. High Blood Pressure

_____

_____

e. Diabetes Mellitus

_____

_____

f. _____ —Over 60 % of American adults are overweight, and 26% are obese. More likely to develop heart disease and stroke.

3. Another Risk Factor Contributing to Heart Disease: _____

_____

_____

Discussion Questions

1. Would you say that your risk of developing heart disease is low, medium, or high? Which of the cardiovascular risk factors mentioned in the selection do you possess? On the basis of what you have learned in this reading, is there anything you can do to decrease your risk of developing heart disease? Explain.

2. The selection lists the benefits that come with physical activity but states that health professionals are amazed that so many Americans refuse to become regularly active. In your view, why don't more Americans get the recommended amount of physical activity?

3. The selection mentions that people who are under stress are more likely to develop negative dependence behaviors—for example, smoking, underactivity, poor dietary practices—to deal with the stress. What are some positive ways that you know of that people use to cope with stress? Have you tried any of them? If so, have you found them to be effective? Why or why not?

4. The selection states that the best time to start protecting and improving one's cardiovascular system is early in life. We can't go back in time, but we can help to influence the younger generation. How can we encourage the younger generation to develop heart-healthy habits? What negative influences must we overcome to do so?

Note: Writing assignments for this selection appear on page 642.

Check Your Performance

CARDIOVASCULAR DISEASE RISK FACTORS

Activity	Number Right	Points	Score
Reading Comprehension Questions			
Vocabulary in Context (2 items)	_____	x 4 =	_____
Central Point and Main Ideas (3 items)	_____	x 4 =	_____
Supporting Details (2 items)	_____	x 4 =	_____
Transitions (1 item)	_____	x 4 =	_____
Patterns of Organization (1 item)	_____	x 4 =	_____
Inferences (3 items)	_____	x 4 =	_____
Purpose and Tone (2 items)	_____	x 4 =	_____
Argument (2 items)	_____	x 4 =	_____
Critical Reading (4 items)	_____	x 4 =	_____
Active Reading and Study (10 items)	_____	x 2 =	_____
		TOTAL SCORE =	_____%

Enter your total score into the **Reading Performance Chart: Ten Reading Selections** on the inside back cover.

6 Exploring the World of Business and Economics

William Pride, Robert Hughes, and Jack R. Kapoor

Preview

Are you considering a career in business? If so, the following selection from the textbook *Business* will reveal what opportunities might be waiting for you after you graduate—and what it takes to succeed in today's corporate world.

Words to Watch

entrepreneur (1): business organizer and risk-taker
pioneered (1): opened up (a new area)
imposed (7): required
compelling (13): powerful
ultimately (15): in the end

inside business

How Amazon Kindles Business Success

1   At the dawn of the Internet age, entrepreneur° Jeff Bezos founded a Web-based bookstore he named Amazon.com to suggest the immense selection of titles on his virtual shelves. His plan was to create a customer-centered company using cutting-edge technology to keep prices low and provide good service. In the course of building his business, Bezos pioneered° many features that have become staples of online retailing, including personalized product recommendations, customer reviews, and free shipping with a minimum order.

2   Today, the once-tiny enterprise with the quirky name has become a giant corporation that rings up more than $24 billion in annual sales worldwide. Amazon owns Zappos, the online shoe retailer known for outstanding service, and now sells everything from televisions, toys, and tools

to computers, cameras and clothing. It has also used its retailing expertise to become a virtual storefront for thousands of companies and individuals who sign up to sell goods and services on the Amazon Web site. In addition, it has used its tech expertise to offer on-demand services such as data storage and extra computing power to businesses of all sizes.

3   As CEO, Bezos continues to move Amazon in new directions. A few years ago, the company introduced the Kindle, an electronic handheld device that allows users to instantly download and read books and magazines when and where they please. The Kindle was innovative because it was the first e-book reader to connect wirelessly for content download without additional subscription or network fees. The initial response was so strong that Amazon struggled to meet the unexpectedly high demand.

4   Over time, Amazon has refined the Kindle by streamlining its design, adding features, making the product more eco-friendly, cutting the price, and expanding the catalog of content available for instant download. Despite competition from bookstore rival Barnes & Noble and electronics giant Sony, which have both launched wireless e-book readers, the Kindle remains popular with buyers in North America and beyond. Thanks to this and other entrepreneurial innovations, Amazon has kept sales growing for more than 15 years, even during the toughest of economic times. Now the challenge for Jeff Bezos is to extend that remarkable record of success and find new ways to kindle future profits.

5   Wow! What a challenging world we live in. Just for a moment, think about the economic problems listed here and how they affect not only businesses but also individuals.

- Unemployment rates hovering around 10 percent
- Reduced consumer spending
- A slowdown in the home-building industry and record home foreclosures
- A large number of troubled banks and financial institutions
- An increasing number of business failures
- Depressed stock values that reduced the value of investment and retirement accounts for most individuals

6   In fact, just about every person around the globe was affected in some way by the economic crisis that began in late 2007. Despite the efforts of the U.S. government and other world governments to provide the economic stimulus needed to stabilize

the economy, it took nearly two years before the economy began to improve. Hopefully, by the time you read this material, the nation's economy will be much stronger. Still, it is important to remember the old adage, "History is a great teacher." Both the nation and individuals should take a look at what went wrong to avoid making the same mistakes in the future. In addition, it helps to keep one factor in mind: Despite all the problems just described, make no mistake about it, our economic system will survive. In fact, our economy continues to adapt and change to meet the challenges of an ever-changing world and to provide opportunities for those who want to achieve success.

7   Our economic system provides an amazing amount of freedom that allows businesses that range in size from the small corner grocer to Amazon. com—the company profiled in the Inside Business opening case for this chapter—to adapt to changing business environments. Within certain limits, imposed° mainly to ensure public safety, the owners of a business can produce any legal good or service they choose and attempt to sell it at the price they set. This system of business, in which individuals decide what to produce, how to produce it, and at what price to sell it, is called **free enterprise**. Our free-enterprise system ensures, for example, that Amazon.com can sell everything from televisions, toys, and tools to computers, cameras, and clothing. Our system gives Amazon's owners and stockholders the right to make a profit from the company's success. It gives

Amazon's management the right to compete with bookstore rival Barnes & Noble and electronics giant Sony. It also gives consumers the right to choose.

8   In this chapter, we look briefly at what business is and how it became that way. First, we discuss what you must do to be successful in the world of business and explore some important reasons for studying business. . . .

YOUR FUTURE IN THE CHANGING WORLD OF BUSINESS

9   The key word in this heading is *changing*. When faced with both economic problems and increasing competition not only from firms in the United States but also from international firms located in other parts of the world, employees and managers began to ask the question: What do we do now? Although this is a fair question, it is difficult to answer. Certainly, for a college student taking business courses or an employee just starting a career, the question is even more difficult to answer. Yet there are still opportunities out there for people who are willing to work hard, continue to learn, and possess the ability to adapt to change. Let's begin our discussion in this section with three basic concepts.

- What do you want?
- Why do you want it?
- Write it down!

10   During a segment on *The Oprah Winfrey Show*, Joe Dudley, one of the world's most successful black business owners, gave the preceding advice

to anyone who wanted to succeed in business. His advice can help you achieve success. What is so amazing about Dudley's success is that he started a manufacturing business in his own kitchen, with his wife and children serving as the new firm's only employees. He went on to develop his own line of more than 400 hair-care and cosmetic products sold directly to cosmetologists, barbers, and beauty schools. Today, Mr. Dudley has built a multimillion-dollar empire—one of the most successful minority-owned companies in the nation. He is not only a successful business owner but also a winner of the Horatio Alger Award—an award given to outstanding individuals who have succeeded in the face of adversity. Although many people would say that Joe Dudley was just lucky or happened to be in the right place at the right time, the truth is that he became a success because he had a dream and worked hard to turn his dream into a reality. Today, Dudley's vision is to see people succeed—to realize "The American Dream." He would be the first to tell you that you have the same opportunities that he had. According to Mr. Dudley, "Success is a journey, not just a destination."

11   Whether you want to obtain part-time employment to pay college and living expenses, begin your career as a full-time employee, or start a business, you must bring something to the table that makes you different from the next person. Employers and our economic system are more demanding than ever before. Ask yourself: What can I do that will make employers want to pay me a salary? What skills do I have that employers need? With these two questions in mind, we begin the next section with another basic question: Why study business?

WHY STUDY BUSINESS?

The potential benefits of higher 12 education are enormous. To begin with, there are economic benefits. Over their lifetimes, college graduates on average earn much more than high school graduates. Although lifetime earnings are substantially higher for college graduates, so are annual income amounts (see Figure 1.1).

The nice feature of education and 13 knowledge is that once you have it, no one can take it away. It is yours to use for a lifetime. In this section, we explore what you may expect to get out of this business course and text. You will find at least five compelling° reasons for studying business.

For Help in Choosing a Career

What do you want to do with the rest 14 of your life? At some place and some time in your life, someone probably has asked you this same question. Like many people, you may find it a difficult question to answer. This business course will introduce you to a wide array of employment opportunities. In private enterprise, these range from small, local businesses owned by one individual to large companies such as American Express and Marriott International that are owned by thousands of stockholders. There are also employment opportunities with federal, state, county, and local governments and with not-for-profit organizations such as the Red Cross and Save the Children. For more information, visit the following sites:

- Career Builder at
  http://www.careerbuilder.com
- Career One Stop at
  http://www.careeronestop.org
- Monster at
  http://www.monster.com
- Yahoo! Hot Jobs at
  http://hotjobs.yahoo.com

15   One thing to remember as you think about what your ideal career might be is that a person's choice of a career ultimately° is just a reflection of what he or she values and holds most important. What will give one individual personal satisfaction may not satisfy another. For example, one person may dream of a career as a corporate executive and becoming a millionaire before the age of 30. Another may choose a career that has more modest monetary rewards but that provides the opportunity to help others. One person may be willing to work long hours and seek additional responsibility to get promotions and pay raises. Someone else may prefer a less demanding job with little stress and more free time. What you choose to do with your life will be based on what you feel is most important. And you are a very important part of that decision.

To Be a Successful Employee

Deciding on the type of career you want   16
is only the first step. To get a job in your chosen field and to be successful at it, you will have to develop a plan, or a road map, that ensures that you have the skills and knowledge the job requires. You will be expected to have both the technical skills needed to accomplish a specific task

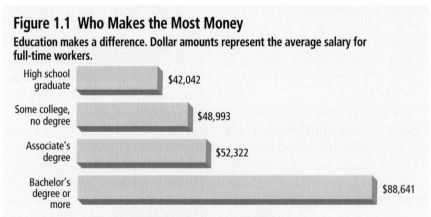

Figure 1.1 Who Makes the Most Money

Education makes a difference. Dollar amounts represent the average salary for full-time workers.

High school graduate	$42,042
Some college, no degree	$48,993
Associate's degree	$52,322
Bachelor's degree or more	$88,641

Source: U.S. Census Bureau, *The 2010 Statistical Abstract of the United States*

and the ability to work well with many types of people in a culturally diverse workplace. **Cultural (or workplace) diversity** refers to the differences among people in a workforce owing to race, ethnicity, and gender. These skills, together with a working knowledge of the American business system and an appreciation for a culturally diverse workplace, can give you an inside edge when you are interviewing with a prospective employer.

17   This course, your instructor, and all the resources available at your college or university can help you to acquire the skills and knowledge you will need for a successful career. But do not underestimate your part in making your dream a reality. In addition to job-related skills and knowledge you need to be successful in a specific job, employers will also look for the following characteristics when hiring a new employee or promoting an existing employee:

- Honesty and integrity
- Willingness to work hard
- Dependability
- Time management skills
- Self-confidence
- Motivation
- Willingness to learn
- Communication skills
- Professionalism

18   The above skills and values are traits you will need to succeed in the workplace—and with work on your part you can learn and develop these traits to improve your chances of getting just the right job.

19   Employers will also be interested in any work experience you may have had in cooperative work/school programs, during summer vacations, or in part-time jobs during the school year. These things can make a difference when it is time to apply for the job you really want.

To Improve Your Management Skills

20   Often, employees become managers or supervisors. In fact, many employees want to become managers because managers often receive higher salaries. Although management obviously can be a rewarding career, what is not so obvious is the amount of time and hard work needed to achieve the higher salaries. Today, managers have demanding jobs. For starters, employers expect more from managers and supervisors than ever before. Typically, the heavy workload requires that managers work long hours, and most do not get paid overtime. They also experience enormous demands on their time and face increased problems created by the economic crisis, increased competition, employee downsizing, the quest for improved quality, and the need for efficient use of the firm's resources.

21   To be an effective manager, managers must be able to perform four basic management functions: planning, organizing, leading and motivating, and controlling. . . . To successfully perform these management functions, managers must possess three very important skills.

- *Interpersonal skills*—The ability to deal effectively with individual employees, other managers within the firm, and people outside the firm.

- *Technical skills*—The skill required to accomplish a specific kind of work being done in an organization. Although managers may not actually perform the technical tasks, they should be able to train employees and answer technical questions.

- *Conceptual skills*—The ability to think in abstract terms in order to see the "big picture." Conceptual skills help managers understand how the various parts of an organization or idea can fit together.

22   In addition to the three skills just described, a successful manager will need many of the same skills that an employee needs to be successful. For example, oral and written communication skills, willingness to work hard, and time-management skills are important for both employees and managers.

To Start Your Own Business

23   Some people prefer to work for themselves, and they open their own businesses. To be successful, business owners must possess many of the same skills that successful employees have, and they must be willing to work hard and put in long hours.

24   It also helps if your small business can provide a product or service that customers want. For example, Mark Cuban started a small Internet company called Broadcast.com that provided hundreds of live and on-demand audio and video programs ranging from rap music to sporting events to business

events over the Internet. Because Cuban's company met the needs of his customers, Broadcast.com was very successful. When Cuban sold Broadcast.com to Yahoo! Inc., he became a billionaire.

25   Unfortunately, many small-business firms fail; approximately 70 percent of them fail within the first seven years. Typical reasons for business failures include undercapitalization (not enough money), poor business location, poor customer service, unqualified or untrained employees, fraud, lack of a proper business plan, and failure to seek outside professional help. . . .

To Become a Better Informed Consumer and Investor

26   The world of business surrounds us. You cannot buy a home, a new Ford Fusion Hybrid from the local Ford dealer, a Black & Decker sander at an ACE Hardware store, a pair of jeans at Gap Inc., or a hot dog from a street vendor without entering a business transaction. Because you no doubt will engage in business transactions almost every day of your life, one very good reason for studying business is to become a more fully informed consumer. Many people also rely on a basic understanding of business to help them to invest for the future. According to Julie Stav, Hispanic stockbroker-turned-author/radio personality, "Take $25, add to it drive plus determination, and then watch it multiply into an empire." The author of *Get Your Share*, a *New York Times* best seller, believes that it is important to learn the basics about the economy

and business, stocks, mutual funds, and other alternatives before investing your money. She also believes that it is never too early to start investing. Although this is an obvious conclusion, just dreaming of being rich does not make it happen. In fact, like many facets of life, it takes planning and determination to establish the type of investment program that will help you to accomplish your financial goals.

Reading Comprehension Questions

Vocabulary in Context

_____ 1. In the sentence below, the word *staples* (stā′pəlz) means
  A. challenges.
  B. office supplies.
  C. drawbacks.
  D. basics.

  "Bezos pioneered many features that have become staples of online retailing, including personalized product recommendations, customer reviews, and free shipping with a minimum order." (Paragraph 1)

_____ 2. In the sentence below, the word *innovative* (ĭn′ə-vā′tĭv) means
  A. standard.
  B. confusing.
  C. new and original.
  D. too expensive.

  "The Kindle was innovative because it was the first e-book reader to connect wirelessly for content download without additional subscription or network fees." (Paragraph 3)

Central Point and Main Ideas

_____ 3. Which point best expresses the central point of the selection?
A. Our economic system rewards hard work, determination, and the ability to adapt to change.
B. Jeff Bezos, Joe Dudley, and Mark Cuban are three examples of men who founded highly successful businesses.
C. A person's choice of a career is ultimately just a reflection of what he or she values and holds most important.
D. Because business is central to our way of life and an attractive career choice, it's a worthwhile subject to study.

_____ 4. The main idea of paragraph 16 is stated in its
A. first sentence.
B. second sentence.
C. third sentence.
D. fourth sentence.

_____ 5. The main idea of paragraph 20 is stated in its
A. first sentence.
B. second sentence.
C. fourth sentence.
D. fifth sentence.

_____ 6. The implied main idea of paragraph 10 is that
A. hard work was the key to Joe Dudley's success.
B. Joe Dudley is an excellent role model for those who want to create and build their own businesses.
C. anyone can make his or her dreams come true.
D. Joe Dudley's hair-care items and his cosmetics are the best-selling products in their field in the United States.

Supporting Details

_____ 7. According to the selection, which of the following is *not* a reason to study business?
A. To help choose a career
B. To improve management skills
C. To learn how to start a savings plan
D. To learn how to start a business

_____ 8. The selection states that the limits put on free enterprise are intended mainly to
   A. reduce global competition.
   B. ensure economic stability.
   C. ensure a level playing field for minority business owners.
   D. ensure public safety.

Transitions

_____ 9. The relationship between the two parts of the sentence below is one of
   A. illustration.
   B. cause and effect.
   C. contrast.
   D. comparison.

   "Despite the efforts of the U.S. government and other world governments to provide the economic stimulus needed to stabilize the economy, it took nearly two years before the economy began to improve." (Paragraph 6)

_____ 10. The relationship of the second sentence below to the first is one of
   A. illustration.
   B. addition.
   C. cause and effect.
   D. contrast.

   "This system of business, in which individuals decide what to produce, how to produce it, and at what price to sell it, is called **free enterprise**. Our free-enterprise system ensures, for example, that Amazon.com can sell everything from televisions, toys, and tools to computers, cameras, and clothing." (Paragraph 7)

_____ 11. The relationship expressed in the sentences below is one of
   A. comparison.
   B. addition.
   C. cause and effect.
   D. contrast.

   "In private enterprise, these range from small, local businesses owned by one individual to large companies such as American Express and Marriott International that are owned by thousands of stockholders. There are also employment opportunities with federal, state, county, and local governments and with not-for-profit organizations such as the Red Cross and Save the Children." (Paragraph 14)

Patterns of Organization

_____12. The main pattern of organization of paragraph 2 is
    A. list of items.
    B. problem and solution.
    C. cause and effect.
    D. time order.

Inferences

_____13. On the basis of paragraph 16, we can infer that
    A. it is more important to possess technical skills than to be able to work well with different types of people.
    B. employees who can't get along with different types of people can harm a company's productivity.
    C. what courses you take in college will have little effect on your future career.
    D. all of the above.

_____14. On the basis of paragraphs 21–22, we can infer that a knowledge of computer programming would be an example of a(n)
    A. interpersonal skill.
    B. technical skill.
    C. conceptual skill.
    D. time-management skill.

_____15. We can infer that the authors of this selection
    A. are scornful of people who don't care much about monetary rewards.
    B. fear that the United States may no longer be able to compete successfully with other nations.
    C. strongly believe in the American system of free enterprise.
    D. long for the days when there were fewer governmental regulations.

Purpose and Tone

_____16. The main purpose of this selection is to
    A. inform people that it's worthwhile to study business.
    B. entertain people with incredible stories of people who went from rags to riches.
    C. persuade people that they, too, can start a successful business.

_____17. Overall, the tone of the selection is
   A. detached and ironic.
   B. straightforward and optimistic.
   C. casual and amused.
   D. praising and appreciative.

Argument

_____18. Which item does *not* support the following point?

Point: Amazon is a company that continually finds new ways to generate profits.

   A. Although Amazon started as an online bookstore, it now sells everything from televisions, toys, and tools to computers, cameras, and clothing.
   B. Amazon faces intense competition from bookstore rival Barnes & Noble and electronics giant Sony.
   C. Amazon now offers on-demand services such as data storage and extra computing power to businesses of all sizes.
   D. Amazon developed the Kindle—the first e-book reader to connect wirelessly for content download without additional subscription or network fees.

Critical Reading

_____19. The statement below is
   A. fact.
   B. opinion.
   C. a mixture of fact and opinion.

   "Both the nation and individuals should take a look at what went wrong to avoid making the same mistakes in the future." (Paragraph 6)

_____20. A person who states, "My dad was a successful manager, and he never had to worry about workplace diversity, so I don't see why I have to" is committing the logical fallacy of
   A. straw man *(an argument is made by claiming an opponent holds an extreme position and then opposing that extreme position).*
   B. false comparison *(the argument assumes that two things being compared are more alike than they really are).*
   C. either-or *(the argument assumes that there are only two sides to a question).*
   D. false cause *(the argument assumes that the order of events alone shows cause and effect).*

Active Reading and Study of a Textbook Selection

Complete the following study notes on paragraphs 12–26 of the selection. Some items are already filled in for you.

Central point: _____

1. For help in choosing a career _____

   a. _____

   b. You'll learn about websites that provide career information.

   Ex. — _____

   c. A person's career choice reflects what he or she values.

2. _____

   a. You'll develop skills and knowledge needed for a successful career.

   b. _____

   Ex. — honesty, integrity, willingness to work hard, time-management skills, self-confidence, motivation, willingness to learn

3. To help improve your management skills _____

   a. _____

   _____

   _____

   b. To perform these functions, managers need interpersonal skills, technical skills, and conceptual skills.

   c. _____

   Ex. — communication skills, willingness to work hard, time-management.

4. To start your own business _____

   a. Business owners need the same skills as successful employees, and they must work hard, put in long hours, and provide something consumers want.

   b. _____

   _____

5. _____

   a. We engage in business transactions almost every day.

   b. _____

   _____

Discussion Questions

1. The authors of this selection present at least five reasons for studying business. Have they convinced you that studying business is worthwhile? Explain your point of view.

2. According to Joe Dudley, "Success is a journey, not just a destination." What do you think he means by this statement? How does his own "success story" illustrate what he is saying?

3. The authors of this selection say, "Make no mistake about it, our economic system will survive." In the light of the economic crisis that began in late 2007, do you share their optimism? Why or why not?

4. As the authors of the selection suggest, it can be highly rewarding but also very difficult to create a successful business. If you were to start a business, what kind of business would you start? What challenges might you meet along the way? How would you go about meeting them?

Note: Writing assignments for this selection appear on page 642.

Check Your Performance

EXPLORING THE WORLD OF BUSINESS AND ECONOMICS

Activity	Number Right	Points	Score
Reading Comprehension Questions			
Vocabulary in Context (2 items)	_____	x 4 =	_____
Central Point and Main Ideas (4 items)	_____	x 4 =	_____
Supporting Details (2 items)	_____	x 4 =	_____
Transitions (3 items)	_____	x 4 =	_____
Patterns of Organization (1 item)	_____	x 4 =	_____
Inferences (3 items)	_____	x 4 =	_____
Purpose and Tone (2 items)	_____	x 4 =	_____
Argument (1 item)	_____	x 4 =	_____
Critical Reading (2 items)	_____	x 4 =	_____
Active Reading and Study (10 items)	_____	x 2 =	_____
		TOTAL SCORE =	_____%

Enter your total score into the **Reading Performance Chart: Ten Reading Selections** on the inside back cover.

7 Abusive Relationships among the Young

Miriam Hill

Preview

It's shocking but true: by the time of high-school graduation, one in three girls will have been involved in an abusive relationship. What begins as a romantic relationship becomes characterized by physical violence, stalking, and emotional abuse. Why are young women so vulnerable to abuse? Why do they stay with and even defend their abusers? What drives young men to hurt and humiliate their girlfriends? And most importantly, how can a girl make the abuse stop? This selection explores a problem that is common but often hidden out of sight, due to the victims' tangled feelings of hurt, guilt, and fear.

Words to Watch

hovering (1): hanging
demographic (4): social group
monitor (9): keep watch over
dysfunctional (11): performing badly
escalates (22): increases rapidly
intimidate (22): persuade by frightening

1   When Sarah first set eyes on Joe at a back-to-school dance, she thought he was really cute. And when they started dating, he showered her with flowers, compliments, and tickets to the movies. But their relationship quickly went downhill, as Joe began to insult, make demands, and then physically abuse her. The final straw came when Joe kicked her, knocking her into a wall, where she hit her head and lost consciousness. "I woke up and he was hovering° over me," Sarah, now 18, recalls. "I just wanted to get away." Four months after their first date, Sarah stood in line at the family division of the Santa Clara County, California court clerk's office, waiting to pick up a copy of a restraining order.

2   Kayla Brown's story began much like Sarah's. At first, her high school boyfriend was highly respectful, even calling Kayla's mom to introduce himself. But then he began calling her every hour to see where she was and what she was doing. Finally, he slammed a chair

into a table and raised a fist to strike her during an argument in the school cafeteria. Kayla confided in her mother, who had also been involved with an abusive man. When her mother advised her to break off the relationship, Kayla did so. But the process took months. To make sure she was never alone with her ex-boyfriend, she had friends accompany her everywhere, even to the school lavatory.

3   Heather Norris wasn't so lucky. She was 17 when she met her boyfriend, Joshua Bean, and 20 when he stabbed her to death.

4   Why does "love" turn so ugly? What is behind what many are calling an "epidemic" of abusive relationships among the young? The statistics are alarming: one in three girls will have an abusive dating relationship by the time she graduates from high school, and females from the ages of 16 to 24 are the most likely demographic° to experience dating violence. And in today's world, social networking sites and texting are only making it easier for abusers to harass, humiliate, and stalk their victims. It's not only men who abuse women; however, when abuse turns physical, it is the women who wind up in the emergency room.

5   One factor that helps make abusive relationships common is the value our society places on being in a relationship. Whether it's on TV, in movies, in magazines, or on the Internet, the message is that being alone is for losers. Teenage girls, in particular, measure their self-worth by having a boyfriend. Think of it: from an early age, girls in our culture are taught that being a "princess" is the ideal state of femininity. Is it any wonder they long for a Prince Charming to come and sweep them off their feet?

6   Dr. Jill Murray, an expert in the field of abusive relationships, puts teenage girls' strong need for social acceptance in psychological terms: "Adolescents are primarily concerned with the way they appear to their peers. That is one reason girls are often desperate for a boyfriend in high school. If their friends are dating, they feel out of place if they are not."

7   Ron Davis agrees. He runs a teen program at a middle school in Walnut Creek, California.

8   "Girls at 16 are looking for love, anybody who's going to show any affection at all," he says. "They fall in love so fast with anybody. That's when they get taken advantage of." Young people whose parents have neglected them emotionally are even more likely to become involved in abusive relationships.

9   Experts also agree that children who are exposed to violence at home often repeat it in their adult relationships. A girl who sees her father or another male abuse her mother learns to view abuse as a natural part of a relationship. Similarly, when a boy observes his father or another male dominate his mother and sister with emotional and physical abuse, he grows up believing that it is "normal" for him to control a woman by abusing her. Such abuse may include touching his girlfriend inappropriately in public in order to prove to others that she "belongs" to him. It may also include

calling her or texting her repeatedly in an attempt to monitor° her behavior.

10 In addition, male abusers often hold a stereotyped idea of male and female relationships. In their view, women are inferior to men, so a girlfriend should "know her place." This macho attitude is reinforced by some religious groups, whose teachings emphasize that a man is the natural head of the household and should always be obeyed. Physical or emotional abuse of a female partner is thus viewed as "discipline."

11 Coming from a home where substance abuse takes place is another strong predictor of involvement in an abusive relationship. Abusers generally have a low tolerance for frustration and turn to alcohol or drugs to escape feelings of failure or powerlessness. Alcohol, in turn, lowers inhibitions and increases aggression. Likewise, chronic use of marijuana or crystal meth causes rage and paranoia. In many cases, children of substance abusers adopt their parents' dysfunctional° pattern of behavior. Undergoing financial difficulties such as the loss of a job only makes it more likely that people will take out their feelings of frustration on those closest to them.

12 Complicating matters is the fact that young women who have very limited experience in relationships often confuse jealousy and possessiveness with love. At first they are flattered when a boy calls or texts them at all hours. "It shows he loves me," they tell themselves. Shockingly, in one recent study, some teens reported receiving 200 to 300 texts *a day* from boyfriends

or girlfriends wanting to know where they were, who they were with, and why. And up to 82 percent of parents had no idea what was happening.

13 "Youths don't recognize that as stalking behavior," says Tatiana Colon, head of the Teen Dating Violence Task Force in Alameda County, California. In other words, it's not about love, it's about control. And control is at the core of abusive behavior.

14 Of course, few girls consciously choose to become involved with an abuser. As in the case of Sarah and Kayla, the relationship usually starts off tenderly. But then a pattern begins to emerge—with abusers emotionally or physically abusive one minute, sweetly apologetic the next.

15 "Honey, I didn't mean it—I'll never do it again," is a common refrain. Furthermore, abusers often have "Dr. Jekyll" and "Mr. Hyde" personalities. That is, they are careful to present only their good "Dr. Jekyll" side to outsiders. It's not unusual for them to be charming and popular—star athletes and good students. In cases such as these, girls are understandably reluctant to confide that they are being abused for fear of not being believed. When Sarah told school authorities that Joe was abusing her, they ordered him to attend a different school. But other girls told Sarah, "How could you do this to him? He's *so cute.*"

16 Another reason girls fail to tell others that they are being abused is that they feel it's their responsibility to fix whatever is wrong in the relationship.

17 "Think of articles in women's magazines," says Dr. Murray. "There is

always at least one in which the tone of the article is how to fix your relationship." As Murray points out, there are basically three types of relationship articles: how to catch a man, how to hold onto a man, and how you must fix whatever is wrong in a relationship.

18   Ever notice that men's magazines don't have similar articles?

19   Girls who come from homes where they have been expected to care for a depressed parent are especially likely to fall into this "caretaker" pattern of thinking. Having been trained as children to be "good little helpers," they hold the mistaken belief that they can rescue the abuser. And since few abusers are abusive all the time, they hold out hope that his good side will win out.

20   "He comes from a bad home. I'm all he's got. I can save him," they often think. Although an abuser may express remorse and swear that he will never do it again, experts warn that abuse involves a cycle that feeds itself. It *will not* stop unless drastic action is taken. In fact, 80% of abusers fail to stop their abuse *even with* therapy. According to Murray, an abused woman will typically go back to her abuser seven to nine times before she leaves for good—if she's still alive.

21   Abuse often begins with insults such as "You're fat, you're ugly and stupid. Nobody else would want you." Such hostility is a form of what psychologists term *projection*. In other words, whatever the abuser dislikes about himself, he will "project" onto his partner. By destroying her self-confidence, he feels his power

increase. Of course, women can also be guilty of projection. For example, a young woman who cheats on her boyfriend may guiltily accuse him of cheating on her.

22   Emotional abuse generally escalates° to physical abuse. At first, an abuser may punch a wall next to his victim or throw something or kick a chair. Such behavior is meant to threaten and intimidate.° An abuser will then graduate to pushing, slapping, pulling hair, kicking, or punching his victim. Sexual abuse is the most serious form of relationship abuse. In fact, date rape accounts for 67% of sexual assaults among teens. Sadly, some young women still believe that it is a male's right to demand sex from his partner whenever he feels like it. Experts disagree. They maintain that if sex is not completely consensual, it is rape.

23   Young women often downplay abuse. "He lost control. It was the alcohol talking, not him," they'll say. Perhaps saddest of all, some young women actually believe their abuser when he insists, "You made me do it."

24   "No one actually loses control," says Scott A. Johnson, author of *When 'I Love You' Turns Violent*. "Rather a conscious decision is made . . . to blame the victim." He adds, "If you are being abused, your significant other is telling you loudly and clearly, 'I do not love you!'"

What To Do

25   If you know a young person who is in an abusive relationship, how do you advise him or her to get out? Experts

agree that it is best *not* to confront the abuser. Such confrontations can become violent, as the abuser seeks at all costs to reestablish control over his victim. "If I can't have you, no one will," is a classic threat, and one that should be taken at face value.

26   Instead of confronting an abuser, victims should confide in someone trustworthy, such as a teacher, guidance counselor, doctor, friend, or parent. Contact the National Teen Dating Abuse 24/7 Helpline at 1-866-331-9474, www.loveisrespect.org or the National Domestic Violence Hotline at 1-800-799-7233. Both organizations help victims of abuse design a personal safety plan to lower the risk of being hurt by an abuser.

27   Remember, there is nothing "loving" about being treated as someone's possession. And no one should have to put up with abusive behavior. So don't be silent if you or someone you know is being abused. You can make it stop, but only if you let others know what's happening.

Reading Comprehension Questions

Vocabulary in Context

_____ 1. In the sentence below, the word *inhibitions* (ĭn-hə-bĭsh′əns) means
   A. restraints.
   B. acceptable choices.
   C. body temperature.
   D. emotions.

   "Alcohol, in turn, lowers inhibitions and increases aggression." (Paragraph 11)

_____ 2. In the excerpt below, the word *consensual* (kən-sĕn′shōō-əl) means
   A. enjoyable.
   B. agreed to by all involved.
   C. risk-free.
   D. within the bonds of marriage.

   "Sadly, some young women still believe that it is a male's right to demand sex from his partner whenever he feels like it. Experts disagree. They maintain that if sex is not completely consensual, it is rape." (Paragraph 22)

Central Point and Main Ideas

_____ 3. Which sentence best expresses the central point of the selection?
   A. Today, modern technology is making it easier for abusers to harass, humiliate, and stalk their victims.
   B. Children who are exposed to violence and substance abuse at home often become involved in abusive relationships.
   C. Abuse involves a cycle that feeds itself and will not stop unless drastic action is taken.
   D. There are a number of factors that cause young people to become involved in abusive relationships.

_____ 4. The implied main idea of paragraphs 5–8 is that
   A. many girls in our culture long for a Prince Charming to come and sweep them off their feet.
   B. psychologists such as Dr. Jill Murray believe that adolescents are primarily concerned with the way they appear to their peers.
   C. because teenage girls in our culture place such a high value on being in a relationship, they are more likely to become involved in abusive relationships.
   D. TV, the movies, magazines, and the Internet all communicate the message that it's important to be in a relationship.

_____ 5. The main idea of paragraph 9 is stated in its
   A. first sentence.
   B. second sentence.
   C. third sentence.
   D. fourth sentence.

_____ 6. The implied main idea of paragraph 15 is that
   A. some abusers are good at disguising their true nature.
   B. most abusers lie about their actions.
   C. most people do not believe girls who complain about date abuse.
   D. if an abuser is good-looking and popular, his victim will forgive him.

Supporting Details

_____ 7. According to the selection, which of the following statements would an abusive male *not* be likely to say?
   A. "She belongs to me."
   B. "Women should know their place."
   C. "It's up to me to fix whatever is wrong in this relationship."
   D. "You made me do it."

_____ 8. According to the selection, a girl who sees her father or another male abuse her mother

    A. is more likely to stay single.

    B. is more likely to demand respectful treatment from her partner.

    C. is more likely to abuse her male partner.

    D. tends to view abuse as natural.

_____ 9. According to the selection, which of the following is *not* mentioned as a contributing factor in abusive relationships?

    A. Coming from a violent home

    B. Coming from a home where substance abuse takes place

    C. Watching violent TV shows and movies

    D. Confusing jealousy and possessiveness with love

Transitions

_____10. The relationship between the two sentences below is one of

    A. cause and effect.

    B. addition.

    C. comparison.

    D. contrast.

> "Alcohol, in turn, lowers inhibitions and increases aggression. Likewise, chronic use of marijuana or crystal meth causes rage and paranoia." (Paragraph 11)

Patterns of Organization

_____11. The main pattern of organization of paragraphs 1 and 2 is

    A. illustration.

    B. list of items.

    C. time order.

    D. cause and effect.

_____12. The main pattern of organization of paragraphs 25–26 is

    A. definition and example.

    B. problem and solution.

    C. contrast.

    D. cause and effect.

Inferences

_____13. We can conclude from paragraphs 5–8 that
  A. most girls who once pretended to be princesses will become involved in abusive relationships.
  B. it is natural for boys to grow up to become "Prince Charming."
  C. it's not good for girls to base their self-worth on having a boyfriend.
  D. all of the above.

_____14. We can infer from paragraph 12 that
  A. in some ways, modern technology is making it more difficult for parents to protect their children.
  B. today, most parents are too busy to care much about who their children are dating.
  C. without cell phones, there would be very few abusive relationships among the young.
  D. there is nothing that parents can do to protect their children from becoming victims of abuse.

_____15. On the basis of paragraphs 16–18, we can conclude that
  A. most of the men who read men's magazines aren't interested in women.
  B. men's magazines would be more popular if they carried stories about how men should fix romantic relationships.
  C. in general, men aren't interested in reading about how to fix romantic relationships.
  D. men's magazines deliberately encourage abuse in relationships.

_____16. We can infer from the selection that
  A. only children who are exposed to violence at home become involved in abusive relationships.
  B. many young people today don't know what a loving relationship looks like.
  C. loving someone means wanting to know what he or she is doing at all times.
  D. young men who are physically unattractive are more likely to become abusive toward women.

_____17. On the basis of the last three paragraphs of the selection, we can conclude that the author
  A. has interviewed many victims of abuse.
  B. was once a victim of abuse herself.
  C. believes that escaping an abusive relationship can be a matter of life or death.
  D. thinks that abusers often make threats that they have no intention of carrying out.

Purpose and Tone

_____ 18. The main purpose of this selection is to
   A. inform readers about what causes abusive relationships and how to escape such relationships.
   B. entertain readers with dramatic stories of how some young women escaped abusive relationships.
   C. persuade readers that it's a waste of time to provide abusers with therapy.

Argument

19. Label the point of the following argument with a **P** and the three statements of support with an **S**.

   ___ A. Girls who have had to care for a depressed parent often think that it's their responsibility to help an abuser.

   ___ B. Young men who are raised to believe that the man is the natural head of the household sometimes view abuse as "discipline."

   ___ C. Our beliefs about relationships can influence how likely we are to become involved in an abusive relationship.

   ___ D. Teenage girls who think that being alone is for losers are more likely to become involved with a young man who will abuse them.

Critical Reading

_____ 20. Girls who believe that they must make a choice between dating someone who abuses them and being thought of as a "loser" are committing the logical fallacy of
   A. false cause *(the argument assumes the order of events alone shows cause and effect).*
   B. circular reasoning *(a statement repeats itself rather than providing a real supporting reason to back up an argument).*
   C. either-or *(the argument assumes that there are only two sides to a question).*
   D. false comparison *(the argument assumes that two things being compared are more alike than they really are).*

Outlining

Complete the following outline of paragraphs 4–20 of the selection by filling in the central point and the missing major and minor details.

Central point: _____

_____

1. _____

   _____

   A. Young people receive the message that being alone is for losers.
   B. Teenage girls feel out of place if their friends are dating, and they are not.
   C. Teenage girls are often desperate for a boyfriend and get taken advantage of as a result.

   D. _____

      _____

2. _____

   _____

   A. A girl who sees her father or another male abuse her mother tends to view abuse as "natural."

   B. _____

      _____

3. Males hold stereotypical ideas of male/female relationships.

   A. _____

      _____

   B. Some religious groups view abuse of a female partner as "discipline."

4. _____

   _____

   A. _____

   B. Chronic use of marijuana or crystal meth causes rage or paranoia.

5. _____

   _____

A. Constant text messaging is not about love; it's about control (stalking behavior).

B. Abusers often have "Dr. Jekyll" and "Mr. Hyde" personalities— hiding their abusiveness from outsiders and making girls reluctant to confide their abuse for fear of not being believed.

6. _____

_____

A. Girls who come from homes where they have had to care for a depressed parent are most likely to fall into this pattern of thinking.

B. Some girls think they can "save" their abuser. However, 80% of abusers fail to stop their abuse even with therapy.

Discussion Questions

1. Was there anything in this selection that surprised you? If so, what was it, and why did you find it surprising? Was there any information that you disagree with? Explain.

2. Think back to when you were in high school. Was it considered normal to be in a relationship? Were kids who weren't in relationships looked on as "losers"? If so, was dating violence ever discussed? Explain.

3. The selection focuses mainly on males who abuse females. Do you think that women abusing men is also a serious problem? Why or why not?

4. Experts believe that dating violence is on the rise. Whether it is or not, it's clearly a serious problem. In your view, is there anything that can be done to reduce the likelihood that young people will become involved in abusive relationships, either as abusers or as victims? If so, what?

Note: Writing assignments for this selection appear on page 643.

Check Your Performance

ABUSIVE RELATIONSHIPS AMONG THE YOUNG

Activity	Number Right		Points		Score
Reading Comprehension Questions					
Vocabulary in Context (2 items)	_____	x	4	=	_____
Central Point and Main Ideas (4 items)	_____	x	4	=	_____
Supporting Details (3 items)	_____	x	4	=	_____
Transitions (1 item)	_____	x	4	=	_____
Patterns of Organization (2 items)	_____	x	4	=	_____
Inferences (5 items)	_____	x	4	=	_____
Purpose and Tone (1 item)	_____	x	4	=	_____
Argument (1 item)	_____	x	4	=	_____
Critical Reading (1 item)	_____	x	4	=	_____
Outlining (10 items)	_____	x	2	=	_____
		TOTAL SCORE		=	_____%

Enter your total score into the **Reading Performance Chart: Ten Reading Selections** on the inside back cover.

8 A Civil War Soldier's Letter to His Wife

Sullivan Ballou

Preview

When the American Civil War began in 1861, citizens on both sides of the conflict were driven by equally passionate convictions. One young volunteer was Sullivan Ballou, a 32-year-old lawyer who joined the Union army shortly after war was declared. On July 14, 1861, he wrote the following letter to his wife, Sarah, as he awaited orders in a camp just outside of Washington, D.C. His letter has achieved fame as both a personal expression of love and a heartfelt statement of one young soldier's devotion to his country. One week after writing the letter, Ballou was killed at the Battle of Bull Run.

Words to Watch

impelled (4): forced
communing (7): sharing my thoughts
wafted (10): passing gently through the air
buffet (11): strike against
frolics (14): playful actions

1 July 14th, 1861

2 Washington, D.C.

3 My very dear Sarah:

4 The indications are very strong that we shall move in a few days—perhaps tomorrow. Lest I should not be able to write you again, I feel impelled° to write lines that may fall under your eye when I shall be no more.

5   Our movement may be one of a few days' duration and full of pleasure—and it may be one of severe conflict and death to me. Not my will, but thine, O God, be done. If it is necessary that I should fall on the battlefield for my country, I am ready. I have no misgivings about, or lack of confidence in, the cause in which I am engaged, and my courage does not halt or falter. I know how strongly American civilization now leans upon the triumph of the government, and how great a debt we owe to those who went before us through the blood and

suffering of the Revolution. And I am willing—perfectly willing—to lay down all my joys in this life, to help maintain this government, and to pay that debt.

6   But, my dear wife, when I know that with my own joys I lay down nearly all of yours, and replace them in this life with cares and sorrows—when, after having eaten for long years the bitter fruit of orphanage myself, I must offer it as their only sustenance to my dear little children—is it weak or dishonorable, while the banner of my purpose floats calmly and proudly in the breeze, that my unbounded love for you, my darling wife and children, should struggle in fierce, though useless, contest with my love of country?

7   I cannot describe to you my feelings on this calm summer night, when two thousand men are sleeping around me, many of them enjoying the last, perhaps, before that of death—and I, suspicious that Death is creeping behind me with his fatal dart, am communing° with God, my country, and thee.

8   I have sought most closely and diligently, and often in my breast, for a wrong motive in thus hazarding the happiness of those I loved, and I could not find one. A pure love of my country and . . . "the name of honor that I love more than I fear death" have called upon me, and I have obeyed.

9   Sarah, my love for you is deathless; it seems to bind me to you with mighty cables that nothing but Omnipotence could break; and yet my love of country comes over me like a strong wind and bears me irresistibly on with all these chains to the battlefield.

10   The memories of the blissful moments I have spent with you come creeping over me, and I feel most gratified to God and to you that I have enjoyed them so long. And hard it is for me to give them up and burn to ashes the hopes of future years, when God willing, we might still have lived and loved together and seen our sons grow up to honorable manhood around us. I have, I know, but few and small claims upon Divine Providence, but something whispers to me—perhaps it is the wafted° prayer of my little Edgar—that I shall return to my loved ones unharmed. If I do not, my dear Sarah, never forget how much I love you, and when my last breath escapes me on the battlefield, it will whisper your name.

11   Forgive my many faults, and the many pains I have caused you. How thoughtless and foolish I have oftentimes been! How gladly would I wash out with my tears every little spot upon your happiness, and struggle with all the misfortune of this world, to shield you and my children from harm. But I cannot. I must watch you from the spirit land and hover near you, while you buffet° the storms with your precious little freight, and wait with sad patience till we meet to part no more.

12   But, O Sarah! If the dead can come back to this earth and flit unseen around those they loved, I shall always be near you; in the garish day and in the darkest night—amidst your happiest scenes and gloomiest hours—always, always; and if there be a soft breeze upon your cheek, it shall be my breath; or if the cool

air fans your throbbing temple, it shall be my spirit passing by.

13   Sarah, do not mourn me dead; think I am gone and wait for thee, for we shall meet again.

14   As for my little boys, they will grow as I have done, and never know a father's love and care. Little Willie is too young to remember me long, and my blue-eyed Edgar will keep my frolics° with him among the dimmest memories of his childhood. Sarah, I have unlimited confidence in your maternal care and your development of their characters. Tell my two mothers I call God's blessing upon them. O Sarah, I wait for you there! Come to me, and lead thither my children.

Sullivan

Reading Comprehension Questions

Vocabulary in Context

_____ 1. In the excerpt below, the word *sustenance* (sŭs′tə-nəns) means
   A. hope for the future.
   B. nourishment.
   C. happy memories.
   D. concern for someone's welfare.

> "But, my dear wife, when I know that with my own joys I lay down nearly all of yours, and replace them in this life with cares and sorrows—when, after having eaten for long years the bitter fruit of orphanage myself, I must offer it as their only sustenance to my dear little children . . ." (Paragraph 6)

_____ 2. In the excerpt below, the word *hazarding* (hăz′ərd-ĭng) means
   A. guessing.
   B. risking.
   C. enjoying.
   D. insuring.

> "I have sought most closely and diligently, and often in my breast, for a wrong motive in thus hazarding the happiness of those I loved, and I could not find one." (Paragraph 8)

Central Point and Main Ideas

_____ 3. Which sentence best expresses the central point of the selection?
  A. The author is willing to suffer as much as other Americans suffered during the Revolution.
  B. The author realizes that if he is killed in battle, his wife and sons will suffer greatly.
  C. The author fully expects to see his wife and sons in eternal life.
  D. The author is willing to sacrifice his life and the happiness of his family to fight for a cause that he believes is just.

_____ 4. The implied main idea of paragraph 14 is that the author
  A. knows that his sons will probably only have dim memories of him.
  B. regrets that his sons will never know a father's love and care.
  C. has confidence that even if he dies in battle, his wife will raise his sons properly so that they all can meet in Heaven.
  D. knows that his wife will need the help of others in raising the couple's two sons should he die in battle.

Supporting Details

_____ 5. The author believes that he and others owe a great debt to
  A. Divine Providence.
  B. the two thousand men who are sleeping around him.
  C. those who bled and suffered during the Revolution.
  D. President Lincoln.

_____ 6. The author regrets that his two sons, like him, may
  A. have bitter memories of their father.
  B. never know a father's love and care.
  C. have a weak, unsupportive mother.
  D. be killed in battle.

Transitions

_____ 7. The relationship between the two sentences below is one of
  A. addition.
  B. cause and effect.
  C. comparison.
  D. contrast.

  "How gladly would I wash out with my tears every little spot upon your happiness, and struggle with all the misfortunes of this world, to shield you and my children from harm. But I cannot." (Paragraph 11)

Patterns of Organization

_____ 8. Paragraph 5 compares

    A. American civilization as it is now with the way it used to be.

    B. the author's willingness to die for his country with the sacrifices of those who suffered and died before him.

    C. the author's own desires with those of his wife and children.

    D. the author's debts with those who came before him.

_____ 9. This selection mainly

    A. lists reasons why the author believes that the Union cause is just.

    B. presents a series of historical events in time order.

    C. contrasts the author's love of his country with the personal sacrifices involved in fighting to preserve his country.

    D. compares his wife's support for the cause with his own.

Inferences

_____ 10. In paragraph 6, the author wants his wife to know that

    A. he considers himself weak and dishonorable.

    B. he regrets that his commitment to the Union cause may hurt his family.

    C. he is as proud and calm as the banner which flies nearby.

    D. his love of country is useless.

_____ 11. The phrase "and I, suspicious that Death is creeping behind me with his fatal dart" suggests that the author

    A. feels he will be struck with a dart.

    B. believes that one of his own men will be responsible for his death.

    C. suspects that he might not have long to live.

    D. is naturally very suspicious.

_____ 12. The "chains" that the author mentions in paragraph 9 refer to

    A. the ties of love that connect him to his wife.

    B. the way that slaves were routinely treated in the Confederacy.

    C. the love that the author feels for his country.

    D. his unwillingness to go to the battlefield.

_____ 13. In paragraph 14, the author concludes that

    A. he was raised by two women.

    B. his sons will remember him forever.

    C. his sons will have bitter memories of him for leaving them fatherless.

    D. due to his wife's influence, his sons will turn out well.

14. On the basis of paragraphs 11 through 14, we can infer that the author
   A. believes that his family might be better off without him.
   B. believes that he and his family will be reunited after death.
   C. believes that the dead are powerless to help the living.
   D. knows that his children will always remember him.

15. A reasonable conclusion we can draw from the reading is that
   A. the author is bitter about being forced to choose between his family and his country.
   B. the author knows that his wife and children can never understand his reasons for fighting.
   C. few men actually shared the author's belief in the Union cause.
   D. the author believes that his duty to his country must outweigh his personal happiness and that of his family.

Purpose and Tone

16. The main purpose of this selection is to
   A. inform Ballou's wife both of his love for her and his need to fight for a cause which he believes is just.
   B. persuade his wife to change her mind about her support for the Union cause.
   C. entertain his wife with amusing stories of life in an army camp.

17. The tone of this selection can be described as
   A. nostalgic and bitter.
   B. affectionate and instructive.
   C. uncertain and worried.
   D. loving and serious.

Argument

18. Label the point of the following argument with a **P** and the three statements of support with an **S**.
   A. In paragraph 6, Ballou speaks of his "unbounded love" for his wife.
   B. Toward the end of the letter, Ballou tells his wife that if the dead can come back to this earth, he will always be near her.
   C. In this letter, Ballou seeks to reassure his wife of his profound love for her.
   D. In paragraph 10, Ballou tells his wife that when his last breath escapes him on the battlefield, it will whisper her name.

Critical Reading

19. The sentence below is one of
    A. fact.
    B. opinion.

    "Lest I should not be able to write you again, I feel impelled to write lines that may fall under your eye when I shall be no more." (Paragraph 4)

20. A housing development near the site of a major Civil War battlefield is called "Liberty Acres." What propaganda technique did the developer use in naming this development?
    A. Testimonial
    B. Transfer
    C. Plain folks
    D. Bandwagon

Summarizing

Add the ideas needed to complete the following summary of "A Civil War Soldier's Letter to His Wife."

Ballou begins his letter by telling his wife that the Union Army will probably move soon. Fearing that he may not be able to write to her again, he says that he is willing to lay down his life for a cause that he feels is just, but struggles with the thought that in laying down his own joys, he must also _____ _____ and leave for his children only the _____ _____.

He goes on to say that even though his love for his wife is deathless, his love of country bears him _____. He tells his wife that should he die in battle, his last thoughts will be of her. He urges her to forgive him his faults and wishes that he could make her happy and shield her and his children from harm. Unable to do that, he will instead _____ and wait with sad patience until they meet again.

He concludes by telling her that he has unlimited _____ in her maternal care and ability to develop their sons' characters. He waits for her and expects her to lead his children to him.

Discussion Questions

1. What does Sullivan Ballou's letter reveal about his character and principles? Does he deserve to be called a hero? Why or why not?

2. Do you agree with Sullivan Ballou's decision to fight for what he believed in, even though it meant risking the happiness and security of his wife and children? Why or why not?

3. The letter makes clear that author Sullivan Ballou believed he was carrying out a tradition of sacrifice in the defense of liberty that others had begun during the American Revolution. Do you believe that the recent wars in which America has been engaged continue this tradition— or depart from it? Explain.

4. Under what circumstances, if any, would you be willing to sacrifice your life for a cause?

Note: Writing assignments for this selection appear on page 643.

Check Your Performance   A CIVIL WAR SOLDIER'S
LETTER TO HIS WIFE

Activity	Number Right	Points	Score
Reading Comprehension Questions			
Vocabulary in Context (2 items)	_____	x 4 =	_____
Central Point and Main Ideas (2 items)	_____	x 4 =	_____
Supporting Details (2 items)	_____	x 4 =	_____
Transitions (1 item)	_____	x 4 =	_____
Patterns of Organization (2 items)	_____	x 4 =	_____
Inferences (6 items)	_____	x 4 =	_____
Purpose and Tone (2 items)	_____	x 4 =	_____
Argument (1 item)	_____	x 4 =	_____
Critical Reading (2 items)	_____	x 4 =	_____
Summarizing (5 items)	_____	x 4 =	_____
		TOTAL SCORE =	_____%

Enter your total score into the **Reading Performance Chart: Ten Reading Selections** on the inside back cover.

9 In My Day

Russell Baker

Preview

class work

To see a parent becoming old and infirm is painful. It is a particularly awkward transition when the parent has been tough-minded and opinionated, as was Russell Baker's mother in her younger years. In this poignant essay from his autobiography *Growing Up*, Baker reflects on the difficulty of negotiating the shifting terrain as one's parent becomes a child.

Words to Watch

debris (15): scattered remains of something broken
drugstore cowboy (15): someone who is all talk and no action
libertine (15): an immoral person
banal (41): uninteresting and trivial
wrest (44): to pull forcibly
interrogators (49): questioners
exemplary (50): serving as a desirable model

1 At the age of eighty my mother had her last bad fall, and after that her mind wandered free through time. Some days she went to weddings and funerals that had taken place half a century earlier. On others she presided over family dinners cooked on Sunday afternoons for children who were now gray with age. Through all this she lay in bed but moved across time, traveling among the dead decades with a speed and ease beyond the gift of physical science.

2 "Where's Russell?" she asked one day when I came to visit at the nursing home.

3 "I'm Russell," I said.

4 She gazed at this improbably overgrown figure out of an inconceivable future and promptly dismissed it.

5 "Russell's only this big," she said, holding her hand, palm down, two feet from the floor. That day she was a young country wife with chickens in the backyard and a view of hazy blue Virginia mountains behind the apple orchard, and I was a stranger old enough to be her father.

6 Early one morning she phoned me in New York. "Are you coming to my funeral today?" she asked.

7 It was an awkward question with which to be awakened. "What are you talking about, for God's sake?" was the best reply I could manage.

8   "I'm being buried today," she declared briskly, as though announcing an important social event.

9   "I'll phone you back," I said and hung up, and when I did phone back she was all right, although she wasn't all right, of course, and we all knew she wasn't.

10   She had always been a small woman—short, light-boned, delicately structured—but now, under the white hospital sheet, she was becoming tiny. I thought of a doll with huge, fierce eyes. There had always been a fierceness in her. It showed in that angry, challenging thrust of the chin when she issued an opinion, and a great one she had always been for issuing opinions.

11   "I tell people exactly what's on my mind," she has been fond of boasting. "I tell them what I think, whether they like it or not." Often they had not liked it. She could be sarcastic to people in whom she detected evidence of the ignoramus or the fool.

12   "It's not always good policy to tell people exactly what's on your mind," I used to caution her.

13   "If they don't like it, that's too bad," was her customary reply, "because that's the way I am."

14   And so she was. A formidable woman. Determined to speak her mind, determined to have her way, determined to bend those who opposed her. In that time when I had known her best, my mother had hurled herself at life with chin thrust forward, eyes blazing, and an energy that made her seem always on the run.

15   She ran after squawking chickens, an axe in her hand, determined on a beheading that would put dinner in the pot. She ran when she made the beds, ran when she set the table. One Thanksgiving she burned herself badly when, running up from the cellar oven with the ceremonial turkey, she tripped on the stairs and tumbled back down, ending at the bottom in the debris° of giblets, hot gravy and battered turkey. Life was combat, and victory was not to the lazy, the timid, the slugabed, the drugstore cowboy°, the libertine°, the mushmouth afraid to tell people exactly what was on his mind whether people liked it or not. She ran.

16   But now the running was over. For a time I could not accept the inevitable. As I sat by her bed, my impulse was to argue her back to reality. On my first visit to the hospital in Baltimore, she asked who I was.

17   "Russell," I said.

18   "Russell's way out west," she advised me.

19   "No, I'm right here."

20   "Guess where I came from today?" was her response.

21   "Where?"

22   "All the way from New Jersey."

23   "When?"

24   "Tonight."

25   "No. You've been in the hospital for three days," I insisted.

26   "I suggest the thing to do is calm down a little bit," she replied. "Go over to the house and shut the door."

27   Now she was years deep into the past, living in the neighborhood where she had settled forty years earlier, and she had just been talking with Mrs. Hoffman, a neighbor across the street.

28   "It's like Mrs. Hoffman said today: The children always wander back to where they come from," she remarked.

29   "Mrs. Hoffman has been dead for fifteen years."

30   "Russ got married today," she replied.

31   "I got married in 1950," I said, which was the fact.

32   "The house is unlocked," she said.

33   So it went until a doctor came by to give one of those oral quizzes that medical men apply in such cases. She failed catastrophically, giving wrong answers or none at all to "What day is this?" "Do you know where you are?" "How old are you?" and so on. Then, a surprise.

34   "When is your birthday?" he asked.

35   "November 5, 1897," she said. Correct. Absolutely correct.

36   "How do you remember that?" the doctor asked.

37   "Because I was born on Guy Fawkes Day," she said.

38   "Guy Fawkes?" asked the doctor. "Who is Guy Fawkes?"

39   She replied with a rhyme I had heard her recite time and again over the years when the subject of her birth date arose:

> *"Please to remember the Fifth of November,*
> *Gunpowder treason and plot.*
> *I see no reason why gunpowder treason*
> *Should ever be forgot."*

Then she glared at this young doctor, so ill informed about Guy Fawkes's failed scheme to blow King James off his throne with barrels of gunpowder in 1605. She had been a schoolteacher, after all, and knew how to glare at a dolt. "You may know a lot about medicine, but you obviously don't know any history," she said. Having told him exactly what was on her mind, she left us again.

40   The doctors diagnosed a hopeless senility. Not unusual, they said. "Hardening of the arteries" was the explanation for laymen. I thought it was more complicated than that. For ten years or more the ferocity with which she had once attacked life had been turning to a rage against the weakness, the boredom, and the absence of love that too much age had brought her. Now, after the last bad fall, she seemed to have broken chains that imprisoned her in a life she had come to hate and to return to a time inhabited by people who loved her, a time in which she was needed. Gradually I understood. It was the first time in years I had seen her happy.

41   She had written a letter three years earlier which explained more than "hardening of the arteries." I had gone down from New York to Baltimore, where she lived, for one of my infrequent visits and, afterwards, had written her with some banal° advice to look for the silver lining, to count her blessings instead of burdening others with her miseries. I suppose what it really amounted to was a threat that if she was not more cheerful during my visits I would not come to see her very often. Sons are capable of such letters. This one was written out of a childish faith in the external strength of parents, a naïve belief that age and wear could be overcome by an effort of will, that all she needed was a good pep

talk to recharge a flagging spirit. It was such a foolish, innocent idea, but one thinks of parents differently from other people. Other people can become frail and break, but not parents.

42   She wrote back in an unusually cheery vein intended to demonstrate, I suppose, that she was mending her ways. She was never a woman to apologize, but for one moment with a pen in her hand she came very close. Referring to my visit, she wrote: "If I seemed unhappy to you at times—" Here she drew back, reconsidered, and said something quite different:

43   "If I seemed unhappy to you at times, I am, but there's really nothing anyone can do about it, because I'm just so very tired and lonely that I'll just go to sleep and forget it." She was then seventy-eight.

44   Now, three years later, after the last bad fall, she had managed to forget the fatigue and loneliness and, in these free-wheeling excursions back through time, to recapture happiness. I soon stopped trying to wrest° her back to what I considered the real world and tried to travel along with her on those fantastic swoops into the past. One day, when I arrived at her bedside, she was radiant.

45   "Feeling good today," I said.

46   "Why shouldn't I feel good?" she asked. "Papa's going to take me up to Baltimore on the boat today."

47   At that moment she was a young girl standing on a wharf at Merry Point, Virginia, waiting for the Chesapeake Bay steamer with her father, who had been dead sixty-one years. William Howard Taft was in the White House, Europe still drowsed in the dusk of the great century of peace, America was a young country, and the future stretched before it in beams of crystal sunlight. "The greatest country on God's green earth," her father might have said, if I had been able to step into my mother's time machine and join him on the wharf with the satchels packed for Baltimore.

48   I could imagine her there quite clearly. She was wearing a blue dress with big puffy sleeves and long black stockings. There was a ribbon in her hair and a big bow tied on the side of her head. There had been a childhood photograph in her bedroom which showed all this, although the colors, of course, had been added years later by a restorer who tinted the picture.

49   About her father, my grandfather, I could only guess, and indeed, about the girl on the wharf with the bow in her hair, I was merely sentimentalizing. Of my mother's childhood and her people, of their time and place, I knew very little. A world had lived and died, and though it was part of my blood and bone I knew little more about it than I knew of the world of the pharaohs. It was useless now to ask for help from my mother. The orbits of her mind rarely touched present interrogators° for more than a moment.

50   Sitting at her bedside, forever out of touch with her, I wondered about my own children, and their children, and children in general, and about the disconnections between children and parents that prevent them from knowing each other. Children rarely want to know

who their parents were before they were parents, and when age finally stirs their curiosity, there is no parent left to tell them. If a parent does lift the curtain a bit, it is often only to stun the young with some exemplary° tale of how much harder life was in the old days.

51   I had been guilty of this when my children were small in the early 1960s and living the affluent life. It galled me that their childhoods should be, as I thought, so easy when my own had been, as I thought, so hard. I had developed the habit, when they complained about the steak being overcooked or the television being cut off, of lecturing them on the harshness of life in my day.

52   "In my day all we got for dinner was macaroni and cheese, and we were glad to get it."

53   "In my day we didn't have any television."

54   "In my day . . ."

55   "In my day . . ."

56   At dinner one evening, a son had offended me with an inadequate report card, and as I leaned back and cleared my throat to lecture, he gazed at me with an expression of unutterable resignation and said, "Tell me how it was in your day, Dad."

57   I was angry with him for that, but angrier with myself for having become one of those ancient bores whose highly selective memories of the past become transparently dishonest even to small children. I tried to break the habit, but must have failed. A few years later my son was referring to me when I was out of earshot as "the old-timer." Between us there was a dispute about time. He looked upon the time that had been my future in a disturbing way. My future was his past, and being young, he was indifferent to the past.

58   As I hovered over my mother's bed listening for muffled signals from her childhood, I realized that this same dispute had existed between her and me. When she was young, with life ahead of her, I had been her future and resented it. Instinctively, I wanted to break free, cease being a creature defined by her time, consign her future to the past, and create my own. Well, I had finally done that, and then with my own children I had seen my exciting future become their boring past.

59   These hopeless end-of-the-line visits with my mother made me wish I had not thrown off my own past so carelessly. We all come from the past, and children ought to know what it was that went into their making, to know that life is a braided cord of humanity stretching up from some time long gone, and that it cannot be defined by the span of a single journey from diaper to shroud.

Reading Comprehension Questions

Vocabulary in Context

_A_ 1. In the excerpt below, the word *dolt* (dōlt) means

+1

    A. stupid person.
    B. spot on the wall.
    C. genius.
    D. son.

> "Then she glared at this young doctor, so ill informed about Guy Fawkes's failed scheme to blow King James off his throne with barrels of gunpowder in 1605. She had been a schoolteacher, after all, and knew how to glare at a dolt. 'You may know a lot about medicine, but you obviously don't know any history,' she said." (Paragraph 39)

_B_ 2. In the sentence below, the word *flagging* (flăg'ĭng) means

+1

    A. terrible.
    B. weakening.
    C. challenging.
    D. definite.

> "This one was written out of a childish faith in the external strength of parents, a naïve belief that age and wear could be overcome by an effort of will, that all she needed was a good pep talk to recharge a flagging spirit." (Paragraph 41)

_A_ 3. In the excerpt below, the word *galled* (gôld) means

    A. puzzled.
    B. amused.
    C. annoyed.
    D. threatened.

— 1

> "If a parent does lift the curtain a bit, it is often only to stun the young with some exemplary tale of how much harder life was in the old days.
>
> "I had been guilty of this when my children were small in the early 1960s and living the affluent life. It galled me that their childhood should be, as I thought, so easy when my own had been, as I thought, so hard." (Paragraphs 50–51)

Central Point and Main Ideas

_C_ 4. Which sentence best expresses the central point of the selection?

A. The author and his mother had many differences of opinion due to her forceful personality and his desire to escape her influence.

B. The author is sad to see his mother become senile due to hardening of the arteries, even though she is happier that way.

C. Children are not usually interested in their parents' past history until they get older themselves.

D. When his mother becomes senile, the author regrets that he never learned much about her early life and suggests that young people should try to learn more about their parents' past.

_A_ 5. The main idea of paragraphs 11–15 is that the author's mother

A. had once been strong-willed, active, and outspoken.

B. was sometimes sarcastic to people who she felt were stupid or foolish.

C. once burned herself badly when she fell down the stairs on Thanksgiving while carrying the roast turkey.

D. looked down on people who disagreed with her.

_C_ 6. Which of the following sentences best expresses the main idea of paragraph 40?

A. The doctors diagnosed the author's mother as being hopelessly senile.

B. After her last bad fall, the author's mother became hopelessly senile.

C. The author's mother's senility made her happy because it allowed her to return mentally to a time when she had been loved and needed.

D. Before becoming senile, the author's mother had spent ten years in a rage because of her old age.

_B_ 7. The main idea of paragraphs 50–57 is that

A. the author is annoyed that his children have easy lives while his was hard.

B. both parents and children are responsible for the disconnections between them.

C. generally speaking, children who grew up in the 1960s had it easy.

D. most parents tend to bore their children with stories of how much harder life was in the old days.

Supporting Details

_____ 8. At first when his mother became senile, the author tried to "wrest her back to the real world," but soon
   A. gave up visiting her entirely.
   B. paid little attention to what she said.
   C. tried to travel along with her on her visits into the past.
   D. challenged her on her recall of key dates and events.

_____ 9. The author's mother remembers her own birthday because
   A. her son, Russell, got married on the same date in 1950.
   B. it was the same date that she began teaching school.
   C. her son, Russell, often reminded her of that date.
   D. she was born on Guy Fawkes Day, the subject of a rhyme she knew by heart.

_____ 10. The selection uses all of the patterns of organization below **except**
   A. definition and example.
   B. cause and effect.
   C. time order.
   D. comparison and contrast.

Inferences

_____ 11. On the basis of paragraph 40, we can infer that the author
   A. believed that the doctors had misdiagnosed his mother's condition.
   B. began to view his mother's senility in a positive manner.
   C. could not understand his mother's desire to be loved and needed.
   D. believed that his mother would gradually come to her senses.

_____ 12. On the basis of paragraph 41, we can infer that the author
   A. knew that all his mother really needed was a good pep talk.
   B. visited his mother less often after he wrote telling her to look for the silver lining.
   C. always thought his mother was foolish and innocent.
   D. regrets the naïve advice he once gave his mother.

_____ 13. On the basis of the selection, we can conclude that the author
   A. regrets that he did not learn more about his mother's youth when she was still in her right mind.
   B. fears that he may become senile like his mother.
   C. recognizes that young people have very little to gain from learning about their parents' youth.
   D. believes that he is closer to his children than his mother was to him.

_B_ 14. The last two paragraphs of the reading suggest that

+1

    A. it is hopeless to try to revisit the past.

    B. a person's life is always connected to the lives of those who came before.

    C. it is hard to predict what will happen in the course of a single life.

    D. the course of most people's lives goes from exciting to boring.

_C_ 15. From the details Baker selects to describe his mother, we can conclude that his description of her is

+1

    A. overly sentimental.

    B. without insight.

    C. realistic.

    D. totally unsympathetic.

Purpose and Tone

_D_ 16. The author's purpose is to

+1

    A. inform us of his struggles to understand the differences in outlook which separate parents and children.

    B. entertain us with colorful stories about his mother, complete with dialog.

    C. persuade us that the past should not be taken lightly.

    D. all of the above.

_D_ 17. The general tone of the reading is

+1

    A. self-pitying and tragic.

    B. ironic and detached.

    C. bitter and bewildered.

    D. remorseful and loving.

Argument

_D_ 18. One of the following statements is the point of an argument. The other statements are support for that point. Write the letter of the point of the argument.

+1

    A. The author realized that he never really learned much about his mother's youth.

    B. His mother became senile and failed to recognize him.

    C. The author often lectured his children about how much harder his childhood was than theirs, but his lectures annoyed them.

    D. The author of the selection felt disconnected from both his mother and his children.

Critical Reading

C 19. The statement below is
    A. a fact.
    B. an opinion.
    C. both fact and opinion.

+1

   "At the age of eighty my mother had her last bad fall, and after that her mind wandered free through time." (Paragraph 1)

A 20. When Russell Baker responds to his children's complaints by telling them how much harder life was in his day, he is committing the fallacy of

—1

    A. straw man (an argument is made by claiming an opponent holds an extreme position and then opposing that extreme position).
    B. either-or (the argument assumes that there are only two sides to a question).
    C. false cause (the argument assumes that the order of events alone shows cause and effect).
    D. false comparison (the argument assumes that two things being compared are more alike than they really are).

Summarizing

Add the ideas needed to complete the following summary of "In My Day."

The author, Russell Baker, writes about his eighty-year-old mother who has become senile after her last bad fall. Confined to a hospital and then a nursing home, the old woman disturbs him by doing such things as _____

_____ and _____

_____.

While visiting his mother at a hospital in Baltimore, Baker recalls what a formidable and opinionated woman she once had been. In response to her flights of senility, Baker tries to bring her back to reality. The doctors come in, question her, and diagnose her as hopelessly senile when she fails their oral quiz. Shortly afterward, Baker comes to realize that his mother's senility has enabled her to

_____

_____. He then recalls the

"naïve" letters he wrote her three years earlier in which he tried to _____

_____, not realizing then that

_____.

Now, three years later, Baker has stopped trying to force his mother to recognize reality and attempts to travel mentally back through time with her as she imagines that she is a young girl again. Sitting at her bedside, however, Baker realizes that he actually _____

_____. He reflects on the disconnections which separate parents and children. His own children, he realizes, are bored when he _____

_____

_____, recollections which he admits are _____

_____. He further regrets that he did not learn more about his mother's youth when she _____

_____. Although children instinctively want to _____

_____, Baker reminds us that "we all come from the past" and that we "ought to know" that "[life] cannot be defined by the span of a single journey from diaper to shroud."

Discussion Questions

1. How would you describe the author's mother, first as a young woman and then as an elderly one? Do you see any similarities between the young Mrs. Baker and the eighty-year-old Mrs. Baker? Between the eighty-year-old Mrs. Baker and her son Russell?

2. When her mind began to wander, Baker at first tried to bring his mother back to the present. Later, however, he played along with her "trips through time." Do you think he was right to stop correcting her mistakes? Why or why not?

3. Baker writes that "one thinks of parents differently from other people. Other people can become frail and break, but not parents." Why do you think people hold their parents to higher standards than they do other people, and find it harder to forgive their parents when they fall short?

4. Baker now regrets not knowing more of his family history. Once he became curious about his mother's past, she was no longer able to tell him about it. What can you—and other parents and children—do to overcome the "disconnections" between generations so that a family's past history can be preserved for the future?

Note: Writing assignments for this selection appear on page 644.

Check Your Performance   IN MY DAY

Activity	Number Right	Points	Score
Basic Skill Questions			
Vocabulary in Context (3 items)	_____	× 4 =	_____
Central Point and Main Ideas (4 items)	_____	× 4 =	_____
Supporting Details (3 items)	_____	× 4 =	_____
Inferences (5 items)	_____	× 4 =	_____
Purpose and Tone (2 items)	_____	× 4 =	_____
Argument (1 item)	_____	× 4 =	_____
Critical Reading (2 items)	_____	× 4 =	_____
Summarizing (10 items)	_____	× 2 =	_____
		TOTAL SCORE =	_____%

Enter your total score into the **Reading Performance Chart: Ten Reading Selections** on the inside back cover.

10 The Spider and the Wasp
Alexander Petrunkevitch

Preview

The tarantula and the digger wasp are creatures linked by destiny. So that baby wasps may live, the tarantula must die. Such cruelties of nature are not uncommon. But what is surprising is the passive way in which the tarantula submits to its fate. In this essay from *Scientific American* magazine, noted naturalist Alexander Petrunkevitch analyzes the spider's cooperation in its own demise.

Words to Watch

progeny (1): offspring
crass (1): crude; not refined
tactile (8): related to the sense of touch
pungent (9): sharp-smelling
gargantuan (9): huge
chitinous (9): concerning the material that makes up an insect's exoskeleton
discriminating (10): selective
girth (11): middle
protruding (12): sticking out
olfactory (14): related to the sense of smell
simulating (15): pretending
initiative (16): power to act before others do
chasm (16): a deep opening in the earth's surface

1   In the feeding and safeguarding of their progeny°, insects and spiders exhibit some interesting analogies to reasoning and some crass° examples of blind instinct. The case I propose to describe here is that of the tarantula spiders and their arch-enemy, the digger wasps of the genus *Pepsis*. It is a classic example of what looks like intelligence pitted against instinct—a strange situation in which the victim, though fully able to defend itself, submits unwittingly to its destruction.

2   Most tarantulas live in the tropics, but several species occur in the temperate zone, and a few are common in the southern United States. Some varieties are large and have powerful fangs with which they can inflict a deep wound. These formidable-looking

spiders do not, however, attack man; you can hold one in your hand, if you are gentle, without being bitten. Their bite is dangerous only to insects and small mammals such as mice; for a man it is no worse than a hornet's sting.

3   Tarantulas customarily live in deep cylindrical burrows, from which they emerge at dusk and into which they retire at dawn. Mature males wander about after dark in search of females and occasionally stray into houses. After mating, the male dies in a few weeks, but a female lives much longer and can mate several years in succession. In a Paris museum is a tropical specimen which is said to have been living in captivity for twenty-five years.

4   A fertilized female tarantula lays from 200 to 400 eggs at a time; thus it is possible for a single tarantula to produce several thousand young. She takes no care of them beyond weaving a cocoon of silk to enclose the eggs. After they hatch, the young walk away, find convenient places in which to dig their burrows, and spend the rest of their lives in solitude. Tarantulas feed mostly on insects and millipedes. Once their appetite is appeased, they digest the food for several days before eating again. Their sight is poor, being limited to sensing a change in the intensity of light and to the perception of moving objects. They apparently have little or no sense of hearing, for a hungry tarantula will pay no attention to a loudly chirping cricket placed in its cage unless the insect happens to touch one of its legs.

5   But all spiders, and especially hairy ones, have an extremely delicate sense of touch. Laboratory experiments prove that tarantulas can distinguish three types of touch: pressure against the body wall, stroking of the body hair, and riffling of certain very fine hairs on the legs called trichobothria. Pressure against the body, by a finger or the end of a pencil, causes the tarantula to move off slowly for a short distance. The touch excites no defensive response unless the approach is from above where the spider can see the motion, in which case it rises on its hind legs, lifts its front legs, opens its fangs, and holds this threatening posture as long as the object continues to move. When the motion stops, the spider drops back to the ground, remains quiet for a few seconds, and then moves slowly away.

6   The entire body of a tarantula, especially its legs, is thickly clothed with hair. Some of it is short and woolly, some long and stiff. Touching this body hair produces one of two distinct reactions. When the spider is hungry, it responds with an immediate and swift attack. At the touch of a cricket's antennae, the tarantula seizes the insect so swiftly that a motion picture taken at the rate of 64 frames per second shows only the result and not the process of capture. But when the spider is not hungry, the stimulation of its hairs merely causes it to shake the touched limb. An insect can walk under its hairy belly unharmed.

7   The trichobothria, very fine hairs growing from disklike membranes on the legs, were once thought to be the spider's hearing organs, but we now know that they have nothing to do with sound. They are sensitive only to air

movement. A light breeze makes them vibrate slowly without disturbing the common hair. When one blows gently on the trichobothria, the tarantula reacts with a quick jerk of its four front legs. If the front and hind legs are stimulated at the same time, the spider makes a sudden jump. This reaction is quite independent of the state of its appetite.

8   These three tactile° responses—to pressure on the body wall, to moving of the common hair, and to flexing of the trichobothria—are so different from one another that there is no possibility of confusing them. They serve the tarantula adequately for most of its needs and enable it to avoid most annoyances and dangers. But they fail the spider completely when it meets its deadly enemy, the digger wasp *Pepsis*.

9   These solitary wasps are beautiful and formidable creatures. Most species are either a deep shiny blue all over, or deep blue with rusty wings. The largest have a wing span of about four inches. They live on nectar. When excited, they give off a pungent° odor—a warning that they are ready to attack. The sting is much worse than that of a bee or common wasp, and the pain and swelling last longer. In the adult stage the wasp lives only a few months. The female produces but a few eggs, one at a time at intervals of two or three days. For each egg the mother must provide one adult tarantula, alive but paralyzed. The tarantula must be of the correct species to nourish the larva. The mother wasp attaches the egg to the paralyzed spider's abdomen. Upon hatching from the egg, the larva is many hundreds of times smaller than its living but helpless victim. It eats no other food and drinks no water. By the time it has finished its single gargantuan° meal and become ready for wasphood, nothing remains of the tarantula but its indigestible chitinous° skeleton.

10   The mother wasp goes tarantula-hunting when the egg in her ovary is almost ready to be laid. Flying low over the ground late on a sunny afternoon, the wasp looks for its victim or for the mouth of a tarantula burrow, a round hole edged by a bit of silk. The sex of the spider makes no difference, but the mother is highly discriminating° as to species. Each species of *Pepsis* requires a certain species of tarantula, and the wasp will not attack the wrong species. In a cage with a tarantula which is not its normal prey, the wasp avoids the spider, and is usually killed by it in the night.

11   Yet when a wasp finds the correct species, it is the other way around. To identify the species, the wasp apparently must explore the spider with her antennae. The tarantula shows an amazing tolerance to this exploration. The wasp crawls under it and walks over it without evoking any hostile response. The molestation is so great and so persistent that the tarantula often rises on all eight legs, as if it were on stilts. It may stand this way for several minutes. Meanwhile the wasp, having satisfied itself that the victim is of the right species, moves off a few inches to dig the spider's grave. Working vigorously with legs and jaws, it excavates a hole eight to ten inches deep with a diameter slightly larger than the spider's girth°.

Now and again the wasp pops out of the hole to make sure that the spider is still there.

12   When the grave is finished, the wasp returns to the tarantula to complete her ghastly enterprise. First she feels it all over once more with her antennae. Then her behavior becomes more aggressive. She bends her abdomen, protruding° her sting, and searches for the soft membrane at the point where the spider's leg joins its body—the only spot where she can penetrate the horny skeleton. From time to time, as the exasperated spider slowly shifts ground, the wasp turns on her back and slides along with the aid of her wings, trying to get under the tarantula for a shot at the vital spot. During all this maneuvering, which can last for several minutes, the tarantula makes no move to save itself. Finally the wasp corners it against some obstruction and grasps one of its legs in her powerful jaws. Now at last the harassed spider tries a desperate but vain defense. The two contestants roll over and over on the ground. It is a terrifying sight, and the outcome is always the same. The wasp finally manages to thrust her sting into the soft spot and holds it there for a few seconds while she pumps in the poison. Almost immediately the tarantula falls paralyzed on its back. Its legs stop twitching; its heart stops beating. Yet it is not dead, as is shown by the fact that if taken from the wasp it can be restored to some sensitivity by being kept in a moist chamber for several months.

13   After paralyzing the tarantula, the wasp cleans herself by dragging her body along the ground and rubbing her feet, sucks the drop of blood oozing from the wound in the spider's abdomen, then grabs a leg of the flabby, helpless animal in her jaws and drags it down to the bottom of the grave. She stays there for many minutes, sometimes for several hours, and what she does all that time in the dark we do not know. Eventually she lays her egg and attaches it to the side of the spider's abdomen with a sticky secretion. Then she emerges, fills the grave with soil carried bit by bit in her jaws, and finally tramples the ground all around to hide any trace of the grave from prowlers. Then she flies away, leaving her descendant safely started in life.

14   In all this the behavior of the wasp evidently is qualitatively different from that of the spider. The wasp acts like an intelligent animal. This is not to say that instinct plays no part or that she reasons as man does. But her actions are to the point; they are not automatic and can be modified to fit the situation. We do not know for certain how she identifies the tarantula—probably it is by some olfactory° or chemo-tactile sense—but she does it purposefully and does not blindly tackle a wrong species.

15   On the other hand, the tarantula's behavior shows only confusion. Evidently the wasp's pawing gives it no pleasure, for it tries to move away. That the wasp is not simulating° sexual stimulation is certain, because male and female tarantulas react in the same way to its advances. That the spider is not anesthetized by some odorless secretion is easily shown by blowing

lightly at the tarantula and making it jump suddenly. What, then, makes the tarantula behave as stupidly as it does?

16   No clear, simple answer is available. Possibly the stimulation by the wasp's antennae is masked by a heavier pressure on the spider's body, so that it reacts as when prodded by a pencil. But the explanation may be much more complex. Initiative° in attack is not in the nature of tarantulas; most species fight only when cornered so that escape is impossible. Their inherited patterns of behavior apparently prompt them to avoid problems rather than attack them. For example, spiders always weave their webs in three dimensions, and when a spider finds that there is insufficient space to attach certain threads in the third dimension, it leaves the place and seeks another, instead of finishing the web in a single plane. This urge to escape seems to arise under all circumstances, in all phases of life and to take the place of reasoning. For a spider to change the pattern of its web is as impossible as for an inexperienced man to build a bridge across a chasm° obstructing his way.

17   In a way the instinctive urge to escape is not only easier but often more efficient than reasoning. The tarantula does exactly what is most efficient in all cases except in an encounter with a ruthless and determined attacker dependent for the existence of her own species on killing as many tarantulas as she can lay eggs. Perhaps in this case the spider follows its usual pattern of trying to escape, instead of seizing and killing the wasp, because it is not aware of its danger. In any case, the survival of the tarantula species as a whole is protected by the fact that the spider is much more fertile than the wasp.

Reading Comprehension Questions

Vocabulary in Context

1. In the excerpt below, the word *formidable* (fôr′mĭ-də-bəl) means
   A. delicate.
   B. inspiring fear or dread.
   C. nervous.
   D. genuine.

   "Some varieties are large and have powerful fangs with which they can inflict a deep wound. These formidable-looking spiders do not, however, attack man . . ." (Paragraph 2)

2. In the excerpt below, the word *appeased* (ə-pēzd′) means
   A. satisfied.
   B. aroused.
   C. affected.
   D. changed.

   "Tarantulas feed mostly on insects and millipedes. Once their appetite is appeased, they digest the food for several days before eating again." (Paragraph 4)

3. In the excerpt below, the word *evoking* (ĭ-vōk′ĭng) means
   A. using.
   B. challenging.
   C. hiding.
   D. bringing out.

   "To identify the species, the wasp apparently must explore the spider with her antennae. The tarantula shows an amazing tolerance to this exploration. The wasp crawls under it and walks over it without evoking any hostile response." (Paragraph 11)

Central Point and Main Ideas

4. Which sentence best expresses the central point of the selection?
   A. Tarantulas are among the stupidest creatures in the natural world.
   B. The female digger wasp will go to great lengths to ensure that her offspring survive.
   C. Even though a digger wasp can disable and kill a tarantula, tarantulas will survive as a species because they are more fertile than wasps.
   D. In the conflict between digger wasps and tarantulas, the seemingly intelligent wasps win out over the tarantulas, which act instinctively.

5. Which of the following expresses the main idea of paragraphs 5–7?
   A. Spiders, particularly hairy ones such as the tarantula, have an extremely delicate sense of touch.
   B. Tarantulas have hair on their bodies as well as on their legs.
   C. The way that the tarantula responds to touch is dependent partly on whether it is hungry and partly on where it is touched.
   D. A hungry tarantula will attack and kill an insect that touches it, but a tarantula that is not hungry will merely shake the touched limb.

_____ 6. Which sentence best expresses the main idea of paragraph 9?

    A. The solitary wasps are extremely beautiful but live only a few months.

    B. The wasps are beautiful but deadly to tarantulas, which they paralyze in order to feed their young.

    C. The sting of these wasps is much worse than that of a bee or common wasp.

    D. All that the wasp larva needs to survive is a disabled tarantula.

Supporting Details

_____ 7. A female tarantula's care of its young consists of

    A. providing them with dead insects to feed on.

    B. hiding them in a below-ground nest.

    C. hovering nearby to defend them from predators.

    D. enclosing them, as eggs, in a silk cocoon.

_____ 8. Immediately after the digger wasp has satisfied itself that its victim is of the right species, it

    A. digs the tarantula's grave.

    B. stings the tarantula in the space where its leg joins its body.

    C. lays eggs.

    D. grasps one of the tarantula's legs in its powerful jaws.

Transitions

_____ 9. The relationship of the second sentence below to the first sentence is one of

    A. cause and effect.

    B. addition.

    C. contrast.

    D. illustration.

> "At the touch of a cricket's antennae, the tarantula seizes the insect so swiftly that a motion picture taken at the rate of 64 frames per second shows only the result and not the process of capture. But when the spider is not hungry, the stimulation of its hairs merely causes it to shake the touched limb." (Paragraph 6)

Patterns of Organization

_____ 10. The main pattern of organization of paragraphs 12–13 is
- A. time order.
- B. list of items.
- C. definition and example.
- D. comparison.

_____ 11. The main pattern of organization of paragraphs 14–15 is
- A. cause and effect.
- B. list of items.
- C. contrast.
- D. time order.

Inferences

_____ 12. On the basis of paragraphs 14 and 15, we can infer that the author
- A. is disgusted by the wasp's behavior.
- B. fully understands the behavior of the tarantula.
- C. is impressed by the behavior of the wasp but not by the behavior of the tarantula.
- D. is disgusted by the behavior of both the wasp and the tarantula.

_____ 13. We might conclude from the reading that
- A. animals that can modify their behavior to fit certain circumstances have an advantage over animals that cannot.
- B. creatures that cannot reason quickly die out.
- C. in a laboratory setting, tarantulas could probably be trained to attack digger wasps.
- D. the author has made documentary films on the behavior of tarantulas and wasps.

Purpose and Tone

_____ 14. The author's main purpose is to
- A. inform readers about a classic example of intelligence pitted against instinct in the animal kingdom.
- B. persuade readers that all creatures, even insects and spiders, have a right to exist.
- C. entertain us with fascinating yet gory examples of the behavior of wasps and tarantulas.

15. In describing the death struggle between the wasp and the tarantula, the author's tone is one of
    A. horror.
    B. detachment.
    C. admiration.
    D. amusement.

_____16. The general tone of the reading is
    A. sentimental.
    B. critical.
    C. instructive.
    D. sympathetic.

Argument

_____17. Write the letter of the statement that is the point of the following argument. The other statements are support for that point.
    A. The digger wasp pumps poison into the tarantula, which quickly paralyzes it.
    B. The tarantula seems helpless to defend itself against the digger wasp's attack.
    C. Although it is smaller than a tarantula, a digger wasp is the tarantula's worst enemy.
    D. The larva of the digger wasp feeds on the paralyzed tarantula until it is dead.

Critical Reading

_____18. The reading is
    A. mainly fact.
    B. all opinion.
    C. about half fact and half opinion.

_____19. The facts of the reading are probably based on
    A. the author's personal observations.
    B. a great deal of scientific research, including the author's.
    C. one or two cases where digger wasps have been observed to disable tarantulas.
    D. popular accounts of human encounters with tarantulas and wasps.

20. People who argue that it's okay for them to engage in ruthless and selfish behavior on the basis of examples from the animal kingdom are illustrating the fallacy of

    A. either-or *(the argument assumes that there are only two sides to a question).*

    B. false cause *(the argument assumes that the order of events alone shows cause and effect).*

    C. false comparison *(the argument assumes that two things being compared are more alike than they really are).*

    D. straw man *(an argument is made by claiming an opponent holds an extreme position and then opposing that extreme position).*

Outlining

Complete the outline of paragraphs 10–13 of the selection by filling in the missing major and minor details.

Central point: The mother wasp finds and paralyzes an adult tarantula so that her offspring can feed on it.

1. _____

    a. When her egg is almost ready to be laid, she locates a tarantula burrow.

    b. To identify the correct species of tarantula, the wasp explores the tarantula with her antennae.

    c. _____

    _____

2. During the attack

    a. The wasp protrudes her sting.

    b. _____

    _____

    c. The tarantula unsuccessfully tries to get away.

    d. The wasp pumps in poison at the spot where the spider's leg joins its body.

    e. The tarantula becomes paralyzed.

3. After the attack

    a. The wasp cleans herself and sucks some blood from the tarantula's wound.

    b. _____

       _____

    c. She lays her egg and attaches it to the tarantula.

    d. She fills in the grave with soil.

    e. She flies away, leaving her descendant to hatch and feed on the tarantula.

Discussion Questions

1. Many people are frightened or disgusted by spiders and wasps. Yet this writer obviously finds both to be beautiful and fascinating creatures. What details about the wasp and the tarantula surprised or interested you most? What similarities to humans do these two species possess? Finally, what conclusions, if any, can we draw about human behavior on the basis of the interactions between the "intelligent" digger wasps and the "instinctual" tarantulas?

2. To us, the behavior of the tarantula with the digger wasp seems suicidal. Yet common sense tells us that the tarantula does not want to die in order to provide food for the wasp's offspring. What alternative explanations might there be for the tarantula's behavior?

3. Books, articles, and television shows about animal behavior are often very popular, with adults as well as children. How would you explain the fascination that animal behavior holds for people?

4. The tarantula, as a creature of instinct, can't choose whether to fight or flee, but people can. Think of a time when you were faced with a threatening situation. Did you choose to flee—or to fight? What factors in the situation helped you make your decision?

Note: Writing assignments for this selection appear on page 644.

Check Your Performance

THE SPIDER AND THE WASP

Activity	Number Right		Points		Score
Reading Comprehension Questions					
Vocabulary in Context (3 items)	_____	×	4	=	_____
Central Point and Main Ideas (3 items)	_____	×	4	=	_____
Supporting Details (2 items)	_____	×	4	=	_____
Transitions (1 item)	_____	×	4	=	_____
Patterns of Organization (2 items)	_____	×	4	=	_____
Inferences (2 items)	_____	×	4	=	_____
Purpose and Tone (3 items)	_____	×	4	=	_____
Argument (1 item)	_____	×	4	=	_____
Critical Reading (3 items)	_____	×	4	=	_____
Outlining (4 items)	_____	×	5	=	_____
		TOTAL SCORE		=	_____%

Enter your total score into the **Reading Performance Chart: Ten Reading Selections** on the inside back cover.

Part Three

Relationships and Combined-Skills Tests

1 Relationships Tests

Understanding relationships between ideas is a key part of good comprehension. The tests that follow will give you practice at mastering the common types of relationships that have been explained in Chapters 4 and 5 of this book.

RELATIONSHIPS: Test 1

For each pair of sentences below, answer the question about the relationship between the sentences.

_____ 1. ● People have chosen to end their lives in a variety of unusual ways.
● In ancient China, people committed suicide by eating a pound of salt.

What does the second sentence do?

A. It gives unexpected information.
B. It sums up the point raised in the first sentence.
C. It provides an example of what is stated in the first sentence.
D. It repeats the information given in the first sentence.

_____ 2. ● Watching a football game or other sports event on television makes more sense these days than going to the game itself.
● Going to a sports event could cost $50 to $100 for parking and an admission ticket.

What does the second sentence do?

A. It gives a solution to the problem stated in the first sentence.
B. It gives evidence to support the claim made in the first sentence.
C. It gives contradictory information.
D. It repeats the same idea.

_____ 3. ● Television has led voters to place more emphasis on a candidate's physical appearance.
● It's nearly impossible for a homely candidate to be elected President of the United States.

What is the relationship between the two sentences?

A. Addition   C. Contrast
B. Problem and solution   D. Cause and effect

_____ 4. ● Many people fear that if they swim in the ocean, they will be attacked by sharks.
● In the United States, more people are killed by pigs on Iowa farms every year than are killed by sharks.

What does the second sentence do?

A. It presents a solution to the problem mentioned in the first sentence.
B. It gives contradictory information.
C. It reinforces the claim made in the first sentence.
D. It provides an example of what is stated in the first sentence.

_____ 5. ● The belief that spinach is packed with iron actually stems from a researcher's reporting error—the decimal point was put in the wrong place.
● For years, people believed that spinach has ten times more iron than it really does.

How are the two sentences related?

A. They contradict each other.
B. They give a cause and an effect.
C. They repeat the same idea.
D. The second sentence analyzes the claim made in the first sentence.

_____ 6. ● The way we think about life's stages is shaped by society.
● During the Middle Ages, children dressed—and were expected to act—just like little adults.

How are the two sentences related?

A. They give a cause and an effect.
B. They contradict each other.
C. The second sentence provides an example that supports the claim made in the first sentence.
D. The second sentence repeats the information given in the first sentence.

_____ 7. ● In India, many people work barefoot in the fields and have no access to the kind of medical care needed for snakebites.
● It is estimated that somewhere between 10,000 and 30,000 Indians die *every year* after being bitten by poisonous snakes.

What does the second sentence do?

A. It states a result.
B. It provides an example of what is stated in the first sentence.
C. It repeats the information stated in the first sentence.
D. It gives a solution to the problem that is stated in the first sentence.

_____ 8. ● Folk wisdom has long held that when answering questions on multiple-choice tests, students should trust their first instincts.
● A research instructor has found that students who change answers that they're unsure of usually improve their scores.

What does the second sentence do?

A. It presents a solution to the problem mentioned in the first sentence.
B. It explains the effect of the cause mentioned in the first sentence.
C. It gives contradictory information.
D. It provides an example of what is stated in the first sentence.

_____ 9. ● There is a tremendous gap between the wages of the average American wage earner and those of top corporate executives.
● In 2010, chief executives at some of the nation's largest companies earned an average of $11.4 million in total pay—343 times more than a typical American worker.

What does the second sentence do?

A. It explains the effect of a cause mentioned in the first sentence.
B. It presents a solution to the problem mentioned in the first sentence.
C. It sums up the points raised in the first sentence.
D. It gives evidence to support the claim made in the first sentence.

_____ 10. ● If left completely untreated, the bite from a brown recluse spider may cause death in children.
● Children who are bitten by brown recluse spiders should receive prompt medical attention because the bites are sometimes fatal.

What does the second sentence do?

A. It gives unexpected information.
B. It provides an example of what is stated in the first sentence.
C. It sums up the points raised in the first sentence.
D. It repeats the information given in the first sentence.

_____ 11. ● Social media sites like Facebook, MySpace, and Twitter are wonderful ways for people to connect with one another.
● Online bullying has become a huge problem due to social media sites like Facebook, MySpace, and Twitter.

What does the second sentence do?

A. It contrasts with the first sentence.
B. It provides an example.
C. It supports the first sentence.
D. It restates the first sentence.

_____ 12. ● Sugary soft drinks have been found to be a major cause of childhood obesity.
   ● School districts have replaced soft drinks in vending machines and lunchrooms with healthier beverage choices.

What does the second sentence do?

   A. It explains the reason for the result mentioned in the first sentence.
   B. It provides an example of what is stated in the first sentence.
   C. It analyzes the claim made in the first sentence.
   D. It gives a solution to the problem that is stated in the first sentence.

_____ 13. ● Certain significant differences exist between the House of Representatives and the Senate.
   ● The most obvious difference, of course, is size—the House has 435 members, while the Senate has 100.

What does the second sentence do?

   A. It gives unexpected information.
   B. It repeats the information given in the first sentence.
   C. It gives evidence to support the claim made in the first sentence.
   D. It draws a conclusion about what is stated in the first sentence.

_____ 14. ● People eat fewer hamburgers today than they did in the past.
   ● Fast-food restaurants have had to develop new items for their menus.

What does the second sentence do?

   A. It repeats the information given in the first sentence.
   B. It gives unexpected information.
   C. It explains the effect of the cause mentioned in the first sentence.
   D. It gives evidence to support the claim made in the first sentence.

_____ 15. ● Some fairy tales are particularly gruesome.
   ● In one version of "Cinderella," Cinderella's cruel stepsisters cut off pieces of their feet to make the glass slippers fit them and later have their eyes pecked out by a flock of birds.

How are the two sentences related?

   A. They give a cause and an effect.
   B. They repeat the same idea.
   C. They contradict each other.
   D. The second sentence provides an example of what is stated in the first sentence.

_____ 16. ● Traffic accidents are the leading cause of death for teenagers.
           ● States have imposed limits on the number of passengers a teenage driver can have.

What does the second sentence do?

A. It gives unexpected information.
B. It gives a solution to the problem stated in the first sentence.
C. It analyzes the claim made in the first sentence.
D. It repeats the information given in the first sentence.

_____ 17. ● After Japan bombed Pearl Harbor in 1941, the U.S. government sent thousands of Japanese-American citizens to live in prison-like internment camps.
           ● The only Americans ever convicted of aiding Japan during World War II were white.

What does the second sentence do?

A. It gives a solution to the problem that is stated in the first sentence.
B. It explains the reason for the result mentioned in the first sentence.
C. It gives unexpected information.
D. It draws a conclusion about what is stated in the first sentence.

_____ 18. ● Airline travel has become unpleasant due to burdensome security measures.
           ● It's no fun to fly anymore because going through airline security is so tiresome.

What does the second sentence do?

A. It gives unexpected information.
B. It repeats the information given in the first sentence.
C. It draws a conclusion about what is stated in the first sentence.
D. It provides an example of what is stated in the first sentence.

_____ 19. ● In America, lawns are an energy-intensive, wasteful, and non-productive form of landscaping.
           ● Achieving a picture-perfect lawn requires gallons of expensive fertilizer and hazardous pesticides that pollute groundwater, lakes, and rivers.

How are the two sentences related?

A. They give a cause and an effect.
B. The second sentence supports the claim made in the first sentence.
C. The second sentence presents a solution to the problem mentioned in the first sentence.
D. The second sentence repeats the information given in the first sentence.

_____ 20. ● A recent study found that television and video games increase teenagers' and young adults' risk of developing attention disorders.
● Some parents are setting limits on the amount of time their children spend watching TV and playing video games.

What does the second sentence do?

A. It gives unexpected information.
B. It sums up the point raised in the first sentence.
C. It gives a solution to the problem that is stated in the first sentence.
D. It provides an example of what is stated in the first sentence.

_____ 21. ● In the 1980s, many manufacturing jobs, especially in the steel and auto industries, were transferred from the United States to Third World countries.
● Millions of blue-collar workers in the Midwest and Northeast became unemployed or underemployed.

What does the second sentence do?

A. It presents a solution to the problem mentioned in the first sentence.
B. It gives contradictory information.
C. It explains the effect of the cause mentioned in the first sentence.
D. It provides an example of what is stated in the first sentence.

_____ 22. ● Dictators often come from the outskirts of a society, rather than from its center.
● French dictator Napoleon Bonaparte came from the Mediterranean island of Corsica, while Adolf Hitler was Austrian, not German.

What does the second sentence do?

A. It provides examples of what is stated in the first sentence.
B. It gives contradictory information.
C. It draws a conclusion about what is stated in the first sentence.
D. It explains the effect of the cause mentioned in the first sentence.

_____ 23. ● In the late 1800s, girls were often discouraged by doctors from taking part in team sports because of fear of injury or illness.
● Many "experts" in the latter decades of the 1800s insisted that girls were not physically strong enough to take part in sports such as baseball and basketball.

How are the two sentences related?

A. They give a cause and an effect.
B. They contradict each other.
C. They repeat the same information.
D. The second sentence analyzes the claim made in the first sentence.

_____ 24. ● For many years grizzly bears were killed for their fur, their skulls, and often just because they looked so fierce.

● Over the past 100 years or so, humans have reduced the grizzly population in the lower 48 states of the U.S. from 50,000 to 1,000.

What does the second sentence do?

A. It gives unexpected information.

B. It provides an example of what is stated in the first sentence.

C. It analyzes the claim made in the first sentence.

D. It states a result.

_____ 25. ● Maternal stress during pregnancy may have negative consequences for the fetus.

● In one well-known study, the risk that a child would grow up to develop schizophrenia was higher when the mother had experienced the death of a close relative during the first trimester of pregnancy.

What does the second sentence do?

A. It presents a solution to the problem mentioned in the first sentence.

B. It gives contradictory information.

C. It reinforces the claim made in the first sentence.

D. It draws a conclusion about what is stated in the first sentence.

RELATIONSHIPS: Test 2

For each pair of sentences below, answer the question about the relationship between the sentences.

___B___ 1. ● Some people work only to pay the bills.
● For others, however, work is a key part of their self-image.

What is the relationship between the two sentences?

A. Time   C. Problem and solution
B. Contrast   D. Cause and effect

___D___ 2. ● Frequently, people who perform a certain job will develop a jargon, or specialized language.
● For instance, air traffic controllers refer to what they do as "pushing tin," while police refer to suspects as "perps."

What is the relationship between the two sentences?

A. Cause and effect   C. Time
B. Addition   D. Statement and example

___C___ 3. ● Jane Goodall was the first researcher to observe chimps in the wild making and using tools.
● Furthermore, Goodall discovered that chimps often kill and eat other animals.

What is the relationship between the two sentences?

A. Cause and effect   C. Addition
B. Statement and example   D. Time

___C___ 4. ● Many Hispanic girls celebrate their fifteenth birthday in a special way.
● Similarly, Anglo girls have a special party for their "sweet" sixteenth birthday.

What is the relationship between the two sentences?

A. Addition   C. Comparison
B. Cause and effect   D. Statement and example

___B___ 5. ● Illegal drug labs can manufacture methamphetamine using ingredients found in over-the-counter cold or allergy medicines.
● Stores now allow customers to purchase only small quantities of such medicines and require customers to show identification before purchasing them.

What is the relationship between the two sentences?

A. Contrast   C. Statement and example
B. Problem and solution   D. Addition

_B_ 6. ● Educational programs such as *Sesame Street* have been shown to improve language and social skills in children aged 3 and up.
   ● But show the same programs to younger children, and their language skills will actually develop more slowly.

What is the relationship between the two sentences?

   A. Cause and effect   c. Addition
   B. Contrast   D. Statement and example

_D_ 7. ● When movies such as *101 Dalmatians* or *Beverly Hills Chihuahua* are released, many people rush out to buy the breed of dog featured in the movie.
   ● Later, many of these same people abandon the dogs after they tire of them.

What is the relationship between the two sentences?

   A. Contrast   c. Addition
   B. Statement and example   D. Time

_____ 8. ● In early America, one image that often appeared on gravestones was the death's head: a grinning skull.
   ● Another common image on gravestones was a cherub: a smiling, baby-faced angel.

What is the relationship between the two sentences?

   A. Contrast   c. Statement and example
   B. Problem and solution   D. Addition

_____ 9. ● Disposable plastic shopping bags fill up landfills and litter vacant lots, parks, and fields.
   ● Supermarkets have begun selling inexpensive, reusable cloth shopping bags.

What is the relationship between the two sentences?

   A. Contrast   c. Statement and example
   B. Problem and solution   D. Addition

_____ 10. ● Lions are fearsome hunters that can tear apart their prey in minutes.
   ● Yet all over the United States, there are people who keep lions and other wild cats as household pets.

What is the relationship between the two sentences?

   A. Cause and effect   c. Comparison
   B. Time   D. Contrast

_____ 11. ● A number of our words are derived from the names of ancient Roman gods and goddesses.
● Specifically, the word *cereal* comes from Ceres, the harvest goddess, while *volcano* comes from Vulcan, the god of fire.

What is the relationship between the two sentences?

A. Contrast   C. Statement and example
B. Problem and solution   D. Addition

_____ 12. ● Our kidneys, using nearly two million tiny filters, remove impurities from our blood.
● Then the liver works to flush those impurities out of our body.

What is the relationship between the two sentences?

A. Cause and effect   C. Comparison
B. Time   D. Contrast

_____ 13. ● The first railroad cars were very similar to horse-drawn carriages.
● Both were called "coaches" and held just six passengers.

What is the relationship between the two sentences?

A. Cause and effect   C. Comparison
B. Time   D. Contrast

_____ 14. ● Because boys are assumed to be better able to provide for their parents, people in rural China and India would often rather have sons than daughters.
● As a result, millions of female fetuses have been aborted, resulting in more boys being born than girls.

What is the relationship between the two sentences?

A. Cause and effect   C. Addition
B. Statement and example   D. Time

_____ 15. ● First of all, walking is excellent exercise.
● Secondly, walking lets you chat with your neighbors and see for yourself what's going on in your community.

What is the relationship between the two sentences?

A. Cause and effect   C. Addition
B. Statement and example   D. Contrast

_____ 16. ● More and more people have been getting their news online, leading many newspapers to experience a decline in readership.
● Newspapers have decided to offer readers subscriptions to online editions at less than the cost of home delivery.

What is the relationship between the two sentences?

A. Comparison   C. Addition
B. Time   D. Problem and solution

_____ 17. ● Many Japanese are turning away from their traditional low-fat diet of rice, fish, chicken, and vegetables and eating more Western foods that are high in fat.
● About a quarter of adult Japanese are now considered significantly overweight.

What is the relationship between the two sentences?

A. Problem and solution   C. Cause and effect
B. Statement and example   D. Time

_____ 18. ● On the night of April 14, 1865, John Wilkes Booth assassinated President Lincoln as Lincoln sat watching a play at Ford's Theater in Washington, D.C.
● Afterward, Booth escaped on horseback to Maryland before heading to Virginia, where he was finally cornered and killed.

What is the relationship between the two sentences?

A. Cause and effect   C. Time
B. Statement and example   D. Addition

_____ 19. ● Heavy drinking has no proven health benefits.
● However, moderate drinking has been connected to reduced risk of cardiovascular disease, the number one killer in the United States.

What is the relationship between the two sentences?

A. Cause and effect   C. Addition
B. Contrast   D. Problem and solution

_____ 20. ● "Why did you leave your last job?" can be a difficult question to answer during job interviews.
● If you were fired, talk about personality conflicts, but without blaming anyone.

What is the relationship between the two sentences?

A. Contrast   C. Statement and example
B. Problem and solution   D. Addition

_____ 21. ● Future Hall of Fame baseball player Jackie Robinson refused to move to the back of a bus while stationed at Fort Hood in Texas in 1944.
● Likewise, in 1955, Rosa Parks of Montgomery, Alabama, refused to obey a local ordinance requiring black people to sit at the back of city buses.

What is the relationship between the two sentences?

A. Cause and effect   C. Comparison
B. Addition   D. Contrast

_____ 22. ● People who smoke generally have more health problems than non-smokers.

● Consequently, large employers such as Walmart have begun requiring smokers to pay much more for health coverage than nonsmokers.

What is the relationship between the two sentences?

A. Cause and effect   C. Statement and example

B. Addition   D. Comparison

_____ 23. ● One thing to avoid when arguing is bringing up unrelated issues from other situations.

● Also, it's wise to avoid using your knowledge of a person to humiliate him or her.

What is the relationship between the two sentences?

A. Cause and effect   C. Time

B. Addition   D. Contrast

_____ 24. ● Human beings often speak of machines as if the machines were alive.

● For instance, cars don't just break down—they die; while computers don't power down—they sleep.

What is the relationship between the two sentences?

A. Contrast   C. Statement and example

B. Problem and solution   D. Addition

_____ 25. ● In 1985, inventor Steve Jobs was fired from the company he had helped to found, Apple Computer.

● Jobs eventually returned to Apple and spearheaded the development of the iPod, iPhone, and iPad.

What is the relationship between the two sentences?

A. Cause and effect   C. Comparison

B. Addition   D. Time

RELATIONSHIPS: Test 3

For each pair of sentences below, answer the question about the relationship between the sentences.

_____ 1. ● A number of Southwestern cities are experiencing water shortages.
      ● Residents of Tucson, Arizona have begun to irrigate their trees and plants with recycled water from their sinks and washing machines.

What is the relationship between the two sentences?

A. Contrast   C. Addition
B. Comparison   D. Problem and solution

_____ 2. ● Researchers have found that the more children are exposed to profanity, the more likely they are to use swear words themselves.
      ● Those who used profanity are also more likely to become aggressive toward others.

What is the relationship between the two sentences?

A. Time   C. Addition
B. Statement and example   D. Contrast

_____ 3. ● Professional athletes tend to be superstitious.
      ● Hoping to continue his college success, Michael Jordan wore his University of North Carolina shorts under his Bulls shorts in every NBA game he played.

What is the relationship between the two sentences?

A. Cause and effect   C. Contrast
B. Statement and example   D. Comparison

_____ 4. ● Many great writers, artists, and musicians were poor and unknown in their own lifetimes.
      ● J. K. Rowling, author of the Harry Potter books, is one of the wealthiest women in the world.

What is the relationship between the two sentences?

A. Cause and effect   C. Contrast
B. Statement and example   D. Comparison

_____ 5. ● In the past forty years, a great many women have entered the workplace.
      ● Wives are much less dependent on men for economic support.

What is the relationship between the two sentences?

A. Comparison   C. Addition
B. Time   D. Cause and effect

6. ● In the first decade of the 1900s, automobile drivers bought gasoline at general stores, hardware stores, and even blacksmith shops.
   ● In 1913, the first "drive-in" gas station opened to the public in Pittsburgh, PA.

   What is the relationship between the two sentences?

   A. Comparison   C. Addition
   B. Time   D. Cause and effect

7. ● All small children need the help of others to feed and clothe themselves.
   ● Many elderly people need help with eating, drinking, and dressing themselves.

   What is the relationship between the two sentences?

   A. Comparison   C. Problem and solution
   B. Time   D. Contrast

8. ● The traffic on Route 417 backs up for miles during rush hour.
   ● The state has approved funds to build a new high-speed rail line that will run parallel to Route 417.

   What is the relationship between the two sentences?

   A. Comparison   C. Problem and solution
   B. Time   D. Contrast

9. ● Despite brawls caused by drunken fans, it is virtually impossible to eliminate alcohol from baseball stadiums.
   ● A major reason is that key sponsors of baseball games are beer manufacturers such as Coors, Miller, and Busch.

   What is the relationship between the two sentences?

   A. Addition   C. Contrast
   B. Problem and solution D. Cause and effect

10. ● A number of fatal car crashes have been caused by drivers who were text-messaging.
    ● Many people continue to text-message while driving.

    What is the relationship between the two sentences?

    A. Comparison   C. Problem and solution
    B. Statement and example D. Contrast

11. ● Mummies can be dried in the sun, with fire or smoke, or with chemicals.
    ● Furthermore, permanent freezing can produce a mummy.

    What is the relationship between the two sentences?

    A. Comparison   C. Time
    B. Addition   D. Cause and effect

_____ C 12.
- At about six months, babies begin to repeat simple sounds.
- At about nine or ten months, babies can repeat sounds and carry on little "conversations."

What is the relationship between the two sentences?

A. Statement and example   C. Time
B. Addition   D. Cause and effect

_____ B 13.
- It appears that humans are not the only creatures who will risk their lives to help others.
- Recently, onlookers watched in amazement as a dog raced out into traffic to pull to safety another dog that had been hit by a car.

What is the relationship between the two sentences?

A. Cause and effect   C. Problem and solution
B. Statement and example   D. Contrast

_____ A 14.
- In England, Charles Dickens' famous novel *Oliver Twist* exposed British readers to the cruel conditions suffered by orphaned children in workhouses.
- Upton Sinclair's shocking novel *The Jungle* exposed American readers to the filthy conditions common in Chicago's meat-packing plants.

What is the relationship between the two sentences?

A. Comparison   C. Problem and solution
B. Contrast   D. Cause and effect

_____ C 15.
- In the 1950s, horror movies such as *Godzilla* and *The Deadly Mantis* featured oversized radioactive monsters.
- *It Came From Beneath the Sea*, another 1950s horror movie, featured a giant octopus that tried to destroy San Francisco.

What is the relationship between the two sentences?

A. Contrast   C. Addition
B. Time   D. Cause and effect

_____ B 16.
- HIV/AIDS is spread when addicts who inject drugs share needles.
- Some health organizations distribute free needles to intravenous drug users.

What is the relationship between the two sentences?

A. Contrast   C. Statement and example
B. Problem and solution   D. Addition

17. ● The heavy use of fertilizers has made it possible for farmers to get a higher yield per acre than ever before.

● Fertilizers run off into rivers, lakes, and bays, polluting them and killing off fish.

What is the relationship between the two sentences?

A. Contrast   C. Addition
B. Problem and solution   D. Statement and example

18. ● Despite their gruesome appearance, maggots have genuine medical uses.

● Maggots have been used to consume dead tissue, kill harmful bacteria, and stimulate healing in sores caused by diabetes.

What is the relationship between the two sentences?

A. Time   C. Problem and solution
B. Statement and example   D. Comparison

19. ● Until the mid-1990s, developers built enclosed shopping malls and renovated older outdoor malls, turning them into enclosed ones.

● Now it is once again fashionable to build open-air malls.

What is the relationship between the two sentences?

A. Time   C. Problem and solution
B. Statement and example   D. Comparison

20. ● Bigger, more aggressive children are more likely to try to bully smaller, quieter children.

● Moreover, exposure to violence in the home is a factor in bullying.

What is the relationship between the two sentences?

A. Time   C. Cause and effect
B. Statement and example   D. Addition

21. ● In the United States the percentage of the population over 65 is expected to rise from about 35 million in 2000 to an estimated 71 million in 2030.

● The number of assisted living facilities has greatly increased, along with the need for nurses, nursing assistants, and home health aides.

What is the relationship between the two sentences?

A. Time   C. Cause and effect
B. Statement and example   D. Addition

_22._ ● The invention of the printing press revolutionized the way people learned news and ideas.

● The Internet has changed the way in which people obtain information and communicate.

What is the relationship between the two sentences?

A. Comparison
B. Cause and effect
C. Statement and example
D. Addition

_23._ ● What you consider a "normal" diet depends on where you live.

● Stink bugs are popular in Indonesia, grasshoppers are eaten in Mexico, and tuna eyeballs are consumed in Japan and China.

What is the relationship between the two sentences?

A. Comparison
B. Cause and effect
C. Statement and example
D. Addition

_24._ ● In 1978, former First Lady Betty Ford became one of the first people in public life to speak openly about her struggles with alcoholism.

● After her recovery, she established the Betty Ford Center in Rancho Mirage, California, for the treatment of chemical dependency.

What is the relationship between the two sentences?

A. Comparison
B. Time
C. Addition
D. Problem and solution

_25._ ● Test scores of American students have fallen behind those of students in other industrialized nations.

● Some schools have increased the number of hours in the school day and reduced the length of summer vacation.

What is the relationship between the two sentences?

A. Time
B. Statement and example
C. Problem and solution
D. Comparison

2 Combined-Skills Tests

Following are twenty-five tests that cover many of the skills taught in Part One and reinforced in Part Two of this book. Each test consists of a short reading passage followed by questions on any of the following: vocabulary in context, central points and main ideas, supporting details, relationships, inferences, purpose and tone, argument, and critical reading.

COMBINED SKILLS: Test 1

Read the passage below. Then write the letter of the best answer to each question that follows.

[1]An abundance of research shows how self-fulfilling prophecies can affect job performance. [2]For example:

- [3]A group of clerks at the U.S. Census Bureau was told they were expected to punch about 550 cards per day. [4]They were also told that processing more cards might cause stress. [5]A second group was not given any limits or warnings; they were told to punch as many cards as they could. [6]The first group averaged 550 cards and indeed reported stress when they tried to do more. [7]The second group averaged almost 2,000 cards a day with no signs of stress.

- [8]Military personnel who were randomly labeled as having high potential performed up to the expectations of their superiors. [9]They were also more likely to volunteer for dangerous special duty.

- [10]A group of welders with relatively equal aptitudes began training. [11]Everyone, including the trainer, was told that five of the welders had higher scores on an aptitude test—even though they were chosen randomly. [12]All five finished at the top of the class. [13]They had fewer absences and significantly higher final test scores. [14]Most impressively, they learned the skills of their trade twice as quickly as those who weren't identified as being so talented.

[15]Many more studies of self-fulfilling prophecies show how managers can help employees become more productive by communicating high expectations. [16]While this is valuable information for supervisors, self-fulfilling prophecies can assist those in nonmanagerial positions as well. [17]Having positive expectations and communicating them confidently is an asset in any field or position. [18]The salesperson who approaches a client or customer with high expectations ("I can succeed here") and then behaves accordingly is more likely to be successful that those with lower hopes. [19]It may sound simple, but research confirms that positive expectations can lead to positive communication, which can lead to positive results.

_____ 1. In sentences 10 and 11, the word *aptitudes* means

    A. ages.   C. skills.

    B. work habits.   D. experience.

_____ 2. According to the selection, which of the following did ***not*** happen after five welders were told that they had higher aptitude scores than others in their group?

    A. All five finished at the top of their class.

    B. They had fewer absences and higher final test scores than the rest of the group.

    C. They were given cash bonuses for outperforming others in the class.

    D. They learned the skills of their trade twice as fast as the other workers.

_____ 3. In general, this passage
    A. contrasts supervisors who communicate high expectations with those who don't.
    B. compares government clerks and military personnel with workers in private industry.
    C. lists various factors that enable some workers to outperform others.
    D. illustrates how self-fulfilling prophecies affect job performance.

_____ 4. The relationship of sentence 4 to sentence 3 is one of
    A. illustration.
    B. addition.
    C. cause and effect.
    D. comparison.

_____ 5. We can conclude from the first paragraph that
    A. government clerks tend to be lazy.
    B. punching cards all day is very stressful.
    C. people tend to perform up or down to whatever is expected of them.
    D. the second group of clerks included naturally faster workers than the first group.

_____ 6. The selection suggests that
    A. people who tend to think positively are more likely to be successful than people who tend to think negatively.
    B. people with high expectations don't need to work hard in order to succeed.
    C. there is not much managers can do to help employees who are not naturally positive.
    D. there has been little research done as to what motivates people to succeed.

_____ 7. The author's main purpose is to
    A. inform readers about the power of self-fulfilling prophecies.
    B. entertain readers with stories about how workers can be manipulated to work harder.
    C. persuade readers to become more positive.

_____ 8. Which statement best expresses the central point of the selection?
    A. Self-fulfilling prophecies can affect job performance.
    B. It is easy to motivate today's workers to succeed.
    C. There has been a great deal of research devoted to self-fulfilling prophecies.
    D. To improve their own job performance, today's managers need to keep up with current research.

COMBINED SKILLS: Test 2

Read the passage below. Then write the letter of the best answer to each question that follows.

[1]Each year, two college sports—football and men's basketball—generate more than $6 billion in revenue. [2]This sum is more than that generated by the entire National Basketball Association. [3]And what portion of this revenue do the athletes get? [4]Nothing. [5]They are supposed to be content with a scholarship that does not even cover the full cost of attending college. [6]The time has come to admit that college football and men's basketball are big business and pay the athletes. [7]The first element to realistically doing so is for college coaches to offer athletes real contracts, just as professional teams do. [8]One school might think a star halfback is worth $40,000 a year; another might think he is worth $60,000. [9]When the player chooses a school, money will inevitably be part of the equation. [10]The second element is a salary cap for every team, along with a minimum annual salary for every scholarship athlete. [11]A realistic salary cap might be $3 million for the salaries for the football team, and $650,000 for basketball, with a minimum salary of $25,000 per athlete. [12]Since college football and basketball players must spend so much of their time on the playing field or court, every athlete who stays in school for four years would also get an additional two-year scholarship, which he could use either to complete his bachelor's degree or get a master's degree. [13]That's the third element. [14]The fourth element would be that each athlete would have lifetime health insurance. [15]This is a reasonable requirement because of the heavy physical toll that playing college football or basketball takes on athletes. [16]Finally, an organization would be created to represent both current and former college athletes. [17]This organization would manage the health insurance, negotiate with the N.C.A.A. to set the salary caps and salary minimums, distribute royalties, and serve as an all-around counterweight to the N.C.A.A. [18]Paying college athletes would probably eliminate most of the scandals that involve players taking money. [19]They wouldn't need to take money "under the table" because they would be paid for their work.

_____ 1. In sentence 9, the word *inevitably* means
   A. certainly.   B. unfortunately.
   C. sometimes.   D. secretly.

_____ 2. Which of the following is **not** mentioned in this passage as something that college athletes should receive?
   A. The right to choose the school that offers him the most money.
   B. Lifetime health insurance.
   C. An additional two-year scholarship if he stays in school for two years.
   D. The right to continue receiving a salary even if he can no longer play college football or basketball.

_____ 3. The relationship of the first part of sentence 12 to the second part is one of
    A. addition.
    B. contrast.
    C. cause and effect.
    D. time.

_____ 4. Sentences 7–19 mainly
    A. present reasons why college football and male basketball players should be paid.
    B. contrast college athletes with professional athletes.
    C. illustrate the challenges college football and male basketball players face in balancing athletics and class work.
    D. list elements of a plan that would pay college football and male basketball players what they are worth.

_____ 5. The author would probably agree with which of the following statements?
    A. The N.C.A.A. currently does a great job of serving the interests of college athletes.
    B. The N.C.A.A. currently serves the business interests of colleges better than it serves college athletes.
    C. The N.C.A.A. should be abolished.
    D. The N.C.A.A. is not as powerful today as it once was.

_____ 6. Sentence 18 is a statement of
    A. fact.
    B. opinion.

_____ 7. The purpose of this selection is to
    A. inform.
    B. persuade.
    C. both inform and persuade.
    D. entertain.

_____ 8. The main idea of this passage is found in its
    A. first sentence.
    B. fifth sentence.
    C. sixth sentence.
    D. seventh sentence.

COMBINED SKILLS: Test 3

Read the passage below. Then write the letter of the best answer to each question that follows.

¹Indulging oneself is a common coping strategy that proves of almost no value in helping us deal with problems. ²Consider the example of Doug, whose girlfriend of 18 months has just broken up with him. ³In response, Doug has dived into a number of self-indulgent habits that he had previously held to a minimum. ⁴He is smoking at least a pack of cigarettes a day. ⁵As soon as he is home from work, he pours himself a slug of Jack Daniels—a beverage he continues to sip throughout the evening until he passes out. ⁶On the weekends, he hits a nearby casino with some fellow single friends and gambles far more than he can afford to lose.

⁷Doug would describe each of these behaviors—smoking, drinking, and gambling—as pleasurable. ⁸And yet, when practiced to excess, each of them has a negative effect on his overall well-being. ⁹None of them addresses the problem that is the source of his stress—why his relationship with his girlfriend has ended.

¹⁰People who respond to stressful events by indulging themselves are attempting to compensate, or make up for, a lack of satisfaction in one area of their lives by providing themselves with an alternate form of satisfaction. ¹¹Drinking, smoking, binge eating, shopping sprees, drug use, and gambling are all forms of self-indulgence commonly used to compensate for stressful events. ¹²Not surprisingly, this form of coping leads to its own problems, in the shape of poor physical health, addiction, and financial problems.

¹³A recent form of this maladaptive coping style is seen in people who respond to the stress of daily life by spending excessive amounts of time online. ¹⁴Some people become so immersed in the virtual world of online games, websites, social networking, and so on, that it seems no exaggeration to call them "Internet addicts." ¹⁵People who spend an inordinate amount of time on the Internet often describe themselves as feeling empty, lost, depressed, and anxious when they are not able to be online. ¹⁶Their real-life relationships, as well as their ability to function at work or at school, suffer as they become more immersed in their online activities. ¹⁷Like other forms of self-indulgence as a coping strategy, Internet overuse can end up creating, rather than solving, problems in the subject's life.

_____ 1. In sentence 15, the word *inordinate* means
   A. modest.   C. excessive.
   B. relaxing.   D. unusual.

_____ 2. According to the selection, the source of Doug's stress is
   A. his excessive drinking.
   B. the fact that he often gambles far more than he can afford to lose.
   C. the fact that he spends so much time online that he has little time for the people in his life.
   D. his breakup with his girlfriend.

_____ 3. According to the selection, smoking, drinking, and gambling
   A. are pleasurable.
   B. always have a negative effect on a person's well-being.
   C. are harmful when practiced to excess.
   D. are less harmful than being addicted to the Internet.

_____ 4. In general, the selection
   A. contrasts people who respond to the stresses of daily life in a positive way with those who do not.
   B. discusses self-indulgence as a coping strategy and explains why it can create problems in one's life.
   C. lists factors that cause people to engage in self-indulgent behavior.
   D. compares addiction to substances such as drugs, alcohol, and food with Internet addiction.

_____ 5. The relationship of sentence 11 to sentence 10 is one of
   A. illustration.
   B. time.
   C. cause and effect.
   D. contrast.

_____ 6. The passage suggests that the author
   A. is himself immersed in the virtual world of the Internet.
   B. is a recovering alcoholic.
   C. knows something about psychology.
   D. has family members who engage in self-indulgent behavior.

_____ 7. The tone of this passage is
   A. anxious and concerned.
   B. straightforward and instructive.
   C. mocking and sarcastic.
   D. warm and encouraging.

_____ 8. Which statement best expresses the central point of the passage?
   A. Self-indulgent behavior such as drinking and smoking can lead to serious health problems.
   B. Just as some people become addicted to drugs or drinking, it is no exaggeration to call other people "Internet addicts."
   C. Self-indulgence as a coping strategy can end up creating rather than solving problems in one's life.
   D. Drinking to excess, smoking, and gambling to excess are all examples of self-indulgent behavior.

COMBINED SKILLS: Test 4

Read the passage below. Then write the letter of the best answer to each question that follows.

[1]Animal researchers are rethinking their belief that play fights between animals are practice for the real thing. [2]A key piece of evidence that play fighting isn't about learning how to win is the fact that all animals both win and lose their play fights. [3]No young animal ever wins all his play fights; if he did, nobody would play with him. [4]When a juvenile animal is bigger, stronger, older, and more dominant than the other animal he is play fighting with, the bigger animal will roll over on his back and lose on purpose a certain amount of the time. [5]That's called *self-handicapping*, and all animals do it, maybe because if they didn't do it, their smaller friends would stop playing with them. [6]This is also called *role reversal*, because the winner and the loser reverse roles.

[7]Role reversal is such a basic part of roughhouse play that animals do it when they play games like tug-of-war, too. [8]A friend told me a story about her mixed-breed dog, when he was a year old and fully grown, playing with the four-month-old Labrador puppy next door. [9]The two dogs liked to play tug-of-war with a rope toy my friend had out on her terrace, but of course my friend's dog was so huge compared to the puppy that it was no contest. [10]If he used all his strength, he'd end up just whipping the puppy around the terrace like a Frisbee.

[11]But that's not what happened. [12]Pretty soon my friend noticed that the puppy was "winning" some of the tugs. [13]First my friend's mutt would pull the puppy across the terrace; then the puppy would pull him back a bit. [14]My friend said her dog was "keeping the puppy in the game," and I'm sure she's right.

[15]Some animal researchers say that the fact that all animals self-handicap might mean that the purpose of play fighting isn't to teach animals how to win, but to teach them how to win and lose. [16]All animals probably need to know both the dominant and the subordinate role, because no animal starts out on top, and no animal who lives to old age ends up on top, either. [17]Even a male who is going to end up as the alpha starts out young and vulnerable. [18]He has to know how to exhibit proper subordinate behaviors.

_____ 1. In sentence 18, the word *subordinate* means
  A. bossy.
  B. lower in rank.
  C. harmful.
  D. playful.

_____ 2. According to some researchers, the fact that animals self-handicap might mean
   A. that they are imitating human behavior.
   B. that no animal starts out on top.
   C. that they need to learn both winning and losing behaviors.
   D. that they need to learn dominant behavior.

_____ 3. What is the relationship of paragraphs 2 and 3 to paragraph 1?
   A. Time order
   B. List of items
   C. Illustration
   D. Cause and effect

_____ 4. We can infer that the author's attitude toward dogs is
   A. amused and carefree.
   B. superior but tolerant.
   C. detached and critical.
   D. understanding and approving.

_____ 5. We can reasonably conclude from this selection that
   A. animal behavior is more complex than researchers previously thought.
   B. dogs dislike losing and will do anything to avoid it.
   C. dogs behave differently with each other when they know they are being watched.
   D. once an animal is dominant, he stays that way for life.

_____ 6. The tone of this passage is best described as
   A. dull and scientific.
   B. informal yet informative.
   C. preachy.
   D. sarcastic.

_____ 7. Which is the most appropriate title for this selection?
   A. Myths about Animals
   B. Two Dogs at Play
   C. Animal Role Reversal during Play
   D. A Kind-Hearted Big Dog

_____ 8. Which statement best expresses the central point of the selection?
   A. A grown dog will occasionally let a puppy win at tug-of-war to "keep him in the game."
   B. Some animal researchers no longer believe that play fights between animals are practice for the real thing.
   C. Animals practice role reversal while play fighting because they need to know both the dominant and subordinate roles.
   D. It can be entertaining and informative to watch two dogs at play.

COMBINED SKILLS: Test 5

Read the passage below. Then write the letter of the best answer to each question that follows.

> [1]While previous generations of American students have had to sit through tests, never have the tests been given so frequently, and never have they played such a prominent role in schooling. [2]Exams used to be administered mostly to decide where to place kids or what kind of help they needed; only recently have scores been published in the newspaper and used as the primary criteria for judging children, teachers, and schools—indeed, as the basis for flunking students or denying them a diploma, deciding where money should be spent, and so on. [3]Tests have lately become a mechanism by which public officials can impose their will on schools, and they are doing so with a vengeance.
>
> [4]This situation is also unusual from an international perspective. [5]"Few countries today give these formal examinations to students before the age of sixteen or so," two scholars report. [6]In the U.S., we give standardized tests to children as young as *six*, despite the fact that almost all experts in early childhood education condemn this practice. [7]And it isn't easy to find other countries that give multiple-choice tests to students of any age.
>
> [8]In short, our children are tested to an extent that is unprecedented in our history and unparalleled anywhere else in the world. [9]Rather than seeing this as odd, or something that needs to be defended, many of us have come to take it for granted. [10]The result is that most of today's discourse about education has been reduced to a crude series of monosyllables: "Test scores are too low. Make them go up."

_____ 1. In sentence 10, the word *discourse* means
    A. warning.
    B. discussion.
    C. curriculum.
    D. agreement.

_____ 2. Paragraph 2
    A. provides reasons why American students take so many standardized tests.
    B. compares former and current American attitudes toward standardized testing.
    C. contrasts American testing of students with practices in other countries.
    D. lists examples of current standardized tests.

_____ 3. According to the selection, public officials use standardized tests to
   A. decide where to place kids or what kind of help they need.
   B. humiliate failing students.
   C. decide where to enroll their own children.
   D. recklessly impose their will on schools.

_____ 4. The passage suggests that administering standardized tests to children as young as six
   A. is helpful in determining whether a particular student should be promoted.
   B. is not beneficial to the children involved.
   C. is crucial to judging their academic ability.
   D. is seldom done in America.

_____ 5. We can infer that the author of this passage believes that standardized tests in America
   A. detract from more important aspects of education.
   B. should play a larger part in judging children, teachers, and schools.
   C. have drawbacks, but are the most accurate method of judging the quality of education.
   D. are entirely without value and should be eliminated.

_____ 6. The author's tone with regard to standardized testing as used today in America can best be described as
   A. sorrowful.
   B. disapproving.
   C. bewildered.
   D. matter-of-fact.

_____ 7. Sentence 6 is a statement of
   A. fact.
   B. opinion.
   C. fact and opinion.

_____ 8. Which of the following statements best expresses the central point of the selection?
   A. American schoolchildren are subjected to far too many standardized tests.
   B. American public officials are overly concerned about standardized test scores.
   C. Children in other countries generally take far fewer standardized tests than American children do.
   D. Scores on standardized tests have been declining for decades.

COMBINED SKILLS: Test 6

Read the passage below. Then write the letter of the best answer to each question that follows.

[1]Some psychologists are interested in resilience: the ability to "bounce back," recovering one's self-confidence, good spirits, and hopeful attitude, after extreme or prolonged stress. [2]In particular, psychologists want to understand why some children who grow up in adverse circumstances (such as extreme poverty, dangerous neighborhoods, abusive parents, and/or exposure to drugs and alcohol) become well-adjusted adults, whereas others remain troubled—and frequently get into trouble—throughout their lives.

[3]One team of researchers identified 240 high-risk children in Hawaii who had experienced stress at birth, poverty, and family conflict, and followed their development for 40 years. [4]Two-thirds of the children became involved in crime, but one-third became confident, competent, caring adults. [5]The resilient members of this sample tended to be affectionate and outgoing from birth, which attracted other people to them. [6]They had interests and talents (intellectual, artistic, athletic) that helped them make friends, develop a sense of purpose, and gain self-esteem. [7]Equally important, they had warm, supportive relationships with at least one adult other than their parents who viewed them as special and important. [8]Compared to their troubled peers—and to a control group of children who grew up in secure environments—the resilient children grew into adults with the highest percentage of stable marriages and lowest proportions of unemployment, divorce, and serious health problems. [9]Another study of adolescents whose parents suffer from depression found that the most resilient teenagers had a strong relationship with an outside adult and a hobby at which they excelled, both of which gave them a sense of value. [10]Taken together, these studies suggest that two ways to foster resilience in high-risk children are mentor programs (such as Big Brother/Sister, which teams an adult volunteer with a needy child) and after-school programs that offer a range of activities.

_____ 1. In sentence 2, the word *adverse* means
    A. financially needy.
    B. desirable.
    C. highly unusual.
    D. unfavorable.

_____ 2. Which of the following is **not** mentioned in this passage as a characteristic of resilient children?
    A. They tend to be outgoing and affectionate from birth.
    B. They tend to mentor younger children.
    C. They have special interests and talents.
    D. They receive encouragement from at least one adult other than their parents.

_____ 3. Sentences 5–7 mainly
   A. contrast resilient with non-resilient children.
   B. list reasons why some high-risk children become confident, caring adults.
   C. provide steps in the process of conducting a psychological survey.
   D. narrate some typical events in the lives of high-risk children.

_____ 4. The relationship of sentence 9 to sentence 8 is one of
   A. illustration.
   B. comparison.
   C. addition.
   D. time.

_____ 5. This passage suggests that a root cause of crime is
   A. poverty.
   B. a lack of self-worth.
   C. exposure to drugs and alcohol.
   D. living in a dangerous neighborhood.

_____ 6. The author of this selection would probably agree with which of the following statements?
   A. Children who grow up under adverse conditions naturally become criminals.
   B. People should be encouraged to mentor high-risk youth.
   C. The ability to "bounce back" is determined at birth.
   D. There is little that society can do to support high-risk youth.

_____ 7. The author's tone can be described as
   A. pessimistic and blaming.
   B. indignant and self-righteous.
   C. sentimental and pitying.
   D. serious and caring.

_____ 8. Which is the most appropriate title for this selection?
   A. Resilience and How to Foster It
   B. The Troubled Environment of Today's Youth
   C. Resilience: Something You're Born With
   D. The Criminal Tendencies of High-Risk Youth

COMBINED SKILLS: Test 7

Read the passage below. Then write the letter of the best answer to each question that follows.

[1]Mention the word "parasite," and most people react by thinking "yuck." [2]A parasite is by definition an organism that grows, feeds, and is sheltered by a "host" organism, to which it contributes nothing in return. [3]In fact, some parasites go beyond "contributing nothing": they actually drive their hosts to suicidal behavior for the benefit of the parasite. [4]For example, ants are sometimes invaded by tiny parasites called liver flukes. [5]The flukes burrow into the ants' brains. [6]In response, the ants do something that is quite insane. [7]They spend the rest of their lives climbing to the tops of blades of grass. [8]They climb, they fall, they climb again. [9]This mad behavior actually makes complete sense, from the parasite's point of view. [10]In order to complete its life cycle, the liver fluke needs to get into the digestive system of a cow or a sheep. [11]The quickest way to accomplish this is to place itself at the top of a blade of grass and wait for a grazing animal to come along. [12]Therefore, what amounts to suicide for the ant insures that the fluke survives and reproduces. [13]A similar example is seen in the three-spined stickleback, a kind of freshwater fish. [14]The stickleback is frequently invaded by a tiny parasite that needs to end up in the belly of a bird in order to complete its life cycle. [15]When the parasite infects the stickleback, it causes several changes in the fish. [16]It turns it a lighter color, causes it to swim on the surface of the water, and darkens its eyes. [17]All these changes make the fish more visible to a bird that happens to be flying overhead. [18]The dark eyes even indicate to the bird in which direction the fish is swimming, thereby letting the bird know which way to dive in order to scoop the fish up. [19]The fish dies, but the parasite lives on.

_____ 1. According to this selection, ants with liver flukes in their brains
   A. are more likely to be eaten by birds.
   B. repeatedly climb to the tops of blades of grass.
   C. turn a lighter color.
   D. attach themselves to cows and sheep.

_____ 2. Both liver flukes and the parasites in sticklebacks cause their hosts' death by
   A. draining off so many nutrients that the hosts die of starvation.
   B. driving the hosts so crazy that the hosts deliberately commit suicide.
   C. making it more likely that their hosts will be eaten by another animal.
   D. exposing them to disease-causing agents.

_____ 3. TRUE OR FALSE? Both the liver fluke and the tiny parasites in stickle-backs complete their life cycles in the digestive systems of other animals.

_____ 4. The main pattern of organization used in the selection is
   A. definition and example.
   B. list of items.
   C. time order.
   D. contrast.

_____ 5. The author of this passage would probably agree with which of the following statements?
   A. The behavior of some parasites is extremely disgusting.
   B. It is tragic that some animals must die so that others can live.
   C. Parasites are vicious animals.
   D. In nature, there are rational reasons for even the strangest behavior.

_____ 6. You may reasonably infer from the examples in the passage that
   A. liver flukes are more intelligent than ants.
   B. the hosts of parasites want to die rather than endure any more torture.
   C. the hosts' life cycles remain intact thanks to the parasites.
   D. the hosts are powerless to resist the parasites' influence.

_____ 7. Which title best summarizes the selection?
   A. The Life Cycle of the Liver Fluke
   B. Tiny but Powerful Parasites
   C. A Stickleback's Worst Enemy
   D. Avoiding Harmful Parasites

_____ 8. The main idea of this passage is found in its
   A. first sentence.
   B. second sentence.
   C. third sentence.
   D. fourth sentence.

COMBINED SKILLS: Test 8

Read the passage below. Then write the letter of the best answer to each question that follows.

¹Clearly, no society can shift from an economy based on manual labor to one based on knowledge unless its people are educated—illiterates cannot process written information. ²The vast transformation of work in industrial societies was based in part on vast changes in educational systems and practices.

³In 1647, only twenty-seven years after they had landed at Plymouth Rock, the Puritans of the Massachusetts Colony enacted a law embodying the very radical idea that all children should attend school—at the time almost no children went to school anywhere in the world. ⁴The Massachusetts School Law required that in any township having fifty households, one person must be appointed to teach the children to read and write, and the teacher's wages were to be paid either by the parents or the inhabitants in general. ⁵Furthermore, in any township having a hundred or more households, a school must be established, "the master thereof being able to instruct youth so far as they may be fitted for the university." ⁶Any community that failed to provide these educational services was to be fined "till they shall perform this order." ⁷As word spread that Massachusetts had passed a compulsory school law, it often was taken as further evidence that the Puritans were crazy.

⁸From these rustic beginnings, the ideal of public schools for all children became part of American culture—as settlers moved west, they took the "one-room schoolhouse" with them. ⁹Nevertheless, even 150 years ago, in most of the world, including Europe, most children were not schooled. ¹⁰Education was reserved for an elite few. ¹¹That America—still largely a frontier—was able to contribute so many important inventions to the Industrial Revolution during the nineteenth century is now seen as a result of its educational efforts. ¹²Moreover, as the Industrial Revolution spread, policies of mass education spread with it.

_____ 1. In sentence 8, the word *rustic* means
   A. relating to city life.
   B. simple.
   C. routine.
   D. complicated.

_____ 2. This selection is mainly about
   A. the Massachusetts School Law enacted by the Puritans.
   B. the vast transformation of work in industrial societies.
   C. American contributions to the Industrial Revolution.
   D. educational practices and policies in early America.

_____ 3. According to this passage, the Massachusetts School Law of 1647
   A. was crazy.
   B. was a failure.
   C. affected only an elite few.
   D. created a new system of public education.

_____ 4. The relationship of sentence 9 to sentence 8 is one of
   A. cause and effect.
   B. illustration.
   C. contrast.
   D. addition.

_____ 5. This passage suggests that as settlers moved west, they
   A. packed up their schoolhouses and took them with them.
   B. concluded that education was a luxury they could not afford.
   C. wanted their children to be educated, but didn't know how to go about it.
   D. found ways to ensure that their children received an education.

_____ 6. The author's tone is
   A. compassionate.
   B. straightforward.
   C. approving.
   D. disapproving.

_____ 7. Which statement can you reasonably infer from the passage?
   A. Small schools do a better job of educating than large schools do.
   B. Education played a significant role in the Industrial Revolution.
   C. Educational reform is needed to improve America's current economy.
   D. The Puritans were poor at school planning.

_____ 8. Which statement best expresses the central point of this passage?
   A. A knowledge-based economy demands educated workers.
   B. The Massachusetts Colony was the first to require children to attend school.
   C. The Puritans were widely regarded to be offbeat in their practices.
   D. The idea that all children should be educated started with the Puritans of Massachusetts and spread with the Industrial Revolution.

COMBINED SKILLS: Test 9

Read the passage below. Then write the letter of the best answer to each question that follows.

¹If you're like many Americans, you're probably consuming far more sugar than you realize. ²In fact, the average American consumes 130 pounds of sugar a year, or 1/3 of a pound a day. ³Much of this sugar comes in the form of high-fructose corn syrup, which the food industry began adding to virtually all processed foods in the 1970s. ⁴This was back when the consumption of fat was first linked to heart disease. ⁵With the best of intentions, the food industry reduced the fat content in many processed foods. ⁶Unfortunately, low-fat foods taste like cardboard, so the food industry added high-fructose corn syrup to make them "tasty" once more. ⁷As a result, while the consumption of table sugar has gone down, the consumption of high-fructose corn syrup has skyrocketed. ⁸The problem is that research now links sugar consumption in *any* form to a host of health problems, including obesity, type 2 diabetes, heart disease, and even cancer. ⁹Some researchers are going so far as to label sugar "toxic."

¹⁰Recent studies at the University of California, Davis, show that when a person consumes too much sugar, the liver gets overloaded with fructose and converts some of it into fat. ¹¹Some of that fat ends up in the bloodstream and helps generate an especially dangerous kind of cholesterol called small dense LDL. ¹²These LDL particles are known to lodge in blood vessels, form plaque, and cause heart attacks. ¹³In addition, sugar has become a major focus in cancer research. ¹⁴Researchers are finding that sugar consumption causes a sudden spike in the hormone insulin, which can serve as a catalyst to fuel certain types of cancers, including those of the breast and colon.

¹⁵Think that you can satisfy your sweet tooth by consuming artificial sweeteners? ¹⁶Think again. ¹⁷A study of rats that were fed artificially sweetened food found that their metabolism slowed down, and they were triggered to consume more calories and gain more weight than rats fed sugar-sweetened food. ¹⁸Similarly, people who consume diet drinks regularly have a 200 percent increased risk of weight gain, a 36 percent increased risk of pre-diabetes or metabolic syndrome, and a 67 percent increased risk of diabetes.

¹⁹What to do? ²⁰An American Heart Association report recommends that men should consume no more than 150 calories of added sugars a day, and women should consume just 100 calories. ²¹That's less than the amount in one can of soda.

_____ 1. In sentence 14, the word *catalyst* means something that
     A. stimulates.   C. distracts.
     B. gets in the way.   D. repeats.

___ 2. According to the selection, the food industry added high fructose corn syrup to processed foods
   A. because high fructose corn syrup was believed to be healthier than regular sugar.
   B. because farmers who grew corn wanted to expand the market for corn products.
   C. because low fructose corn syrup had been linked to heart disease.
   D. to make up for the loss of taste caused by reducing the fat content of processed foods.

___ 3. The relationship of sentence 18 to sentence 17 is one of
   A. contrast.
   B. cause and effect.
   C. comparison.
   D. illustration.

___ 4. In general, this selection
   A. contrasts sugar consumption with the consumption of artificial sweeteners.
   B. lists the negative effects of consuming sugar and artificial sweeteners.
   C. defines the term *high fructose corn syrup* and explains how it is made.
   D. provides a brief history of the modern American food industry.

___ 5. The passage suggests that
   A. eating sugary foods is less risky than eating fatty foods.
   B. consuming artificially sweetened foods is a good way to avoid consuming too much sugar.
   C. Americans need to drastically reduce their intake of all forms of sugar.
   D. it's better to consume table sugar than high fructose corn syrup.

___ 6. The tone of the selection can be described as
   A. pleading.
   B. bitter.
   C. sarcastic.
   D. concerned.

___ 7. Which is the most appropriate title for this selection?
   A. Changing Patterns of Sugar Consumption
   B. How to Lower Your Chances of Getting Cancer
   C. The Case Against Sugar and Artificial Sweeteners
   D. Toxic Substances

___ 8. Which statement best expresses the central point of this selection?
   A. It was a mistake for the food industry to add high fructose corn syrup to processed foods.
   B. Both sugar in all its forms and artificial sweeteners carry significant health risks.
   C. Eating too much high fructose corn syrup is just as bad as eating too much table sugar.
   D. A number of recent studies have explored the consequences of consuming sugar and artificial sweeteners.

COMBINED SKILLS: Test 10

Read the passage below. Then write the letter of the best answer to each question that follows.

[1]Research reveals that males and females exhibit both similarities and differences in what they look for in a marital partner. [2]Many characteristics, such as emotional stability, dependability, and pleasant disposition, are rated highly by both sexes. [3]However, a few crucial differences between men's and women's priorities have been found, and these differences appear to be nearly universal across cultures. [4]Women tend to place a higher value than men on potential partners' socioeconomic status, intelligence, ambition, and financial prospects. [5]In contrast, men consistently show more interest than women in a potential partner's youthfulness and physical attractiveness.

[6]Most theorists explain these gender disparities in terms of evolutionary concepts. [7]According to evolutionary theories, all organisms, including humans, are motivated to enhance their chances of passing on their genes to subsequent generations. [8]Human females supposedly accomplish this end not by seeking larger or stronger partners, as in the animal kingdom, but by seeking male partners who possess or are likely to acquire more material resources that can then be invested in children. [9]Men, on the other hand, are assumed to maximize their reproductive outlook by seeking female partners with good breeding potential. [10]Thus, men are thought to look for youth, attractiveness, good health, and other characteristics presumed to be associated with higher fertility. [11]These evolutionary analyses of gender differences in mating are speculative, and there are alternative explanations, but they fit with the evidence quite well.

_____ 1. In sentence 11, the word *speculative* means
  A. interesting.
  B. unproved.
  C. helpful.
  D. surprising.

_____ 2. According to the selection, men and women place an equally high value on
  A. socioeconomic status.
  B. physical attractiveness.
  C. youth.
  D. a pleasant disposition.

_____ 3. TRUE OR FALSE? A key concept of evolution is that all organisms are driven to try to pass on their genes to later generations.

_____ 4. The relationship of sentence 3 to sentence 2 is one of
  A. list of items.
  B. contrast.
  C. cause and effect.
  D. problem and solution.

_____ 5. The main patterns of organization of this selection are comparison-contrast and
  A. time order.
  B. list of items.
  C. cause and effect.
  D. definition and example.

_____ 6. You can reasonably conclude from this passage that women
  A. are more likely to marry older, more financially stable men.
  B. often seek mates who are young, healthy, and attractive.
  C. don't care about a potential partner's emotional stability or dependability.
  D. prefer to marry men who are already supporting another woman's children.

_____ 7. The main purpose of this selection is to
  A. inform readers about what men and women look for in a mate and why.
  B. entertain readers by highlighting differences between the sexes.
  C. persuade readers to be more selective when choosing a mate.

_____ 8. Which statement best expresses the central point of the passage?
  A. Males and females exhibit similarities and differences in what they look for in a mate.
  B. Evolutionary theories explain reasons for women's preferences when selecting a reproductive partner.
  C. There are differences in the way men and women seek potential partners.
  D. Human mating rituals are complex and resemble what happens in the animal kingdom.

COMBINED SKILLS: Test 11

Read the passage below. Then write the letter of the best answer to each question that follows.

[1]One common sales trick, the foot-in-the-door technique, relies on getting the potential customer to grant an initial small request, which prepares the customer psychologically to grant a subsequent larger request. [2]To my chagrin, I was outwitted—once—by a clever gang of driveway sealers who used this technique on me. [3]One day while I was raking leaves in front of my house, these men pulled up in their truck and asked if they could have a drink of water. [4]I, of course, said yes; how could I say no to a request like that? [5]Then they got out of the truck and one said, "Oh, if you have some lemonade or soda, that would even be better; we'd really appreciate that." [6]Well, all right, I did have some lemonade. [7]As I brought it to them, one of the men pointed to the cracks in my driveway and commented that they had just enough sealing material and time to do my driveway that afternoon, and they could give me a special deal. [8]Normally, I would never have agreed to a bargain like that on the spot; but I found myself unable to say no. [9]I ended up paying far more than I should have, and they did a very poor job. [10]I had been taken in by what I now see clearly was a novel twist on the foot-in-the-door sales technique.

[11]The basis of the foot-in-the-door technique is that people are more likely to agree to a large request if they have already agreed to a small one. [12]The driveway sealers got me twice on that: Their request for water primed me to agree to their request for lemonade, and their request for lemonade primed me to agree to their deal about sealing my driveway. [13]One researcher has argued that the foot-in-the-door technique works largely through the principle of cognitive dissonance. [14]Having agreed, apparently of my own free will, to give the men lemonade, I must have justified that action to myself by thinking, *These are a pretty good bunch of guys*, and that thought was dissonant with any temptation I might have had a few moments later, when they proposed the driveway deal, to think, *These people may be cheating me.* [15]So I pushed the latter thought out of my mind before it fully registered.

_____ 1. In sentence 2, the word *chagrin* means
    A. delight.   C. confusion.
    B. horror.   D. embarrassment.

_____ 2. The author states that he found himself unable to say no to the driveway sealers because
    A. his driveway was in very poor condition, and he badly needed the work done.
    B. he was afraid of angering them.
    C. he had convinced himself that they were good people.
    D. the price they offered him was extremely low.

_____ 3. Paragraph 1 mainly
  A. defines and gives an example of the foot-in-the-door technique.
  B. contrasts the author's generous behavior with the trickiness of the workmen.
  C. explains why the driveway sealing job turned out poorly.
  D. compares an honest selling technique with a dishonest one.

_____ 4. You can infer from this passage that
  A. agreeing to a small request always leads to a larger request.
  B. driveway sealers are among the most dishonest salespeople.
  C. the author did not fall a second time for the foot-in-the-door technique.
  D. the author called the police to complain about the driveway sealers.

_____ 5. The passage suggests that the author
  A. knows something about psychology.
  B. has learned from his experience with the driveway sealers.
  C. is a nice person.
  D. all of the above.

_____ 6. The tone of this passage is
  A. lighthearted and humorous.
  B. bitter and vengeful.
  C. sad and resentful.
  D. instructive and casual.

_____ 7. Which statement best expresses the central point of the passage?
  A. Many tradespeople use the foot-in-the-door technique to cheat unwitting customers.
  B. The foot-in-the-door technique is a common sales strategy in which the customer agrees to a small request and then cannot refuse a larger one.
  C. Many people are victimized by clever sales techniques.
  D. Do not trust tradespeople who offer you special deals.

_____ 8. What is the most appropriate title for this selection?
  A. Outwitted!
  B. An Embarrassing Experience
  C. Beware of the Foot-in-the-Door Technique
  D. Sneaky Sales Tricks

COMBINED SKILLS: Test 12

Read the passage below. Then write the letter of the best answer to each question that follows.

[1]Until recently, most researchers believed the human brain followed a fairly predictable developmental arc. [2]It started out open and versatile, gained shape and intellectual muscle as it matured, and reached its peak of power and nimbleness by age 40. [3]After that, the brain began a slow decline, clouding up little by little until, by age 60 or 70, it had lost much of its ability to retain new information and was fumbling with what it had. [4]But that was all right because late-life crankiness had by then made us largely resistant to new ideas anyway.

[5]That, as it turns out, is hooey. [6]More and more, neurologists and psychologists are coming to the conclusion that the brain at midlife—a period increasingly defined as the years from 35 to 65 and even beyond—is a much more elastic, much more supple thing than anyone ever realized.

[7]Far from slowly powering down, the brain as it ages begins bringing new cognitive systems on line and cross-indexing existing ones in ways it never did before. [8]You may not pack so much raw data into memory as you could when you were cramming for college finals, and your short-term memory may not be what it was, but you manage information and parse meanings that were entirely beyond you when you were younger. [9]What's more, your temperament changes to suit those new skills, growing more comfortable with ambiguity and less susceptible to frustration or irritation. [10]Although inflexibility, confusion and even later-life dementia are very real problems, for many people the aging process not only does not batter the brain; it actually makes it better.

[11]"In midlife," says UCLA neurologist George Bartzokis, "you're beginning to maximize the ability to use the entirety of the information in your brain on an everyday, ongoing, second-to-second basis. [12]Biologically, that's what wisdom is."

_____ 1. In sentence 8, the word *parse* means
   A. reject.
   B. figure out.
   C. emphasize.
   D. review.

_____ 2. According to this passage, as people age, they
   A. grow more susceptible to frustration and irritation.
   B. gain in short-term memory.
   C. grow more skilled at managing information.
   D. pack more raw data into their memory.

_____ 3. This selection primarily
   A. contrasts what researchers used to believe about the brain as it ages with what they believe now.
   B. defines the term "developmental arc."
   C. lists the biological effects of aging on the brain.
   D. explains why some people become confused and develop dementia in later life while others do not.

_____ 4. The main organizational pattern of paragraph 1 is
   A. cause and effect.
   B. definition and example.
   C. comparison.
   D. time order.

_____ 5. This passage suggests that
   A. old people have a difficult time absorbing new ideas.
   B. wisdom is closely associated with maturity.
   C. later-life dementia is inevitable.
   D. the brain begins powering down during midlife.

_____ 6. The author's attitude towards aging seems to be one of
   A. fear.
   B. distaste.
   C. respect.
   D. worry.

_____ 7. The writer uses a tone that is
   A. dry and scholarly.
   B. optimistic.
   C. bitterly critical.
   D. undecided.

_____ 8. Which statement best expresses the central point of the passage?
   A. In contrast to what researchers previously believed, current research indicates that the brain actually improves as it ages.
   B. People at midlife lose short-term memory but gain the ability to manage information.
   C. Inflexibility, confusion, and late-life dementia are serious problems of old age.
   D. As people enter midlife, they often become less susceptible to frustration or irritation.

COMBINED SKILLS: Test 13

Read the passage below. Then write the letter of the best answer to each question that follows.

[1]Suppose that you and three other individuals apply for a part-time job in the parks and recreation department, and you are selected for the position. [2]How do you explain your success? [3]Chances are, you tell yourself that you were hired because you were the most qualified for the job. [4]But how do the other people interpret their negative outcome? [5]Do they tell themselves that you got the job because you were the most able? [6]Unlikely! [7]Instead, they probably attribute their loss to "bad luck" or to not having had time to prepare for the interview. [8]These different explanations for success and failure reflect the *self-serving bias*, or the tendency to attribute one's successes to personal factors and one's failures to situational factors.

[9]Research indicates that people are likely to take credit for their successes and to disavow their failures. [10]To illustrate: In an experiment, two strangers jointly took a test. [11]They then received bogus success or failure feedback about their test performance and were asked to assign responsibility for the test results. [12]Successful participants claimed credit, but those who failed blamed their partners. [13]Still, people don't always rush to take credit. [14]In another experiment in the just-cited study, participants were actual friends. [15]In this case, participants shared responsibility for both successful and unsuccessful outcomes. [16]Thus, friendship places limits on the self-serving bias.

[17]Although the self-serving bias has been documented in a variety of cultures, it seems to be prevalent in individualistic Western societies, such as those in North America and Europe, where the emphasis on competition and high self-esteem motivates people to try to impress others as well as themselves. [18]In contrast, Japanese subjects exhibit a *self-effacing bias* in explaining successes, as they tend to attribute their successes to the help they receive from others or to the ease of the task, while downplaying the importance of their ability. [19]When they fail, Japanese subjects are more self-critical than subjects from individualistic cultures. [20]They are more likely to accept responsibility for their failures and to use their setbacks as an impetus for self-improvement. [21]Studies have also failed to find the Western self-serving bias in Nepalese and Chinese samples.

_____ 1. In sentence 9, the word *disavow* means
   A. believe in.
   B. deny responsibility for.
   C. doubt the truth of.
   D. promise to correct.

_____ 2. According to the passage, people in Western societies tend to attribute their failures to
  A. the negative influence of friends.
  B. personal shortcomings.
  C. situational factors.
  D. bias on the parts of others.

_____ 3. In contrast to people in Western societies, the Japanese tend to attribute their successes to
  A. high self-esteem.
  B. the help they receive from others or the ease of the task.
  C. a strong desire for self-improvement.
  D. their own superior skills.

_____ 4. The main pattern of organization used in paragraph 1 is
  A. time order.   C. comparison.
  B. list of items.   D. contrast.

_____ 5. The relationship of sentence 16 to sentence 15 is one of
  A. time.
  B. addition.
  C. definition and example.
  D. cause and effect.

_____ 6. You could reasonably conclude from the passage that
  A. Japanese society places responsibility for success or failure on the group, rather than on the individual.
  B. Western societies place little value upon friendship.
  C. the lower one's self-esteem, the more likely one is to blame situational factors for one's failure.
  D. self-effacement is valued in Asian societies generally.

_____ 7. Sentence 19 is a statement of
  A. fact.
  B. opinion.
  C. both fact and opinion.

_____ 8. Which statement best expresses the central point of the selection?
  A. Whereas Western societies generally exhibit a self-serving bias, the Japanese and other Eastern cultures tend to exhibit a self-effacing bias.
  B. Most people take credit for success but not for failure.
  C. The Japanese take more responsibility for failure than Westerners do.
  D. Researchers have uncovered some interesting facts with regard to people's attitudes toward success and failure.

COMBINED SKILLS: Test 14

Read the passage below. Then write the letter of the best answer to each question that follows.

¹Sociologists have discovered a number of causal factors in child abuse. ²One is the *intergenerational transmission of violence:* Parents are likely to abuse their children if they have learned in childhood that it is all right to use violence in dealing with child-rearing problems. ³This learning may come from *the experience of being abused as children*.

⁴Indeed, research has shown that child-abusing parents are more likely than nonabusing parents to have been abused themselves as children. ⁵More specifically, about 30 percent of child abusers have been abused themselves, while only 3 or 4 percent of nonabusers had the same experience in the past. ⁶But this should not be taken to mean that receiving early abuse inevitably leads to later abuse-giving because, contrary to popular belief, the *majority* (about 70 percent) of child-abuse victims do *not* grow up to become abusers. ⁷A history of the abuser being abused is only one of the causal influences on child abuse, and not its only cause. ⁸The other learned influence—the legitimacy of using violence to deal with problems—also comes from *having observed as children how parents and other significant adults use violence* to express anger, to react to stress, or to deal with marital problems. ⁹This explains why researchers often find that child abusers are more likely than nonabusers to have been raised in homes with a great deal of marital conflict and violence.

¹⁰Another contributing factor to child abuse is the acceptance of the very popular view that physical punishment is a proper way of disciplining children. ¹¹Nearly half of all U.S. parents resort to physical punishment in an attempt to correct a child's misbehavior. ¹²But there is a tendency for physical punishment (say, spanking or slapping) to spill over into child abuse (punching or kicking). ¹³As a researcher has found, parents who approve of physical punishment are four times more likely to abuse their children than are parents who disapprove of such physical discipline. ¹⁴Because of the social acceptance of physical punishment, child abusers tend to see their abusive behavior as good and proper. ¹⁵This can be illustrated by the case of a father who had severely beaten his two boys, one five years old and the other only eighteen months old. ¹⁶In the hospital where the boys were brought in for treatment of multiple bruises, lacerations, and fractures, the father said to the examining physician, "Children have to be taught respect for authority and be taught obedience. ¹⁷I would rather have my children grow up afraid of me and respecting me than loving me and spoiled."

_____ 1. In sentence 8, the word *legitimacy* means
   A. primary method.
   B. acceptability.
   C. dislike.
   D. sincerity.

_____ 2. According to the selection, parents who approve of physical punishment
     A. almost always abuse their children.
     B. are 30 percent more likely to abuse their children than are other parents.
     C. rarely abuse their children.
     D. are four times more likely to abuse their children than are other parents.

_____ 3. How many main causes of child abuse are mentioned in paragraph 2?
     A. One
     B. Two
     C. Three
     D. Four

_____ 4. In general, this selection
     A. contrasts parents who abuse their children with parents who do not.
     B. defines the term *child abuse* and gives examples of it.
     C. illustrates the long-term effects of child abuse.
     D. lists the factors which cause parents to abuse their children.

_____ 5. This selection is mostly based on
     A. fact.
     B. opinion.
     C. a mixture of fact and opinion.

_____ 6. The tone of the third paragraph can be described as
     A. enthusiastic.
     B. tolerant.
     C. ambivalent.
     D. serious.

_____ 7. Which of the following titles would be most suitable for this passage?
     A. The Case against Physical Discipline
     B. An Abusive Father
     C. The Roots of Child Abuse
     D. Let's Stamp Out Child Abuse

_____ 8. Which statement best expresses the central point of the passage?
     A. Many Americans wrongly believe that physical punishment is a good way to discipline children.
     B. Contrary to popular belief, the majority of child abuse victims do not grow up to abuse their own children.
     C. The root causes of child abuse include being abused as a child, observing adults react to stressful situations with violence, and believing in physical punishment as a form of discipline.
     D. There are better ways to discipline children than physical punishment.

COMBINED SKILLS: Test 15

Read the passage below. Then write the letter of the best answer to each question that follows.

[1]Italian Renaissance noblewoman Lucrezia Borgia (1480–1519) remains infamous today for using the poison arsenic to dispose of her personal and political enemies. [2]Recent research, however, has cast doubt on whether Lucrezia actually poisoned anyone, arguing instead that her family's political enemies in Rome ruined her reputation. [3]But whether or not Lucrezia Borgia actually used poison, few historians will dispute that the weapon was a great equalizer. [4]Murder required administering a poison in repeated or large doses, tasks that women could conveniently perform since they were trusted with the preparation of food and the administration of medicines. [5]As a group, women had plenty of reasons to commit murder, too—lack of economic opportunity, limited property rights, and difficulty in escaping the marriage bond. [6]In his recent book *Elements of Murder: A History of Poison*, John Emsley describes multiple cases of women who killed to gain political power, get rid of husbands, collect insurance, cover up swindling and theft during domestic employment, and receive inheritances. [7]In France, arsenic came to be called *poudre de succession*, "inheritance powder." [8]One noblewoman, a true experimentalist, tested what dosages of arsenic would cause illness and death by sending gifts of food containing the substance to patients at a local hospital. [9]She then poisoned her father to inherit his wealth and knocked off her two brothers so she would not have to share it.

[10]The favored poisons of the late 19th century were also an appealing instrument of murder, at least for the villain, because their effects on the body were gruesome. [11]Mercury, arsenic, antimony, lead, and thallium—some of the most common poisons—induced repeated vomiting and diarrhea and turned the body into wasting, stench-ridden flesh. [12]Furthermore, the advantage to the murderer was that symptoms of poison closely resembled those of common diseases. [13]Victims were usually consigned to their graves as dead of natural causes rather than objects of foul play.

[14]Poisoning was also relatively easy to get away with for centuries because possession of the murder weapon was by no means a clear indicator of guilt. [15]Would-be poisoners could easily obtain the necessary materials from the shops of apothecaries or chemists, under the guise of using them in small doses for a cosmetic or medical purpose. [16]In ancient times, stibnite powder, an antimony compound, was used as mascara. [17]In the 19th century, a popular arsenic-based medication was used to treat syphilis, epilepsy, and skin disorders. [18]During the 19th century, however, improved methods of chemical analysis increased the risk that a poisoner would be caught. [19]The expert testimony of academic chemists, based on post-mortem detections of poisons in corpses, led to convictions.

_____ 1. In sentence 19, the word *post-mortem* means
    A. before death.
    B. after death.
    C. causing death.
    D. preventing death.

_____ 2. According to the author, poison in times past was
    A. usually traced in the dead victim's body.
    B. inconvenient to obtain at times.
    C. commonly given to hospital patients.
    D. administered in food and medicine.

_____ 3. The relationship of sentences 8 and 9 to sentence 7 is one of
    A. list of items.
    B. time order.
    C. cause-effect.
    D. illustration.

_____ 4. The main pattern of organization used in this passage is
    A. time order.
    B. cause and effect.
    C. comparison.
    D. contrast.

_____ 5. Paragraphs 2 and 3 mainly
    A. list reasons why poison was an appealing murder instrument.
    B. contrast 19th century methods of murder with earlier methods.
    C. compare the effects on the body of various types of poison.
    D. all of the above.

_____ 6. The tone of this selection is
    A. shocked.
    B. apologetic.
    C. concerned.
    D. objective.

_____ 7. The author suggests that poisoners
    A. often enjoyed seeing their victims suffer.
    B. typically killed people they did not know well.
    C. were generally caught and convicted of their crimes.
    D. were mentally ill.

_____ 8. Which title is most appropriate for the selection?
    A. Famous Poisoners
    B. Evil Women Throughout History
    C. Poison: A Popular Murder Weapon
    D. The Decline of Poison as a Murder Weapon

COMBINED SKILLS: Test 16

Read the passage below. Then write the letter of the best answer to each question that follows.

[1]In today's society, having a baby is nearly always associated with doctors and hospitals. [2]But in the early days of America's independence, babies were born at home, and mother and baby were cared for by a midwife. [3]Why, then, did doctors begin delivering babies? [4]And what does this tell us about theories of social inequality?

[5]Martha Ballard was a midwife from 1785 to 1812. [6]During that time, she delivered 816 babies and treated a wide variety of illnesses. [7]According to historian Laurel Thatcher Ulrich, who used Ballard's diary to write her Pulitzer-Prize-winning *A Midwife's Tale*, the midwife's extensive knowledge was gained not through attendance at a medical school but on the job, working with other women and by herself to care for others in her community. [8]Ballard's personal competitor was a young physician named Benjamin Page, who charged $6 to deliver a baby while she charged $2.

[9]Page was clearly less experienced and less capable than Ballard at delivering babies. [10]For example, he misused the newly popular drug laudanum, a form of opium, putting one laboring woman into a stupor that stopped her labor completely. [11]In Ballard's opinion, Page was the cause of more than one infant's death. [12]Furthermore, records indicate that deaths of mothers and babies increased rather than decreased when physicians began routinely attending births in the 19th century. [13]Why, then, would people employ young, inexperienced physicians such as Page? [14]Ulrich explains Page's appeal: "Ben Page had certain advantages: a gentlemanly bearing, a successfully completed apprenticeship, and credit with certain younger members of the educated elite. [15]At this time, from the late 1700s to the 1840s, women who wished to start a career in midwifery did not have the option of going to medical school and making the kind of social connections with the elite that male physicians could."

[16]The case of Martha Ballard and Benjamin Page provides a clear example of the constraints that operate in the labor market. [17]The change from a reliance on midwifery to employment of physicians occurred not because physicians were better than midwives at what they did, but because they were men and as such were already connected to other powerful institutions, including law, education, business, and politics. [18]Young physicians such as Benjamin Page were employed—and paid higher rates—to do something they weren't very good at. [19]Though midwives were as competent as or more competent than any physician at prenatal care and delivering babies, men had more power and were able to drive the women out of their traditional role.

_____ 1. In sentence 16, the word *constraints* means
      A. opportunities.   C. restrictions.
      B. descriptions.   D. time limits.

_____ 2. According to medical records,
    A. Benjamin Page was responsible for more infant deaths than Martha Ballard.
    B. the use of drugs during labor was the primary cause of infant deaths.
    C. death rates increased when physicians started delivering babies.
    D. more infant and mother deaths occurred during the late 1700s than any other time period.

_____ 3. According to the passage, women in Martha Ballard's day
    A. seldom cared for mothers and babies.
    B. did not have the option of attending medical school.
    C. could have gone to medical school, but preferred on-the-job training.
    D. often used laudanum to aid laboring women.

_____ 4. Which of the following is **not** a reason why people chose Benjamin Page to deliver their babies?
    A. He had a gentlemanly bearing.
    B. He had successfully completed an apprenticeship.
    C. He charged less than a midwife for performing the same services.
    D. He knew other members of the young social elite.

_____ 5. This selection's main pattern of organization is
    A. comparison.   C. illustration.
    B. time order.   D. cause-effect.

_____ 6. The relationship of sentence 10 to sentence 9 is one of
    A. addition.   C. contrast.
    B. definition and example.   D. illustration.

_____ 7. The passage suggests that
    A. women are naturally much better at delivering babies than men are.
    B. medical schools in Page's time did not adequately prepare physicians to perform prenatal care and deliver babies.
    C. pregnant women preferred that midwives deliver their babies, but their husbands preferred male physicians.
    D. it would eventually become illegal to practice midwifery in the United States.

_____ 8. Which statement best expresses the central point of this selection?
    A. Whether to employ a doctor or midwife to deliver a baby remains an important decision for women.
    B. Midwives traditionally have been more competent at delivering babies than physicians.
    C. Martha Ballard and Benjamin Page were competitors in the labor market in the late 1700s.
    D. The cases of Martha Ballard and Benjamin Page illustrate the truth that historically, men's dominance in the labor market has relied more on power and connections than on competence.

COMBINED SKILLS: Test 17

Read the passage below. Then write the letter of the best answer to each question that follows.

[1]In 1998, Karla Faye Tucker, age 38, was executed in Texas for murdering two people with a pickax 15 years earlier. [2]She was the first woman put to death by the state since the Civil War and the second woman in the United States officially killed since 1976, the year when the U.S. Supreme Court reinstated the death penalty. [3]Most Americans believe that the death penalty is an effective deterrent to murder. [4]Many sociologists, however, have for a long time found otherwise, given the following forms of evidence.

[5]First, the homicide rates in states that have retained the death penalty law are generally much higher than in states that have abolished it. [6]Southern states which still practice the death penalty generally have higher murder rates than the states in other regions, which have mostly abolished capital punishment. [7]This suggests that the death penalty does not appear to deter murder.

[8]Secondly, within the same states, murder rates generally did not go up after the death penalty was abolished. [9]Moreover, the restoration of capital punishment in states that had abolished it earlier did not lead to a significant decrease in homicides.

[10]A third piece of evidence came from comparing the number of homicides shortly before and shortly after executions of convicted murderers that had been widely publicized. [11]If the death penalty has a deterrent effect, the execution should so scare potential criminals that they would refrain from killing, and the number of homicides in the area should decline. [12]This may sound logical, but reality contradicts it. [13]In Philadelphia during the 1930s, for example, the number of homicides remained about the same in the period from 60 days before to 60 days after a widely publicized execution of five murderers. [14]This finding, among others, suggests that the death penalty apparently does not prevent potential killers from killing even when the state shows people that it means business.

[15]Why doesn't the death penalty seem to deter murder? [16]One reason is that murder is a crime of passion, most often carried out under the overwhelming pressure of volcanic emotion, namely, uncontrollable rage. [17]People in such a condition cannot stop and think about the death penalty. [18]Another reason is that the causal forces of murder, such as severe poverty and child abuse, are simply too powerful to be neutralized by the threat of capital punishment.

_____ 1. In sentence 3, the word *deterrent* means

    A. cure.   C. stimulus.

    B. something that prevents.   D. excuse.

_____ 2. This selection mainly
  A. narrates the history of the death penalty in America.
  B. lists evidence that the death penalty does not prevent murder.
  C. contrasts murder rates in several Southern states with murder rates in several Northern states.
  D. compares the effectiveness of the death penalty to the effectiveness of life in prison.

_____ 3. The relationship of sentence 9 to sentence 8 is one of
  A. addition.   C. time.
  B. illustration.   D. cause and effect.

_____ 4. According to the passage, the homicide rates in states that have retained the death penalty are
  A. significantly lower than in states which have abolished the death penalty.
  B. slightly higher than in states which have abolished the death penalty.
  C. about the same as in states which have abolished the death penalty.
  D. generally much higher than in states that have abolished the death penalty.

_____ 5. The selection suggests that
  A. if the United States abolished the death penalty, the murder rate would rise.
  B. it is a mistake to believe that the death penalty prevents murder.
  C. if the United States abolished the death penalty, the murder rate would decline.
  D. Karla Faye Tucker was wrongly convicted.

_____ 6. On the basis of paragraph 5, we can infer that
  A. people who grow up in impoverished, abusive circumstances are more likely to commit murder than those who do not.
  B. people who commit murder usually coolly plan their crimes.
  C. there is nothing society can do to stop poverty and child abuse.
  D. people who commit murder have made a conscious decision to risk being executed.

_____ 7. Sentence 2 is a statement of
  A. fact.   B. opinion.   C. both fact and opinion.

_____ 8. Which title is most suitable for this passage?
  A. Let's Abolish the Death Penalty
  B. The Death Penalty: No Deterrent to Murder
  C. Women on Death Row
  D. Murder: A Crime of Passion

COMBINED SKILLS: Test 18

Read the passage below. Then write the letter of the best answer to each question that follows.

[1]Today it is commonly assumed that the roots of violence in American society lie in our frontier heritage of violence and lawlessness. [2]A popular vision of the frontier has grown up and been disseminated by dime novels, pulp newspapers, and television and movie Westerns. [3]This vision is of a lawless land populated by violent men: outlaws, stagecoach robbers, gunslingers, vigilantes, claim jumpers, cattle rustlers, horse thieves, Indian fighters, border ruffians, and mule skinners. [4]Most popular accounts of Western banditry, however, appear to be grossly exaggerated and romanticized. [5]According to legend, Bat Masterson killed 30 men in gunfights. [6]Actually he killed only three. [7]Billy the Kid, who supposedly killed 21 men in his 21 years of life, also apparently killed only three.

[8]Legend holds that Kansas's brawling cattle towns witnessed a killing every night. [9]But in fact, the towns of Abilene, Caldwell, Dodge City, Ellsworth, and Wichita recorded a grand total of 45 homicides during a 15-year span. [10]That worked out to 1.5 murders per cattle traveling season, never exceeding five in one year. [11]In Deadwood, South Dakota—infamous for being the town where Wild Bill Hickok was shot in the back while playing poker in 1876—only four homicides (and no lynchings) took place in the town's most violent year. [12]And even in Tombstone, Arizona, the site of the famous shoot-out at the O.K. Corral (where Marshal Virgil Earp, his brothers Wyatt and Morgan, and gambler Doc Holliday hurled the Clanton brothers "into eternity in the duration of a moment"), only five men were killed during the city's deadliest year.

[13]Despite the omnipresence of rifles, knives, and revolvers and the prevalence of saloons, gambling houses, and bordellos, crimes such as rape, robbery, and burglary were relatively rare. [14]One miner wrote, "We could go to sleep in our cabins with our bag of gold dust under our pillows, minus locks, bolts, or bars, and feel a sense of absolute security."

_____ 1. In sentence 13, the word *omnipresence* means
  A. scarcity.
  B. illegality.
  C. reputation.
  D. existence everywhere.

_____ 2. According to popular legend, Kansas's cattle towns
  A. were not nearly as violent as other towns.
  B. were centers of rape, robbery, and burglary.
  C. witnessed a killing every night.
  D. were places of absolute security.

_____ 3. Wild Bill Hickok
   A. actually killed only three men in gunfights, not 30.
   B. hurled the Clanton brothers "into eternity in the duration of a moment."
   C. was a gold miner.
   D. was shot in the back while playing poker.

_____ 4. This selection mainly
   A. contrasts the mythology of the American frontier with the reality.
   B. describes in chronological order important gun battles of the American West.
   C. explores the effects of a lawless frontier culture.
   D. compares the early American West to the present-day American West.

_____ 5. This passage suggests that
   A. the roots of violence in American society do not lie in our frontier heritage.
   B. most Americans have little interest in the history of their country.
   C. most Americans have never believed the popular mythology of a violent West.
   D. the American West is less violent today than it was in frontier times.

_____ 6. You can infer from this passage that
   A. most citizens of the frontier West did not own guns.
   B. the Clanton brothers were outlaws.
   C. gold miners were frequently the victims of crime.
   D. liquor was illegal in many Western towns.

_____ 7. The primary purpose of this passage is to
   A. inform readers about the actual degree of violence in the frontier West.
   B. persuade readers that Billy the Kid and Bat Masterson do not deserve their reputations as killers.
   C. entertain readers with colorful stories about the old West.

_____ 8. The central point of this passage is found in
   A. sentence 1.
   B. sentence 2.
   C. sentence 3.
   D. sentence 4.

COMBINED SKILLS: Test 19

Read the passage below. Then write the letter of the best answer to each question that follows.

[1]In James Thurber's classic short story, "The Secret Life of Walter Mitty," the meek, painfully shy central character spends much of his time weaving elaborate fantasies in which he stars as a bold, dashing adventurer. [2]Few people live in their imaginations to the extent Walter Mitty does, but everyone has daydreams: apparently effortless, spontaneous shifts in attention away from the here and now into a private world of make-believe.

[3]The urge to daydream seems to come in waves, surging about every 90 minutes and peaking between noon and 2 p.m. [4]According to some estimates, the average person spends almost half of his or her waking hours fantasizing, though this varies from person to person and situation to situation. [5]Typically, we daydream when we would rather be somewhere else or be doing something else, so daydreaming is a momentary escape.

[6]Are daydreams random paths your mind travels? [7]Not at all. [8]Studies show that most daydreams are variations on a central theme: thoughts and images of unfulfilled goals and wishes, accompanied by emotions arising from an appraisal of where we are now compared to where we want to be. [9]Some people imagine pleasant, playful, entertaining scenarios, uncomplicated by guilt or worry. [10]By contrast, people who are extremely achievement-oriented tend to experience recurring themes of frustration, guilt, fear of failure, and hostility, reflecting the self-doubt and competitive envy that accompanies great ambition. [11]While most daydreaming is quite normal, it is considered maladaptive when it involves extensive fantasizing, replacing human interaction and interfering with vocational or academic success.

[12]Does daydreaming serve any useful function? [13]Some psychologists view daydreaming as nothing more than a retreat from the real world, especially when that world is not meeting our needs. [14]Other psychologists stress the positive value of daydreaming and fantasy. [15]Daydreams may provide a refreshing break from a stressful day and serve to remind us of neglected personal needs. [16]Freudian theorists tend to view daydreams as a harmless way of working through hostile feelings or satisfying guilty desires. [17]Cognitive psychologists emphasize that daydreaming can build problem-solving and interpersonal skills, as well as encourage creativity. [18]Moreover, daydreaming helps people endure difficult situations. [19]Prisoners of war have used fantasies to survive torture and deprivation. [20]Daydreaming and fantasy, then, may provide welcome relief from unpleasant reality and reduce internal tension and external aggression.

_____ 1. In sentence 11, the word *maladaptive* means

    A. long and boring.   C. not promoting healthy development.

    B. filled with errors.   D. overly complicated.

_____ 2. According to the passage,
   A. daydreaming is relatively rare.
   B. people generally daydream for two hours a day.
   C. daydreams usually contain a central theme.
   D. daydreams are random paths the mind travels.

_____ 3. For the most part, sentences 15–19
   A. provide examples of the usefulness of daydreaming.
   B. contrast the views of Freudian theorists with the views of others.
   C. compare dated views of daydreaming with modern views.
   D. explain the biological causes of daydreaming.

_____ 4. The main pattern of organization used in the final paragraph is
   A. list of items.
   B. definition and example.
   C. illustration.
   D. comparison.

_____ 5. The author's main purpose is to
   A. inform readers about daydreaming.
   B. persuade readers that too much daydreaming can have negative effects.
   C. entertain readers with examples of Walter Mitty's elaborate fantasies.

_____ 6. Sentences 4 and 5 are statements of
   A. fact.
   B. opinion.
   C. both fact and opinion.

_____ 7. Which is the most appropriate title for this selection?
   A. Those Ridiculous Daydreamers
   B. The Dangers of Daydreaming
   C. Strange Daydreams
   D. The Functions of Daydreaming

_____ 8. Which of the following statements best expresses the central point of the selection?
   A. Daydreams are not random fantasies, but are usually variations on a central theme.
   B. Whereas some people daydream about pleasant situations, other people's daydreams involve frustration, guilt, and hostility.
   C. James Thurber's creation, Walter Mitty, represents the daydreamer in all of us.
   D. Daydreams are a normal imaginative outlet and can serve a useful purpose.

COMBINED SKILLS: Test 20

Read the passage below. Then write the letter of the best answer to each question that follows.

¹How many computers have you or your family gone through in the past ten years? ²How about televisions? ³Cell phones? ⁴Stereos? ⁵If you're like many Americans, you buy a new computer or other piece of electronic equipment as soon as new technology makes the one you own seem out of date. ⁶What do you do with your old electronic equipment when you buy something new? ⁷E-waste, or electronic waste, is currently the most rapidly growing waste problem in the world, with amounts of E-waste increasing nearly three times more quickly than amounts of other municipal wastes. ⁸And E-waste is toxic waste: computers and other electronic equipment contain lead, mercury, cadmium, barium, chromium, beryllium, PCBs, dioxins, and other pollutants. ⁹Consumers and business users have to pay recyclers to take E-waste off their hands.

¹⁰Recycling materials from electronic equipment is time-consuming and unprofitable—at least in industrialized nations. ¹¹So Americans ship it to other countries where the lack of environmental, health, and safety regulations make recycling E-waste profitable—and dangerous. ¹²For example, in Guiyu, China, about 100,000 men, women, and children are employed in taking computers apart—mostly by hand—and extracting copper from wiring, gold from capacitors, and other valuable products. ¹³Employees work with no protection for their hands, eyes, skin, and respiratory systems. ¹⁴Plastics are burned in the open air, acids are poured into canals and rivers, and lead-laden monitor glass and other components are dumped where heavy metals can leach into groundwater.

¹⁵Global inequality is at the root of E-waste exportation. ¹⁶In the wealthy industrialized United States, protected by multiple layers of regulations, wastes are generated and exported. ¹⁷In developing nations with few or no environmental and health regulations, on the other hand, poor people are willing and eager to work for $1.50 a day to handle toxic materials. ¹⁸As the authors of *Exporting Harm: The High-Tech Trashing of Asia* point out: "E-waste exports to Asia are motivated by brute global economics. . . . ¹⁹A free trade in hazardous wastes leaves the poorer people of the world with an untenable choice between poverty and poison—a choice that nobody should have to make."

_____ 1. In sentence 19, the word *untenable* means
   A. not capable of being understood.
   B. worthy of being envied.
   C. unpredictable.
   D. unthinkable.

_____ 2. According to the selection, the number of people in Guiyu, China, who are employed in taking computers apart is
   A. 1,000.   C. 100,000.
   B. 10,000.   D. 1,000,000.

_____ 3. Which of the following statements best expresses the main idea of paragraph 1?
   A. Most Americans buy new electronic equipment when new technology makes the equipment they own seem out of date.
   B. Electronic waste is increasing three times faster than other municipal wastes.
   C. Electronic waste, which is toxic, is the most rapidly growing waste problem in the world.
   D. Consumers and businesses pay recyclers to remove E-waste.

_____ 4. The relationship of sentence 11 to sentence 10 is one of
   A. contrast.   C. cause and effect.
   B. illustration.   D. addition.

_____ 5. The relationship between sentences 16 and 17 is one of
   A. definition and example.   C. time order.
   B. addition.   D. contrast.

_____ 6. The selection suggests that
   A. it is unfair to expect people in developing nations to recycle our dangerous E-waste without adequate safeguards.
   B. poor people in developing nations should be grateful for the opportunity to earn money recycling E-waste.
   C. people in developing countries don't really care if their air and water is contaminated by E-waste.
   D. There is nothing anyone can do about the problem of E-waste.

_____ 7. The tone of this selection is
   A. concerned and critical.
   B. detached and instructive.
   C. scornful and sarcastic.
   D. straightforward and tolerant.

_____ 8. The most appropriate title for this selection would be
   A. The Roots of Global Inequality
   B. America's Trash Is Asia's Cash
   C. Industry in Asia
   D. The Problems of E-Waste

COMBINED SKILLS: Test 21

Read the passage below. Then write the letter of the best answer to each question that follows.

[1]Researcher Mary Koss drew heavy criticism when she published her findings that more than a quarter of all college women have experienced an act that met the legal definition of rape. [2]Her estimate was 10 to 15 times higher than comparable rates reported by the Bureau of Justice in statistics from their National Crime Victimization Survey (NCVS). [3]Why are the numbers so different?

[4]In cases of rape, it seems that how the data are gathered is critical. [5]The NCVS questions used to determine these rates do not actually ask a woman if she has ever been raped. [6]Rape itself is never mentioned: it is up to the person being questioned to volunteer the information.

[7]An obvious way to get more information is to ask people directly whether they have been raped. [8]A national survey that asked this question of both men and women found that 9.2 percent of women and less than 1.0 percent of men had ever been raped in their lifetimes. [9]Both numbers are significantly higher than those that appear in the National Crime Survey.

[10]Even higher rates are obtained when the question is asked in a different way. [11]When respondents were asked if anyone had ever forced them to do something sexual, 22 percent of women and 4 percent of men responded yes. [12]A study that Bonnie Fisher and her colleagues conducted of nearly 5,000 women attending U.S. colleges and universities also found that what is asked makes a big difference. [13]This study included a comparison component that used methods similar to those used in the NCVS. [14]The main study, which used extremely detailed questions about "unwanted sexual experiences," found rates of rape and attempted rape that were 11 and 6 times higher, respectively, than the rates found by the comparison study. [15]These rates are in line with those reported by Mary Koss for college women and by others for the general population. [16]The Fisher survey responses showed that 1.7 percent of the college women had experienced a rape and 1.1 percent an attempted rape during an average period of about seven months. [17]Projected over the five years that most students now spend getting an undergraduate degree, one-fifth to one-quarter of all college women would experience a rape or attempted rape.

[18]How many rapes we believe occur seems to depend primarily on how victims are asked about their experiences. [19]Fisher and her colleagues concluded, "The use of graphically worded screen questions . . . likely prompted more women who had experienced a sexual victimization to report this fact to the interviewer."

_____ 1. In sentence 13, the word *component* means

    A. viewpoint.   C. part of a whole.

    B. conflict.   D. recommendation.

_____ 2. According to the selection, the National Crime Victimization Survey
   A. was highly accurate.
   B. encouraged women to volunteer information by using extremely detailed questions.
   C. disregarded the legal definition of rape.
   D. never actually asked women if they had been raped.

_____ 3. According to the Fisher survey, the percentage of college women who would experience rape or attempted rape during their college careers is
   A. 1.7%.   C. 9.2%.
   B. 2.8%.   D. 20 to 25%.

_____ 4. Sentence 12 is a statement of
   A. fact.   C. both fact and opinion.
   B. opinion.

_____ 5. We can conclude from this selection that
   A. the legal definition of rape needs to be changed.
   B. college women often invent stories of attempted rape.
   C. victims of rape or attempted rape are often reluctant to volunteer information about their experience.
   D. the incidence of rape is increasing in America.

_____ 6. You can infer from this passage that
   A. rape occurs on college campuses more often than anywhere else.
   B. many of the subjects who talked to Mary Koss were not really raped.
   C. the authors of the NCVS deliberately designed their questions so as to make their rape findings artificially low.
   D. many women who are sexually victimized do not report the incident to the police.

_____ 7. Which title would best summarize this passage?
   A. Rape Data Depends Upon Questioning
   B. Rape on College Campuses
   C. Researcher Is Criticized for Methods Used
   D. Men, Too, Are Sometimes Rape Victims

_____ 8. Which statement best expresses the central point of the passage?
   A. The National Crime Victimization Survey results conflict with other reports and therefore may not be accurate.
   B. The reliability of data on rape depends on the types of questions victims are asked.
   C. Mary Koss and Bonnie Fisher conducted research on sexual victimization.
   D. Rape is a difficult subject for many people to talk about.

COMBINED SKILLS: Test 22

Read the passage below. Then write the letter of the best answer to each question that follows.

[1]Before a German submarine launched two torpedoes at the U.S. destroyer *Greer*, heading for Iceland on September 4, 1941, the American ship had stalked the submarine for hours. [2]Twice the *Greer* signaled the German submarine's location to British patrol bombers, one of which dropped depth charges on the submarine. [3]After the torpedo attack, which missed its mark, the *Greer* also released depth charges. [4]But when President Roosevelt described the encounter in a dramatic radio "Fireside Chat" on September 11, he declared that the German submarine, without warning, had fired the first shot, and he protested German "piracy" as a violation of the principle of freedom of the seas.

[5]Roosevelt did not tell the American people the full truth about the events of September 4, and what he did tell was misleading. [6]The incident had little to do with freedom of the seas—which related to neutral merchant ships, not to U.S. warships operating in a war zone. [7]Roosevelt's words amounted to a call to arms, yet he never asked Congress for a declaration of war against Germany. [8]The president believed that he had to deceive the public in order to move hesitant Americans toward noble positions that they would ultimately see as necessary. [9]Public opinion polls soon demonstrated that the practice worked, as most Americans approved the shoot-on-sight policy Roosevelt announced as a consequence of the *Greer* incident.

[10]Several years later, in his book *The Man in the Street* (1948), Thomas Bailey defended Roosevelt. [11]The historian argued that "because the masses are notoriously short-sighted, and generally cannot see danger until it is at their throats, our statesmen are forced to deceive them into an awareness of their own long-term interests." [12]Roosevelt's critics, on the other hand, even those who agreed with him that Nazi Germany had to be stopped, have seen in his methods a danger to the democratic process, which cannot work in an environment of dishonesty and a usurping of congressional powers.

[13]Following Roosevelt, presidents have found it easier to exaggerate, distort, withhold, or even lie about the facts of foreign relations in order to shape a public opinion favorable to their policies. [14]One result: the growth of the "imperial presidency"—the president's grabbing of power from Congress, and use of questionable means to reach his objectives. [15]The practice of deception—for an end the president calls noble—was one of Roosevelt's legacies for a people and a nation.

_____ 1. In sentence 12, the word *usurping* means
   A. criticizing.   C. influencing.
   B. supporting.   D. seizing without legal authority.

_____ 2. An immediate consequence of the *Greer* incident was that
   A. the U.S. declared war on Germany.
   B. Germany declared war on the United States.
   C. Roosevelt announced a shoot-on-sight policy against Germany.
   D. Congress demanded that Roosevelt tell the truth about the event.

_____ 3. According to the passage, President Roosevelt
    A. denied that the *Greer* had encountered a German submarine.
    B. said that the *Greer* had stalked the German submarine for hours.
    C. misled the American people when he told them that the German submarine had fired the first shot.
    D. realized that it was impossible to deceive the American people.

_____ 4. According to the selection, one long-term consequence of President Roosevelt's handling of the *Greer* incident was
    A. a demand for greater congressional oversight of foreign policy.
    B. that many Americans learned to mistrust much of what future presidents told them.
    C. the growth of the "imperial presidency."
    D. U.S.-German diplomatic relations were permanently damaged.

_____ 5. In this selection, the author mainly
    A. contrasts what really happened in the encounter between the *Greer* and the German submarine with what Roosevelt told the American people.
    B. lists reasons why our leaders are forced, at times, to deceive us.
    C. uses time order to provide a history of presidential deceptions since World War II.
    D. compares recent presidential deceptions with Roosevelt's deception concerning the *Greer* incident.

_____ 6. We can infer that the U.S. destroyer *Greer* stalked the German submarine for hours because it
    A. realized the German submarine was close to the American coast.
    B. wanted to provoke a German attack.
    C. feared the submarine would attack the British patrol bombers.
    D. believed that the submarine was about to launch a torpedo against an American passenger liner.

_____ 7. The author's tone in this passage can best be described as
    A. admiring.   C. bitter.
    B. critical.   D. remorseful.

_____ 8. Which sentence best expresses the central point of this selection?
    A. Roosevelt's version of the *Greer* incident, however well-intentioned, had disturbing long-term consequences for the democratic process.
    B. It is impossible for presidents to rally support for important causes without occasionally resorting to deception.
    C. If Roosevelt had not deceived the American public with regard to the *Greer* incident, we never would have won the war with Germany.
    D. Although Roosevelt is remembered as a great president, he does not deserve his reputation.

+13

COMBINED SKILLS: Test 23

Read the passage below. Then write the letter of the best answer to each question that follows.

¹If we define drugs broadly to include caffeine, tobacco, and alcohol, then most people throughout the world use some type of drug on an occasional or a regular basis. ²Most of these people use such drugs in moderation and do not suffer ill effects. ³But for some, substance use escalates into abuse or dependence. ⁴*Substance abuse* is a pattern of drug use that diminishes a person's ability to fulfill responsibilities, results in repeated use of the drug in dangerous situations, or leads to legal difficulties related to drug use. ⁵For example, people whose drinking causes ill health and problems within their families or on their jobs are abusing alcohol. ⁶Substance abuse is America's leading health problem.

⁷The ongoing abuse of drugs, including alcohol, may lead to compulsive use of substances, or *substance dependence*, which is also known as *addiction*. ⁸Although not everyone who abuses a substance develops dependence, dependence usually follows a period of abuse. ⁹Dependence often includes *tolerance*, the phenomenon whereby higher doses of the drug are required to produce its original effects or to prevent *withdrawal symptoms*. ¹⁰Many organizations publicize self-tests based on these and other elements in the definition of substance abuse. ¹¹For example, a self-test from the National Council on Alcoholism includes the questions, "Can you handle more alcohol now than when you first started to drink?" and "When drinking with other people, do you try to have a few extra drinks the others won't know about?"

¹²The causes of substance abuse and dependence are a complex combination of biological, psychological, and social factors that varies for each individual and for each substance. ¹³Also, the development of substance dependence does not follow an established timetable. ¹⁴One person might drink socially for years before abusing alcohol, whereas someone else might become addicted to cocaine in a matter of days.

_____ 1. In sentence 7, the word *compulsive* means
     A. moderate.
     B. uncontrollable.
     C. casual.
     D. gradual.

_____ 2. According to the selection, if someone has *tolerance* for a substance, he or she
     A. can consume large quantities of that substance without suffering any harmful effects.
     B. refuses to judge others on the basis of their use of that substance.
     C. requires higher doses of that substance to produce its original effect or to prevent withdrawal symptoms.
     D. can only consume that substance in small quantities.

_B_ 3. According to the selection, which of the following is **not** a characteristic of substance abuse?
   A. Being unable to fulfill one's responsibilities at home or work because of one's use of a drug or alcohol.
   B. Getting drunk once in a while at parties.
   C. Repeated use of a drug in dangerous situations.
   D. Drug or alcohol use that leads to legal difficulties.

_D_ 4. In general, this selection
   A. explains why some people become substance abusers.
   B. contrasts addiction to drugs with alcoholism.
   C. lists the consequences of substance abuse.
   D. defines and illustrates terms connected with substance abuse.

_A_ 5. The relationship of sentence 13 to sentence 12 is one of
   A. addition.
   B. illustration.
   C. cause and effect.
   D. contrast.

_D_ 6. We can infer from paragraphs 2 and 3 that
   A. some people are not sure whether or not they are substance abusers.
   B. a person who can handle more alcohol now than when he or she first started to drink has developed a tolerance for alcohol.
   C. substance dependence can take place gradually.
   D. all of the above.

_A_ 7. The tone of this passage is
   A. informal.
   B. disapproving.
   C. instructive.
   D. worried.

_C_ 8. What is the most appropriate title for this selection?
   A. Whatever You Do—Don't Abuse Drugs
   B. The High Cost of Substance Abuse
   C. Defining Substance Abuse
   D. Are You an Alcoholic?

$\times 20$

COMBINED SKILLS: Test 24

Read the passage below. Then write the letter of the best answer to each question that follows.

¹"Congress shall make no law . . . abridging the freedom of speech." ²These important words, found in the First Amendment to the U.S. Constitution, sound pretty straightforward. ³However since they were written at the end of the 18th century, they have been subject to numerous interpretations and have been at the heart of countless decisions handed down by the U.S. Supreme Court.

⁴Perhaps one of the most far-reaching and controversial of these decisions was the one in the 2010 case of *Citizens United vs. Federal Election Commission*. ⁵In that decision, the Court overturned a law passed by Congress in 2002, saying it violated the free speech rights guaranteed by the First Amendment. ⁶That law had prohibited corporations, labor unions and non-profit organizations from broadcasting any "electioneering communication" for or against a political candidate 60 days before a general election or 30 days before a primary election.

⁷"So, what's wrong with that?" you might ask. ⁸Isn't more freedom of speech always better than less? ⁹Well, not necessarily. ¹⁰The *Citizens United* case has opened the floodgates to unlimited spending by interest groups and wealthy individuals in our political campaigns. ¹¹Unlike people or groups who contribute directly to political candidates, these so-called "independent" entities are permitted to spend unlimited amounts of money, frequently without any disclosure of where the funding has come from. ¹²Further undermining the integrity of the political process, they most often use their substantial resources to air highly negative—and frequently untrue—commercials about one or more of the candidates. ¹³Because the law prohibits these groups from "coordinating" with a candidate, those running for office can deny knowledge of what is being done to benefit them and can escape responsibility for any misrepresentation of their opponent's record, character or political agenda.

¹⁴When candidates are not required to take responsibility for what is being done in their name, it becomes extremely difficult for voters to hold them accountable or even assess their honesty. ¹⁵If the expansion of freedom of speech creates that situation, then maybe it has gone too far.

_____ 1. In sentence 12, the word *integrity* means
  A. smooth functioning.
  B. safety.
  C. honesty.
  D. excitement.

2. According to the selection, the *Citizens United* case permits special interest groups to
   A. contribute directly to political campaigns, as long as they disclose where the money is coming from.
   B. spend unlimited amounts of money on a candidate without disclosing where the funding is coming from.
   C. coordinate electioneering communication with a political candidate.
   D. assess the honesty of each candidate in a primary or general election.

3. The relationship of sentence 3 to sentence 2 is one of
   A. cause and effect.   C. definition and example.
   B. addition.   D. contrast.

4. The passage suggests that
   A. most people pay little attention to political commercials.
   B. special interest groups have too much influence over our political process.
   C. most politicians are opposed to special interest groups that spend money to air highly negative commercials.
   D. the *Citizens United* decision will soon be overturned.

5. The author would probably agree that
   A. the Supreme Court made an unwise decision in the case of *Citizens United vs. Federal Election Commission.*
   B. more freedom of speech is always better than less.
   C. the First Amendment is not subject to interpretation.
   D. candidates should not be held accountable for what is being done in their name.

6. The purpose of this selection is to
   A. entertain.   C. inform.
   B. persuade.   D. both inform and persuade.

7. The tone of this selection is
   A. depressed.   C. outraged.
   B. concerned.   D. matter-of-fact.

8. Which is the most appropriate title for this selection?
   A. Freedom of Speech
   B. The Effect of Negative Commercials on Elections
   C. Why Money Matters
   D. *Citizens United:* An Unwise Decision

COMBINED SKILLS: Test 25

Read the passage below. Then write the letter of the best answer to each question that follows.

[1]Virtually everyone is familiar with the Golden Rule, which most of us learned in the form "Do unto others as you would have them do unto you." [2]By obliging us to treat others as well as we would treat ourselves, this maxim seems to offer the foundation for a civil society in which everyone would behave with consideration.

[3]Some ethicists have pointed out that the Golden Rule doesn't work well in situations where others don't want to be treated the same way you would. [4]You may like to blast hip-hop music at top volume at 3 A.M., but appeals to the Golden Rule probably won't placate neighbors who don't share your musical tastes or late-night hours. [5]Likewise, just because you enjoy teasing banter, you aren't entitled to banter with others who might find this type of humor offensive or hurtful.

[6]The Golden Rule presents special problems in cases of intercultural contacts, where norms for what is desirable vary dramatically. [7]For example, most speakers from low-context cultures where English is the first language value honesty and explicit communication, but this level of candor would be offensive in the high-context cultures of Asia or the Middle East. [8]A naïve communicator following the Golden Rule might justify social blunders by claiming, "I was just communicating the way I'd like to be treated." [9]This sort of selfish thinking is a recipe for unsuccessful communication and perhaps for very unpleasant consequences.

[10]In response to the challenge of differing wants, Milton Bennett proposed a "Platinum Rule": "Do unto others as they themselves would have done unto them." [11]Unlike the Golden Rule, this rule requires us to understand how others think and what they want before we can determine how to act ethically. [12]Put differently, the Platinum Rule implies that empathy is a prerequisite for moral sensitivity.

[13]Despite its initial appeal, the Platinum Rule poses its own problems. [14]There are certainly cases where doing unto others what they want might compromise our own needs or even our ethical principles. [15]It is easy to imagine cases in which the Platinum Rule would oblige us to cheat, steal, or lie on others' behalf.

[16]Even if acting on the Platinum Rule is problematic, the benefit of thinking about it seems clear. [17]An essential requirement for benign behavior is the ability to empathize, helping us recognize that what others want may be different from what we would want under the same circumstances.

_____ 1. In sentence 2, the word *maxim* means
   A. question.   C. enlargement.
   B. wise saying.   D. misbehavior.

_____ 2. According to the selection, the Golden Rule requires us to
   A. compromise our own needs or ethical principles.
   B. understand how others think and what they want.
   C. refrain from teasing banter.
   D. treat others as we would wish to be treated.

3. The relationship of sentence 5 to sentence 4 is one of
   A. addition.   C. comparison.
   B. illustration.   D. contrast.

4. In general, this selection
   A. lists various ways that people in different cultures communicate with one another.
   B. states the problems involved with the Golden Rule and proposes a solution.
   C. provides examples of selfish thinking.
   D. compares American and Asian cultures.

5. We can infer that if an American practiced the Platinum Rule in Asia, he or she would
   A. be brutally honest at all times.
   B. keep in mind that his or her hosts would probably be offended by direct criticism.
   C. justify any social blunders he or she might make by claiming, "I was just communicating the way I'd like to be treated."
   D. engage in teasing banter and outright dishonesty.

6. You could reasonably conclude from the selection that the author believes that
   A. the Golden Rule is superior to the Platinum Rule.
   B. the Platinum Rule is superior to the Golden Rule, especially when interacting with other cultures.
   C. there is little value in either the Golden Rule or the Platinum Rule.
   D. selfish thinking can be a valuable tool when interacting with other cultures.

7. The tone of this passage is
   A. optimistic and appreciative.
   B. pleading and compassionate.
   C. ambivalent and worried.
   D. straightforward and tolerant.

8. Which statement best expresses the central point of the passage?
   A. Because of cultural as well as language differences, communication with non-English speakers presents difficulties.
   B. Although both the Golden Rule and the Platinum Rule pose their own problems, the Platinum Rule reminds us to think about other people's needs and wants.
   C. Despite the fact that most people are familiar with the Golden Rule, it doesn't work well in every situation.
   D. Norms for what is desirable very dramatically from culture to culture.

Sample Answer Sheet

Use the form below as a model answer sheet for the twenty-five combined-skills tests.

Name _____ Date _____

Section _____ SCORE: (Number correct) _____ x 12.5 = _____ %

COMBINED SKILLS: Mastery Test ____

1. _____

2. _____

3. _____

4. _____

5. _____

6. _____

7. _____

8. _____

Part Four

Readings in Science and Mathematics

Doing Well in Science and Mathematics

Follow these tips if you want to do well in science and math courses:

🏷 **TIP 1   Don't fall behind.** Most of what you learn in science and math courses builds in a methodical, step-by-step way upon what you have already learned. It's very important, then, that you not miss class. If you do, rely upon a classmate to find out what you missed, or ask your instructor for help. And if you have trouble understanding concepts early on, do not hesitate to visit your school's tutoring center in order to get one-on-one instruction.

🏷 **TIP 2   Sit down with your textbook and carefully note headings and subheadings, definitions, explanations, enumerations, and examples.** Look at the excerpt that follows on pages 611–618 from the first chapter of a science book titled *Human Anatomy and Physiology*. The chapter introduces you to its subject by using definitions, enumerations, headings and subheadings, and examples. You know just by looking at the chapter title "The Human Body: An Orientation" that you'll be getting an overview of the human body. You'll then get definitions of anatomy and physiology, lists (enumerations) of anatomy topics and physiology topics, and other enumerations, including a list of "Necessary Life Functions" and a list of "Survival Needs." The excerpt illustrates how a good textbook can really help you understand a subject if you take the time to patiently read and study it.

Also look at the excerpt on pages 620–627 from the first chapter of a mathematics book titled *Introduction to Statistics*. The chapter begins with definitions of commonly used statistical terms and then goes on to present basic principles of statistical thinking. In a step-by-step way, it provides explanations and examples that make those terms and principles very clear. As with the science excerpt, a great deal of information is presented in a very clear and organized way. The key to understanding is to take the time needed to read carefully through all the information.

TIP 3   Next, to study the material, take notes on it. As a general rule in science and mathematics courses, write down definitions, key concepts (set off in **boldfaced** type), examples of those definitions and concepts, and enumerations. Then recite your notes to yourself until you can repeat them without having to look at them.

For example, with the science excerpt, you might write down on one side of a flashcard the words *Survival Needs*. Then, on the other side of the flashcard, list the five survival needs:

> 1. Nutrients
> 2. Oxygen
> 3. Water
> 4. Normal Body Temperature
> 5. Appropriate Atmospheric Pressure

You should then study this list until you can recite all five survival needs without looking at the back of the flashcard.

Also, with the *Introduction to Statistics* excerpt, you might write down on a flashcard the terms being defined (*data, statistics, population, census, sample*) and then their definitions on the back of the flashcard:

> Data—collections of observations (such as measurements, genders, survey responses)
>
> Statistics—science of planning studies and experiments, obtaining data, and then organizing, summarizing, presenting, analyzing, interpreting, and drawing conclusions based on the data
>
> Population—complete collection of all individuals (scores, people, measurements, and so on) to be studied
>
> Census—collection of data from <u>every</u> member of the population
>
> Sample—<u>subcollection</u> of members selected from a population

TIP 4   Remember there is no shortcut. You must read through mathematics and science materials slowly and patiently. Understanding will come gradually as you continue to work on the material. Taking notes—flashcards are recommended—will help you master the material.

With all the above in mind, carefully read the science and mathematics selections that follow and see if you can answer the questions that follow each selection.

2 The Human Body: An Orientation

Elaine N. Marieb and Katja Hoehn

The following selection is from the introductory chapter of *Human Anatomy and Physiology*, Eighth Edition, by Elaine N. Marieb and Katja Hoehn.

1 Welcome to the study of one of the most fascinating subjects possible—your own body. Such a study is not only highly personal, but timely as well. We get news of some medical advance almost daily. To appreciate emerging discoveries in genetic engineering, to understand new techniques for detecting and treating disease, and to make use of published facts on how to stay healthy, you'll find it helpful to learn about the workings of your body. If you are preparing for a career in the health sciences, the study of anatomy and physiology has added rewards because it provides the foundation needed to support your clinical experiences.

2 In this chapter we define and contrast anatomy and physiology and discuss how the human body is organized. Then we review needs and functional processes common to all living organisms. Three essential concepts—*the complementarity of structure and function, the hierarchy of structural organization,* and *homeostasis*—will unify and form the bedrock for your study of the human body. The final section of the chapter deals with the language of anatomy—terminology that anatomists use to describe the body or its parts.

AN OVERVIEW OF ANATOMY AND PHYSIOLOGY

- Define anatomy and physiology and describe their subdivisions.
- Explain the principle of complementarity.

3 Two complementary branches of science—anatomy and physiology—provide the concepts that help us to understand the human body. **Anatomy** studies the *structure* of body parts and their relationships to one another. Anatomy has a certain appeal because it is concrete. Body structures can be seen, felt, and examined closely. You don't need to imagine what they look like.

4 **Physiology** concerns the *function* of the body, in other words, how the body parts work and carry out their life-sustaining activities. When all is said and done, physiology is explainable only in terms of the underlying anatomy.

5   To simplify the study of the body, when we refer to body structures and/or physiological values (body temperature, heart rate, and the like) we will assume that we are talking about a healthy young (22-year old) male weighing about 155 lb (the *reference man*) or a healthy young female weighing about 125 lb (the *reference woman*).

Topics of Anatomy

6   Anatomy is a broad field with many subdivisions, each providing enough information to be a course in itself. **Gross**, or **macroscopic, anatomy** is the study of large body structures visible to the naked eye, such as the heart, lungs, and kidneys. Indeed, the term *anatomy* (derived from the Greek words meaning "to cut apart") relates most closely to gross anatomy because in such studies preserved animals or their organs are dissected (cut up) to be examined.

7   Gross anatomy can be approached in different ways. In **regional anatomy**, all the structures (muscles, bones, blood vessels, nerves, etc.) in a particular region of the body, such as the abdomen or leg, are examined at the same time.

8   In **systemic** (sis-tem′ik) **anatomy**, body structure is studied system by system. For example, when studying the cardiovascular system, you would examine the heart and the blood vessels of the entire body.

9   Another subdivision of gross anatomy is **surface anatomy**, the study of internal structures as they relate to the overlying skin surface. You use surface anatomy when you identify the bulging muscles beneath a bodybuilder's skin, and clinicians use it to locate appropriate blood vessels in which to feel pulses and draw blood.

10   **Microscopic anatomy** deals with structures too small to be seen with the naked eye. For most such studies, exceedingly thin slices of body tissues are stained and mounted on glass slides to be examined under the microscope. Subdivisions of microscopic anatomy include **cytology** (si-tol′o-je), which considers the cells of the body, and **histology** (his-tol′o-je), the study of tissues.

11   **Developmental anatomy** traces structural changes that occur in the body throughout the life span. **Embryology** (em′bre-ol′o-je), a subdivision of developmental anatomy, concerns developmental changes that occur before birth.

12   Some highly specialized branches of anatomy are used primarily for medical diagnosis and scientific research. For example, *pathological anatomy* studies structural changes caused by disease. *Radiographic anatomy* studies internal structures as visualized by X-ray images or specialized scanning procedures.

13   Subjects of interest to anatomists range from easily seen structures down to the smallest molecule. In *molecular biology*, for example, the structure of biological molecules (chemical substances) is investigated. Molecular biology is actually a separate branch of biology, but it falls under the anatomy umbrella when we push anatomical studies to the subcellular level.

14   One essential tool for studying anatomy is a mastery of anatomical

terminology. Others are observation, manipulation, and, in a living person, *palpation* (feeling organs with your hands) and *auscultation* (listening to organ sounds with a stethoscope). A simple example illustrates how some of these tools work together in an anatomical study.

15   Let's assume that your topic is freely movable joints of the body. In the laboratory, you will be able to *observe* an animal joint, noting how its parts fit together. You can work the joint (*manipulate* it) to determine its range of motion. Using *anatomical terminology*, you can name its parts and describe how they are related so that other students (and your instructor) will have no trouble understanding you. The list of word roots (at the back of the book) and the glossary will help you with this special vocabulary.

16   Although you will make most of your observations with the naked eye or with the help of a microscope, medical technology has developed a number of sophisticated tools that can peer into the body without disrupting it.

Topics of Physiology

17   Like anatomy, physiology has many subdivisions. Most of them consider the operation of specific organ systems. For example, **renal physiology** concerns kidney function and urine production. **Neurophysiology** explains the workings of the nervous system. **Cardiovascular physiology** examines the operation of the heart and blood vessels. While anatomy provides us with a static image of the body's architecture, physiology reveals the body's dynamic and animated workings.

18   Physiology often focuses on events at the cellular or molecular level. This is because the body's abilities depend on those of its individual cells, and cells' abilities ultimately depend on the chemical reactions that go on within them. Physiology also rests on principles of physics, which help explain electrical currents, blood pressure, and the way muscles use bones to cause body movements, among other things. We present basic chemical and physical principles in Chapter 2 and throughout the book as needed to explain physiological topics.

Complementarity of Structure and Function

19   Although it is possible to study anatomy and physiology individually, they are really inseparable because function always reflects structure. That is, what a structure can do depends on its specific form. This key concept is called the **principle of complementarity of structure and function.**

20   For example, bones can support and protect body organs because they contain hard mineral deposits. Blood flows in one direction through the heart because the heart has valves that prevent backflow. Throughout this book, we accompany description of a structure's anatomy with an explanation of its function, and we emphasize structural characteristics contributing to that function.

LEVELS OF STRUCTURAL ORGANIZATION

- Name the different levels of structural organization that make up the human body, and explain their relationship.

- List the 11 organ systems of the body, identify their components, and briefly explain the major function(s) of each system.

21 The human body has many levels of structural organization. The simplest level of the structural hierarchy is the **chemical level**, which we study in Chapter 2. At this level, *atoms*, tiny building blocks of matter, combine to form *molecules* such as water and proteins. Molecules, in turn, associate in specific ways to form *organelles*, basic components of the microscopic cells. *Cells* are the smallest units of living things. We examine the **cellular level** in Chapter 3. All cells have some common functions, but individual cells vary widely in size and shape, reflecting their unique functions in the body.

22   The simplest living creatures are single cells, but in complex organisms such as human beings, the hierarchy continues on to the **tissue level.** *Tissues* are groups of similar cells that have a common function. The four basic tissue types in the human body are epithelium, muscle, connective tissue, and nervous tissue.

23   Each tissue type has a characteristic role in the body, which we explore in Chapter 4. Briefly, epithelium covers the body surface and lines its cavities. Muscle provides movement. Connective tissue supports and protects body organs. Nervous tissue provides a means of rapid internal communication by transmitting electrical impulses.

24   An *organ* is a discrete structure composed of at least two tissue types (four is more common) that performs a specific function for the body. The liver, the brain, and a blood vessel are very difference from the stomach, but each is an organ. You can think of each organ of the body as a specialized functional center responsible for a necessary activity that no other organ can perform.

25   At the **organ level**, extremely complex functions become possible. Let's take the stomach for an example. Its lining is an epithelium that produces digestive juices. The bulk of its wall is muscle, which churns and mixes stomach contents (food). Its connective tissue reinforces the soft muscular walls. Its nerve fibers increase digestive activity by stimulating the muscle to contract more vigorously and the glands to secrete more digestive juices.

26   The next level of organization is the **organ system level.** Organs that work together to accomplish a common purpose make up an *organ system*. For

example, the heart and blood vessels of the cardiovascular system circulate blood continuously to carry oxygen and nutrients to all body cells. Besides the cardiovascular system, the other organ systems of the body are the integumentary, skeletal, muscular, nervous, endocrine, lymphatic, respiratory, digestive, urinary, and reproductive systems. (Note that the immune system is closely associated with the lymphatic system.)

27   The highest level of organization is the *organism*, the living human being. The **organismal level** represents the sum total of all structural levels working together to keep us alive.

CHECK YOUR UNDERSTANDING

3. What level of structural organization is typical of a cytologist's field of study?

4. What is the correct structural order for the following terms: tissue, organism, organ, cell?

5. Which organ system includes the bones and cartilages? Which includes the nasal cavity, lungs, and trachea?

MAINTAINING LIFE

- List the functional characteristics necessary to maintain life in humans.

- List the survival needs of the body.

Necessary Life Functions

28   Now that you know the structural levels of the human body, the question that naturally follows is: What does this highly organized human body do?

29   Like all complex animals, humans maintain their boundaries, move, respond to environmental changes, take in and digest nutrients, carry out metabolism, dispose of wastes, reproduce themselves, and grow. We will introduce these necessary life functions here and discuss them in more detail in later chapters.

30   We cannot emphasize too strongly that all body cells are interdependent. This interdependence is due to the fact that humans are multicellular organisms and our vital body functions are parceled out among different organ systems. Organ systems, in turn, work cooperatively to promote the well-being of the entire body. This theme is repeated throughout the book.

Maintaining Boundaries

31   Every living organism must **maintain its boundaries** so that its internal environment (its inside) remains distinct from the external environment surrounding it (its outside). In single-celled organisms, the external boundary is a limiting membrane that encloses its contents and lets in needed substances while restricting entry of potentially damaging or unnecessary substances. Similarly, all the cells of our body are surrounded by a selectively permeable membrane.

32   Additionally, the body as a whole is enclosed and protected by the integumentary system, or skin. This system protects our internal organs from drying out (a fatal change),

bacteria, and the damaging effects of heat, sunlight, and an unbelievable number of chemicals in the external environment.

Movement

33   **Movement** includes the activities promoted by the muscular system, such as propelling ourselves from one place to another by running or swimming, and manipulating the external environment with our nimble fingers. The skeletal system provides the bony framework that the muscles pull on as they work. Movement also occurs when substances such as blood, foodstuffs, and urine are propelled through internal organs of the cardiovascular, digestive, and urinary systems, respectively. On the cellular level, the muscle cell's ability to move by shortening is more precisely called **contractility**.

Responsiveness

34   **Responsiveness**, or **irritability**, is the ability to sense changes (which serve as stimuli) in the environment and then respond to them. For example, if you cut your hand on broken glass, a withdrawal reflex occurs—you involuntarily pull your hand away from the painful stimulus (the broken glass). You don't have to think about it—it just happens! Likewise, when carbon dioxide in your blood rises to dangerously high levels, chemical sensors respond by sending messages to brain centers controlling respiration, and you breathe more rapidly.

35   Because nerve cells are highly irritable and communicate rapidly with each other via electrical impulses, the nervous system is most involved with responsiveness. However, all body cells are irritable to some extent.

Digestion

Digestion is the breaking down of   36
ingested foodstuffs to simple molecules that can be absorbed into the blood. The nutrient-rich blood is then distributed to all body cells by the cardiovascular system. In a simple, one-celled organism such as an amoeba, the cell itself is the "digestion factory," but in the multi-cellular human body, the digestive system performs this function for the entire body.

Metabolism

Metabolism (me-tab′o-lizm; "a state of   37
change") is a broad term that includes all chemical reactions that occur within body cells. It includes breaking down substances into their simpler building blocks (more specifically, the process of *catabolism*), synthesizing more complex cellular structures from simpler substances (*anabolism*), and using nutrients and oxygen to produce (via *cellular respiration*) ATP, the energy-rich molecules that power cellular activities. Metabolism depends on the digestive and respiratory systems to make nutrients and oxygen available to the blood and on the cardiovascular system to distribute them throughout the body. Metabolism is regulated largely by hormones secreted by endocrine system glands.

Excretion

Excretion is the process of removing   38
wastes, or *excreta* (ek-skre′tah), from the

body. If the body is to operate as we expect it to, it must get rid of nonuseful substances produced during digestion and metabolism.

39   Several organ systems participate in excretion. For example, the digestive system rids the body of indigestible food residues in feces, and the urinary system disposes of nitrogen-containing metabolic wastes, such as urea, in urine. Carbon dioxide, a by-product of cellular respiration, is carried in the blood to the lungs, where it leaves the body in exhaled air.

Reproduction

40   **Reproduction** occurs at the cellular and the organismal level. In cellular reproduction, the original cell divides, producing two identical daughter cells that may then be used for body growth or repair. Reproduction of the human organism, or making a whole new person, is the major task of the reproductive system. When a sperm unites with an egg, a fertilized egg forms and develops into a baby within the mother's body. The reproductive system is directly responsible for producing offspring, but its function is exquisitely regulated by hormones of the endocrine system.

41   Because males produce sperm and females produce eggs (ova), there is a division of labor in reproduction, and the reproductive organs of males and females are different. Additionally, the female's reproductive structures provide the site for fertilization of eggs by sperm, and then protect and nurture the developing fetus until birth.

Growth

42   **Growth** is an increase in size of a body part or the organism. It is usually accomplished by increasing the number of cells. However, individual cells also increase in size when not dividing. For true growth to occur, constructive activities must occur at a faster rate than destructive ones.

Survival Needs

43   The ultimate goal of all body systems is to maintain life. However, life is extraordinarily fragile and requires several factors. These factors, which we will call *survival needs*, include nutrients (food), oxygen, water, and appropriate temperature and atmospheric pressure.

Nutrients

44   **Nutrients**, taken in via the diet, contain the chemical substances used for energy and cell building. Most plant-derived foods are rich in carbohydrates, vitamins, and minerals, whereas most animal foods are richer in proteins and fats.

45   Carbohydrates are the major energy fuel for body cells. Proteins, and to a lesser extent fats, are essential for building cell structures. Fats also provide a reserve of energy-rich fuel. Selected minerals and vitamins are required for the chemical reactions that go on in cells and for oxygen transport in the blood. The mineral calcium helps to make bones hard and is required for blood clotting.

Oxygen

46   All the nutrients in the world are useless unless **oxygen** is also available.

Because the chemical reactions that release energy from foods are *oxidative* reactions that require oxygen, human cells can survive for only a few minutes without oxygen. Approximately 20% of the air we breathe is oxygen. The cooperative efforts of the respiratory and cardiovascular systems make oxygen available to the blood and body cells.

Water

47   **Water** accounts for 60–80% of our body weight and is the single most abundant chemical substance in the body. It provides the watery environment necessary for chemical reactions and the fluid base for body secretions and excretions. We obtain water chiefly from ingested foods or liquids. We lose it from the body by evaporation from the lungs and skin and in body excretions.

Normal Body Temperature

48   If chemical reactions are to continue at life-sustaining rates, **normal body temperature** must be maintained. As body temperature drops below 37°C (98.6°F), metabolic reactions become slower and slower, and finally stop. When body temperature is too high, chemical reactions occur at a frantic pace and body proteins lose their characteristic shape and stop functioning. At either extreme, death occurs. The activity of the muscular system generates most body heat.

Appropriate Atmospheric Pressure

49   **Atmospheric pressure** is the force that air exerts on the surface of the body. Breathing and gas exchange in the lungs depend on *appropriate* atmospheric pressure. At high altitudes, where atmospheric pressure is lower and the air is thin, gas exchange may be inadequate to support cellular metabolism.

50   The mere presence of these survival factors is not sufficient to sustain life. They must be present in *appropriate* amounts. Excesses and deficits may be equally harmful. For example, oxygen is essential, but excessive amounts are toxic to body cells. Similarly, the food we eat must be of high quality and in proper amounts. Otherwise, nutritional disease, obesity, or starvation is likely. Also, while the needs listed above are the most crucial, they do not even begin to encompass all of the body's needs. For example, we can live without gravity if we must, but the quality of life suffers.

CHECK YOUR UNDERSTANDING

6. What separates living beings from nonliving objects?
7. What name is given to all chemical reactions that occur within body cells?
8. Why is it necessary to be in a pressurized cabin when flying at 30,000 feet?

PRACTICE

Textbook authors use headings and subheadings, definitions (often **boldfaced**), examples, and enumerations in the text to signal important ideas. Take advantage of such signals to answer the following questions about "The Human Body: An Orientation."

1. What is the difference between anatomy and physiology?

   _____

   _____

   _____

_____ 2. How many terms and principles are **boldfaced** under the heading "An Overview of Anatomy and Physiology"?
   A. 10
   B. 15
   C. 20

3. What is an example of the principle of complementarity of structure and function?

   _____

   _____

   _____

_____ 4. How many levels of structural organization are explained in the selection?
   A. 3
   B. 6
   C. 12

_____ 5. How many necessary life functions are explained in the selection?
   A. 4
   B. 8
   C. 12

3 Introduction to Statistics
Mario F. Triola

The following selection is from the introductory chapter of *Elementary Statistics,* Eleventh Edition, by Mario F. Triola.

REVIEW AND PREVIEW

1 The first section of each of the Chapters 1 through 14 begins with a brief review of what preceded the chapter, and a preview of what the chapter includes. This first chapter isn't preceded by much of anything except the Preface, and we won't review that (most people don't even read it in the first place). However, we can review and formally define some statistical terms that are commonly used. For example, polls collect data from a small part of a larger group so that we can learn something about the larger group. This is a common and important goal of statistics: Learn about a large group by examining data from some of its members. In this context, the terms *sample* and *population* have special meanings. Formal definitions for these and other basic terms are given here.

Statistics is the science of planning studies and experiments, obtaining data, and then organizing, summarizing, presenting, analyzing, interpreting, and drawing conclusions based on the data.

A **population** is the complete collection of all individuals (scores, people, measurements, and so on) to be studied. The collection is complete in the sense that it includes *all* of the individuals to be studied.

A **census** is the collection of data from *every* member of the population.

A **sample** is a *subcollection* of members selected from a population.

DEFINITIONS

Data are collections of observations (such as measurements, genders, survey responses).

2 In this book we demonstrate how to use sample data to form conclusions about populations. It is *extremely* important to obtain sample data that are representative of the population from which the data are drawn. As

we proceed through this chapter and discuss types of data and sampling methods, we should focus on these key concepts:

- **Sample data must be collected in an appropriate way, such as through a process of *random* selection.**

- **If sample data are not collected in an appropriate way, the data may be so completely useless that no amount of statistical torturing can salvage them.**

STATISTICAL THINKING

3   **Key Concept** This section introduces basic principles of statistical thinking used throughout this book. Whether conducting a statistical analysis of data that we have collected, or analyzing a statistical analysis done by someone else, we should not rely on blind acceptance of mathematical calculations. We should consider these factors:

- Context of the data
- Source of the data
- Sampling method
- Conclusions
- Practical implications

In learning how to think statistically, common sense and practical considerations are typically much more important than implementation of cookbook formulas and calculations.

4   Statistics involves the analysis of data, so let's begin by considering the data in Table 1-1.

Table 1-1	**Data Used for Analysis**				
x	56	67	57	60	64
y	53	66	58	61	68

After completing an introductory statistics course, we are armed with many statistical tools. In some cases, we are "armed and dangerous" if we jump in and start calculations without considering some critically important "big picture" issues. In order to properly analyze the data in Table 1-1, we must have some additional information. Here are some key questions that we might pose to get this information: What is the context of the data? What is the source of the data? How were the data obtained? What can we conclude from the data? Based on statistical conclusions, what practical implications result from our analysis?

Context As presented in Table 1-1, 5 the data have no context. There is no description of what the values represent, where they came from, and why they were collected. Such a context is given in Example 1.

EXAMPLE 1

Context for Table 1-1 The data in Table 1-1 are taken from Data Set 3 in Appendix B. The entries in Table1-1 are weights (in kilograms) of Rutgers students. The x values are weights measured in September of their freshman year, and the y values are their corresponding weights measured in April of the following spring semester. For example, the first student had a September weight of 56 kg and an April weight of 53 kg. These weights are included in a study described in "Changes in Body Weight and Fat Mass of Men and Women in the First Year of College: A Study of the 'Freshman 15,'" by Hoffman, Policastro, Quick, and Lee, *Journal of American College Health*, Vol. 55, No. 1. The title of the article tells us the goal of the study: Determine whether college students actually gain 15 pounds during their freshman year, as is commonly believed according to the "Freshman 15" legend.

6   The described context of the data in Table 1-1 shows that they consist of matched pairs. That is, each *x-y* pair of values has a "before" weight and an "after" weight for one particular student included in the study. An understanding of this context will directly affect the statistical procedures we use. Here, the key issue is whether the changes in weight appear to support or contradict the common belief that college students typically gain 15 lb during their freshman year. We can address this issue by using methods presented later in this book.

7   If the values in Table 1-1 were numbers printed on the jerseys of Rutgers basketball players, where the *x*-values are from the men's team and

the *y*-values are from the women's team, then this context would suggest that there is no meaningful statistical procedure that could be used with the data (because the numbers don't measure or count anything). *Always consider the context of the data, because the context affects the statistical analysis that should be used.*

Source of Data   Consider the source   8 of the data, and consider whether that source is likely to be objective or there is some incentive to be biased.

EXAMPLE 2

Source of the Data in Table 1-1 Reputable researchers from the Department of Nutritional Sciences at Rutgers University compiled the measurements in Table 1-1. The researchers have no incentive to distort or spin results to support some self-serving position. They have nothing to gain or lose by distorting results. They were not paid by a company that could profit from favorable results. We can be confident that these researchers are unbiased and they did not distort results.

Not all studies have such unbiased   9 sources. For example, Kiwi Brands, a maker of shoe polish, commissioned a study that led to the conclusion that wearing scuffed shoes was the most common reason for a male job applicant to fail to make a good first impression.

Physicians who receive funding from drug companies conduct some clinical experiments of drugs, so they have an incentive to obtain favorable results. Some professional journals, such as *Journal of the American Medical Association,* now require that physicians report such funding in journal articles. We should be vigilant and skeptical of studies from sources that may be biased.

10   **Sampling Method** If we are collecting sample data for a study, the sampling method that we choose can greatly influence the validity of our conclusions. Sections 1-4 and 1-5 will discuss sampling methods in more detail, but for now note that voluntary response (or self-selected) samples often have a bias, because those with a special interest in the subject are more likely to participate in the study. In a *voluntary response sample*, the respondents themselves decide whether to be included. For example, the ABC television show *Nightline* asked viewers to call with their opinion about whether the United Nations headquarters should remain in the United States. Viewers then decided themselves whether to call with their opinions, and those with strong feelings about the topic were more likely to call. We can use sound statistical methods to analyze voluntary response samples, but the results are not necessarily valid. There are other sampling methods, such as random sampling, that are more likely to produce good results.

EXAMPLE 3

Sampling Used for Table 1-1

The weights in Table 1-1 are from the larger sample of weights listed in Data Set 3 of Appendix B. Researchers obtained those data from subjects who were volunteers in a health assessment conducted in September of their freshman year. All of the 217 students who participated in the September assessment were invited for a follow-up in the spring, and 67 of those students responded and were measured again in the last two weeks of April. This sample is a voluntary response sample. The researchers wrote that "the sample obtained was not random and may have introduced self-selection bias." They elaborated on the potential for bias by specifically listing particular potential sources of bias, such as the response of "only those students who felt comfortable enough with their weight to be measured both times."

Not all studies and articles are so   11
clear about the potential for bias. It is very common to encounter surveys that use self-selected subjects, yet the reports and conclusions fail to identify the limitations of such potentially biased samples.

12   **Conclusions** When forming a conclusion based on a statistical analysis, we should make statements that are clear to those without any understanding of statistics and its terminology. We should carefully avoid making statements not justified by the statistical analysis. For example, Section 10-2 introduces the concept of a *correlation*, or association between two variables, such as smoking and pulse rate. A statistical analysis might justify the statement that there is a correlation between the number of cigarettes smoked and pulse rate, but it would not justify a statement that the number of cigarettes smoked *causes* a person's pulse rate to change. Correlation does not imply causality.

EXAMPLE 4

Conclusions from Data in Table 1-1 Table 1-1 lists before and after weights of five subjects taken from Data Set 3 in Appendix B. Those weights were analyzed with conclusions included in "Changes in Body Weight and Fat Mass of Men and Women in the First Year of College: A Study of the 'Freshman 15,' " by Hoffman, Policastro, Quick, and Lee, *Journal of American College Health*, Vol. 55, No. 1. In analyzing the data in Table 1-1, the investigators concluded that the freshman year of college is a time during which weight gain occurs. But the investigators went on to state that in the small nonrandom group studied, the weight gain was less than 15 pounds, and this amount was not universal. They concluded that the "Freshman 15" weight gain is a myth.

Practical Implications In addition   13
to clearly stating conclusions of the statistical analysis, we should also identify any practical implications of the results.

EXAMPLE 5

Practical Implications from Data in Table 1-1 In their analysis of the data collected in the "Freshman 15" study, the researchers point out some practical implications of their results. They wrote that "it is perhaps most important for students to recognize that seemingly minor and perhaps even harmless changes in eating or exercise behavior may result in large changes in weight and body fat mass over an extended period of time." Beginning freshman college students should recognize that there could be serious health consequences resulting from radically different diet and exercise routines.

The *statistical significance* of a study   14
can differ from its *practical significance*. It is possible that, based on the available

sample data, methods of statistics can be used to reach a conclusion that some treatment or finding is effective, but common sense might suggest that the treatment or finding does not make enough of a difference to justify its use or to be practical.

EXAMPLE 6

Statistical Significance versus Practical Significance In a test of the Atkins weight loss program, 40 subjects using that program had a mean weight loss of 2.1 lb after one year (based on data from "Comparison of the Atkins, Ornish, Weight Watchers, and Zone Diets for Weight Loss and Heart Disease Risk Reductions," by Dansinger et al., *Journal of the American Medical Association*, Vol. 293, No. 1). Using formal methods of statistical analysis, we can conclude that the mean weight loss of 2.1 is statistically significant. That is, based on statistical criteria, the diet appears to be effective. However, using common sense, it does not seem worthwhile to pursue a weight loss program resulting in such relatively insignificant results. Someone starting a weight loss program would likely want to lose considerably more than 2.1 lb. Although the mean weight loss of 2.1 lb is statistically significant, it does not have practical significance. The statistical

analysis suggests that the weight loss program is effective, but practical considerations suggest that the program is basically ineffective.

Statistical Significance *Statistical significance* is a concept we will consider at length throughout this book. To prepare for those discussions, Examples 7 and 8 illustrate the concept in a simple setting. 15

EXAMPLE 7

Statistical Significance The Genetics and IVF Institute in Fairfax, Virginia developed a technique called MicroSort, which supposedly increases the chances of a couple having a baby girl. In a preliminary test, researchers located 14 couples who wanted baby girls. After using the MicroSort technique, 13 of them had girls and one couple had a boy. After obtaining these results, we have two possible conclusions:

1. The MicroSort technique is not effective and the result of 13 girls in 14 births occurred by chance.

2. The MicroSort technique is effective, and couples who use the technique are more likely to have baby girls, as claimed by the Genetics and IVF Institute.

When choosing between the two possible explanations for the results, statisticians consider the *likelihood* of getting the results by chance. They are able to determine that if the MicroSort technique has no effect, then there is about 1 chance in 1000 of getting results like those obtained here. Because that likelihood is so small, statisticians conclude that the results are statistically significant, so it appears that the MicroSort technique is effective.

EXAMPLE 8

Statistical Significance Instead of the result in Example 7, suppose the couples had 8 baby girls in 14 births. We can see that 8 baby girls is more than the 7 girls that we would expect with an ineffective treatment. However, statisticians can determine that if the MicroSort technique has no effect, then there are roughly two chances in five of getting 8 girls in 14 births. Unlike the one chance in 1000 from the preceding example, two chances in five indicates that the results could *easily occur by chance*. This would indicate that the result of 8 girls in 14 births is *not statistically significant*. With 8 girls in 14 births, we would not

conclude that the technique is effective, because it is so easy (two chances in five) to get the results with an ineffective treatment or no treatment.

What Is Statistical Thinking? Statis- 16
ticians universally agree that statistical thinking is good, but there are different views of what actually constitutes statistical thinking. In this section we have described statistical thinking in terms of the ability to see the big picture and to consider such relevant factors as context, source of data, and sampling method, and to form conclusions and identify practical implications. Statistical thinking involves critical thinking and the ability to make sense of results. Statistical thinking might involve determining whether results are statistically significant, as in Examples 7 and 8. Statistical thinking is so much more than the mere ability to execute complicated calculations. Through numerous examples, exercises, and discussions, this book will develop the statistical thinking skills that are so important in today's world.

BASIC SKILLS AND CONCEPTS

Statistical Literacy and Critical Thinking

1. **Voluntary Response Sample** What is a voluntary response sample?

2. **Voluntary Response Sample** Why is a voluntary response sample generally not suitable for a statistical study?

3. **Statistical Significance versus Practical Significance** What is the difference between statistical significance and practical significance?

4. **Context of Data** You have collected a large sample of values. Why is it important to understand the *context* of the data?

5. **Statistical Significance versus Practical Significance** In a study of the Weight Watchers weight loss program, 40 subjects lost a mean of 3.0 lb after 12 months (based on data from "Comparison of the Atkins, Ornish, Weight Watchers, and Zone Diets for Weight Loss and Heart Disease Risk Reduction," by Dansinger et al., *Journal of the American Medical Association*, Vol. 293, No. 1). Methods of statistics can be used to verify that the diet is effective. Does the Weight Watchers weight loss program have statistical significance? Does it have practical significance? Why or why not?

6. **Sampling Method** In the study of the Weight Watchers weight loss program from Exercise 5, subjects were found using the method described as follows: "We recruited study candidates from the Greater Boston area using newspaper advertisements and television publicity." Is the sample a voluntary response sample? Why or why not?

In Exercises 7–14, use common sense to determine whether the given event is (a) impossible; (b) possible, but very unlikely; (c) possible and likely.

7. **Super Bowl** The New York Giants beat the Denver Broncos in the Super Bowl by a score of 120 to 98.

8. **Speeding Ticket** While driving to his home in Connecticut, David Letterman was ticketed for driving 205 mi/h on a highway with a speed limit of 55 mi/h.

9. **Traffic Lights** While driving through a city, Mario Andretti arrived at three consecutive traffic lights and they were all green.

10. **Thanksgiving** Thanksgiving Day will fall on a Monday next year.

11. **Supreme Court** All of the justices on the United States Supreme Court have the same birthday.

12. **Calculators** When each of 25 statistics students turns on his or her TI-84 Plus calculator, all 25 calculators operate successfully.

13. **Lucky Dice** Steve Wynn rolled a pair of dice and got a total of 14.

14. **Slot Machine** Wayne Newton hit the jackpot on a slot machine each time in ten consecutive attempts.

PRACTICE

Textbook authors use headings and subheadings, definitions (often **boldfaced**), examples, and enumerations in the text to signal important ideas. Take advantage of such signals to answer the following questions about "Introduction to Statistics."

_____ 1. How many definitions and key concepts are presented under the heading "Review and Preview"?
   A. 5
   B. 7
   C. 10

_____ 2. How many key factors are presented under the heading "Statistical Thinking"?
   A. 3
   B. 5
   C. 7

_____ 3. How many of these key factors are explained with an example?
   A. 3 of them
   B. 5 of them
   C. 7 of them

4. What is the difference between statistical significance and practical significance?

_____

_____

_____

_____

_____ 5. How many examples are provided to help explain statistical significance?
   A. 2
   B. 3
   C. 4

Appendixes

Pronunciation Guide

Each item in Chapter 3 of the Introduction, "Notes on Vocabulary in Context," is followed by information in parentheses that shows you how to pronounce the word. (There are also pronunciations for the vocabulary items that follow the readings in Parts One and Two.) The guide below and on the next page explains how to use that information.

Long Vowel Sounds

ā	pay
ē	she
ī	hi
ō	go
ōō	cool
yōō	use

Short Vowel Sounds

ă	hat
ĕ	ten
ĭ	sit
ŏ	lot
ŏŏ	look
ŭ	up
yŏŏ	cure

Other Vowel Sounds

â	care
ä	card
îr	here
ô	all
oi	oil
ou	out
ûr	fur
ə	ago, item, easily, gallop, circus

Consonant Sounds

b	big
d	do
f	fall
g	dog
h	he

Consonant Sounds

j	jump
k	kiss
l	let
m	meet
n	no
p	put
r	red
s	sell
t	top
v	have
w	way
y	yes
z	zero
ch	church
sh	dish
th	then
th	thick
zh	usual

Note that each pronunciation symbol above is paired with a common word that shows the sound of the symbol. For example, the symbol ā has the sound of the *a* in the common word *pay*. The symbol ă has the sound of the *a* in the common word *hat*. The symbol ə, which looks like an upside-down *e* and is known as the schwa, has the unaccented sound in the common word *ago*. It sounds like the "uh" a speaker often says when hesitating.

Accent marks are small black marks that tell you which syllable to emphasize as you say a word. A bold accent mark (′) shows which syllable should be stressed. A lighter accent mark (′) in some words indicates a secondary stress. Syllables without an accent mark are unstressed.

Writing Assignments

A Brief Guide to Effective Writing

Here in a nutshell is what you need to do to write effectively.

Step 1: Explore Your Topic through Informal Writing

To begin with, explore the topic that you want to write about or that you have been assigned to write about. You can examine your topic through **informal writing**, which usually means one of three things.

First, you can **freewrite** about your topic for at least ten minutes. In other words, write, for ten minutes, whatever comes into your head about your subject. Write without stopping and without worrying at all about spelling or grammar or the like. Simply get down on paper all the information about the topic that occurs to you.

A second thing you can do is to **make a list of ideas and details** that could go into your paper. Simply pile these items up, one after another, like a shopping list, without worrying about putting them in any special order. Try to accumulate as many details as you can think of.

A third way to explore your topic is to **write down a series of questions and answers** about it. Your questions can start with words like *what, why, how, when,* and *where.*

Getting your thoughts and ideas down on paper will help you think more about your topic. With some raw material to look at, you are now in a better position to decide on just how to proceed.

Step 2: Plan Your Paper with an Informal Outline

After exploring your topic, plan your paper, using an informal outline. Do two things:

- **Decide on and write out the point of your paper.** It is often a good idea to begin your paragraph with this point, which is also known as the *topic sentence.* If you are writing an essay of several paragraphs, you will probably want to include your main point somewhere in your first paragraph. In a paper of several paragraphs, the main point is called the *central point, central idea,* or *thesis.*

- **List the supporting reasons, examples, or other details that back up your point.** In many cases, you should have at least two or three items of support.

Step 3: Use Transitions

Once your outline is worked out, you will have a clear "road map" for writing your paper. As you write the early drafts of your paper, use **transitions** to introduce each of the separate supporting items (reasons, examples, or other details) you present to back up your point. For instance, you might introduce your first supporting item with the transitional words *first of all.* You might begin your second supporting item with words such as *another reason* or *another example.* And you might indicate your final supporting detail with such words as *last of all* or *a final reason.*

Step 4: Edit and Proofread Your Paper

After you have a solid draft, edit and proofread the paper. To evaluate your paper, ask yourself these questions:

1 Is the paper **unified**? Does all the material in the paper truly support the main point?

2 Is the paper **well supported**? Is there plenty of specific evidence to back up the main point?

3 Is the paper **clearly organized**? Does the material proceed in a way that makes sense? Do transitions help connect ideas?

4 Is the paper **well written**? When the paper is read aloud, do the sentences flow smoothly and clearly? Has the paper been checked carefully for grammar, punctuation, and spelling mistakes?

Writing Assignments for the Twenty Readings

Note: The discussion questions accompanying the twenty readings can also make good topics for writing. Some of the writing assignments here are based on these questions.

Part One Readings

Getting a Good Night's Sleep

1. Write a paragraph in which you suggest three common reasons why people might not get enough sleep. Provide some detail that makes it clear why, for many people, these reasons take precedence over sleeping.

2. What changes would you have to make in your own daily routine in order to consistently get eight hours of sleep a night? Write a paragraph in which you explain those changes.

3. This essay explains how Americans would benefit from getting more regular sleep. Write an essay about another change in lifestyle that you think Americans would benefit from. In your essay, describe three ways that you believe people's lives would be improved if they would follow your recommendation.

Alcohol

1. Alcohol can damage the individual and society, just as many illegal drugs can. Why do you think alcohol remains so much more socially acceptable than other drugs? Write a paragraph explaining some possible reasons for its social acceptance.

2. Unlike the authors of this selection, advertisers portray alcohol in a very positive light. Write a paragraph about some of the ways advertisers make alcohol seem attractive to consumers.

3. Why do you think people in the 18- to 29-year-old age group drink so much? Write an essay in which you identify three possible reasons. Explain why those reasons might be especially powerful for people at this stage in life.

"Extra Large, Please"

1. The author suggests that childhood obesity affects more than just a child and his or her family—it is a problem that society should be addressing. Do you agree? Write a paragraph explaining why you think childhood obesity should be regarded as a social problem. Alternatively, write a paragraph explaining why it should be seen as a private, individual issue.

2. Write a paragraph about the environment you lived in as a child and what opportunities for physical exercise were available.

3. What can parents do to encourage their children to eat healthy foods and get more exercise? Write an essay in which you suggest several ideas and how parents might put them into practice.

Skills of Effective Face-to-Face Conversationalists

1. Write a paragraph about someone you know who is, in your opinion, a good conversationalist. In the paragraph, describe two or three things about this person's conversational style that you think are particularly effective.

2. In a paragraph, explain what you think are your strongest point *and* your weakest point as a conversationalist. Give examples of each.

3. Along with *good* conversationalists, there are *poor* ones. Write an essay in which you describe three types of bad conversationalists. Use specific examples so your reader can understand why each type of person is boring, annoying, or otherwise difficult to talk to.

Hoover and Hard Times

1. What piece of information in this reading surprised or interested you the most? Write a paragraph that answers that question and explains your response.

2. Write a paragraph explaining how, in your opinion, current attitudes about women in the workforce compare to or contrast with the attitudes that existed during the Depression.

3. Write an essay in which you describe how racism *or* sexism seems to have been a factor in how people fared during the Depression. In your opinion, is racism or sexism still as great a factor in people's economic success today? Why or why not?

The Ugly Truth about Beauty

1. While many people are, like Barry, critical of the influence of Barbie dolls, the dolls are still extremely popular. Write a paragraph in which you explain why you would or would not encourage your own young daughter to "play Barbies."

2. The selection focuses on women's insecurity about their appearance. What kind of insecurities do you think are especially common among men? Write a paragraph in which you describe one such common male insecurity.

3. Looks are certainly part of why we find another person attractive, but they're not the only part. Write an essay in which you name three *non*-physical qualities that are important to you in a potential romantic partner. Explain why each of them matters to you.

Self-Help Books

1. Do you sometimes read self-help books or articles, or watch self-help shows like *Dr. Phil*? Write a paragraph about what attracts you to them.

2. The authors write, "Research suggests that narcissism levels have increased among recent generations of college students." Write a paragraph in which you describe examples of narcissism that you have observed in real life.

3. The selection states that "in recent decades Americans' average anxiety level has moved upwards, and the prevalence of depression has increased as well. The multitude of self-help books that crowd bookstore shelves represent just one more symptom of our collective distress and our search for the elusive secret of happiness." Write an essay in which you explore why Americans might be more anxious and depressed now than they were in the past. Begin with a thesis statement something like this: "I believe there are three reasons people are more anxious and depressed than ever before."

Diamonds Aren't Forever

1. Regardless of your gender or marital status, if you were to become engaged right now, would you want to give or receive a diamond engagement ring? Why or why not? Write a paragraph explaining your answer.

2. The author points out that advertisers manipulate us into feeling that we should want certain things, even if we don't need them. What are some examples of non-essential products that are heavily advertised? Write a paragraph about one or more of those products and how consumers are persuaded to want them.

3. The diamond engagement ring is only one part of planning a wedding that many people accept as a necessity. Write an essay about three other customs that have become an expected part of an engagement or wedding. In your essay, discuss both the positive and the negative aspects of these customs.

A Scary Time to Raise a Daughter

1. Write a paragraph in which you defend one of the following topic sentences: "Steve Lopez is right in saying that young teens today are strongly pressured to have sex" *or* "Steve Lopez is exaggerating the pressure on young teens to have sex."

2. Imagine you had a friend, a boy or girl in his or her early teens, who confided in you that he or she was feeling "out of it" and "like a loser" because he or she was a virgin. Your friend was thinking about "getting it over with" by taking the next sexual opportunity that came along and wanted to know what you thought about that plan. Write a paragraph explaining how you would respond.

3. Some people believe that being sexually active defines them as adults. But there are far more meaningful measures of maturity. Write an essay in which you name three characteristics that you believe define a true adult. Describe how those characteristics are demonstrated in an adult's life.

Personal Conflict Styles

1. "Crazy-making" is a very good description of passive-aggressive behavior. Write a paragraph about a time you've been subjected to someone's passive aggression, what the person said or did, and how you responded.

2. Of the approaches to handling personal conflict described in this reading, which best describes your own style? Are you satisfied with your own approach, or would you like to learn to get better at one of the others described here? Write a paragraph in which you answer both questions.

3. The selection describes five approaches to handling personal conflict: non-assertive behavior, direct aggression, passive aggression, indirect communication, and assertion. Write an essay in which you describe how a person might deal with the same situation three different ways—that is, using three of those techniques. You might begin with a thesis statement similar to the following: "If your boss keeps giving you extra work to do without extra pay, you have three possible responses."

Part Two Readings

Understand Your Nervousness

1. If you had to speak in public, would you be very nervous, somewhat nervous, or not particularly nervous? Write a paragraph in which you describe the feelings you have before, during, and after giving a speech.

2. Other than public speaking, what is a situation that makes you feel a high degree of anxiety? Write a paragraph in which you identify that situation and describe the physical response you experience.

3. The authors refer to the "fight or flight" response to anxiety, during which the body produces more adrenaline, increases its breathing rate, and quickens its heart rate. Aside from public speaking, what are some circumstances in which the fight or flight response might be helpful? Write an essay in which you identify three such circumstances and how those physical changes might assist you.

Consequences of Social Class

1. Does the author's description of the different approaches to child-rearing by upper and lower classes (paragraphs 26–27) seem accurate to you? Write a paragraph in which you explain why you do or do not agree with the author's assessment.

2. Unlike the United States, most industrialized countries provide universal health care for their citizens. Do you think the U.S. should do the same? Or do you prefer the current system, where health care is available based on employment or income? Write a paragraph in which you state the reasons for your answer.

3. This selection describes how class affects many areas of life. Write an essay about your everyday observations of class differences. Choose three areas, such as in your neighborhood, at school, at work, or on the street. Write an essay in which you describe, for each area, behavior and attitudes that you believe are rooted in class differences.

Types of Nonverbal Symbols

1. Think of a person you have met who seemed socially awkward, in ways that revealed themselves nonverbally. Write a paragraph that analyzes that person's unspoken communication.

2. What are some gestures that are a common part of your nonspoken communication? Write a paragraph describing these gestures in detail and explaining what they express. Imagine that you are writing for a visitor from another planet who knows nothing about human gestures.

3. Write an essay that compares and contrasts the nonverbal behavior of two people you know. Choose people who have very different styles: perhaps a very dominant man and a quiet, passive man; an outgoing, athletic woman and a socially withdrawn woman, etc.

The Roots of Happiness

1. Of the findings reported in this study, which one surprised you the most? Why? Write a paragraph in which you explain your answer.

2. Think of a person you know whom you would describe as either exceptionally happy or exceptionally unhappy. Write a paragraph with the topic sentence "_____ is one of the happiest/unhappiest people I know." To support your statement, give examples of the person's behavior, and then draw a conclusion about what might cause that person to be more or less happy than other people.

3. On the basis of what you learned from this selection, what advice would you give a person who wanted to lead a happy life? Write an essay with a thesis statement similar to this: "In order to live a happy life, you should keep these three things in mind." Be specific about how the person should incorporate the three things into his or her life.

Cardiovascular Disease Risk Factors

1. What is a health problem that seems to run in your family? Write a paragraph about this problem: whom it currently affects, what effect it has on this person, and whether you are concerned that you will be affected.

2. Do you smoke? Have you smoked in the past? Are you a militant non-smoker? Write a paragraph in which you describe your personal relationship (or non-relationship) with cigarettes.

3. Write an essay in which you analyze your own risk of developing heart disease, based upon what you have learned in this reading. Name some of the risk factors that you possess; how serious you believe they are; and what, if anything, you are planning to do about them.

Exploring the World of Business and Economics

1. The United States has long been thought of as the land of opportunity, where anyone who was willing to work hard could make a success of himself or herself. Do you think this idea is as true today as it was a generation or more ago? Write a paragraph defending your answer.

2. This selection describes several successful entrepreneurs and the businesses they have established. If you were to develop a business of your own, what would it be? What attracts you to that idea? Write a paragraph describing the business you would like to set up and why it appeals to you.

3. The selection points out that whatever your career goals may be, "you must bring something to the table that makes you different from the next person." As you think of your own career plan, what specific talent, skills, or abilities do you "bring to the table"? Write an essay in which you state your career goals and then discuss three reasons why you will be a more desirable employee than the average person.

Abusive Relationships among the Young

1. Have you ever known someone who was in an abusive relationship? (Alternately, have you ever been in such a relationship?) Is the relationship still going on, or did it end? Write a paragraph in which you describe the relationship, the nature of the abuse, and the current state of the relationship.

2. This selection states: "[F]rom an early age, girls in our culture are taught that being a 'princess' is the ideal state of femininity. Is it any wonder they long for a Prince Charming to come and sweep them off their feet?" Do you agree that girls in today's culture get this message? Write a paragraph in which you state your position, supporting it with specific examples.

3. Most people would say, "I would never stay with anyone who abused me." Yet once they are in such a relationship, many women *do* stay. Why do you think a woman might remain with a partner who hurts her physically or emotionally? Write an essay in which you explore three possible reasons.

A Civil War Soldier's Letter to His Wife

1. Choose the one single adjective that you think best describes Sullivan Ballou's letter. Write a paragraph explaining your choice.

2. We do not know how Sarah Ballou responded to her husband's letter. Write an essay in which you compare and contrast two different ways she may have felt when she received it.

3. Do you believe dying for your country can be a noble act? Or are people like Sullivan Ballou, who believe that they are giving their lives for a good cause, only fooling themselves? Write a paragraph or an essay in which you explore this question.

In My Day

1. Baker describes his mother vividly, calling her, among other things, "formidable," "fierce," and "sarcastic." Think of an older person of your acquaintance, and write a paragraph describing his or her character.

2. What is one wise or helpful lesson that an older person has imparted to you? Write a paragraph about this lesson and the person who taught it to you.

3. If you had a time machine, which aspects of your own family's history would you like to learn more about? Write an essay about three times and places where you would go and what you would try to learn there.

The Spider and the Wasp

1. The dictionary defines *instinct* as "an inborn pattern of behavior that is characteristic of a species." Write a paragraph in which you provide several examples of human instincts—behaviors that we seem to be born with, rather than learn.

2. Write a paragraph about a time when you were confronted in an aggressive way, either physically or verbally. How did you feel—physically *and* mentally—and what did you do?

3. Petrunkevitch describes the appearance, habits, and behaviors of the spider and the wasp in extremely fine detail, giving even readers who have never seen the creatures a very good idea of how they look and act. Write an essay in which you provide an equally detailed description of another animal—even one as common as a cat or dog or squirrel. Observe the animal closely and record your observations, so that your essay could make even someone who had never seen such an animal imagine it vividly.

Limited Answer Key

An important note: To strengthen your reading skills, you must do more than simply find out which of your answers are right and which are wrong. You also need to figure out (with the help of this book, the teacher, or other students) *why* you missed the questions you did. By using each of your wrong answers as a learning opportunity, you will strengthen your understanding of the skills. You will also prepare yourself for the review and mastery tests in Part One, the reading comprehension questions in Part Two, and the relationships tests and combined-skills tests in Part Three, for which answers are not given here.

Answers to the Practices in Part One

1 Main Ideas

Practice 1

1. S		6. S	
S		S	
S		S	
P		P	
2. S		7. S	
S		P	
S		S	
P		S	
3. S		8. S	
P		P	
S		S	
S		S	
4. S		9. S	
S		P	
P		S	
S		S	
5. S		10. S	
S		S	
P		P	
S		S	

Practice 2 *(Wording of topics may vary.)*

1. Topic: Halloween
   Main idea: Sentence 2

2. Topic: The American criminal justice system
   Main idea: Sentence 1

3. Topic: The ability to empathize
   Main idea: Sentence 1

4. Topic: Drive-in movies
   Main idea: Sentence 1

Practice 3

1. 3
2. 1
3. 6
4. 7

2 Supporting Details

Practice 1 *(Wording of answers may vary)*

A. **Main idea:** [Non-human] animals communicate in their own ways.
   1. Nonverbal sounds
   2. Chemical signals
   3. Touch
   4. Visual signals

B. **Main idea:** Human diseases can be classified into a number of basic types.
   2. Hereditary
      Minor detail: Sickle-cell anemia
   3. Degenerative
      Minor detail: Arthritis
   4. Hormonal
      Minor detail: Diabetes
   5. Environmental
      Minor detail: Allergies and lead poisoning
   6. Deficiency
      Minor detail: Scurvy and pellagra

Practice 2 *(Wording of answers may vary)*

A. Photography was a serious business.
   People could not keep smiling for a long time.
   People didn't want to show their teeth.

B. *Major detail:* Debt
   Major detail: Crime
   Major detail: War and conquest
      Minor detail: Romans enslaved Greeks.

Practice 3

1. Passage A: C
2. Passage B: B

3 Implied Main Ideas

Practice 1

Paragraph 1
1. B
2. A

Paragraph 2
1. B
2. B

Paragraph 3
1. C
2. A

Practice 2

1. D
2. C
3. C

Practice 3 *(Wording of answers may vary.)*

A. *Topic:* Schools and colleges
   Implied main idea: Schools and colleges serve a number of functions in our society.

B. *Topic: Body temperature*
   Implied main idea: Several factors affect body temperatures in humans.

C. *Topic:* The current economic crisis
   Implied main idea: Regular Americans are also to blame for the current economic crisis.

Practice 4

Passage 1: *Implied central idea:* B
Passage 2: *Implied central idea:* C

4 Relationships I

Practice 1 *(Answers may vary.)*

1. also
2. moreover
3. second
4. in addition
5. Another

Practice 2 *(Answers may vary.)*

1. after
2. When
3. By
4. Before
5. until

Practice 3 *(Wording of answers may vary.)*

A. Main idea: There are three important lists people should make before going to the doctor.
1. All the medications they are taking
2. The symptoms they are experiencing
3. Any specific questions they may have

B. Main idea: . . . a variety of techniques for tattoo removal.
1. Dermabrasion
2. Cryosurgery
3. Laser removal

Practice 4 *(Wording of answers may vary.)*

Main idea: A furious Hitler quickly went on the attack against Britain.
1. Used submarines against British shipping
2. Sent air force to destroy Britain's military defenses
3. Bombed civilian targets in London and other British cities

Practice 5 *(Wording of answers may vary.)*

Main idea: To write effectively, practice four rules of thumb.
1. Decide what point you want to make.
2. Provide sufficient support for that point.
3. Organize your support.
4. Write clear, error-free sentences.

Practice 6

1. B
2. A
3. A
4. B
5. A
6. B
7. B
8. A
9. A
10. B

5 Relationships II

Practice 1 *(Answers may vary.)*

1. for example
2. such as
3. For instance
4. including
5. illustration

Practice 2 *(Wording of answers may vary.)*

A. *Scripts*; definition—2; example—3
B. *Enculturation; definition*—2; example 1—3; example 2—4; example 3—5

Practice 3 *(Answers may vary.*

1. In the same way
2. just as
3. Both
4. Just like
5. same

Practice 4 *(Answers may vary.)*

1. while
2. However
3. but
4. Although
5. On the other hand

Practice 5 *(Wording of answers may vary.)*

A. Comparison: Abraham Lincoln and Frederick Douglass
B. Contrast: personal distress and empathy

Practice 6 *(Answers may vary.)*

1. because
2. lead to
3. As a result
4. caused
5. since

Practice 7 *(Wording of answers may vary.)*

A. **Main idea** *(the effect):* Victorian women often fainted.
   Major supporting details (the causes):
   1. Their tight undergarments cut off air supply and blood flow.
   2. They knew that fainting made them seem delicate and feminine.

B. **Main idea** *(the cause):* Rising sea levels would result in global problems.
   Effect: Drastic change in existing coastlines
   Effect: Threat to dikes and sea walls
   Effect: Increase in global warming

Practice 8

1. D
2. A
3. B
4. E
5. C

Practice 9

A. Problem—3; solution—5
B. Problem: Relief workers have been frustrated by their inability to help victims of famine. Solution: A nutritionist developed a paste of peanut butter enriched with vitamins and minerals.

Practice 10

1. B	6. B
2. C	7. A
3. A	8. B
4. A	9. A
5. C	10. C

6 Inferences

Practice 1

1. A, B	4. B, D
2. A, C	5. B, D
3. C, D	

Practice 2

A. 1. B	D. 10. C
2. C	11. A
3. B	12. B
B. 4. C	E. 13. A
5. C	14. B
6. B	15. A
C. 7. A	
8. B	
9. A	

Practice 3

1. C, metaphor
2. B, simile
3. A, simile
4. A, metaphor
5. C, metaphor

Practice 4

B, E, G, H, I

Practice 5

B, C, F

7 Purpose and Tone

Practice 1

1. I	6. P
2. P	7. E
3. I	8. I
4. E	9. P
5. I	10. E

Practice 2

1. I+P
2. I
3. E

Practice 3

A. 1. B	B. 6. B
2. C	7. D
3. D	8. E
4. A	9. A
5. E	10. C

Practice 4

1. B
2. C
3. H
4. D
5. F

8 Argument

Practice 1

1. I agree: A, C, D
   I disagree: B, E, F

2. I agree: C, D, F
   I disagree: A, B, E

3. I agree: A, C, E
   I disagree: B, D, F

4. I agree: C, D, E
   I disagree: A, B, F

5. I agree: A, C, E
   I disagree: B, D, F

Practice 2

1. A, B, E
2. B, D, E
3. B, C, F
4. A, D, E
5. B, C, E

Practice 3

1. C	4. C
2. A	5. B
3. D	

9 Critical Reading

Practice 1

1. O	6. F
2. F	7. O
3. F	8. F
4. O	9. O
5. F+O	10. F+O

Detecting Propaganda

- *Bandwagon:* 2
- *Testimonial:* 2
- *Transfer:* 1
- *Plain Folks:* 2
- *Name Calling:* 1
- *Glittering Generalities:* 1

Practice 2

1. B	6. E
2. C	7. C
3. A	8. A
4. D	9. B
5. F	10. D

Fallacies That Ignore the Issue

- *Circular Reasoning:* 1
- *Personal Attack:* 2
- *Straw Man:* 1

Fallacies That Oversimplify the Issue

- *False Cause:* 1
- *False Comparison:* 1
- *Either-Or:* 2

Practice 3

A. 1. A	B. 6. C
2. B	7. A
3. C	8. B
4. B	9. A
5. C	10. B

10 Active Reading and Study

Practice 1 *(Wording of answers may vary.)*

1. Selection from a History Text
Point: Three factors explain why the United States experienced falling birth rates in the 19th century.
Support:
1. America was becoming urban—birth rates are historically lower in cities.
2. Infant mortality fell—families did not have to bear as many children.
3. For a better quality of life, people decided to limit family size.

2. Selection from a Communications Text
Point: There are at least three different types of noise.
Support:
1. Semantic—different people have different meanings for words and phrases
Example: A "soda" in New York is called "pop" in the Midwest.
2. Mechanical—problem with a machine used to assist communication
Example: A pen running out of ink; a static-filled radio
3. Environmental—noise that interferes with the communication process
Example: A noisy restaurant; someone drumming fingers

3. Selection from a Biology Text
Point: Chemical element—one of 92 naturally occurring kinds of matter that cannot be separated chemically into similar substances
Support:
1. Each element has specific properties that make it different from other elements: physical state, color, odor, texture, boiling/freezing points, etc.
2. SPONCH—six familiar elements (sulfur, phosphorus, oxygen, nitrogen, carbon, and hydrogen) that make up 99% of living matter

Practice 2 *(Wording of answers may vary.)*

1. Selection from a Health Text
Reasons for anger:
1. Time—working longer hours
2. Technology—cell phones and pagers make us available 24/7/365
3. Tension—we're always running
Danger in venting anger: Makes anger worse; doesn't deal with underlying causes of anger
Results of anger: Sabotages physical as well as mental health—increased risk of stroke and heart attack

2. Selection from a Business Text
Point: Three factors help us differentiate between work and play.
1. Purpose: Work has a definite purpose (something being accomplished). Play does not have to have a definite purpose.
2. Attitude: A task may be work or play depending on the attitude of the person performing the task (example: professional baseball players).
3. Reward: External rewards are given for work (example: money); internal rewards are received for play (example: enjoyment).

3. Selection from a Sociology Text
Point: Social class has a significant impact on how people behave and think and affects people in almost every area of life.
1. Determines life chances—people's level of living and options for choice
   Ex.—Higher class = more education (go farther; do better)
2. Affects health and life expectancy—lower-class people die sooner
   Ex.—Lower class = more obesity; more exposure to environmental hazards
3. Affects exposure to dangerous situations
   Ex.—Lower class = 80% of soldiers in Vietnam; most victims on *Titanic*
4. Affects people's style of life—consumption of goods and services
   Ex.—Lower class = more convenience foods and beer
5. Is associated with certain patterns of behavior
   Ex.—Higher classes are more likely to vote

Answers to the Practices in Part Four

2 The Human Body: An Orientation

Practice *(Wording of answers may vary.)*
1. Anatomy studies the structure of body parts; physiology concerns the function of these body parts.
2. B
3. Bones can support and protect body organs because they contain hard mineral deposits. *Or:* Blood flows in one direction through the heart because the heart has valves that prevent backflow.
4. B
5. B

3 Introduction to Statistics

Practice *(Wording of answers may vary.)*
1. A
2. B
3. B
4. Statistical significance means that a result was reached, using the available data and sampling methods, that could not be due to chance. Practical significance means that the result has value in the real world.
5. A

Acknowledgments

Adler, Ronald B., Russell F. Proctor II, and Neil Towne, "Personal Conflict Styles." From *Looking Out, Looking In*, 11th edition. Copyright © 2005 Wadsworth, a part of Cengage Learning, Inc. Reproduced by permission. www.cengage.com/permissions

Baker, Russell, "In My Day." From *Growing Up* by Russell Baker. Copyright © 1982 by Russell Baker. Reprinted by permission of Don Congdon Associates, Inc.

Baldwin, Mike. Cartoon on page 99. Copyright © by Mike Baldwin. Reproduced with permission of CartoonStock Ltd. www.cartoonstock.com

Barry, Dave, "The Ugly Truth about Beauty." From the *Miami Herald*, February 1, 1998. Copyright © 1998 by Dave Barry. Reprinted by permission of the author.

Beebe, Steven A., and Susan J. Beebe, "Understand Your Nervousness." From *Public Speaking Handbook*, 3rd edition, copyright © 2010. Printed and Electronically reproduced by permission of Pearson Education, Inc., Upper Saddle River, NJ.

Davies, Alice M., "'Extra Large, Please.'" Used with the permission of Alice M. Davies.

Drafke, Michael W. Selections on pages 380–381 and 407 and "Types of Nonverbal Symbols." From *The Human Side of Organizations*, 9th edition, copyright © 2006. Printed and Electronically reproduced by permission of Pearson Education, Inc., Upper Saddle River, NJ.

Draughon, Dennis. Cartoon on page 255. Copyright © 2003 by *The Scranton Times/ Shamrock Communications*. Reprinted by permission of the artist.

Glasbergen, Randy. Cartoons on pages 23, 63, and 257. Copyright © 2003, 2004 by Randy Glasbergen. Reprinted with permission of the artist.

Hales, Dianne. Selections on pages 367 and 383 and graph on page 243. From *An Invitation to Health*, 11th edition. Copyright © 2005 Wadsworth, a division of Cengage Learning. Inc.

Henslin, James M. Selections on pages 231 and 330. Used with the permission of James M. Henslin.

Henslin, James M., "Consequences of Social Class." From *Essentials of Sociology: A Down-to-Earth Approach*, 9th edition, copyright © 2011. Printed and Electronically reproduced by permission of Pearson Education, Inc., Upper Saddle River, NJ.

Hill, Miriam, "Abusive Relationships among the Young." Reprinted by permission of the author.

Lopez, Steve, "A Scary Time to Raise a Daughter." From the *Los Angeles Times*, October 26, 2003. Copyright © 2003 by the *Los Angeles Times*. Reprinted with permission.

Lyon, Bill. Selection on pages 240–241. From the *Philadelphia Inquirer*, April 29, 2003. Used with the permission of Bill Lyon.

Marieb, Elaine N., and Katja Hoehn, "The Human Body: An Orientation." From *Human Anatomy and Physiology*, 8th edition, copyright © 2010. Printed and Electronically reproduced by permission of Pearson Education, Inc., Upper Saddle River, NJ.

McCourt, Frank. Selection on page 262. Reprinted with the permission of Scribner, a Division of Simon & Schuster, Inc., from *Teacher Man: A Memoir* by Frank McCourt. Copyright © 2005 by Green Peril Corp. All rights reserved.

Moehringer, J. R. Selection on page 248. From *The Tender Bar*. Copyright © 2005 by J. R. Moehringer. Reprinted by permission of Hyperion. All rights reserved.

Morris, Charles G., and Albert A. Maisto, "Alcohol." From *Understanding Psychology*, 10th edition, copyright © 2013. Printed and Electronically reproduced by permission of Pearson Education, Inc., Upper Saddle River, NJ.

Morris, Charles G., and Albert A. Maisto. Selections on pages 574 and 592. From *Psychology: An Introduction*, 12th edition, copyright © 2005. Printed and Electronically reproduced by permission of Pearson Education, Inc., Upper Saddle River, NJ.

Morris, Charles G., and Albert A. Maisto. Selection on page 566. From *Understanding Psychology*, 7th edition, copyright © 2006. Printed and Electronically reproduced by permission of Pearson Education, Inc., Upper Saddle River, NJ.

Norton, Mary Beth, et al. Selection on page 598 and "Hoover and Hard Times." From *A People and a Nation: A History of the United States*, 7th edition. Copyright © 2005 Wadsworth, a part of Cengage Learning, Inc. Reproduced by permission. www.cengage.com/permissions

Payne, Wayne A., Dale B. Hahn, and Ellen B. Lucas, "Cardiovascular Disease Risk Factors." From *Understanding Your Health*, 9th edition, copyright © 2006. Reprinted with permission of The McGraw-Hill Companies.

Petrunkevitch, Alexander, "The Spider and the Wasp." From *Scientific American*, August 1952. Reprinted with permission. Copyright © 1952 Scientific American, Inc. All rights reserved.

Photograph on page 265. From a collection of photographs of caskets at Dover Air Force Base publicly released by the United States Air Force.

Pride, William M., Robert J. Hughes, and Jack R. Kapoor, "Exploring the World of Business and Economics." From *Business*, 11th edition. Copyright © 2012 South-Western, a part of Cengage Learning, Inc. Reprinted by permission. www.cengage.com/permissions

Rooney, Andy. Excerpt on page 297. From *60 Minutes,* CBS, May 30, 2004.

Rouff, Ruth A. "Diamonds Aren't Forever." Reprinted by permission of the author.

Russell, Bertrand. Excerpted from *The Three Passions* by Bertrand Russell. Reprinted by permission of Taylor & Francis Books, Ltd. and The Bertrand Russell Peace Foundation.

Schulz, Charles M. Cartoons on pages 237, 371, and 386. From PEANUTS copyright © 1995, 1997, and 1963 by Peanuts Worldwide LLC and distributed by UNIVERSAL UCLICK. Reprinted with permission. All rights reserved.

Song, Sora, "Getting a Good Night's Sleep." *Time* Magazine, January 16, 2006. Copyright © 2006 Time Inc. Reprinted by permission.

Thaves, Bob. Cartoon on page 275. From "Frank and Ernest," copyright © 1995 by Thaves. Reprinted with permission.

Triola, Mario F., "Introduction to Statistics." From *Elementary Statistics Technology Update*, 11th edition, copyright © 2012. Printed and Electronically reproduced by permission of Pearson Education, Inc., Upper Saddle River, NJ.

Twohy, Mike. Cartoon on page 227. From "That's Life," copyright © 2005 by Mike Twohy. Used with the permission of Mike Twohy and the Cartoonist Group. All rights reserved.

Verderber, Rudolph F., and Kathleen S. Verderber. Selection on page 399 and "Skills of Effective Face-to-Face Conversationalists." From *Communicate!*, (with CD-ROM, Non-InfoTrac Version), 10th edition. Copyright © 2002 Wadsworth, a part of Cengage Learning, Inc. Reproduced by permission. www.cengage.com/permissions

Weiten, Wayne, and Margaret A. Lloyd. Selection on page 580. From *Psychology Applied to Modern Life, Adjustment in the 21st Century*, 8th edition, by Weiten/Lloyd. Copyright © 2006 Wadsworth, a part of Cengage Learning, Inc.

Weiten, Wayne, Dana S. Dunn, and Elizabeth Yost Hammer. "The Roots of Happiness: An Empirical Approach" and "Self-Help Books." From Weiten/Dunn/Hammer, *Psychology Applied to Modern Life,* 10th edition. Copyright © 2012 Wadsworth, a part of Cengage Learning, Inc. Reproduced by permission. www.cengage.com/permissions

Wise, Gary, and Lance Aldrich. Cartoon on page 299. From "Real Life Adventures," copyright © 2005 GarLanco. Reprinted with permission of UNIVERSAL UCLICK. All rights reserved.

Index